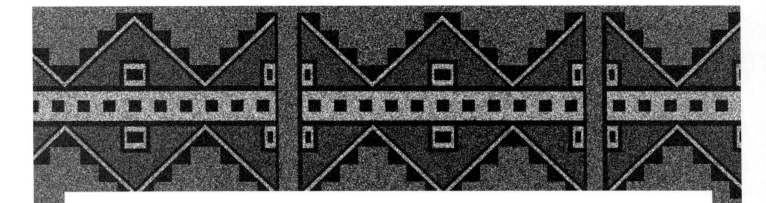

Reference Library of

NATIVE

NORTH

AMERICA

Reference Library of

NATIVE

NORTH

AMERICA

VOLUME

IV

Edited by
Duane Champagne

Distributed exclusively by:

**African American Publications
Proteus Enterprises**

Rebecca Parks, *Editor*
Shelly Dickey, *Managing Editor*
William Harmer, *Contributing Editor*
Laura L. Brandau, *Associate Editor*
Brian J. Koski, *Associate Editor*
Jeffrey Wilson, *Associate Editor*
Mark Springer, *Technical Training Specialist*

Mary Beth Trimper, *Composition and Electronic Prepress Manager*
Evi Seoud, *Assistant Composition and Electronic Prepress Manager*

Kenn Zorn, *Product Design Manager*
Jennifer Wahi, *Art Director*
Barbara Yarrow, *Manager, Imaging and Multimedia Content*
Randy Bassett, *Imaging Supervisor*
Pamela A. Reed, *Imaging Coordinator*
Leitha Etheridge-Sims, Mary K. Grimes, David G. Oblender, *Image Catalogers*

The Reference Library of Native North America/ edited by Duane Champagne
Cover artwork: *The Veteran*, courtesy of Richard Glazer-Danay. *White Hopi Clown Child*, courtesy of
Owen Seumptewa.

Copyright © 2001
Gale Group
27500 Drake Rd.
Farmington Hills, MI 48331–3535
http://www.galegroup.com
800–877-4253
248–699-4253

ISBN 0–7876-5615–1 (set)
ISBN 0–7876-5616–X (volume 1)
ISBN 0–7876-5617–8 (volume 2)
ISBN 0–7876-5618–6 (volume 3)
ISBN 0–7876-5618–94 (volume 4)

1. Indians of North America—Encyclopedias.   I. Champagne, Duane.
E76.2 .R43 2000
970.004'97—dc21   00-046599

Printed in the United States of America
10 9 8 7 6 5 4 3 2 1

Board of Advisors

John Aubrey, *Librarian, The Newberry Library, Chicago, Illinois*
Cheryl Metoyer-Duran, *Librarian, Mashantucket Pequot Research Center and Museum, Mashantucket, Connecticut*
G. Edward Evans, *University Librarian, Loyola Marymount University, Los Angeles*
Hanay Geiogamah, *Professor of Theater, University of California, Los Angeles*
Carole Goldberg-Ambrose, *Professor of Law, University of California, Los Angeles*

Editorial Team at the American Indian Studies Center, University of California, Los Angeles

Editor: Duane Champagne, *Director, American Indian Studies Center, and Professor of Sociology, University of California, Los Angeles*
Assistant Editors: Amy Ware, Alexandra Harris, Tim Petete, Elton Naswood, Jacob Goff, Demelza Champagne, and Garrett Saracho.
Photographic Editor: Roselle Kipp
Bibliographic Editor: Ken Wade
Graphic Artist: James Perkins

Biographers

Angela Aleiss, *American Indian Studies Center, University of California, Los Angeles*
Paola Carini, *English Department, University of California, Los Angeles*
Duane Champagne, *American Indian Studies Center, University of California, Los Angeles*
James Coulon, *Coulon, Ink., San Diego, California*
Troy Johnson, *American Indian Studies Department, California State University, Long Beach*
Richard Keeling, *Ethnomusicology Department, University of California, Los Angeles*
Patrick Macklem, *Faculty of Law, University of Toronto, Toronto, Ontario, Canada*
Tim Petete, *American Indian Studies Center, University of California, Los Angeles*
Amy Kathleen Simmons, *American Indian Studies Center, University of California, Los Angeles*
Amy Ware, *American Indian Studies Center, University of California, Los Angeles*

Contributing Authors

Frances Abele, *School of Public Administration, Carleton University, Ottawa, Ontario, Canada*
Gerald Alfred, *School of Public Administration, The University of Victoria, Victoria, Canada*
Karen Baird-Olson, *Department of Sociology and Anthropology, University of Central Florida, Orlando, Florida*
Russel Lawrence Barsh, *Native Studies, University of Lethbridge, Lethbridge, Alberta, Canada*
Janet Berlo, *Department of Art History, University of Rochester, New York*
Peggy Berryhill, *Native Media Resource Center (NMRC), Bodega Bay, California*
Ted Binnema, *History Department, The University of Northern British Columbia, Prince George, British Columbia, Canada*
Nancy Bonvillain, *Simon's Rock College of Bard, Great Barrington, Massachusetts*
Daniel Boxberger, *Department of Anthropology, Western Washington University, Bellingham, Washington*
Simon Brascoupe, *Department of Sociology and Anthropology, Carleton University, Ottawa, Ontario, Canada*
William Bright, *Department of Linguistics, University of Colorado, Boulder, Colorado*
Tara Browner, *Department of Ethnomusicology, University of California, Los Angeles, California*
Gregory Cajete, *Center for Research and Cultural Exchange, University of New Mexico, Albuquerque, New Mexico*
Edward Castillo, *Native American Studies, Sonoma State University, Rohnert Park, California*
Katherine Beatty Chiste, *Department of Social Sciences, University of Lethbridge, Lethbridge, Alberta, Canada*

Anthony Clark, *Department of Sociology, University of Kansas, Lawrence, Kansas*
Richmond Clow, *Native American Studies, University of Montana, Missoula, Montana*
Heather Coleman, *Faculty of Social Work, University of Calgary, Calgary, Alberta, Canada*
David de Jong, *Prescott High School, Arizona*
Henry Dobyns, *Independent Consultant, Tucson, Arizona*
Leroy Eid, *Department of History, University of Dayton, Dayton, Ohio*
Jo-Anne Fiske, *Anthropology Department, The University of Northern British Columbia, Prince George, British Columbia, Canada*
Donald Fixico, *Department of History, The University of Kansas, Lawrence, Kansas*
Hanay Geiogamah, *Theater Department, University of California, Los Angeles, California*
Douglas George-Kanentiio, *Journalist, Oneida Iroquois Territory, Oneida, New York*
Ian Getty, *Research Director, Stoney Tribe, Nakota Institute, Calgary, Alberta, Canada*
Carole Goldberg-Ambrose, *School of Law, University of California, Los Angeles, California*
Charlotte Heth, *Department of Ethnomusicology, University of California, Los Angeles, California*
Ann Marie Hodes, *Health Services Center, University of Alberta, Edmonton, Alberta, Canada*
Felicia Schanche Hodge, *University of California, San Francisco, and University of Minnesota, Minneapolis*
Cornelius Jaenen, *Department of History, University of Ottawa, Ottawa, Ontario, Canada*
Jennie Joe, *Native American Research and Training Center, University of Arizona, Tucson, Arizona*
Clara Sue Kidwell, *Native American Studies, University of Oklahoma, Norman, Oklahoma*
Rita Ledesma, *Department of Social Welfare, California State University, Los Angeles*
John D. Loftin, *Loftin & Loftin, Hillsborough, North Carolina*
Carol Lujan, *American Indian Studies Program, Arizona State University, Tempe, Arizona*
John A. (Ian) Mackenzie, *Centre for Indian Scholars, Terrace, British Columbia, Canada*
David C. Mass, *Department of Political Science, University of Alaska, Anchorage, Alaska*
Donald McCaskill, *Department of Native Studies, Trent University, Peterborough, Ontario, Canada*
Alan McMillan, *Department of Archaeology, Simon Fraser College, Burnaby, British Columbia, Canada*
Dorothy Lonewolf Miller, *Native American Studies, University of California, Berkeley, California*
C. Patrick Morris, *Department of Native American Studies, Salish Kootenai College, Pablo, Montana*
Ken Morrison, *Religious Studies, Arizona State University, Tempe, Arizona*
Bradford Morse, *Faculty of Law, University of Ottawa, Ottawa, Ontario, Canada*
Joane Nagel, *Department of Sociology, University of Kansas, Lawrence, Kansas*
Elton Naswood, *American Indian Studies Center, University of California, Los Angeles*
David Newhouse, *Department of Native Studies, Trent University, Peterborough, Ontario, Canada*
Brigid O'Donnell, *Department of Ecology and Evolutionary Biology, University of Connecticut*
James H. O'Donnell III, *Department of History, Marietta College, Marietta, Ohio*
Michael O'Donnell, *Director of Distance Education, Salish Kootenai Community College, Pablo, Montana*
Darren Ranco, *Department of Ethnic Studies, University of California, Berkeley*
Audry Jane Roy, *School of Public Administration, The University of Victoria, Victoria, Canada*
Kathryn W. Shanley, *Department of English, Cornell University, Ithaca, New York*
Leanne Simpson, *Department of Native Studies, University of Manitoba, Winnipeg, Manitoba, Canada*
Gerald Slater, *Vice President of Academic Affairs, Salish Kootenai Community College, Pablo, Montana*
Dean Smith, *College of Business Administration, Northern Arizona University, Flagstaff, Arizona*
C. Matthew Snipp, *Department of Sociology, Stanford University, Stanford, California*
Rennard Strickland, *School of Law, University of Oklahoma, Norman, Oklahoma*
Paul Stuart, *School of Social Welfare, University of Alabama, Tuscaloosa, Alabama*
Imre Sutton, *Professor Emeritus, Department of Geography, California State University, Fullerton, California*
Karen Swisher, *College of Education, Arizona State University, Tempe, Arizona*
Steve Talbot, *Department of Sociology and Anthropology, San Joaquin College, Stockton, California*
Wesley Thomas, *Department of Anthropology, Idaho State University, Pocatello, Idaho*
Loretta Todd, *Film Maker, Vancouver, British Columbia, Canada*
Clifford Trafzer, *Department of Ethnic Studies, University of California, Riverside, California*
Ronald Trosper, *Department of Forestry, Northern Arizona University, Flagstaff, Arizona*
Daniel Usner, *History Department, Cornell University, Ithaca, New York*
Joan Vastokas, *Department of Anthropology, Trent University, Peterborough, Ontario, Canada*
Tarajean Yazzie, *School of Education, Harvard University, Cambridge, Massachusetts*

Brother,

   When you first came to this island

   you were as children, in need of food and shelter,

   and we, a great and mighty nation.

   But we took you by the hand

   and we planted you and watered you

   and you grew to be a great oak,

   we a mere sapling in comparison.

   Now we are the children

   (in need of food and shelter).

An opening speech often used by Northeastern Indian leaders at conferences with Europeans during the early colonial period.

Highlights

Persons interested in a comprehensive reference providing information on all aspects of the Native American and Canadian experience can turn to one accurate source: *The Reference Library of Native North America.* The first seventeen chapters are composed of signed essays, annotated directory information, and documentary excerpts; the final chapter presents more than 500 concise biographies of prominent Native North Americans. *The Reference Library of Native North America* covers a broad scope of topics, including:

- History and historical landmarks
- Health
- Law and legislation
- Major culture areas
- Activism
- Environment
- Urbanization and non-reservation populations
- Administration
- Education
- Economy
- Languages
- Demography
- Religion
- Arts
- Literature
- Media
- Women
- Gender Relations

Arrangement Allows for Quick Information Access

The Reference Library of Native North America provides a wealth of information, and its logical format makes it easy to use. The chapters contain subject-specific bibliographies and are enlivened by close to 350 photographs, maps, and charts. Other value-added features include:

- Contents section details each chapter's coverage, including directories and bibliographies
- Alphabetical and geographical lists of tribes
- Multimedia bibliography of sources for further reading and research
- Glossary of Native terms
- Comprehensive keyword index listing tribe and band names (with alternate spellings), personal names, important events, and geographic locations
- Detailed occupational index giving insight into Natives who have excelled in their field of endeavor

Contents

Acknowledgments

The undertaking of the update and revision of this set was a far greater task than originally anticipated, and a great many people contributed to its compilation, writing, editing, and production. I am greatly honored to express thanks to my numerous colleagues who contributed their updated and revised manuscripts, and provided the inspiration for a reference work about contemporary Native North American peoples. The contributors were enthusiastic about updating the *Reference Library;* most thought that over the past seven years many events and changes occurred in Indian Country that required new interpretations and additional material. The set benefits greatly from these many contributors who bring their expertise and understanding into four volumes. We all share the same vision and the understanding of having put forth our best efforts for a worthy cause.

Great credit and thanks are due to people at the Gale Group for their vision and support. Chris Nasso deserves special recognition for developing the idea and groundwork for the set; our readers and the Native peoples are indebted to her for her sympathetic foresight. The Gale editors made workable a long and difficult project. Rebecca Parks deserves special and heartfelt recognition for taking on a difficult and complicated project. With her patience, guidance, and perseverance, the second edition is made possible.

Special mention must also be made of our advisory board. I fondly remember the two days in early summer 1991 when we hammered out the outline and basic entry assignments for the entire set. These sessions are a testament that hard work and engaging company need not be separate events. G. Edward Evans, in particular, provided many insights and a guiding hand, and for this we are grateful. Since the first edition, board member Vee Salabiye passed away, and we miss her insight, knowledge and understanding. She made many comments and contributions that shaped the philosophy and direction of the *Reference Library*.

Many of my friends and associates provided valuable contributions, and I take this opportunity to give them thanks. Roselle Kipp provided greatly needed help in securing photographs and producing digital images; Kenneth Wade worked diligently on the bibliographies, glossaries and some directories; Amy Ware worked cheerfully and tirelessly throughout the entire project in copyediting the manuscript, and we all give thanks for her care, understanding, and concern in creating a quality product. Many students had an opportunity to contribute on parts of the *Reference Library*, and I thank them for their help and effort. In particular I wish to thank Jacob Goff, Demelza Champagne, and Alexandra Harris for their hard work on difficult tasks. Too numerous to thank are the people who helped collect the many illustrations and photographs, but special mention must be made to Ilka Hartmann, Sara Wiles, Carole Lujan, Mary Wentz, Sara Loe, and Mike McClure who all generously made available their artistic and informative photographs and images. Special thanks to Garrett Saracho whose help was indispensable for bringing the entire project to a happy conclusion.

Duane Champagne
March 2001

Preface

The *Reference Library of Native North America* provides historical and contemporary information about the Native peoples of North America. Too often reference books about Native North Americans stop providing information after the 1890s. Consequently, many people cannot find accurate, accessible, and systematic information about contemporary Native culture, art, communities, life, and legal relations. Furthermore, many reference works have given little attention to Canadian Natives, even though Canadian Natives often play a more central role in Canadian constitutional issues and politics than do Native peoples in the United States. In this set, special efforts were made to gather together experts on many aspects of U.S. and Canadian Native life, as well as to include as many U.S. and Canadian Native authors as possible. This effort paid off greatly, since these authors provided many points of view and information that could only come from individuals continually engaged in Native life and issues. In this way, the set represents an overview of the history of Native peoples in North America and provides new and probing perspectives not found in comparable reference works.

At the beginning of the twentieth century, many people believed that Native Americans would disappear and assimilate into Canadian or U.S. society. The experience of the twentieth century, however, has shown that Native communities have survived, and are strongly entrenched in their traditions and institutions. At the beginning of the twenty-first century Native Nations continue to struggle to protect their land, political rights, religions, and cultures. The *Reference Library* informs the reader about the struggle of contemporary Native North Americans and gives considerable insight into their present conditions regarding health, education, economy, politics, art, and other areas. This work is devoted to the student who has had little background or knowledge about Native Americans, and we hope it will inspire, inform, and educate students and the general public about Native peoples. If this set creates greater understanding and appreciation between the peoples of North America and peoples around the world it will have served one of its primary purposes.

Terminology: Is Indian the Right Name?

Throughout the set, a variety of terms are used interchangeably for Native North Americans, such as Indian, American Indian, Native, aborigine, First Nations, First Peoples, and others. The Native peoples of the Americas have the unfortunate distinction of having been given the wrong name, Indians, since the Native people of the Americas were not from the country or civilization of India, the subcontinent in southern Asia. The search for a single name, however, has not been entirely successful. In the United States, Native American has been used but has recently fallen out of favor, and American Indian is now preferred. Nevertheless, American Indian still retains the unfortunate Indian terminology and consequently is not an entirely satisfactory term. Native American also has serious difficulties since anyone born in North or South America may claim to be a "native American."

The Canadians have wrestled with this question of names, and many Native Canadians reject the appellation of Indian. Métis (mixed bloods) and Inuit (often called Eskimos) in Canada will not answer to the name Indian. Similarly, in Alaska the Inuit, Yupik, and Aleut peoples consider themselves distinct from Indian peoples, and do not wish to be called Indian. The Canadians have developed a range of terms such as Native, aboriginal, First Nations, and First Peoples, which in many ways more accurately describes the Native peoples. Throughout the text, we have tried to respect the Canadian preference for avoiding the inclusive term "Indian" for denoting all Native peoples. Many Native people in Canada are called "Indian," and it is appropriate for most Native peoples below the subarctic region, except for the Métis, who consider themselves a distinct ethnic group from Native as well as non-Native Canadians.

The ultimate problem in these terminological difficulties is that Native peoples in North America do not form a single ethnic group but are better understood as thousands of distinct communities and cultures. Many Native peoples have distinct languages, religious beliefs, ceremonies, and sociopolitical organization. Characterizing this diverse array of cultures and peoples with one inclusive name presents serious difficulties from the start, and no one word can characterize such diversity. The inclusive word "Indian" must be seen as something akin to "European," where there is clear recognition of peoples who occupy a contiguous geographic area but have a wide variety of language, culture, and sociopolitical organization. The same applies in Native North America: the term "Indian" or other generic terms can denote only the collection of people who occupied the North American continent, but it says little about the diversity and independence of the cultures.

The best way to characterize Native North Americans is by recognizing their specific tribal or community identities, such as Blackfeet, Cherokee, or Cree. Such identifications more accurately capture the unique and varied tribal and cultural distinctions found among Native North American peoples.

Every effort has been made to keep Native tribal and community identities distinct, but when broader tribal designations were appropriate we allowed the many authors to use their own terms. We do not wish to offend anyone, and we offer our apologies to anyone who is offended, but for ease of presentation and because our many authors used a variety of terms, we have decided not to favor one particular term but rather hoped to see that the various terms were used appropriately in all situations.

The Native North American Peoples

Native North Americans occupied their continent for at least the last ten thousand years, if not for a considerably longer period. Unlike all other groups that live in North America, Natives do not have a recent immigrant experience but rather live in cultures that predate the present institutions and societies of Canada and the United States. Native peoples have legal, cultural, and political claims to priority over Canada and the United States for use of the land, for rights to self-government, and for the practice of their cultures and religions. Over the past five hundred years Native people have experienced considerable change and dislocation, yet most Native communities have survived and will continue as communities into the next centuries. Native North Americans live in thousands of small communities and exhibit considerable differences in culture, language, religion, and social organization. Perhaps the strongest unifying force among these diverse cultures and communities is the general insistence by U.S. and Canadian societies and governments to treat Natives as a homogeneous ethnic group. Nothing could be further from the truth, but since they are treated as homogeneous, there are many situations in which Natives can act collectively to pursue their economic and political goals. Consequently, Natives have operated in mass North American society in increasingly well-organized national organizations and interest groups. These trends will most likely continue and become a major force in contemporary Native affairs.

Scope and Content

The Reference Library of Native North America covers the range of Native history and culture in the United States and Canada, providing a chronology, demographic and distribution descriptions and histories, and discussions of religion and religious change, art, music, theater, film, traditional arts, history, economy, administration, and law and legal issues.

Eighteen chapters were written by over sixty scholarly contributors while students worked to collect information for wide-ranging directories of Native North American communities, major Native cultural events and major writings, films, and videos produced by Native peoples. The range of topics provides an overview and introduction to the history and present-day life of Native North Americans. Each chapter has an ample bibliography for those users interested in further reading or who wish to conduct more specialized studies. Chapter 18 comprises biographical essays on significant Native North Americans, about one-third of whom are historical figures.

An extensive glossary provides definitions of words and concepts that are commonly used in Native affairs and history.

The index provides a quick means to find information on special topics that are discussed throughout the *Reference Library.*

Close to four hundred illustrations—including photographs, line drawings, tables, maps, and figures—complement the text. Every effort was made to use Native photographers and to present views of everyday Native life and scenes.

Suggestions Are Welcome

A work as large as *The Reference Library of Native*

North America may contain oversights and errors, and we appreciate any suggestions for correction of factual material or additions that will make future editions more accurate, sympathetic, and useful. Please send comments to:

Editor
The Reference Library of Native North America
The Gale Group
27500 Drake Rd.
Farmington Hills, MI 48331
Toll Free: (800) 347–4253

Duane Champagne
March 2001

Duane Champagne has been teaching at the University of California, Los Angeles, since 1984. In 1986, he became editor of the *American Indian Culture and Research Journal* and went on to be named professor in 1997.

Dr. Champagne received a doctoral degree in sociology from Harvard University in 1982, and accepted a postdoctoral award from the Rockefeller Foundation in 1982–83. During this time, he completed fieldwork trips to the Tlingit of southeast Alaska and to the Northern Cheyenne in Montana.

Most of Dr. Champagne's writings focus on issues of social, cultural, and political change in American Indian societies as they adapted to European political, cultural, and economic incorporation. He has published in both the sociology and American Indian studies fields, including his two books *American Indian Societies: Strategies and Conditions of Political and Cultural Survival* (1989) and *Social Order and Political Change: Constitutional Governments Among the Cherokee, the Choctaw, the Chickasaw, and the Creek* (1992). He is an active writer and has produced over sixty papers and book publications.

Dr. Champagne is also the director of the UCLA American Indian Studies Center, which carries out research, conducts a master's degree program in American Indian studies, and publishes books for both academic and Indian communities.

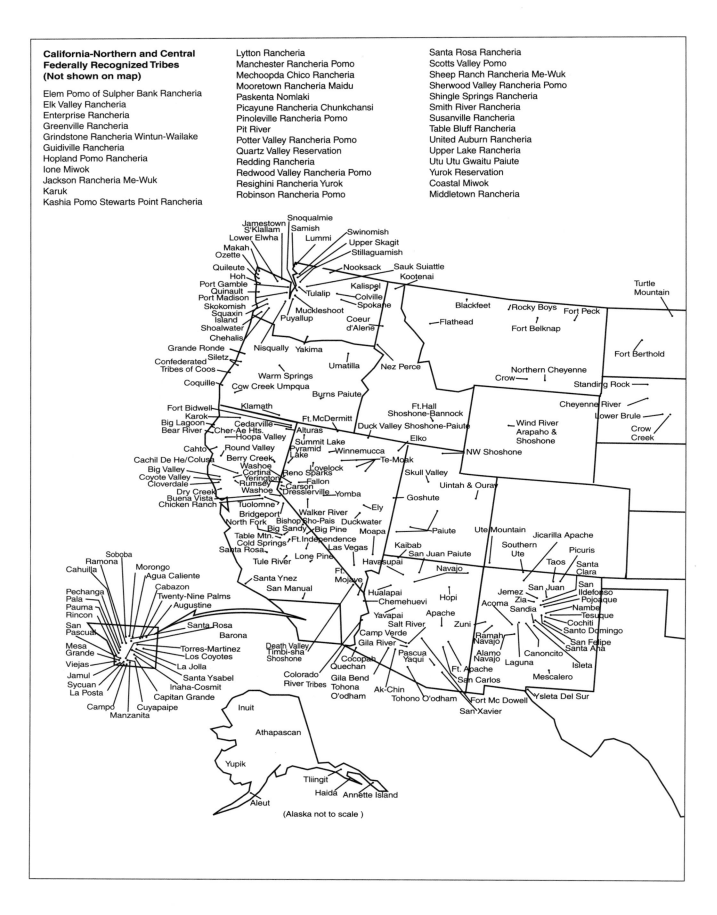

California-Northern and Central Federally Recognized Tribes (Not shown on map)

Elem Pomo of Sulpher Bank Rancheria
Elk Valley Rancheria
Enterprise Rancheria
Greenville Rancheria
Grindstone Rancheria Wintun-Wailake
Guidiville Rancheria
Hopland Pomo Rancheria
Ione Miwok
Jackson Rancheria Me-Wuk
Karuk
Kashia Pomo Stewarts Point Rancheria

Lytton Rancheria
Manchester Rancheria Pomo
Mechoopda Chico Rancheria
Mooretown Rancheria Maidu
Paskenta Nomlaki
Picayune Rancheria Chunkchansi
Pinoleville Rancheria Pomo
Pit River
Potter Valley Rancheria Pomo
Quartz Valley Reservation
Redding Rancheria
Redwood Valley Rancheria Pomo
Resighini Rancheria Yurok
Robinson Rancheria Pomo

Santa Rosa Rancheria
Scotts Valley Pomo
Sheep Ranch Rancheria Me-Wuk
Sherwood Valley Rancheria Pomo
Shingle Springs Rancheria
Smith River Rancheria
Susanville Rancheria
Table Bluff Rancheria
United Auburn Rancheria
Upper Lake Rancheria
Utu Utu Gwaitu Paiute
Yurok Reservation
Coastal Miwok
Middletown Rancheria

Federally Recognized Native American Tribes

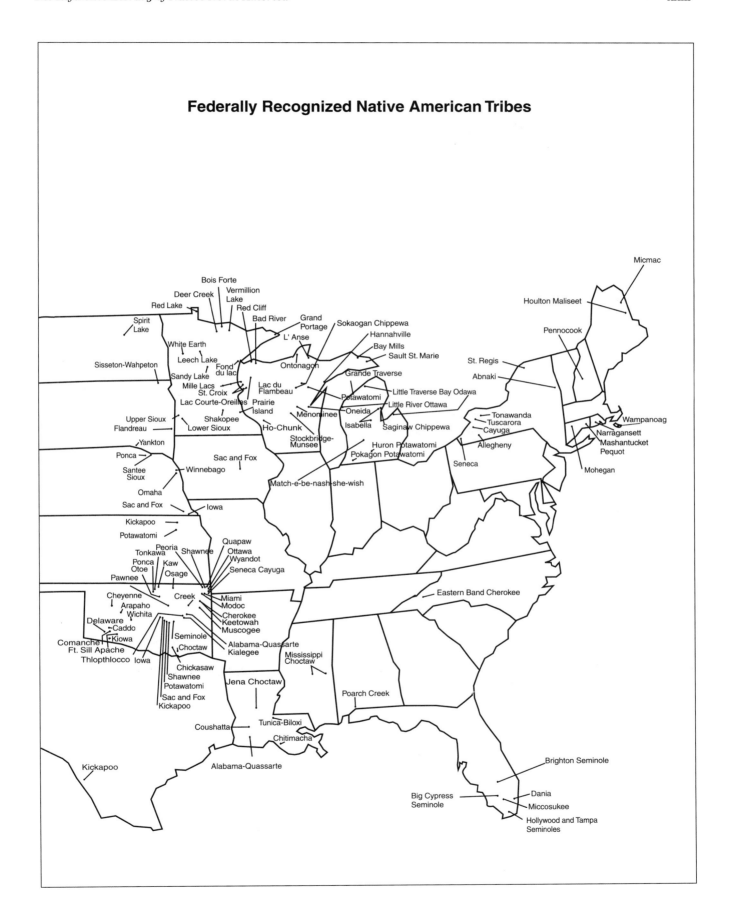

Canadian Native

Culture Groups

Major Native Nations

UNITED STATES

◆ NORTHEAST

Abenaki
Brotherton
Cayuga
Chickahominy
Chippewa (Ojibway)
Fox
Huron
Maliseet
Mattaponi
Menominee
Miami
Mohawk
Mohegan
Montauk
Nanticoke
Narragansett
Nipmuc-Hassanamisco
Oneida
Onondaga
Ottawa
Pamunkey
Passamaquoddy
Paugusset
Penobscot
Pequot
Piscataway
Poosepatuck
Potawatomi
Rappahanock
Sauk
Schaghticoke
Seneca
Shawnee
Shinnecock
Sioux
Stockbridge-Munsee
Tuscarora
Wampanoag

Winnebago

◆ SOUTHEAST

Alabama
Biloxi
Catawba
Cherokee (Eastern)
Chitimacha
Choctaw (Mississippi)
Coharie
Coushatta
Creek
Edisto
Haliwa
Houma
Lumbee
Miccosukee
Santee
Saponi
Seminole
Texas Kickapoo
Tunica
Waccamaw

◆ OKLAHOMA

Apache
Caddo
Cherokee
Cheyenne-Arapaho
Chickasaw
Choctaw
Comanche
Creek
Delaware
Iowa
Kaw
Kickapoo

Kiowa
Miami
Modoc
Osage
Otoe-Missouri
Ottawa
Pawnee
Peoria
Ponca
Potawatomi
Quapaw
Sac and Fox
Seminole
Seneca-Cayuga
Shawnee
Tonkawa
Wichita
Wyandotte

◆ PLAINS

Arikara
Assiniboine
Blackfeet
Cheyenne
Chippewa
Crow
Delaware
Gros Ventre
Hidatsa
Iowa
Kickapoo
Mandan
Omaha
Plains Ojibwa
Potawatomi
Sac and Fox
Sioux
Winnebago
Wyandotte

◆ ROCKY MOUNTAIN AREA

Arapaho
Bannock
Cayuse
Coeur d'Alene
Confederated Tribes of
  Colville
Flathead
Gosiute
Kalispel
Klamath
Kootenai
Nespelem
Nez Percé
Paiute (Northern)
Sanpoil
Shoshoni (Northern)
Spokane
Umatilla
Ute
Walla Walla
Warm Springs
Wasco
Washo
Yakima

◆ SOUTHWEST

Apache
Chemehuevi
Havasupai
Hopi
Hualapai
Maricopa
Mohave
Navajo
Paiute
Pima
Pueblo
Tohono O'Odham (Papago)
Yaqui
Yavapai
Yuma
Zuni

◆ CALIFORNIA

Achumawi
Atsugewi
Cahuilla
Cupeño
Diegueño
Gabrielino
Hupa
Karok
Luiseño
Maidu
Miwok
Mohave
Mono
Ohlone
Paiute
Patwin
Pomo
Serrano
Shasta
Shoshoni (Western)
Tolowa
Washo
Wintu
Wiyot
Yana
Yokuts
Yuki
Yurok

◆ NORTHWEST COAST

Bella Bella
Bella Coola
Chehalis
Chinook
Clallam
Coos
Coquille
Gitksan
Haida
Heiltsuk
Hoh
Kalapuya

Kwakiutl
Lillooet
Lummi
Makah
Molala
Muckleshoot
Nisgha
Nisqually
Nooksack
Nootka
Puyallup
Quileute
Quinault
Rogue River
Sauk-Suiattle
Shasta
Siletz
Siuslaw
Skagit
Skokomish
Snohomish
Squaxin Island
Stillaguamish
Suquamish
Swinomish
Tillamook
Tlingit
Tsimshian
Tulalip
Twana
Umpqua
Wishram

◆ ALASKA

Ahtena
Aleut
Athapascan
Eyak
Haida
Inuit
Tlingit
Tsimshian
Yupik

CANADA

Abenaki
Algonquin
Assiniboine
Beaver
Bella Bella
Bella Coola
Blackfoot
Blood
Carrier
Chilcotin
Chipewyan
Chippewa (Ojibway)
Comox
Cowichan
Cree
Dakota
Dogrib

Gitksan
Gros Ventre
Haida
Haisla
Hare
Heiltsuk
Huron
Inuit
Kootenay
Kutchin
Kwakiutl
Lillooet
Loucheux
Maliseet
Micmac
Mohawk
Montagnais

Nahani
Naskapi
Nisgha
Nootka
Ntlakyapamuk
Okanagon
Potawatomi
Sarsi
Sekani
Shuswap
Slave
Songhees
Squamish
Tagish
Tahltan
Tsimshian

Economy

- ◆ U.S. Indian Business and Enterprise ◆ Modern Tribal Economic Development
- ◆ American Indian Labor
- ◆ An Overview of U.S. Government Assistance and Restitution to American Indians
- ◆ Aboriginal Economic and Business Activity in Canada
- ◆ Government Assistance and Restitution for Natives in Canada
- ◆ An Overview of Economic Development History on Canadian Native Reserves
- ◆ Economic Organizations ◆ Native Owned Businesses
- ◆ Indian Gaming Casinos & Organizations

◆ U.S. INDIAN BUSINESS AND ENTERPRISE

In the five hundred years since the first contact between old and new worlds, the characteristics of world and local markets have changed. These changes help in understanding the changing conditions of Indian business. When the two worlds first met, their technologies were at similar levels, but had different capabilities and products. Europeans had long-distance transport capability over the world's oceans; Indians had long-distance transportation networks over land, based on the river network. Indians had advanced agricultural crops, such as corn, cotton, and potatoes. Gold, silver, and fur-bearing animals also existed in the new world. Europe could offer useful animal power, in horses, oxen, and cattle, as well as metal tools. Consequently, very productive trade could start immediately, as each side acquired the new products available from the other. The influx of gold and silver to Europe drove an expanding mercantile economy based on trade by merchants and large trading companies, within controls by governments of the time.

This mercantilist trading period lasted from 1500 to 1750, characterized by relative equality on the two sides. The Indian side diminished for a noneconomic reason—the loss of population due to disease. The European side grew because of its agricultural revolution, which during the 1700s consisted of rapid increases in agricultural productivity as potatoes were introduced to cold parts of Europe, and cropping patterns changed.

Partly as a consequence of the capital provided by the agricultural revolution and partly due to technological and organizational developments, the industrial revolution began in England in the middle of the eighteenth century. By 1750 England had discovered the usefulness of factory organization, had a productive agriculture, and had a trade network with the New World that could provide raw materials. England learned how to harness coal in the production of energy for factory production. It began to move toward less governmental control of trade.

The resulting industrial revolution changed the characteristics of the world market. Newly industrializing countries began rapid expansion of their market needs. Political power, armies, and navies were put to work securing sources of supply for the growing industrial center. In North America, conversion of land from its uses in the mercantile economy (food, furs, and forage) to commercial agriculture fueled a rapid growth in the geographic area of the United States. In the South, additional land was needed for cotton starting in the early 1800s for sale to English textile mills. In the North, timber could be used for building cities, and agriculture could produce food for those cities.

Until 1750 Indians retreated gradually from the Atlantic Coast. Even as late as 1800, Indians were holding their own militarily and economically with the European merchants. The industrial revolution created a juggernaut, however, that overwhelmed Indians over the course of the nineteenth century. In 1870 the United States had completed a rail network; Indian businesses were precarious. Indians lacked the political power to retain ownership of valuable resources and without a resource base their businesses shrank or failed to grow.

The expansion of the American economy continued in the twentieth century, with rapid growth having only one major setback, the Great Depression of the 1930s. World War II restarted the economic engine, which did not falter again until the mid-1970s, when the golden age of capitalism ended. In the 1970s, during the time of the two OPEC (an international alliance of oil-producing nations) oil embargoes, the rate of increase in worker productivity in the United States slowed suddenly and mysteriously. The price of energy rose for a time, which added to the difficulties. The economies of Asia, Africa, and Latin America became more important. Because the U.S. government overspent, the United States became a debtor nation as debt to foreign nations rose higher than the value of U.S. credit to foreign nations. The collapse of the Soviet Union in 1989, however, was followed by a revitalization of the American economy even as other regions of the world, including the former Soviet Union, continued to have economic difficulties. At the start of the new millienium, emerging ecological problems such as global warming present new difficulties to capitalism.

As the general American economy weakened, some American Indians began to develop businesses of their own within the newly changed system. The change in capitalism coincided with a political change, the acceptance of Indian self-government. By the late 1980s, as Indians began to assert greater control over their tribal governments, they began to control the economies on their reservations. The weakened U.S. capitalist market began to show niches into which Indian enterprise could squeeze. Indians began to hold onto their marketable natural resources (land, oil, minerals), and in some cases reclaim them, thus strengthening resource-based business. Tribes near large population-centers developed gaming enterprises in spite of opposition from state governments. Widespread economic growth on Indian reservations, however, has not occurred, because substantial barriers remain for non-gaming tribes. A major obstacle is U.S. government trust responsibility and regulatory control over Indian land and resources, which has resulted from two centuries of sustained subordination to industrial capitalist forces.

The Consequences of Contact

American Indians had markets, meaning they traded goods, before contact with Europeans. Particular types of sea shells, called wampum, were used as money. Goods produced in one part of the continent have been found in homesites and old cities far from the place of production, such as Cahokia, a large city near present-day St. Louis, and many cities in what is now Mexico. In such trades, one type of good, such as pottery, was exchanged directly for another, such as leather. Trading also occurred in which money, in the form of processed strings of sea shells, would be obtained by selling one good and later used to purchase another.

When two different economies begin to trade with one another, both can benefit considerably. Trade with Europe opened up new possibilities for Indians. They could sell goods to be transported to Europe, and they could purchase useful European goods, particularly metal ones. A consequence of the opening of trade between Europe and the Native Americas was an increase in the income levels of both Europeans and Native Americans. The improved position of American Indians, however, was masked by the rapid depopulation that occurred as a result of disease. American Indians were unable to withstand large-scale epidemics of small-pox and other communicable diseases brought over by Europeans. Between 1500 and 1800, the Native population fell from more than 5 million to less than 1 million people. This freed a great deal of land for use by European colonists, whose population increased to 5 million.

American Indians and the Mercantile Economy

Throughout the sixteenth century, Europe's economy grew as its merchants increased their levels of trading. The largest part of this pattern in North America was the sale of fur. Beaver was especially valuable, and both the French and English sought to purchase cured and processed beaver pelts from Indians.

During the entire mercantile era, three different ways of managing natural resources coexisted: community property, private property, and open-access. Indians conceived of a hunting area as the property of a whole community, which set up rules that limited the amount of harvest. Usually someone in a community who understood the resource advised everyone on its use. Lands between Indian community-controlled land were open-access areas. Europeans saw resources in one of two ways: either as private property, owned by an individual, or as open-access, in which anyone could take food without concern for resource limitations or traditional Indian hunting areas. The difficulty for Indians was to maintain their community control of hunting areas in the face of the open-access desires of Europeans. During the mercantile era, Indians were able to maintain their control to a great degree. Europeans, familiar only with the concepts of private property and open-access, failed to understand the management methods of the Native peoples. Because the words *enterprise* and *corporation* assume well-defined businesses based on private property, one must recognize that Indian business activity during this period was not organized as enterprises or corporations.

The nature of economic activity differed with the complexity of the Indian communities. Indian "enterprise" was connected to the family, clan, or town structure of each Indian nation. When families controlled territory, "business" was conducted by the family. When a town controlled a territory, business was conducted by the leadership of the town.

In the southeastern part of what became the United States, Indian tribes such as the Cherokee, Choctaw, Chickasaw, and Creek lived in towns. The chiefs of these towns collected a share of products from the members of the town and could use the corn, squash, and other products collected both to care for people who needed food and to trade for needed goods from Europe. They could buy from whichever European colony offered the best trade values, often alternating between trading with the French and English. Indians traded corn and deerskins, purchasing muskets, pots, axes, and blankets. By serving as economic intermediaries, chiefs maintained their political positions as well. They could distribute the European goods to the members of their towns. Indian society was based on giving and receiving gifts, with the leaders being those who gave the most.

Another example of community resource management was the hunting areas of the Cree east of James Bay in Canada. These were organized into family hunting areas, with a "boss" responsible for allocating harvest in each area. When beaver were valuable, the authority of the bosses increased. A non-family member could harvest for food, but the hide belonged to the family or group that controlled the area. At various trading posts, the hides were traded with Europeans for manufactured goods.

In the Pacific Northwest, land and resources were partitioned into areas controlled by "houses." The heads of these houses, the titleholders, regulated salmon harvest as well as other harvesting activities on the lands controlled by his or her house. Title-holding lineages maintained their resource management rights by hosting periodic feasts or potlatches in which they distributed significant amounts of goods to other titleholders. Prestige, power, and access to resources depended upon the ability to share the product of the land with other houses.

European and American approaches to resource-based business differed also in the methods used to distribute the product of hunts. Indians gave each other gifts. A successful hunter was obligated to share his good fortune with his community. Leaders in villages or towns were expected to give more gifts than other people. In the Pacific Northwest, the practice of gift-giving was conducted through potlatches. Indian gift-giving was not a one-way affair, however; the person receiving gifts became obligated to give gifts in return. In the European approach, individuals owned what they harvested. They sold, rather than gave away, surplus. Prestige and power came from owning and holding much property, not from giving it away.

In exchanging goods, both cultures came to understand the ways in which the other side traded. Europeans gave gifts in return for beaver, the amount of gifts being determined by prices set in the European market. Indians understood the effect of prices; if the French were giving fewer gifts for beaver pelts than the English, Indians would take their beaver pelts to the English.

During the mercantile era, Indians did not have to cede control of resources to Europeans. They harvested in their traditional hunting areas and traded furs, hides, and other products of the land for the clothing, guns, and tools available from Europe. Despite disease, Indian populations were equal to European populations. In particular areas of the continent, hunting by Europeans in Indian areas did lead to excessive harvests by both Indians and non-Indians. Some Indians also hunted in other Indians' areas without control. When no one had clear control of an area, its resources were in danger of overuse.

The distinctive feature of market organization in the mercantile era (1600–1750) is that Indian governments retained considerable power over large areas of North America. The European methods of organizing land use and trade, through private property and selling goods for prices determined by markets also under government control, were limited to coastal areas controlled by the colonial government. Indian methods of using land through community control were strong in other areas, where trade involved exchange of gifts. The area between was mixed, with both approaches compromising with each other, or simply competing for resources in an open-access manner.

American Indians and the Industrial Revolution

The relatively even balance of power between non-Indian colonies and confederations of Indians, such as the Iroquois in New York or the Cherokee and Choctaw in the American South, began to change in the middle of the eighteenth century. Indian business remained based on agriculture and the products of wild lands, forest, and prairies. Non-Indian business increasingly began to

How They Till the Soil and Plant (1591). Drawing by Le Moyne from an engraving by Theodore de Bry, *America* part II, plate XXIII. (Public Domain)

be based on a growing industrial sector. The English used cotton and wool to weave new, cheaper, and better cloth. Textile mills were established in America as well. As the mills' ability to purchase cotton increased, plantation owners in the South began to expand their operations.

The Cherokee in Georgia managed to stay in their homeland for many decades after the Industrial Revolution. They developed plantations, selling cotton also. They built a strong economy on their own lands, which made neighbors envious. Non-Indians developed a pattern of using military force to remove Indians, enabling them to take over Indian enterprises and land. This happened throughout the South. The policy of removal, formally adopted by the United States in 1830, allowed forceful removal of Indians from the entire Eastern United States to areas across the Mississippi River, in present-day Oklahoma and Kansas.

By 1850 Indians in different parts of North America had different types of market relationships with non-Indians. In the West and Pacific Northwest, the pattern

of trade that had existed during the mercantile era continued. Indians sold food, furs, and deerskins for manufactured goods. But population pressure from the expanding United States had forced many Indian nations onto lands west of the Mississippi River. They had to turn to agriculture and developed large herds of cattle and horses. Indian enterprise consisted of family activities confined to these new lands.

Later in the nineteenth century, non-Indians entered lands controlled by Indians; common pool management changed from community property to an open-access system. Indians had been able to protect resource stocks against extinction by limiting harvests. Where anyone, Indian or non-Indian, could harvest buffalo, for instance, large herds were wiped out, and by 1890 the American bison narrowly escaped extinction.

The industrial era right after the Civil War coincided with the establishment of many reservations, exclusively for Indian occupancy. They offered the possibility of development of Indian enterprise, based on indigenous organizational principles. The process of reservation development ended abruptly in the late 1880s. Congress passed the General Allotment Act, which authorized the division of reservation lands among the Indians living on the reservation and supposedly imposed ownership of private property as a way to manage land. The amount of land given to each Indian was small, between forty and 160 acres. Many families found that their parcels of land were not contiguous. In addition, Indians did not have the funds to purchase the cattle or farm equipment needed.

Non-Indians moved onto the reservations, and they had advantages in the industrial economy. They had access to equipment and money for economic investment. The court system was on their side. Non-Indians usually controlled the stores on reservations. As a result, non-Indians established farms more easily than Indians. This was a period in which Indian enterprise had great difficulty. Individual Indians found working as laborers in non-Indian businesses easier than operating their own firms.

Patterns established during this period on agricultural reservations remained in place at the end of the twentieth century. Lands were allotted to individuals during the period from 1887 to 1934. On reservations such as the Umatilla Reservation in Oregon, the Crow Reservation in Montana, and many Sioux reservations, the result was severely checker-boarded land, because it had been divided among several joint owners, the descendants of an original allottee. Since the joint Indian owners owned such small portions of land, the Bureau of Indian Affairs (BIA) leased many of these individual allotments in large groups to non-Indian ranchers and farmers, who thereby gain actual control over much of the best grazing and agricultural land on the reservations.

In the Pacific Northwest, Indians who had lived by harvesting salmon found that very few salmon were surviving long enough to reach the fishing sites they traditionally used. Non-Indians, using boats, harvested at sea and caught the fish first. By mid-century, Indians were pushed out of the fishery, and states justified limiting Indian river-mouth harvesting by appeals to conservation.

A few tribal enterprises, such as the Menominee lumber mill in Wisconsin, managed to survive the allotment era; but these are special cases, dependent on favorable political circumstances. Because of support from a senator and because they had forested lands, the federal government did not force the Menominee to divide up the land. This is in contrast to the Quinault Reservation in Washington, where pressure from some Indians assigned to the reservation, not Quinaults, forced division of the forested lands among everyone. The consequence was massive clear-cuts of timber,

encouraged by the Bureau of Indian Affairs, and little development of Indian enterprise based on the forest.

In summary, the expansion of the industrial revolution throughout North America from 1750 to 1930 caused massive declines in Indian land ownership and business activity. Indians were denied an opportunity to participate in the expanding industrial economy because non-Indians obtained ownership of the most productive lands. Even after enormous Indian land cessions occurred, with reservations remaining, the reservation lands were often entered and partially conveyed to non-Indians. Commercial agriculture on irrigated lands was primarily non-Indian. Indians were left on the margins, as ranchers, laborers on commercial farms, and workers in non-Indian enterprises.

Although formal transfers of land to non-Indians decreased dramatically in the 1930s, because of the Indian Reorganization Act of 1934 (IRA), other forms of transfer grew in importance. Energy companies leased Indian land for oil and gas, and timber companies purchased Indian timber. Commercially valuable locations were leased with fifty- and one hundred-year leases at low rental rates. The federal government inundated tribal lands with water from reservoirs behind federally owned dams. While title to land remained held in trust for Indians, Indians had little control over the land and its resources.

American Indian Enterprise in the Post-Golden Age Era

During difficult times for the dominant capitalist economy, such as in the 1930s and from the mid 1970s to the mid 1990s, Indian enterprise was able to advance. When the general economy shrinks, pressure at the edges is reduced. Even though marketing products is difficult when the general economy is weak, the reduction of competition from non-Indians opens opportunities for Indians. Indian enterprise survives if it can become well-established in niches in the world economy. These niches are created by resource endowment, Indian skills, or jurisdictional openings. Examples of resource endowments are tribal timber stands and the presence of oil and gas reserves under reservation lands such as the Osage Reservation in Oklahoma. Indian skills support jewelry production in the Southwest. Smoke shops, which sell cigarettes without state tax, bingo halls, and casinos can operate because of jurisdictional openings that restrict application of state law to reservation governments and communities.

In 1987 the U.S. Census Bureau estimated that approximately 60,000 Indian firms existed throughout the United States. In 1992 the number of American Indian firms had risen to 103,386. The Census Bureau found an

A Navajo shepherd makes his living raising sheep, which are used to make the world-famous Navajo rugs. (Photo by Sara Wiles)

additional 2,738 Aleut-managed firms and 4,493 firms run by Inuit. In its economic censuses, the Census Bureau defines *firm* narrowly: nonagricultural business activities operated by individuals who declared business income on their federal tax form. All Indians are subject to federal income tax if they earn enough income. To become a potential respondent to the bureau's survey, individuals had to have enough income to require submission of the income tax form and had to be identifiable as Indian in some way. The survey form was sent to 21,380 American Indians and Alaska Natives. The Census Bureau estimated that an additional 31,600 nonagricultural firms were not identified. Agricultural firms were counted in the census of agriculture, which reported 7,134 Indian-owned farms and ranches in 1987, and 8,346 such farms in 1992. These numbers are included in the totals above.

The census definition of *firm* excludes corporations, including tribal corporations, as well as enterprise operated directly by tribal governments. A tribal corporation is not operated directly by a tribal government, since it has a board of directors between the

manager and the tribal council. Nonprofit corporations, such as the intertribal organizations concerned with assisting tribal enterprise, were also not counted. The Council of Energy Tribes (CERT), for instance, would not have been counted in this survey. CERT assists tribal groups that have mineral or energy resource endowments to manage and market their holdings. Economic activity organized in traditionally Indian ways, such as through family hunting activities, would be counted only if an Indian head of household sold products and reported them as sales receipts on a federal tax form.

In spite of these omissions, the 1987 survey provided information about Indian economic activity. (In 1992 Indians and Alaskan Native data by industry was combined with data on Asian and Pacific Islanders.) The 60,114 individually owned and operated firms were primarily in agriculture, forestry and fisheries, construction, retail trade, and services. These businesses consist of farmers, ranchers, logging truck operators, salmon fishers, carpenters, electricians, owners of small retail shops, accountants, and other enterprises typical of single-owner firms in a capitalist economy. The ranchers, farmers, and loggers are primarily located on reservations. Those with more mobile jobs, such as long-haul truckers, construction workers, and providers of services could be anywhere, on or off reservations. Because these firms are so diverse and are everywhere, specific information on them is difficult to obtain and hard to summarize. About 9,000 of the 21,000 firms surveyed had one or more employees other than the owner of the firm, indicating that most Indian firms are small.

How have Indians managed to create more than 100,000 firms by 1992? Many of the on-reservation firms were developed during the industrial era. Indians retained control of range land and timber land. As a result, individuals established ranches, and a great many Indians own herds of cattle. Some individuals worked as loggers, selling their harvesting and transport services to non-Indian firms that purchased timber sale contracts for tribally owned timber. Work maintaining the productivity of the forest—thinning, planting, controlled burning—could be done with subcontracts to the federal government under buy-Indian regulations, which mandate that government contracts for work on or near Indian reservations be awarded to Indian firms or laborers.

On allotted reservations, where small parcels of land are jointly owned by many individuals, few Indians were able to succeed as farmers. Although some Indian farmers had equipment and land needed to operate at a large enough scale to do well, the general pattern remained—the legacy of allotment was that non-Indian farming operations dominated use of productive land, even if it was Indian owned.

Another area that developed for Indians was manufacture of jewelry. On the Zuni and Hopi reservations particularly, distinctive styles developed that generated a large market. As a result, individual artisans pursued jewelry making. Other artistic pursuits, such as pottery, painting, and beadwork, also provided ways to earn a living.

A new development in recent times is tribal self-determination, where tribal governments increasingly make decisions without interference from the BIA. This opportunity creates ways for tribal government to encourage development of private and tribal enterprises. To do so, an Indian tribe must overcome a substantial number of barriers inherited from earlier periods. The administration of Indian affairs was purposely set up in ways that removed Indian control over their own resources and territory. In order to develop economically, a tribe needs to restructure its polity and economy in ways that benefit Indians rather than non-Indians. This is a long and hard struggle, not made easier by the high levels of unemployment, extensive poverty, and dependence on U.S. government sources for support and survival.

If it wishes to support business, a tribe must reorient its government toward support of economic enterprise. The key general principle is to provide a climate of relative certainty and stability. If a tribal court system will enforce contracts made by Indians, then an Indian can promise to repay a loan and be believed. If a non-Indian bank takes an Indian entrepreneur into tribal court, and the Indian in fact does owe the bank money, the tribal court makes him pay. When that happens, banks are willing to support individual Indians who are able to make money in business. This has happened on some reservations. Among the Confederated Salish and Kootenai Tribes of the Flathead Indian Reservation in western Montana, the tribal council respects an independent judiciary, where court decisions are not unduly pressured by private or government intervention. A great deal of economic development on the Flathead Reservation occurs as private enterprise by tribal members. There are smoke shops, retail stores, construction companies, logging operations, restaurants, ranches, and farms. The private sector is probably stronger than the public sector, which consists of about three tribal enterprises.

In the Southwest, tribes needed to obtain control of water and to regain control of land leased to non-Indians. In the Pacific Northwest, Indians needed to regain the right to fish. Tribes owning oil, gas, and minerals needed to obtain better prices for their resources or better enforcement of leases already made by the federal government. The Passamaquoddy and Penobscot in Maine succeeded in regaining title to 300,000 acres of land in Maine as well as $80.6 million to offset claims to additional land.

The immediate consequence of tribal success in the legal area is an increase in opportunity for Indian enterprise. Tribes that had lost their right to fish were able to develop new fishing enterprises. In Washington State, under the Boldt decision, the federal courts upheld Indian treaty rights to half of all salmon entering Washington state rivers. In the Southwest, tribes who won water rights were able to develop agricultural activities. The Navajo set up the Navajo Agricultural Products Enterprise, a large-scale, irrigated farming operation south of Farmington, New Mexico. It is the largest of the tribal farming enterprises. Others exist in Arizona, with the AkChin enterprise on the AkChin Reservation particularly well known. These farms use as much equipment and advanced technology as any industrial farming operation in the United States.

The development of separate jurisdictional space on reservations allowed the development of two special kinds of businesses: smoke shops and gambling enterprises. Both businesses present economic opportunity because they are not subject to state law on the reservation. The U.S. Constitution and many legal decisions uphold direct federal and Indian government relations, while excluding state jurisdiction over Indian affairs. For cigarette sales, individual Indians set up retail stores selling cigarettes without charging state taxes, thus having lower prices and higher volume sales. States objected and took the cases to court. The result of the cases was that tribal governments had to intervene and regulate cigarette sales in order to protect the rights of individual reservation entrepreneurs. As a result in the 1970s many Indians were able to get started in retail sales. Many smoke shops have grown into full-service convenience stores, selling food and gasoline, renting video-tapes, and offering gambling machines to the general public. Battles between states and tribes over cigarette sales continue, however, because states think up new ways to attempt to tax the cigarettes.

Another continuing battle occurs over gambling. The same jurisdictional void that allows cigarette sales also provides a space for tribes to engage in gambling. The first establishments were large bingo halls. The Seminole tribe of Florida, located near Miami, set up a bingo operation that drew huge crowds. Other tribes near large population centers rapidly followed. The courts left the operations open and established the rule that a tribe could do anything that a state permitted, even if the state limited the activity severely. Many states allowed charitable organizations to use bingo as money-raising programs. Indians expanded the bingo games to enormous sizes. State opposition created federal legislation, which required that states and tribes write compacts to regulate gambling on reservations. The principle that a tribe could engage in any type of gambling that was allowed under state law remained in the legislation.

The data from the survey by the Bureau of the Census found substantial numbers of Indian firms in the categories that include smoke shops: food stores (895) and miscellaneous retail stores (5,350). These counts exclude tribal enterprise. All tribes that are running gambling operations should be added to the 1,476 private Indian firms providing amusement and recreation services.

The Nez Percé tribe in Idaho obtained the right to purchase timber from their own lands, enabling them to resell the timber for higher prices than the Bureau of Indian Affairs was receiving, by shipping logs to Japan. Other tribes, such as the White Mountain Apache Tribe and the Confederated Tribes of the Warm Springs Reservation, owned lumber mills that cut tribal timber.

A visitor to the Navajo Reservation would see all types of Indian enterprise. Individual Indians make jewelry and sell the jewelry in roadside stands. They have sheep herds and continue to make wool rugs. The tribe once operated a lumber mill, and at the end of the twentieth century operated an electric utility, a large farming operation, and many small enterprises. Individuals had smoke shops near the borders. The old pattern, in which non-Indians operated the retail shops and the trading posts, was superseded by large retail outlets. On the Navajo Reservation, these are in some cases operated by outside companies. But individual Indians are also operating retail stores.

The White Mountain Apache Reservation in Arizona has a ski resort, a lumber mill, a casino, a construction company, many retail outlets, and a tribal herd of cattle. The White Mountain Apache, much more than many other tribes, have organized their economy with tribal enterprise.

Alaska presents some major differences from the rest of the United States. The relationship between tribal governments and enterprise are different because of the Alaska Native Claims Settlement Act (ANCSA) of 1971. This act settled Alaska Native land claims, left Alaska Natives with 44 million acres, and created thirteen regional for-profit corporations and about two hundred village corporations. Unlike in the rest of the United States, Alaska Natives have been forced to organize their economic enterprises as profit-making corporations. The Census Bureau survey identified four thousand American Indian and Alaska Native firms in Alaska in 1987. Because of the definitions used in the census survey, none of the thirteen regional or more than two hundred village corporations created by ANCSA should have been counted in the survey. Even if they were, there is considerable business enterprise in Alaska by Natives that is outside of the corporations set up by the ANCSA.

Between 1971 and 1989, the regional corporations did not have good profit records. Considerable debate has occurred about the causes of the poor performance; and the debate is nearly unresolvable with the information presently available. On one hand, the corporations were not set up like normal corporations in the capitalist world, because shares could not be sold. Supporters of capitalism point to this flaw as a complete explanation for the poor performance. On the other hand, the corporations also did not have clear title to their land for many years. Even after obtaining title, subsurface and surface rights are held by regional and village corporations, respectively. They do not have shareholders experienced in methods of corporate governance. Corporate structures cost at least

$100,000 a year to administer. The corporations have been involved in many legal battles concerning the authority of other federal agencies, such as the Securities and Exchange Commission, to regulate their behavior. Village corporations are more concerned with preserving subsistence rights, while regional corporations are profit oriented. This creates disagreement between long-term goals of sustainable resource management and short-term goals for profits. The complexity of circumstances surrounding Alaska Native corporations makes it difficult to determine which are the true causes of poor performance.

Starting in 1992, the Northern Pacific Fisheries Council allocated a portion of the fish harvested from the Bering Sea to Alaska Native communities. The communities formed six Community Development Corporations, which were financed with quotas from the fishery; hence the program was called the Community Development Quota program (CDQ). Building on lessons learned from the failures and problems with Alaska Native Corporations under the settlement act, the new corporations utilized village governing structures instead of creating entirely new entities. The State of Alaska provided initial financial and management oversight, creating incentives for good management. The CDQ program created considerable community participation in economic development and benefited Alaskan Natives living on the Bering Sea.

Conclusion

Historic and contemporary individual and tribal entrepreneurs on Indian reservations are inseparable from political events and political development. In the mercantile era, tribal political power protected traditional economic organization. The struggle over Indian property dates from the expansion of capitalism to reservations. Often legal rights were retained by Indians, in the process of ceding actual control over resources. This political history then colors all development activities. Tribes are fighting to regain control of reservation resources and to maintain or expand their powers to regulate economic activity on reservations.

When a tribe makes progress toward regaining control over reservation resources, it then can create a framework of relative security regarding government policy in order to allow economic development to occur. A stable judicial system can support development of individual Indian businesses. Clear divisions of power between council, judiciary, and chairman within a tribal government can support tribal enterprise. Because many tribes place maintenance of political autonomy and cultural distinctiveness equal in importance to economic development, some types of economic activity are limited, especially if outside interests are involved.

At the end of the twentieth century, the weakening of capitalism as a political force on reservations has allowed tribes to establish institutions that combine capitalist ideas with traditional Indian ones. While the hybrid institutions are not a return to pre-1750 patterns, they are distinctly Indian in their formulation.

Ronald L. Trosper
Northern Arizona University

◆ MODERN TRIBAL ECONOMIC DEVELOPMENT

Within the United States a large number of distinct cultures are present among the aboriginal population. However, these populations face severe social and economic problems due to past treatment by the federal government. As a result, many of the distinct values and traditional practices of Native American tribes are threatened. But hope is available and cultural, social, and economic progress is being made. As such, a manifest imperative in Indian Country is maintaining the cultures and strengthening sovereign powers. One of the methods of achieving this goal is developing tribal resources within a cultural context. Modern tribal governments face the challenges of moving their communities from the status quo of high unemployment rates, low educational achievement levels, and serious social problems.

Many scholars maintain that economic development is a means to the end of sustaining tribal character, and as such it is vital to formulate all development plans with an understanding of how they impact the overall societal makeup. Only when the individual tribe has control of its resources and sustains its identity as a distinct civilization does economic development make sense; otherwise, the tribe must choose between cultural integrity and economic development. A common misconception involves the seeming conflict between maintaining a tribe's cultural heritage and increased economic activity on the reservation. However, it has been shown that developing the economy increases the potential for strengthening and developing the tribal culture.

The economy is the production mechanism of society. Economic activity is not the end result of anything; rather it is the engine that drives society to higher culture levels. The quest is to design an economic structure that allows the rest of society to maintain its cultural integrity and develop new and improved methods of living. In many cases, the cultural issues outweigh economic activity.

Tribes are interested in developing their economies as a means to self-determination. In other words, developing natural and human resources can strengthen their culture. Clearly, conflicts between culture and economic activity can arise, but this is the common vision only because past development strategies have either been conducted by outside interests for the benefit of outsiders, or the strategies were designed with the goal of assimilating the tribes into the mainstream capitalist styled economy. What is necessary is a rethinking of the potential gains from activities designed by and for Native Americans, while reducing the negative aspects of those activities. These gains include increasing opportunities for and interest by tribal members in their traditions, heritage, language, and identity. Reducing the negative aspects includes designing environmentally sound and culturally sensitive activities. This combination of more positive and fewer negative conditions aims the community toward cultural development as a result of the economic development. This is the first step in achieving healthy communities.

Cultural development involves an ever-evolving system of cultural subsystems, including the spiritual, economic, familial, and ceremonial, among others. This dynamic collection of subsystems and the compatibility among the various sectors defines not only the society as a whole, but also the individuals within that society. This social compatibility paradigm dictates that these subsystems are always changing to bring about a compatible equilibrium. Understating the situation on many Native American reservations, the current cultural system has spiraled downward due to federal policies and governance. The main reason for the current situation is the fact that these societies have undergone drastic changes in several vital subsystems. Most importantly, the federal interference in these communities essentially destroyed many economic and political subsystems. Instead of progressive change being determined within the existing culture, the changes came about as imposed changes by outsiders. One current challenge is to reinvigorate the economic subsystem to help elevate the culture systems of indigenous communities.

Economic development is the engine for overall social development. As Native America integrates into the global economy, decisions have to be made regarding economic activity such that a cohesive structure develops within a cultural context. Using these terms,

we can think of culture as holding together the communities on reservations. The shared property and common experiences provide the feeling of connectedness. Tribal governments are in positions to either better improve the overall community, or cause increased isolation among their members. The social difficulties together with continued isolation extend the problems facing tribal governments. Alternatively, activities that increase the feelings of community, specifically economic ones improve the overall social structure.

The Economic Development Process

It is very important to understand that economic development—the development of jobs and incomes—is a complex process. Instead of looking at a single project at a time, an overall plan of action must be viewed to understand how the different pieces fit together. The development process can be thought of as a cycle of four stages. Although it is not necessary that all four stages occur for any one community, the stages do tend to lead from one to the next. It is also important to recognize that once set into action, the different stages can—and usually do—occur simultaneously in different directions. For simplicity, these four stages can be termed *import earning, import-replacing, development of new and better products*, and *export generation*.

The first stage of the cycle of growth involves an initial export industry earning imports. At first glance it might be said that an economy facing an excess of a 50 percent unemployment rate and the concomitant dire poverty does not have many such export industries; however, reservation economies clearly have the ability to import products. Tribes do earn revenues from extractive enterprises such as mines, forestry projects, and water sales. Other tribal and private enterprises provide some degree of earnings. A variety of federal, state, and tribal government activities provide additional employment. Besides these salaries, royalties, and profits earned from tribal activities, other major sources of funds are transfer payments and trust account earnings. Recently, many tribes have begun to earn imports with the profits from their gaming facilities. In a few cases, these profits are substantial. Therefore most tribes do satisfy the requirement of earning imports. Moreover, residents typically purchase private imports from the border towns on day trips. Thus, the first stage of the cycle is initially satisfied.

The second stage, and one of primary importance in the current context, is the development of import-replacing industries within the local economy. In this stage the reservation economy begins to produce locally hitherto imported products. The import-replacing phase allows for a drastic reduction of the leakages to

An Anishinabe man and woman gather wild rice from a canoe in Minnesota. (Courtesy of the Minnesota Historical Society)

border communities. In terms of reservation economies, this primarily means an increase in retail and service activity. An extension of this idea is the advent of actually producing some of the products previously imported.

Two of the best examples of this import-replacement can be seen within the economies of the Hualapai and Navajo nations. Both of these First Nations have made specific efforts at developing the retail sectors within their communities. So now instead of driving many miles to border towns, residents can shop at local stores for groceries and other such items. Another example is Cochiti Pueblo where they opened a laundromat in the early 1990s. This new facility was soon overwhelmed with business.

Another important avenue for import-replacing is the local provision of services such as plumbing, electrical, and construction. Some reservations are developing their own road divisions for paving and repairing road systems. Other examples include hair care, accounting and tax services and all the other types of services available in non-reservation communities.

The import-replacement phase expands the understanding that trade patterns should follow well-known economic fundamentals. Reducing transport distances, and developing new and improved technology—not to mention lowered wage rates on the reservation—may well allow a tribe to import-replace some previously imported products at a cost savings. The problem is to properly identify those products that can be successfully produced by the tribe, which of course is the question any development plan must answer. Regional science analysis has produced various techniques to help determine the sectors and industries potentially ripe for expansion, but these problems are beyond the scope of the current discussion. Clearly, the activities to be import-replaced are reservation specific, but once the products and services are identified and the tribe begins to domestically produce the product, it is then possible that the direction of the trade actually reverses through the process, which is the next stage in the cycle.

The third stage involves developing new and innovative products and production techniques during the import-replacing phase. For example, modern Navajo arts and crafts industries include world-renowned techniques for weaving and silversmithing. Techniques for dying, spinning, and weaving wool have progressed from rudimentary ones to advanced techniques allowing for intricate designs and patterns. Originally, Navajos developed these industries for domestic consumption of blankets and jewelry; however, these industries are now significant sources of income for individual artisans and the tribally managed Navajo Arts and Crafts Enterprise.

The fourth stage encompasses developing these new techniques and products into new export industries, which provide increased or substitute import earning income. At this stage, the process cycles: new import-replacing takes place, which develops new products, which cultivates a new phase of exports. Thus a cycle of vigorous growth is obtained.

A community can become involved with the development process by engaging in a series of strategies that lead to a more prosperous future. In order for the process to be successful all that is necessary is for a community to be a cohesive entity as a central identity. Nowhere is this identity more pronounced than on and near reservations. Political borders are unimportant in the development process, except for defining sovereignty, and legal and tax systems and their impacts. What makes a reservation and the border towns a cohesive whole is the cultural and economic linkages existing within a definable region with a definable population. The development cycle begins with no other precondition other than an initial earning of imports, which currently occurs within reservation economies.

Growth and development are a process, and not a static burst of energy. Explosive episodes in Indian Country will start small and grow over time. The initial episode will likely evolve over the next fifteen to twenty years. This follows 100 to 500 years of stagnation and deterioration during the periods of colonization and federal oversight.

Growth occurs from the import-replacing and export development process due to five interwoven considerations. First, as import-replacing occurs an increased number and diversity of employment opportunities develop. Second, as employment earnings increase and the multiplier effect obtains, the region has enlarged import markets providing imports of new and different kinds. Third, as activity and employment increases, jobs and activity spread throughout the community, thereby increasing economic activity in the surrounding areas. Fourth, as the process continues there will be new uses for existing technology and new technological developments as entrepreneurial activity occurs. And last, as the process proceeds and new businesses are opened, there will be an increase in the capital stock of the community. These five forces of growth lead to increased economic activity and employment, and lead towards the development of the cycling of growth: new exports earning increased and new imports.

Constraints on Growth

While it is difficult to generalize across such a wide range of different cultures and events, it does seem evident that the policies of the federal government toward Native Americans have not reflected a sincere concern for Indian communities or their economic interests. On the contrary, federal government regulations and management have inhibited Indian use of human and natural resources for economic growth.

It is possible to identify the several important factors constraining reservation development: (1) fluctuating federal policies, such as containment of most Indian people on reservations, the division of tribal communal lands into small private allotments (the General Allotment Act of 1887 and others), reconstitution of tribes by the Indian Reorganization Act of 1934, termination of reservations during the 1950s, and self-determination, have led to fragmented resources and populations; (2) loss of self-sufficiency and imposed dependency on the federal government through Indian wardship to the Bureau of Indian Affairs (BIA) led to mismanagement of resources and loss of local control; (3) lost self-esteem through cultural genocide brought about by European-based education in schools and the conversion of many Indians to Christianity and other non-Indian worldviews led to cultural incoherence; (4) low expectations based on a history of U.S. interference under laws created to divest Indians of their land and resources further reduced the economic and social assets of the communities; (5) lack of access to capital for investing in productive economic ventures limits potential development; (6) disrupted political institutions that breed nepotism and politicize economic management cause instability and limit long-term planning; (7) subjugated and impoverished reservation communities that do not foster success, social acceptance, and cultural identity among school age populations reduce educational achievement; and (8) bureaucratic and political stultification of initiative resulted in generations of frustrated and restrained tribal leaders.

School board members tour the construction site of a new school building on the Wind River Reservation. (Photo by Mike McClure)

Current Economic Activities

Although much of Indian history is a tragic tale recounting suffering, changes are taking place that suggest that the cycles of poverty and despair can be broken. The Indian Self-Determination and Education Assistance Act (P.L. 93–638) passed in 1975 has empowered tribal governments to contract for the provision of services that were formerly provided by the BIA. This change combined with the growing levels of professional expertise in all areas of tribal program administration is bringing about major changes in the intention and outcomes of economic development efforts. In other words, tribal leaders are now making their own decisions based on their own ideals instead of federal bureaucrats making decisions for questionable, at best, reasons.

Indian reservations face the major task of using their existing natural and human resource base to create jobs, provide higher standards of living, and improve social welfare for their tribal members. Apart from vigorously import-replacing retail and service sectors, reservation economic development efforts at increasing exports fall into the areas of energy and mining, agriculture and livestock raising, forestry, gaming, cultural tourism, arts and crafts, and manufacturing and assembly. As these sectors increase, additional import-replacement can take place in terms of retail and various services in the cycle of vigorous growth.

Energy and Mining.   In 1973 OPEC, an international cartel of oil-producing states, imposed an oil embargo on most Western nations and created a crisis that called attention to the strategic importance of Indian-owned energy resources. Over 200 billion tons of coal, 4.2 billion barrels of oil, and 17.5 trillion cubic feet of natural gas are located on Indian reservations in the West.

These energy resources are significant sources of tribal income for the forty-two members of the Council of Energy Resource Tribes (CERT), an organization of energy resource-rich Indian tribes. CERT monitors and negotiates resource contracts for the sale of oil, coal, gas and minerals found on reservation lands. CERT was organized because BIA leasing policies caused much controversy when the BIA often sold Indian coal, oil, and other natural resources at less than fair market value.

On the Navajo and Hopi reservations, for example, coal companies were granted fifty-year leases at prices of less than 50 cents per ton at a time when the market price was over $70 per ton. Recently, a stunning legal decision was reached regarding the negotiations for this coal. A federal judge determined that the Interior Department is not bound by federal law to uphold the best interests of the Navajo Nation regarding the lease negotiations. Although it was clear that the negotiations between the Interior Department and Peabody Coal Company clearly harmed the Navajo Nation, no remedy is forthcoming.

Royalties that should have been paid to the tribes on the basis of the resource's market value have been underreported or stolen. The Wind River Reservation in Wyoming lost over $750,000 in oil royalties during a nine-year period. Related to this is the fact that energy-resource royalties have not been as beneficial as hoped in terms of improving employment opportunities for tribal members. In part, this is due to the nature of jobs in the oil drilling and coal mining industries, which require fairly high skill levels. Most reservation Indians do not have training in the right skills for employment in these industries. Furthermore, many high-paying jobs are controlled by unions which promote the interests of their members over opportunities to hire local qualified residents.

More recently, tribal self-governance has resulted in several leases being re-negotiated in favor of the tribes. The development of these exports and the improved incomes allows Indian tribes to earn imports.

Farming and Ranching.   Several Indian tribes, such as the Cherokee, Creek, and Hopi, have long traditions as farmers. Organized around common land use, families and clans worked together and shared the produce. Between 1887 and 1934 the allotment of reservation land to individual Indians destroyed traditional tribal obligations and ownership and led to a widespread pattern of fractionated reservation land ownership. The Indian Reorganization Act of 1934 prohibited further allotment and alienation of Indian lands.

The general patterns of land ownership on reservations vary. For example, there is "fee simple" land that belongs to individuals; "trust land" that belongs to the tribe but is held in trust by the BIA; and land that belongs to individuals that is BIA-regulated. Of the more than 54 million acres of Indian land, 42.1 million acres, or 77 percent, is tribally owned, and 10.6 million (20 percent) is owned by individuals under BIA trust relations.

Because of the complications arising from the inheritance of allotted lands, parcels of land that could be commercially valuable are often broken up into small disconnected tracts. Such disparate land holdings and the fact that trust land cannot be used as collateral to back up a loan, make it difficult for Indian landowners to get loans for investing in farm equipment, seeds, and fertilizer. Moreover, because of low investment levels, average productivity is much lower than comparable nonreservation farmland. In 1983 Congress enacted the Indian Land Consolidation Act to help reduce the fractionalization of Indian land ownership. Under this law, tribes can establish inheritance codes to govern the disposition of real property. Over time this power may help improve and consolidate Indian land.

Tribes like the Mille Lacs Band of Chippewa in Minnesota are trying to overcome the land fractionation problem by starting a Land Purchase Trust Fund to restore their 61,000-acre reservation. Some of this land was lost to competing claims by non-Indian farmers and timber companies, who purchased fee simple allotted lands from Indian owners, removing it from control and ownership by the Mille Lacs Band.

Leasing trust lands is a strategy used to induce non-Indians to invest and generate income for reservation job creation. About 7 million acres of Indian trust land is leased to non-Indian farmers and ranchers. Another 8 million acres are under mineral leases to large non-Indian companies. The leasing of Indian land resulted in about $68 million in 1984. Of this, $16.8 million was generated by business leases, while $48.4 million was gained from agricultural leases. Oil, gas, coal, and other mineral leases produced over $230 million. While an important source of revenue, the leasing strategy often focuses too narrowly on income generation while ignoring the economic, social, and environmental impacts on the reservation community.

Today, tribal leaders on reservations are starting to recognize the importance of economic development projects that preserve the integrity of their traditional cultures. For example, five Indian Pueblos in New Mexico established a confederation to grow and sell their traditional foodstuff, blue corn. The organization contracts with individual farmers and processes the corn into consumer products, which it sells at fairs and through organic-gardening magazines. In light of this, activities that complement cultural practices such as cattle and sheep ranching, fishing, and truck farming offer jobs and ways to increase the incomes of Indian families. Some tribes also have been managing buffalo, elk, and other game herds for both traditional uses and the sale of hunting licenses.

The lack of available capital funding can be clearly seen by comparing farms and ranches on Indian lands with those on neighboring non-Indian lands. For example, driving along Highway 2 in Montana shows very capital intensive farming and ranching where many of the fields have various watering systems. Then a sign announces that you have entered the Fort Belknap Indian Community and the watering systems are not present and the apparent quality of the fields distinctly lessens.

However as tribal governments gain control of their resources, more capital funding is becoming available. For example, the Colorado River Indian Tribes run and operate a system of farms that produce a variety of crops. This profitable enterprise earns the tribes substantial imports.

Forestry. American Indians own about 54 million acres, or about 2 percent of the total land area in the country. Of this, about 5.3 million acres contain commercially valuable timber resources. This translates into approximately 40 billion board feet, or 1.5 percent of the country's total supply.

Forestry contributes substantial revenues for many reservations. Tribes engaged in forestry operations are largely harvesters of raw timber, which is sent to mills outside the reservations. Some reservations such as the Warm Springs and White Mountain Apache operate their own mills. The forestry industry, however, is subject to major cycles of fluctuating demand and profit, which contributes to the difficulty of creating a long-term stable economy around this enterprise.

Since timber-harvesting activities were historically supervised by the BIA there is considerable bureaucratic red tape and opportunity for mismanagement. A government audit of the Red Lake Chippewa of Minnesota discovered that the BIA had misplaced as much as $500,000 per year. In other instances, BIA timber sale accounts have not been balanced in over seventy years. Forestry is a good example of how BIA over-regulation of Indian resources often interferes with reservation economic growth.

As with the Peabody Coal Company case, federal officials have been found to ignore the best interests of the tribes for which they are responsible for. In a classic case, the Quinault tribe sued because the BIA was selling timber for as low as $16 per thousand board feet when the market price exceeded $1,000. And as with the Peabody Coal case, the BIA indicated that managing the resources in the best interest of the Quinault tribe was not mandated by federal law.

More recently, more tribes are taking control of their own resources under the auspice of PL 638. A study in the early 1990s showed very clear evidence of BIA mismanagement. Comparing seventy-five forests being harvested with either BIA management or self-management, it was found that Indian managed forests were far more productive and profitable than BIA managed forests. One startling result, although not that surprising after all, was that adding a highly skilled BIA employee actually *reduced* the productivity of the timber enterprise. As seen with other types of economic activity, tribal management is far more successful than having the federal government managing resources.

Gaming. The issue of Indian gaming is particularly important today. As late as 1979 there were no significant bingo or gaming establishments on Indian reservations. By 1999 gaming income to Indian reservations was estimated at about $8.6 billion, or about 10 percent of all national gaming revenues. Gaming has become a leading source of income for some Indian tribes. Of 558 federally recognized tribes, 198 are engaged in gaming with 326 gaming operations. The Indian gaming industry employs roughly 200,000 people of which 75 percent are non-Indians: many gaming tribes are net importers of employment. A 1997 study showed that in Minnesota, gaming generated over $180 million in payroll and

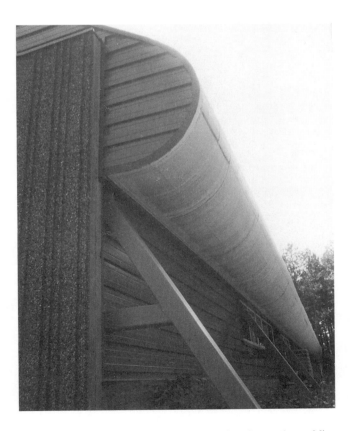

The casino on the Vermilion Reservation in northern Minnesota. (Courtesy of the UCLA American Indian Studies Center)

over $50 million in taxes. Indian gaming has become a major new export industry for several tribes.

Although only a small number of tribes have successful gaming operations, the new export industry is allowing for increased import earning. Several of the successful tribes are using the increased availability of funds to begin a round of import-replacement and development of alternative enterprises by diversifying their economic systems. Thus, for a few tribes, gaming operations are leading toward more successful community structures. The diversification and import-replacing involves several types of activities.

For example, some have used gaming as a means of generating income to support the elderly and sick, and to pay for health care, sanitation, and housing improvements. Some tribes have bought back ancient land, restored sacred and religious sites, worked to preserve traditional culture, created scholarship funds, and created numerous jobs. A good example of community benefits gained from bingo income is the Sycuan Indian community of Southern California. Most of the Sycuan gaming revenues go directly to financing health care, housing, and general assistance to Sycuan community members. In 1997 Caifornia gaming resulted in a $50 million reduction in AFDC payments with a reduction of $21 million to tribal members. As one tribal leader indicated, tribes are becoming taxpayers instead of tax users.

The success of the gaming facilities is allowing tribes to diversify in much the same way that Las Vegas has diversified. The completion of golf courses, resort hotels and entertainment facilities complements the gaming operations. These expanded facilities offer more employment and income potentials.

Cultural Tourism. Another export sector earning imports for tribes is the increasing market for cultural tourism. The idea of marketing selected aspects of Indian culture and traditions for the tourist trade can be an important business activity if properly managed. As long as the activities are self-determined by the tribes themselves with regard to sacred sites and cultural rituals, substantial economic activity can be garnered by developing tourism.

Some tribes have been successful, such as the Eastern Cherokee of North Carolina, who annually produce a pageant play, *Onto these Hills*, which portrays Cherokee life during forced removal to the West in the late 1830s. This also helps communicate Cherokee history and culture to large non-Indian audiences. Powwows and ceremonies performed before public audiences have been favorite tourist attractions for many years. Several Pueblo villages have long traditions of opening some ceremonies to public attendance. Major powwows, like the Crow Fair held near the Custer Battle Ground in southeastern Montana, are open to the public and are well attended by Indians and non-Indians alike. Another example is the new hotel operated by the Hualapai Nation. Combining the hotel operations with their river trips through the Grand Canyon and a visitation site on the rim of the Grand Canyon provides this tribe with substantial revenue. Many tribes use tourism revenues to finance tribal museums, art galleries, and annual powwows.

An important aspect of these cultural tourism activities is the increased demand for tribal members who can provide these services. As a result, there is increasing interest in traditional cultural activities and languages. In addition, the increased income among tribal members is allowing for the rejuvenation of traditional ceremonies and activities.

Arts and Crafts. Various types of Indian arts and crafts, such as jewelry, pottery, and woven textiles have become familiar to most Americans. In many instances the sale of these items plays an important role in supplementing limited household income, but only rarely have Indian arts and craft productions become more than small-scale industries.

There is often controversy within reservation communities over whether Indian artisans should make objects for sale to non-Indians, especially if the objects have had traditional sacred or ceremonial significance. Many items produced by Indian artists are not produced for sale, but for specific religious or ceremonial purposes. After the ceremony, the objects were usually destroyed, having served their purpose. For example, among the Hopi of Arizona, representations of ceremonial and ancestral rain spirits called kachinas are painted on the walls of kivas, circular ceremonial rooms below ground. The paintings of the Kachina spirits are made for one ceremony only and then are destroyed. They are not saved for posterity or for artistic display.

Among the Navajo of the Southwest, paintings made from different colored sands have special sacred or purification powers. The sand paintings often depict Navajo sacred beings or represent the order and balance of the universe. Sand paintings are used in curing ceremonies, where they help an Indian doctor restore harmony and balance to a patient, who sits within the sand painting. After the curing ceremony, the sand paintings are destroyed, and each new ceremony demands fresh sand paintings. Many sand paintings, however, are visually attractive, and upon seeing them, tourists have offered to buy them. Needing money, some Navajo started selling sand paintings but included small mistakes in the paintings so they would not desecrate the sacred power of the healing ceremonies. To those who objected to selling sand paintings to tourists, the sellers argued they were not selling sacred powers because they "broke" the painting's power by leaving deliberate mistakes in them, thereby preserving sacred knowledge and powers.

While there are development opportunities for the promotion of Indian arts and crafts, any tribally owned enterprise or cooperative seeking to capitalize on the growing demand faces tremendous competition from the existing brokers and from Indian art copies imported from foreign countries. Many reservations and co-operative enterprises between tribes have been successful in developing marketing enterprises. One example is the Navajo Arts and Crafts Enterprise. This vertical diversification essentially import-replaces the marketing aspect of the industry and provides employment and income for individuals not directly producing the artwork.

In addition to artifacts, several Native American artists are reaching levels of international success in literature and music. Sherman Alexie is a well-known writer and Joanne Shenandoah is a well-known musician. The popularity of these artists then stimulates further demand for cultural tourism and arts and crafts.

Manufacturing and Assembly.   Developing Indian reservations is frequently understood in terms of creating jobs. The federal government has attempted to induce private companies to expand manufacturing facilities to impoverished reservations. As a result, thousands of new jobs have been created in industries that manufacture consumer goods, electronic components, clothing, and the like.

It is very important that many tribes are exploring alternative economic development approaches. Often the capital for economic development comes from land claims suits against the federal government, mineral royalties, or large federal grants. After receiving $81.5 million to settle disputed land claims, the Passamaquoddy and Penobscot Indians in Maine invested in several commercial enterprises to promote tribal economic development. Dozens of other tribes have followed suit and aggressively pursued manufacturing opportunities. The Blackfeet tribe of Montana founded the Blackfeet Indian Writing Company, which makes pens, pencils, and markers. The company has generated millions of dollars in sales and provided badly needed jobs on the Blackfeet reservation, where unemployment ranged between 55 and 65 percent.

Many tribal governments see light industry as a means to providing long-term jobs and economic growth on Indian reservations. A few reservations, such as the Turtle Mountain and Devils Lake reservations of North Dakota and the Mississippi Choctaw near Philadelphia, Mississippi, have had significant success at managing electronic assembly plants, building military equipment, or manufacturing greeting cards. Indian reservation manufacturing and entrepreneurship is only a beginning, but light manufacturing may hold the greatest promise for ameliorating the deep economic poverty of many Indian reservations.

Another example is Apache Manufacturing. This tribal enterprise on the Whiteriver Apache Reservation produced various parts on a contract for McDonnell-Douglas. Following several attempts at manufacturing difference items, the manager approached McDonnell-Douglas, a major aircraft company recently bought by the Boeing aircraft company, and negotiated from the perspective that if McDonnell-Douglas was producing the Apache Helicopter, a highly successful military attack gunship, then they should at least buy some inputs from Apaches.

Conclusion

Even today, historical aspects of colonialism shape the progress of Indian economic development. The trust relationship designed to help prevent the continuing exploitation of Indians and further loss of their lands tends to inhibit reservation economic development. Several layers of BIA bureaucracy must approve tribal business decisions, which adds to the cost of doing business. Resource-owning tribes are saddled with unprofitable long-term leases negotiated by the BIA. Indian lands cannot be sold or encumbered without express congressional authorization, which inhibits its chances for raising working capital for business investment. Non-Indian businesses are often reluctant about locating on Indian reservations, and tribal councils may lack the business experience to oversee tribal business operations.

Another significant problem is the lack of economic linkages that sustain the benefits of economic development projects. Because there are few reservation businesses, Indians usually drive many miles to buy needed goods and services. Without a local economic base, most local income and revenues accruing to Indian communities are passed on to non-Indian businesses without much impact within the reservation economy. In order to capture income and employment enhancing effects, known as "multipliers," Indians must spend more income with businesses that hire Indian employees and invest in Indian communities.

As more and more tribes begin the process of self-determined economic activities the population is becoming more and more self-sufficient. The process of economic development via the cycle of vigorous growth is leading Indian nations to greater success. Import-replacing retail and service sectors allows the multiplier effect to reverberate the importance of incomes and employment. Vertically diversifying existing enterprises, such as mills for processing timber, is another example of import-replacement. Developing new products for export, such as cultural tourism, earns more imports and leads to further income and employment. When these activities are designed and managed by the indigenous populations, then not only do they tend to be more productive, they avoid conflicts between traditional cultures and resource management.

Over time, with complementary improvements in education and health care and increased political stability, more tribal communities are demonstrating economic successes. The history of American Indians demonstrates that the most important factor is that they do it on their own terms.

Dean Howard Smith
Northern Arizona Unversity

◆ AMERICAN INDIAN LABOR

Historical Background

Before Columbus. Not much is known about how the Natives of North America labored before Europeans arrived. There was probably a great deal of variety in their work and in the way they organized their labor. It certainly required complex division of labor to sustain the large complex societies that once occupied the Southwest and the Mississippi River valley. Certain types of work were probably assigned by gender and others by social position such as family or clan memberships. Presumably, these societies were organized hierarchically, so that the most unpleasant and disagreeable tasks were delegated to those in the lowest social positions. Some of these societies might have taken slaves from enemy villages who were then employed to perform the most undesirable labor.

Much of North America also was inhabited by small, nomadic hunting-and-gathering societies. Although these societies had simpler divisions of labor, gender and social position were probably still important for allocating work duties. These people probably spent most if not all their working lives in activities related to providing adequate food, shelter, and clothing for survival. Unlike larger complex societies, small populations cannot ordinarily produce economic surpluses large enough to allow some members to engage full-time in practicing art, medicine, or religion. Nor do they have the means to encourage long distance trade with other communities.

The Arrival of Capitalism. Although none of this may sound very surprising, and may even mirror societies in parts of the world today, capitalism as a system of economic organization was unknown in the western hemisphere; the arrival of the Europeans changed this. Capitalism introduced new ways of organizing economic production and conducting trade. In particular, capitalism is an economic system designed to maximize personal wealth by maximizing business profits. Profits are greatest when it is possible to exploit labor through low wages and to gain advantage over trading partners such as suppliers, customers, and competitors.

We do not know much about indigenous economies before 1492, but it is quite possible that in many Native societies, economic production was not aimed exclusively at personal gain. If anything, economic production promoted the well-being of the village or community. Similarly, personal wealth was not a measure of personal status as it is in capitalist societies. In fact, it is possible that some societies regarded personal wealth as a reflection of individual greed and that social status was acquired through demonstrations of generosity. Even today in American Indian communities—in potlatches or giveaways, ceremonies in which one person or family presents gifts to others at the ceremony—personal status is enhanced by giving away material goods, not by acquiring them.

The expansion of capitalism into the New World together with the introduction of novelties from the Old World—such as horses, guns, and metal goods—completely reshaped the way Native North Americans sustained themselves. American Indians' incorporation into the expanding world market first changed their work ways by introducing new tools and techniques. Guns, metal knives, traps, and other implements made Indian hunters more efficient, allowing them to kill game more easily and possibly more quickly. Metal pots, needles, and other domestic goods also changed women's work.

The introduction of trade initiated a subtler, more profound change in the nature of work among American Indians. Archaeological evidence indicates that trade and exchange had been prevalent among American Indian societies for thousands of years. However, because trade and exchange in these societies were not guided exclusively by the desire for personal gain, trade with Euro-Americans brought a new cultural ethos to the work of American Indians. As American Indians worked and produced goods for trade with Euro-Americans, new motives and rationales gradually leeched into older cultural beliefs about the meaning and importance of work, creating conflicts that are still visible today.

The incorporation of American Indians into the world economy also changed their work by fostering new markets for Native goods and by creating flourishing trade networks. The Spanish, French, and English, among others, launched far flung trading operations that were driven by the heavy demand in Europe for fur and other animal skins. Deerskin, for example, was highly valued for making breeches.

The establishment of the fur trade in the sixteenth and seventeenth centuries depended heavily on the labor of American Indians. Indian hunters, using guns, traps, and knives manufactured in Europe, exploited animal populations for the enrichment of the fur companies. It is important to remember, however, that the Indians were not employees of the fur companies. Nonetheless, it was not unusual for traders to extend credit and manage these accounts in ways that kept Indian hunters perpetually in debt. Traders frequently held a near monopoly over manufactured goods which allowed them to dictate trade terms: they set high prices for manufactured goods and low prices for furs. Fraud and usury were also commonly employed to keep Indian hunters in debt. In many ways, these practices made the relationship between fur traders and Indian hunters resemble an employer-employee relationship.

The fur trade had an impact on other aspects of the working lives of American Indians. For example, in some tribes, it accentuated the division of labor between men and women. During the mid-seventeenth century, in the Southeast, there was a thriving trade for deerskins. As a result, the Indian men in this region devoted most of their energies to deer hunting and other activities related to this trade. While women helped process the skins, they also took over responsibility for tending the home and garden, assuming duties that had previously been performed by the men who were now occupied with hunting.

The fur trade was an important source of work for American Indians; while it was important as a first experience in providing labor for a capitalist economy, the fur trade was relatively short lived. The fur trade declined because animal resources dwindled and because the demand for furs in Europe declined. The demise of colonialism in the Americas, marked by the emergence of the United States as a political sovereign, signaled a new era in the economic role of American Indians. While the fur trade did not entirely disappear, U.S. citizens increasingly took over. The American Fur Company was a major corporation in the nineteenth century. In the first century of the U.S. republic, however, Indian labor did not have a place.

The Expanding American Economy. Until the late nineteenth century, the United States economy was decidedly agrarian. Economic expansion meant clearing additional land for agricultural production. Consistent with this policy, the nation adopted a political ideology known as Manifest Destiny that called for populating the country with settlers from coast to coast. European immigration to the United States exploded in this century and many immigrants migrated West in search of agricultural land. The immigrant farmers' desire for land ultimately required that the people living on the land be removed and resettled. Ironically, some Indians, such as those living in the Southeast, were already farmers, but this made no difference to the immigrant settlers. At this time, the idea that American Indians could have a productive economic role was considered ridiculous by the dominant society.

The removal and resettlement of American Indians to reservations and places in Oklahoma was complete by the late nineteenth century, and it was devastating to these people who had once been self-sufficient and self-governing. Hunting and fishing no longer provided a comfortable living, and many traditional agricultural practices were either not viable or were discouraged by federal Indian agents. Reservation settlement created the abject poverty that persists today.

The late nineteenth century was also a time when the United States was quickly becoming an urban industrial society. Reformers concerned about past treatment of Indians believed that it was time to "civilize" them by encouraging and often forcing them to give up their traditional tribal culture. For nearly forty years, from the early 1890s to 1934, the federal government tried to accomplish this by forcing Indians to adopt Euro-American farming practices. Such efforts generally failed, and Indian men, accustomed to hunting or fishing, rejected farming. A few Indians took up farming or ranching like their non-Indian neighbors, and, like their neighbors, were often economic failures.

Entering the Work Force. By the early twentieth century, American Indians began increasingly to look outside the reservation for employment. Because they often had few skills, they often settled for unskilled labor such as farm work, clearing brush, or digging ditches. The Navajo, for example, sometimes provided unskilled labor for the Southern Pacific Railroad. A very small number of American Indians obtained an education, and a handful went on to become noted doctors, lawyers, and writers, such as Charles Eastman (Ohiyesa) or Carlos Montezuma.

By 1930 American Indians had in large measure adopted modern occupations. In the 1930 Census, more than 80 percent of the men over the age of eighteen were counted as "gainful workers," most of whom (63 percent) were agricultural workers. In the early 1930s, the federal government reconsidered its efforts to "civilize" American Indians and turned its attention to helping Indians find work in the midst of the Great Depression. The Indian New Deal (legislation enacted during the Roosevelt Administration in the early 1930s to promote tribal government and economic recovery programs for reservations) was enacted through a series of laws, the first of which passed in 1933. Among its many provisions, the Indian New Deal established programs aimed at providing jobs and income to desperately needy reservations. For example, federal projects employed many Indians to prevent soil erosion, for flood control, and for road and bridge construction.

The Indian New Deal was important through the 1930s, but the coming of World War II curtailed many of its programs, and it was not reinstated after the war. Reservations languished in intense poverty and unemployment while the rest of the nation prospered in the postwar years. In the early 1950s, federal officials proposed eliminating reservations to move Indians to cities where they might find work. In 1951 the federal government established the Direct Employment Assistance program to encourage reservation Indians to move to preselected urban areas such as Los Angeles. This, together with subsequent programs, came to be known as Relocation. Federal relocation programs moved thousands of American Indians—often long distances from their former homes—to cities such as Los Angeles and Seattle.

The relocation programs were not very successful in helping Indians find work. The American Indians who benefited most from relocation were those with the education, job skills, and desire to compete in urban labor markets. However, many relocated Indians had a limited education and few skills. These Indians benefited little from relocation as they went from being unemployed on the reservation to being unemployed in the city.

Jobs and Reservation Development. The federal government abandoned relocation programs in the late 1960s and have since implemented efforts to revitalize reservation economies. Through job training, the government has attempted to help American Indians qualify for semi-skilled and skilled jobs. Roads, sewage systems, and industrial parks were built to attract new businesses to reservations. Tribal governments also vastly increased in size as tribes became more involved in governing their own reservations. Efforts to attract business to reservations and to provide education and job training were at best a mixed success. American Indians are better educated today than twenty years ago, but relatively few industries have located permanently on reservations.

In the absence of private industry, the largest single sources of reservation employment have without question been tied to the growth in tribal government and related services. This has made American Indian reservations extremely vulnerable to changing federal policies that affect local government spending. Predictably, massive cutbacks in federal spending in the early 1980s produced massive increases in unemployment on reservations across the country.

Since the early 1980s, the federal government has focused on helping private enterprise develop on reservations. While some reservations have successfully promoted private development, the outlook for many others is not good. Due to a lack of resources, capital, or location, reservations are not often fertile grounds to nurture new business. One possible exception has been the advent of reservation gambling.

Reservation gambling, sometimes described as Indian bingo, has generated tremendous sums of money for some, but not all reservations. Reservation gambling initially began on a few reservations as high stakes bingo, with prizes exceeding $100,000 (the Florida Seminole tribe were the first to adopt reservation gambling). Bingo operations soon spread to reservations across the country as tribes searched for ways to provide jobs and income. These establishments soon moved beyond bingo to include other types of gambling such as blackjack, roulette, and slot machines.

Although not universally successful, reservation gambling has been an important source of tribal revenue and employment. However, most jobs directly related to gaming are low-wage service positions such as cashier, attendant, and waitress. While gambling creates employment in spin-off industries such as restaurants and motels, these are not highly desirable jobs in terms of wages and fringe benefits. At this time, it is unclear whether gambling and related developments will act as an economic panacea to provide workers with desperately needed employment and a decent standard of living.

American Indians in the Labor Force

Information about the experience of American Indians in the labor force is scarce, and up-to-date information becomes available only once every ten years: the only good source of statistical information about American Indians is the U.S. Census, which is conducted once every decade. As of this writing, information from the most recent census, taken in 2000, is not yet available. We must therefore rely on data from 1990; these data, however, should be adequate since economic conditions for American Indians have scarcely changed in the past forty years, and since there is little to suggest

The Pacific Auto Mechanic Center in California's Bay Area trains Indian people in the skills and trade of auto mechanics. (Photo by Ilka Hartmann)

that conditions in the early 2000s will differ much from those of the early 1990s.

Labor-Force Participation.   One of the most common ways of describing the status of any group in the labor market is in terms of labor-force participation rates. To participate in the labor force one must be employed or be actively seeking employment. Persons outside the labor force are either not able to work or have abandoned hope of finding employment and have become discouraged workers. Because American Indians face many obstacles to becoming employed, such as their geographic location, they experience relatively high rates of unemployment and low rates of labor-force participation. It should be noted that this is in terms of the percentage of the labor force without employment; unemployed persons who have given up their search for work are not counted in this statistic because they are not considered part of the labor force. In 1990 for example, about 15 percent of American Indian men were unemployed. In the same year, only about 5 percent of white men were jobless. Similarly, in

1990, about 31 percent of adult American Indian men were not part of the labor force, while this figure was 25 percent for white men.

These figures clearly indicate that American Indians are more jobless than whites. However, these numbers gloss over another important element in labor-force participation for employed American Indians, including time at work and recent episodes of unemployment. Many American Indians who are employed do not necessarily have a full-time job, or a job that consistently provides them with full-time work. Other American Indians, although considered employed, do not work during much of the year because they are employed in seasonal industries such as construction or tourism.

From the standpoint of employment, most American Indians are not employed in year-round jobs. In fact, 50 percent of American Indians who worked in 1989 worked less than fifty weeks. This is very different from the experience of non-Hispanic white workers, of whom only 35 percent spent less than fifty weeks on a job.

Navajo woman teacher at a school for auto mechanics, 1972. (Photo by Ilka Hartmann)

Likewise, the time spent at work is very different for Indians than for whites. Full-time employment for American Indians, defined as working thirty-five hours or more a week, tends to be sporadic. In 1979, only 47 percent of American Indians who found full-time work reported working for the entire year. On the other hand, 65 percent of white workers held full-time, full-year jobs.

Worker Characteristics and Labor-Force Participation. Gross statistics on unemployment or hours worked obscure a much more complicated situation. Of course, American Indians are not all alike and some spend more time working than others. Opportunities to secure full-time, full-year work depend heavily on the personal qualifications of workers, and on-the-job supply in the local labor market.

Gender, age, education, and family circumstances each have an important role in helping or hindering American Indian's participation in the labor force, just as it plays a role in the employment of most workers, regardless of race. Gender plays a very important role because, not surprisingly, employment opportunities for women differed markedly from those for men. The subject of American Indian women in the work force merits a more detailed discussion, which will follow shortly.

Age also affects access to employment. Older American Indians sometimes have obsolete job skills or physical infirmities that limit their employability, while younger American Indians often lack the work experience desired by employers. American Indians who are at the prime working age, between twenty-five and fifty-four years old, are most often employed, least often outside of the labor force, and are less likely to be unemployed than older or younger American Indians. For example, about 73 percent of Indian men aged twenty-five to fifty-four were employed in 1989, compared to approximately 54 percent of Indian men over age fifty-five.

Education is another obvious prerequisite for labor-force participation. Employers understandably desire employees who are capable of reading and performing basic math, and who can follow instructions. Unfortunately, many American Indians are severely handicapped by their lack of schooling. The educational deficit among American Indians often begins at the high school level. American Indian youths leave school before graduating at much higher rates than other youths. In 1990, 19 percent of American Indians ages sixteen to nineteen had dropped out of school, compared to 10 percent of white youths. The employment prospects for these youths are bleak: only 36 percent of American Indian dropouts have any type of employment. Predictably, American Indians have a lower rate of high school completion than whites: 56 percent of American Indians finish high school compared to 69 percent of white students. Of the American Indians who successfully finish high school, relatively few attend college.

It is clear that well-educated American Indians have considerably more success in the job market than their poorly educated brethren. In 1990, for example, college-educated American Indian men had average earnings exceeding $30,000, while Indian men who had dropped out of high school had average earnings of less than $15,000. It is clear that American Indians benefit economically from continued education.

A stable family environment also is a powerful incentive to Indian men to stay in the labor force. Married American Indian men have higher employment rates and lower unemployment than single or divorced men. For the same reasons, married American Indian women tend not to work, especially if there are children at home. Family disruptions such as death or divorce also work against labor-force participation; men have less incentive to stay at work, while women have more incentive to find work, especially if they must support their children.

Local Economies and American Indian Labor-Force Participation. The role of personal characteristics in shaping labor-force participation is certainly important. The cure for unemployment among American

Table 17.1
Percent Distribution of Time at Work and Unemployment in 1989 for American Indians and Alaska Natives Aged Sixteen and Over*

Residence and Gender	Worked 26 Weeks or Less	Worked 35 Hours or Less	Unemployed
Metropolitan			
Male	21.0	15.4	11.9
Female	25.7	28.0	10.8
Non-Metropolitan			
Male	32.1	15.1	20.3
Female	34.0	28.4	16.3

*1 percent of persons did not work 35 or more hours per week for a period of 6 months or more.
Source: 1990 Census of Population, Social and Economic Characteristics, United States.

Indians does not merely entail measures such as providing job experience for younger workers, encouraging them to stay in school and go on to college, and promoting family stability. If there are no jobs available in the local economy, no amount of education will help secure employment. In fact, some experts contend that American Indian youths drop out of school because they see no opportunity for work in their community, and no reason for staying in school. There is no question that for many American Indians, especially those living in rural reservation areas, opportunities are limited.

For reasons explained here and elsewhere in this volume, American Indian reservations often present few economic opportunities and extreme economic hardship. On many large reservations, unemployment rates hovered around 20 to 30 percent while unemployment in the rest of the nation settled at 6 to 7 percent. Some of these reservations are severely distressed: the Pine Ridge Reservation in South Dakota, for example, had an unemployment rate of 33 percent in 1980.

For American Indians who have some job skills or a good education, urban areas offer more opportunities. Urban Indians typically have higher rates of labor-force participation and lower unemployment rates than reservation Indians. American Indians living in cities had an unemployment rate of approximately 11 percent in 1990; this figure is lower than that of many reservations, but is still about six points higher than white unemployment rates. While urban areas may provide better opportunities for a select number of American Indians, moving to these locations often entails other costs in terms of leaving behind family, friends, and a familiar culture.

The labor markets in which American Indians seek employment vary regionally. Since some regions of the United States are economically healthier than others,

American Indians seeking work in these areas are more likely to find employment than those who seek work in regions with weak economies. Until very recently, the West, especially the so-called Sunbelt, has been the most economically vigorous region in the United States. Predictably, American Indians living in this region find more employment than those living in other areas of the United States, especially those living in the hard-hit Northeast Rust Belt region. American Indian employment rates also reflect declines in the U.S. agricultural economy. Relatively few Indians work in agriculture, but the economic depression of regions that depend on agriculture ultimately translates to a decrease in the number of jobs available to American Indian workers.

American Indians at Work

Occupations. We can view the work performed by American Indians from several perspectives. We can simply group together the kinds of jobs or occupations filled by American Indians; jobs that entail similar activities are grouped together into distinct categories such as manual or nonmanual occupations, for example. We can also look at American Indian workers in relation to the places where they work; that is, whether they work on farms, in offices, or in manufacturing plants. A third perspective can focus on ownership to consider whether American Indians are self-employed, employed by privately owned businesses, or employed by a government agency. Each of these perspectives provides a unique picture of American Indians at work.

The occupations of American Indians vary considerably depending on gender, job location, and education. About 69 percent of American Indian men, for example, are in employed manual occupations. This partially

Table 17.2
Percent Distribution of the Labor-Force Participation of American Indians
Aged Sixteen and Over Residing on the Sixteen Largest Reservations in 1990

Reservation	1980		1990	
	In Labor Force %	Unemployment Rate %	In Labor Force %	Unemployment Rate %
Navajo (AZ, UT, NM)	58.3	23.7	43.7	29.5
Pine Ridge (SD)	61.8	35.8	48.1	32.7
Gila River (AZ)	61.5	29.5	44.7	30.6
Papago (AZ)	58.6	20.4	36.1	23.4
Fort Apache (AZ)	64.1	20.3	54.9	35.3
Hopi (AZ)	54.7	20.5	48.0	26.8
Zuni Pueblo (NM)	79.7	23.2	64.4	13.8
San Carlos (AZ)	59.1	21.1	59.1	21.1
Rosebud (SD)	65.0	28.7	50.6	29.5
Blackfeet (MT)	72.2	37.0	56.2	31.1
Yakima (WA)	70.1	32.5	49.8	24.5
Eastern Cherokee (NC)	73.7	21.1	66.2	17.7
Standing Rock (ND, SD)	65.8	36.0	50.2	33.1
Osage (OK)	65.9	14.2	56.9	10.2
Fort Peck (MT)	75.7	39.3	57.6	29.7
Wind River (WY)	68.2	30.2	50.5	32.4

Sources: "American Indians, Eskimos, and Aleuts on Identified Reservations and in the Historic Areas of Oklahoma," *1980 Census of Population, Subject Report*; and "Social and Economic Characteristics, American Indian and Alaska Native Areas," *1990 Census of Population, Subject Report*.

accounts for the frequent disruptions of work that trouble many American Indians. Manual occupations are subject to disruptions of work due to weather, seasonal variations in production schedules, and economic downturns. On the other hand 61 percent of American Indian women work in nonmanual occupations. These women primarily hold lower-status white collar positions such as teachers, secretaries, and nurses; few are doctors, lawyers, or executives.

The socioeconomic disadvantages that hinder the competitiveness of Indian workers are also reflected in their occupational status. In 1990 27 percent of white men were employed in high-status professional and technical occupations while only 15 percent of American Indian men held such jobs. The gap in the occupational status between American Indian women and white women is nearly as large as it is for men. Significantly, American Indian women are substantially more concentrated in so-called service occupations than either white women or American Indian men. Approximately one-fourth of Indian women are employed in occupations such as motel maid or waitress.

The occupations of American Indians also vary according to whether they are employed in urban labor markets or in rural reservation areas; the differences are predictable. American Indians who work in an urban labor market are much more likely to hold a white collar job—in an office or a similar setting—than their counterparts in rural areas. This reflects the fact that there are many more white collar jobs for both men and women in urban areas. On the other hand, jobs as fishermen, farm workers, and loggers are more common in rural areas; rural American Indians are naturally more apt to be employed in these and related occupations than are American Indians in urban areas.

Although many American Indians continue to practice their traditional tribal culture, relatively few are able to sustain themselves in an exclusively traditional manner. Hunting, fishing, and gardening are important, especially for reservation Indians. However, American Indians living on reservations and in urban areas rely on a cash economy for certain goods and services. Most find that this work for income is not closely related to traditional tribal activities. American Indians who earn their living as hunting and fishing guides, trappers, or artisans who make pottery, jewelry, or rugs are uncommon exceptions.

Industries.   Because certain kinds of industries (defines here as groups of firms that produce similar goods or services) tend to employ certain kinds of occupations, patterns of industrial employment closely parallel occupational patterns. For example, American Indians are more often employed in extractive industries such as agriculture, forestry, or mining than either whites or African Americans. Not surprisingly, Indian men living in rural areas are most likely to be employed in these industries. Construction companies are also an important source of employment, although this is true primarily for American Indian men and not for Indian women. The overwhelming majority of American Indians, especially men, tend to be concentrated either in service or manufacturing jobs.

American Indian women, on the other hand, are not concentrated in manufacturing or in other industries that typically demand arduous physical labor. In 1990 nearly one-half (45 percent) of all employed Indian women worked in the so-called service sector of the economy, in establishments that provide social services, health care, and education. In this respect, American Indian women are not very different from other women insofar as they often find themselves working in places with large concentrations of female workers. They often work in companies that have many so-called female jobs such as secretaries, clerk-typists, nurses, physician's assistants, teachers, and teacher's aides.

Public Sector Employment.   Due to the lack of job opportunities for American Indians, especially for those living on reservations, American Indians depend heavily on the federal and tribal governments for employment. The federal government, by virtue of its legal and treaty obligations, exercises a substantial role in day-to-day reservation affairs. The Bureau of Indian Affairs and the Indian Health Service employ many workers in jobs ranging from law enforcement, road construction, and logging, to health care, law, and real estate. Similarly, tribal governments increasingly have assumed a greater role in managing community affairs, employing a variety of workers, especially in tribal enterprises such as tourist developments or manufacturing establishments.

American Indians depend substantially on public sector employment. While it is true that a higher percentage of American Indians are hired by private sector employers than by the federal or tribal governments (more than two-thirds of Indian workers were employed in the private sector in 1980), a lower percentage of American Indians—compared to both whites and African Americans—are employed in the private

sector. In 1990 approximately 14 percent of the American Indian work force held jobs in federal and state government, compared to only 7.5 percent of the white labor force. Most of these jobs held by American Indian workers were probably with agencies such as the Indian Health Service or the Bureau of Indian Affairs (BIA). Similarly, in 1990 about 9 percent of the Indian work force were employed by local governments. With respect to reservations, the term *local government* means tribal government. It is also interesting to note that between 1980 and 1990 the percentage of American Indians working in local government decreased from 12 percent to 9 percent, reflecting the cutbacks in tribal government that took place during the 1980s and job growth in other sectors of the economy.

American Indians' heavy dependence on public sector employment reflects the scarcity of employment available to them, especially to those living on reservations. There are relatively few opportunities for productive employment in the private sector. In fact, in many of these areas, jobs with the BIA or with the tribe may be the best employment available. While such jobs may be desirable in terms of wages and working conditions, they are often highly insecure. These jobs are often created by soft money, that is, funds that have been appropriated for various kinds of social programs.

These programs appear and disappear, depending on the political agenda set by the federal government. Workers in such programs are seldom covered by civil service rules and find themselves jobless when federal support for a program or project is reduced or eliminated. American Indians' dependence on public sector employment also makes them vulnerable to changes in the national political climate that are reflected in terms of support for public policy initiatives. In the early 1980s, in the wake of massive federal budget reductions, unemployment skyrocketed on many reservations.

Tribal leaders are acutely aware that their communities' dependency on public sector employment makes them vulnerable to shifting political fortunes in Washington, D.C. Many tribes promote economic development in order to lessen this dependence. For the foreseeable future, however, jobs with federal agencies and tribal government will continue to be a major source of employment, especially for skilled and professional workers.

American Indian Women in the Work Force

Like other women, American Indian women face certain obstacles in the labor market that men do not. American Indian women participate in the labor market under somewhat different circumstances from other

Table 17.3
Percent Distribution of Blacks, Whites, and American Indians Aged Sixteen and Over Employed in Manual and Non-Manual Occupations, 1980–1990

	1980		1990	
	Males	Females	Males	Females
Blacks				
Manual	73.1	48.3	66.5	39.9
Non-Manual	26.9	51.7	33.5	60.1
Whites				
Manual	55.5	30.3	51.1	26.0
Non-Manual	44.5	69.7	48.9	74.0
American Indians				
Manual	72.1	43.6	69.1	38.7
Non-Manual	27.9	56.4	30.9	61.3

Sources: 1980 Census of Population, General Social and Economic Characteristics, United States Summary; 1990 Census of Population, Social and Economic Characteristics, United States.

women. Indian women also live in remote areas, may have fewer opportunities, and may face special problems finding work because the few existing jobs may be in industries—such as logging or fishing—that are traditionally dominated by men. Furthermore, by virtue of tribal culture, American Indian women may also have special obligations to their families and community that may limit their ability to work outside the home.

Nonetheless, the constraints that limit the labor-force participation of American Indian women are similar to those that hinder women of other races. Family obligations, especially child-rearing duties, often determine whether Indian women join the labor force. In 1990 46 percent of American Indian women with children under age six were not active in the labor force. However, as children spend more time at school, the reduction in child care duties allows many of these women to resume their jobs or to enter the labor force. Only 31 percent, approximately, of women with children ages six to seventeen are not participating in the work force. Predictably, women with no children have the highest rates of labor-force participation.

The fact that Indian women often have large families further limits their participation in the labor force. American Indian women tend to have more children than either white or African-American women and hence are burdened with more child care responsibilities. This may explain, in part, why the labor-force participation rates of American Indian women are lower than the rates for either whites or African Americans.

Finally, the relationship between child-bearing and labor-force participation is further complicated by the fact that less-educated Indian women tend to have more children and lower rates of labor-force participation. Without question, poorly educated Indian women have a difficult time finding work. It is not clear, however, whether these women abandoned their education to have children or whether a low level of education somehow contributes to their having larger families. Both explanations probably have some merit.

Providing economic support is another important element determining the labor-force participation of American Indian women, especially in cases where the woman's partner is absent or unable to find work. For most American Indian women, the decision to work is a complex calculation that takes into account the need to provide child care, the presence of a husband or partner, and the opportunities available in the local job market. We know little about how Indian women prioritize and sort through these competing contingencies.

We might expect American Indian women with young children to stay home to provide child care regardless of whether they live with the children's father. If the father is present, we might assume that he will support the family, or, if he is unemployed, that welfare assistance will allow the mother to remain at home. However, research indicates that women with young children under age six who are married and living with their husbands are only slightly less likely to be active in the

Table 17.4
Percent Distribution of Class of Worker
of Employed Blacks, Whites, and American Indians, 1980–1990

Class	Blacks		Whites		American Indians	
	1980	1990	1980	1990	1980	1990
Private Wage and Salary Worker	70.2	73.2	76.0	77.6	66.3	71.1
Federal and State Government Worker	14.2	13.0	7.7	7.5	16.9	13.6
Local Government Worker	13.1	10.8	8.2	6.8	11.6	9.1
Self-employed Worker	2.4	2.8	7.5	7.6	4.8	5.8
Unpaid Family Worker	0.1	0.2	0.6	0.5	0.4	0.4

Sources: 1980 Census of Population, General Social and Economic Characteristics, United States Summary; 1990 Census of Population, Social and Economic Characteristics, United States.

labor force than are women with young children who are unmarried or living alone.

Whether her husband is employed and whether her husband's earnings meet household needs also affect an American Indian woman's decision to work. We might consider the labor-force participation of American Indian women to be compensatory: that is, Indian women work when their husbands are unemployed or do not earn enough to meet household needs. On the other hand, men and women often marry spouses who have similar backgrounds and characteristics. Consequently, Indian women with unemployed or poorly paid husbands face similar, if not more difficult, hardships than their spouses.

One study suggests that the labor-force participation of American Indian women does not compensate for the disadvantages faced by their husbands. On the contrary, American Indian women who are married to poorly educated and unemployed men tend to be poorly educated and either unemployed, or simply not active in the labor force. By the same token, relatively well-educated American Indian women often have relatively well-educated husbands, both of whom are considerably more successful in finding well-paid employment than are couples with less education. Contrary to popular wisdom, opposites do not attract; the result is that husbands and wives do not compensate but compound whatever advantages or disadvantages each has in the labor market.

Concluding Observations

American Indians' current position in the U.S. labor market reflects a complex mix of long-term historical processes with recent developments in the United States and international economy. American Indians have always—even prior to the arrival of Europeans—worked, in the broadest sense of the word. While all societies require some division of labor, the complexity of this division, and the norms for allocating its products can vary enormously. The norms by which American Indians govern the distribution of economic resources were unquestionably very different from those common among sixteenth-century Europeans.

The arrival of Europeans introduced mercantile capitalism to the New World, and with this system came a new set of conditions, expectations, and norms governing economic transactions. Today we take the terms of this system for granted in our everyday lives; for the indigenous cultures of North America, however, a market economy organized by capitalist principles was an entirely alien system. Such elements of capitalistic trade as credit, interest rates, and profits were utterly foreign. And although Natives who dealt regularly with the mercantile traders soon learned about these concepts, they did not readily accept them. Capitalism as a system designed to maximize personal material gain has never meshed well with traditional tribal cultures that value communal well-being above personal avarice.

The emergence of large-scale industrial capitalism in the nineteenth century, characterized by large-scale factory production, confronted Native cultures with yet another alien element. The organization of large-scale factories requires a submissive work force comprised of workers who are willing to accept industrial discipline, and who will order their lives around the passage of time on a clock. Traditional tribal cultures do not measure time by the clock and are often highly egalitarian, and this did not mesh well with industrial capitalism. These are among the many reasons why the expansion of capitalism in the United States depended on the exploitation of Indian lands, while it did not depend on

Table 17.5
Percent Distribution of Employed Blacks, Whites, and American Indians
and Alaska Natives in Selected Occupations, 1990

Occupation	Blacks		Whites		American Indians	
	Males	Females	Males	Females	Males	Females
Managerial and Professional	14.5	21.3	26.8	29.3	15.4	21.7
Technical, Sales, and Administrative Support	19.0	38.7	22.1	44.7	15.6	39.6
Service	18.8	25.1	8.8	15.4	14.2	23.4
Farming, Forestry, and Fishing	2.7	0.3	3.8	0.9	5.3	1.1
Precision Production, Craft, and Repair	14.6	2.4	19.5	2.2	22.9	3.1
Operators, Fabricators, and Laborers	30.4	12.1	18.9	7.5	26.7	11.1

Source: 1990 Census of Population, Social and Economic Characteristics, United States.

the exploitation of Indian labor. American Indians were considered to be unfit for work because they were economically self-sufficient, especially before they were moved to reservations; they were seldom inclined to submit to the kinds of industrial exploitation that European and Chinese immigrants suffered. As a matter of deliberate policy, the federal government sought to isolate American Indians from the mainstream of the U.S. economy; in retrospect, they were highly successful.

Today, despite periodic attempts to resettle American Indians away from reservations, many continue to live in Indian Country, often in places that are extremely remote and isolated. After generations of living at the margins of the U.S. economy, it should be no surprise that American Indians face some of the greatest economic hardships known in American society. And relocation should not be seen as a simple way to ease these hardships. Without the resources to compete successfully in a modern urban labor market, American Indians have few prospects for success. The marginal areas where many American Indians live often lack the resources required to succeed in the labor market. Lack of education is often a serious impediment to Indians who seek work. On the other hand, it is difficult to encourage American Indian youth to pursue an education when the lack of employment opportunities offers little incentive to stay in school.

American Indians who find employment still face a number of hurdles, at least by the standards of mainstream American society. American Indian men are typically employed in blue collar jobs that entail physical labor in difficult working conditions, and they often work in industries, such as construction, that are plagued by mandatory stretches of unemployment. Compared to men, relatively few American Indian women are employed in blue collar jobs, but many hold menial jobs as service workers. Better qualified Indian women often find jobs in low status white collar jobs such as teachers, nurses' aides, or social service workers, but relatively few attain professional and technical occupations.

The experience of American Indians in the labor market has improved over the past several decades, but much improvement is still needed. American Indians continue to need more vital resources such as education and training to help them to compete in the labor market. At the same time, job opportunities must be created in the places where American Indians live. Unless these objectives are addressed American Indians' traditional role as the nation's poorest of the poor will continue indefinitely.

C. Matthew Snipp
Stanford University

◆ AN OVERVIEW OF U.S. GOVERNMENT ASSISTANCE AND RESTITUTION TO AMERICAN INDIANS

This section examines the relationship between U.S. government assistance and restitution programs to American Indians and American social welfare policies and programs. The roots of federal assistance and restitution programs arose from the appropriation of Indian lands by the European colonists and frontier settlers. Contact between the indigenous people of this

Three affiliated tribes participate in a giveaway in North Dakota, 1989. (Photo by Ilka Hartmann)

continent and non-Indians resulted in dramatic social and cultural changes associated with the loss of the traditional land base. Guarantees of services were proffered to American Indians in recognition that the blatant takeover of Indian lands required some level of compensation. The final annexation of land was accomplished with the establishment of the reservation system and the passage of the General Allotment Act. This section will discuss the current demographic and socioeconomic status of American Indians and the subsequent need for services; issues associated with the Temporary Assistance to Needy Families program; and the range of assistance programs currently available to American Indians.

Consequences of Contact

Worse and worse have become reservation conditions under a system that was bad from the beginning. Such a deplorable state of affairs could only continue to exist because of several reasons, mainly, because of slight public concern for the Indian; because the declaration of President Coolidge on June 5, 1924, presumably made the Indian a citizen of the United States; and because the mass of people think and say, 'The Government takes care of the Indian.'

—Luther Standing Bear, 1933

Although American Indians experience similar problems to those confronted by other minority groups in the United States, the American Indian experience cannot be compared with the experiences of any other ethnic or racial minority in the United States. Every aspect of American Indian life—all resources, opportunities, and struggles—are influenced by the special political and legal relationships that exist between Indian tribes as sovereign nations and the federal and state governments. Contemporary American Indian life is affected by the social, historical, political, and cultural conditions that are the result of contact between American Indians and Euro-Americans.

Bringing in Wild Animals, Fish, and Other Stores (1591). Drawing by Le Moyne, from an engraving by Theodore de Bry, *America*, part II, plate XXIII. (Public Domain)

Five hundred years ago, European explorers and settlers discovered and began to explore a world that was new to them. This so-called New World was inhabited by various groups of people, indigenous tribes and nations, whose lives were shaped by cultural, social, spiritual, and political systems that differed radically from those of the Europeans. Every part of the continent was populated. The ecological environment and physical geography offered the natural resources necessary for the construction of life and influenced culturally based behaviors and practices. For example, the buffalo influenced the construction of life for the Plains tribes and the salmon, whale, and other marine life influenced life for the coastal tribes of the Northwest. Cultural, social, spiritual, and political life was organized with reference to the natural resources and the ecological environment that was home to a given Indian community. In the Southwest, Navajo were hunters and gatherers and Pueblo were farmers, because the physical and biological geography predisposed different sociocultural structures that would support group survival. Despite the diversity of physical environments

and culturally based practices that reflected the interactions between the people and the place where they resided, there were similarities across these indigenous tribes who populated the New World. Typically, the social structures and lifestyles of each group developed in ways that recognized balance, harmony, and mutuality with the environment. Similarities are evident in the fundamental belief systems, in the history and consequences of contact with non-Indians and in the processes of accommodation and survival. For example, most indigenous people believed that humans are composed of spirit, mind, and body; that plants, animals, and nature have equal status to humans in the natural world; that a Creator exists who is the giver and sustainer of life; that spirit-helpers exist who model appropriate behavior and provide support and guidance; that each individual is responsible for his or her own behavior; and that harmony, balance, and reciprocity are necessary for supporting life.

There existed a family and a collective orientation that can be found in the origin stories, tribal histories, and rituals of American Indians. The legacy of contact is visible in the social and cultural shifts that occurred as a result of the many losses and challenges experienced as Native people interacted with non-Indians. Yet many American Indian communities managed to resist, accommodate, and survive despite the brutal consequences of contact with non-Indians. These similarities across groups that lived in a large and diverse geographical territory, allow discussion of issues that are the consequence of contact with non-Indians from a broader intertribal or pan-Indian perspective.

As the American frontier experience and sensibility evolved, it became important for the dominant society to minimize the numbers of American Indians and groups whose lives and communities were destroyed and disrupted as a result of contact with non-Indians. It became equally important to judge, dehumanize, and render insignificant the lifestyles and social and cultural structures of American Indians and declare American Indians savage, lazy, and ignorant. These ideas were necessary in order for non-Indians to justify and rationalize the elimination of native opposition to the annexation and the take-over of life sustaining resources, the imposition of different lifestyles and social structures, the removal of Indians from traditional lands, and the eventual confinement of American Indians on reservations in the 1800s.

The expropriation of Indian territories began with the colonists and settlers who obtained land by force, fraud, and treaty. Subsequently, the governments of France, England, and the United States appropriated land through treaties. Through the treaty mechanism, a legal, formal, and binding agreement entered into between two nations, American Indians ceded land in exchange for money and services. As the nineteenth century unfolded, non-Indians promoted the policy of removal, which allowed the exploitation of native resources.

The Indian Removal Act of 1830 provided for "an exchange of lands with any of the Indians residing in any of the states and territories and for their removal west of the river Mississippi." By 1850 much of the American Indian territory east of the Mississippi River was no longer inhabited by Native people. The infamous Trail of Tears, which can rightfully be described as one of the most shameful events in American history, is the most renowned example of the removal policy. The Cherokee who survived this death march were relocated in what is now the state of Oklahoma and what was then territory occupied by other indigenous groups.

The General Allotment Act (Dawes Act of 1887) represented another intrusion into the social, political, and cultural fabric of Native life. The traditional land base that had been historically held in common by the

group was redistributed in forty, eighty, and 160 acre shares. American Indians who accepted shares were required to use the land for agricultural purposes. The General Allotment Act was proclaimed a mechanism for introducing American Indians to the American farming lifestyle. This legislation also introduced the system of blood quantum, land trusts, and federal recognition of individual Indians. It was an overt effort to expropriate the traditional land base and exploit natural resources. It resulted in the separation of American Indians from their land and traditional way of life and resulted in the loss of approximately two-thirds of the traditional land holdings to the federal government. The establishment of reservations by the federal government completed the seizure of the traditional American Indian land base and the disruption of traditional life.

The history of Native and non-Native interactions can be summarized as a history of contact, conflict, anguish, accommodation, and adjustment. Contemporary issues confronting American Indians on and off the reservation are the consequences of this history. Disease, death, dependence, and sociocultural disorganization are the consequences of contact, conquest, removal, and reservation policies. Disease has decimated American Indian communities for centuries. Dependence was fostered when tribes were disenfranchised from life-sustaining land bases and when the practice of life-affirming spiritual and cultural rituals was forbidden. Disorganization was promoted when traditional political and cultural structures were changed as a result of the removal and reservation policies. The current assistance initiatives and the contemporary issues confronting Indian Country must be understood as consequences of this history of Native and non-Native interaction.

Treaties forced upon and entered into by Indian nations ratified the dual policies of removal and reservation and offered guarantees for assistance and restitution via the provision of multiple services. Treaties were the end result of contact, force, brutality, and military conquest. The sovereign nation status of American Indian groups is recognized in treaties, and treaties mandate that the government of the United States provide assistance and restitution to American Indian nations. Therefore, the first forms of assistance and restitution can be understood as examples of foreign policy rather than social welfare policy. Contemporary programs providing services to American Indian communities and individuals must be understood as examples of the historical guarantees that were originally set forth in the various treaties that exist between American Indian sovereign nations and the United States government. This concept was operationalized in the Snyder Act of 1921, which guaranteed health, welfare, and education services to every American Indian on and off the reservation.

American Social Welfare Policy

Many of the services mandated by treaty and the Snyder Act are now included in the national social welfare policy debates that are defined by federal legislation and implemented under state jurisdiction. The American social welfare system developed independent of the treaty obligations that offer guarantees of the social welfare services to American Indians. For example, treaties in the eighteenth century typically mandate peace, education, health, family, and community support services in exchange for land, and the federal government provided these services. However, the English Poor Law traditions and values, which made available local resources to the needy only when the family could not meet its care-giving responsibilities, influenced American social welfare policies.

In the English Poor Law tradition, government overseers were required to collect taxes from property owners and to distribute relief to the impoverished. The laws required that able-bodied recipients work in exchange for assistance. The provision of assistance was based on the overseer's assessment of need and the assessment of the personal responsibility/culpability for the needy condition. Assistance was discretionary; individuals might be provided with direct relief or assigned to work for another or placed in a workhouse or almshouse. In the latter half of the nineteenth century, attention was focused on the mentally ill, on physically abused children, and on freed slaves and veterans. This resulted in the development of federal legislation and services and led to the development of the formal American social welfare system. This system evolved at a rather slow pace through the beginning of the twentieth century. Most assistance came from private sources that were dependent upon the goodwill of individual citizens. By the end of the century, private charities were the main source of assistance and the main mechanism for the delivery of social welfare. The Great Depression, however, promoted the dramatic growth of the social welfare system.

Historically, social welfare policies that influence the design and delivery of health, educational, nutritional, and social services in the United States reflect traditions associated with the English Poor Laws. There are two philosophical perspectives that influence social welfare in the United States: the *residual* and the *institutional* approaches. Most social welfare interventions reflect the residual perspective. The residual concept of social welfare is based on the idea that individual and family needs should be met in the marketplace and that social welfare is required only during times of market disruption. In theory, social welfare services are withdrawn because they are no longer needed, when the marketplace is stabilized and restored to healthy functioning. Therefore, various forms of government assistance can be made available to individuals and families during periods of economic recession or depression. Eligibility for services is generally determined by individuals offering proof that there is a need that cannot be met by the family. The philosophical values that support this orientation assume that everyone in society has equal access to the resources and opportunities needed to interact with the market place and that chronic dependence on social welfare services is indicative of individual failure to exercise proper moral or personal choice.

The institutional concept of social welfare is based on the idea that social welfare is a legitimate function of modern society. It is assumed that there are naturally occurring conditions that will limit the individual or the family from meeting all needs. Philosophically, social welfare is perceived to be a necessary, permanent, and desirable part of the social structure. Currently, in most western European countries, the institutional model dominates. The American social welfare philosophy has been described as reluctant, because of its failure to provide universal access for the range of social services that are required to maintain a healthy society. Unfortunately, there are multiple barriers that undermine access to the marketplace. Therefore, there is a great burden that is placed on those sectors of the population that lack sufficient discretionary income to purchase the social welfare services required for survival. The reluctance of the American social welfare system to policies from the institutional perspective mirrors the reluctance of the federal government to assume responsibility for the multiple hazards that undermine contemporary American Indian life. These hazards are the direct and lingering result of contact and the loss of the traditional land bases that sustained life. Further, there is reluctance to focus on restitution in lieu of assistance to American Indian communities.

Federal legislation defines the parameters of social welfare policies. Assistance and restitution services for American Indians are influenced by social welfare policies, despite the fact that the promises for these services originally reflected foreign policy to the extent that they operationalized provisions of treaties. Therefore, the federal government is involved in the management of two parallel systems of assistance. One system, directed toward American Indians, mandated by treaties and typically managed by the Bureau of Indian Affairs or other federal departments, is driven by the

A group of Lakota children at a Catholic Indian Mission boarding school, circa 1940. (Photo by Rita Ledesma)

legal obligations incurred as a result of the appropriation of land to provide assistance and restitution. The other system, directed primarily toward all citizens, is driven by the traditions of the English Poor Laws, the general reluctance of the federal government to step into the private family arena, and a preference for intervening only when the family, the marketplace, or local institutions cannot effectively manage the caregiving needs of the citizenry. Each system of care is influenced by the values articulated in the English Poor Laws and the dominant society.

Boundaries between the two systems have blurred over the years for three reasons. American Indians are eligible for services that are available to all citizens. Each system responds to similar needs and issues, and the same federal departments administer services directed specifically toward American Indians. Finally, the values associated with the English traditions have influenced the evolution and development of social welfare policies within the United States. This has resulted in tension and contradiction between the federal government's obligation to American Indian peoples and the American social welfare traditions that

favor the most minimal levels of assistance. These include a preference for the pull-yourself-up-by-your-bootstraps mentality, minimal encroachment into the marketplace and family life, and the provision of services on a temporary basis. The subtext of federal assistance initiatives to American Indians also has been historically influenced by the belief that assistance initiatives can be used to create fundamental change in the structure and fabric of American Indian societies. For example, as early as 1790 the federal government allocated at least $10,000 to a Civilization Fund that supported economic development and education among Indians in order to promote the transformation of Indians into farmers and citizens.

This orientation of American social welfare policies fails to account for federal policies that have consistently eroded and stressed the fabric of American Indian life and the federal obligation to provide assistance and restitution for the loss of land. Equally important, the residual approach that characterizes American social welfare policies does not adequately address issues of restitution. The residual approach is directed toward the provision of temporary assistance to those who demonstrate that they meet specific eligibility criteria. With regard to American Indians, social welfare policies reflect the need to minimize the magnitude of the disruptions to American Indian societies as a result of the removal, reservation, and relocation policies. There is also a preference within the residual approach for attributing the cause of the current distress confronting American Indians solely to personal deficits. The social and economic status of American Indians and contemporary social welfare policy debates illustrate these issues.

Contemporary Social and Economic Issues

Multiple problems have resulted from the losses incurred by American Indians as a result of contact with non-Indians, despite the federal guarantees to provide assistance and restitution. These problems include substandard housing, low educational attainment, poverty, substance abuse, toxic and hazardous environments, compromised health status, high mortality rates, interpersonal violence, despair, and depression. Current federal social welfare assistance programs direct interventions at these problems.

The concentration of American Indians in the western United States reflects the conquest of Indian nations, the decimation of the indigenous population, and the federal policies of removal and relocation. The increasing urbanization of the population reflects the relocation policies of the 1950s and the search for employment and educational opportunities in environments. Although American Indians are mobile, moving on and off the reservation, the distribution of the population has remained and is projected to remain, relatively stable. This means that solutions to the current social problems that are fueled by environmental conditions are not likely to be solved with geographic cures. Assistance and intervention initiatives for American Indians must acknowledge the physical geography, environmental conditions, and cultural considerations in the design and implementation of social welfare policy. For example, the current welfare-to-work policies mandate that recipients work in exchange for receiving unearned income benefits. This mandate assumes that the environment has jobs available for welfare recipients and the jobs sites are accessible. For the welfare recipient who lives in one of the districts on Pine Ridge Reservation, this assumes that there is a local job available and that transportation to the job is accessible. Both assumptions may be incorrect, not only on Pine Ridge, but also on other reservations. On many reservations, employment opportunities are extremely limited and public transportation is almost nonexistent. The relative stability of the residential patterns of American Indians indicates that urban Indians are at risk of being disconnected from reservation-based assistance programs, such as those provided by the Bureau of Indian Affairs (BIA) and the Indian Health Service (IHS).

Although there are more than 500 recognized tribes, 50 percent of the American Indian population identifies with one of the eight largest tribes. These are the Cherokee, Navajo, Chippewa, Sioux, Choctaw, Pueblo, Apache, and Iroquois. Membership in a large tribe does not offer protections or access to the social and economic benefits that are associated with American life in this new century.

For example, Pine Ridge reservation, home to the Lakota, is located in Shannon County, which has long been the poorest county in the United States. One-half of American Indian homes on the Navajo Reservation and trust lands lack complete plumbing. Nationally, about 20 percent of American Indian homes lack complete plumbing, and approximately 18 percent of American Indian homes on the reservation and 3 percent of American homes off the reservation lack complete kitchen facilities (a sink with piped water, a cook stove, and a refrigerator). Although telephones are considered as common as air to the average American adolescent, 53 percent of American Indian homes do not have a telephone. The telephone is such a staple of American life that it is difficult to conceptualize the multiple ways that access to a telephone can constrain daily life—from calling 9-1-1 in an emergency, to following up on a job interview, to crossing the digital divide.

These material deficits that characterize American Indian life reflect the deep poverty that impacts Indian Country and the residual approach to social welfare to the degree that the accouterments of modern industrial life—telephones and indoor plumbing—are expected to be purchased in the market place. These deficits symbolize the failure of this approach to adequately support federal obligations to American Indians for assistance and restitution.

Educational attainment is consistently associated with economic opportunity and personal independence. The federal government and its agents have a long history as providers of educational services to Indian children. The earliest boarding schools and federal educational initiatives were quite harsh and dedicated to separating Indian children from their families, communities, and cultures by educating the Indian out of Native children. Current Population Survey data provides the following information about the educational attainment of American Indians between the ages of twenty-five and forty-four years: 18 percent have less

Children from the Campos family around 1940 at Holy Rosary Boarding School, Rosebud Reservation in South Dakota, circa 1940. (Photo by Rita Ledesma)

than a high school education; 41 percent have a high school education; 26 percent have some college education; and 15 percent have a bachelor's degree or higher.

With regard to American Indians and poverty the same data indicated that: 25 percent live in poverty; 13 percent live in extreme poverty (below 50 percent of the official poverty threshold); and 50 percent received some form of welfare (Temporary Assistance to Needy Families, Supplemental Security Income, Medicaid, food stamps, free or reduced school lunches and housing, or rent subsidies). Further, 88 percent of the poor American Indian population received some form of welfare assistance. Thus, American Indians are well represented as consumers of federal assistance/social welfare programs that are designed to support all citizens.

The poverty and educational status of American Indians is associated with federal policies that have unfolded in the last two centuries; however, current social welfare assistance programs do not in any way acknowledge this. Thus, the root causes of the problems that plague American Indians are not addressed in the contemporary social welfare arena, even as sanctions and limitations are developed for those sectors of the community who continue to need assistance. For example, the assistance program for poor families, Temporary Assistance for Needy Families (TANF), has mandated strict work requirements, established time limits for services, and instituted sanctions for failures to adhere to program requirements. In California, for example, parenting minors must be enrolled and making satisfactory progress in order to continue to receive benefits. Nationally, aid is limited to not more that five years in a lifetime. Welfare reform, as demonstrated in the TANF initiative, illustrates the residual approach and assumes that the root causes of poverty resides within the individual. Clearly, welfare reform is potentially devastating to American Indian children and families for these reasons.

Poverty is overcome when structural and institutional changes support individual growth and development. Economic development is one mechanism for promoting the structural changes to eradicate poverty

Los Angeles urban Indians drum to prevent the closing of a drug rehabilitation center. (Photo by Mary G. Wentz)

and its consequences in the American Indian community. However, in Indian Country economic development is chronically underdeveloped. Gambling operations have constituted the major form of economic growth since the passage of the 1988 Indian Gaming Regulatory Act. Gambling represents an indigenous response to the pervasive problems that have become entrenched across generations. It also reflects the absence of federal leadership in fostering assistance and restitution initiatives that honor historical obligations. For a small number of gaming tribes, gambling operations have been the engine driving economic success, but it is not a panacea. The Navajo have consistently opposed gambling on religious/ceremonial grounds, and many reservations are located too far away from the large population centers needed to generate and sustain profitability.

Other tribes have explored different routes to economic development. The Havasupai have focused on tourism to promote economic development. The Oneida of Wisconsin and the Mississippi Band of Choctaw Indians have promoted the development of factories. The work ethic and commitment to care for their own

families is as strong in American Indian communities as it is in other communities. Tribal governments must continue to look to federal sources of support in order to address the educational, health and social services needs of their constituents. Major funding for these programs comes from federal sources. The income support assistance programs are developed and funded in the social welfare arena, while health, education and social services are typically housed within the BIA and IHS, whose budgets are annually the subject to debate and cutback. The rate of Indian poverty, the absence of economic development in reservation communities, the residual orientation in social welfare, and the long history of federal ambivalence with regard to providing assistance and restitution undermine the lives and opportunities of many American Indians.

Assistance and Restitution Programs

The Bureau of Indian Affairs was the first major provider of assistance to American Indians. Originally housed in the War Department, its mission was to direct and manage all Indian affairs. It established a system of boarding schools, provided subsistence services and managed land issues as determined necessary by a network of agents, supervisors, and the Indian commissioner.

On the national level, many states in 1911 began to provide Mothers' Pensions to widows with children. This was the first indicator that federal and local governments were willing to assume responsibility for citizens and insure a minimum standard of living. Although there was always opposition to these programs from social conservatives, the Great Depression forced a reevaluation of the government's role as a provider of assistance, because so many citizens were poor and unemployed. The Social Security Act of 1935 marks the entry of the federal government as a central provider of assistance. The Social Security Act included economic assistance programs, federal and state unemployment insurance, a national system for retirement benefits, and social services. The economic assistance programs included Aid to Families with Dependent Children, Aid to the Blind, Aid to the Permanently and Totally Disabled, and Old Age Assistance.

The 1928 Meriam Report documented the plight of American Indians and the crisis conditions on reservations, resulting in a reorganization of the Office of Indian Affairs. The Great Depression had a critical impact on reservations. However, tribes had to fight throughout the 1940s to receive the benefits of these programs. Arizona and New Mexico were the last states to accord the rights enjoyed by other citizens to Indians, including access to federal and state economic assistance programs. The terrible impact of the Depression on reservations was buffered temporarily with the creation of public works jobs. Beginning in the 1940s, the BIA instituted a cash assistance program to offset the extreme poverty on reservations. The first assistance was provided in the form of vouchers that could be exchanged for food at trading posts. By the late 1940s the administration of general assistance programs was placed in Bureau agency offices on or near the reservation. The BIA general assistance program can include families who do not meet the eligibility criteria for state administered programs.

In the 1960s poverty was rediscovered as an issue that continued to affect non-Indians and a War on Poverty was declared. The Economic Opportunity Act of 1964 (EOA) established a number of initiatives designed to give people the opportunities and assistance necessary for overcoming poverty. These initiatives included the Head Start program, which gave economically disadvantaged children educational opportunities, and Community Action Programs, which were designed to give local communities the opportunity to identify needs and develop solutions. Indian tribes, like

states and cities could apply to administer programs funded by the EOA, thus, tribes could exercise more control over these social welfare initiatives as compared to those that were under federal jurisdiction. Health care and social services amendments were added to the Social Security Act during this period, which included Medicaid for the elderly and the impoverished. The federal government committed to funding up to 75 percent of these services. However, as costs escalated in the 1970s, new amendments were passed that placed spending caps on states and that stipulated eligibility for services. These limitations continued into the 1980s when huge cuts in social welfare programs and block grant funding were instituted. These changes were driven by the desire to limit federal spending and the affirmation of the residual approach to social welfare.

Independent of the national assistance program available to all citizens, the last fifty years have seen the birth of three changes with regard to the provision of assistance to Indians only. The Bureau of Indian Affairs was reorganized in the late 1940s and given oversight responsibility for implementing federal policies and programs, all federal lands and all Indian affairs. The Indian Health Service was established in 1955 as a part of the Public Health Service, and charged with the responsibility for the health of all Indian people. The passage of the Indian Self Determination and Education Assistance Act of 1975, Public Law 638, encouraged tribal administration of programs previously administered by the BIA. There was some opposition to this act as it could be used to terminate a tribe's special trust status and thus, the authority of treaty agreements. Tribes could hardly be self-supporting without adequate federal funding for contracts. Since the 1950s, administration of the primary federal programs developed for tribes and Indians living off the reservation have been divided between two federal agencies: the Department of the Interior and the Department of Health and Human Services. As noted, tribal members are also eligible for services available to all citizens. Therefore, American Indians may interact with assistance programs administered by the federal, state, BIA and IHS agencies. There are also special programs for Indian people in all twelve cabinet level departments, as well as hundreds of local and privately funded programs. The complexity associated with accessing all these programs is staggering. Another issue continues to surface that makes this complexity even more challenging.

The federal government continues to confront contradictions in the efforts to devise programs that adhere to the American social welfare value orientations and treaty obligations. Many of the programs offered to Indian communities that fall under the mantle of the

Social Security Act and the poverty initiatives of the 1960s are neither supportive of nor compatible with tribal ways and environmental conditions. Programs may conflict with community values or contain provisions that are unrealizable in the local community. The preceding discussion on Temporary Assistance to Needy Families illustrates this, as program directives assume that jobs are locally available and that a community infrastructure exists (plumbing, utilities, transportation, child care) to support work. One outcome of this contradiction is that programs cannot achieve intended results. Although the federal government had invested heavily in assistance programs the lack of attention to the root causes that drive the need for assistance programs and the lack or attention to cultural and environmental considerations consistently undermine efforts. The income assistance program designed for needy families illustrate these issues.

Temporary Assistance to Needy Families

Passage of the *Personal Responsibility and Work Opportunity Reconciliation Act of 1996 (PL 104–193)*, commonly known as welfare reform, solidified the residual approach to income assistance for poor children and their families and marks a retreat from the federal responsibility to insure a minimum standard of living for all families. A year after passage of the welfare reform legislation, Congress amended the law by establishing *Welfare to Work* legislation. These laws create significant change in the provision of welfare assistance to needy individuals, children, and families. Aid to Families with Dependent Children (AFDC) has been dismantled and transformed into the Temporary Assistance for Needy Families program (TANF). TANF is now funded via discretionary block grants to the states and mandates strict work participation requirements for all participants. All welfare-related assistance programs and service—Food Stamps, Medicaid, Medicare, child care, and children's programs—are impacted as state and local governments are now charged with responsibility for program implementations and given spending authority. In the process, the residual approach that promotes temporary assistance, minimal intrusion from the federal government, and personal responsibility is affirmed as the federal government shed much of its fiscal and jurisdictional responsibilities for income assistance to poor children and families. Vocational training, job search activities, and employment are mandatory for recipients of Temporary Aid to Needy Families.

As noted earlier in this discussion, Indian Country is significantly impacted by poverty and its consequences. As such, the potential impact of welfare reform is especially hazardous to the health and well being of Indian communities. The contradictions associated with American social welfare policy and American Indians are glaringly apparent. There are few provisions within the welfare reform legislation that address the unique status or issues of Indians in American society. Tribal governments now have less standing, rights, and privileges in the design and implementation of welfare reform programs than do states. The long-standing problems of tribal and reservation economic development significantly undermine the capacity of Indian recipients to meet eligibility criteria and the mandatory requirements; therefore, they are at great risk of being sanctioned for non-compliance. Tribes are able to operate their own tribal TANF programs, and many are doing so. However, the resources available to the states for implementation are not available to tribal governments. Therefore, tribes are burdened in the earliest stages of development because they lack the resources needed to develop and sustain TANF programs. States have partnered with the federal government for many years to provide income assistance programs. Because tribes have not been provided with the support required for a fair and equal collaboration with federal government, their TANF initiatives will likely be plagued with special problems in the initial phases of implementation. It appears that it will be extremely difficult for tribes to mount locally controlled TANF programs without state fiscal support. Yet states are not required to match tribal resources; therefore, there is little motivation for them to do so. As tribes are offered the opportunity to develop tribal TANF initiatives, they must be prepared to assume the costs for enormously expensive welfare programs and to provide comprehensive services to a historically needy population. TANF recipients are required to meet strict work requirements and eligibility for assistance is limited to a period of not more that two consecutive years and not more than five years in a lifetime. These provisions clearly reiterate the residual approach to social welfare, and the assumption that poverty is a personal choice, that jobs are available and that infrastructure supports exist to promote and enhance employability. A special provision is provided for Indians who reside on reservations where the unemployment rate is at least 50 percent in a designated reporting period. However, unemployment rates fluctuate over time and an unemployment rate of 48 percent does not eliminate work requirements, so this provision does not offer significant relief. As noted previously, there is a significant relationship between economic development and poverty. The chronic absence of economic development fuels chronic poverty. True welfare reform on reservations requires jobs and economic development. True welfare reform on and off the reservation would acknowledge the unique legal relationships that exist between Indians and the federal government and recognize that the root causes of poverty must be addressed.

Federal Programs for American Indians

There are eleven cabinet-level federal departments, the BIA under the Department of the Interior, and a number of independent federal agencies that provide programs designed to serve Indian tribes and/or off-reservation Indian people. The BIA has five major divisions—Office of Administration, Office of Indian Education Programs, Office of Tribal Services, Office of Trust and Economic Development, and Area Offices—and each has a number of subdivisions and programs. Information about some of these programs is provided. Readers can access more detailed and specific information about these programs via the Internet and in federal documents and reports on federal assistance programs written for the Senate Committee on Indian Affairs. Since both houses of Congress are responsible for Indian policy and for funding and overseeing programs for Indians, special committees are appointed to carry out these responsibilities, such as the Senate Committee on Indian Affairs. Committee staff persons become knowledgeable about Indian programs, and the committee holds special hearings to acquire information needed by members of Congress and the general public.

The Department of Agriculture administers programs designed to enhance utilization of natural resources (soil conservation, for example) and technical assistance programs designed to aid persons engaged in farming and forestry, in addition to the food programs described in the preceding section.

The Department of Commerce administers programs to stimulate economic development and alleviate unemployment, such as loans and technical assistance to develop small businesses to determine feasibility of a proposed enterprise. The Minority Business Development Agency provides financial assistance for business development to American Indian businesses, business owners, and tribes. The department administers special programs related to the fishing industry. Indian tribes, like states, can apply for grant monies for the construction of public facilities to encourage long-term economic growth in communities where economic growth is seen to be lagging behind.

The Department of Defense sponsors a program to recruit American Indians into the National Guard. The Air Force's Affirmative Employment American Indian/ Alaskan Native Special Emphasis Program assesses barriers in the recruitment process and in the work place to American Indian participation. The Defense Department shares the cost of running Procurement Technical Assistance programs to tribally based businesses to increase tribal opportunities to obtain Defense Department contracts. The Army's Corps of Engineers may assist in assessing the feasibility of developing tribal land areas for income producing recreational purposes.

The Department of Education has many programs related to American Indians. Central goals are to establish and enrich Indian-controlled schools and projects that meet the educational and cultural needs of Indian children. Formula grants are available to tribes, local educational agencies, and tribal schools to provide financial assistance in the development, establishment, and operation of elementary and secondary school programs that meet the culturally related academic needs of Indian children. Resources also are available to develop adult education programs to increase basic academic skills of American Indian adults; increase the number of adults who earn a high school equivalency diploma; and support the heritage of American Indian adults. All these funds are allocated using a competitive, grant proposal process. In addition, the department provides technical assistance and training to education agencies, parent committees, and tribes and Indian organizations in the design, management, implementation, and evaluation of education programs in which more than 5,000 Indian children are enrolled. Fellowships are available to Indian persons admitted to undergraduate or graduate programs in engineering, business administration, natural resources, and related fields and to Indian students in graduate programs in medicine, psychology, law, education, and related fields.

The Department of Energy offers a state formula grant program for energy-efficient homes to low-income homeowners, especially the aged and handicapped, and offers programs designed to conserve energy. The department assists minority financial institutions, such as banks, by providing long-term capital to increase the funds available for loans and investments in minority communities.

The Department of Housing and Urban Development provides funds for housing construction in Indian communities. Most of these funds are used to subsidize privately owned family homes.

The Department of Health and Human Services is the key department of the executive branch of the U.S. government responsible for income support and social service programs. Its diverse programs are administered by a number of subdivisions within the department. The Administration for Children, Youth, and Families administers several programs for which tribes

The American Indian clubhouse in downtown Los Angeles serves Native students in an after–school program. (Photo by Mary G. Wentz)

may apply, two of which are the Head Start program, which provides health, educational, nutritional, and social services to economically disadvantaged preschool-aged children and their families, and the Child Welfare Services program, which establishes and strengthens the child welfare services provided by state and local public welfare agencies to enable children to remain in their own homes or, when that is not possible, to provide alternate permanent homes. Funds are available to Indian tribal organizations to provide child welfare services.

The Administration for Native Americans (ANA) places a priority on funding innovative projects that will, in the administration's opinion, have the greatest impact on promoting economic, political, and social self-sufficiency for Native peoples to increase their independence from U.S. programs. ANA-funded projects assist tribal governments to exercise control over their resources; to foster development of stable, diversified local economies to increase jobs, promote economic well-being, and reduce dependency on public

funds and social services; and to foster social development to support access to, control of, and coordination of services and programs that safeguard the health and well-being of people.

The Office of Policy, Planning, and Legislation funds small grants to prevent family violence and alleviate its effects.

The Indian Health Service of the Public Health Service was established in 1955 to improve the health of American Indians and Alaska Natives by providing a full range of curative, preventive, and rehabilitative health services. In addition, IHS is supposed to build the capacity of tribes to manage their own health programs. Tribes may contract with IHS to provide direct services to tribal members. Funds are available for recruitment and scholarship support to increase the number of Indian health care professionals.

The Office of Community Services of the Family Support Administration can fund tribes to assist low-income families to meet their costs of home energy. This program office also can award block grants to tribes to ameliorate poverty by providing a number of services to low-income members, including employment, education, improved use of their available income, housing, emergency assistance, removal of obstacles to self-sufficiency, community participation, better use of other programs related to decreasing poverty, improved coordination of service delivery, and increased use of private sector resources to fight poverty.

The Department of the Interior houses the Bureau of Indian Affairs (BIA), the major agency responsible for Indian programs. The BIA serves as the intermediary between tribes and the federal government. Most of the BIA's attention is focused on land and resource management. However, within the several divisions some attention is given to social welfare issues. Authorized by the Snyder Act of 1921, the Division of Education provides financial aid to enable Indians to attend college and to enable adults to increase their basic skills and to obtain a high school equivalency degree.

The BIA Division of Self-Determination Services, Office of Tribal Services, can provide grants to the governing bodies of federally recognized tribes to improve tribal governing capacities, prepare for contracting of bureau programs, enable tribes to provide direction to the bureau and to other federal programs intended to serve Indian people. These are called self-determination grants, and Public Law 93–638, the Self-Determination and Education Assistance Act of 1975 authorizes them. Provided in the form of project grants, and thus competitive, projects must be designed to improve a tribe's capacity to enter into contracts, including the purchase of third party technical assistance, the acquisition of land, and the designing, monitoring, and evaluation of federal programs serving Indian tribes. The funds requested for 1991 were less than one-third the funding request for 1990 (one-third of $13.5 million). Again, resources available for these programs are decreasing. The number of programs alone, without assessing the amount of funds available, does not tell us the value of the support to American Indians.

The BIA initiated cash General Assistance Program on reservations in the early 1940s. In addition, the BIA administers social service programs for families and children and awards funds competitively through a grant application process for tribal Indian child welfare service programs. The BIA has a guaranteed loan program designed to increase the number of lending institutions that will loan money to Indian organizations and individuals residing on or near a federally recognized reservation and to Indian-run business ventures.

The Department of Justice, Civil Rights Division, enforces the civil rights of American Indians defined in federal statute, the Constitution, and civil rights acts. The latter includes protection of equal rights to federal programs. Also, funds are available to improve reporting of child abuse and services to victims.

The Department of Labor administers Indian training and employment efforts.

The Department of Transportation provides assistance toward increasing Native employment opportunities in transportation linked projects and toward assuring Indian access to Department of Transportation contracts.

The Department of Veteran Affairs offers assistance toward Indians receiving earned benefits.

The massive number of programs can be deceptive if the actual program size and available funding for each program are not assessed. For example, substandard housing, family violence, and substance abuse prevention continue to impact Indian communities. On paper there is a program through the Department of Health and Human Services, Office of Policy, Planning and Legislation, yet 85 percent of the available funds are designated for states, thus monies for tribes to address this critical issue are very limited. Assistance initiatives to American Indians must address the multitude of issues that erode the fabric of American Indian communities and that support comprehensive, coordinated and well-funded service delivery systems.

Indian families consistently receive less support than non-Indian families. For example, state support for day care for low-income families commonly is not available to the same extent to families living on reservations. Since states will only reimburse state-licensed day care providers if such providers are not accessible to Indian families, the families cannot receive subsidized day care services. A number of tribes continue to have the lowest per capita income levels in the United States, with large numbers of families falling well below national poverty levels. Overall the average income for Indian families is lower than the incomes of other families, including minority of color populations such as African American families; the unemployment rates are higher; and the employment resources, housing, sanitation, and life expectancy rates are all lower.

Government agencies provide subsistence-level public assistance to tribal communities, but the federal government has historically been unwilling to launch the major economic development programs that could lead to economic independence and that would compensate for the social and economic disorganization and dependence that is a consequence of the contact between Indians and non-Indians. Economic assistance and restitution initiatives to American Indians must address the root causes of the poverty in Indian Country and all the social, cultural, material, and psychological consequences. Assistance initiatives must be connected with restitution and disconnected from the residual philosophies that characterize American social welfare policies.

Rita Ledesma
California State University, Los Angeles

◆ ABORIGINAL ECONOMIC ACTIVITY IN CANADA

Aboriginal economic activity has been important to the early survival of European settlers and the development of Canada throughout its history as a country. Trade with aboriginal peoples sustained many of the early settlers. In later years, aboriginal labor helped build the railway, harvest crops, bring in the hay, herd cows, pick fruit, can salmon, transport furs along waterways, and guide settlers through unknown territory, among myriad other activities. Yet, by any statistical standard one wishes to apply, aboriginal peoples have come to occupy the lowest rung on the economic ladder in Canada. Through several decades of the welfare state and various state initiatives to address the economic problems of aboriginal peoples, levels of income, labor force participation, and education remain stubbornly and significantly below that of the general population.

Aboriginal peoples have been seen as a people somehow ill suited to commercial or capitalist activity and hence unable to participate effectively in a capitalist economy. The communal nature of aboriginal culture, the absence of institutions of private property, and the lack of a profit motive, the argument runs, has rendered aboriginal peoples unable to compete in a competitive marketplace and limited the community's ability to adjust to rapidly changing times.

A quick historical profile of indigenous economic activity reveals that these generalizations are not supportable. Long before Europeans arrived in North America, aboriginal people maintained extensive and productive trade networks, exchanging surplus products, securing supplies of necessary items, and distributing new materials and products. Trade in North America was not, therefore, a European innovation or import.

The Royal Commission on Aboriginal Peoples (1996) describes aboriginal economic history in four periods which correspond roughly to the development of the relationship between aboriginal peoples and Canadians.

The Pre-Contact Period (Before 1500)

Prior to the arrival of Europeans, most aboriginal peoples in Canada were hunters, fishers, and gatherers. Those who lived near the Pacific, Arctic, and Atlantic oceans had an economy that involved sea harvesting; those on the St. Lawrence valley and Great Lakes engaged in agriculture.

Aboriginal peoples were thinly scattered with two principal concentrations: the Pacific Northwest and the Lower Great Lakes Regions. For the most part, economic activity varied according to the seasons and the availability of fish, wildlife, and vegetation. The emphasis was on living in balance with nature rather than on accumulating economic surpluses or wealth. For most this meant paying close attention to the food needs of the group, the ability of the land or sea to sustain future inhabitants.

Robin Riddington, an anthropologist at the University of British Columbia, theorizes that the technology used as the basis of aboriginal economies was based upon knowledge rather than tools. More than material technology, he argues, it was intimate knowledge of the ecosystem, developed over thousands of years, and aboriginal ingenuity that enabled aboriginal peoples to survive in the harsh northern environment.

Extensive trade networks were used for the movement of goods and technology across the country: fish from the Northwest Coast were transported to the interior; obsidian (a volcanic rock used in tools), originating in British Columbia, was found in the western plains; abalone from California was found in the interior.

Aboriginal economic activity was undertaken for a number of reasons: profit or material gain, prestige, to build or maintain alliances, or cement agreements. In some aboriginal societies, particularly those of the Pacific the accumulation of wealth was accompanied by ceremonies for giving it away: the potlatch. Prestige and status accrued to those who were most generous.

The Fur Trade (1500–1814)

In this period, aboriginal peoples and Europeans regarded each other as distinct and autonomous, left to govern their own internal affairs but cooperating in areas of mutual interest and occasionally and increasingly linked in various trading relationships and other forms of nation-to-nation alliances.

In the initial period of contact, aboriginal peoples were able to continue their traditional patterns of economic activity. In the early 1500s, Mi'kmaq began to trade furs for European goods: knives, iron goods, foodstuffs, and clothing. Across the continent, aboriginal peoples' early encounters with Europeans were primarily as potential trading partners and occasionally as suppliers of local goods, contractors (trappers) who harvested local wildlife in exchange for European goods, and middlemen between aboriginal suppliers and European trading companies. The fur trade began to expand; Maliseet, Montagnais, Iroquois, Cree, and Ojibwa, among others were actively engaged in the trade as either trappers or middlemen.

Aboriginal people initially adapted well to the demands of the fur trade, which built upon and supported traditional lifestyles rather than displacing them. Aboriginal peoples were also important players in the economies of the time. They were excellent harvesters and negotiators, seeking the best deals for their furs, and they were adept at playing off the English and French, or one boat against another, to get the best prices. The Hudson Bay Company had to develop a standard of exchange for furs and European goods to counter aboriginal negotiating prowess.

Métis people were also important actors in the fur trade. The Métis lived in and around trading posts; some worked as independent laborers, as freighters on boat brigades, or in clerical or supervisory jots at trading posts. The merger of the North West Company and the Hudon's Bay Company in 1821 reduced labor requirements somewhat, but many Métis people were still employed in the fur trade and in new opportunity areas of buffalo hunting and exporting of buffalo hides and furs to the United States. The continuing arrival of European settlers and the growth of towns and villages led to the emergence of a small Métis merchant class and Métis skilled craftsmen who built churches, housing, and commercial establishments and manufactured carts.

The fur trade also had negative consequences, including the depletion of fur-bearing animals as new technologies permitted greater harvests and European market demands rose; conflict among aboriginal groups as they pushed into new territories in search of resources; exposure to the boom and bust cycle for staple production and its resultant unemployment, first in the fur trade but then in other areas such as whaling, forest production, fishing, sealing, and mineral mining; and exposure to contagious disease which devastated aboriginal populations and caused much social, economic, and cultural disruption.

The Settler Period (1814–1930)

In this period, non-aboriginal society was for the most part no longer willing to respect the distinctiveness of aboriginal communities. Non-aboriginal society made repeated attempts to recast aboriginal peoples and their institutions to conform to the expectations of mainstream Canada. Aboriginal peoples remained determined to maintain their distinctiveness and conduct their relations in line with their original and agreed upon understandings as outlined in treaties and other agreements.

As Europeans created new and permanent communities, they came to see aboriginal peoples as a hindrance to the development of Canada's lands, waters, and other natural resources. Aboriginal peoples were pushed to the margins and the alienation of aboriginal peoples from their lands and resources began. In many cases, Europeans simply assumed that they had title to these new lands and resources (or were given title by those whom they assumed had the authority to grant it). In some cases, Europeans recognized that some form of negotiation and compensation was necessary. This recognition lead to and informed a period of treaty making which transferred large amounts of land and resources from aboriginal peoples to Canada. In some cases, particularly in British Columbia, no treaties were offered and there is no agreement on the sharing of lands and resources. The Canadian government has established a treaty claims process aimed at rectifying problems with treaties (through specific claims) and at dealing with areas and aboriginal peoples who did not sign treaties.

The decline of the fur trade and the continued development of the settler economy led to extreme disruption of aboriginal economies to the point where aboriginal peoples experienced severe economic deprivation. For example, Métis people on the prairies saw their overland hauling routes undermined by railroads and steamboats; the decline of the buffalo damaged both Indian and Métis livelihoods; and all experienced the depletion of forbearing animals in the woodland areas of the Great Lakes and the overfishing of lakes and streams.

The new government of Canada in 1867, through the Constitution Act, assumed the exclusive responsibility for Indians and lands reserved for Indians. The Gradual Enfranchisement Act of 1869 replaced traditional Indian governments with elected chiefs and councilors whose decisions required the approval of a federally appointed Indian agent acting on behalf of a minister of the Crown. The transfer of control from Indian people to the government of Canada caused enormous disruptions in the socioeconomic development of communities which last into today. Laws which restricted mobility, the ownership of property, and the extension of credit, among others, impeded economic development.

In the late nineteenth and early twentieth century, Canada made significant attempts to persuade Indian people to become farmers. The goal was to have Indian and Métis people settle down and adopt a European way of life. For the most part these efforts were unsuccessful; government policies did not permit sufficient resources, either land, equipment, or seed, while drought, overproduction of land, and low prices hindered success. More often than not, non-Indian farmers persuaded the government to sell productive Indian lands to them, place restrictions on the sale of Indian produce, and limit Indian use of new technologies.

As Canada industrialized, aboriginal people began to participate in the market economy, mostly on the margins and in manual occupations. Aboriginal peoples again began to develop a measure of self-sufficiency, although at low levels of income. They participated in the new industries springing up, worked their own farms or as hired hands on others, constructed houses, and established businesses in such areas as crafts.

Rolf Knight, in his book *Indians at Work: An Informal History of Native Labor in British Columbia, 1858–1930* (1978), documents the various ways in which aboriginal peoples in British Columbia participated in logging, transportation, construction, long shoring, commercial fishing, and canning, among other industries since the arrival of Europeans; Fred Wein in *Rebuilding the Economic Base of Indian Communities: The Micmac in Nova Scotia* (1986) documents the participation of Mikm'aq people in the Atlantic economy in road construction, ship loading, pip prop cutting for coal mines, and arts and crafts production. Many traveled to Maine for seasonal harvesting of blueberries and potatoes; when unable to find employment locally, they took up jobs in the emerging manufacturing industries of New England.

There is some evidence that aboriginal peoples were successfully making a transition from a traditional to a modern economy, albeit this transition has been difficult and uneven.

The Period of Dependence (1930–)

Aboriginal participation in the settler economy was tenuous, marginal, and vulnerable. The great depression of the 1930s led to a large decline in aboriginal participation in the labor force as businesses and jobs disappeared. Aboriginal peoples, as a result of their vulnerable position, were often the first to lose their jobs or businesses. Labor force participation increased temporarily as a result of labor shortages during the Second World War, but the end of the war and the return of soldiers displaced these peoples again. Indian people increasingly turned to governments to assist in

dealing with the effects of economic distress and to take advantage of economic opportunity.

Aboriginal people were viewed as existing outside local society and, therefore, also beyond the responsibility of the federal government. Local municipalities and provinces did not seem to take any responsibility for assisting local Indian populations, particularly those living on reserves. Local services were not available, banks were reluctant to do business with people on reserves without federal guarantees on loans, and businesses saw the reserve community primarily as a market for their goods and services, not thinking of a reciprocal obligation to provide employment or other types of community support.

In an effort to address problems of Indian poverty and unemployment, the federal government began to act to try to improve the situation. It began to relocate and consolidate reserves in order to create larger communities and to locate near more suitable land or natural resources. This approach did not work: it ignored the social effects of relocation, and the jobs created were often short-term and only available at the start of the relocation. Once the work of building and housing the members was over, the jobs disappeared.

The government also put into place an extensive welfare system. Starting in the 1960s, this was supplemented by on-reserve job creation programs. While these programs were helpful in dealing with the immediate problem of poverty and unemployment, they did not address the problem of building an economic base for the community. They were developed with little aboriginal involvement and often worked against local economic recovery. As the aboriginal population grew, the demand for jobs increased. With the rate of job creation much below the demand, the demand for social assistance increased. Over time, communities unable to meet the demand for jobs from their members grew to depend significantly on social assistance funding.

At the same time, private sector companies engaged in a series of actions that hampered the development of aboriginal economies. In the northern areas, major resource companies established operations in areas where aboriginal peoples were trying to continue to live a traditional lifestyle. Mining, forestry, oil, and gas projects were highly disruptive of aboriginal land use and harvesting patterns. In this period of expanding government, federal and provincial governments adopted whole new regimes of regulations with a wide variety of objectives: to preserve fish and game, to register tramlines, and to control access to Crown lands. They ignored aboriginal and treaty rights or interpreted them very narrowly. Starting in the 1970s, courts began to interpret these rights more broadly.

The period of dependence started in the 1930s and continues for the most part to the present. It has a number of roots, including the disruption of traditional ways of making a living; dispossession from a rich land and resource base; laws, regulations, and government policies that blocked the rebuilding of economies; failure of an education system to provide an appropriate education for aboriginal children; shifts in the mainstream economy as labor-saving technology replaced people and required more highly educated people to operate it; lack of capital to purchase this technology for their own enterprises; and the general racism exhibited toward aboriginal peoples.

Displacement Over Time

As the Canadian industrial economy continued to evolve, aboriginal people generally discovered that there was little room for them within the mainstream. Deeply entrenched patterns of racial discrimination limited the options of many otherwise qualified people. The arrival of Oriental workers on the west coast, for example, led to the displacement of substantial numbers of aboriginal workers from the fishing fleets and canneries. Few aboriginal people found work in the industrial plants and factories or in the growing number of mining and lumber operations springing up across the country. It is misleading to suggest, however, that aboriginal people did not adjust to the changing economic order, although the opportunity to do so was often circumscribed by non-Native assumptions and actions.

The economic situation of aboriginal peoples reflects a complex mix of Native choice, discrimination, and a poor fit between aboriginal skills and the changing needs of the national economy. Where possible, aboriginal people tended to preserve the harvesting option as long as they could, even if this meant only casual and seasonal involvement with the wage economy. Over time the very skills that made aboriginal people so economically important during the early days of the fur trade, commercial fishery, Arctic whaling, and other sectors were devalued by the advent of new technology or the decline of the industry. Without adequate education and still wishing to retain a substantial connection to the land, aboriginal people found themselves trapped on the outside of the evolving market economy. When groups made concerted efforts to join the new order, however, as in the case of the Plains Indians who took up commercial agriculture in the late nineteenth century, they often found that government policy and non-Native discrimination stood in their way.

A fundamental transition had occurred. In the first period of contact, aboriginal skills and knowledge had been highly valued and were essential to the success of non-Native economic development. By the late nineteenth century, reliance on aboriginal peoples had declined precipitously, and by the middle of the next century aboriginal people had been rendered essentially irrelevant to the Canadian economy. Aboriginal people attempted to adapt to the new realities but found that the newcomers had erected substantial barriers to full participation. Aboriginal peoples suffered from discrimination, which denied them access to employment and other economic opportunities. A flawed missionary-based education system was coupled with the self-serving belief that aboriginal peoples should be kept separate from non-Native peoples until they were "ready" for full integration. Not surprisingly, a variety of social and cultural difficulties accompanied the loss of autonomy and economic freedom that accompanied the loss of aboriginal lands, access to resources, and commercial opportunities. By the 1950s, when the Canadian government decided that it had an obligation to take substantial measures to address the economic gap between aboriginal and non-aboriginal peoples, the First Nations found themselves on the margins of the Canadian economy.

Renewal

Since the 1960s there have been consistent and continual efforts to try to improve the economic circumstances of aboriginal peoples. The federal government has been a key actor in this effort. Over the forty-year period starting in the 1960s, there has been a consistent evolution of the approach to aboriginal economic development. The primary focus of the early efforts was business development. In order to facilitate the start up of businesses, the federal government established the Indian Revolving Loan Fund in 1960. It provided loans and assistance (business advice and training, and small equity contributions to Indian individuals who wished to start small businesses). In the mid-1960s, this focused approach on individuals was broadened to include communities and, in 1963, the Community Development Program was established. This program increased the scope of the development effort by including social development as part of a comprehensive approach.

The Hawthrone Report (1966) recommended "that economic development should be based on a comprehensive program on many fronts besides the purely economic." This thinking was to form the basis of economic development policy for the 1970s and 1980s.

These two decades saw the development of an increasing broader set of economic development programs. These programs, NEED (Native Economic and Employment Development) and NEDP (Native Economic Development Program) in the early 1980s and CAEDS (Canadian Aboriginal Economic Development Strategy) in the late 1980s, were comprehensive and broad on a number of fronts.

First, the scope of assistance has increased from direct loans and equity contributions to include loan guarantees, provision of management and technical assistance directly by the federal government and then by nongovernmental organizations such as CESO (Canadian Executive Services Overseas now Canadian Executive Services Organization), FBDB (Federal Business Development Bank), Frontiers Foundation, and many others. Second, the number of target groups has increased from exclusively Indians on-reserve, to Inuit, Métis, and off-reserve Indian people, women, and youth. Third, the scope of program objectives has widened. The objectives were initially focused narrowly on small business development through the Indian revolving loan fund, then included community development through the community development program; economic sector development through support and assistance to arts and crafts, agriculture, fishing, and forestry; institutional development through the NEED and CAEDS program; and human resource development through the NEED, ICHRS (Indian Community Human Resource Strategy), and CAEDS programs. Fourth, the number of government departments involved has also increased. There has been a shift from the single-agency approach centered on INAC (Indian and Northern Affairs Canada) in the 1960s to a multi-department approach of the 1990s, which now includes Human Resources Canada, Aboriginal Business Canada, and Health Canada. In addition, there is now a more coordinated approach among the various federal departments involved. Fifth, the degree of participation and control by aboriginal people has also increased. In the 1960s and early 1970s, the federal government retained control over all aspects of economic development: planning, setting priorities, and developing and approving projects. Since then, aboriginal peoples and their institutions have assumed larger and larger roles in all of these processes. Finally, significant growth in the institutional capacity of aboriginal communities has furthered their socioeconomic development.

Aboriginal people have demonstrated a remarkable consistency in their preferred approach to economic development. This approach was set out in the *Wahbung: Our Tomorrows*, a report prepared by the Manitoba Indian Brotherhood in response to the White Paper[1] of 1969. This report called for development to proceed, not in bits and pieces, but according to a comprehensive plan. This plan consisted of three essential elements: (1) a plan to help individuals and communities recover from the pathological consequences of poverty and powerlessness; (2) a plan for the protection of Indian interests in lands and resources; and (3) a concerted effort toward human resource and cultural development. The report argued that any change that was to be beneficial would have to directed and evaluated by Indian people themselves, who could take individual and communal interests into consideration better than the federal government. It also argued that Canadian governments would have to relinquish some powers to Indian people to enable self-government and that Indian people would also have to link Canadian and local cultures.

Wahbung, while it may have been a reaction against government policy, was a positive statement of principle and value by aboriginal leaders. It outlined a vision of how they wanted the future to unfold. It was an act of a human agency. This act had an enormous effect. Over the next thirty years, aboriginal leaders were to advocate for these principles in almost all areas.

The Royal Commission on Aboriginal Peoples (1991–1996) undertook significant research into aboriginal economies and their future development. This effort was one of the first in contemporary times to examine in great detail what had gone wrong in Native economic development and how to rectify it. The research was one of the first efforts to focus on a distinct entity called an *aboriginal economy*. In this sense, it represented a shift in thinking about aboriginal peoples, causing a shift in public policy away from a project-oriented approach to a community-development approach based on long term agreements for resources and assistance.

Aboriginal leaders and Canadian policymakers have started to think about something called an *aboriginal economy* or *aboriginal economies* and to explore the nature and functioning of that economy and the appropriate micro economic policies to develop it. There is now an understanding that these economies are enormously varied across a number of different spectra, from predominately traditional economies to modern market economies. Each has varying levels of natural and human resources, varying economic, social and political goals, and differing institutional capacities to facilitate, encourage, advocate, assist in and direct the development of local economies.

The Report of the Royal Commission on Aboriginal Peoples and Economic Development (1996)

The commission concluded, on the basis of its hearings, community visits, and research during the 1991–1996 period that current conditions and approaches to economic development would bring little improvement in the conditions and prospects for aboriginal peoples. Achieving a more self-reliant economic base for aboriginal peoples would require significant, even radical, departures from business as usual.

While the current situation was bleak, the commission found that the situation was not static and that there were some promising new directions. Over the past two decades, several major comprehensive claims agreements have been signed. These provide access to new human, financial, and natural resources for economic development. There has been much growth in the number of aboriginal businesses, especially those started by women. There have been significant improvements in the institutional base to support economic development as evidenced by the emergence of personnel and organizations specializing in economic development and providing capital, education, and training programs.

The commission also found a realistic appreciation of the challenges that lie ahead as well as a spirit of determination to regain stewardship of aboriginal economies and to develop them in accordance with the values and priorities of particular nations and communities. Strategies for change, the commission argues, must be rooted in an understanding of the forces that have created economic marginalization in the first place. Factors essential for economic development, such as the economic provisions in historical treaties, the freedom for aboriginal peoples to manage their own economies, and a fair share of the land and resource base that sustained aboriginal economies in the past were ignored and now needed to be addressed.

The problem of economic development is often defined as an individual based problem (i.e., aboriginal individuals do not have access to opportunities for employment or business development in the larger Canadian society). This approach ignores the collectivity in aboriginal society. It overlooks the fact that economic development is the product of interaction of many factors: health, education, self-worth, functioning communities, stable environments, and the like. While economic development must support individuals, it must also support collectives. Some of the most important steps that need to be taken involve this collectivity, for example regaining control over decisions affecting the economy, and regaining greater ownership and control over economic development.

Economic development is also a process that can be supported or frustrated. The role of aboriginal and non-aboriginal governments should be to support the process, help create the conditions under which economic development can thrive, and remove the obstacles that stand in its way.

Aboriginal economies are diverse, ranging from comprehensive claims regions such as the Inuvialuit regions of the western Arctic, Nunavut, and James Bay; Métis settlements in northern Alberta; reserves such as Six Nations which have a dynamic small business sector; and rural and urban communities where a self-sustaining economic base is far from being achieved or where traditional pursuits such as hunting, fishing, or trapping are interwoven into the wage economy. This means that a policy developed and issued in Ottawa to be applied uniformly across the diversity of economies would not be helpful to aboriginal peoples.

Aboriginal Economic Goals.   The commission also reported on the economic goals that aboriginal people want to achieve. These include:

1. Respect for the treaties, the comprehensive claims, and other agreements made with the Crown and to remedy past injustices concerning land and resources, including securing a land base for all aboriginal people, including Métis;

2. Jobs that provide a decent income that do not necessarily require moving from aboriginal communities and that provide meaning to people's lives, contributing to the development of self-esteem and aboriginal identity. Aboriginal economies should provide choices for people rather than dictating directions;

3. Economies capable of supporting those who wish to continue traditional pursuits while enabling those who wish to participate in a wage and market economy to do so;

4. Economies that are largely self-reliant and sustaining, not in the sense of being independent from trade networks and other economic systems, but in the sense of being in a position to give and receive fair value in economic exchanges;

5. Economies providing not only the basis for survival but also an opportunity to prosper and help build a sense of accomplishment and self-worth for the individual and the collective;

6. Choices about the nature of this economy, its structure, and processes made to the largest extent possible by aboriginal peoples and their institutions;

7. Economic development that will contribute to the development of aboriginal peoples as distinct peoples within Canada and to permit them to exercise, in a significant and substantial manner, governance in their communities and stewardship of lands and resources. In short, economic development is expected to enable aboriginal peoples to govern themselves; and

8. Economies structured in accordance with aboriginal values, principles, and customs, contributing to the development and affirmation of aboriginal culture and identity.

In the view of aboriginal peoples, the commission notes, economic development is more than just individuals striving to maximize incomes and prestige. It is about maintaining and developing culture and identity; supporting self-governing institutions, and sustaining traditional ways of making a living. It is about giving people choice in their lives and maintaining appropriate forms of relationships with their own and other societies.

The Commission's Critical Issues. The commission highlights three critical economic issues facing aboriginal peoples: (1) the need to develop stronger, more self-reliant aboriginal economies to accompany and sustain self-government; (2) the need to eliminate the sharp inequalities in employment and incomes that separate aboriginal people from Canadian standards; and (3) the need to come to grips with the rapid increase in the aboriginal population, which will need 300,000 new jobs by the year 2016.

The commission sees the economic development as a process with three principal participants: aboriginal individuals, communities, and nations. It sees governments, both aboriginal and non-aboriginal, as facilitators of the process of change. They can set the stage for economic development, remove barriers, create opportunities and provide support. In some cases, they may also own and manage business ventures on behalf of their communities.

The commission underlines the importance of understanding the goals that aboriginal peoples are trying to achieve and using this understanding as the basis for action by non-aboriginal and aboriginal governments.

The Call for a New Relationship. The economic development recommendations of the Royal Commission on Aboriginal Peoples (RCAP) are made within the context of its call for a new relationship between Canada and aboriginal peoples. This new relationship, in the commission's view, should be a nation-to-nation one, based upon the restoration of aboriginal nations.

The sixty or so aboriginal nations would have governments with a wide range of powers and authorities and constitutionally situated as a third-order of government. One of the powers of these new governments would be over the development of its economy.

The commission concludes that the transformation of aboriginal economies from dependence on government transfers to interdependence and self-reliance is fundamental to the development of self-government. Aboriginal nations and communities must be able to generate sufficient wealth to provide an acceptable quality of life for their members. They also state that this type of transformation will require a concerted, comprehensive effort over an extended period of time. It will take a deliberate commitment of time and resources by Canada and aboriginal peoples. Given the diversity of aboriginal economies across the country, no single approach to their development is possible. Each must be allowed, encouraged, and supported to find and follow their own path.

Key Issues. The commission has identified six key issues which it felt it was necessary to address in order to support economic development. These issues are:

1. The restoration of fair shares in the lands and resources of Canada through the recognition of aboriginal rights and treaty provisions and the negotiation of new or renewed treaties;

2. The development of effective institutions of governance and economic development whereby aboriginal peoples regain control of key decisions concerning economic strategy;

3. The creation and management of enterprises that can harvest resources and manufacture the resources and services that generate income and wealth;

4. The mastery of professional and technical skills necessary to work in modern economy and influence the way business is conducted;

5. A concerted national effort in job creation and training to achieve aboriginal employment rates similar to those of other Canadians; and

6. New approaches to the use of social assistance for aboriginal communities which link income supplements to productive activity.

The commission makes fifty-two recommendations regarding aboriginal economic development in the areas outlined above. While the government has not yet responded to all of them, it is important to understand that what was proposed is consistent with aboriginal thinking on these issues over the last three decades and lays a foundation for future economic development efforts.

The fundamental view of the commission is that aboriginal economic development is a process that needs to be under the control and guidance of aboriginal peoples and their institutions of governance for it to be successful. The economic goals which aboriginal peoples pursue are broad and not narrowly focused on income or the creation of individual wealth. Economic development is expected to further the movement toward self-government.

In the commission's view, there are a number of critical but highly interrelated tasks which need to be undertaken. The high level of interrelatedness of the tasks themselves, the links between aboriginal economies and the mainstream economies, and the enormity of the development task indicate the need for a concerted and coordinated long-term development effort.

Aboriginal Business Development in Canada

One of the areas in economic development that tends to be ignored is the area of business development. Relatively little attention is paid to the nature and extent of business development within aboriginal communities. The popular conception is that aboriginal economies consist mainly of occasional wage work, employment in government and administrative service, and reliance on transfer payments. However, contrary to this conception, aboriginal businesses are becoming important elements in the economic realm of aboriginal peoples in Canada and an important part of the economic development strategies of aboriginal communities.

The 1991 Aboriginal Peoples' Survey indicated that 25,275 aboriginal people in Canada reported current business ownership and/or income from self-employment. Another 12,575 reported prior business ownership. The 1996 Aboriginal Business Survey reported that 20,000 aboriginal people were self-employed. The growth in self-employment from the period 1991 to 1996 was 2.5 times that of the Canadian national increase in self-employment. Aboriginal entrepreneurs are active in every sector of the economy, from the old economy to the new economy. Fifty percent of aboriginal businesses are located in urban centers. The same 1996 investigation of aboriginal businesses found that the vast majority of these enterprises were profitable, contributed about 5,000 new jobs in aboriginal communities and provided many other spin-off benefits. This is still a far cry from the 300,000 new jobs needed by the year 2016 to accommodate the growth in the aboriginal labor force population.

Business activity by Indians was limited by the legal restrictions under which Canadian Indians[2] live. Under the terms of the Indian Act, first passed in 1867, status Indians living on an Indian reserve were prevented from owning reserve land as a private holding, taking out a mortgage, securing a bank loan, or otherwise taking the steps necessary to establish a business. These limitations, coupled with government paternalism and non-aboriginal discrimination, prevented many aboriginal people from participating fully in the commercial arena. A few who wished to capitalize on commercial opportunities were forced to seek enfranchisement, which required surrendering their Indian status in order to be freed from the restrictions. While some of these constraints remain in place—reserve lands, for example, are held in trust by the federal government and hence cannot be used as collateral for loans (although there have been changes to the Indian Act that permit First Nations to designate lands for development and create a separate legal regime for them)—the post–Second World War period saw significant barriers lifted to aboriginal business prospects.

Since the 1950s, aboriginal people have been aided by a variety of government support programs to start small businesses. The initiatives started in a limited fashion, through the provision of small loans to purchase trucks for wood-cutting or other such ventures. By the 1960s, full-fledged national programs were in place, providing development capital, formal advice and oversight, and ongoing government support for aboriginal peoples (individuals and communities) interested in starting a business as well as special programs in sectors such as agriculture, mining, forestry, and arts and crafts. Programs like the Indian Business Development Fund provided financial support for Indian-owned businesses. Application and approval procedures were often cumbersome and the success rate (defined in terms of long-term, profitable operations) was quite low. These early business development programs evolved into larger economic development programs NEED, NEDP, ICHRS, and CAEDS, in which business development become a part of a larger more comprehensive development strategy.

Government support efforts were also supplemented by other efforts both within and outside aboriginal communities. Aboriginal organizations made similar efforts to assist individuals wishing to establish commercial ventures. There were efforts in the 1970s to establish a national Indian Business Association whose goal was to assist business startup and to advocate on behalf of aboriginal businesses. Business advice was provided through organizations like CESO which established the Canadian Native Business Program and recruited retired business people to provide management and technical advice to aboriginal businesses. Universities across the country, through their business schools, provided expertise through the Indian Business Assistance Program (later the Indian Management Assistance Program). Local community economic development organizations also provided support in the form of training, advice, and small loans. A group of Canadian business leaders formed the Canada Council for Aboriginal Business to provide advice and support for aboriginal entrepreneurs and to encourage Canadian businesses to assist in establishing aboriginal businesses.

Aboriginal peoples over the past two decades have challenged the popular conception that engaging in business activity is not part of aboriginal culture and that individuals would not be supported if they started businesses or that collectively owned enterprises would not work and could not be profitable. There is now a small but solid foundation of aboriginal businesses, both individually and collectively owned. There is a great determination to move away from the culture of dependency that has characterized many aboriginal communities over the past half century. Aboriginal businesses are now seen as much a part of the movement towards self government as is the reestablishment of aboriginal governments.

Aboriginal Entrepreneurs in Canada, a 1999 study by Aboriginal Business Canada reported that an active business sector of privately owned Native-run businesses is emerging. Although this sector is relatively small in the overall context of Canadian business, it is growing. This report found that aboriginal businesses parallel other Canadian business: they are relatively small (54 percent have no full-time employees versus 60 percent of Canadian businesses that have no employees; 46 percent versus 40 percent have at least one full-time employee); more and more aboriginal women are establishing their own businesses; the majority (62 percent) of aboriginal businesses are profitable, but their profitability is less (approximately two-thirds that of Canadian businesses) and aboriginal businesses tend to be concentrated in recreational/personal services, construction, and transportation industries. Only a few are in the new economy. The survey indicated a high level of awareness among aboriginal entrepreneurs of the skills and knowledge necessary to survive in businesses as well as a desire to constantly improve their own skill levels.

There are still many problems facing aboriginal businesses, particularly those located in areas where markets are small or financing is not readily available, or where there are insufficient numbers of educated and trained people to fill managerial and technical positions. The small size of many businesses means that they are more vulnerable to changes in economic and market conditions. The high demand by communities for employment places great pressure on aboriginal businesses for rapid growth. Racism against aboriginal peoples continues to be a factor in many places. Government assistance programs tend to ignore aboriginal peoples living off reserve or Métis people, focusing primarily on status Indians. All pose challenges that need to be addressed if the aboriginal business sector is to continue to grow. Yet it is a tribute to the perseverance and ingenuity of aboriginal people coupled with the assistance of the Canadian state and some members of the private sector that they have been able to create this small but central business community after Natives peoples' forced exclusion from the Canadian economy.

David Newhouse
Trent University

Notes

1. In 1969, the government of Canada introduced for discussion a policy paper entitled "Statement of Indian Policy of the Government of Canada." It proposed, among other measures, the repeal of the Indian Act, the termination of Indian status, the dissolution of Indian reserves, and the shift of responsibilities for Indians to provinces. Governments release policy statements for discussion in what are termed *white papers*. The government policy paper became know as The White Paper, an ironic title given its Anglo- centric perspective.

2. The Indian Act creates a category of person called Status Indian; that is, a person registered in the official Indian registry maintained by the Indian Registrar. There are non-status Indians, i.e. people who are Indians but not entitled to be officially registered. The government of Canada limits its legal obligations only to those 400,000-plus status Indians and then mainly to those 225,000-plus living on Indian reserves.

◆ GOVERNMENT ASSISTANCE AND RESTITUTION FOR NATIVES IN CANADA

Canada covers the northern part of North America except for Alaska. As a former colony of Great Britain, Canada is now an independent country, although it is a member of the British Commonwealth. Canada became a country in 1867. It is now a federation of ten provinces and three territories and is bordered by the Atlantic Ocean on the east, the Pacific Ocean to the west and the Arctic Ocean to the north. The geography of Canada is very diverse and most of the population lives within a couple hundred miles of the Canada-United States border. In 1982 the Constitution Act transferred constitutional power from the British Parliament to the Canadian government. The population of Canada in 2000 was estimated to be 31,281,092. It covers 3,851,781 square miles. The federal and provincial governments are responsible for social services to Native people as outlined in the British North American Act (1867), the Canadian Constitution (1982) and the Indian Act (1876).

The number of Native people in Canada ranges from 2 to 3 percent of the total population, depending on what definition of *Indian* is used. By some estimates, the total Native population (status and non-status and Inuit) is over 1 million. The term *Indian* means different things, depending on who is doing the defining. The three groups of Indian in Canada are status Indian, non-status Indian, and Treaty Indian. The Inuit are the original inhabitants of northern Canada who reside north of the sixtieth parallel as well as in northern Labrador and Quebec. They are generally considered to be status Indians. On the other hand, the Métis are people of mixed Native and European ancestry. They have a unique culture based on their ancestral origins. The recognition and status of Métis people across Canada varies from province to province. All groups are collectively referred to as *aboriginal* or *Native* people. Detailed information about the Métis and non-status Indians is unavailable because of problems of definition and the failure to collect this information; however, population estimates for these people range between 500,000 and 1 million. In addition, 25,000 Inuit live in Canada's northern regions.

Almost two-thirds of status Indians live on reserves, which are often referred to as First Nations. Reserves are assigned to different bands and the average population of reserves is 450. Reserves are located in all provinces and territories in Canada, with the exception of Newfoundland. Most status Indians live in areas that are remote from urban centers and the non-Indian world.

History

Sadly, our history with respect to the treatment of Aboriginal people is not something in which we can take pride. Attitudes of racial and cultural superiority led to a suppression of Aboriginal culture and values. As a country, we are burdened by past actions that resulted in weakening the identity of Aboriginal peoples, suppressing their languages and cultures, and outlawing spiritual practice. . . . The Government of Canada formally expresses to all Aboriginal people in Canada our profound regret for past actions of the federal government which have contributed to these difficult pages in the history of our relationship together.

—excerpt from the Statement of Reconciliation

Before the arrival of the Europeans, many unique cultures of aboriginal peoples existed in what is now Canada. They consisted of many different peoples, with unique languages and cultures. These peoples shared a deep spiritual connection to the land as well as the shared goal of living in harmony with nature.

In 1534 Jacques Cartier claimed Canada on behalf of France. In 1604 Samuel de Champlain established a French settlement. Champlain was followed by French settlers who were enticed by the seemingly limitless supply of fish and furs. In 1670 the English established the Hudson's Bay Company to compete with the French for the fur trade. Conflict erupted between the French and the English over the land and abundant resources. The fur trade and pressure for Native-European alliances aggravated the existing animosity and conflicts between certain tribes. In 1763 the English won a battle against France, gaining control over Canada.

By the end of the eighteenth century and the beginning of the nineteenth century, the population of settlers increased significantly. Between 1763 and 1800 many treaties of land surrender were signed with the Indians of Upper Canada (now Ontario). The underlying motive of the government was to give land to the settlers. At the same time, the fur trade also wiped out fur-bearing animals in eastern Canada, causing a movement West, where the buffalo soon also faced decimation.

Native people were forced off their land and the agricultural needs of the settlers interfered with the traditional use of the land. More treaties were signed with various tribes from Ontario to Alberta. In 1871 British Columbia entered the Confederation on the condition that a railway be built. The railroad brought an influx of settlers and the government took more land from the Native people. Between 1871 and 1921 the Numbered Treaties were signed.

The fate of the northern Inuit shares a similar history. Canada's north, which is the homeland of the

Inuit, is unique. Before the arrival of the white man, Inuit lived a subsistence existence by harvesting fish, plants, and wildlife. Their survival depended on sharing. Throughout recent Canadian history, the traditional lifestyle of the Inuit has been eroded by the economic and political development of the north.

The Hudson's Bay Company established a monopoly over all the lands draining into Hudson Bay, subordinated the Native people, and produced a continuous supply of resources to the southern part of the country. The Northwest Mounted Police entered the northern lands and enforced southern laws. The new ways hurt traditional Inuit culture. Mining also brought settlement to the north. Furthermore, the north played a strategic military role in World War II. When vanishing wildlife threatened the survival of many Inuit, the federal government attempted to relocate them and in the process created dependency on the federal government. To this day, the main industry of the north is its primary industries. In many northern regions, government provision of housing, education, health, defense, law enforcement, and public works continues to be a significant chunk of the northern economy.

Canada became a country in 1867. This era is known as Confederation. The pre-Confederation period was dominated by military and missionary activities directed toward Native peoples. The missionaries believed they were morally superior and used this belief to convert Native people to Christianity and to impose their European cultural traditions.

In 1850 the first statutory definition of who was considered Indian was enacted. The concept of enfranchisement was first introduced in 1857 whereby an aboriginal *man* with the correct qualifications could relinquish his heritage and become a full citizen. Responsibility for assimilation moved to the civilian sector, where the imposition of European ways and confinement of Native people to rural communities were attempted. Following the Indian Act of 1867, the government started the Indian Register, which is the official record identifying all status Indians in Canada. Later legislation redefined who is and is not an Indian.

The Canadian government policy toward its Native peoples has been protection, civilization, and assimilation. It must be remembered that degradation is the other side of assimilation because the underlying belief of assimilation is that certain cultures are inferior. The outgrowth of these activities was that the Indian assumed special status in the political and social fabric of Canada. This unique status became enshrined in the constitutional structure of Canada in 1867, when the federal government assumed exclusive jurisdiction over Indians and Indian land.

Recently, the federal government has started to change its approach to Native peoples. Two incidents sparked this shift: disclosures of residential school abuse and the Oka Crisis. Residential schools started out of the missionary zeal of various Christian churches. They were located in almost every province and territory. At its apex, there were approximately one hundred such schools in operation. The federal government operated most residential schools in conjunction with various churches until 1969, when the government assumed full responsibility. Most schools were closed by the mid-1970s, with only seven remaining open through the 1980s. The last school closed in the 1980s.

In recent years, former students have come forward with tragic stories of physical and sexual abuse at residential schools. Many continue to struggle with the aftermath of this abuse. Currently as many as twenty lawsuits are being filed every week against the government and churches, and they now number about six thousand.

In 1998 the government of Canada released Canada's Aboriginal Action Plan, calling for a renewed partnership with Native people. The government signaled its intentions to rectify past mistakes and injustices, and move toward reconciliation and support healing. As part of this initiative, the federal government committed $350 million to support a community-based strategy for healing arising from the legacy of physical and sexual abuse at residential schools. This money is known as the Healing Fund. The government also renewed its commitment to Native self-government.

Legislation

The rights of Native peoples in Canada are legislated primarily by the Indian Act (1876) and three other pieces of legislation: the British North America Act (BNA 1867), the Canadian Constitution (1982), and the Canadian Charter of Rights and Freedoms (1984). The Indian Act, discussed in more detail in the next section, provides the legal definition of *Indian* in Canada, outlines Native rights, and details the responsibility of the federal government toward them. The British North America Act determined that "Indians and lands reserved for Indians fell under the jurisdiction of the Canadian Parliament," thereby assigning fiduciary responsibility for the Native people to the Canadian government. This responsibility has been the foundation of the development of social programs for Native people in Canada. Finally the Charter of Rights and Freedoms is a document that supersedes any other Canadian legislation that denies equality because of race, national origin, color, religion, or sex. Ultimately, it is the Indian Act that defines Native rights in a practical way and is the main legislation that affects Native people in Canada. The Indian Act has also been the primary instrument through which the federal government has oppressed Native people in the past.

The implementation of Canada's public policy concerning Native people primarily resides within one government department. While most federal departments play a role in assisting and supporting Native peoples, implementation of policy is the responsibility of the Department of Indian Affairs and Northern Development (DIAND). DIAND, in its current form, was created in 1966 to focus specifically on the delivery of programs and services to the Indian and Inuit peoples. Now its role is intended to be advisory. It also provides basic services in the form of funding and supporting various programs for status Indians.

The federal and provincial governments disagree about their respective roles and obligations toward Native people. While the federal government has exclusive legislative responsibility for Native people, some social services available to other Canadians fall within provincial mandates. Moreover, Native people are subject to the same laws and benefits as other Canadians.

Typically, the provinces are responsible for education, health, and social services and under usual arrangements, the federal government transfers funds to the provinces for these services. Both levels of government share the cost of these provincially mandated services. Because of the legislation giving the federal government exclusive jurisdiction over Native people, it carries the brunt of the cost. Fund transfer is based on the status Indian composition of a provincial population. To date, the provinces have refused to provide social services on reserves. In this vacuum, DIAND bears the complete financial burden for on-reserve services in all provinces.

Treaties

Some restitution is made to Native people according to the conditions of treaties, especially the more recent ones. A treaty is a signed agreement between the Crown and a specified group or groups of Native people. Treaties are legal documents outlining promises, obligations, and benefits of the parties to the treaty. Approximately seventy historic treaties have been made to date in Canada, with new treaties being negotiated yearly. The interpretation of historic treaties have assumed greater importance because they are protected in the Constitution Act of 1982. Current questions about the meaning of older treaties often pertain to the definition and extent of promised benefits. Promised benefits typically concern fishing, hunting and trapping rights, educational and health services, taxation exemption, mandatory military service, eligibility for treaty annuities and portability of treaty rights. Every treaty is unique, as are the promised benefits. Historically, the government and Native people have had different intentions and viewpoints when signing treaties. Today, some suggest that the former treaty process was fraudulent and exploitive of Native people.

The Indian Act

The first Indian Act was passed in 1876 as a consolidation of existing legislation with some new sections. For example, it brought forward the idea of enfranchisement from the Act to Encourage Civilization of Indian Tribes (1857). Enfranchisement was a mechanism through which Native men could renounce Indian status and become part of the dominant society. It also defined "Indianess" by introducing the designation of "status" and "non-status" Indians. Since then, the Indian Act has been amended many times, often becoming more restrictive. The main advantages of Indian status fall into the areas of education, health care, tax benefits and housing. To this day, the word *status* separates those who were entitled to reside on Indian lands and qualify for federal government programs from those who could not.

Historically, the Indian Act has been a racist and oppressive piece of legislation. Native women lost Indian status when they married a non-Indian. By comparison, Native men kept their status when they married a non-Native and their non-Native spouses acquired Indian status. Moreover, earlier versions of the act defined a person as "someone other than an Indian." Only by voluntarily enfranchisement could an Indian become a person. Finally, Native peoples were denied the right to vote well into the twentieth century.

The definition of who could legally be called Indian continues to create tension and conflict. Some people are denied the benefits derived from Indian status because they do not qualify for status although they have similar Native ancestry as those who do have status. Non-status Indians generally include Indian peoples and their descendants who lost their rights to be registered as defined by the Indian Act. They are therefore excluded from claiming rights and services. Those opposed to the special status claim that the Indian Act violates normative standards of equality. These critics are usually non-aboriginal. The federal government argues that its major aim is to preserve Native culture and to provide Indians with additional rights and safeguards guaranteed by the Canadian Constitution as well as various treaties. Among the many complaints about the Indian Act is the argument that it still assigns too much power and authority to the government. This government control prevents Native communities from developing their lands and resources in their own ways.

With the implementation of Bill C-31 in 1985, Native women who lost their status by marrying a non-Indian could apply to have their status restored, as could their children. The bill also abolished enfranchisement. Finally bands could set their own criteria for membership so long as the criteria does not conflict with the rights of existing First Nations members or with the rights of those who had their status restored under Bill C-31. One criticism of Bill C-31 is that it is infused with a European value-base that encourages a legislated notion of "Indianess."

Today all matters impacting status and membership fall under the Indian Act. The act continues to define who is Indian. It also endorses the maintenance of the Indian Registry (which is the list of status Indians), and band lists of First Nations members who have not yet passed their own membership codes.

While the Indian Act was apparently designed both to protect Native peoples and, earlier, to facilitate assimilation, it has not weathered the storms of time well. The Indian Act is blamed for the creation of structural inequality, poverty, massive social problems, and lack of achievement among Native people. It has also undermined the freedom and morale of Native people across Canada. On one hand, it accorded Indians special status, legally and constitutionally; on the other, it denied them equality in other realms of Canadian life (Berger 1981).

Department of Indian and Northern Affairs

In 1966 the Department of Indian Affairs and Northern Development (DIAND) was created to deliver programs and services to the status Indians and Inuit peoples. The minister of Indian affairs and northern development is responsible for Indian and Inuit affairs. DIAND supports band and tribal councils and helps them offer on-reserve programs. It also fulfills legislative and treaty obligations. Money is transferred by means of funding agreements with reserves. Much criticism has been leveled at this department, in part because of the historical connection to colonial domination and assimilation as well as the fact that it has such a wide mandate, which makes it an easy target.

The amount of funding transferred to bands is based on a formula that uses band membership numbers, location, on-reserve population size, type, and value of programs and services delivered by the band, and the number of band employees who administer services. After a century of discriminatory and oppressive policies, DIAND is changing its role from that of a direct service provider to that of program funding and facilitation. The welfare of status Indians is its primary mandate and as such is shifting its policy toward giving decision-making power to the people.

Demographics and Social Problems

Whatever the social or economic indicator you wish to choose, the situation of the Indian people in Canada constitutes an inexcusable embarrassment to all Canadians.

—David Ahenakew, national chief of the Assembly of First Nations, 1983

In 1996 and 1997 DIAND administered 2,406 reserves for 608 bands across Canada, covering 2.6 million hectares of land. The largest concentration of Native peoples is in the North, accounting for 62 percent of the population of the Northwest Territories and 20 percent in the Yukon. In addition, it is estimated that 85 percent of the new territory of Nunavut is Native or Inuit. The greatest numbers of Native people live in Ontario, whereas in Alberta the Métis population is largest.

Native people experience high rates of problems that social programs are designed to address. For example, social programs are designed to ameliorate problems such as poverty, unemployment, child abuse, crime, illiteracy, and inadequate housing. As discussed below, the standard of living of many Native people in Canada is well below the living conditions of most other Canadians. Economic impoverishment and personal and structural social dependency contribute to high rates of social problems among Canada's Native peoples.

The Native population is growing faster than the general Canadian population. Between 1986 and 1991, the aboriginal population increased by 43 percent, a figure that includes an estimated 80,000 people who gained Indian status from Bill C-31. The non-status Indian population is also experiencing rapid growth. This growth compares to the much smaller increase of 7 percent for the non-Native population.[1]

The number of children in Native communities is large—almost twice that of the general population. Almost one-half of the Native population is younger than fifteen years, and two-thirds are younger than twenty-five. Because of this, the aboriginal population, on average, is ten years younger than the general population.[2] Much concern has been focused on the young people who are the hope for the future in many Native communities, which are in crisis. They experience disproportionate rates of suicide and substance abuse. In addition, proportionally more Native young people are in care, fewer complete secondary school, and they have the highest suicide rates in the country.

Many have compared the living conditions of Native peoples in Canada to those of Third World countries. In comparison to other groups in Canada, Native people experience greater difficulty in terms of employment, housing, health, education, and poverty. In addition, houses on reserves are overcrowded and substandard, and incomes and employment rates fall short of national standards. Equally troublesome, a disproportionate number of Native people face incarceration and Native people are overrepresented in federal and provincial prisons, a trend most evident in Western Canada.

Between 1986 and 1991 movement between reserves and urban centers increased. Information about mobility is important because census data on mobility is used to set transfer payments from the federal government to the provinces. Mobility is particularly high for young people between the ages of fifteen and twenty-four, leading to decreasing numbers of on-reserve status Indians.[3] This mobility sometimes results in cultural conflicts, gaps in services, and a variety of social problems. The situation is further complicated by distrust of service providers in urban centers because most are non-Native professionals. This cultural insensitivity has been a major flaw of urban services. While greater appreciation for culturally sensitive services is starting to develop, there is much work to be done.

Federal Programs and Services

The BNA Act of 1867 outlined the responsibilities of the provincial and federal governments. Provinces assume the primary responsibility for health, welfare, and education and offer these services to their provincial citizens. However, under the Indian Act, the responsibility for status Indians resides with the federal government. While the federal government contends that Indian people are subject to the same laws as the general population unless they conflict with treaties or the Indian Act, provinces have refused to provide provincially mandated services to status Indians on reserves. The provinces argue that the welfare of status Indians is the responsibility of the federal government. In response, the federal government claims that because it already transfers money to the provinces for status Indians, the provinces should shoulder their

responsibilities. The outcome of this disagreement is that the Department of Indian and Northern Development still shoulders the bulk of the responsibility for providing support and administering services to status Indians. Status Indians are eligible for the benefits provided through the social service division of DIAND in addition to the social welfare benefits available to all Canadians.

DIAND transfers funds through different funding arrangements with bands. Comprehensive Funding Arrangements (CFA) involve the basic transfer of money from DIAND to Native bands for programs and services. Alternative Funding Arrangements (AFA) expand the authority of band councils to develop programs. There are fewer conditions attached to Alternative Funding Arrangements and bands can keep carryover to finance other programs. Bands with a successful history of administering programs and have the administrative structure in place and mechanisms for accountability are eligible for Alternative Funding Arrangements. CFAs cover a one-year period while AFAs last for five years and are subject to audit. Over one-half of the bands currently receive AFA funding.

In light of provincial reluctance to provide services for status Indians, the federal government is obligated to fill this void. It provides a range of direct services discussed later in this chapter. The paternalistic and bureaucratic approach is starting to change in recent years as federal policy is starting to value client involvement and self-determination.

As citizens of Canada, all Native people benefit from the same general federal programs available to everyone, regardless of status. The major programs available to all Canadians are discussed below. They include Old Age Security, Guaranteed Income Supplement, Employment Insurance, Workers Compensation, Canada Pension, and Health Care. In addition to these widely available programs, there are specific programs arising out of Canada's constitutional and statutory obligations to status Indians and Inuit. Some programs in this latter category are also available to status Indians living off-reserve. These two types of social programs are discussed separately.

Programs Available to all Canadians

Under the Canada Assistance Plan (CAP 1966), the federal government shares the cost of provincial welfare programs and social services with the provinces. Because of the expense of these programs, the federal government is trying to find ways to slash costs, but it is encountering resistance from the provinces as well as the Canadian population. CAP assists provinces to provide comprehensive social programs. As mentioned before, however, the provinces do not provide these services to status Indians who live on reserves.

Employment Insurance (EI) is a federal social program designed to assist individuals who are unable to work due to illness, pregnancy, or loss of a job for other reasons. The benefits are tied into the labor force; that is, only those individuals who have worked for a specified number of weeks prior to losing their job are entitled to collect Employment Insurance. In addition, the amount and length of eligible EI benefits is based on how much a worker has contributed to the plan. Recipients are also required to register for work or attend an approved course for upgrading while collecting benefits.

Canadians are very proud of their health care system, which is a universal program. Individuals can receive most health care services at no cost to the individual. Instead, they pay a small monthly premium to the province for individual or family coverage, and in return, the cost of health services, including hospitalization, is covered. Individuals are free to select the doctor of their choice. Individuals who are unable to pay the monthly premium can apply for a subsidy from the province. Health care is legislated by the Canada Health Act, which is federal legislation. The federal government transfers money to the provinces for part of the cost of health care, under the condition that the provinces meet the stipulations of the federal policies. For example, no province can set up a private health care system. The federal government enacts the national policies for health care while the provinces are responsible for implementing them. Through this system, all Canadians have equal access to health care. Some provinces also cover other services, such as optometrists, chiropractors, home care, and prescription drugs. Health care, together with the Canada Assistance Plan, can also cover glasses, prostheses, dental care, and prescriptions for qualifying individuals. Health care spending by the government is very costly, and governments are trying to find better ways to provide quality health care services.

All people over the age of sixty-five receive Old Age Security (OAS). Individuals must live in Canada for ten years prior to receiving OAS. For those seniors who have little or no other income besides OAS, they are eligible for the Guaranteed Income Supplement (GIS). The spouse of an individual who receives OAS is also entitled to receive the Spouse's Allowance provided their combined income is less than a specified amount determined by the government.

The Canada Pension Plan (CPP) covers individuals who are over the age of sixty-five or disabled and who paid into the plan while working. CPP also pays benefits to widows and survivors. Finally, the Child Tax Credit Benefit Program assists families with low and middle incomes with children under the age of eighteen.

Services for Status Indians

In addition to the social programs discussed above, the federal government also funds programs and services specifically for status Indians who live on reserves. It funds the delivery of a broad spectrum of services including Social Assistance and is responsible for ensuring that basic services are provided to communities it serves. Other programs available to status Indians include (1) exemption from income tax earned on reserves; (2) partial exemption from federal and provincial sales tax; (3) medical benefits not covered by the universal medical insurance of provinces, including dental care; (4) subsidized on-reserve housing; (5) post-secondary education support and scholarships; (6) elementary and secondary school education; (7) housing; (8) community infrastructure support; and (9) band administration costs.

Many reserves are starting to administer the programs themselves, according to their unique priorities and policies. A few programs are offered to status Indians who do not live on a reserve. These include assistance for post-secondary education and some non-insured health benefits. While the federal government provides some services directly to Natives who do not live on reserves, its view is that provincial governments should provide the same basic services to this group that are provided to other provincial residents. However, provinces typically consider status Indians a federal responsibility regardless of where they live. Although the provinces, in practice, will usually provide needed services, certain services such as welfare and childcare are only available after a specified residency off-reserve.

Education: Elementary, Secondary and Post-Secondary. Elementary and secondary educational programs are available to status Indian children living on reserves. Three different educational systems may exist: band-operated schools, provincially administered schools off reserves, and federal schools operated by DIAND. The federal government is responsible for a full range of elementary and secondary educational services for school-aged Native students. Additional educational services include the provision of teachers, school supplies, administrative and paraprofessional support, and curriculum development. Education services to Native children in the territories (Yukon, Northwest Territory and Nunavut) are provided by the respective territorial governments. In addition, post-secondary funding is available from DIAND for eligible status Indians and Inuit regardless of where they live in Canada. Full-time post-secondary students receive financial assistance for tuition, travel, living expenses, and books. Currently DIAND sponsors more than 15,000 students in post-secondary education programs across Canada.

While the retention of Native children in secondary schools is increasing, the school completion rate is still well below the national rate. Nevertheless the educational attainment of Native people is increasing. For example, the number of Native people with less than grade nine education decreased to 18 percent in 1991 from 26 percent five years earlier. The proportion of Native people with some secondary schooling also increased in 1991 to 43 percent from 34 percent during the same period. This compares favorably with the non-aboriginal rate, which rose to 39 percent from 27 percent.[4] The failure of school systems to provide culturally appropriate and language-specific education is cited as a major reason for the poor educational attainment of Native people. In addition, the high rate of social problems on reserves also interferes with the education of young Native people.

Health. The federal government funds a range of health services to status Indians beyond what the provincial health systems offer. Federally funded health services include community health services, environmental health and surveillance, non-insured health benefits, the National Native Alcohol and Drug Abuse Program (NNADAP), hospital services, and capital construction. NNADAP was created as a community-based program for alcohol treatment facilities. Responsibility for delivery of these special health services resides in Health and Welfare Canada, Medical Services Branch (MSB). Bands and tribal councils can apply to Medical Services Branch for financial resources to assess community health care needs, prepare a health development plan, and develop a health management structure, in preparation for self-government of health services.

Medical Services Branch also delivers Public Health services, including health education, nutrition, mental health, dental services, medical and dental advice and assistance, counseling, and federal hospital or alcohol treatment services. The federal government also pays hospital insurance premiums. Through the Medical Services Branch, the federal government also provides treatment and public health services in remote areas. MSB may also assist with certain non-insured health benefits such as prescription drugs, dental services, glasses and medical transportation not covered by provincial health insurance plans. Most of the conflict surrounds the non-insured services.

The federal government is trying to pass the responsibility for health services directly to the bands. Criticism of health services provided to status Indians has partially focused the failure to consult communities as well as insufficient funding. With the shift to self-government, some also fear that the hidden agenda of the federal government is to eliminate the parts of Indian health care services unavailable to non-Native Canadians. Others suspect that the federal government is intending to withdraw special health services because they are a provincial responsibility. A final concern is that a condition of health care transfer to the bands is a "no enrichment" clause. This means that health services cannot be enhanced once they are in band control. However, this is a problem because the present services are underfunded. In addition, because transfer payments are based on the number of registered band members living on the reserve, it can exclude band members who are mobile and live off the reserve. Another potential problem is that band health by-laws must align with provincial health care policies, producing potential conflict between the band and the province.

Nevertheless, the federal government has committed to a long-term goal of a "more integrated, culturally relevant community health care program and improved health conditions for Indian people." The transfer process seems to have increased community interest in community health issues, but it has not been without controversy. Some Native leaders suspect that the ultimate aim of the government is to reduce spending on health and social services, abdicate legal and fiduciary responsibility for the delivery of health care services to Native people, and deny treaty rights. The long history of injustice at the hands of the government makes their suspicion easy to understand.

The previous approach to the provision of health care services to Native peoples has been a dismal failure and the health of Canadian Native peoples remains a concern. Their health status is affected by poor living conditions such as housing, economic impoverishment, availability of safe drinking water, and nutrition. Obviously, improved health status of Canada's Native peoples will only be improved through a holistic approach to health. Currently, life expectancy remains below the national average, mainly because of high infant and youth mortality. Substance abuse is also a significant health problem and over half of all of illnesses and deaths may be alcohol-related. Stories of the horrific health problems of Native people abound, involving alcohol and drug abuse, gas sniffing, infectious diseases, and mental health problems such as depression, stress, and high suicide rates. Deaths by suicide, homicide, and accident accounted for over one-third of the deaths of Native people. In response, Native communities are demanding involvement in the planning and delivery of health and mental health services. They would like to blend traditional methods of healing with Western medicine, and many bands have started along this path. Ultimately, the effectiveness of the health transfer policies will only be revealed by the next generation.

Social Assistance. The social services division of DIAND is obligated to guarantee that services offered to Native people are equivalent to provincial services available to non-Indians. As with other social services and programs, it is seeking the participation of Native peoples in the design and implementation of social assistance programs. An important part of this process has been the transfer of financial responsibility for the implementation and operation of programs to band councils. This objective seems to be working since most bands now administer the delivery of social assistance. The federal government would also like social services to be provided by other government and private agencies. This point remains contentious in federal-provincial relationships.

Social assistance provides money to single persons or heads of families to meet basic needs, for food, clothing, and shelter. Another category of social assistance targets disabled individuals who are unable to work. The amount paid for social assistance depends on the rate set by each province. The cost of social assistance to status Indians is rising significantly. For example, federal expenditures almost tripled between 1981 and 1994. During the same period, the number of recipients rose from 39,000 to almost 68,000.[5] Social assistance comprises 10 percent of the DIAND budget. Because the amount of social assistance paid is determined through specified provincial eligibility criteria and benefit rates in each of the provinces, the federal government is unable to control the costs of social assistance paid to status Indians. In addition, because of the socioeconomic conditions on reserves, the amount paid for social assistance is only expected to rise.

Transfer of responsibility is also occurring in direct services. DIAND has implemented a program providing basic material needs to status Indians. In recent years, this has been expanded to include day-care services and institutional and special care for the aged, the physically infirm, and the mentally handicapped. Again, where possible, responsibility for these services has entailed training Native peoples to plan and operate them. As the trend away from the reserves continues, DIAND is striving to ensure that services are available in urban centers. A function of these urban services is helping needy Indians connect with existing provincial, municipal, and voluntary services.

The government relationship with Native peoples has created a situation whereby Native peoples are one of the most economically disadvantaged groups in Canada. While the situation is improving slightly, much progress remains to be made. For example, while the average individual income for non-Native people increased by 7 percent between 1986 and 1991, it rose by almost one-third for Native people over the same time.[6] This increase did little to rectify the gap in income between non-Native and Native peoples, whose income remains significantly lower than other groups. Many still live in such dire poverty that the Human Rights Commission urged that poverty be acknowledged as a human rights issue.

Approximately 40 percent of status Indians currently receive government transfer payments. The average income for off-reserve status Indians, Inuit, and Métis in 1991 was $12,000, while the income of on-reserve status Indians plummeted to $9,000. In addition, the unemployment rate for aboriginal people is about double that of non-aboriginal people. While unemployment rates are decreasing, the rates are still distressing and unacceptable. For example, the unemployment rate for off-reserve status Indians was 25 percent in 1991 and 31 percent for on-reserve status Indians. Unemployment has produced reliance upon social assistance and this reliance is increasing. DIAND provided approximately $60 million in 1993 for social assistance for aboriginal people (Frideres 1998).

As with other social problems, poverty, unemployment, and dependence on social assistance cannot be addressed in a piecemeal fashion. Unemployment is related to education, gender, age, experience, language, and area of residence as well as institutional discrimination. These factors—considered alongside national unemployment rates, poverty, and long-term reliance on social assistance—depict a bleak life for many Native people.

Housing. Because of restrictions imposed by the Indian Act, most people who live on reserves cannot obtain conventional mortgages to purchase or build houses. The restrictions in the Indian Act make it impossible for bands or individuals to use their land as collateral. They are consequently unable to obtain mortgages without a government guarantee of repayment in case of default. Therefore, government assistance is required to build and maintain adequate housing because of the limited economic opportunities on many reserves.

While the federal government is not bound by legislation or treaties to provide housing, it continues to do so out of historical obligation (Frideres 1998). Consistent with the shift in government policy in other social programs, Indians and bands are encouraged to take control of the administration of the housing program. The long-term objective is to have housing meet national building standards. In addition, housing programs must now include local involvement, cost effectiveness, and linkages between home construction and community economic development and employment. Canada Mortgage and Housing Corporation (CMHC) in partnership agreements under the National Housing Act with government and nonprofit corporations builds social housing across Canada. CMHC contributes up to 90 percent of the capital cost and 50 percent of continued operations costs for new construction and rehabilitation projects.

Three basic programs are included in this agreement. The On-Reserve Rental Housing Program provides First Nations with suitable, affordable rental housing in First Nations communities. CMHC provides interest-free repayable loans for proposal development for rental housing projects. It also ensures loans by approved lenders for housing projects and annually subsidizes the project's operating costs for the duration of the loan. The Emergency Repair Program assists homeowners who live in rural areas to implement emergency repairs to make their homes safe and covers the cost of materials and labor. The Homeowner Residential Rehabilitation Assistance Program Helps Native homeowners living in substandard housing by allowing them to repair their homes and upgrade them to a minimum level of health and safety.

Similar to other initiatives, the federal government is shifting the emphasis for the housing program to First Nations control, using local resources for on-reserve home building. Under this policy, communities can also build expertise through on-the-job formal training. A five year and $160 million commitment on the part of the federal government, combined with $300 million in ongoing annual housing support, are helping reserves develop the skills and organizational ability to address the conditions of housing.[7] CMHC and DIAND also fund training, management, and technical expertise to help communities administer their own housing programs. Today most bands deliver their own housing programs. Programs are accountable to band councils and new houses must meet the residential standards of the national building code.

DIAND can approve housing proposals submitted by bands for housing development. The policy enables First Nations to develop community housing programs, create jobs, and improve housing conditions in a single initiative. The funding is split between DIAND and Canada Mortgage Housing Corporation. This new policy links housing to other community assets and needs such as training and and social assistance.

The rapid birth rate of First Nations peoples is creating pressure for affordable and appropriate housing on reserves across Canada. Chronic housing shortages have led to overcrowding, which exacerbates and contributes to social, familial, and health problems. Houses on reserves have short life spans because of overcrowding and poor construction. Consequently, many of the new houses being built are replacing dilapidated houses instead of freeing up new houses to accommodate the population growth. By one estimate, over one-half of the houses on reserves are substandard.

While housing conditions on reserves are notoriously poor, they are improving. On average, 90 percent of houses have central electricity and 75 percent have running water. By 1990 86 percent had an adequate water supply and 77 percent had adequate sewage disposal. (Friederes 1998, 171). Houses on reserves are relatively new with 93 percent built between 1961 and 1991. Two decades ago, only one-half of the houses on reserves were considered adequate. While the number of houses increased between 1989 and 1996, still only one-half were considered adequate. In the same period, many other houses on reserves were renovated.[8] However, housing shortages continue on reserves where lack of affordable housing remains a problem. The percentage of dwellings on reserves with more than one person per room (an indicator of overcrowding) is decreasing but there is room for improvement. The situation is complicated by the fact that many reserves are remote, making housing costs higher than for urban centers. In addition, Crown ownership of reserve lands makes it difficult for Native people to finance housing and mortgages. Those who live in northern regions also have the added burden of threatening weather conditions that require extra housing costs.

Tax Benefits. Canadians pay some of the highest taxes in the industrialized world. However, under the Indian Act, status Indians do not pay any federal and provincial taxes on personal and real property on a reserve. Income is considered personal property. Status Indians who earn income and live on reserves do not have to pay taxes. In addition, for the purposes of taxation, post-secondary scholarships provided by DIAND for status Indians are considered to be "situated on a reserve." Payment of the Goods and Services Tax (a federal tax on purchases) depends on where the goods and services are consumed or purchased.

Community Infrastructure Support. DIAND provides financial assistance for infrastructure support on reserves. This assistance pertains to building, operating, and maintaining community facilities and schools.

Money is also allocated to address problems with water, sanitation, electrical, and road systems, fire protection facilities, and flood and erosion control.

Law Enforcement. Policing on reserves is provided by the provincial police forces. The Royal Canadian Mounted Police (RCMP) are responsible for rural areas where there is no provincial force. DIAND assists the Royal Canadian Mounted Police (RCMP) for a RCMP Special Constable Program on reserves. Constables are accountable to local RCMP detachments. Special constables offer police enforcement under the jurisdiction of the Indian Act and other federal statutes. Other funded policing arrangements include the Ontario Indian Constable Program, which is co-funded under a federal-provincial agreement with the solicitor general in Ontario.

In other law enforcement initiatives, the federal solicitor general funds programs to improve Native policy and programs through research, pilot projects, and information. Two final initiatives are available. The Native Law Students Program helps Native people enter the legal profession and the Native Court Workers Program provides paralegal support to Native defendants.

Culture. Together with the secretary of state, DIAND funds support Native culture and educational activities. This initiative covers friendship centers, the development of Native political lobby associations, the promotion of traditional and contemporary art forms, language maintenance and revitalization, and the adaptation of modern communication tools for Native use. There is now a high quality aboriginal television station that is available across the country.

Small Business Loan Program. The Small Business Loan Program helps Native entrepreneurs involved in a variety of businesses. Federal funds offer loans, loan guarantees and financial planning services, investment banking facilities and management services. These funds are used to promote businesses. The Indian Economic Development Guarantee Order guarantees bank loans for Native businesses.

The oil and gas deposits on Alberta Reserve have created a situation where massive royalty payments accrue to the affected bands. Thus, there are isolated pockets of some very wealthy Native bands, such as the Samson band (Hobbema) and the Ermineskin and Louis Bull bands from the same reserves. The Inuvialuit of the western Arctic has also settled on a range of benefits and rights in recognition of the non-fulfillment of the original treaty.

Child Welfare. Child welfare falls under provincial jurisdiction and until recently Native people were subjected to culturally insensitive child welfare practices.

In earlier years Native children were taken from their families and placed for adoption with white families, even to families outside of Canada. This loss of Native children has been the source of much grief for Indian bands. Many bands have made valiant efforts to repatriate these children, which means returning these children to their home reserves.

Now in some provinces, there are branches of the Child Welfare Department specifically targeting Native child welfare services. Native overrepresentation in child welfare is particularly evident in western Canada where Native children comprise more than one-fifth of the children in substitute care. In the western provinces, the ratio of Native children in care to the provincial total is particularly high, and at times accounted for as many as one-half of the children in care.

The implementation of new child welfare agreements with bands is the first step in the restoration of Native control over their child welfare services. Previously, child welfare services were carried out within the context of colonization. These efforts devalued or ignored Native culture and aimed to assimilate Native children into the dominant culture. Newly designed child welfare agreements challenge the colonization philosophy of the past. To Native peoples, gaining control over their own child welfare services is as significant as other rights including health, education, land claims, and economic development. To date, most Native child welfare services follow a delegated authority model whereby Native agencies administer provincial child welfare legislation and procedures with the provincial government retaining ultimate authority. These Native child welfare agencies have executive rather than legislative authority. The Blood band in Alberta is in the process of developing their own legislation, which may serve as a prototype for other bands across the country.

Services for Inuit

Although the federal government delivers some services directly to Inuit in the north, most programs are delivered by the respective territorial governments. Territorial governments receive approximately 80 percent of revenues in transfer payments from the federal government. Similar agreements have been made between the Inuit and the government of Quebec. The federal government contributes a share of the funding for these services. In Labrador, the Newfoundland provincial government exercises primary responsibility for administering services to Inuit, again under a cost-sharing agreement with the federal government.

Programs for Aboriginal People Provided by Other Federal Departments

The list of programs specifically targeting Native peoples in Canada is extensive. At least eleven federal departments have Native-specific programs designed to preserve, maintain, and enhance the cultural heritage of Native peoples across Canada. Examples of these programs include the Northern Native Broadcast Access Program, the Aboriginal Friendship Centre Program, and Spiritual Services for Federal Inmates. Human Resources Development Canada works with Native people to help them assume control of the employment services and skills development.

Self-Government and Land Claims. Native peoples in Canada have fought for self-government and economic independence for many years. In particular, they are eager to control their own destiny and make decisions about the preservation of their unique cultures. A number of highly organized Native political organizations in Canada have been at the forefront of this struggle. Land claims and accompanying benefits is an important form of government assistance and restitution to Native peoples. Natives are struggling to reclaim the land and resources promised to them by previous Canadian governments. The federal government has failed to recognize or honor these aspirations until recent years. The federal government was criticized recently by the Canadian Human Rights Commission, which called for an independent and evenhanded system of dealing with Native land claims.

There are two types of land claims in Canada: comprehensive and specific. Comprehensive land claims acknowledge that there are continuing unresolved Native rights to their lands. Comprehensive claims occur where Native title has not yet been assigned through a treaty or legal settlement. They are comprehensive because of their wide scope, which typically includes land title, fishing, and trapping rights and financial compensation. Specific claims deal with existing treaties that have not been honored, and with how their lands and other assets under the Indian Act are administered. A particular problem with past settlements is that many echoed the belief that assimilation was a desirable inevitable—a prevailing government attitude toward the indigenous peoples of Canada.

There is now a glimmer of hope in the form of a shift in government thinking. The previous way in which the federal government has dealt with Native peoples has been a dismal failure. This is especially evident because of the high rate of social problems among Canada's Native peoples. Recently, a process was started whereby the federal government, in partnership with First Nations communities, would strive for self-government, which refers to governments designed, established, and administered by Native peoples. This seems to be the wave of the future. Each agreement will be unique in terms of the special historical, cultural, political, and economic circumstances of each community. Areas of self-government will typically fall into the areas of health care, child welfare, education, housing, and economic development. Negotiations in this new process would ideally include provincial and territorial governments, but the extent of provincial involvement remains to be seen. The right to self-government is protected through the constitution as well as through changes in existing treaties or as part of land claim settlements.

There is reason to be optimistic. The federal government has publicly recognized the importance and necessity of Native self-government and has vowed that it will not end its fiduciary relationship with Native peoples. Ideally, self-government should be a shared financial responsibility between federal, provincial, and territorial governments.

Conclusion

Government assistance and restitution attempts have failed Native people in Canada in the past. Earlier attempts have been blamed for fostering dependency of Native people on the government. The historical impact of colonization as well as racist and assimilationist policies reinforces the need for special social and economic rights for Canada's Native peoples. The political ideology of assimilation reflected in the attempts of missionaries and early settlers to "civilize" Native people has been evident throughout Canadian history. Nevertheless, Native people in Canada have held onto their proud heritage and have refused to relinquish their claim to sovereignty and their unique rights and benefits, despite a hostile and oppressive environment making it difficult to do so.

Their battle is for the preservation of separate and distinct Native cultures. However, efforts for self-government, sovereignty, and cultural continuity have been eroded by lack of control over the political and social institutions that affect them. This is very evident in the social services that affect them. Increasingly, Native peoples are questioning the value and effectiveness of these social programs and institutions.

The political activism of Native peoples combined with distrust of government around such issues as land claims, aboriginal rights, and the legal status and definition of the word *Indian* has been the impetus for greater self-government. Native peoples have shown increasing interest in assuming control of the formal social services now provided by the established health and welfare system. Out of this has evolved a commitment to the development of services designed by and administered for Native peoples.

The present situation dictates that social policies concerning Native people be designed and administered by Native people themselves. Moreover, these policies demand recognition of their unique position in the Canadian social fabric. Social policies must move beyond the present obstacles to offer services that support the right to Native self-determination through self-government. In this shift, the government cannot withhold needed financial resources to help make their dream come true.

After centuries of domination and discrimination, the dominant society is starting to become sensitive to Native peoples and their issues. However, there is more work to be done. Indian activism will continue to confront the status quo. Goals for the future include strengthening and affirming the identity of Native peoples and redressing historical wrongs.

Despite some progress, many problems continue as a result of the legacy of Native people's treatment in Canada. Native people remain over-represented in most social problems and they still carry the wounds of culturally insensitive and blatantly discriminatory social programs. Discriminatory attitudes and actions negate the basic premise of cultural and human respect and serve to credit the negative stereotyping that still exists.

The Native peoples of Canada have a strong and proud heritage. They also have the strength and resources to overcome historical injustices done to their culture and well being, but they need support from the dominant society to improve their situation. At the very least, their aspirations should not be thwarted. Canada owes them the best it has to offer.

Heather Coleman
University of Calgary

Don Collins
University of Calgary

Notes

1. Statistics obtained from "Indian and Northern Affairs Canada," <http://www.inac.gc.ca/stats/facts/1995/howdo.html>, 1995.

2. "1996 Census: Aboriginal Data," <http://www.statscan.ca/Daily/English/980113/d980113.html>, 1995.

3. "Indian and Northern Affairs Canada," <http://www.inac.gc.ca/stats/facts/1995/abocon.html>, 1995.

4. Ibid.

5. Ibid.

6. Ibid.

7. "Housing," <http://www.inac.gc.ca/index>.

8. Ibid.

◆ AN OVERVIEW OF ECONOMIC DEVELOPMENT HISTORY ON CANADIAN NATIVE RESERVES

The historical evolution of the economic development of Indian communities has gone through profound changes since the arrival of Christopher Columbus five hundred years ago. This section will examine how the indigenous peoples of Canada have adjusted, adapted, accommodated to, and resisted the various social, political, cultural, and economic institutions introduced by the waves of European newcomers settling in their respective homelands. Many indigenous populations declined drastically from the ravages of diseases and dislocation due to warfare. Many indigenous institutions were altered or replaced by European models and, over time, Native societies became powerless and unable to control their fate. Nevertheless, the Native people of Canada remain undefeated and continue to resist assimilation into mainstream Canadian society.

This overview will examine the primary political events that have shaped the institutions and circumstances of Canada's First Nations, the original peoples in the North American continent, in their dealings with the British Crown and Canada's federal government. A political transition occurred from 1850 to the early twentieth century when twelve numbered and several other treaties were signed covering most territory within central and western Canada. Upon conclusion of the treaty-making process, Indian nations unwittingly came under the paternalistic guidance of the Indian Act, first enacted in 1876. It defined Canadian Indian rights and status under the bureaucratic management of the Department of Indian Affairs established in 1880. These factors remain the determinant forces in Indian policy to the present day.

The Newcomers' Legacy

Canadian Indians signed a series of "peace and friendship" treaties with the European newcomers starting with the French in the early sixteenth century during the settlement of New France. After decades of warfare, the French were displaced by the British after the conquest of 1760. Subsequently, the British government granted the Royal Proclamation of 1763, the fundamental document setting out Indian political and land rights, in order to effect a lasting peace with the Indian First Nations. The unique constitutional status of Canada's aboriginal peoples has its beginnings in the Royal Proclamation whereby the British Crown, the British head of state, officially recognized the Indian peoples' interest in the land of this "Great Island" (which the English named British North America). It was soon apparent that the Indian nations had little input into defining British-Indian affairs as European settlement proceeded westward into Indian territory. The aboriginal peoples were treated as subjects of the colonizing state, but they remained sovereign allies economically and militarily until the early eighteenth century.

During the seventeenth and eighteenth centuries, the focus of both the French and British colonial governments was regulation of the fur trade commerce. The Indian nations controlled access to the resources of the country including furs, timber, fish, and agricultural goods. In turn, the indigenous population became conspicuous consumers of European goods and developed a growing dependency on modern technology and manufactured goods, such as guns and metal utensils. Inevitably the Indian nations and the colonizers clashed over land use and the exploitation of the natural resources.

The progressing commercial trade was paralleled by a growing European military presence as the newcomers' settlements expanded into the interior of North America. The Indian nations were either potential allies or enemies, because global politics did not recognize neutrality, and the First Nation confederations welcomed alliance with the technologically powerful newcomers in their struggles with other confederacies. Numerous peace and friendship treaties were signed to ensure the protection of commerce and the vulnerable European settlements. The newcomers' population remained relatively small and largely dependent on the indigenous people, and the colonial governments reaffirmed the friendship agreements through a system of presents or annuities. Thus treaty payments and promises regarding the sharing of resources became the foundation of colonial Indian policy during the eighteenth and nineteenth centuries.

The economics of the New World trade, based on the transatlantic shipment of fish, timber, and furs to the European mercantile nations, became bound up with the imposition of European values and standards— whether religious conversion to Christianity, formal education, or social-political institutions. The Native people were expected to become "civilized" according to European standards. Conflicts arose over land use and ownership, and these remained the root of much misunderstanding when treaties were signed. The British Crown interpreted the treaties as land "surrenders" and "extinguishment" of aboriginal title and certain rights. Indian First Nations invariably regarded a treaty as a promise to keep the peace and to share the bountiful resources from the land. A land sale or exchange or proprietary ownership was contrary to the philosophy and attitudes of most indigenous peoples about their relationship with Mother Earth; land was not a possession that could be sold. Natural resources were provided for all people to share for their survival.

Traditional Indian Economies

Indian nations across Canada at the time of first prolonged contact with European explorers in the sixteenth century enjoyed a diversity of economies. The sea coast peoples living in British Columbia along the Pacific Ocean coast, the northern Arctic Ocean peoples, and the Atlantic east coast maritime nations utilized the rich marine life and fisheries in their resource-based economies. The rich plant life of the sea, shorelines, and forest supplied all the necessary raw material for food, clothing, transportation, fuel, and shelter. Life was generally easier than in the harsher and less-productive regions of the interior plains. Complex and sophisticated social, economic, religious, and political institutions developed to suit their respective environments during the centuries before European contact.

We may generalize to describe pre-contact economic development as seasonal resource management revolving around hunting, trading, fishing, and gathering. The use of natural resources, however, varied from culture to culture. The Woodlands people, in the large forested lands of central Canada used the canoe for transportation and raised crops. The Plains people of the great western prairie lands traveled on foot and used dog travois until their culture was radically transformed by the introduction of the horse onto the prairies in the early eighteenth century. Indigenous technology included the spear, hook, bow and arrow, snare, deadfall, buffalo jumps, and pounds. Shelter was easily constructed out of tree materials or hides. Social groupings varied from the large one-house villages of the Eastern Iroquois to small wandering bands of less than one hundred members characteristic of the plains buffalo hunting camps.

The great Iroquois Confederacy, composed of the Cayuga, Mohawk, Oneida, Onondaga, Seneca, and later the Tuscarora, developed a horticultural economy in southeastern Ontario and upstate New York based on corn, squash, beans, and tobacco. Their sedentary lifestyle was augmented by trading surplus food to neighboring tribes whose lifestyle was centered around a hunting and trapping economy. There was an overlap of seasonal activities revolving around fishing, hunting, preparing fields, planting, harvesting, trading, gathering wild crops and firewood, socializing, making new articles, and conducting special ceremonies throughout the year.

The hunting and gathering economies characterized the traditional way of life for the large number of tribes living in the forest belts, parkland and the prairies covering much of Canada. All enjoyed their own language, customs, ceremonies, songs and institutions. The largest group was the Algonkian-speakers, the dominant Indian language group, represented by the Mi'kmaq (Micmac) and Maliseet of the Maritimes, the Innu (Montagnais) and Cree-Naskapi of Quebec, and the large Plains bands of the Cree, Blood, Peigan, and Siksika (Blackfeet) of the prairies.

Within the span of a few generations after the arrival of European traders and settlers in North America, modern warfare, epidemics, alcohol, and the depletion of fur animals and game had reduced most First Nations to considerable dependence on the European way of life. The coexistence that characterized initial contact gradually gave way to a growing reliance on imported manufactured goods. The local economy became enmeshed in a continent-wide trading system. A growing number of Indian communities began to rise near trading posts and the rapidly expanding European settlements. The traditional gathering, fishing, hunting, and local subsistence lifestyle was gradually replaced by working for wages, barter, and demand for goods and services found only in urban settlements.

European settlements expanded across British North America, starting on the East Coast in the 1600s and extending across the North American continent over the next two hundred years. The newcomers came to exploit the natural resources including the fisheries, timber, and the fur trade. This exploitation-settlement pattern started an unstoppable chain of events. To the Indian Nations, the European settler was a visitor to an already occupied homeland. The normal procedure was to establish a "peace and friendship" treaty to allow mutual sharing of the land and its resources. The subsequent cross-cultural contact in time significantly altered the Indian way of life, customs, and institutions.

The main focus of contact in much of Canada, notably around the Great Lakes and across the prairies and the wooded north, was the fur trade industry. Formally initiated by a royal charter granted by the king

of England in 1670, the Hudson's Bay Company promptly precipitated a new economic relationship based on a barter exchange system, which eventually altered Indian social structures and living patterns and gradually created a dependence on new manufactured products imported from Europe. The Hudson's Bay Company dominated the fur trade in western Canada until the late eighteenth century when rival independent traders formed the North West Company from the 1790s until 1821, when the two companies merged as the reorganized Hudson's Bay Company.

The Native peoples accepted what the newcomers had to offer, and, with acceptance, their traditional way of life changed. Equipment such as guns and metal traps, and new transportation methods made it possible to kill more animals for food and for trading of the skins. This included beaver and fur-bearing animals in the eastern and northern forests, sea otter on the West Coast, and buffalo on the great plains. Indian families from the Mi'kmaq (Micmac), Iroquois, Ojibwa (Chippewa), and Cree nations gained wealth as "middlemen" in the new trade economy. Members of these tribes closest to the trading centers served as distributors for the trader and the trappers living in the interior forests. Some tribes, such as the Ojibwa, Cree, and Athabaskan people of Northwest Canada, exploited the new technology of metal traps, metal tools, and guns. The more efficient traps were a better guarantee against starvation; furs were exchanged for food and luxuries; and weapons were more effective and increased security. The value of furs was based on the value of a prime beaver pelt (known as a made beaver), and credits from the trade of pelts were used to purchase trade goods from the distributors or the trading factor employed by the Hudson's Bay Company. The most discernible impact of the fur trade on indigenous societies was in their material culture and social organizations. The rifle replaced spears and arrows; metal utensils displaced bone, wooden, stone, and leather tools; manufactured goods dominated hand-produced products.

Among the Indians of the Northwest Pacific, potlatch ceremonies grew bigger and more elaborate as a result of the influx of new goods as hosting clans distributed or destroyed personal possessions to enhance their status. The potlatch ceremonies helped to define the economic and social status of families and might be held to validate an inherited position or the adoption of a name or ceremonial title. On the prairies, a hunter had the means and reason to kill many more buffalo and attain more new possessions to fill his larger tipi. Families would settle near the forts and towns to obtain more easily European tools, clothing, food, and resources. Many became entrapped in a new economy as dependent consumers rather than as self-sufficient suppliers of trade goods.

The fierce commercial competition for furs lasted for two centuries until the union of the Hudson's Bay Company and the North West Trading Company in 1821. When beaver became scarce due to overtrapping, a band of families either moved into new trapping territory or became impoverished dependents residing near the forts.

Increased contact between the various Indian nations brought further change in territorial boundaries and intertribal trade patterns. The Mi'kmaq (Micmac) expanded throughout the Atlantic maritime provinces and New England states and were key allies in the British-French battle for domination in North America. The Six Nations Iroquois Confederacy displaced the Huron, one of the greatest Iroquois tribes known for their farm villages, as the dominant people around the Great Lakes of Ontario. In the Hudson's Bay Company territory of western Canada, the Cree Nation emerged as dominant traders with their new wealth of guns, metal tools, and highly valued trade wares. The Cree tribes along the prairie waterways spread north into the lands of the Chipewyan, the Slave, and the Beaver people who shared the great forest lands of the Northwest Territories. The horse-oriented buffalo hunt of the Plains Cree culture flourished until the buffalo herds, once numbering in the tens of millions, were reduced to a few hundred by the 1880s.

In the Canadian West, the economic cycles of the fur economy changed the tribal system, and the family-based band system broke down for many people. The trade in alcohol led to social disintegration for families tied to the traditional economy. The struggle for power and wealth was irrevocably imbalanced by the spread of new diseases from Europe, which killed thousands of Natives. Measles, smallpox, influenza, fevers, and venereal disease swept across North America carried by traders, explorers, and intertribal contact. It is speculated that up to half (sometimes entire bands) of the original peoples on the prairies were killed by the epidemics of the 1780s and 1830s. The leadership, ceremonial practices, and oral history lost in these epidemics could never be regained. The loss of confidence in Native healers and spiritual powers further encouraged acceptance of the Christian teachings and some acceptance of schools.

The fur trade posts became centers of social and commercial activity. As Indian families accepted more European customs and adopted more manufactured goods, the indigenous economy was no longer self-sufficient (producing for immediate family or tribal needs), but eventually became bound to the ever-demanding European trading market.

An elaborate trade ritual reaffirmed the basis of peace and friendship between the cultures. The trade ceremony would begin with a presentation to the head man of a gift of tea, tobacco, or alcohol, or colorful cloth or ribbon for the women and candy for the children. Then followed a lengthy discussion and haggling, often extending over several days, over the comparative value of furs and trade goods. After business was completed, there was an exchange of parting presents to re-confirm the bonds of friendship. A spirit of cooperation and mutual exploitation characterized the Hudson's Bay Company's relationship with its indigenous partners. The trade ritual was also a political ceremony to cement the company-Indian alliance. These early ceremonies and protocol rituals were later adopted during the treaty negotiations of the nineteenth century.

By the mid-nineteenth century, with the fur trade era in rapid decline, a new economy based on agricultural settlement and ranching began to shape the Canadian West. This period of European-Native coexistence was characterized by rapid cultural adjustment among all tribes and by the corresponding destabilization of the traditional indigenous economy based on hunting of game and trading of furs. By the end of that century, there was little game left to hunt and few fur animals to trap. The once-populous beaver, muskrat, otter, and forest fur-bearing animals had been reduced to dangerously low levels. The large game such as bison, moose, elk, and deer were in rapid decline from overhunting and loss of habitat to agriculture and forest fires. For Canada's indigenous peoples, the consequences were catastrophic. Their traditional food supplies were severely reduced or totally gone, notably the buffalo. Disease had killed tens of thousands of Natives and alcohol threatened many others. Economic trade evolved into political-social colonization. The political-economic consequences are still felt today.

Whereas during the fur trade era, the Indian people had some measure of control and the reciprocal trade patterns created an interdependency among the participants, during the post-1870s settlement period, the newcomers completely disrupted the traditional way of life. Settlers, ranchers, and urban residents did not depend on mutual cooperation and did not respect the original inhabitants. Indeed, Native society was typified as a hindrance to "progress," and Native people were viewed as the government's "problem." Euro-Canadian culture not only began to dominate, but a new economy and lifestyle were also forced on the Natives by the actions of missionaries and by the surrounding communities of farmers, ranchers, and townspeople. Nation-to-nation relations originally founded on coexistence and sharing of resources was gradually replaced in the nineteenth century by Euro-Canadian dominance based on paternalism, assimilation, and subjugation.

The Treaties and Economic Self-Determination

The legal, political, social, and economic basis of Indian First Nation government relations are governed by the Canadian Constitution and by a variety of legislative acts passed by the Canadian Parliament and by provincial legislatures. The First Nations of central Canada began negotiating modern treaties in 1850, starting with the Robinson-Superior and Robinson-Huron treaties covering the north shore of the Great Lakes of Ontario. Subsequently, Treaties 1 to 11 were signed between 1871 and 1923 covering mostly western Canada. It is important to understand the terms and conditions, as well as the spirit and intent, of these modern numbered treaties to appreciate the socioeconomic and political evolution of First Nation governments over the past two centuries.

Treaties between the Crown and the First Nations confirmed their separate status, and the documents set out certain obligations for their future benefit now commonly referred to as "treaty rights." Throughout the treaty process, the First Nations were dealt with on a nation-to-nation basis, which is recognized today in constitutional law and in government-to-government protocol. This bilateral relationship was assured when the Canadian Parliament was given the power by the 1867 Constitution Act (formerly the British North America Act) for "Indians and Lands reserved for the Indians" under section 91(24), which Parliament has interpreted as its authority to make laws for Canadian registered or "status" Indians, who were defined by the act. Most First Nations assert that they never surrendered their sovereignty and that they enjoy an inherent (inalienable) right to self-determination. The right to self-government is now widely accepted in Canada, a reversal of events starting over 125 years ago.

Soon after the first numbered treaties were negotiated in the 1870s the traditional economy of Indian nations was wiped out when the great bison herds were completely decimated by the early 1880s. Indian treaty negotiators focused on securing the economic future of their people. The first request was a guarantee to continue their traditional hunting and trapping economy, but government commissioners insisted these rights be made subject to the queen's regulations. The establishment of Indian reserves, lands set aside for Indian occupation, was not intended to maintain the traditional way of life in the new economic order, but rather to assist Native people toward assimilation into Canadian society. Treaty negotiations often covered the terms and conditions whereby an Indian agricultural economy could be encouraged, including the provision of plows, agricultural implements, seeds, and stock to build up community herds as Natives settled on reserve lands. The stated object of the government's policy was to prepare the Indian people for a new way of life centered on the industrial arts and agriculture. To facilitate this goal Parliament passed the 1876 Indian Act, which enforced regulations for protecting Native people from exploitation by the white majority and for managing the affairs of Indians until they became "civilized." The end result, however, was economic dependency and underdevelopment. Indian reserve economies did not flourish and social assistance became a prevalent means of subsistence. Native reserves became pockets of poverty surrounded by expansive and wealthy non-Native communities.

In part, the treaties were economic agreements to share the land and its resources, and in return, the federal government agreed to provide compensation in various ways. The government did operate a number of demonstration farms to serve as models for training. However, as the official government authority, the local Indian agent controlled all commercial activities and business conducted on the reserve. Later the "pass system," requiring a letter of permission to cross the reserve's border, was instituted to control Native movement off the reserve. Government policy was directed toward breaking down the Indian culture through education and encouraging integration and eventual assimilation into Canadian society.

Early Economic Programs

Among the severe limitations on Indian economic development are the various sections of the Indian Act dealing with management of reserve lands, Indian monies, and tribal governments operating through an elective band council system. In addition, hundreds of federal statutes, federal provincial agreements, administrative rules and regulations, and by-laws must be considered in land transactions, economic development loan funds, taxation, and financial management. Today, there are numerous publications dealing with the legal complexities of operating business enterprises on Indian reserves.

The powers of Indian band councils, which are reserve governments specified in the Indian Act, are not clearly identified, and the role of local government has shifted dramatically over the past century. From the 1870s to the 1920s, the Canadian government extended control over every aspect of life on Indian reserves. Some First Nations, such as the Iroquois on the Six Nations Reserve in Brantford, Ontario, and the Kahnawake in the province of Quebec, retain much of their traditional form of governance and leadership. But on most Indian reserves, the Indian agent dominated political and economic decision making. Official policies for assimilating Native peoples were supported by a combination of power groups within Canadian society, especially the Christian denominations. The denominational churches sought to convert the band members, and Roman Catholic, Anglican, and Methodist-United Church mission societies also operated day schools and boarding or industrial schools. The Christian boarding schools combined year-round residence facilities with practical training in agriculture, carpentry, and manual work taught half the day and the traditional subjects (reading, writing, and arithmetic) taught in the second half.

After World War I, national and provincial Native organizations were formed across Canada, such as the League of Indian Nations. Native leaders began to question the Canadian government's unilateral management of Native political, economic, and cultural affairs. Year after year, resolutions were passed at annual assemblies calling for changes to the Indian Act and demanding recognition of aboriginal and treaty rights. With Indians stereotyped as a dying race until the 1930s, the poor quality of life evident on Indian reserves could not be dismissed or corrected with paternalistic policies. The high unemployment, short life expectancy, high infant mortality, systemic poverty, shoddy housing, inadequate community services and facilities, and open discrimination became controversial issues in the public press and legislative debates. There were calls for legal inquiries, royal commissions, and just treatment of Canada's Native peoples.

From 1946 to 1948, the joint Senate and House parliamentary committees held hearings and recommended massive revision of the Indian Act. The revised act passed in 1951 removed over fifty sections, including the most blatant discriminatory policies such as the pass system, prohibition on religious ceremonies, and restrictions on property ownership. Still the government and the minister of Indian affairs retained final authority on all land matters and severely limited the powers of local Native government. Indeed the basic policy of controlling Indian socioeconomic development and integrating people into Euro-Canadian institutions remained unchanged. During the 1960s, the Black Power movement gained momentum in the United States, and a corresponding Red Power movement

raised the political profile of Native issues all across North America. A push for radical change gained momentum during the activist 1960s decade, and there was renewed pressure to radically amend the Indian Act and to realign the long-entrenched policies of the Department of Indian Affairs headquartered in Ottawa. Residential boarding schools were closed, and education evolved toward local community control. Churches became more supportive of Indian issues, and support groups such as the Indian-Eskimo Association allied with provincial Native organizations and militant Red Power groups such as AIM (American Indian Movement).

When problems reach crisis proportions, the government's response is invariably to set up an inquiry. The federal government commissioned a broadly mandated but detailed "Survey of the Contemporary Indians of Canada: Economic, Political, Educational Needs and Policies," commonly known as the Hawthorn Report, after its chairman, Harry Hawthorn, an anthropologist. Through intensive interviews with local community leaders and by compiling massive statistics, the report presented an embarrassing indictment of the social and economic conditions of Canada's first citizens. Nothing had changed since reserves were established—low life expectancy (although populations were rising), poor education and health services, inferior housing, high unemployment coupled with demoralizing welfare, high levels of incarceration often rooted in alcohol abuse, inadequate capital funds, and endemic discrimination at every level of interaction with Canadian society and institutions continued. Few Indians could get business or personal loans, credit was limited, and the right to vote in federal elections came only in 1960 with passage of the Canadian Bill of Rights. The Hawthorn Report noted the dismal failure of government efforts to achieve assimilation and suggested many innovative changes in policies and programs. Perhaps the most controversial recommendation was to extend provincial services to Indians contrary to the historically based bilateral treaty relationship between federal and Indian governments.

Recent Strategies for Socioeconomic Development

During the 1960s, the Indian leadership in bands, councils, and provincial organizations demanded greater control over their own affairs. They wanted to develop their own programs, administer their own monies, control their internal affairs, and plan their own future. The major hindrance was the Indian Act, but there was no consensus on how to amend or abolish the archaic piece of legislation. Many community members were under the misunderstanding that the act was the basis of their rights. A growing number called on the Canadian government to honor the spirit and intent of the modern treaties rather than following its legal obligations limited to the strict written terms with the narrowest of responsibility. Gaining confidence and organizational lobbying skills from the social action movement of the 1960s, a new generation of Indian leaders gained the public's attention, and the government was forced to pay attention.

The most popular concept for promoting development in rural and remote communities took the form of community development. The provinces of Ontario, Manitoba, and Alberta were the first to experiment with this new grassroots approach to self-help change. Community members were encouraged to define their own problems and solutions for attaining their own goals. The next phase involved finding the resources necessary to implement long-term development. The federal administration yielded to the mounting pressure and introduced its own community development program in 1963, and coincidentally in the late 1960s, the provinces began to withdraw support or transfer resources to local Native organizations. A new spirit, pride, and vitality was evident in Native communities. They challenged government goals and methods and, typically, the government was unprepared to meet the heightened expectations and limited its commitment to the community development process. The century-old policy of assimilation and paternalism was finally under severe attack for its ineffective and antiquated approach in dealing with the clearly identified social and economic problems endemic to Canada's Indian communities.

As an alternative, the Department of Indian Affairs established a number of regional advisory boards to discuss revision of the Indian Act. A consultation process commenced with the National Indian Advisory Board comprised of prominent Indian leaders from across Canada, which expanded its mandate to investigate budgeting, program evaluations, and administration policy. This new assertiveness was paralleled by a rise in power of provincial Indian political organizations such as the Indian Association of Alberta led by Harold Cardinal, the Federation of Saskatchewan Indians led by Walter Deiter, the Manitoba Indian Brotherhood led by Dave Courchene, the powerful Union of Ontario Chiefs, and the long-established Indian Brotherhoods in British Columbia, the North West Territories, and the Maritimes. One manifestation of the increased sophistication of Indian political organization and communication was the revival of a national body, the National Indian Brotherhood (NIB). During the 1980s, the NIB fostered the growth of Indian leadership and gained momentum and credibility under its president, George Manual, from the Shuswap Nation of British Columbia. In 1981, the NIB reorganized itself as the Assembly of First Nations (AFN).

The electrifying selection of Pierre Elliott Trudeau as the Liberal Party leader in 1968 heralded a new era of hope for aboriginal peoples who were initially attracted to his vision of a "just society." The 1969 White Paper entitled "Statement of the Government of Canada on Indian Policy," has become a landmark in Native resistance to Indian affairs policy makers. The underlying assumption remained: the bureaucratic solution to economic advancement was assimilation into mainstream society. The federal government proposed to eliminate the special status (or rights) of Indians; it projected the disappearance of reserves; and it planned to transfer responsibility for Indians to the provinces albeit under cost-sharing programs. The Indian Act and the Department of Indian Affairs would be terminated, and special legislative, administrative, and judicial rights would give way to equality within modern Canadian society. Indians were to receive the same services as other Canadians through the provincial or municipal delivery systems. The long-honored trust responsibility of the federal government, whereby the minister of Indian Affairs is ultimately responsible to Parliament, was to be abrogated, and management of Indian lands transferred to local control. The Liberal government's policy reflected its ideological emphasis on individual equality and opportunity, but this threatened the collective communal survival of distinct Indian societies in Canada. The historic and cultural uniqueness of the aboriginal peoples, their special constitutional status, their belief in treaty rights, the sovereignty of Indian lands, and the validity of outstanding aboriginal land claims and inherent rights were arbitrarily rejected by the policy makers in Ottawa. The reaction to this bureaucratic reformulation of old assimilationist goals was fast and furious from the "New Indians" of the Red Power movement.

The government White Paper galvanized the local, provincial, and national Native organizations into a united rejection of the proposed changes to federal Indian policy. Under the leadership of the charismatic Cree leader from the Sucker Creek reserve in Alberta, Harold Cardinal, the chiefs of the forty-four Indian bands in Alberta presented their own vision for future development in a counter-publication called the "Red Paper" (1971). Similarly, the Manitoba Indian Brotherhood responded with "Wahbung: Our Tomorrows" (1971), and the Council for Yukon Indians published their terms and conditions for a comprehensive land claim, called "Together Today for our Children Tomorrow" (1973). These and other position papers stressed the cultural and spiritual heritage of their peoples and called for a new relationship based on their special status as "Citizens Plus," as the Alberta Red Paper was retitled.

Indian communities required money and resources to implement self-government. Existing support programs for office administration, health services, recreation, and most importantly social welfare funds could be redirected toward education and training programs. Community infrastructures—roads, utilities, housing, power, heat, recreation, schools, and administration buildings—would require long-term planning and training programs. Nevertheless, it was generally acknowledged that the key to success was the special relationship with the land, their cultural identity, as reflected in the Yukon Indian vision published in their land claim statement in 1973: "Without land Indian people have no soul—no life—no identity—no Purpose. Control of our land is necessary for our Cultural and Economic Survival." During the first half of the twentieth century, surplus or underdeveloped reserve land was "surrendered" to government officials. Some reserves in western Canada lost as much as one-third of their most productive farmland. The Canadian government is currently undertaking to return much of this land where available or providing cash compensation to Indian bands.

During the 1960s, the main source of funds for local economic development was the Indian Revolving Fund, created by the Department of Indian Affairs to provide start-up capital on reserves, which was limited in scope to small business. The 1970s may best be characterized as the experimental decade to jumpstart economic development in Indian communities across Canada. Although the controversial White Paper of 1969 was withdrawn, the White Paper's economic plan was instituted in 1971 through the Indian Economic Development Fund, which in the 1970s made available over $100 million for economic investment on Indian reserves. About $70 million was dispensed by direct loans through the Department of Indian Affairs and Northern Development (DIAND), the national office for administering Canadian Indian affairs; about $30 million was distributed by financial institutions in the form of guaranteed loans; and approximately $10 million was made available in outright grants. Hundreds of projects were funded through the Canadian employment programs and the Department of Regional Economic Expansion with priority given to small independent business ventures such as retail stores, gas stations, handicraft shops, and service outlets.

Unfortunately, the centralized bureaucratic administrators selected economic development projects that

had little relevance to the social, cultural, or political needs of the indigenous communities. Red tape and endless reporting requirements, progress reports, and financial statements thwarted local control. But as young leaders gained experience, local communities benefited from a variety of federal development programs, such as LIP (Local Initiative Program), LEAP (Local Employment Assistance Program), cultural/education centers, and other federally funded enterprises. Hundreds of communities gained short-term economic benefits while funds lasted. Some large industrial schemes were dismal failures but the debate continues whether the lessons learned were worth the investment. Many training programs were targeted for Natives but the results were variable. In terms of community self-esteem, adoption of planning procedures, and political awareness, some short-term benefits accrued to the reserve economies. Yet the social problems associated with poverty, unemployment, under-education, and self-identity are still major hurdles to community development. To the Indian leadership, economic development in the 1970s was tied to the government's policy of assimilation and therefore was viewed as a threat to Indian culture and traditional lifestyle. The federal government's economic development plans, policies, and programs have not been seen as effective in solving the root problems of underdevelopment and poverty on Indian reserves.

The late 1970s witnessed a series of independent national studies, inquiries, and reports on the future direction of Indian self-determination, most critical of the federal government's progress. The governments' limited economic approach to development problems continued to ignore the social, cultural, educational, and political realities on Indian reserves. Its shortcomings were critically analyzed by the National Indian Brotherhood (NIB) in 1973 at a federal-provincial economic conference when the NIB released its "Statement on Economic Development of Indian Communities." In 1976 and 1977, the NIB released "A Strategy for the Socioeconomic Development of Indian people." Both NIB reports criticized the lack of an overall socioeconomic development program that was integrated, well-coordinated, and meaningful to local communities. The Indian Economic Development Fund was criticized as another experiment in problem solving conceived, designed, and managed by government bureaucrats. The government, the reports said, denigrated the viability of an Indian economy and failed to link economic development with community development. The National Indian Brotherhood suggested that a more realistic approach was to encourage the planning process at the community level, which would incorporate the social, cultural, education, and political factors into long-range goals. Local community leaders argued that they had to have control over decision making in consultation with the elders and band members if real community development was to succeed. New policies for self-government and community-based planning were the only realistic alternative to the existing program structures based on federal-Native power relationships. There was a sense of optimism that the federal government was finally willing to listen to its critics and commissioned reviews of its failed policies.

At the national level, the National Indian Brotherhood called for the economic emancipation of Indian communities so that local control could be a reality. The brotherhood proposed transfer and equalization payments to Indian governments similar to that given to provincial governments. This implied political autonomy and the establishment of new institutions better suited to reflect each First Nation's culture, tradition, capitalization, and resource base. Although new fiscal arrangements would need to be negotiated, much of the planning and infrastructure could be assumed through the settlement of land claims, honoring treaty rights, and recognizing the inherent rights of Indian First Nations. Flexibility would be essential to meet the differing economic, cultural, and political evolution of almost six hundred Indian bands occupying over two thousand reserves scattered across Canada. The NIB recommendation reinforced local Native government and traditional economic relations. The strategy report made sixty-eight recommendations, of which the primary starting point was transfer of all authority and decision-making powers to local band governments. DIAND would be merely the financial conduit and fulfill the trust responsibility of the federal government.

Unfortunately, the growing entrenchment of the federal agencies shelved many of the ideas, theories, and approaches discussed among the Indian organizations and its leadership during the 1970s. The federal government's attention was focused on negotiating the massive comprehensive land claim known as the James Bay and Northern Quebec Agreements, signed in 1975. This coincided with the public hearings into the Mackenzie Valley gas pipeline chaired by one of Canada's most noted jurists, Mr. Justice Thomas Berger. He was appointed by the federal government to undertake a comprehensive analysis of the environmental and socioeconomic impacts of a proposed oil and natural gas pipeline extending twenty-six hundred miles from the Beaufort Sea in the Canadian Arctic southward along the Mackenzie River valley of the Northwest Territories to link up with the existing pipelines in Alberta that served markets in the United States. During nineteen months of hearings, listening to over a thousand witnesses including professionals but also people from twenty-six Dene communities, Judge Berger was told that the Dene feared that their survival as a race was at stake. The environment would be damaged, but the influx of southern construction workers would irrevocably alter Dene aspirations for self-determination as eloquently articulated in the famous Dene Declaration of July 1975. In their statement of rights the Dene people declared: "What we seek then is independence and self determination within the country of Canada (as a distinct people and as a nation). This is what we mean when we call for a just land settlement for the Dene Nation."

The Dene people challenged the Canadian government and the Canadian people to recognize their unique culture and the right to self-determination as a nation within Canada. The federal minister swiftly rejected the declaration as a separatist statement prompted by radical back-room academic advisors. Nevertheless, Justice Berger recommended a ten-year moratorium on development, and land claim settlement negotiations continue into the 1990s in northern Canada.

In the 1970s, the Liberal government under Prime Minister Pierre Elliot Trudeau responded to Native issues by sponsoring community and regional studies. The government provided funding for housing, community services and infrastructure, career training, natural resource development, band government, cultural education centers, health and welfare programs, and capital investment programs.

During the 1970s to mid-1980s, the Indian Economic Development Fund provided $150 million to Indian business, comprising about half of the total funding for economic development. This averaged out to about $40,000 per band annually and was not adequate to meet the growing demand from bands and individuals. During the 1980s the federal government shifted its priority to funding regional and tribal programs, and it created a new all-Native advisory board called the Native Economic Development Program (NEDP). A fund of $345 million was allocated over a four-year period commencing in April 1984 with the specific task "to assist the development of economic self-reliance among Canada's Aboriginal people." The programs were open to all status and non-status Indian, Métis, and Inuit. The NEDP called for creation of: (1) Native-operated financial and economic institutions organized to fund Native entrepreneurial business; (2) community-based economic development to enhance Native economic self-reliance; (3) special projects for marketing research and analysis, and sponsoring special studies on Native business issues; and (4) greater Native accessibility to other federal agencies and federal departments.

NEDP funds proved difficult to obtain. The full amount available was never committed, and many projects simply died from neglect. The bands were rewarded with attractive grants and government loan guarantees, only if the band councils persevered and completed the research on market feasibility, raised enough equity investment, justified the social and economic costs and benefits, and provided land and economic infrastructure such as roads, water, and electricity.

In 1989, the NEDP was replaced by the Canadian Aboriginal Economic Development Strategy (CAEDS). As in previous federally sponsored programs of the 1970s, the economic development approach was encouraged through entrepreneurship and individual enterprise rather than community-based employment strategies. Increasingly DIAND wanted to concentrate on community-based economic development and focus on employment-intensive major resource projects, maximizing the use of traditional resources. The objective of CAEDS is to mobilize the resources of several government departments within a single economic development proposal. The Department of Employment and Immigration funds job training and skill development, while the Department of Industry, Science and Technology provides technical assistance to Native-owned businesses, joint ventures, and financial institutions.

The promotion of the entrepreneurial spirit and work ethic among the Native business community is best represented by the Canadian Council for Native Business (CCNB) established by business leaders in 1984 (in 1993 the organization changed its name to the Canadian Council for Aboriginal Business [CCAB]). The organization encourages the involvement and participation of aboriginal people in the mainstream workforce by offering business education internships for Natives to work in large corporate offices. CCNB-CCAB business members also provide business development advice to prospective Native entrepreneurs with the hope that they will succeed in developing the economic self-sufficiency of Canada's First Nations. Corporate employers are assisted in recruiting post-secondary students, and the private sector is encouraged to develop joint venture partnerships with Native corporations in order to share their business, financial, and management expertise while perhaps gaining some beneficial tax exemptions by operating on Indian lands.

The CCNB-CCAB has a high profile with federal government departments including DIAND, Employment and Immigration Canada, the CAEDS, and the Aboriginal Workforce Participation Initiative (AWPI). The government wants Canadian corporations to open their doors to the ninety-two thousand Native graduates with post-secondary (university/college) education and over thirty thousand graduates from job skills training programs each year. The federal government has promised to improve the socioeconomic conditions among Native communities and it has targeted business and natural resource ventures. These are the most promising areas for aboriginal peoples to gain "the skills and experience needed to become full participants in the Canadian economy." The CCNB-CCAB has hosted several high-profile networking conferences to bridge the gap between job opportunities and the growing Native business community and Native professionals. The organization publishes a newsletter called *Contact* with the objective of sharing "information and experiences about Aboriginal employment and develop more effective hiring, promotional and retention strategies."

Numerous Native communities and entrepreneurs are utilizing the CAEDS program to gain valuable skill development and managerial experience within the private sector and the Canadian public service. While demonstrating some success in the 1980s, the number of Native workers in the public service continued to decline in the 1990s, perhaps as a reflection of disillusionment with the federal government's objective of integrating Native graduates into mainstream society. The trend toward favoring business enterprise and entrepreneurship is welcomed by some Indian communities but feared by others as part of a suspected "hidden agenda" to undermine traditional aboriginal culture. The paternalistic approach of earlier government objectives has practically disappeared, and options to Native communities and individuals are expanding as self-confidence and experience grows. Economic self-reliance and the desire to control their own destiny are seen as the fundamental basis for political self-determination in the 1990s.

One of the provincial organizations most active in promoting Native economic well being is the Federation of Saskatchewan Indian Nations (FSIN). FSIN utilizes a series of boards to plan for the future. An indication of future directions is suggested by the responsibility given to the Economic Development Board, which includes the Saskatchewan Indian Resource Council; the Northern Economic Council; the Economic Action Resource Management Program; the Institute for Management, Energy, and Business; small businesses; and trade and commerce.

Federal and Native organizations typically enter into a long-term (usually three to five year) economic development framework agreement, which may be part of a comprehensive socioeconomic package called an Alternate Funding Arrangement (AFA). Indian governments are assured of their base funding for business management training and entrepreneurship and once into the agreement, they can shift funds among their programs and projects. Thus long-range planning and funding contributions provide a basis for stability and predictability in expenditures with the realistic prospect of reducing unemployment and achieving self-sufficiency.

Modern Land Claim (Comprehensive) Settlements

Comprehensive land claims negotiations covering northern Canada across British Columbia, Yukon, North West Territories, and the Arctic have focused on four major aboriginal organizations: the Council of Yukon Indians (CYI), the Dene/Métis groups of the Mackenzie River Valley; the Committee for Original Peoples' Entitlement (COPE), representing the Beaufort Sea area; and the Tungavik Federation of Nunavut (TFN) in the central and eastern Arctic covering the new territory of Nunavut, which means "Our Land" in the Inuktitut language. Not unexpectedly, since the discovery of massive gas pools in the Beaufort Sea, a settlement was reached with COPE in 1984 and was quickly implemented. The same year, the CYI reached an agreement in principle on its land claims, but not all bands are ready for ratification. Economic development was interconnected with political self-determination and cultural identity. Access to lands and natural resources to meet present and future needs was written into the comprehensive land claims settlement negotiated by the Council of Yukon Indians (CYI) in 1991 and 1992.

In 1982, a territory-wide plebiscite approved (by 56 percent of the territory's voters) the division of the vast North West Territories into two jurisdictions: the Western Arctic dominated by the Dene and Métis with a large non-Native population centered in Yellowknife, and the eastern Arctic, homeland to twenty thousand Inuit, in Nunavut. The Dene, Métis, and Inuit agreed to negotiate a political boundary based on their respective but overlapping land claims areas. The idea of division was widely discussed during the Berger Inquiry into the Mackenzie Valley gas pipeline in the mid-1970s by the Inuit, who combined political issues of self-determination with the federal government's comprehensive land claims policy.

In 1988, the Dene/Métis land claim was tentatively settled with the federal government. Two years later when debated at their chiefs assembly representing twelve thousand people throughout the Mackenzie Valley, the Dene leadership rejected a clause that referred to the "extinguishment" of their aboriginal rights. Moreover, the proposed settlement made the Dene relinquish rights to 225 square miles of land in Nunavut territory where they hunted caribou and other wildlife. A fierce debate arose over the urgency to gain a measure of political and economic control over their own affairs

rather than deferring to the federal or territorial governments.

The federal government proceeded to negotiate separate comprehensive land claims agreements with the Gwich'in Indians from the North West Territories and the Inuit. Native leaders, who were forced to agree with one group against the other, voiced objections to Ottawa's "divide-and-conquer" tactics. The Gwich'in Nation of two thousand members retained title to 9,200 square miles in the Yukon and North West Territories as well as receiving $75 million in compensation over fifteen years. In return they relinquished their claim (and perhaps rights) to 18,500 square miles of traditional lands rich in natural resources already under development by international corporations.

In December 1991, the Inuit of the Arctic signed a self-government agreement with the federal government returning ownership of over 140,000 square miles, while conceding their claim to 640,000 square miles in return for $1.1 billion dollars paid over fourteen years.

Subsequently, several Dene bands from northern Saskatchewan filed a statement of claim in the Federal Court of Canada seeking affirmation of their historical presence in 9,600 square miles of land included in the Nunavut territory. Their forefathers served as middlemen traders with the Hudson's Bay Company and regularly trapped fur, and hunted caribou and other game animals in the Nunavut Territory. The ongoing debate may be settled in court if the political impasse is not resolved between the Inuit and Dene.

Political control and self-determination will inevitably be a key determinant in the scope, direction, and intensity of economic development in Canada's newest northern territories. They also will be vital factors in their preparation toward provincehood within confederation in the twenty-first century.

Statutory Limitations on Indian Business

Under the terms of the Canadian Constitution, section 91(24), the treaties, and the Indian Act, the federal government holds "lands reserved for Indians" in a trust relationship. The legal title is vested in Her Majesty the Crown and reserve lands are not legally "Indian property" but remain under the guardianship of the federal government. Reserve land is managed for "the use and benefit of a band" in a communal sense. Reserve land can only be leased or sold after a "surrender" is agreed to by a vote or referendum of eligible voters, and approved by the minister of Indian affairs.

Band-controlled businesses or band members wanting to start a business have to carefully define their type of proprietorship. Some reserves, mainly in eastern

Canada, do issue a "certificate of possession" through the Department of Indian Affairs, but any business operation that is legally incorporated or has non-Indian investment will require a surrender, permit, or lease, and the entrepreneurs will lose their tax-exemption privileges. Reserve property cannot be seized or mortgaged; consequently, capital investment or loans are practically impossible to arrange. This places another limit on the ability of reserve-based enterprises to borrow or attract capital investment.

Even after many of the most blatant discriminatory aspects of Indian policy were removed in 1951 when the Indian Act was revised, federal economic development schemes have been short-term, stop-gap measures entangled in bureaucratic red tape. Special loan funds for Indians date back to 1938, but the current regulations were adopted in the early 1970s. The Department of Indian Affairs has adopted two approaches to encourage reserve business development. Direct loans may be granted by the department to start a business and to purchase assets. Alternatively the government may guarantee a loan from a bank or financial institution. The usual procedures and criteria are applied, such as developing a business plan, in order to assure an enterprise's viability, profitability, and ability to ensure repayment of any loans.

Requests for government loans or grants from band councils, individuals, or Native groups may take months or even years to go through the bureaucratic approval process. Once a band council resolution detailing the economic request is passed, it goes to the departments' district office or to the regional office and finally to headquarters to await the minister's signature. At each level of bureaucracy, the request is analyzed and questions are raised requiring answers from the band council or the local-regional office. At headquarters other federal departments may be involved in the decision making, such as the Justice Department, Treasury Board, and Canada Employment, and secretary of state and cabinet approval may be required for politically sensitive projects or programs.

Economic Self-Determination for Aboriginal People

The urgency of change is apparent in light of the poverty, unemployment, and social-economic conditions on most Indian reserves. Many economic programs are available, but often times information on policy shifts is not effectively communicated to band leaders and members. All too often, economic change has been imposed on local reserve communities. Urbanization, assimilation pressures, and political developments off the reserves may give rise to conflicts, loss of values and culture, depression, social problems, frustration, and lack of hope. The interface of Indian government with the federal and provincial governments is extremely complex. Band governments must deal with several departments managing hundreds of services and programs. Band councils must serve and be accountable to their community members, but must also prepare, negotiate, and account for their annual operations with the government. This dual accountability may be streamlined in the future as self-government is implemented to reflect local needs, priorities, culture, and economic base for the community and individual enterprises.

Across Canada, there are close to four hundred thousand status Indians in about six hundred bands living on about twenty-five hundred reserves and "Crown Land" settlements. Generally, the reserves are small, scattered in rural lands, and lack the administrative infrastructure or resources to economically sustain their rapidly growing population. About one hundred bands are described as resource producing (with oil and gas production or timber and mining), and several large prosperous reserves are located adjacent to metropolitan centers, such as Vancouver, Calgary, Saskatoon, Brantford, Montreal, Quebec City, Fredericton, and Sydney.

A common analytical approach sees post-treaty economic developments as the fault of "colonial exploitation" and "underdevelopment," where Indian reserves have become pockets of poverty and unemployment. The land base of First Nations has been severely limited, and the indigenous people increasingly have been denied access to natural resources. We have seen how the Indian Act and legislation has limited the powers of band councils and in fact has served to entrench the Department of Indian Affairs' control over every aspect of an individual's life and band administration. Combined with the paternalistic nature of the Indian Act, the creation of Indian reserves has kept Indian people from participating in the political and economic processes of the dominant Canadian society and from significantly improving their socioeconomic position.

Indian communities are largely dependent on government transfer payments—social welfare programs— or they find their traditional economies replaced by a system based upon wage labor and market competition. The depletion of natural resources, the static land base, increase in population, and lack of jobs, housing, and work opportunities have prompted an ever-increasing migration from reserves to urban centers. The demands of urban living based on a wage economy and resulting different lifestyle have had profound effects on traditional Indian culture, values, and expectations.

Acculturation pressures have forced the Native population to move from a relatively independent subsistence economy to involvement in an economic market place requiring formal education, technical training, and structured work styles.

When taking note of the socioeconomic and cultural environment on an Indian reserve, an individual entrepreneur or tribal corporation (small business) is faced with a number of institutional constraints unique to Canadian Indians. The legal aspects of economic development on Indian reserves are key determinant factors as to what can be done and how it can be achieved.

There are also numerous factors within a reserve community external to the economic environment that will help or hinder change. Some of these include (1) political and legal frameworks (government policy and laws, financial regulations); economic marketplaces (markets, supply and demand, operational costs, capitalization, competition, availability of resources); financial institutions (access to loans); sociocultural constraints (cultural attitudes, collective versus individual values, spiritual values); education (level of education and dropout rate); and physical limitations (community infrastructure for communications, housing, roads, services, and available natural resources)

The fundamental goal is to create jobs on the reserve for band members and coincidentally to take control of economic development in order to assure control over decision-making (whether planning, hiring and firing, creating income, or assuming self-determination). Resource-rich bands have demonstrated initiative and diversification during the 1980s. In 1984, production of oil and gas on Indian land amounted to $346 million, but by 1991 the economic returns had declined to $56 million, according to Indian Oil and Gas Canada (IOGC). Much of the investment activity in the oil and gas industry is centered on Indian reserves in the province of Alberta and some in the province of Saskatchewan. Bands have established development trust funds to enter into joint ventures with established oil companies and thereby gain technical and managerial expertise and provide employment opportunities. The enticement for non-Native corporations are enhanced tax exemptions and a positive corporate image.

In the spring of 1992, the newly formed Canadian Indian Energy Corporation (IEC) hosted the All Chiefs Oil and Gas Conference in Calgary, Alberta, to promote a closer working relationship between Indian nations and the major oil and gas companies. A Memorandum of Understanding and Statement of Principles was signed by IEC chair Joe Dion and Canadian Petroleum Association president Ian Smyth to ensure joint planning and joint ventures and cooperation in developing

employment, investment, training and business opportunities. The conference theme, "Working with Industry," highlighted the importance of economic development to coordinate the human, financial, and productive resources of the IEC First Nations. The IEC will focus on resource control and management while serving as a business advisory body to new locally controlled entrepreneurial ventures.

On less affluent reserves, economic development is motivated by the need to earn an income and is often centered around traditional work (producing handicrafts) or a family project. Community development is similarly motivated by the desire to create employment and is more likely to follow a business plan with well-defined goals and detailed accounting projections provided by outside advisors/consultants.

Community development is not gauged by economic factors alone. Projects are commonly judged according to whether the community or individual will retain its special character and resist assimilation into Canadian culture; whether the project will further self-esteem, affirm their pride, protect land ownership, enhance community values, and respect the sacredness of the land and environment are all considerations.

To some, dealing with bureaucratic red tape and an endless line of civil servants at local, regional, and national offices is simply another hurdle in creating employment on the reserve. DIAND support ranges from seed money for market studies, subsidizing construction costs or purchase of fixed assets, providing loan guarantees or lines of credit, offering work capital, and providing wage subsidies or technical assistance through advisors. These incentives are offset by the administrative delay in the approval process, unrealistic financing structures relating to cash flow, and the threat of termination of tax exemptions.

In recent years, many aboriginal communities have initiated change; they are preparing long-range plans, setting down goals and objectives, and forming a vision for the future. In the past, the most contentious issue has been over control and political change and pressure for change is increasing as the twenty-first century approaches. Political self-determination will depend on economic self-reliance, and the political-economic framework must reflect the cultural values of each indigenous society. Canada's aboriginal peoples have gained recognition in the Constitution for "the inherent right to self-government" as a "third order government" equal in stature to the federal and provincial governments within Canada. This fundamental human right, the inherent right to aboriginal self-government, means that aboriginal communities will have control within their own reserve lands or settlement areas. Aboriginal governments will be jurisdictionally autonomous over all economic, social, political, and cultural aspects of their lives. Ultimately, if properly implemented, the exercise of self-government will empower each aboriginal community to practice its traditional form of government outside the current limitations imposed by the Indian Act. Many of the current restraints are under review by government-sponsored committees, involving subjects such as lands management, Indian monies, taxation, and financing of Indian government, in order to resolve or remove the various alien rules and regulations imposed by Parliament. Now, instead of being necessarily reactive to government proposals or resistant to unexpected change, aboriginal peoples can take the initiative in planning and decision making.

Entering the Twenty-First Century

If the 1980s were dominated by constitutional First Minister's Conferences and comprehensive land claims negotiations, the 1990s have been marked by unprecedented growth in economic development opportunities for Canada's First Nations as they continued their strident advancement towards self determination and laid the foundations for political, economic, and professional growth. More than ever, economic power has reinforced political power and influence. The expansive growth of self-government since the 1970s has been the key catalyst at the local, regional, and national levels, which has made economic development a priority on many fronts. As their economies grow due to land claim settlements, Supreme Court of Canada decisions, and entrepreneurial expansion, First Nations have seen corresponding rise in their political strength and influence on decision making at the corporate levels to complement their legal and political gains.

Some of the systemic impediments to establishing and sustaining the economic viability of First Nations communities have been successfully challenged. There is a growing recognition that First Nations must have access to financial capital and better education and training. First Nations must also benefit from natural resource development in order to rebuild their communities and sustain self governance, preferably without taxation revenue. Formerly denied access to off-reserve lands and to traditional sources of food, clothing, housing, jobs, and training, Native peoples today have unlimited opportunities.

For example, since 1985 there have been about fifty Supreme Court of Canada decisions involving First Nations rights. The *Guerin* decision of 1985 ruled that the federal government of Canada did owe a fiduciary trust to Indian bands to ensure that they received equitable economic compensation for surrendered lands. The landmark decision in *Regina v. Apsassin* (1995

Blueberry River Indian Band) resulted in a $147 million settlement involving compensation for oil and gas mineral rights located under allegedly surrendered reserve lands.

Other far-reaching judgments made by the Supreme Court of Canada in November 1997 known as *Delgamuukw/Gisdayway* and in the 1999 *Donald Marshall* decision have confirmed that First Nations all across Canada do have aboriginal jurisdiction over traditional lands and natural resources such as forestry, fisheries, and the right to a reasonable level of livelihood utilizing the natural resources in their traditional territories. The courts at all levels continue to grapple with the reality of post-contact aboriginal economies and what aboriginal and treaty rights are essential for making a livelihood. Nevertheless, the federal Crown continues to ignore aboriginal history and pursues legal challenges in a seemingly endless series of litigation aimed at denying First Nations commercial access to wildlife, fisheries, forestry, and natural resources.

In an attempt to avoid costly litigation, the federal government originally adopted a policy on specific claims in 1973 as an alternative dispute resolution mechanism. Research monies were increased in 1990 following the "Oka Crisis" which has resulted in the submission of 1,014 submitted specific claims of which over 500 remain unsettled or ignored. The economic spin-off of the settlements is estimated in the hundreds of millions of dollars and one study estimated the total cost might reach $5 billion. In the past decade there have been about fifty Treaty Land Entitlement agreements implemented in the prairie treaty areas of Alberta, Saskatchewan, and Manitoba, which has pumped millions of dollars into the economy. While it is the Canadian society that benefits the greatest from these kind of settlements, the addition of Indian reserve lands and cash settlements put into trust agreements has begun to provide a sound economic foundation for the beneficiary First Nations. Similar economic results will eventually flow from the Treaty Process in British Columbia and the Comprehensive Land Settlements covering northern Canada. The economic impact of all these land claim settlements will be critical to the self-determination and self-reliance of Canada's aboriginal peoples in the future.

A major undertaking of the federal government arising out of the failed attempts at constitutional reform in the 1990 Meech Lake Accord and the 1992 Charlottetown Accord, was the appointment of the Royal Commission on Aboriginal Peoples (or RCAP). After five years of hearings, interviews and round table consultations at an expenditure of about $60 million, the Royal Commission released its five-volume report in November 1996. The reports not only create a historical baseline for the treaties, Indian Act, residential schools, governance, lands and resources, economic development, social policy, health, housing, education, and a constitutional framework, but it also made 440 recommendations to lay the foundation of a renewed relationship between Canada and the First Nations peoples.

The general recommendations call for a spirit of reconciliation and reinforce the need for mutual respect and recognition of wrongdoing. But some of the recommendations are dramatic and call for the complete overhaul of existing policies and structures. The Commission's recommendations span all levels of aboriginal life as it currently exists in Canada, ranging from the formation of an Aboriginal Parliament to detailed recommendations on revamping child care, social policy, membership codes, and policies affecting elders, women, and youth. Many proposals are innovative and creative, calling for the acknowledgment of past injustices, treaty obligations, oral testimony, and the importance of financial resources. In some respects, however, the proposals would reinforce the status quo by encouraging a top-down approach to programming and continue to include health and education within the mainstream systems. Many critics resent the amalgamation of combining all aboriginal groups (Indian, Métis, and Inuit) under one policy while conspicuously avoiding contentious political hot issues such as international status, sovereignty, and fiscal resourcing for First Nations governance.

Release of the long awaited RCAP in November 1996 prompted both First Nations and the Department of Indian Affairs to commence a lengthy process of technical analysis, consultation meetings, and months of silence interspersed with calls for extreme caution and further study and analysis of the 440 recommendations. The recommendations on Economic Development are covered in Volume 2, "Restructuring the Relationships" which emphasizes that there must be "mutual and shared responsibility" for resource development based upon "co-jurisdiction and co-management arrangements" to attain the predicted 300,000 additional jobs needed over the next twenty years to attain a comparable employment level with mainstream Canadians. The Commission made fifty-two recommendations (out of 440 in total) on how to begin restructuring the employment, programming, training, social development, and social assistance programs which have historically fostered dependence on governmental institutions and were premised on a colonial mentality. The RCAP report discusses the transformation of economic development programs by developing a diverse strategy that responds to local community needs, goals and priorities developed cooperatively based upon capacity building, financing, and self-reliance, and grounded in long

term economic development agreements. To achieve these changes, First Nations governments, businesses, and entrepreneurs need less bureaucratic access to business advice, trade promotion opportunities, government support programs designed to support self development initiatives, and business financing. In fact, resource management and fiscal arrangements for economic development continue to be an important part in ongoing treaty and land claim settlements.

In summary, RCAP concludes that aboriginal economies require access to land and resources based on historic and modern treaties; that each community is unique and diverse; that economic participation must be enhanced, facilitated, and self-empowering; that plans be made to motivate young people through training and promoting new approaches to commercial activity; and that the development of economies must cross several sectors such as health, education, governance, and social services in an integrated holistic manner. Finally, the commission recommends the creation of economic institutions which reflect aboriginal values and be accountable primarily to its membership without political interference; the establishment of capital corporations to serve aboriginal people with loan guarantees and limited subsidies; the inauguration of a national development bank to provide financing and technical assistance, raise capital investments, and create leadership opportunities; and the creation of a special employment and training initiative to provide training, identify employment sectors, and place permanent employment in collaboration with government agencies, private sector corporations, and employment service agencies.

Despite the initial public fanfare upon the release of the long delayed and anxiously anticipated RCAP in five volumes, and hundreds of commissioned background research reports (available on CD-ROM), it took the federal government a further two years of "analysis" to prepare its official response to a selection of the 440 RCAP recommendations.

Meanwhile there was a parallel analysis being undertaken by Native organizations and groups which were questioning the non-critical emphasis on healing, reconciliation, new partnership, and strengthening self-governance themes which were prominently featured in a national program entitled "Gathering Strength: Canada's Aboriginal Action Plan" launched in January 1998 by then Indian Affairs Minister Jane Stewart along with a statement of apology and reconciliation. The "Gathering Strength" program focuses on four core areas of community development: a healing and reconciliation strategy; social development; fiscal relations; and economic development.

The plan generally adopted the principles set out in RCAP of mutual respect, recognition of rights, and political responsibility combined with accountability and sharing. The key objectives were to review the Canada-First Nations partnerships, strengthen community-based governance, develop a new fiscal model, and provide support for strong communities and economies.

At the same time the government established a healing foundation with a grant of $350 million to support healing initiatives such as counseling, spiritual guidance, workshops, and other processes to begin addressing the detrimental legacy of physical, cultural, and emotional abuse suffered at residential schools and government-sponsored institutions.

In July 2000, federal ministers Robert Nault and Ralph Goodale issued "A Progress Report" on the initial two years of the program which lauded the "Gathering Strength" action plan. The report concluded that (1) aboriginal peoples and governments should work together to build jobs, growth, stability, and standard-of-life improvements for all Native people and (2) strong aboriginal communities depend on partnership, good governance, and a new fiscal relationship. The 2000 progress report identified several achievements in strengthening communities and economic development opportunities, including:

- completion of 100 professional development projects to strengthen skills of native administrators;
- settlement of sixteen specific claims and implementation of the precedent setting Nishga'a Final Agreement in northern British Columbia;
- completion of income security reform projects involving more than 350 First Nations (out of 610 communities); and
- participation of more than eighty First Nations in community-based housing initiatives.

The progress report concludes that the government is successful in promoting self-sufficiency and the quality of life. The vision captured in Gathering Strength is fairly straightforward. They plan:

- a new partnership among aboriginal people and other Canadians that reflects mutual interdependence and enables people to work together to build a better future;
- financially viable aboriginal governments able to generate their own revenues and able to operate with secure, predictable government transfers;
- aboriginal governments reflective of their communities' needs and values; and

- a quality of life for aboriginal people like other Canadians.

In hindsight, the obstacles and barriers to participating and implementing economic development programs in First Nation communities are thoroughly identified now in academic publications, government studies, and in the 1996 RCAP study.

There are numerous conferences and workshops held by government agencies and Native organizations and business agencies on every aspect of economic development. Typically the conference/workshop themes include: economic self-reliance; Native business opportunities in the new reality; financing First Nations; investing in self-reliance; First Nations tourism and resort development; financing the aboriginal economy in the twenty-first century; manufacturing on aboriginal lands; the future of aboriginal gaming in Canada; creatively developing aboriginal lands; and Native women's business issues.

The significant advances and strength of economic development activity in the 1990s culminated in May 2000 with an announcement by the Canadian government to triple its economic development funds to $75 million for that fiscal year with the promise of an additional $100 million for 2001. Promoted as " building on the significant success of Gathering Strength—Canada's Aboriginal Action Plan." the infusion of funds especially for economic growth very much reflects Indian Affairs Minister Robert Nault's belief in the restorative value of economic projects to lay the foundations for community self-sufficiency into the next century.

Aside from government policies, there is a demonstrable growth in professional organizations such as the Council for the Advancement of Native Development Officers (CANDO). Under their first president, Charles Sampson, they began publishing in 1993 an educational journal called *Mawio'mi Journal* to share information among economic development officers. Then in 1995 the organization established the Economic Developer Recognition Award to promote awareness of entrepreneurs and organizations in the field of aboriginal economic development. Another professional magazine entitled *First Nations Business—Canada's Aboriginal Business Magazine* was started in 1996 to feature individual and business profiles, interviews, financial markets, policy analyses, and general business advice on "exciting developments in the world of business development in Aboriginal Canada."

This growth in professionalism is also reflected in the formation of national and provincial organizations such as the Alberta Indian Economic Development Officers Network (AIEDON) established in 1997. The

AIEDON officers adopted as their mission statement: "Achieving self-sufficiency for grassroots First Nations peoples and First Nations through a collective economic development voice." The organization's goals and objectives emphasize networking and maximizing their access to programs, services, and institutions.

Conclusion

Economic development combined with self-reliance and self-governance is clearly one of the essential building blocks to the renewal of First Nations' communities. Many social, political, and economic problems will continue to challenge First Nations leaders, such as inadequate housing, under capitalization, restricted access to financing, lack of training programs, high suicide rates, health problems, racism, bureaucracy, and political disempowerment. But there are also new community based programs, healing foundations, more post-secondary graduates, professional networking, support for individual entrepreneurs and businesses, and greater economic opportunities through land claims settlements than ever before at the turn of the new millennium. Despite a century of many frustrations, disappointments, and incredible hurdles, many of Canada's First Nations are well positioned to enter the twenty-first century ready for the political and economic challenges they face to become truly self-reliant and self-governing.

Ian Getty
The Stoney Tribal Administration

Economic Organizations

UNITED STATES

ALASKA NATIVE INC.
2600 Cordova Street, Suite 211
Anchorage, AK 99503
(907) 263–7013

ALASKA VILLAGE ELECTRIC
COOPERATIVE, INC.
4831 Eagle St.
Anchorage, AK 99503–7431
(907) 561–1818

ALASKA VILLAGE INITIATIVE
1577 C St. Plaza, Suite 304
Anchorage, AK 99501
(907) 274–5400

AMERICANS FOR INDIAN OPPORTUNITY
681 Juniper Hill Rd.
Bernalillo, NM 87004
(505) 867–0278

ARIZONA NATIVE AMERICAN ECONOMIC
COALITION
P.O. Box 22247
Flagstaff, AZ 86002–2247
(520) 523–7320

BERING SEA FISHERMEN'S ASSOCIATION
725 Christensen Dr.
Anchorage, AK 99501
(907) 279–6519

COUNCIL OF ENERGY RESOURCE
TRIBES (CERT)
695 S. Colorado Blvd., Suite 10
Denver, CO 80246
(303) 282–7576

FIRST NATIONS DEVELOPMENT INSTITUTE
11917 Main St.
Fredericksburg, VA 22408
(540) 371–5615

LAKOTA FUND
P.O. Box 340
Kyle, SD 57752
(605) 455–2500

NATIONAL AMERICAN INDIAN CATTLEMAN'S
ASSOCIATION
1541 Foster Rd.
Toppenish, WA 98948
(509) 854–1329

NATIONAL CENTER FOR AMERICAN INDIAN
ENTERPRISE DEVELOPMENT
Head Quarters
953 East Juanita
Mesa, AZ 85204
(480) 545–1298

NATIVE AMERICAN FINANCE OFFICERS
ASSOCIATION
Marlene Lynch
P.O. Box 170
Fort Defiance, AZ 86504
(520) 729–6211

NEW MEXICO INDIAN BUSINESS
DEVELOPMENT CENTER
123 Fourth St. Southwest, P.O. Box 400
Albuquerque, NM 87103
(505) 889–9092

NORTHWEST REGIONAL OFFICE
934 N 143 St.
Seattle, WA 98133
(206) 365–7735

PACIFIC REGIONAL

Pacific Regional
11138 Valley Mall, Suite 200
El Monte, CA 91731
(626) 442–3701

THE PUEBLO OF SANTA ANA

2 Dove Road
Bernalillo, NM 87004
(505) 867–3301

UIDA CONSULTING GROUP

430 Commeres Park Dr., SE
4th FL 424
Marietta, GA 30063
(770) 494–0117

UPPER TANANA DEVELOPMENT
   CORPORATION

P.O. Box 459
Tok, AK 99780
(907) 883–5158

WORLD VISION INTERNATIONAL

800 West Chestnut Ave
Monrovia, CA 91016
(818) 303–8811

CANADA

ABORIGINAL BUSINESS CANADA OFFICES

To obtain more information about how ABORIGINAL BUSINESS CANADA can work with Aboriginal firms, please contact the office nearest you.

◆ HEAD OFFICE

ABORIGINAL BUSINESS CANADA

Industry Canada
1st Floor West
235 Queen Street
Ottawa, ON K1A 0H5
(613) 954–4064

◆ ALBERTA & NORTHWEST TERRITORY

ABORIGINAL BUSINESS CANADA

Industry Canada
Canada Place Room 725
9700 Jasper Avenue
Edmonton, AB T5J 4C3
(780) 495–2954

◆ ATLANTIC

ABORIGINAL BUSINESS CANADA

Industry Canada
1505 Barrington Street
Maritime Centre, Suite 1605
P.O. Box 940, Station M
Halifax, NS B3J 3K5
(902) 426–2018

◆ BRITISH COLUMBIA & YUKON TERRITORY

ABORIGINAL BUSINESS CANADA

Industry Canada
300 West Georgia Street, 21st Floor
Vancouver, BC V6B 6E2
(604) 666–3871

◆ MANITOBA

ABORIGINAL BUSINESS CANADA

Industry Canada
4th Floor, 400 St. Mary Avenue
Winnipeg, MB R3C 4K5
(204) 983–7316

◆ ONTARIO

ABORIGINAL BUSINESS CANADA

Industry Canada
3rd Floor, 151 Yonge Street
Toronto, ON M5C 2W7
(416) 973–8800

ABORIGINAL BUSINESS CANADA

Industry Canada
c/o Indian and Northern Affairs Office
1760 Regent Street South
Sudbury, ON P3E 3Z8
(705) 522–5100

◆ QUEBEC & NUNAVUT

ABORIGINAL BUSINESS CANADA
Industry Canada
5 Place Ville-Marie, 8th Floor
P.O. Box 289
Montreal, QC H3B 2G2
(514) 283–1828

◆ SASKATCHEWAN

ABORIGINAL BUSINESS CANADA
Industry Canada
7th Floor
123–2nd Avenue South
Saskatoon, SK S7K 7E6
(306) 975–4329

External Delivery Organizations

A number of Aboriginal business organizations across the country also deliver program services. For a list of these organizations, please call your nearest Aboriginal Business Canada office.

ABORIGINAL CAPITAL CORPORATIONS

Aboriginal Capital Corporations (ACCS) are Aboriginal-owned and controlled business lending organizations. A listing of the ACCs throughout Canada can be found below.

◆ ALBERTA & NORTHWEST TERRITORY

ALBERTA INDIAN INVESTMENT CORPORATION
Box 180
Enoch, AB T7X 3Y3
(780) 470–3600

APEETOGOSAN (Métis) DEVELOPMENT INC.
12527–129th Street
Edmonton, AB T5L 1H7
(780) 452–7951

INDIAN AGRI-BUSINESS CORPORATION
210–2720-12th St. N.E.
Calgary, AB T2E 7N4
(403) 291–5151

NORTHWEST TERRITORY COOPERATIVE
Business Development Fund
321-C Old Airport Road
Yellowknife, NT X1A 3T3
(867) 873–3481

NWT METIS-DENE DEVELOPMENT FUND
P.O. Box 1805
5125–50th Street
Yellowknife, NT X1A 2P4
(867) 873–9341

SETTLEMENT INVESTMENT CORPORATION
10339–124th Street, Suite 777
Edmonton, AB T5N 3W1
(780) 488–5656

◆ ATLANTIC

ULNOOWEG DEVELOPMENT GROUP INC.
139 Esplanade Street
P.O. Box 1259
Truro, NS B2N 5N2
(902) 893–7379
(888) 766–2376

◆ BRITISH COLUMBIA & YUKON

ALL NATIONS TRUST COMPANY
Suite 208 West
345 Yellowhead Highway
Kamloops, BC V2H 1H1
(250) 828–9770

BELLA BELLA COMMUNITY DEVELOPMENT SOCIETY
P.O. Box 880
Waglisia, BC V0T 1Z0
(250) 957–2381

DANA NAYE VENTURES
409 Black Street
Whitehorse, YK Y1A 2N2
(867) 668–6925
(800) 661–0448

FIRST NATIONS AGRICULTURAL LENDING
ASSOCIATION
Suite 200–345 Yellowhead Highway
Kamloops, BC V2H 1H1
(250) 828–9751

NATIVE FISHING ASSOCIATION
Suite 102–1500 Howe Street
Vancouver, BC V6Z 2N1
(604) 684–0699

NUU-CHAH-NULTH ECONOMIC
DEVELOPMENT CORPORATION
7563 Pacific Rim Highway
P.O. Box 1384
Port Alberni, BC V9Y 7M2
(250) 724–3131

TALE'AWTXW ABORIGINAL CAPITOL
CORPORATION
Units 29 & 30
6014 Vedder Road
Chilliwack, BC V2R 5M4
(250) 824–2088

TALE'AWTXW ABORIGINAL CAPITOL
CORPORATION
(Branch Office)
R.R. #1, Trans Canada Highway
Ladysmith, BC V0R 2E0
(250) 245–9903

TRIBAL RESOURCES INVESTMENT
CORPORATION
217–3rd Avenue West
Prince Rupert, BC V8J 1L2
(250) 624–3535

◆ QUEBEC & NUNAVUT

CORPORATION DE DEVELOPMENT
ECONOMIQUE MONTAGNAIS
1005, boul. Laure, suite 110
Sept-;les, QC G4R 4S6
(418) 968–1246
(800) 463–2216

KAHNAWAKE LOAN GUARANTEE FUND INC.
P.O. Box 1110
Kahnawake, QC J0L 1B0
(450) 638–4280

NUNAVIK INVESTMENT CORPORATION
C.P. 239
Kuujjuaq, QC J0M 1C0
(819) 964–2035

SOCIETE DE CREDIT COMMERCIAL
AUTOCHTONE
Native Commercial
Credit Corporation
265–201, Place Chef Michel Laveau
Wendake, QC G0A 4V0
(418) 842–0972
(800) 241–0972

◆ MANITOBA

ANISHINABE MAZASKA CAPITOL
CORPORATION
300–208 Edmonton Street
Winnipeg, MB R3C 1R7
(204) 957–0045

LOUIS RIEL CAPITAL CORPORATION
24–1635 Burrows Avenue
Winnipeg, MB R2X 3B5
(204) 586–8474 ext. 275

TRIBAL WI-CHI-WAY WIN CAPITAL
CORPORATION
203–400 St. Mary Avenue
Winnipeg, MB R3C 4K5
(204) 988–1888

◆ ONTARIO

INDIAN AGRICULTURAL PROGRAM OF
ONTARIO
P.O. Box 100
220 North Street
Stirling, ON K0K 3E0
(613) 395–5505

NISHNAWBE-ASKI DEVELOPMENT FUND
P.O. Box 20119, Green Acres
Thunder Bay, ON P7E 6P2
(807) 623–5397

OHWISTHA CAPITAL CORPORATION
P.O. Box 1394
Cornwall, ON K6H 5V4
(613) 933–6500

OMAA DEVELOPMENT CORPORATION
452 Albert Street East
2nd Floor-Walrus Building #1
Sault Ste. Marie, ON P6A 2J8
(705) 949–8220

TECUMSEH DEVELOPMENT CORPORATION
R.R. #1
Muncey, ON N0L 1Y0
(519) 289–2122

TWO RIVERS COMMUNITY
    DEVELOPMENT CENTRE
P.O. Box 225
Ohsweken, ON N0A 1M0
(519) 445–4567

◆ SASKATCHEWAN

SASKATCHEWAN INDIAN EQUITY FUND
224B-4th Avenue South
Saskatoon, SK S7K 5M5
(306) 955–4550

SASKATCHEWAN INDIAN LOAN COMPANY
224B-4th Avenue South
Saskatoon, SK S7K 5M5
(306) 955–8699

SASKNATIVE ECONOMIC DEVELOPMENT
    CORPORATION
#108–219 Robin Crescent
Saskatoon, SK S7L 6M8
(306) 477–4350

Native Owned Businesses

◆ ALASKA

AHTNA, INC.
Glennallen Office
P.O. Box 649
Glennallen, AK 99588
(907) 822–3476

ALEUT CORPORATION
4000 Old Seward Hwy., Suite 300
Anchorage, AK 99503
(907) 561–4300
www.aleutcorp.com

BERING STRAITS NATIVE CORP.
P.O. Box 1008
Nome, AK 99762
(907) 443–5252

BRISTOL BAY NATIVE CORP.
P.O. Box 100220
800 Cordova St., Suite 200
Anchorage, AK 99510–6299
(907) 278–3602
www.bbnc.net

CALISTA CORP.
301 Calista Court, Suite A
Anchorage, AK 99518
(907) 279–5516
www.calistacorp.com

CHUGACH ALASKA CORP.
560 E. 34th Ave., Suite 200
Anchorage, AK 99503
(907) 563–8866

COOK INLET REGION, INC.
203 W. 15th Ave., Suite 102
Anchorage, AK 99501
(907) 274–8638

DOYON, LTD.
1 Doyon Place, Suite 300
Fairbanks, AK 99701
(907) 452–4755
www.doyon.com

KONIAG, INC.
4300 B St., Suite 407
Anchorage, AK 99503
(907) 561–2668
www.koniag.com

NANA REGIONAL CORPORATION
P.O. Box 49
Kotzebue, AK 99752
(907) 442–3301
www.nana.com

SEALASKA CORP.
One Sealaska Plaza, Suite 400
Juneau, AK 99801
(907) 586–1512
www.sealaska.com

◆ ARIZONA

FORT APACHE TIMBER COMPANY (FATCO)
P.O. Box 1090
1 Fatco Rd.
Whiteriver, AZ 85941
(520) 338–4931

◆ MINNESOTA

NATIVE TOURS & TRAVEL
6875 Highway 65, NE
Minneapolis, MN 55432
(763) 571–8184
www.nativetours.com,

◆ MISSISSIPPI

CHAHTA Development Company (CHOCTAW)
201 James Billy Rd.
Philadelphia, MS 39350
(601) 656–7350

CHAHTA Enterprise Plant I & II (CHOCTAW)
390 Industrial Rd.
Philadelphia, MS 39350
(601) 656–7350

CHOCTAW ELECTRONICS
404 Industrial Rd.
Philadelphia, MS 39350
(601) 656–3650

CHOCTAW MANUFACTURING ENTERPRISE
Rte. 7, Box 3-D
Carthage, MS 39051
(601) 267–5681

◆ MONTANA

A & S TRIBAL INDUSTRIES
P.O. Box 308
Industrial Park
Poplar, MT 59255
(406) 768–5151

BLACKFEET NATIONAL BANK
P.O. Box 730
Browning, MT 59417
(406) 338–7000

WEST ELECTRONICS
P.O. Box 577
Industrial Park
Poplar, MT 59255
(406) 768–5511

◆ NEW MEXICO

LAGUNA INDUSTRIES, INC.
P.O. Box 1001
Laguna, NM 87026
(505) 552–6041

NAVAJO AGRICULTURAL PRODUCTS
   INDUSTRIES (NAPI)
P.O. Drawer 1318
Farmington, NM 87499
(505) 327–5251

2-D
P.O. Box 1669
Crownpoint, New Mexico 87313
(505) 208–5973

◆ OKLAHOMA

FIRST OKLAHOMA BANK OF SHAWNEE
130 East MacArthur
Shawnee, OK 74801
(405) 275–8830

◆ OREGON

KAH-NEE-TA RESORT
Box Office K
Warm Springs, OR 97761
(541) 553–1112

WARM SPRINGS FOREST PRODUCTS
   INDUSTRIES
P.O. Box 810
Warm Springs, OR 97761
(541) 553–1131

◆ NORTH DAKOTA

FORT BERTHOLD DEVELOPMENT
   CORPORATION
THREE AFFILIATED TRIBES
Box 867
New Town, ND 58763
(701) 627–4828

MANDAREE ELECTRONICS
   CORPORATION (MEC)
1 Community Center Rd.
P.O. Box 425
Mandaree, ND 58757
(701) 759–3399

TURTLE MOUNTAIN MANUFACTURING
Highway 5 W.
Belcourt, ND 58316
(701) 477–6404

UNIBAND CORPORATION
P.O. Box 1059
Belcourt, ND 58316
(701) 477–6445
www.uniband.com

◆ WASHINGTON

KALISPEL CASE LINE
P.O. Box 267
Cusick, WA 99119
(509) 445–1121

SPOKANE TRIBAL WOOD PRODUCTS
P.O. Box 100

Wellpinit, WA 99040
(509) 258–7431

◆ WISCONSIN

MENOMINEE TRIBAL ENTERPRISES (M.T.E.)
P.O. BOX 10
Neopit, WI 54150
(715) 756–2311

Indian Gaming Casinos & Organizations

◆ UNITED STATES

INSTITUTE FOR THE STUDY OF GAMBLING
AND COMMERCIAL GAMING
College of Business Administration
Reno, NV 89557–0208
(775) 784–1442

NATIONAL INDIAN GAMING ASSOCIATION
224 Second Street, SE
Washington, DC 20003
(202) 546–7711
1–800–286–6442

NORTH AMERICAN GAMING REGULATORS
ASSOCIATION
P.O. Box 21886
Lincoln, NE 68542–1886
(402) 474–4261

NATIONAL INDIAN GAMING COMMISSION & REGIONAL OFFICES

NATIONAL INDIAN GAMING COMMISSION
NATIONAL HEADQUARTERS
1441 L Street NW, 9th Floor
Washington, DC 20005
(202) 632–7003

REGION 1
Solomon Building, Suite 212
620 Main Street
Portland, OR 97205
(503) 326–5095

REGION 2
501 I Street, Suite 12400
Sacramento, CA 95814
(916) 930–2230

REGION 3
One Columbus Plaza Suite 880
Phoenix, AZ 58012
(602) 604–2951

REGION 4
190 E. 5th St., Suite 170
St. Paul, MN 55101
(651) 290–4004

REGION 5
224 South Boulder
Tulsa, OK 74103
(918) 581–7924

STATE GAMING ORGANIZATIONS

◆ ARIZONA

ARIZONA DEPARTMENT OF GAMING
202 E. Earl, Suite 200
Phoenix, AZ 85012
(602) 604–1801

◆ COLORADO

CENTRAL CITY–BLACK HAWK OFFICE
142 Lawrence Street (location address)
P.O. Box 721
Central City, CO 80427–0721
(303) 582–0529

COLORADO DIVISION OF GAMING
Lakewood (Headquarters) Office
1881 Pierce Street, Suite 112
Lakewood, CO 80214–1496
(303) 205–1355

CRIPPLE CREEK OFFICE
433 E. Carr Avenue (location address)
P.O. Box 1209 (mailing address)
Cripple Creek, CO 80813–1209
(719) 689–3362

◆ CALIFORNIA

CALIFORNIA COUNCIL ON PROBLEM
    GAMBLING
121 S. Palm Canyon Drive, Suite 225
Palm Springs, CA 92262
(760) 320–0234
Helpline: (800) GAMBLER

CALIFORNIA NATIONS INDIAN GAMING
    ASSOCIATION
1130 K Street, Suite 150
Sacramento, CA 95814
(916) 448–8706

U.S. INDIAN GAMING CASINOS &
BINGO HALLS

◆ ALABAMA

CREEK INDIAN BINGO PALACE
Poarch Band of Creek Indians
5811 Jack Springs Road
Atmore, AL 36502
(334) 368–9136

◆ ALASKA

KLAWOCK COOPERATIVE ASSOCIATION
P.O. Box 430
Klawock, AK 99925
(907) 755–2265

METLAKATLA INDIAN COMMUNITY
P.O. Box 8
Metlakatla, AK 99926
(907) 886–4441

◆ ARIZONA

APACHE GOLD CASINO
San Carlos Apache Tribe
P.O. Box 1210
San Carlos, AZ 85550
(520) 475–2361

BLUEWATER CASINO
Colorado River Indian Tribes
Route 1, Box 23-B
Parker, AZ 85344
(520) 669–9211

BUCKY'S CASINO
Yavapai-Prescott Indian Tribe
530 East Merritt St.
Prescott, AZ 86301
(602) 445–8790

CASINO IN THE SUN
Pascua Yaqui Tribe of Arizona
7474 S. Camino De Oeste
Tucson, AZ 85746
(520) 883–2838

CLIFF CASTLE CASINO
Yavapai Apache Tribe
P.O. Box 1188
Camp Verde, AZ 86322
(602) 567–3649

COCOPAH CASINO
Cocopah Indian Tribe
15136 South Ave. B
Somerton, AZ 85350
(602) 627–2102

FORT MCDOWELL CASINO
Fort McDowell Mohave-Apache Indian Community
P.O. Box 17779
Fountain Hills, AZ 85269
(602) 837–5121

GILA RIVER CASINO
Gila River Indian Community
P.O. Box 97
Sacaton, AZ 85247
(602) 963–4323

HARRAH'S PHOENIX AK-CHIN
Ak Chin Indian Community
42507 W. Peters & Nall Rd.
Maricopa, AZ 85239
(520) 568–2227

HONDAH RESORT, CASINO, AND
    CONFERENCE CENTER
White Mountain Apache Tribe
P.O. Box 700
Whiteriver, AZ 85941
(602) 338–4346

MAZATZAL CASINO
Tonto Apache Tribe
Tonto Apache Reservation #30
Payson, AZ 85541
(602) 474–5000

QUECHAN INDIAN TRIBE
P.O. Box 11352
Yuma, AZ 85366
(760) 572–0213

SALT RIVER PIMA-MARICOPA INDIAN
COMMUNITY
10005 Osborn Road
Scottsdale, AZ 85256
(602) 850–8000

TOHONO O'ODHAM NATION
P.O. Box 837
Sells, AZ 85364
(602) 383–2221

◆ CALIFORNIA

AUBERRY BIG SANDY RANCHERIA
P.O. Box 337
Auberry, CA 93602
(209) 855–4003

BARONA CASINO
Barona Band of Mission Indians
1095 Barona Road
Lakeside, CA 92040
(619) 443–6612

BIG PINE PAIUTE TRIBE OF THE
OWENS VALLEY
545 Butcher Lane
Big Pine, CA 93513
(619) 938–3359

BLACK BART CASINO
Sherwood Valley Rancheria
190 Sherwood Hill Drive
Willits, CA 95490
(707) 459–9690

CAHTO TRIBE OF THE LAYTONVILLE
RANCHERIA
P.O. Box 1239
Laytonville, CA 95454
(707) 984–6197

CAHUILLA BAND OF MISSION INDIANS
P.O. Box 391760
Anza, CA 92539
(909) 763–5549

CASINO MORONGO
Morongo Band of Mission Indians
11581 Potrero Road
Banning, CA 92220
(909) 849–4697

CHERAE HEIGHTS BINGO AND CASINO
Trinidad Rancheria
P.O. Box 630
27 Scenic Drive
Trinidad, CA 95570
(707) 677–0211

CHICKEN RANCH BAND OF ME-WUK
INDIANS
P.O. Box 1159
Jamestown, CA 95327
(209) 984–4806

CHUMASH CASINO
Santa Ynez Band of Mission Indians
P.O. Box 517
Santa Ynez, CA 93460
(805) 688–7997

COAST INDIAN COMMUNITY OF THE
RESIGHINI RANCHERIA
P.O. Box 529
Klamath, CA 95548
(707) 482–2431

COLUSA CASINO
Colusa Band of Wintun Indians
50 Wintun Road #D
Colusa, CA 95932
(916) 458–8231

EAGLE MOUNTAIN CASINO
Tule River Tribe of the Tule River Indian
Reservation
P.O. Box 589
Porterville, CA 93258
(209) 781–4271

ELK VALLEY CASINO
Elk Valley Rancheria
440 Mathews Street, P.O. Box 1042
Crescent City, CA 95531
(707) 464–1020

FANTASY SPRINGS CASINO
Cabazon Band of Mission Indians
84–245 Indio Spring Drive
Indio, CA 92201
(619) 342–5000

FEATHER FALLS CASINO
Mooretown Rancheria
#1 Alverda Drive
Oroville, CA 95966
(916) 533–3625

FORT MOJAVE TRIBAL COUNCIL
500 Merriman Avenue
Needles, CA 92363
(760) 326–4591

GOLD COUNTRY CASINO
Tyme Maidu Tribe of the Berry Creek Rancheria
5 Tyme Way
Oroville, CA 95966
(916) 534–3859

GOLDEN BEARS CASINO
Resighini Rancheria
158 E. Klamath Beach Road
Klamath, CA 95548
(707) 482–5501

HAVASU LANDING RESORT AND CASINO
Chemehuevi Indian Tribe
P.O. Box 1976
Havasu Lake, CA 92363
(619) 858–4219

HOOPA VALLEY TRIBE
P.O. Box 1348
Hoopa, CA 95546
(916) 625–4211

HOPLAND CASINO
Hopland Band of Pomo Indians
P.O. Box 610
Hopland, CA 95449
(707) 744–1647

JACKSON RANCHERIA CASINO
Jackson Rancheria Band of Miwuk Indians
P.O. Box 429
Jackson, CA 95642
(209) 223–1935

KONOCTI VISTA CASINO AND BINGO
Big Valley Rancheria of Pomo Indians
P.O. Box 955
Lakeport, CA 95453
(707) 262–0629

LUCKY SEVEN CASINO
Smith River Rancheria
250 North Indian Road
Smith River, CA 95567
(707) 487–9255

MONO WIND CASINO
Big Sandy Rancheria Band of Western Mono Indians
P.O. Box 337
Auberry, CA 93602
(559) 855–2703

NORTHERN LIGHTS CASINO
SYCUAN CASINO:
Sycuan Band of Mission Indians
5459 Dehesa Road
El Cajon, CA 92019
(619) 445–6002

PAIUTE PALACE CASINO
Bishop Paiute Tribe
P.O. Box 548
Paiute Professional Bldg.
Bishop, CA 93515
(760) 873–3584

PALACE BINGO INDIAN GAMING CENTER
Santa Rosa Band of Tachi Indians
17255 Jersey Ave.
Lemoore, CA 93245
(800) 942–6886

PECHANGA CASINO
Pechanga Indian Nation
P.O. Box 1477
Temecula, CA 92593
(909) 694–3333

PIT RIVER CASINO
Pit River Tribe
20265 Tamarack Avenue
Burney, CA 96013
(916) 335–2334

RINCON RIVER OATS CASINO
Rincon Indian Reservation
33750 Valley Center Rd.
Valley Center, CA 92082
(619) 749–2100

ROBINSON RANCHERIA CASINO
Robinson Rancheria of Pomo Indians
1545 E. Highway 20
Nice, CA 95464
(707) 275–9000

RUMSEY INDIAN RANCHERIA
P.O. Box 18
Brooks, CA 95606
(916) 796–3400

SAN MANUEL CASINO
San Manuel Band of Mission Indians
5795 Victoria Ave.
Highland, CA 92346
(909) 864–5050

SHINGLE SPRINGS RANCHERIA
P.O. Box 1340
Shingle Springs, CA 95682
(530) 676–8010

SHODAKI COYOTE VALLEY CASINO
Coyote Valley Band of Pomo Indians
P.O. Box 320
Calpella, CA 95418
(707) 485–8723

SOBOBA CASINO
Soboba Band of Mission Indians
P.O. Box 817, 23333 Soboba Rd.
San Jacinto, CA 92581
(909) 654–2883

SPA HOTEL AND CASINO
Agua Caliente Band of Cahuilla Indians
600 E. Tahquitz Way
Palm Springs, CA 92262
(760) 325–3400

SPOTLIGHT 29 CASINO
Twenty Nine Palms Band of Mission Indians
46–200 Harrison Street
Coachela, CA 92236
(760) 775–5566

SUSANVILLE INDIAN RANCHERIA
745 Joaquin Street
Susanville, CA 96130
(559) 257–6264

TABLE MOUNTAIN CASINO AND BINGO
Table Mountain Rancheria
8184 Table Mountain Road
Friant, CA 93626
(800) 541–3637

TWIN PINE CASINO
Lake Miwok Indian Nation of the Middletown
    Rancheria
P.O. Box 1035
Middletown, CA 95461
(707) 987–0197

VIEJAS CASINO
Viejas Band of Mission Indians
5000 Willows Road
Alpine, CA 91901
(619) 445–5400

WINRIVER CASINO BINGO
Redding Rancheria
2100 Redding Rancheria Road
Redding, CA 96001
(916) 243–3377

♦ **COLORADO**

SKY UTE CASINO AND LODGE
Southern Ute Indian Tribe
P.O. Box 737
Ignacio, CO 81137
(970) 569–3000

UTE MOUNTAIN CASINO
Ute Mountain Ute Tribe
P.O. Box V
Cortez, CO 81321
(970) 565–8800

♦ **CONNECTICUT**

FOXWOODS CASINO
Mashantucket Pequot Tribe
P.O. Box 410, Route 2
Ledyard, CT 06339
(800) PLAY-BIG

MOHEGAN SUN
Mohegan Tribe of Indians of Connecticut
1 Mohegan Sun Blvd.
Uncasville, CT 06382
(860) 204–8000

◆ FLORIDA

MICCOUSUKEE TRIBAL INDIANS OF
    FLORIDA
500 SW 177 Avenue
Miami, FL 33194
(305) 222–4600

SEMINOLE TRIBE OF FLORIDA
506 S. First Street
Immokalee, FL 34142
(941) 658–1313

◆ IDAHO

CLEARWATER RIVER CASINO
It'se Ye-Ye Casino
Nez Percé Tribe
7463 N. And S. Highway
Lewiston, ID 83501
(208) 746–0723

COEUR D'ALENE TRIBAL BINGO AND
    CASINO
Coeur d'Alene Tribe
P.O. Box 236, U.S. Highway 95
Worley, ID 83876–0236
(208) 686–5048

KOOTENAI RIVER INN
Kootenai Tribe of Idaho
River Plaza, 7160 Plaza St.
Bonner's Ferry, ID 83805
(800) 346–5668

SHOSHONE BANNOCK CASINO
Shoshone-Bannock Tribes
P.O. Box 868
Fort Hall, ID 83203
(208) 237–8765

◆ IOWA

CASINOMAHA
Omaha Tribe of Nebraska
P.O. Box 89
Inawa, IA 51040
(800) 858-UBET

MESKWAKI BINGO AND CASINO HOTEL
Sac & Fox Tribe of Mississippi in Iowa
1504 305 Street
Tama, IA 52339
(515) 484–2108

WINNAVEGAS CASINO AND BINGO
Winnebago Tribe of Nebraska
1500 330 St.
Sloan, IA 51055
(800) 468–9466

◆ KANSAS

GOLDEN EAGLE CASINO
Kickapoo Nation in Kansas
1121 Goldfinch
Horton, KS 66439
(785) 486–6601

IOWA TRIBE PARTY GAMES
Iowa Tribe of Kansas and Nebraska
Route 1, Box 58A
White Cloud, KS 66094
(913) 595–6640

PRAIRIE BAND CASINO
Prairie Band Potawatomi
12305 150 Rd.
Mayetta, KS 66509
(913) 966–7777

SAC AND FOX NATION OF MISSOURI
P.O. Box 105-A
Powhatan, KS 66527
(913) 742–7438

◆ LOUISIANA

CYPRESS BAYOU CASINO
Chitimacha Tribe of Louisiana
832 Martin Luther King Road
Charenton, LA 70523
(800) 284–4386

GRAND CASINO AVOYELLES
Tunica-Biloxi Indian Tribe of Louisiana
711 Grand Blvd.
Marksville, LA 71350
(318) 253–1946

GRAND CASINO COUSHATTA
Coushatta Tribe of Louisiana
P.O. Box 1510, 777 Coushatta Dr.
Kinder, LA 70648
(800) 584–7263

◆ MICHIGAN

BIG BUCKS BINGO AND OJIBWA CASINO
Keweenaw Bay Indian Community
797 Michigan Ave.
Baraga, MI 49908
(906) 353–6333

BINGO PALACE
EAGLE'S VIEW CASINO
LEELANAU SANDS CASINO
TURTLE CREEK CASINO
Grand Traverse Band of Ottawa and Chippewa
    Indians
2649 N. West Bayshore Drive
Suttons Bay, MI 49682
(616) 271–7333

CHIP IN'S ISLAND RESORT AND CASINO
Hannahville Indian Community
P.O. Box 351-W399 Hwy 2 and 41
Harris, MI 49845–0351
(906) 466–2941

KEWADIN CASINO, HOTELS, AND
    CONVENTION CENTER
Sault Ste. Marie Tribe of Chippewa Indians
2186 Shunk Road
Sault Ste. Marie, MI 49873
(800)KEWADIN

KING'S CLUB CASINO
BAY MILLS CASINO
Bay Mills Indian Community
12140 W. Lakeshore Dr.
Brimley, MI 49715
(906) 248–3715

LAC VIEUX DESERT CASINO
Lac Vieux Desert Band of Lake Superior Chippewa
    Indians
P.O. Box 129 N45
Watersmeet, MI 49969
(906) 358–4226

LITTLE RIVER BAND OF OTTAWA INDIANS
P.O. Box 214
Manistee, MI 49660
(231) 723–1535

SOARING EAGLE CASINO AND RESORT
Saginaw Chippewa Indian Tribe
6800 Soaring Eagle Blvd.
Mt. Pleasant, MI 48858
(517) 775–5777

VICTORIES CASINO ENTERTAINMENT
    CENTER
Little Traverse Band of Odawa Indians
101 Greenwood
Petoskey, MI 49770
(231) 439–6807

◆ MINNESOTA

BLACK BEAR CASINO AND HOTEL
FOND-DU-LUTH CASINO
Fond du Lac Band of Lake Superior Chippewa
1785 Hwy. 210; Box 777
Carlton, MN 55718
(218) 878–2327

FIREFLY CREEK CASINO
Upper Sioux Community
P.O. Box 96
Granite Falls, MN 56241
(320) 564–2121

FORTUNE BAY RESORT CASINO
Bois Forte Band of Chippewas
1430 Bois Forte Road
Tower, MN 55790
(218) 753–6400

GRAND CASINO HINCKLEY
Mille Lacs Band of Chippewa Indians
777 Lady Luck Dr., Rt. 3, Box 15
Hinckley, MN 55037
(800) 472–6321

GRAND CASINO MILLE LACS
Mille Lacs Band of Ojibwe
777 Grand Ave., HCR 67
(HWY 169 W Shore of Mille Lacs Lake)
Onamia, MN 56359
(800) 626–5825

GRAND PORTAGE CASINO
Grand Portage Band of Chippewa Indians
70 Casino Drive
Grand Portage, MN 55605
(218) 475–2401

JACKPOT JUNCTION CASINO HOTEL
Lower Sioux Indian Community
39375 Co., Hwy 24, P.O. Box 420
Morton, MN 56270
(507) 644–3000

LAKE OF THE WOODS CASINO AND BINGO
RIVER ROAD CASINO
RED LAKE CASINO AND BINGO
Red Lake Band of Chippewa Indians
1012 E. Lake Street
Warroad, MN 56763
(218) 386–3381

LITTLE SIX CASINO AND MYSTIC
    LAKE CASINO
Shakopee Mdewakanton Sioux Community
Country Road 83
Prior Lake, MN 55372
(612) 445–8982

NORTHERN LIGHTS CASINO
PALACE BINGO CASINO HOTEL
Leech Lake Band of Chippewa Indians
HCR73 Box 1003
Walker, MN 5663–3484
(218) 547–2744

SHOOTING STAR CASINO
White Earth Band of Chippewa Indians
P.O. Box 418
Mahnomen, MN 56557
(218) 935–2711

TREASURE ISLAND RESORT AND CASINO
Prairie Island Indian Community
5734 Sturgeon Lake Road
Red Wing, MN 55066
(651) 388–6300

◆ MISSISSIPPI

SILVER STAR RESORT AND CASINO
Mississippi Band of Choctaw Indians
P.O. Box 6048, Highway 16 West
Philadelphia, MS 39350
(800) 557–0711

◆ MISSOURI

BORDER TOWN BINGO
Eastern Shawnee Tribe of Oklahoma
P.O. Box 350
Seneca, MO 64865
(918) 666–8702

◆ MONTANA

BLACKFEET TRIBAL BINGO
Blackfeet Tribe of Indians
P.O. Box 850
Browning, MT 59417
(406) 338–5751

CHARGING HORSE CASINO AND BINGO
Northern Cheyenne Tribe
P.O. Box 128
Lame Deer, MT 59043
(406) 477–6677

FT. BELKNAP CASINO
Gros Ventre and Assiniboine Tribes
Ft. Belknap
Rt. 2, Box 66
Ft. Belknap, MT 59526
(800) 343–6107

FOUR C'S CASINO
Chippewa Cree Tribe of the Rocky Boy's
    Reservation
Rocky Boy Route, Box 544 RR1
Box Elder, MT 59521
(406) 395–4863

KWATAQNUK RESORT AND CASINO
Confederated Salish & Kootenai Tribes of the
    Flathead Nation
303 US Hwy 93 East
Polson, MT 59860
(406) 883–3636

LITTLE BIG HORN CASINO
Crow Indian Tribe
Box 1–580
Crow Agency, MT 59022
(406) 638–4444

SILVER WOLF CASINO
Assiniboine & Sioux Tribes of the Fort Peck
    Reservation
P.O. Box 726, Hwy 13 W
Wolf Point, MT 59201
(406) 653–3476

◆ NEBRASKA

OMAHA TRIBE OF NEBRASKA
P.O. Box 368
Macy, NE 68039
(402) 837–5391

ROSEBUD CASINO
Rosebud Sioux Tribe
HC 14 Box 135
Valentine, NE 69201
(605) 378–3800

SANTEE SIOUX TRIBE OF NEBRASKA
Route 2, Box 163
Niobrara, NE 68760
(402) 857–2393

◆ NEVADA

AVI RESORT AND CASINO
Ft. Mohave Indian Tribe
10000 Aha Macav Parkway
Box 77011
Laughlin, NV 89028–7011
(702) 535–5555

MOAPA BAND TRIBAL ENTERPRISE CASINO
Moapa Band of Paiutes
Moapa Indian Reservation, Box 340
Moapa, NV 89025
(702) 864–2601

SMOKE MOUNTAIN SMOKE SHOP
Las Vegas Paiute Tribe
11515 Nu-Way Kaiv Blvd.
Las Vegas, NV 89124
(702) 645–2957

◆ NEW MEXICO

APACHE NUGGET CASINO
Jicarilla Apache Tribe
Narrow Gage Rd.
Dulce, NM 87528
(505) 759–3777

CASINO APACHE
Mescalero Apache Tribe
P.O. Box 205
Mescalero, NM 88340
(505) 630–4100

CITIES OF GOLD CASINO
Pueblo of Pojoaque
10 B Cities of Gold Road
Santa Fe, NM 87501
(505) 455–3313

ISLETA GAMING PALACE
Pueblo of Isleta
11000 Broadway, SE
Albuquerque, NM 87105
(505) 869–2614

OH KAY CASINO
Pueblo of San Juan
P.O. Box 1270
San Juan Pueblo, NM 87566
(505) 747–1668

PUEBLO OF SANDIA
Box 10188
Albuquerque, NM 87184
(505) 897–2173

PUEBLO OF TESUQUE
Route 5 Box 360-T
Santa Fe, NM 87501
(505) 983–2667

SANDIA CASINO
SANTA ANA STAR CASINO
Pueblo of Santa Ana
54 Jemez Canyon Dam Road
Bernalillo, NM 87004
(505) 867–0000

SAN FELIPE CASINO HOLLYWOOD
Pueblo of San Felipe
25 Hogan Rd., P.O. Box 4152
San Felipe, NM 87001
(505) 867–6700

SKY CITY CASINO
Pueblo of Acoma
P.O. Box 519
San Fidel, NM 87049
(505) 552–6017

TAOS MOUNTAIN CASINO
Pueblo of Taos
P.O. Box 777
Taos, NM 87571
(505) 737–0777

◆ NEW YORK

AKWESASNE MOHAWK CASINO
MOHAWK BINGO PALACE
St. Regis Mohawk Tribe
Akwesasne Community Building
Rt. 37, Box 670
Hogansburg, NY 13655
(518) 358–2222

SENECA NATION OF INDIANS
P.O. Box 231
Salamanca, NY 14779
(716) 945–1790

TURNING STONE CASINO
Oneida Nation of New York
P.O. Box 126, Patrick Road
Vernon, NY 13478
(315) 361–7711

◆ NORTH CAROLINA

HARRAH'S CHEROKEE CASINO
Eastern Band of Cherokee Indians
P.O. Box 455
Cherokee, NC 28719
(828) 497–7777

◆ NORTH DAKOTA

4 BEARS CASINO AND LODGE
Three Affiliated Tribes of the Fort Berthold
  Reservation
Mandan, Hidatsa & Arikara Nation
P.O. Box HC 3, Box 2
New Town, ND 58763
(701) 627–4018

PRAIRIE KNIGHTS CASINO AND LODGE
Standing Rock Sioux Tribe
7932 Hwy 24
Fort Yates, ND 58538
(701) 854–7777

SPIRIT LAKE CASINO AND RESORT
Spirit Lake Sioux Nation
7889 Highway 57
St. Michael, ND 58370–9000
(701) 766–4747

TURTLE MOUNTAIN CHIPPEWA CASINO
Turtle Mountain Band of Chippewa Indians
P.O. Box 1449, Hwy 5 West
Belcourt, ND 58316
(701) 477–3281

◆ OKLAHOMA

CHEROKEE CASINO
Cherokee Nation of Oklahoma
P.O. Box 948
Tahlequah, OK 74465
(918) 456–0671

CHICKASAW GAMING CENTER
Chickasaw Nation of Oklahoma
1500 North Country Club Rd.
Ada, OK 74820
(405) 436–3740

CHOCTAW GAMING CENTER
Choctaw Nation of Oklahoma
3735 Choctaw Rd., P.O. Box 1909
Durant, OK 74702
(580) 920–0160

CIMARRON BINGO CASINO
Iowa Tribe of Oklahoma
W. Freeman Ave.
Perkins, OK 74059
(405) 547–5352

CITIZEN BAND POTAWATOMI INDIANS OF
  OKLAHOMA
1601 S. Gordon Cooper Dr.
Shawnee, OK 74801
(405) 273–2242

COMANCHE RED RIVER CASINO
Comanche Indian Tribe
P.O. Box 231
Randlett, OK 73501
(580) 281–3580

DELAWARE TRIBAL GAMES
Delaware Tribe of Western Oklahoma
P.O. Box 806
Anadarko, OK 73005
(405) 247–6979

FOX FIRE BINGO
Sac & Fox Nation of Oklahoma
Route 2 Box 246
Stroud, OK 74079
(918) 968–3526

KAW NATION BINGO
Kaw Nation of Oklahoma
Drawer 271
Kaw City, OK 74641
(405) 269–2552

KEETOOWAH BINGO
United Keetoowah Band of Cherokee Indians
2450 S. Muskogee
Tahlequah, OK 74464
(918) 456–6131

KICKAPOO TRIBE OF OKLAHOMA
P.O. Box 70
McLoud, OK 74851
(405) 964–2075

KIOWA TRIBE OF OKLAHOMA
P.O. Box 369
Carnegie, OK 73015
(580) 654–2300

LUCKY STAR BINGO
Cheyenne and Arapaho Tribes of Oklahoma
7777 N Hwy 81
Concho, OK 73022
(405) 262–0345

MIAMI TRIBE ENTERTAINMENT
Miami Tribe of Oklahoma
202 South Eight Tribes Trail
P.O. Box 1326
Miami, OK 74355
(918) 542–1445

MODOC TRIBE OF OKLAHOMA
517 G Southeast
Miami, OK 74354
(918) 542–1190

MUSCOGEE (CREEK) NATION
121 W. Lincoln
Bristow, OK 74010
(918) 367–9168

NAISHA GAMES
Apache Tribe of Oklahoma
P.O. Box 768
Anadarko, OK 73005
(405) 247–3260

OTOE BINGO
Otoe Missouria Tribe of Oklahoma
Box 2585
Red Rock, OK 74076
(405) 723–4444

PONCA TRIBAL BINGO
Ponca Tribe of Oklahoma
20 White Eagle Drive
Ponca City, OK 74601
(580) 762–8104

SEMINOLE NATION BINGO
Seminole Nation of Oklahoma
P.O. Box 1484
Seminole, OK 74868
(405) 382–7922

SENECA-CAYUGA TRIBE OF OKLAHOMA
Rt. 4, Box 374 S. 50
Grove, OK 74344
(918) 542–6609

THLOPTHLOCCO TRIBAL TOWN
Box 188
Okemah, OK 74859
(918) 623–0072

THUNDER BIRD ENTERTAINMENT CENTER
Absentee-Shawnee Tribe of Oklahoma
2025 S. Gordon Cooper Drive
Shawnee, OK 74801
(405) 360–9270

TONKAWA TRIBAL BINGO
Tonkawa Tribe of Oklahoma
P.O. Box 70
Tonkawa, OK 74653
(405) 628–2561

◆ OREGON

**CHINOOK WINDS CASINO &
  CONVENTION CENTER**
Confederated Tribes of the Siletz Indians of Oregon
1777 NW 44th Street
Lincoln City, OR 97367
(541) 996–5825

CONFEDERATED TRIBES OF THE GRAND
    RONDE INDIAN COMMUNITY
9615 Grand Ronde Road
Grand Ronde, OR 97347
(503) 879–2350

INDIAN HEAD CASINO AT KAH-NEE-T
    RESORT
Confederated Tribes of the Warm Springs
    Reservation of OR
P.O. Box 1240
Warm Springs, OR 97761
(541) 553–6122

KLAMOYA CASINO
Klamath Tribes
P.O. Box 490
34333 Hwy. 97 N.
Chiloquin, OR 97624
(541) 783–7529

THE MILL CASINO
Coquille Indian Tribe
3201 N. Tremont
North Bend, OR 97459
(541) 756–8800

THE OLD CAMP CASINO
Burns Paiute Tribe
2205 W. Monroe Street
Burns, OR 97720
(541) 573–1500

SEVEN FEATHERS HOTEL AND CASINO
Cow Creek Band of Umpqua Indians
146 Chief Miwaleta Lane
Canyonville, OR 97417
(541) 839–1111

WILDHORSE CASINO RESORT
Confederated Tribes of the Umatilla Indian
    Reservation
72777 Highway 331
Pendleton, OR 97801
(541) 278–2274

◆ SOUTH DAKOTA

CHEYENNE RIVER SIOUX TRIBE
P.O. Box 590
Eagle Butte, SD 57625
(605) 964–4155

DAKOTA SIOUX CASINO
Sisseton-Wahpeton Sioux Tribe
I-29 & E. Hwy. 10 Exit 232
Sisseton, SD 57262
(605) 698–4273

FORT RANDALL CASINO AND HOTEL
Yankton Sioux Tribe
West Hwy. 46, Box 756
Wagner, SD 57380–0756
(605) 487–7871

GRAND RIVER CASINO
Standing Rock Sioux Tribe
W. Hwy. 12
Mobridge, SD 57601
(800) 475–3321

LODE STAR CASINO
Crow Creek Sioux Tribe
P.O. Box 140
Fort Thompson, SD 57339
(605) 245–6000

LOWER BRUTE CASINO
Lower Brule Sioux Tribe
P.O. Box 204
Lower Brule, SD 57548
(605) 473–5577

PRAIRIE WIND CASINO
Oglala Sioux Tribe
HC 49, Box 10
Pine Ridge, SD 57770
(605) 535–6300

ROSEBUD CASINO
Rosebud Sioux Tribe
P.O. Box 430
Rosebud, SD 57570
(605) 747–2381

ROYAL RIVER CASINO, BINGO, AND MOTEL
Flandreau Santee Sioux Tribe
607 S. Veterans St.
P.O. Box 326
Flandreau, SD 57028
(605) 997–3746

◆ TEXAS

KICKAPOO TRADITIONAL TRIBE OF TEXAS
P.O. Box 972
Eagle Pass, TX 78853
(210) 773–2105

SPEAKING ROCK CASINO
Ysleta Del Sur Pueblo Indian Tribe
119 S. Old Pueblo Road
P.O. Box 17579-Ysleta Station
El Paso, TX 79917
(915) 860–7777

♦ **WASHINGTON**

EMERALD QUEEN RIVERBOAT
Puyallup Tribe of Indians
2002 East 28th Street
Tacoma, WA 98404
(253) 597–6200

HARRAH'S SKAGIT VALLEY CASINO
Upper Skagit Indian Tribe
590 Dark Lane
Bow, WA 98232
(360) 724–7777

LITTLE CREEK CASINO
Squaxin Island Tribe
West 91, Hwy. 108
Shelton, WA 98584
(360) 427–7711

LUCKY EAGLE CASINO AND BINGO
Confederated Tribes of the Chehalis Reservation
12888 188th Street, SW
Rochester, WA 98579
(360) 273–2000

MAKAH TRIBAL BINGO
Makah Indian Tribe of the Makah Indian Reservation
P.O. Box 115
Neah Bay, WA 98357
(360) 645–2264

MILL BAY CASINO
Confederated Tribes of the Colville Reservation
455 Wapato Lake Rd.
Manson, WA 98831
(509) 687–2102

MUCKLESHOOT CASINO
Muckleshoot Indian Tribe
2402 Auburn Way S.
Auburn, WA 98002
(206) 804–4444

NISQUALLY INDIAN TRIBE
12819 Yelm Highway SE
Olympia, WA 98513
(360) 412–5000

NOOKSACK RIVER CASINO
Nooksack Indian Tribe
5048 Mt. Baker Hwy
Deming, WA 98244
(360) 592–5472

PORT GAMBLE S'KLALLAM TRIBE
31912 Little Boston Road NE
Kingston, WA 98346
(206) 297–2646

SEVEN CEDARS CASINO
Jamestown S'Klallam Tribe
270756 Hwy 101
Sequim, WA 98382
(360) 683–7777

SHOALWATER BAY CASINO
Shoalwater Bay Indian Tribe
4112 State Hwy 105 (P.O. Box 560)
Tokeland, WA 98590
(360) 267–2048

SUQUAMISH CLEARWATER CASINO
Suquamish Tribe
15347 Suquamish Way, NE
Suquamish, WA 98392
(360) 598–6889

SWINOMISH CASINO
Swinomish Indian Tribal Community
P.O. Box 817
LaConner, WA 98257
(360) 466–3163

TULALIP CASINO BINGO
Tulalip Tribes of Washington
6410 33rd Ave, NE
Marysville, WA 98271
(360) 651–1111

TWO RIVERS CASINO
Spokane Tribe of Indians
61–828 B. Hwy 25, S.
Davenport, WA 99122
(509) 722–4000

YAKAMA LEGENDS CASINO
Confederated Tribes and Bands of the Yakama
Indian Nation
580 Fort Road
Toppenish, WA 98948
(509) 865–8800

◆ WISCONSIN

BAD RIVER CASINO
Bad River Band of Lake Superior Tribe of Chippewa
Indians
P.O. Box 8, Hwy 2
Odanah, WI 54861
(715) 682–7121

GRINDSTONE CREEK CASINO
Lac Courte Oreilles Band of Lake Superior
Chippewas
13767 West County Road B
Hayward, WI 54843
(715) 634–2430

HO-CHUNCK CASINO
Ho-Chunk Nation
S 3214 A Highway 12
Baraboo, WI 53913
(608) 356–6210

HOLE IN THE WALL CASINO
St. Croix Chippewa Indians of Wisconsin
Hwy 35 and 77
Danbury, WI 54830
(800) BET-U-WIN

ISLE VISTA CASINO
Red Cliff Band of Lake Superior Chippewas
P.O. Box 1167-Lucky Hwy. 13 N.
Bayfield, WI 54814
(715) 779–3712

LAKE OF THE TORCHES RESORT CASINO &
CONVENTION CENTER
Lac du Flambeau Band of Lake Superior Chippewa
Indians
P.O. Box 550—510 Old Abe Rd.
Lac du Flambeau, WI 54538
(715) 588–7070

MENOMINEE CASINO
Menominee Indian Tribe of Wisconsin
P.O. Box 910
Keshena, WI 54135
(715) 799–5114

MOHICAN NORTH STAR CASINO AND BINGO
Stockbridge-Munsee Community
W 12180A Country Road A
Bowler, WI 54416
(715) 787–3110

MOLE LAKE CASINOS AND BINGO
Sokaogon Chippewa Community
Route 1, Box 277
Crandon, WI 54520
(715) 478–5290

ONEIDA BINGO/CASINO
Oneida Tribe of Indians of Wisconsin
2020/2100 Airport Drive
Green Bay, WI 54313
(920) 494–4500

POTAWATOMI BINGO AND CASINO
Forest County Potawatomi Community
1721 W. Canal Street
Milwaukee, WI 53233
(414) 645–6866

◆ WYOMING

WIND RIVER INDIAN RESERVATION CASINO
10369 Highway 789 S.
Riverton, WY 82501
(307) 332–6120

CANADA

GAMING REGULATORY AGENCIES

ALBERTA GAMING AND LIQUOR
COMMISSION
50 Corriveau Avenue
St. Albert, AB T8N 3T5
(403) 447–8818

ALCOHOL AND GAMING COMMISSION
OF ONTARIO
20 Dundas Street West, 7th floor
Toronto, ON M5G 2N6
(416) 326–0381

BRITISH COLUMBIA GAMING COMMISSION
P.O. Box 9310, Stn Provincial Government
844 Courtney Street
Victoria, BC V8W 9N1
(250) 387–5311

BRITISH COLUMBIA: REGIONAL OFFICES

Lower Mainland
300–601 West Broadway
Vancouver, BC V5Z 4C2
(604) 660–6970

Northern British Columbia
1044 Fifth Avenue
Prince George, BC V2L 3H9
(250) 565–6997

Southern Interior
108–347 Leon Avenue
Kelowna, BC V1Y 8C7
(250) 861–7363

Vancouver Island
204–2100 LaBieux Rd.
Nanaimo, BC V9T 6E9
(250) 751–7009

CANADIAN CENTRE ON SUBSTANCE ABUSE

75 Albert Street, Suite 300
Ottawa, ON K1P 5E7
(613) 235–4048

CASINO REGINA, SASKATCHEWAN GAMING CORPORATION

1880 Saskatchewan Drive, 3rd Floor
Regina, SK S4P 0B2
(306) 787–1592

GAMING POLICY SECRETARIAT

Province of British Columbia
P.O. Box 9311
506 Government Street
Victoria, BC V8W 9N1
(250) 953–4482

MANITOBA GAMING CONTROL COMMISSION

215 Gary Street, Suite 800
Winnipeg, MB R3C 3P3
(204) 954–9400

RÉGIE DES ALCOOLS, DES COURSES ET DES JEUX

Minist;re de la sécurité publique
1 rue Notre-Dame Est
Montréal, QC H2Y 1B6
(514) 864–2088

SASKATCHEWAN LIQUOR AND GAMING AUTHORITY

North Canadian Oils Building
P.O. Box 5054
2500 Victoria Avenue
Regina, SK S4P 3M3
(306) 787–1762

CASINOS

◆ ALBERTA

ARKAY CASINO
Elbow River Inn
1919 McCloud Trails SE
Calgary, AB T2G 4S1
(403) 266–4355

BACCARAT CASINOS
10128 104 Avenue
Edmonton, AB T5J 4Y8
(780) 413–3178

CASH CASINO PALACE
4040 Blackfoot Trails SE
Calgary, AB T2G 4E6
(403) 287–1635

CASH CASINO–RED DEER
6350 67th St.
Red Deer, AB T4P 3L9
(403) 346–3339

CASINO ABS
1251 3rd Avenue South
Lethbridge, AB T1K 0K1
(403) 381–9467

CASINO ABS–CITY CENTRE
12464 153rd St.
Edmonton, AB T5V 1S5
(780) 424–9467

EDMONTON'S KLONDIKE DAYS
Box 1480
Edmonton, AB T5J 2N5
(780) 471–7210

GOLD DUST CASINO
24 Boudreau Rd.
St. Albert, AB T8N 6K3
(780) 460–8092

MEDICINE HAT LODGE-HOTEL & CASINO
1051 Ross Glen Drive SE
Medicine Hat, AB T1B 3T8
(403) 529–2222

PALACE CASINO
170th St., Suite 2710–8882
Edmonton, AB T5T 4J2
(780) 444–2112

WINNERS CIRCLE CASINO
9725 Hardin St.
Fort Mcmurray, AB T9H 4G9
(780) 790–9739

◆ BRITISH COLUMBIA

BILLY BARKER CASINO AND HOTEL
308 Maclean Street
Quesnel, BC V2J 2N9
(250) 992–7763

BINGO NETWORK GAMING INTERNATIONAL
535 Thurlow, Suite 510
Vancouver, BC V6E 3L2
(604) 681–3864

CASINO HOLLYWOOD
494 George St.
Prince George, BC V2L 1R6
(250) 561–2421

GRAND CASINO
206–5050 Kingsway
Burnaby, BC VH5 4H2
(604) 437–1696

GREAT CANADIAN CASINO
Attn: Marketing
350–13775 Commerce Parkway
Richmond, BC V6V 2V4
(604) 303–1000

GREAT CANADIAN CASINO
620 Terminal Ave
Nanaimo, BC V9R 5E6
(250) 753–3033

GREAT CANADIAN CASINO
709 West Broadway
Vancouver, BC V5Z 1G5
(604) 872–5543

GREAT CANADIAN CASINO MAYFAIR
3075 Douglas St.
Victoria, BC V8T 4N3
(250) 380–3998

KAMLOOPS CASINO
540 Victoria St.
Kamloops, BC U2C 2B2
(250) 372–3336

KELOWNA CASINO
Landmark Square
1007–1708 Dolphin Ave.
Kelowna, BC V1Y 9S4
(250) 860–9467

ROYAL DIAMOND CASINO
Plaza of Nations
B106–750 Pacific Boulevard South
Vancouver, BC V6B 5E7
(604) 685–2340

◆ MANITOBA

CLUB REGENT CASINO
1415 Regent Ave., West
Winnipeg, MB R2C 3B2
(204) 957–2700

CRYSTAL CASINO
Hotel Fort Garry
222 Broadway
Winnipeg, MB R3C 0R3
(204) 942–8251
(800) 665–8088

MCPHILIPS STREET STATION CASINO
484 McPhilips Street
Winnipeg, MB R2X 2H2
(204) 957–3900

◆ NOVA SCOTIA

SHERATON CASINO NOVA SCOTIA
1983 Upper Water Street
Halifax, NS B3J 3Y5
(902) 425–7777

SYDNEY'S CASINO NOVA SCOTIA
525 George Street
Sydney, NS B1P 1K5
(902) 563–7777

◆ ONTARIO

CASINO NIAGARA
P.O. Box 300
5705 Falls Avenue
Niagara Falls, ON L2E 6T3
(888) 946–3255

CASINO WINDSOR
377 Riverside Drive West
Windsor, ON N9A 7H7
(519) 258–7878

GOLDEN EAGLE CHARITABLE CASINO
P.O. Box 2860
Kenora, ON P9N 3X8
(807) 548–1332

GREAT BLUE HERON CHARITABLE CASINO
21777 Island Rd.
Port Perry, ON L9L 1B6
(905) 985–4888

ONTARIO LOTTERY AND GAMING
   CORPORATION
70 Foster Dr., Suite 800
Saulte St. Marie, ON P6A 6V2
(416) 326–0076

◆ QUEBEC

CASINO DE HULL
1, boulevard Casino
Hull, PQ J8Y 6W3
(819) 772–2100

◆ SASKATCHEWAN

BEAR CLAW CASINO & LODGE
White Bear First Nation
P.O. Box 1210
Carlyle, SK S0C 0R0
(306) 577–4577

EMERALD CASINO
P.O. Box 6010
Saskatoon, SK S7K 4E4
(306) 683–8848

GOLD EAGLE CASINO
11902 Railway Avenue
North Battleford, SK S9A 3K7
(306) 446–3833

LLOYDMINSTER EXHIBITION ASSOC.
Box 690
Lloydminster, SK S9V 0Y7
(306) 825–5571

NORTHERN LIGHTS CASINO
44 Marquis Rd West
Prince Albert, SK S6V 7Y5
(306) 764–4777

PAINTED HAND CASINO
30 Third Avenue North
Yorkton, SK S3N 1B9
(306) 786–6777

SWIFT CURRENT
Swift Current Exhibition Assoc.
Box 146
Swift Current, SK S9H 3V5
(306) 773–2944

References

U. S. Indians and the Economy

Anders, Gary. "Social and Economic Consequences of Federal Indian Policy: A Case Study of the Alaska Natives." *Economic Development and Cultural Change* 37, no. 2 (1989): 285–303.

Anderson, Terry L., ed. *Property Rights and Indian Economies.* Lanham, Md.: Rowman & Littlefield, 1992.

Barrington, Linda, ed. *The Other Side of the Frontier: Economic Explorations into Native American History.* Boulder, Colo.: Westview Press, 1999.

Carlson, Leonard A. *Indians, Bureaucrats, and Land: The Dawes Act and the Decline of Indian Farming.* Westport, Conn.: Greenwood Press, 1981.

Cohen, Fay G. *Treaties on Trial: The Continuing Controversy over Northwest Indian Fishing Rights.* Seattle: University of Washington Press, 1986.

Committee to Review the Community Development Quota Program. *The Community Development Quota Program in Alaska.* Washington, D.C.: National Academy Press, 1999.

Cornell, Stephen and Joseph Kalt. "Pathways from Poverty: Economic Development and Institution-Building on American Indian Reservations." *American Indian Culture and Research Journal* 14, no. 1 (1990): 89–125.

Gerdes, Karen, Maria Napoli, Clinton M. Pattea, and Elizabeth A. Segal. "The Impact of Indian Gaming on Economic Development." *Pressing Issues of Inequality and American Indian Communities*, edited by Elizabeth A. Segal, and Keith M. Kilty, 17–30. New York: Haworth Press, 1998.

Hosmer, Brian C. *American Indians in the Marketplace: Persistence and Innovation Among the Menominees and Metlakatlans, 1870–1920.* Lawrence, Kan.: University Press of Kansas, 1999.

———. "Creating Indian Entrepreneurs: Menominees, Neopit Mills, and Timber Exploitation, 1890–1915." *American Indian Culture and Research Journal* 15, no. 1 (1991): 1–28.

Huff, Delores J. "The Tribal Ethic, The Protestant Ethic, and American Indian Economic Development." In *American Indian Policy and Cultural Values: Conflict and Accomodation*, edited by Jennie R. Joe, 75–89. Los Angeles: American Indian Studies Center, UCLA, 1986.

Karpoff, Jonathan M. and Edward M. Rice. "Structure and Performance of Alaska Native Corporations." *Contemporary Policy Issues* 10 no. 3 (1992): 71–84.

Marglin, Stephen A., and Juliet B. Schor, eds. *The Golden Age of Capitalism: Reinterpreting the Postwar Experience.* Oxford: Clarendon Press; New York: Oxford University Press, 1990.

McCool, Daniel. *Command of the Waters: Iron Triangles, Federal Water Development, and Indian Water.* Berkeley and Los Angeles: University of California Press, 1987.

Miner, H. Craig. *The Corporation and the Indian: Tribal Sovereignty and Industrial Development in Indian Territory, 1865–1907.* Columbia, Mo.: University of Missouri Press, 1976.

Oberg, Kalervo. *The Social Economy of the Tlingit Indians.* Vancouver: J.J. Douglas, 1973.

Trosper, Ronald L. "That Other Discipline: Economics and American Indian History." In *New Directions in American Indian History*, edited by Colin G. Calloway, 199–222. Norman: University of Oklahoma Press, 1981.

Van Hoak, Stephen P. "Untangling the Roots of Dependency: Choctaw Economics, 1700–1860." *American Indian Quarterly* 23, no. 3 & 4 (1999): 113–128.

Vinje, David L. "Cultural Values and Economic Development on Reservations." In *American Indian Policy in the Twentieth Century*, edited by Vine Deloria, Jr., 155–175. Norman: University of Oklahoma Press, 1985.

Weatherford, Jack. *Indian Givers: How the Indians of the Americas Transformed the World.* New York: Crown, 1988.

———. *Native Roots: How the Indians Enriched America.* New York: Crown, 1991.

White, Richard. *The Middle Ground: Indians, Empires, and Republics in the Great Lakes Region, 1650–1815.* Cambridge: Cambridge University Press, 1991.

———. *The Roots of Dependency: Subsistence, Environment, and Social Change among the Choctaws, Pawnees, and Navajos.* Lincoln: University of Nebraska Press, 1983.

White, Robert H. *Tribal Assets: The Rebirth of Native America.* New York: H. Holt, 1990.

Ronald L. Trosper

U.S. Reservation Economic Development

Anderson, Joseph and Smith, Dean Howard; "Managing Tribal Assets: Developing Long Term Strategic Plans." *American Indian Culture and Research Journal* 22, no. 2 (1999): 139–156.

Barsh, Russell L. "Indian Resources and the National Economy: Business Cycles and Policy Cycles." In *Native Americans and Public Policy*, edited by Fremont J. Lyden and Lyman H. Legters, 193–222. Pittsburgh: University of Pittsburgh Press, 1992.

Cornell, Stephen and Joseph P. Kalt. "Pathways from Poverty: Economic Development and Institution-Building on American Indian Reservations." *American Indian Culture and Research Journal* 14, no. 3 (1990): 89–125.

———. "Reloading the Dice: Improving the Chances for Economic Development on American Indian Reservations." Cambridge: Harvard Project on American Indian Economic Development, John F. Kennedy School of Government, 1992.

———. *What Can Tribes Do? Strategies and Institutions in American Indian Economic Development.* Los Angeles: American Indian Studies Center, UCLA, 1992.

———. "Where's the Glue? Institutional Bases of American Indian Economic Development." Cambridge: Harvard Project on American Indian Economic Development, John F. Kennedy School of Government, 1991.

Guyette, Susan. *Planning for Balanced Development: A Guide for Native American and Rural Communities.* Santa Fe, N.M.: Clear Light Publishers, 1996.

Hurt, R. Douglas. *Indian Agriculture in America: Prehistory to the Present.* Lawrence: University Press of Kansas, 1987.

Jacobs, Jane. *Cities and the Wealth of Nations: Principles of Economic Life.* New York: Random House, 1984.

———. *The Nature of Economies.* New York: Modern Library, 2000.

———. *Systems of Survival: A Dialogue on the Moral Foundations of Commerce and Politics.* New York: Vintage Books, 1992.

Kalt, Joseph. "The Redefinition of Property Rights in American Indian Reservations: A Comparative Analysis of Native American Economic Development." Cambridge: Harvard Project on American Indian Economic Development, John F. Kennedy School of Government, 1987.

Krepps, Matthew B. "Can Tribes Manage Their Own Resources? A Study of American Indian Forestry and the 638 Program." Cambridge: Harvard Project on American Indian Economic Development, John F. Kennedy School of Government, 1991.

Langdon, Steve J., ed. *Contemporary Alaskan Native Economies.* Lanham, Md.: University Press of America, 1986.

Legters, Lyman H. *American Indian Policy: Self-Governance and Economic Development.* Westport, Conn.: Greenwood Press, 1994.

Miner, H. Craig. *The Corporation and the Indian: Tribal Sovereignty and Industrial Civilization in Indian Territory, 1865–1907.* Columbia: University of Missouri Press, 1976.

Ortiz, Roxanne D., ed. *Economic Development in American Indian Reservations.* Albuquerque: Native American Studies, University of New Mexico, 1979.

Reno, Philip. *Mother Earth, Father Sky, and Economic Development: Navajo Resources and their Use.* Albuquerque: University of New Mexico Press, 1981.

Smith, Dean Howard. "Apache Manufacturing Company: A Teaching Case Study in Tribal Management." Teaching Case C-8. Cambridge: Harvard Project on American Indian Economic Development, 1996.

———. "The Issue of Compatibility Between Cultural Integrity, and Economic Development Among Native American Tribes." *American Indian Culture and Research Journal* 18, no. 3 (1994): 177–206.

———. *Modern Tribal Development: Paths to Self-Sufficiency and Cultural Integrity in Indian Country.* Walnut Creek, Calif.: Altamira Press, 2000.

———. "Native American Economic Development: A Modern Approach." *Review of Regional Studies* 24, no. 1 (1994): 87–102.

Smith, Dean Howard, and Jon Ozmun. "Fort Belknap's Community Development Plan: A Teaching Case Study in Tribal Management." Teaching Case C-5. Cambridge: Harvard Project on American Indian Economic Development, John F. Kennedy School of Government, 1994.

Stanley, Sam, ed. *American Indian Economic Development.* The Hague: Mouton: Chicago: distributed by Aldine, 1978.

Trosper, Ronald L. "Multicriterion Decision Making in a Tribal Context." In *Native Americans and Public Policy,* edited by Fremont J. Lyden and Lyman H. Legters, 223–242. Pittsburgh: University of Pittsburgh Press, 1992.

Wilkinson, Charles F. *Fire on the Plateau: Conflict and Endurance in the American Southwest.* Washington: Island Press/Shearwater Books, 1999.

Dean Howard Smith

U.S. Indian Labor

Ambler, Marjane. *Breaking the Iron Bonds: Indian Control of Energy Development.* Lawrence, Kan.: University Press of Kansas, 1990.

Driver, Harold E. *Indians of North America.* 2d ed. Chicago: University of Chicago Press, 1969.

Fixico, Donald L. *Termination and Relocation: Federal Indian Policy, 1945–1960.* Albuquerque: University of New Mexico Press, 1986.

Gundlach, James H. and Alden E. Roberts. "Native American Indian Migration and Relocation: Success or Failure." *Pacific Sociological Review* 21, no. 1 (1978): 117–128.

Gwartney, James D. and James E. Long. "The Relative Earnings of Blacks and Other Minorities." *Industrial and Labor Relations Review* 31, no. 3 (1978): 336–346.

Hackenberg, Robert A. and C. Roderick Wilson. "Reluctant Emigrants: The Role of Migration in Papago Indian Adaptation." *Human Organization* 31, no. 2 (1972): 171–186.

Jacobsen, Cardell K. "Internal Colonialism and Native Americans: Indian Labor in the United States from 1871 to World War II." *Social Science Quarterly* 65, no. 1 (1984): 158–171.

Sandefur, Gary D., Ronald R. Rindfus, and Barney Cohen (eds.). *Changing Numbers, Changing Needs: American Indian Demography and PublicHealth.* Washington, D.C.: National Academy Press, 1996.

Snipp, C. Matthew. *American Indians: The First of This Land.* New York: Russell Sage, 1989.

———. "A Portrait of American Indian Women and Their Labor Force Experience." In *The American Woman, 1990–91: A Status Report,* edited by Sara E. Rix. New York: Norton, 1990.

Snipp, C. Matthew, and Isik Aytac. "The Labor Force Participation of American Indian Women." In *Research in Human Capital and Development,* edited by Ismail Sirageldin, vol. 6, 189–211. Greenwich: JAI Press, 1990.

Snipp, C. Matthew, and Gary D. Sandefur. "Earnings of American Indians and Alaska Natives: The Effects of Residence and Migration." *Social Forces* 66, no. 4 (1988): 994–1008.

C. Matthew Snipp

U.S. Assistance and Restitution

Blanchard, Evelyn Lance. "The Growth and Development of American Indian and Alaska Native Children." In *The Psychosocial Development of Minority Group Children* edited by Gloria Johnson Powell, 115–130. New York: Brunner/Mazel, 1983.

Brookings Institution. Institute for Government Research. *The Problem of Indian Administration.* Baltimore, Md.: John Hopkins University, 1928. This work is commonly referred to as the *Merriam Report.*

Cooper, Mary H. "Native Americans Future: Do U.S. Policies Block Opportunities for Progress?" *CQ Researcher* 6, no. 26 (1996): 601–624.

Chambers Donald E. *Social Policy and Social Programs: A Method for the Practical Public Policy Analyst.* 3rd ed. Boston: Allyn and Bacon, 2000.

Jansson, Bruce S. *The Reluctant Welfare State: American Social Welfare Policies—Past, Present, and Future.* Pacific Grove, Calif.: Brooks/Cole, 1997.

Johnson, Troy R. "The State and the American Indian: Who Gets the Child?" *Wicazo Sa Review* 14, no. 1 (1999): 197–214.

Kopp, Judy. "Crosscultural Contacts: Changes in the Diet and Nutrition of the Navajo Indians." *American Indian Culture and Research Journal* 10:4 (1986): 1–30.

Kunitz, Stephen J. *Disease Change and the Role of Medicine: The Navajo Experience.* Berkeley: University of California Press, 1983.

Philp, Kenneth R., ed. *Indian Self-Rule: First-Hand Accounts of Indian-White Relations from Roosevelt to Reagan.* Logan, Utah: Utah State University Press, 1995.

Pollard, Kelvin M. and William P. O'Hare. "America's Racial and Ethnic Minorities." *Population Bulletin* 54, no. 3 (1999).

Rosaldo, Renato. *Culture and Truth: The Remaking of Social Analysis.* Boston: Beacon Press, 1989.

Sandefur, Gary D., Ronald R. Rindfuss, and Barney Cohen, eds. *Changing Numbers, Changing Needs: American Indian Demography and Public Health.* Washington, D.C.: National Academy Press, 1996.

Standing Bear, Luther. *Land of the Spotted Eagle.* Lincoln: University of Nebraska Press, 1933.

———. *My Indian Boyhood.* Lincoln: University of Nebraska Press, 1931.

Stewart, Paul H. "Government Agencies." In *Native America in the Twentieth Century: An Encyclopedia,* edited by Mary B. Davis, 210–214. New York: Garland, 1994.

———. *The Indian Office: Growth and Development of an American Institution, 1865–1900.* Ann Arbor, Mich.: UMI Research Press, 1979.

Stiffarm, Lenore and Phil Lane. "The Demography of Native North America: A Question of American Indian Survival." In *The State of Native America: Genocide, Colonization and Resistance,* edited by M. Annette Jaimes, 23–53. Boston: South End Press, 1992.

U.S. American Indian Policy Review Commission. *Final Report: Submitted to Congress May 17, 1977.* 2 vols. Washington, D.C.: GPO, 1977.

U.S. General Accounting Office. *Food Assistance Programs: Nutritional Adequacy of Primary Food Programs on Four Indian Reservations. Report to Congressional Requesters.* Washington, D.C., 1989.

Walke, Roger. *Federal Programs of Assistance to Native Americans: A Report Prepared for the Senate Select Committee on Indian Affairs of the United States Senate.* Washington, D.C.: GPO, 1991.

Rita Ledesma

Canadian Native Economic Development

Barrington, Linda, ed. *The Other Side of the Frontier: Economic Explorations into Native American History.* Boulder, Colo.: Westview Press, 1999.

Canada. Royal Commission on Aboriginal Peoples. *Report of the Royal Commission on Aboriginal Peoples.* Ottawa, 1996.

Carter, Sarah. *Lost Harvests: Prairie Indian Reserve Farmers and Government Policy.* Montreal: McGill-Queen's University Press, 1990.

Elias, Peter Douglas. *Development of Aboriginal People's Communities.* North York, Ont.: Captus Press, 1991.

Evans, Simon M., Sarah Carter and Bill Yeo, eds. *Cowboys, Ranchers and the Cattle Business: Cross-border Perspectives on Ranching History.* Calgary: University of Calgary Press; Boulder, Colo.: University Press of Colorado, 2000.

Cornell, Stephen and Joseph P. Kalt. *What Can Tribes Do? Strategies and Institutions in American Indian Economic Development.* Los Angeles: American Indian Studies Center, UCLA, 1992.

Knight, Rolf. *Indians at Work: An Informal History of Native Labour in British Columbia, 1848–1930.* Vancouver: New Star Books, 1996.

Littlefield, Alice, and Martha C. Knack, eds. *Native Americans and Wage Labor Ethnohistorical Perspectives.* Norman: University of Oklahoma Press, 1996.

Notzke, Claudia. *Aboriginal Peoples and Natural Resources in Canada.* North York, Ont.: Captus University Publications, 1994.

Savoie, Donald J. *Aboriginal Economic Development in New Brunswick.* Moncton, N.B. : Canadian Institute for Research on Regional Development, 2000.

Sloan, Pamela and Roger Hill. *Corporate Aboriginal Relations: Best Practice Case Studies*. Toronto: Hill Sloan Associates Inc., 1995.

Tough, Frank. *'As Their Natural Resources Fail': Native Peoples and the Economic History of Northern Manitoba, 1870–1930*. Vancouver, B.C.: UBC Press, 1996.

Wien, Fred C. *Rebuilding the Economic Base of Indian Communities: The Micmac in Nova Scotia*. Montreal, Quebec: The Institute for Research on Public Policy, 1986.

Wuttunee, Wanda A. *In Business for Ourselves: Northern Entrepreneurs: Fifteen Case Studies of Successful Small Northern Businesses*. Montreal: McGill-Queen's University Press, 1992.

David Newhouse

Overview of Government Assistance and Restitution

Bartlett, Richard. *The Indian Act of Canada*. 2nd ed. Saskatoon: University of Saskatchewan, Native Law Centre, 1988.

Berger, Thomas R. *Fragile Freedoms: Human Rights and Dissent in Canada*. Toronto: Clarke, Irwin, 1981.

Canada. *The Annotated Indian Act, Including Related Treaties, Statutes and Regulations*. Scarborough, Ont.: Carswell, 1988.

Canada. Department of Indian Affairs and Northern Development. *Basic Departmental Data*. Ottawa, 1997.

———. *Federal programs for Status Indians, Métis, Non-Status, and Inuit: Major National Programs*. Ottawa, 1980.

———. *Growth in Federal Expenditures on Aboriginal Peoples*. Ottawa, 1993.

Getty, Ian & Lussier, Antoine, eds. *As Long as the Sun Shines and Water Flows: A Reader in Canadian Native Studies*. Vancouver: University of British Columbia Press, 1983.

Fleras, Augie, and Elliott, Jean. *The "Nations Within": Aboriginal-State Relations in Canada, the United States, and New Zealand*. Toronto: Oxford University Press, 1992.

Frideres, James. *Native People in Canada: Contemporary Conflicts*. 5th ed. Prentice-Hall: Scarborough, Ont., 1998.

Howlett, Michael. "Policy Paradigms and Policy Changes: Lessons From the Old and New Canadian Policies Towards Aboriginal Peoples." *Policy Studies Journal*, 22, no. 4 (1994): 631–649.

Hylton, John (ed.). *Aboriginal Self-Government in Canada: Current Trends and Issues*. Saskatoon, Sask.: Purich Publishing, 1994.

Johnston, Patrick. *Native Children and the Child Welfare System*. Toronto: Canadian Council on Social Development in association with James Lorimer, 1983.

Long, J. Anthony and Menno Boldt, eds. *Governments in Conflict?: Provinces and Indian Nations in Canada*. Toronto: University of Toronto Press, 1988.

McKenzie, Brad. "Social Work Practice with Native People." In *An Introduction to Social Work Practice in Canada*, edited by Shankar Yelaja, 272–288. Scarborough, Ont.: Prentice-Hall, 1985.

Miller, James Rodger. *Skyscrapers Hide the Heavens: A History of Indian-White Relations in Canada*. Toronto: University of Toronto Press, 1989.

Morrison, Bruce and Roderick Wilson, eds. *Native Peoples: The Canadian Experience*. Toronto: McClelland and Stewart, 1995.

Patterson, E. Palmer. "Native Peoples and Social Policy." *Canadian Social Policy*. rev. ed., edited by Shankar A. Yelaja, 175–194. Waterloo, Ont.: Wilfred Laurier University Press, 1987.

Turner, Joanne C. and Francis J. Turner, eds. *Canadian Social Welfare*. 3rd ed. Scarborough, Ont.: Allyn and Bacon, 1995.

Heather Coleman

Canadian Native Economic Development on Reserves

Boldt, Menno, J. Anthony Long, and Leroy Little Bear, eds. *The Quest for Justice: Aboriginal Peoples and Aboriginal Rights*. Toronto: University of Toronto Press, 1985.

Canada. Royal Commission on Aboriginal Peoples. *Report of the Royal Commission on Aboriginal Peoples*. Ottawa, 1996.

Cardinal, Harold. *The Rebirth of Canada's Indians*. Edmonton: Hurtig, 1977.

———. *The Unjust Society: The Tragedy of Canada's Indians*. Edmonton: Hurtig, 1969.

Cassidy, Frank, ed. *Aboriginal Self-Determination*. Lantzville: Oolichan Books, 1991.

Elias, Peter D. *Development of Aboriginal People's Communities*. North York, ON: Captus Press, 1991.

Frideres, James S. *Native Peoples in Canada: Contemporary Conflicts*. 3rd edition. Scarborough: Prentice-Hall Canada, 1988.

Hawthorn, Harry B. *A Survey of the Contemporary Indians of Canada: A Report on Economic, Political, Educational Needs and Policies*. 2 vols. Ottawa: Queen's Printer, 1966–67.

Kariya, Paul, ed. *Native Socio-Economic Development in Canada: Adaptation, Accessibility and Opportunity*. Institute of Urban Studies, Native Issues 1. Winnipeg: University of Winnipeg, 1989.

National Round Table on Aboriginal Economic Development and Resources. *Sharing the Harvest: The Road to Self-Reliance*. Ottawa: Royal Commission on Aboriginal Peoples, 1993.

Native Investment & Trade Association. [Online] Available: http://www.native-invest-trade.com/ [2001 January 28].

Ponting, J. Rick, ed. *Arduous Journey: Canadian Indians and Decolonization*. Toronto: McClelland and Stewart, 1986.

Ian Getty

18

Prominent Native North Americans

Abby Abinanti (1947–)
Yurok attorney and activist

Abby Abinanti is president of the Tribal Law and Policy Institute. She is also a California juvenile dependency judge. Born in San Francisco, California, Abinanti received her law degree from the University of New Mexico in 1973. She later became a specialist in education, tribal development, and social services. She has developed model tribal court systems and codes, trained Indian Child Welfare Act workers, and taught seminars at the National American Indian Court Judges Association.

Since 1977 Abinanti has been active in the national Women and the Law Conferences and has become a strong advocate for women's rights in the areas of educational equity, child abuse, day care, affirmative action, and ratification of the Equal Rights Amendment (ERA). She has previously served as the chair of the California Indian Legal Services board of directors and as trustee of the Humboldt County Law Library. Her publications include *The Indian Child Welfare Act: Strategies for Implementation* (1981) and *Three Optional Tribal Court Structures* (1981).

Abraham (d. 1780)
Mohawk tribal leader

Abraham was the son of Old Abraham and adopted brother and successor to Hendrick, a prominent Mohawk leader. In 1755, when Hendrick was killed in the Battle of Lake George, Abraham became a Mohawk chief. Like Hendrick, Abraham was a renowned orator and diplomat. He served as spokesman for the Iroquois League, an alliance of six Iroquoian speaking nations including the Mohawk, at the Albany Conference of 1754, where colonial leaders gathered to discuss a possible union. During these negotiations Abraham met with Benjamin Franklin and William Johnson. In 1775 the colonists turned to Abraham once again. In that year treaty commissioners from the Continental Congress met with the sachems of the Iroquois League, to acquaint them with what he termed the "United Colonies dwelling upon this Island." The commissioners, according to protocol, selected Abraham as the representative speaker for the Iroquois. Late in the summer of 1775, the colonists appealed to Abraham and his people to remain neutral during the American Revolution. Abraham conveyed to the colonists that his people would remain neutral during the conflict. Later, however, under the leadership of Mohawk Joseph Brant, who had strong personal and political ties to the British, some Mohawk villages gave their support to the British in the American Revolution.

George Abrams (1939–)
Seneca anthropologist, author, and arts administrator

George Abrams is an anthropologist who specializes in the Seneca and other Iroquoian peoples. He is a member of the Seneca tribe, which originally occupied an extensive territory in eastern Canada (from Lake Ontario southward) and the United States. He is a member of the Blue Heron clan.

Abrams was born on the Allegany Indian Reservation near Salamanca, New York, on 4 May 1939. He received his bachelor's degree in anthropology from the State University of New York at Buffalo in 1967 and obtained his master's degree from the University of Arizona in 1967 and studied in the university's doctoral program from 1968 to 1971. His general interests include Native American ethnology, Indian education, applied anthropology, ethnohistory, and museum science. He has published several works, including "The Cornplanter Cemetery," published in *Pennsylvania Archeologist* (1965); "Moving the Fire: A Case of Iroquois Ritual Innovation," published in *Iroquois Culture, History, and Prehistory* (1967); "Red Jacket," published in the *World Book Encyclopedia* (1976); and *The Seneca* (1976).

From 1990 until 1992, he served as special assistant to the director of the National Museum of the American Indian in New York City. He has won many academic awards and has served as a member of several advisory boards and committees, both at the national and state levels. For over ten years, Abrams was chairman of the American Indian Museums Association. Since early 1998, he is director of the Yager Museum, Hartwick College, in Oneonta, New York.

Andrew Acoya (1943–)
Laguna Pueblo architect and urban planner

Andrew Acoya is a facilities planner for the Bureau of Indian Affairs in Albuquerque, New Mexico. He is registered as an architect in the state of New Mexico and is a member of the American Institute of Architects.

Born at Fort Wingate, New Mexico, on 24 June 1943, Acoya obtained his bachelor's degree in Architecture at the University of New Mexico (1968) and earned a master's degree in Architecture at the Massachusetts Institute of Technology (MIT) in 1970. He is said to be the first full-blooded Native American to graduate from the MIT School of Architecture. He was awarded scholarships and awards from the Laguna Pueblo tribe, the Bureau of Indian Affairs, the John Hay Whitney Foundation, and the Massachusetts Institute of Technology.

Acoya completed his master's thesis at MIT with a study entitled "Community Planning for the Acoma Tribe of New Mexico," which examines the relevance of Pueblo village life as form givers in the planning of new Pueblo communities.

He has held the positions of professor of architecture at the University of New Mexico and director of planning for the All Indian Pueblo Council. He assisted in the design of the Pueblo Indian Cultural Center in Albuquerque, New Mexico and the San Juan Pueblo Arts and Crafts Cooperative Building, and influenced a decision to provide space for Native healing ceremonies in a new hospital designed for the Laguna Pueblo

and Acoma Pueblo tribes. He lives in Corrales, New Mexico, with his wife, Maria, of San Felipe Pueblo, and their son, Andrew.

Clarence Acoya (1930–)
Laguna Pueblo business administrator

Clarence Acoya, a business administrator and member of Laguna Pueblo, was born in Albuquerque on 20 October 1930. Acoya attended Albuquerque Indian School, Bacone College, the University of New Mexico, and Yale University. On completing his education, he served in the United States Marine Corps (1951–1954) and later went on to hold a number of important positions as a planner and administrator. He has served as executive director for the New Mexico Commission on Indian Affairs, treasurer for the Pueblo of Laguna, director of Ford Foundation projects for the National Congress of American Indians, and administrative assistant to the mayor of Tucson, Arizona.

Acoya has also been a member of various advisory boards, such as the National Indian Training and Research Center in Washington, D.C. He is a member of the National Congress of American Indians and was president of the American Athletic Hall of Fame.

Evan Tselsa Adams (contemporary)
Coast Salish actor and writer

Born to the Sliammon Band (located near Powell River, British Columbia) of the Coast Salish people, Evan Adams has become a well-known actor and writer in recent years. Reared on the Sliammon Reserve, Adams graduated from St. Michael's University School and Lester B. Pearson College of the Pacific, which are both located in Victoria.

Adams began his acting career early, at age nineteen, when he performed a cameo role in *Toby McTeague*, a movie about a dog sled race. Adams stars in the Emmy-winning television movie *Lost in Barrens* and its sequel *The Curse of the Viking Grave*.

Most recently, Evan Adams starred in the popular movie *Smoke Signals*, which was based on a short story by Sherman Alexie and directed by Chris Eyre. Adams plays Thomas Builds-the-Fire in the film and won an award for Best Debut Performance at the Independent Spirit Awards in Los Angeles.

Architect Andrew Acoya.

Hank Adams (1944–)
Assiniboine/Sioux activist

Hank Adams was born on the Fort Peck Indian Reservation in Montana at a place known as Wolf Point, commonly referred to as Poverty Flats. He graduated from Moclips High School in 1961, where he was student-body president, editor of the school newspaper and annual, and a starting football and basketball player. Following graduation he developed an interest in politics and moved to California where he was a staunch supporter of President John F. Kennedy and a campaign worker for the president's brother, Robert F. Kennedy, in the 1968 Democratic primary.

In 1964 Adams played a behind-the-scenes role when actor Marlon Brando and one thousand Indians marched on the Washington State capitol in Olympia to protest state policies toward Indian fishing rights. Indians reserved the right to take fish in "the usual and accustomed places" in numerous treaties negotiated in the 1850s. State officials, commercial, and sports fisherman tried to restrict the amount, time, and places where Indian people could fish, thus prompting the treaty/fishing-rights battles.

Adams began his activist career in April 1964 when he refused induction into the U.S. Army until Indian treaty rights were recognized. His attempt failed and he ultimately served in the U.S. Army.

In 1968 Adams became the director of the Survival of American Indians Association, a group of 150 to 200 active members primarily dedicated to the Indian treaty/fishing rights battle. Late in 1968, he actively campaigned against state regulation of Indian net fishing on the Nisqually River near Franks Landing, Washington. For this and his role in the fishing-rights battles, Adams was regularly arrested and jailed from 1968 to 1971. In January 1971, on the banks of the Puyallup River near Tacoma, Washington, Adams was shot in the stomach by an unknown assailant. He and a companion, Michael Hunt, had set a fish trap about midnight and remained to watch it. That section of the Puyallup River had been the scene of recent altercations as Indian people claimed fishing rights guaranteed by treaties despite state laws to the contrary. Adams recovered from the gunshot

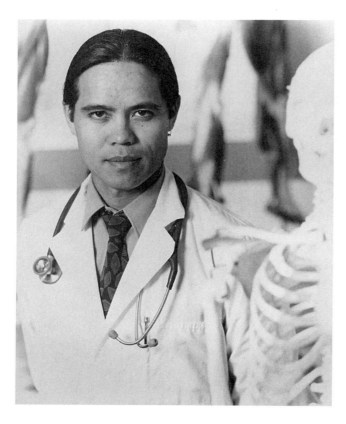

Evan Tselsa Adams.

wound and continued to fight for Indian fishing rights in the state of Washington into the mid-1970s.

Margaret B. Adams (1936–)
Navajo anthropologist and museum director

Margaret Adams is a retired anthropologist of Navajo descent, formerly associated with several museums in the Monterey, California area. Born in Toronto, Ontario, Canada, on 29 April 1936, Adams attended college in California at Monterey Peninsula College and San Jose State University, from which she received her bachelor's in 1971. She completed her master's degree at the University of Utah in 1973. She then returned to Monterey and became chief of the museum branch at Fort Ord Military Complex and head curator of the Fort Ord and Presidio of Monterey Museums, a position she held from 1974 until 1988.

Adams has been a strong advocate of higher education for Native Americans throughout her career, serving on the Indians in Science Panel of the American Association for the Advancement of Science from 1972 until 1985. Adams is involved in protecting Native American burial and ceremonial sites and in conducting research on Native American diet and food preparation methods. She is a member of the National Indian Education Association, the California Indian Education Association, the American Anthropological Association, and the American Association of Museums.

Rebecca Adamson (1949–)
Cherokee economist

Rebecca Adamson has been active in many Native American concerns, particularly education and economic development. From 1972 to 1976, Adamson was a member of the board of directors of the Coalition of Indian-Controlled School Boards in Denver, Colorado, and her efforts were directed toward synthesizing and facilitating policy reform issues at the national level. In 1982 she founded and became president of First Nations Development Institute in Falmouth, Virginia, whose purpose is to promote economic development and the founding of commercial enterprises on reservation lands. She has always worked directly with grassroots tribal communities, advocating local tribal issues on a national level.

Rebecca Adamson, president of First Nations Development Institute.

In 1986 Adamson served as an advisor to the United Nations (UN) on rural development during the United Nations Decade of Women. In 1988 and 1989, she was advisor for the UN's International Labor Organization for International Indigenous Rights. She has served on the board of directors of several organizations, including the National Center for Enterprise Development, the Calvert Social Investment Fund, and the Council on Foundations.

Her interests in economic development of Indian communities led her in 1992 to become an advisor for the Catholic Conference's Campaign for Human Development on strategic planning for economic development. She has served on the President's Council on Sustainable Development/Sustainable Communities Task Force. She was awarded the 1996 Robert W. Scrivner Award from the Council on Foundations for creative and innovative grantmaking and the National Center for American Indian Enterprise Development's 1996 Jay Silverheels Award. In addition, she was named by *Ms. Magazine* as one of their seven Women of the Year (1997), and in 1998 she was named as one of the top ten Social Entrepreneurs of the Year by *Who Cares* magazine.

Adamson holds a Master's of Science in Economic Development from New Hampshire College in Manchester, New Hampshire, where she teaches a graduate course on indigenous economics within the Community Economic Development Program. She also writes a monthly column for *Indian Country Today* devoted to alternative economic development and other issues.

Edward Ahenakew (1885–1961)
Plains Cree minister and author

Edward Ahenakew was one of the first people to collect and transcribe Cree legends. Born at Sandy Lake in Saskatchewan, Canada, in June 1885, he was named after Edward Matheson, an Anglican missionary who had taught at Sandy Lake. Ahenakew attended the missionary school until he reached the age of eleven, when he was sent to boarding school at Prince Albert, Saskatchewan. Upon graduation, Ahenakew returned to Sandy Lake, where he taught at local mission schools until his acceptance as a ministry candidate at Wycliffe College in Toronto. Throughout his years studying, Ahenakew returned to Saskatchewan during the summers to work in the Diocese of Saskatchewan. He completed his religious studies at the University of Saskatoon in 1912.

Following his ordination, Ahenakew traveled to a mission at Onion Lake, Saskatchewan, to assist Matheson's brother, the Reverend John Matheson, who

had fallen ill. Ahenakew proved a vital assistant and friend to John Matheson and remained close to his family after Matheson's death in 1916. In the winter of 1918, a flu epidemic swept the reserves, and Ahenakew resolved to study medicine to help his people. Soon after beginning his new studies, however, Ahenakew himself fell very ill, partly because he had so little money to spend for food.

Ahenakew eventually recovered, but was unable to return to medical school. Instead, he set out to collect and transcribe Cree legends and stories, which were published in 1925 as *Cree Trickster Tales*. Ahenakew also helped to publish a Cree-English dictionary and edited a monthly journal in Cree syllabics. Another collection of Ahenakew's writings, *Voices of the Plains Cree*, was published posthumously in 1974. At the age of seventy-six, Ahenakew died while traveling to Dauphin, Manitoba, to help establish a summer school.

Freda Ahenakew (1932–)
Cree scholar

Freda Ahenakew is a renowned scholar of Cree language and literature, known for her careful transcription and translation of Cree stories and biographies. She was born in 1932 and raised on the Ahtahkakoop Reserve at Sandy Lake in central Saskatchewan. After raising twelve children of her own, Freda Ahenakew became a Cree language teacher. Her formal education includes a bachelor's of education degree from the University of Saskatchewan (1979), and a master's degree in Cree linguistics from the University of Manitoba (1984). She has taught at the Saskatchewan Indian Cultural College (1976–1981) with the Lac La Ronge Band (1979–1980) and the Saskatoon survival school (1980–1981). From 1983 to 1985, she was assistant professor of Native studies at the University of Saskatchewan and later served as associate professor of Native studies at the University of Manitoba and was head of the department from 1990 to 1995.

In addition to technical studies, an introductory book (*Cree Language Studies: A Cree Approach* [1987]), and a series of illustrated children's books, Ahenakew has published several volumes of Cree texts, including *Stories of the House People*, told by Peter Vandall and Joe Duquette (1987). In recent years, Ahenakew has devoted most of her time and energy to the careful transcription, analysis, and translation of traditional stories and autobiographical accounts of Cree people, especially Cree women. She has been preparing such stories and accounts for publication in Cree with English translation. In 1992 Freda Ahenakew received the Citizen of the Year Award from the Federation of

Saskatchewan Indian Nations, a province-wide organization of aboriginal nations aimed at the advancement of aboriginal rights. For her work in education, Ahenahew was appointed in 1998 to the Order of Canada, which recognizes outstanding achievement and service in various fields of human endeavor.

Martha Aiken (1926–)
Inupiaq educator and translator

Martha Aiken is an educator and bilingual curriculum developer of Inupiaq descent. Born at Barrow, Alaska, on 12 July 1926, Martha Aiken is the author of seventeen bilingual books for the North Slope Borough School District in Barrow. She has also translated eighty hymns of the Presbyterian Church and was a major contributor to an Inupiaq dictionary. In the course of this work she also designed and developed an IBM typing element for the Inupiaq language.

Aiken has been a member of the board of the Arctic Slope Regional Corporation and has also served on the Alaska State Committee on Services to the Elderly. She testified at recent hearings on sea mammal hunting, mainly to offer a woman's perspective on these Native traditions. She also volunteered as a cultural consultant for KBRW Broadcasting Company in Barrow. Aiken is active in the movement to preserve Inupiaq language among children and educators and makes public lectures encouraging cultural and linguistic retention.

Sherman Alexie (1966–)
Spokane-Coeur d'Alene poet, novelist, and screenwriter

Sherman Alexie grew up in Wellpinit, Washington, on the Spokane Indian Reservation. Winner of a 1991 Washington State Arts Commission poetry fellowship and a 1992 National Endowment for the Arts poetry fellowship, Alexie has published more than two hundred poems, stories, and translations in publications such as *Another Chicago Magazine, Beloit Poetry Journal, Black Bear Review, Caliban, Journal of Ethnic Studies, New York Quarterly, Red Dirt, Slipstream, ZYZZYVA*, and others.

His first book of poetry and short stories, *The Business of Fancydancing*, was published by Hanging Loose Press in January 1992 and quickly earned a favorable front-page review from *The New York Times Book Review*. This first poetry book was the result of poems and stories written in Alexie's first creative writing workshop at Washington State University in Pullman. Alexie soon published a second collection, *I Would Steal Horses*, which was the winner of Slipstream's

Writer Sherman Alexie.

fifth annual Chapbook Contest in March 1992. In January 1993 he published a third poetry book, *Old Shirts & New Skins* with the UCLA American Indian Studies Center. In 1994, his first collection of short stories, *The Lone Ranger and Tonto Fistfight in Heaven*, was published and received a citation for the PEN/Hemingway Award for Best First Fiction.

In 1995 Alexie won the Before Columbus Foundation's American Book Award and the Murray Morgan Prize for his first novel, *Reservation Blues*. His second novel, *Indian Killer*, published in 1996, was named one of *People Magazine*'s Best of Pages and a *New York Times* Notable Book.

In 1997 Alexie and Chris Eyre, a Cheyenne/Arapaho filmmaker, agreed to collaborate on a film project based on Alexie's short story, "This is What it Means to Say Phoenix, Arizona." Produced by Shadow Catcher Entertainment and released as *Smoke Signals*, the film premiered at the Sundance Film Festival in January 1998, where it won the Audience Award and the Filmmakers Trophy, and was distributed nationwide by Miramax Films.

In June of 1998, he competed in his first World Heavyweight Poetry Bout competition. He went on to win the title the next two years in a row, becoming the first poet to hold the title for three consecutive years. He is the current reigning World Heavyweight Poetry Bout Champion.

Alexie has been widely acknowledged as one of the top writers for the twenty-first century. He resides with his wife and son in Seattle, Washington, and has published fourteen books to date, including his most recent collection of short stories, *The Toughest Indian in the World*, and his newly released poetry collection, *One Stick Song*.

Paula Gunn Allen (1939–)
Laguna Pueblo and Sioux novelist, poet, and professor emerita

Paula Gunn Allen is a distinguished literary figure of mixed ancestry. She was born in Cubero, New Mexico, in 1939. Her father is a Lebanese-American and a former lieutenant-governor of New Mexico, and her mother is Laguna Pueblo on one side and Sioux-Scottish on the other. Thus, she grew up in a multicultural household where Spanish, German, Laguna, English, and Arabic were all spoken and understood. This mixture of ancestry—with all its blessings and difficulties—has been a primary fact of life for Allen and a theme that figures in various writings such as her novel *The Woman Who Owned the Shadows* (1983).

As a scholar and literary critic, Allen has worked to encourage the publication of Native American literature and to educate others about its themes, contexts, and structures. Her book *The Sacred Hoop: Recovering the Feminine in American Indian Traditions* (1986) analyzes the fiction of several Indian writers and has done much to improve understanding of this new literature. She has also introduced the reading public to emergent Native American writers in anthologies such as the award-winning collection *Spider Woman's Granddaughters: Traditional Tales and Contemporary Writing by Native American Women* (1989). These are only a few titles to her credit, as Allen has been an extremely prolific critic and has also published several volumes of poetry.

Allen has won several awards, including fellowships from the National Endowment for the Arts (1978) and the American Indian Studies Program at UCLA (1981), and has also been appointed an associate fellow at the Stanford Humanities Institute. She has served on the faculties at San Francisco State University, the University of New Mexico, the University of California, Berkeley, and the University of California, Los Angeles, until her retirement in 1999.

The mother of three children, Allen is also a dedicated feminist who has stated that her convictions can be traced back to the woman-centered structures of traditional Pueblo society. She has been active consistently in American feminist movements and in antiwar and antinuclear organizations. She is the sister of the Laguna Pueblo writer Carol Lee Sanchez and cousin of the novelist Leslie Marmon Silko. Her most recent publications include *Off the Reservation: Reflections on Boundary-Busting, Border-Crossing Loose Canons* (1998) and *Outfoxing Coyote: Poems*, edited by Allen and Carolyn Dunn (2000).

Thomas Almojuela (1943–)
Squamish army officer

Thomas Almojuela is a retired United States Army Lieutenant Colonel and a member of the Squamish tribe. Born in Seattle, Washington, on 24 April 1943, Almojuela was the first Native American from the Pacific Northwest to graduate from the United States Military Academy at West Point. After attending Olympic College in Washington State, he came to the academy as a congressional appointee and went on to become a member of the dean's honor list at West Point. In addition to these academic honors, Almojuela was also an outstanding athlete who lettered in four sports and was an all-state basketball player two years in a row while attending high school in the Seattle area.

Before his service in Vietnam, Captain Almojuela commanded a tank company in Germany. In Vietnam, he flew the AHIG Cobra gunship and was also in ground combat. His military honors include the Silver Star, two Distinguished Flying Crosses, the Bronze Star, the Air Medal with thirty-three oak clusters, the Army Commendation Medal, the National Defense Medal, the Vietnamese Campaign Medal, and the Combat Infantryman's Badge. He retired in 1992 and is now living in Chile.

Lori Arviso Alvord (1958–)
Navajo surgeon

Lori Arviso Alvord, M.D., is the first Navajo female surgeon. She currently holds the positions of associate dean for student and minority affairs and assistant professor of surgery at Dartmouth Medical School. She is also a practicing general surgeon.

Widely regarded for combining modern medicine with the traditions of her Navajo heritage, Alvord graduated cum laude from Dartmouth and Stanford Medical School (1985), and she trained in surgery at Stanford University Hospital, serving as chief resident in 1990 and 1991. When her training was complete, she worked for the Indian Health Service as general surgeon at the

Gallup Indian Medical Center in Gallup, New Mexico, from 1991 to 1997.

She has served on numerous committees and panels, including the National Committee on Foreign Medical Education and Accreditation, U.S. Department of Education (2000–2001); the Office of Research on Women's Health (ORWH) (1997); the working group for the conference "Beyond Hunt Valley: Research on Women's Health for the Twenty-first Century"; the National Institute of Health (NIH) Task Force on Recruitment and Retention of Women in Clinical Trials, Office of Research on Women's Health (1993); and the NIH Concept Review Panel for the Community Randomized Trial Component of the Women's Health Initiative (1992).

In 1999 Alvord delivered the convocation keynote address at Dartmouth College. She also co-authored a book, with Elizabeth Cohen Van Pelt, entitled *The Scalpel and the Silver Bear: The First Navajo Woman Surgeon Combines Western Medicine and Traditional Healing*, which was published in 1999. Alvord is married to Jonathan Alvord and has two children, Kodiak (Kodi) and Kaitlyn (Katie-bear).

American Horse (1840–1876)
Oglala Sioux tribal leader

In the 1860s and 1870s, American Horse was a Sioux leader in Red Cloud's War, which was fought for control of the Bozeman Trail, a major passage through the present states of Wyoming and Montana. He was a cousin of Red Cloud, another major Sioux leader and, until his death, remained a militant opponent to U.S. settlement of the western Plains.

In the mid-1860s, U.S. settlers and military attempted to build a string of forts along the Bozeman Trail. Settlers and miners had traveled the important passageway illegally since its discovery by John Bozeman in 1863. Much of the trail crossed land that was reserved by treaty for the Sioux and Cheyenne, and from 1866 to 1888 the Sioux and Cheyenne tried to maintain control of the region. American Horse, the son of Smoke, participated in many of the skirmishes and battles of Red Cloud's War.

Despite the temporary land concessions made to Red Cloud in the Fort Laramie Treaty of 1868 and the momentary peace that agreement procured, American Horse remained contentious and militant. In 1870 he accompanied Red Cloud to Washington, D.C., for a meeting with government officials, but diplomatic relations were short-lived. In 1874, after discovery of gold in the Black Hills, an area sacred to the Sioux and located in present-day South Dakota, U.S. miners and speculators streamed into the area. In 1876 American Horse once again took up arms in the fight for the Black Hills and was present at the Battle of the Little Bighorn in 1876.

In September 1876 American Horse took a band of Oglala and Minniconjous southward to present-day South Dakota. Their encampment was attacked by General George Crook. The ensuing Battle of Slim Buttes resulted in the capture of American Horse. Alerted to American Horse's capture, the prominent Sioux leaders Sitting Bull and Gall gathered a rescue party to secure American Horse's release. Although he had been badly wounded from a shot to the abdomen, American Horse refused help from army surgeons. His rescuers were unable to come to his aid or negotiate his release, and American Horse died.

The capture and death of American Horse was one in a series of defeats for the Sioux after the Battle of the Little Bighorn and foreshadowed the Sioux surrender in 1877.

Jack Iyerak Anawak (1950–)
Inuit minister and member of Parliament

The Honorable Jack Anawak is a member of Parliament for Rankin Inlet North and minister of Community Government and Transportation of Nunavut. Born in 1950 in a tent on the Arctic Circle near Repulse Bay to Donat and Margaret Anawak, Jack Anawak was later adopted by Lionel Angotingoar and Phillipa Piova. Raised on the land, Anawak acquired all the traditional Inuit survival skills before attending school in Chesterfield Inlet and Churchill, Northwest Territories. He went on to undertake business management certificate coursework from the Western Canada Co-op College in Saskatoon, Saskatchewan.

After completing his studies, Anawak combined a successful business career with public service. During the 1970s and 1980s, he held a number of high-profile positions in the business community in the Northwest Territories, including the executive director of the Keewatin Chamber of Commerce in Rankin Inlet and the chief executive officer of the hamlet of Repulse Bay. For four years in the 1980s, Anawak was the president and owner of Kivalliq Consulting, Management, and Training Services, Ltd., in Rankin Inlet. Anawak also served as mayor of the hamlet of Rankin Inlet in 1985 and 1986, sitting on numerous committees, including the Repulse Bay Education Committee. He sat on the boards of several organizations devoted to northern economic development, including the Federal Native Economic Development Board. In November 1988, Anawak was elected to the Canadian House of Commons in Ottawa and was appointed in 1989 the official opposition critic for northern affairs. Anawak was still a member of the House of Commons in April 1997, when he accepted the position of interim commissioner to oversee the creation of a territorial government for Nunavut. His term as interim commissioner expired when Nunavut gained territorial status in April 1999.

Owanah Anderson (1926–)
Choctaw administrator and author

Born in Choctaw County, Oklahoma, on 18 February 1926, Owanah Anderson has been an important advocate for advancing the status of American Indian women, especially in the areas of business and media. She was a member of President Carter's Advisory Committee on Women from 1978 to 1981 and chaired the National Committee on Indian Work of the Episcopal Church in 1979 and 1980. She has also served on the Health, Education, and Welfare Advisory Committee on Rights and Responsibilities of Women.

Anderson founded the Ohoyo Resource Center in 1979. Ohoyo means "woman" in Choctaw, and this organization is a women's employment network service, which, among others things, produces national

Owanah Anderson.

directories of Native American women with professional skills in various areas. She also served as project director with National Women's Program Development, Incorporated, in Wichita Falls, Texas. She is chair and interim volunteer executive director of the Indigenous Theological Training Institute of North America, Incorporated.

Anderson was a recipient of the Ann Roe Howard Award from the Graduate School of Education at Harvard University (1981). She has authored *Resource Guide of American Indian and Alaska Native Women* (1980) and *400 Years: Anglican/Episcopal Mission Among American Indians* (1997). She retired in 1998.

Mary Ann Martin Andreas (1945–)
Cahuilla/Serrano political leader and activist

Having been elected tribal chair of the Morongo Band of Mission Indians four times, Mary Ann Andreas has become an effective leader on both state and federal fronts in the battle to protect tribal sovereignty and American Indian interests.

Born Mary Ann Eileen Martin in Soboba, California, to John Martin and Marjorie Saubel in 1945, Andreas grew up on the Morongo Reservation, located at the foot of the San Gorgonio Mountains, just west of Palm Springs. Formerly named the Malki Reservation, Morongo was named after Andreas' great-grandfather, Captain John Morongo, a tribal leader who was fluent in five languages. She is a member of the Coyote Clan.

In 1963 Andreas graduated from high school in Banning, California, and soon after moved to the San Francisco Bay Area under the federal government's relocation program. She stayed in northern California for eight years, during which time she attended Heald Business College.

When she returned home, she became involved in tribal politics. She became active, participating in the housing commission, the scholarship commission, and the enrollment committee, just to name a few. Soon she was elected chair, and the tribe has experienced great economic success since her election.

As chairwoman, Andreas worked closely with her tribal council to oversee the growth of Casino Morongo, one of the most successful gaming operations in California. What started as a modest bingo hall in 1983 now hosts more than 3,000 guests each day and is the largest employer in the region.

During Andreas' tenure as chairwoman, welfare and unemployment have been eliminated on her reservation. She also uses her status to speak out on the importance of her people's traditions and cultural beliefs. While some Cahuilla and Serrano words and concepts are no longer known, Andreas believes that the tribe must cling to their traditions harder than ever. She focuses on children's cultural development and teaches the importance of understanding both tribal and non-Indian worlds.

She also became a media spokeswoman for Proposition 5, the ballot measure overwhelmingly passed by California in a landslide victory in 1998. Featured in the campaign's television commercials, she works countless hours educating state, national, and international reporters and helped to organize grassroots get-out-the-vote efforts.

To reinforce the importance of tribal self-government, Andreas and her council issued the Morongo Sovereignty Bar, a unique chocolate bar with a label explaining the importance of Indian self-sufficiency. The bars are passed out to legislators as well as to children across the country as a teaching tool. Other tribes from throughout the United States write to the Morongo tribe to request donations of the Sovereignty Bar for educational and political events.

In more than two decades as a tribal leader Andreas has received many awards and honors. In 1998 she received the California National Indian Gaming Association Award for Tribal Leader of the Year, and in 2000 Andreas was named California's Woman of the Year by the state's lieutenant governor. She also recently became the first member of her tribe to attend Harvard University where she completed a special studies program for senior executives in local and state governments.

Anne (Queen Anne) (d. 1725)
Powhatan tribal leader

As a Powhatan leader, Anne was a forceful defender of her people's rights. Anne's husband Totopotomoi had allied himself with Virginia colonists to fight an alliance of inland tribes. Upon his death in battle about 1655, Anne assumed leadership of her husband's band. She and her people lived at the junction of the Pamunkey and Mattapony rivers in present-day Virginia. This land was under the jurisdiction of the Powhatan Confederacy, a large Indian confederacy whose power had significantly declined by the 1670s.

Anne played a pivotal role in the Virginia Colony's internal dispute known as Bacon's Rebellion, after Nathaniel Bacon who, in the mid-1670s, tried to overthrow the Virginia colonial government. In 1675, the governor of the colony, William Berkeley, came to Anne for military assistance. With her son at her side, Anne addressed the Virginia legislators and responded to their request for aid. She chastised the surprised

body for neglecting her people after her own husband had given his life in defense of the colony. Only after the colony promised to redress these grievances did Anne offer the services of her warriors. After the rebellion, the Virginia government proclaimed her "Queen of Pamunkey." She remained a forceful advocate for her people in negotiations with the Virginia colonists during her rule. In 1715 Anne again addressed the Virginia legislature and outlined the interests of her people within the Virginia Colony.

Will Antell (1935–)
Chippewa trustee and educator

Will Antell is currently a trustee for the Minnesota State colleges and universities, the fifth largest higher education system in the United States. The board has policy responsibility for system planning, academic programs, fiscal management, personnel, admissions requirements, tuition and fees, and rules and regulations.

Born on the White Earth Reservation in Minnesota on 2 October 1935, Antell attended Bemidji State College in Minnesota, where he received a bachelor's of science degree, Mankato State College in Minnesota, where he received a master's of science, Northern

Will Antell.

Michigan University, and St. Cloud State University of Minnesota, where he received his doctorate in education in 1973.

Early in his career, Antell was a teacher of social sciences at the high school level and a human relations consultant for the state of Minnesota. He has also taught courses on Native American culture and history and he recently retired from the Minnesota Department of Children and Families.

Besides his activities as a professional consultant in the field of education, Antell has served on numerous boards and commissions relating to Indian affairs and has been a lecturer at the Harvard Graduate School of Education, St. Mary's University (Halifax, Nova Scotia), and Wisconsin State University. He also has several publications to his credit, including *American Indian Leadership Training Programs* (1974) and *Culture, Psychological Characteristics, and Socio-Economic Status in Educational Program Development for Native Americans* (1974).

He is the owner of Antell Companies, a consulting firm and insurance agency specializing in service to the American Indian community.

Paul Apodaca (1951–)
Navajo scholar and artist

Paul Apodaca was born in Los Angeles, California, of Navajo, Mexican Indian (Mixton), and Spanish descent. Apodaca is currently associated with Chapman University as a professor of American studies in the Social Sciences Division. He has taught for Cal State Fullerton (CSUF), University of California, Irvine (UCI), and is a visiting professor at the University of California, Los Angeles (UCLA). For seventeen years, Apodaca served with the Bowers Museum, the largest museum in Orange County, California, as an exhibiting artist, artist-in-residence, curator of the Native American art, folk art, and California history collections, and contributing writer and illustrator for Bowers Museum Press publications including *Images of Power*. He is a member of the Autry Museum of Western Heritage Native Voices Advisory Board and a consultant for the Smithsonian Institution National Museum of the American Indian. The state of California hired Apodaca to design state-funded arts programs and to develop a new administrative plan for the California State Indian Museum.

Apodaca works with many arts and academic agencies and funders including the California Arts Council (CAC), the California Council for the Humanities (CCH), the Arizona Commission on the Arts, the Los Angeles Cultural Affairs Department, the Corporation for Public Broadcasting, the National Endowment for the

Paul Apodaca.

Humanities (NEH), and the Fulbright Senior Scholar Program. His work includes consultations for Knott's Berry Farm in Buena Park, California, the Disney Imagineering Group, and Universal Pictures. In 1990, Apodaca worked as committee member and consultant for the Los Angeles Festival as well as master of ceremonies for the Pacific Rim arts and culture event. He is the book review editor for *News From Native California*, teacher-consultant for the Scott-Foresman textbook, *California—Our State, Its History*, and the editor of the *Journal of California and Great Basin Anthropology*. He writes articles and museum exhibition reviews for the *Journal of American Anthropology* and the *Chronicle of Higher Education*.

Throughout his career, Apodaca has been honored with numerous awards and grants including the Smithsonian Institution Minority Museum Professional Fellowship, the Orange County Human Rights Award, and the Daughters of the American Revolution Mary Smith Lockwood Medal for Education. He was part of a team that won the Academy Award for the 1985 feature documentary, *Broken Rainbow* which helped stop the forced relocation of Navajo and Hopi families. The California State Legislature adopted an 8,000-year-old stone carving of a bear found in San Diego County as an official state symbol, recognizing California's indigenous population in response to efforts made by Apodaca, Jon Erickson of UCI, and Henry Koerper of Cypress College.

Apodaca received a master's degree in American Indian studies and a doctorate in folklore and mythology from UCLA. Chancellor Charles Young presented Apodaca with the UCLA Alumni Outstanding Graduate Student Medal in 1995.

Raymond "Ray" Duran Apodaca (1946–)
Ysleta del Sur Pueblo Tribe of Texas administrator

Raymond Apodaca is currently employed as Temporary Assistance to Needy Families' tribal team leader and executive officer for the Division of Tribal Services, Administration for Children and Families, U.S. Department of Health and Human Services. He also serves on the board of directors for the Indian Law Resource Center. He once served as executive director of the Texas Indian Commission, an agency of the state of Texas. Born at Las Cruces, New Mexico, on 15 October 1946, Apodaca obtained his bachelor's degree (1969) and a master's degree in public administration (1976) from New Mexico State University. In the period after graduating and before returning to the university for advanced studies, he served in the United States Air Force from 1969 to 1972.

Apodaca's interests include history, government, theology, and education, and he is the author of *Directory of Information on Health Careers for American Indians* (1977). Apodaca has been an active member of several advisory boards, committees, and other organizations over the years, including the National Indian Education Association, the National Congress of American Indians, the North American Indian Museums Association, and the Texas State Committee on the Protection of Human Remains and Sacred Objects. He was the national president of the Governors' Interstate Indian Council in 1985 and 1986.

Anna Mae Aquash (1945–1976)
Micmac activist

Anna Mae Aquash, nee Pictou, a Micmac Indian from Nova Scotia, Canada, was active in the American Indian Movement (AIM), an organization aimed at advancing the rights of Indian people in North America. Originally formed in 1968 to address the problems of Indian people living in urban areas, the organization quickly expanded to address issues surrounding housing, education, and treaty rights. In the early 1970s, AIM became involved in events on the Pine Ridge Reservation in South Dakota, home to approximately 14,000 Oglala Sioux and mixed-blood Indians. Charges of corruption had been leveled against the Pine Ridge Tribal Council, and AIM members, together with members of the reservation committed to the impeachment of the tribal chairman Richard Wilson, occupied the town of Wounded Knee, located within the Pine Ridge Reservation. Wounded Knee is identified in American Indian history as the 1890 site at which an estimated three hundred Indian men, women, and children were massacred by federal cavalry as they were surrendering their arms. Although the 1973 siege resulted in a negotiated settlement, AIM's occupation of the town also ended in tragedy. Two Indians were killed by government fire.

Anna Mae Aquash was born and raised by her mother, Mary Ellen Pictou, on a Micmac Reserve five miles outside the town of Shubenacadie, Nova Scotia. The Micmac people traditionally have occupied lands located in eastern Canada. After attending school in Nova Scotia, Aquash left her reserve and lived in Boston for several years, where she had two children, became involved in political causes aimed at improving the life of urban Indians, and worked at a low-income day care center. In Boston, she met Nogeeshik Aquash, a Chippewa artist from Ontario, and in 1973, they traveled to Wounded Knee to show solidarity with AIM. They married in Wounded Knee in April 1973 in a traditional Sioux ceremony. Their marriage lasted little more than a year, and Anna Mae became increasingly involved in AIM's activities.

In 1975 the Pine Ridge Reservation again was the site of a confrontation between AIM and federal authorities. Two FBI agents were killed. Anna Mae was found dead five months later, her body abandoned in a field on the Pine Ridge Reservation. According to autopsy reports, she died from a bullet wound to the head. This homicide has not been solved.

Dave Leon Archambault (contemporary)
Standing Rock Sioux educational administrator

Dave Archambault is the former president of Standing Rock College in Fort Yates, North Dakota. He obtained his bachelor's degree in secondary education from Black Hills State College in South Dakota (1976) and went on to complete the master's program in educational administration at Pennsylvania State University in 1982. Archambault's major interest is educational reform, and his master's research focused on ways of changing kindergarten through twelfth-grade curricula to better meet the needs of Indian learners.

On completing his graduate studies, he became a principal at Little Wound School in Kyle, South Dakota, and served in this capacity for eight years. He later became acting recreation director at United Tribes Technical College in Bismarck, North Dakota.

Archambault has been active in many public service boards and organizations, including the American Indian Higher Education Consortium and the North Dakota Humanities Council. He has also won several awards, particularly in the area of athletics; he was named South Dakota Cross Country Coach of the Year (1980), South Dakota Indian Educator of the Year (1982), and National Indian Basketball Coach of the Year (1980).

Joallyn Archambault (1942–)
Standing Rock Sioux anthropologist, administrator, and artist

Joallyn Archambault is director of the American Indian Program, an outreach program to Indian communities established by the National Museum of Natural History, Smithsonian Institution, Washington, D.C.

Born in Claremore, Oklahoma, on 13 February 1942, Archambault received her bachelor's (1970), master's (1971), and doctoral (1984) degrees at the University of California, Berkeley, in anthropology.

Her primary scholarly interests are in the areas of art and material culture, modern social movements, political systems, ethnic relations, and patronage systems. Her dissertation was entitled "The Gallup Ceremonial: A Study of Patronage within a Contemporary Context of Indian-White Relations."

Archambault held several teaching positions early in her career, serving on the faculties at the University of California, Berkeley (1976–1979); California College of Arts and Crafts (1979–1983); California State University, Hayward, and the University of Wisconsin at Milwaukee (1983–1986). She was a research associate for the Center of Race, Crime, and Social Policy at Cornell University (1980–1982) and a field ethnographer for the Sonoma State Foundation in Rohnert Park, California (1983–1984). Archambault became director of American Indian Programs at the Smithsonian Institution in 1986.

She has given many conference papers and organized conference sessions on a wide variety of topics. Most recently, she won a Smithsonian Scholarly Studies Fellowship and an America in Berlin fellowship, which allowed her to conduct research on early Plains ethnographic collections in German museums.

As program director, she has organized numerous outreach activities that served tribal priorities and hosted many individual Indian researchers at the National Museum of Natural History. She organized the

first professional organization for American Indian anthropologists and the Ella Deloria Award for Indian graduate students of anthropology.

Besides her academic accomplishments, Archambault received many awards as an artist and her work is part of the permanent collections at the Navajo Tribal Museum, the Indian Arts and Crafts Board, the Red Cloud Cultural Center, the Gilcrease Museum, and other private collections.

Annette Arkeketa (1958–)
Otoe-Missouria/Creek poet, playwright, journalist, and scriptwriter

Annette Arkeketa is currently working on her master's in interdisciplinary studies at Texas A;M University. Arkeketa is a poet and playwright whose work is widely anthologized. She is the author of a book of poems, *The Terms of a Sister*, published in 1997. She received the Wordcraft Circle Award for Playwright of the Year (1998) for her play *HOKTI*, which has been performed by the Tulsa Indian Actors' Workshop in Tulsa, Oklahoma, and at Haskell Indian Nations University. Arkeketa has taught playwriting at Cornell University, Truman State University, Kansas University, and

Writer Annette Arkeketa.

Red Mesa High School. She participates in numerous community activities: she is a board member for the Native American arts organization ATLATL, a caucus member for Wordcraft Circle of Native Writers and Storytellers, president of the Literary Guild at Texas A;M, and a member of Sigma Tau Delta. In 2000 she was presented with a Wordcraft Circle Award for *Mentor of the Year.*

Arkeketa is daughter to Benjamin Arkeketa (Buffalo Clan) and Mary E. Freeman-Arkeketa (Tiger Clan). She is married with three children and one granddaughter.

Ruth Arrington (1924–)
Creek scholar and administrator

Ruth Arrington has been a major influence in advancing cultural awareness and educational importance among young Indian people. She was professor of speech and coordinator of Indian studies at Northeastern Oklahoma State University in Tahlequah, Oklahoma, until her retirement in 1988.

Born in Tulsa, Oklahoma, on 15 October 1924, Arrington received her doctorate in speech from Louisiana State University in 1971. She produced and directed an influential film entitled *The American Indian and His Government* and has also published numerous professional articles and reviews. Arrington was named Outstanding Oklahoma Woman of the Year by the Oklahoma Federation of Indian Women in 1972, and served as a member of the Oklahoma Indian Affairs Commission from 1982 until 1987.

John H. Artichoker (1930–)
Winnebago and Oglala Sioux educator and administrator

John H. Artichoker is an educator and administrator who dedicated his career to helping young Indian people complete their college education. He was born in Pine Ridge, South Dakota, on 17 January 1930. Artichoker received his bachelor's and master's degrees in education from the University of South Dakota.

His first professional position was as director of Indian education for the state of South Dakota and he later served as tribal affairs chairman for the Bureau of Indian Affairs and the United States Public Health Service. He served as superintendent of the Northern Cheyenne Agency in Montana and of the Colorado Indian Agency, in both cases bringing extensive development programs to rural Indian communities.

Over the years, Artichoker has conducted much research on the special problems of Native American college students, and the results appear in his publication *The Sioux Indian Goes to College* (1959).

Atironta (seventeenth century)
Huron tribal leader

Three chiefs of the Ahrendarrhonon (Rock) Nation—one of five nations that comprised the Huron confederacy (the others being the Attignawantan [Bear], Attigneenongnhahac [Cord], Tahontaenrat [Deer], and the Ataronchronon [Beyond the Silted Lake] Nations)—bore the name Atironta in the seventeenth century, following the Huron custom of resurrecting the name of a deceased chief. The first was a chief of a village near what has become Hawkstone, Ontario. The village is said to have consisted of over two hundred longhouses. According to many scholars, Atironta had been the first Indian chief to make contact with Samuel de Champlain, a French voyager and administrator known in Quebec as the Father of New France. When Champlain sailed up the St. Lawrence River into what is now the Province of Quebec in 1611, he reportedly was met by Atironta and a party of Huron at the Lachine Rapids just west of Montreal and presented with strings of beads from each of the Huron tribes and a beaver pelt from each of the chiefs in the confederacy. Relations between the French and the Huron, which developed into a historic alliance for war and trade, thereafter became the special responsibility of Atironta.

In 1615 Atironta participated in a war party of Huron and Algonkian led by Champlain in an attack on an Iroquois village south of Lake Ontario. On the return journey, Atironta shared a cabin and provisions with Champlain. The next summer, Champlain brought Atironta to Quebec City, where he was entertained and referred to as the "host" of the French people.

Carolyn L. Attneave (1920–1992)
Delaware and Cherokee psychologist

Carolyn Attneave was a professor of psychology and a noted authority on the cross-cultural adaptation of mental health services for Native Americans of the United States and Canada.

Born in El Paso, Texas, on 2 July 1920, Attneave obtained her doctorate in psychology from Stanford University in 1952. Over the years, she worked as a consultant to numerous tribal and urban mental health programs. She was the president of the American Indian Psychologists from 1978 to 1980 and was also an expert witness in federal and state legislative hearings on Indian child custody cases. She was a professor of psychology and adjunct professor of psychiatry and behavioral sciences at the University of Seattle.

Attneave advocated women's rights and educational equity. During World War II, while serving as a naval officer, she developed curricula and training programs for women. She later served on the National Advisory Council on Women's Educational Programs (1980–1981) and was also a campus ombudsman for sexual harassment cases (1978–1981). She produced numerous publications, including the *Bibliography of North American Indians in Mental Health* (1982).

Awashonks (ca. 1670s)
Wampanoag tribal leader

In 1675, when the so-called King Philip's War broke out between New England colonists and the Wampanoag Confederacy, an alliance of Algonkian-speaking nations living in present-day New England, Awashonks was the leader of the Saconnet Indian Band of the Wampanoag Confederacy living near present-day Little Comptom, Rhode Island. It is believed that Awashonks's husband, Tolony, died before the outbreak of the war, and the Saconnet chose Awashonks to succeed her husband as leader.

It appears that Awashonks was initially undecided about which side to support during the war. The Wampanoag Confederacy was led by Metacom, whom the colonists called King Philip. A number of Awashonks's warriors joined King Philip's forces early in the conflict. It is believed, however, that Awashonks was persuaded to side with the colonists after a meeting with Benjamin Church, a colonial militia officer who led the British forces in the conflict against Metacom. Awashonks lent more than her moral support. A number of Saconnet warriors, including Awashonks's son Peter, joined with the colonists. The colonial recruitment of Indian groups, including warriors, during the war was a significant factor in King Philip's eventual defeat. During the war, Awashonks took her people to a safe haven in Sandwich, Massachusetts. After the conflict, and Metacom's defeat, Awashonks remained an ally of Church. According to colonial records she met often with Church and the two became friends.

Elgin Bad Wound (1946–)
Oglala Sioux educator

Elgin Bad Wound, whose Sioux name is Tasunke Kokipapi, is an educator and former president of Oglala Lakota College. Born on the Pine Ridge Reservation in South Dakota on 19 April 1946, Elgin Bad Wound was raised in his tribal community and graduated first in his class from Pine Ridge High School in 1965. He joined the army and served in Vietnam from 1969 until 1971. On returning home, Bad Wound went to work as an adult education instructor at Oglala Lakota College on the Pine Ridge Reservation from 1972 to 1975. Deciding then on a career in education, he obtained his bachelor's degree in secondary education from Black Hills State University (1977) and a master's degree in higher education from the University of Colorado (1978). He then returned home and took over the leadership of Oglala Lakota College, serving as the vice-president from 1978 to 1979 and as president from 1979 until 1986.

At that point Bad Wound returned to school again and completed the doctoral program in higher education at Pennsylvania State University (1990). While he was still a graduate student, he worked on a Ford Foundation research project to examine the factors contributing to the success of Native American students in transferring from local, tribally controlled colleges to major colleges and universities. He became a member of Phi Delta Kappa (PDK), a professional education fraternity, and was one of two winners of the 1988 Kozak Memorial Fellowship, an award presented each year to PDK graduate students demonstrating the highest potential for research, teaching, and public service. He published *Teaching to Empower: Tribal Colleges Must Promote Leadership and Self-Determination in Their Reservations* in 1990.

Since returning to the Pine Ridge area, Bad Wound has been even more actively involved in a variety of other community service programs. He has received awards and recognition for his distinguished scholarship and dedicated public service.

Louis W. Ballard (Honganozhe) (1931–)
Quapaw and Cherokee composer and educator

Louis Ballard is the first person to hold the position of Distinguished Professor of Music at William Jewell College in Liberty, Missouri. As the preeminent Native American composer of classical music, Ballard's innovative music curriculum guides and cultural resources are widely used in public schools, colleges, and universities. He earned his bachelor of arts, bachelor of music education, and master of music degrees from the University of Tulsa and studied privately with Darius Milhaud and Mario Castel-Nuovo Tedesco in Hollywood. He received numerous awards for his musical contributions and an honorary doctorate from the College of Santa Fe.

As a contemporary and classical composer, Ballard expanded the percussion and orchestral vocabulary of western music while introducing and integrating new

Composer and flutist Louis Ballard.

idioms of Native American expression to the concert hall. He collected Indian songs from various tribes in continental North America, and was inspired to create his own original style for piano preludes, chamber music, symphonic, and other classical forms. He wrote the first American Indian ballet (*Koshare*), which premiered in Barcelona, Spain, in 1966 and was first presented in the United States in 1967. His ballet *The Four Moons* also premiered in 1967, and in 1969 he won the Marion Nevins MacDowell Award for the chamber ensemble composition, *Ritmo Indio*.

He was honored as the first American composer to present a concert of his own music in the new Beethoven-House Chamber Music Hall adjoining Beethoven's birthplace in Bonn, Germany. Ballard is also an educator and has written classroom materials aimed at helping all singers and students reinforce musical skills through mastery of tribal songs. He is perhaps the first composer to develop a philosophy of ethnic music education. He was the first dean of the music department at the Institute of American Indian Arts in Santa

Fe, New Mexico. In his own words, "It is not enough to acknowledge that American Indian music is different from other music and that the Indian, somehow, 'marches to a different drum,' as a way of paying obeisance to the unique culture of our Native American people. What is needed in America is an awakening and re-orienting of our total spiritual and cultural perspective to embrace, understand, and learn from the aboriginal American what it is that motivates his musical and artistic impulses."

Dennis J. Banks (Nowacumig) (1932–)
Anishinaabe activist

Dennis Banks was born on the Leech Lake Indian Reservation in northern Minnesota. In 1968 he founded the American Indian Movement (AIM), which was established to protect the traditional ways of Indian people and to engage in legal cases protecting treaty rights of Natives, such as treaty and aboriginal rights to hunt and fish, trap, and gather wild rice.

AIM has been quite successful in bringing Native American issues to the public. Among other activities, AIM members participated in the occupation of Alcatraz Island, where demands were made that all federal surplus property be returned to Indian control. In 1972 AIM organized and led the Trail of Broken Treaties Caravan across the United States to Washington, D.C., calling attention to the plight of Native Americans. The refusal of congressional leaders to meet with the Trail of Broken Treaties delegation led to the 1972 takeover of the Bureau of Indian Affairs offices in the nation's capital.

Under the leadership of Banks, AIM led a protest in Custer, South Dakota, in 1973 against the judicial process that found a non-Indian innocent of murdering an Indian. As a result of his involvement in the 71-day occupation of Wounded Knee, South Dakota, in 1973, and his activities at Custer, Banks and 300 others were arrested. Banks was acquitted of charges stemming from his participation in the Wounded Knee takeover, but was convicted of riot and assault stemming from the confrontation at Custer. Refusing to serve time in prison, Banks went underground but later received amnesty from Governor Jerry Brown of California.

Between 1976 and 1983, Banks earned an associate of arts degree at the University of California, Davis, and taught at D-Q University (an Indian-controlled institution), where he became the first American Indian university chancellor. In the spring of 1979, he taught at Stanford University in Palo Alto, California.

After Governor Brown left office, Banks received sanctuary on the Onondaga Reservation in upstate New

York in 1984. While living there, Banks organized the Great Jim Thorpe Run from New York City to Los Angeles. This spiritual run ended in Los Angeles, where the Jim Thorpe Memorial Games were held and where the gold medals that Thorpe had previously won in the 1912 Olympic games were restored to the Thorpe family.

In 1985 Banks left the Onondaga Reservation to surrender to law enforcement officials in South Dakota, and served eighteen months in prison. When released, he worked as a drug and alcohol counselor on the Pine Ridge Reservation in South Dakota. Banks was active in passing laws in Kentucky and Indiana against desecration of Indian graves and human remains. He organized reburial ceremonies for over 1,200 Indian grave sites that were disturbed by grave-robbers in Uniontown, Kentucky.

In 1988 Banks organized and led a spiritual run called the Sacred Run from New York to San Francisco, and then across Japan from Hiroshima to Hakkaido. Also in 1988, his autobiography *Sacred Soul* was published in Japan, and won the 1988 Non-fiction Book of the Year Award. In 1994, in order to bring attention to Native issues, Banks led the four-month Walk for Justice from Alcatraz Island in San Francisco to Washington, D.C.

Bank's autobiography, *The Longest Walk* was published in 1997. He played roles in several movies, including *War Party*, *The Last of the Mohicans*, and *Thunderheart*. Banks stays involved in American Indian issues, lecturing, teaching, and sharing his experiences.

Thomas Banyacya Sr. (1910–1999)
Hopi tribal and spiritual leader

Thomas Banyacya Sr. was a Hopi elder and traditionalist who spoke out against the relocation of the Navajo and other possible effects of U.S. Public Law 93531, which mandated that the Navajo be relocated, ostensibly so that the land could be returned to the Hopi. The Hopi are a Pueblo tribe whose Native territory is located in northeastern Arizona.

Born in the village of New Oraibi around 1910, Banyacya was one of four young men chosen by Hopi elders in 1948 to be their "ears and tongue"; that is, they were selected as interpreters to tell the outside world of certain direful warnings contained in the ancient Hopi prophecies. According to Banyacya, the depredations of the Americans and their ultimate self-destruction were all revealed ages ago in certain traditional Hopi prophecies. The prophecies mentioned a "gourdful of ashes" (the atomic bomb), predicting the world would end in a global explosion or "purification" unless human beings changed their destructive ways and prayed to the Great Spirit.

Banyacya was the last surviving member of the group, and in recent years he became recognized as a major spokesman for the traditionalist viewpoint on controversial issues, such as the future of a huge expanse of land in the area of Black Mesa in northeast Arizona.

The Hopi-Navajo Land Dispute involves an area of 1.8 million acres of high desert plateau where Navajo herders have lived on little-used Hopi land for generations. In 1972, the Congress passed Public Law 93531, which involved the forced removal of more than ten thousand Navajo and the erection of a barbed wire fence 285 miles long.

When the Navajo protested during the 1970s, many others joined them, including Hopi traditionalists such as Thomas Banyacya and his son, Thomas Banyacyas Jr. The Banyacyas and others believe that the government is mainly interested in clearing the land so that puppet tribal councils can be established and mining companies can gain access to the area's immense deposits of coal, uranium, and oil shale.

Barboncito (1820–1871)
Navajo tribal leader

In the 1860s, under government orders the U.S. military with the government's backing tried to resettle or exterminate the Navajo. Barboncito, along with Delgadito (his brother) and Manuelito, led the Navajo resistance from 1863 to 1866.

Barboncito was born at Canyon de Chelly in present-day Arizona. He was both a military and religious Navajo leader. In 1846, Barboncito signed a treaty pledging friendship with the United States. Peace would soon become impossible. In the early 1860s the U.S. military waged an ongoing mixed campaign of warfare and negotiation to halt Apache and Navajo raids on U.S. settlements in the Southwest. The raids were a response to settler encroachment on Indian land. One important area of contention was the grazing lands around Fort Defiance located in present-day eastern Arizona. In 1860, after soldiers shot a number of Navajo horses, Barboncito and Manuelito led Navajo warriors in retaliation against the soldiers at Fort Defiance. After nearly taking the fort, the Indians were pushed back into their mountain strongholds. Stalemated, U.S. military leaders and Indians agreed to a short-lived peace council.

In early 1862, Barboncito made peace overtures, but these efforts were short-lived. That year, the military chose a barren parcel of land located in present-day eastern New Mexico, called Bosque Redondo, as a Navajo relocation site. The relocation plans pushed Barboncito into open warfare with the United States. In 1864 at Canyon de Chelly, Barboncito was taken prisoner by soldiers commanded by Colonel Kit Carson. He was taken to the relocation camp at Bosque Redondo, where living conditions could barely sustain survival. In 1865, Barboncito rejoined Manuelito after escaping with about five hundred followers. He later surrendered and in 1868, Barboncito signed a treaty that established the Navajo Reservation in present-day New Mexico and Arizona. The Navajo leader died three years later.

Jim Barnes (1933–)
Choctaw poet, translator, and university professor

Jim Barnes is a poet and translator of Choctaw descent. Born near the San Bois Mountains in eastern Oklahoma in 1933, Barnes migrated to Oregon in 1951 and worked as a lumberjack there until 1960. He then returned to Oklahoma and entered Southeastern Oklahoma State University, where he majored in English, French, and drama, receiving his bachelor's in 1964. He

Jim Barnes.

later earned his master's degree and a doctorate in comparative literature from the University of Arkansas.

Barnes began writing fiction and poetry in the 1950s and began publishing in the 1960s. Professor Barnes has published numerous books of poetry, criticism, fiction, and translations (from German and French). His poems have also appeared in numerous anthologies, most notably *Carriers of the Dream Wheel: Contemporary Native American Poetry* (1975) and *Heartland II: Poets of the Midwest* (1975). Barnes continues to be a prolific writer. He wrote an autobiography entitled *On Native Ground: Memoirs and Impression*, and published *Paris: Poems* in 1998.

In 1978, he was awarded a fellowship for poetry by the National Endowment for the Arts, and in 1980 the Translation Center at Columbia University awarded him a prize for his translation of a volume of poetry by the German Dagmar Nick. He has won an Oklahoma Book Award and an American Book Award. He is currently editor of *The Chariton Review* and professor of comparative literature at Northeast Missouri State University.

Irene Bedard (1967–)
Inupiat/Cree Actress

Born in Anchorage, Alaska, Bedard became interested in acting young in life. Convincing the neighborhood children to perform the Beatles' *Yellow Submarine* and other such skits, Bedard heard her calling early. Since then the actress has performed in many highly regarded films including *Smoke Signals* and *Grand Avenue*.

Bedard grew up visiting and participating in potlatches and powwows as a youngster. Her father was politically active during Bedard's youth, and her family insured that she was knowledgeable about her heritage. After studying at a Pennsylvania College for a few years, where she majored in physics and philosophy, Bedard transferred to the University of the Arts in Philadelphia. She changed her major to theater and graduated.

Although she thought she would work in theater her entire life, she was introduced to television and film when Disney offered her a role in its 1994 movie *Squanto: A Warrior's Tale*. Bedard played Squanto's wife in the movie opposite Adam Beach. The same year she also starred in *Lakota Woman: Siege at Wounded Knee*, a Turner Network Television (TNT) movie based on the autobiography of Mary Crow Dog, which chronicles one woman's journey through the 1973 occupation of Wounded Knee.

While on location in Nova Scotia filming *Squanto*, Bedard and her husband Dennis Wilson were married on the movie's set. Her husband grew up in Ohio, but spent part of his childhood in the Southern California area. He is a musician and the couple moved to Ojai when they returned from the shoot.

Since her debut on-screen acting performances, Bedard has been busy working on several film and television projects. Among these projects are *Pocahontas* (1995), for which she performed the voice for the film's title character (she also provided the voice for the movie's sequel); *Grand Avenue* (1996), a HBO movie based on the book by Greg Sarris; *Smoke Signals* (1998), based on a short story by author Sherman Alexie; *Naturally Native* (1998), a movie describing the trials of three California Indian women searching for their identity; and *Tortilla Heaven* (2000), a film based on a New Mexican myth.

Bedard still dabbles in theater performance and founded her own theater company, Chukalukoli Theater Ensemble. In fact, she has written a play for the group entitled *Point Hope*. In addition, Bedard formed a production company titled The Half Moon. Among other projects, the company is involved with film score production.

Bedard has received numerous awards for her performances. She accepted the American Indian Film Festival's Best Supporting Actress Award for her role as Suzy Song in *Smoke Signals*. In addition, she received a Golden Globe nomination, a First Americans in the Arts Award for Best Actress, and the Cowboy Hall of Fame Award for Best Actress for her role as Mary Crow Dog. In 1995 she was named one of *People Magazine*'s Fifty Most Beautiful People.

Tom Bee (1947–)
Santee Sioux (Dakota) performing artist, songwriter, music producer, and record company executive

Born at Gallup, New Mexico, on 8 November 1947, Tom Bee is best known as founder and featured artist of the Native American popular music group XIT, which first appeared in 1970. During the early years of the group, Bee's composition "We've Got Blue Skies" was recorded by Michael Jackson and the Jackson Five. Soon after, XIT was signed by Motown Records. While under contract with Motown, the group released two widely acclaimed albums entitled *Plight of the Redman* and *Silent Warrior*, and their single "Reservation of Education" was among the five best-selling records in France in 1973.

Tom Bee, president of the Soar Corporation.

The political overtones of XIT's music has kept them from achieving superstar status in the United States, but the group has developed a cult status in America and Europe that has allowed their music to survive for the last twenty years.

In 1989, Bee founded a Native American recording company called SOAR (Sound of America Records). The first two releases by SOAR featured the music of XIT, but Bee's company soon expanded to include various other traditional and contemporary forms of music. SOAR now has over 300 quality titles including flute music, powwow music, peyote songs, Navajo music, and round dance songs, as well as their familiar rock-and-roll.

Fred Begay (1932–)
Navajo experimental physicist

Fred Begay is a nuclear physicist and currently is senior staff physicist at the Los Alamos National Laboratory with research interests in the controlled thermonuclear fusion problem and related phenomena, assistant for science and technology to the president and vice-president of the Navajo government, and president of the Seaborg Hall of Science. The Seaborg Hall of

Physicist Fred Begay.

Science, named after the late Nobel chemistry laureate Glenn T. Seaborg, is an independent nonprofit education and research institution dedicated to provide public services to the Navajo community in science and technology matters. The volunteer core members include Navajo professionals who have established distinguished careers in science, engineering, and medicine. Begay is a member of the American Physical Society, the American Association of Physics Teachers, and the American Nuclear Society.

Born on the Ute Mountain Indian Reservation in Towaoc, Colorado, in 1932, Begay attended the Bureau of Indian Affairs-managed Vocational Indian Schools at Ignacio from 1942 to 1946, where his training was in farming. As a non-commissioned officer Begay served in the U.S. Air Force (1951–1955) and was assigned to an air-rescue squadron in Korea during the Korean Conflict.

Without the benefit of a solid pre-college science and mathematics background, Begay attended the University of New Mexico (1955–1956; 1959–1963) and was awarded a bachelor's of science degree in physics and mathematics (1961), a master's of science degree in physics (1963), and a doctorate degree in nuclear physics (1972). Begay was invited to join a NASA-funded

space physics research team at the University of New Mexico to conduct fundamental studies on the origin of high energy gamma rays and solar neutrons.

Since 1971 Begay has been employed at the Los Alamos National Laboratory where he has participated in numerous controlled thermonuclear fusion programs. He has held research and teaching appointments at Stanford University and University of Maryland. Begay has published numerous articles on the progress of the controlled thermonuclear fusion problem and related fundamental problems.

Begay has provided expert advice in science and technology issues as the chairman to the Navajo Nation's Environmental Protection Commission (1974–1976), as principal investigator for the NSF-funded Navajo Research Committee at Navajo Community College (1972–1976), as an advisor to the Board of Science and Technology for International Development, U.S. National Academy of Sciences (1979–1981), as a member of the National Research Council (1979–present), and as an advisor for the Center for Research on Education in Science, Mathematics, Engineering, and Technology, Arizona State University (2000–present).

Begay's life as a physicist and as a Navajo has been documented in various televisions films and documentaries, including *Nation within a Nation* (1972); *In Our Native Land* (1973); *The Long Walk of Fred Young-Begay* (1978); and *Dancing with Photons* (1997). In addition, numerous articles have been published on the physicist in newspapers, magazines, and textbooks, including a feature piece in *National Geographic* (1987).

Because of his groundbreaking work in science, and his contributions to science education and public service, Begay has received various awards, including the Ely Parker Award from the American Indian Society for Engineering and Science (1992); the Lifetime Achievement Award from the National Science Foundation (1994); and the Distinguished Scientist Award from the Society for the Advancement of Chicanos and Native Americans in Science (1999). In addition, Begay has received awards from the Department of Energy and the Navajo government for his work.

Begay is involved with efforts to improve public literacy regarding science and technology. He supports the work of the Los Alamos National Laboratory's Community Relations Office, whose primary objective is improve the quality of Navajo human resources who can improve the quality of the Navajo human and natural environment. Navajo socioeconomic indicators show that the Navajo exist in a human and natural environment which is similar to that of a Third World country. Begay has given numerous lectures on the Navajo and modern perspectives of nature.

Notah Ryan Begay III (1972–)
Navajo professional golfer

Notah Begay is expanding the range of sports icons for Native Americans in the twenty-first century. Born in Albuquerque, New Mexico, he began playing golf at the age of six. Because his family was impoverished, Begay saved spare change to purchase golf balls. His hard work paid off, and he is now a rising star on the Professional Golf Association Tour.

A three-time All-American selection at Stanford University, Begay was a member of the school's 1994 NCAA championship team, and a member of the 1995 United States Walker Cup team, winner of fifteen major junior and amateur titles. He holds the record for lowest eighteen-hole score in NCAA championship history with sixty-two in the second round of the 1994 tournament.

In 2000, Begay won multiple titles for the second straight year, posting back-to-back victories at the St. Jude Classic and Greater Hartford Open. He also went 3–2 for the victorious United States Presidents Cup team.

John Kim Bell (1953–)
Mohawk symphony conductor and composer

John Kim Bell has been making music and history ever since he was a child. Born on the Kahnawake Mohawk Reserve in Quebec, Bell studied since he was eight and was conducting Broadway musicals for such luminaries as Gene Kelly and Vincent Price in New York City at the young age of eighteen, becoming the youngest professional conductor in the United States. Bell completed his musical training at Ohio State University and later at the Academia Musicale Chigiana in Sienna, Italy. In 1980, after conducting numerous Broadway musicals, Bell was appointed apprentice conductor with the Toronto Symphony, becoming the first American Indian to become a symphony conductor.

In 1984, the Canadian Broadcasting Corporation produced a documentary profile of Bell, which sparked a large response from the Native community. Bell received a number of requests seeking information and assistance about musical training for aboriginal youth. In response to these requests and because of his ongoing concern about the many difficulties facing Native

John Kim Bell, president of the National Aboriginal Achievement Foundation.

youth, Bell created the Canadian Native Arts Foundation (CNAF). CNAF is a privately and publicly sponsored national charity that provides scholarships for Native youth so they may be trained in the arts. Between 1988 and 1992, CNAF has awarded approximately $1 million in scholarships to Native youth across Canada. The CNAF raises funds for scholarships through the production of concerts and events. The most ambitious production recently undertaken by CNAF was the staging of the first Native ballet produced by John Kim Bell, entitled *In The Land of The Spirits*. Bell also co-wrote the ballet's orchestral score. The ballet was premiered at the National Arts Centre in Ottawa, Canada's capital, and was a huge artistic and financial success.

CNAF has now awarded over $10 million in scholarships to more than 1,000 recipients and operates a national series of career fairs targeting aboriginal youth. In 1993, Bell established the National Aboriginal Achievement Awards, an awards system celebrating career achievement in the aboriginal community. Bell is an officer of the Order of Canada and he has received four honorary doctorates. He also serves on the boards of the Canadian Broadcasting Corporation, the Canada Millennium Scholarship Foundation, the Aboriginal

Human Resource Development Council of Canada, and the Toronto 2008 Olympic Bid Committee.

Clyde Bellecourt (1939–)
Ojibwa activist

Born on the White Earth Reservation in Minnesota in 1939, Clyde Bellecourt is a founder and director of the American Indian Movement. He was one of the leaders during the 1973 occupation of Wounded Knee. Clyde has been an active participant in the Sun Dance since the early 1970s, and he played a role in organizing the Big Mountain movement that brought attention to the situation of displaced Navajo who were forced by government policy to move from the Hopi-Navajo joint use land in the 1970s. He also played a key role in organizing the Legal Rights Center and the International Indian Treaty Council. He is also directing the Peacemaker Center for Indian Youth and working with the National Coalition on Racism in Sports and the Media. He is also founder and currently chairman of American Indian OIC, an innovative job program that has assisted the transition of over 14,000 people from welfare to full-time employment.

Patricia Benedict-Phillips (1956–)
Abenaki editor and administrator

Patricia Benedict-Phillips was born in Waterbury, Connecticut. She earned an associate degree in drug and alcohol rehabilitation counseling from Mattatuck Community College in Waterbury. She served as executive director for six years at American Indians for Development, a social service agency. She was also a member of the Energy Assistance Program policy-making board in Meriden, the American Indian Committee in New Haven, chair of Eagle Wing Press Pow-wow Committee, as well as board member of the Eagle Wing Press. In addition, she was co-editor of American Indians for Development Newsletter, and editor of *May Wutche Aque'ne: American Indians for Development Journal*. She was appointed by the governor of Connecticut to the Connecticut Legislative Task Force on Indian Affairs where she served three years. She also helped incorporate the New England Indian Task Force and was chair of the Waterbury Title IV Indian Education program. She lives in Waterbury, Connecticut.

Ramona Bennett (1938–)
Puyallup administrator and activist

Ramona Bennett served as the principal administrator for the Puyallup tribe for eleven years, controlling a maximum budget of $9 million annually. From 1971 until 1978 she was the elected chair of the Puyallup Tribal Council. The Puyallup are a Northwest Coast tribe whose original territory was located along the Puyallup River and Commencement Bay in northwestern Washington.

Born in Seattle, Washington, on 28 April 1948, Bennett received her bachelor's degree from Evergreen State College in Washington State and went on to obtain a master's degree in education from the University of Puget Sound.

Besides her tribal activities Bennett is a well-known spokeswoman for Indian rights at the national level, particularly in the areas of fishing rights, Indian child welfare, and Indian health and education. She is an officer of the Survival of American Indians Association, a Native American advocate group, and is a board member of the National Coalition to Support Indian Treaties. As an activist for Indian rights she has often been profiled in the broadcast media and in national publications such as *Redbook*, *The Socialist Worker's Forum*, *National Geographic*, and the *New York Times*. Bennett remains active in local tribal issues.

Robert L. Bennett (1912–)
Oneida commissioner of Indian affairs

Robert L. Bennett is a distinguished administrator and legal professional. He is a member of the Oneida Nation, an Iroquoian tribe whose territory is located mainly in New York, though some Oneida also live in Wisconsin and Ontario, Canada.

Born at Oneida, Wisconsin, on 16 November 1912, Bennett attended Haskell Institute in Kansas and went on to obtain his degree in law from Southeastern University School of Law in Washington, D.C. in 1941. He then served as a Bureau of Indian Affairs administrative assistant on the Navajo Reservation and remained there until serving as a marine during World War II. Following the war he worked at the Veteran's Administration, and in this capacity he helped literally hundreds of Indian veterans obtain an education under the GI Bill.

Bennett later returned to the Bureau of Indian Affairs and served in a variety of positions before his appointment as commissioner of Indian affairs in 1966. In the early 1960s, he served as an area director in Juneau, Alaska, and while working there successfully blocked the state of Alaska from selecting certain lands prior to settling the land claims of Alaska Native peoples. Bennett became known as an extremely vigorous commissioner; he traveled all over the United States helping tribes establish and direct their own social programs and fighting against the movement to exclude tribes from federal assistance.

He retired as commissioner in 1969, and then served as director of the American Indian Law Center at the University of New Mexico until 1975. Bennett has since worked as a legal consultant for various tribal groups and as a lecturer in seminars on American Indian affairs for legal professionals and administrators. He is retired and lives in Albuquerque.

Ruth Bennett (1942–)
Shawnee educator

Ruth Bennett, a Shawnee, is a bilingual education specialist. Born on 12 December 1942, she graduated from Indiana University in 1964 and obtained a master's degree in English at the University of Washington in 1968. She later received a Standard Secondary Teaching Credential from California State University, San Francisco (1973), and finally went on to complete a Ph.D. program in education at the University of California, Berkeley (1980). She also conducted post-doctorate research at the Universidad de Yucatan in Mexico (1994).

Bennett held various teaching positions in the San Francisco Bay Area during the early years of her career, but gradually her work became focused on the tribes of northwestern California. In 1978, she started working with bilingual education programs at the Center of Community Development at Humboldt State University in Arcata, California. In 1980, Bennett became director of a Title VII Bilingual Education Program offering a bilingual teaching credential in Yurok, Hupa, Karok, and Tolowa. Since 1993, she has been an ethnographic researcher, and has served as a Hupa language consultant for the Hoopa Valley Tribe.

Bennett has been involved in creating innovative curriculum materials for many years and has published many articles and books, including *Four Hupa Songs by Alice Pratt* (1994), *Dundi Ne:sing? Dixwe:di 'Unt'e:n? (Who is It? What are You Doing?)* (1997), "It Really Works," (1998) and "Does Writing Have a Place in Preserving an Oral Language?" (1999).

William Beynon (1888–1958)
Tsimshian cultural researcher

William Beynon conducted important cultural research on his own Tsimshian culture and that of other neighboring tribes, for which he has gone almost unrecognized. Born in Victoria, British Columbia, in 1888,

Beynon was the son of a Welsh steamer captain and a Tsimshian woman from Port Simpson. The Tsimshian are a Northwest Coast tribe located along the Nass and Skeena rivers and adjacent coastal areas in western British Columbia (Canada) and also on Metlakatla Island in Alaska.

Far from having a traditional upbringing, he was raised in the city of Victoria and was the only one of six brothers to learn the Tsimshian language from his mother. As a young man, he worked for the Canadian Public Railroad and the Department of Public Works. But in 1913, he went to his mother's home of Port Simpson and developed a strong interest in his Indian heritage. For the rest of his life, when not working in the fishing or canning industries, he devoted himself to cultural research and served as a collector and interpreter of ethnographic data for several well-known anthropologists.

Beynon started working for ethnomusicologist Marius Barbeau in 1914, collecting song-texts, speeches, narratives, and other types of information from elderly Tsimshian speakers and translating the texts into English. For the most part this was done quite independently, as Beynon would write the material in field notebooks and mail these to Barbeau in Ottawa. Over the years between then and his death in 1958, Beynon also worked in a similar fashion for the linguist Edward Sapir and for cultural anthropologists Franz Boas and Philip Drucker.

Beynon's actual contributions to anthropology have been badly slighted, as he is usually identified in the literature only as an "informant and interpreter." He published only one short article under his own name ("The Tsimshians of Metlakatla, Alaska," *American Anthropologist*, 1941), but several hundred pages of his unpublished texts and fieldnotes are among the holdings at the Canadian Centre for Folk Culture Studies (National Museum of Man, Ottawa) and other archives. Perhaps the most important manuscript is a 544-page typescript entitled "Ethnographic and Folkloristic Texts of the Tsimshian," which is part of the Boas Collection at the American Philosophical Society in Philadelphia. This contains rare and important texts that are different from those published in Boas's classic study *Tsimshian Mythology* (1916).

Big Bear (1825?–1888)
Cree tribal leader

Big Bear (Mistahimaskwa) was born near Fort Carlton, Saskatchewan, and became head man and chief of approximately sixty-five Cree lodges. Concerned about the disappearance of the buffalo and the effects of European settlement on traditional Indian life, Big Bear fought for better treaty terms for his people until he died in 1888. He refused to sign his consent to Treaty Six, one of several treaties that Canada entered into with First Nations, because in his view it did not provide his people with sufficient compensation and protection against further settlement and development. Big Bear constantly spoke out against the relocation of First Nations onto reserves and the turn toward agriculture by Indian people. He maintained this view until the buffalo were gone and starvation took hold in his community.

Big Bear also strove to unite the Northern Cree people, and he once succeeded in attracting more than two thousand Indians to join him in his thirst dance at the Poundmaker Reserve near Battleford, Saskatchewan. Late in life, Big Bear began to lose the support of many of his followers who became more militant. Led by Little Bad Man (Ayimisis) and Wandering Spirit (Kapapamahchakwew), the militants killed several white settlers when they became involved in what is known as the second Northwest Rebellion. The rebellion was led by Louis Riel, leader of the Métis people, who sought to establish a provisional government in Saskatchewan against the wishes of Canadian authorities. They were captured shortly thereafter, and Big Bear subsequently surrendered. Big Bear was tried for treason-felony, found guilty, and imprisoned for three years in Stony Mountain Penitentiary. Big Bear became ill in prison and was released after serving two years of his sentence. He died within a year of his release.

Samuel Billison (1925–)
Navajo WWII code talker and education administrator

Samuel Billison is a WWII code talker and veteran, a delegate to the Navajo tribal council, and the first Navajo to receive a doctorate degree in education.

Born at Ganado, Arizona, on 14 March 1925, Billison was raised on the reservation by parents who had no formal education. His grandfather, Hosteen Gani, was a medicine man. He studied at Albuquerque Indian School, Bacone College, East Central State College, and completed the master's program at the University of Oklahoma. He served as a high school principal in Oklahoma and in Texas, and returned to the Navajo Reservation where he held various administrative positions including director of public services for the Navajo tribe before he pursued a doctoral degree in education at the University of Arizona.

Billison had a distinguished military career. He served in the U.S. Marines during World War II as a Code Talker and participated in the landing on Iwo Jima. The code talkers were specially trained Navajo Marines who translated radio communications into unbreakable codes using the Navajo language during World War II.

As one of approximately 150 surviving Navajo code talkers, Billison supplied his voice for the Navajo Code Talker G.I. Joe, an action figure created by the Hasbro Toy Company. The toy, which went on sale in January 2000, speaks seven Navajo phrases and comes with a short history of the Navajo code talkers.

Black Hawk (1767–1838)
Sac (Sauk) tribal leader

During his lifetime Black Hawk resisted the expansion of U.S. settlement into his homeland, located near the Rock River in present-day Illinois. As a young man, Black Hawk showed interest in forming a confederation of Indian tribes to protest the many dubious treaties that were the basis of U.S. settlement in the region. In 1832, he fought a series of ill-fated engagements with U.S. forces, known as Black Hawk's War.

In 1829, when Black Hawk and his followers returned to their homeland in the Rock River country from a hunting trip, they found it occupied by white squatters. Some settlers had even moved into Indian dwellings. For the next few years Black Hawk and his people lived an uneasy coexistence with the U.S. intruders. In June 1831, the U.S. Army tried to dislodge Black Hawk from his village. Black Hawk and his people escaped by crossing the Mississippi River.

Black Hawk and about two thousand followers remained on the western side of the Mississippi River until 5 April 1832. As he crossed the Mississippi, U.S. Army troops were hurriedly deployed to meet him. On May 14, the two forces met and Black Hawk's men won the first battle with U.S. forces.

For the next few months, Black Hawk and his followers moved northward into Wisconsin. Meanwhile, the U.S. troops were put under the command of General Winfield Scott who organized a large army in Chicago. Two U.S. military forces caught up with Black Hawk and his followers after months of traveling and subsistence living. On 21 July 1832, at the battle of Wisconsin Heights, a number of Black Hawk's people were killed. Black Hawk hoped to escape via the Mississippi. His path was blocked on 1 August 1832, by the cannon-laden steamship *Warrior*. With reinforcements of thirteen hundred U.S. regular troops, on August 3 the U.S. forces attacked and killed about three hundred of Black Hawk's people. Black Hawk and a few followers escaped to northern Wisconsin.

On August 27, Black Hawk and about fifty companions were persuaded to surrender. Black Hawk was imprisoned at Fort Monroe, Virginia. In 1833, the defeated leader was taken to Washington, D.C., where he met President Jackson. In the ensuing years, Black Hawk became something of a media celebrity. Many authors vied to write his biography, which he dictated in 1833. In 1837, Charles Bird King painted his now-famous portrait of Black Hawk. Black Hawk died in 1838 in a land that was not his own and among people he barely knew.

Black Kettle (1803–1868)
Southern Cheyenne tribal leader

Black Kettle was a Cheyenne tribal peace leader whose band was attacked in the infamous Sand Creek Massacre during the Cheyenne and Arapaho War of 1864 and 1865. During his youth, Black Kettle was actively engaged as a warrior against the Ute and Delaware, who were enemies of his tribe. He, however, advocated good relations with the Americans and ratified a treaty maintaining peace in Colorado and along the Santa Fe Trail. After traveling to Washington, D.C., in 1863, he met with President Abraham Lincoln.

Events such as the rapid settlement of Kansas and Nebraska territories after 1854 and the Colorado gold rush of 1859 promoted uneasiness between Indians and Americans, and reprisals on each side were not uncommon. Black Kettle and other Cheyenne and Arapaho chiefs met with the governor of Colorado near Denver and were assured that if each band would camp near army installations and regularly report to military officers, they would be safe from attack. Black Kettle moved his people to Sand Creek near Fort Lyon in present-day Colorado and informed the garrison of their peaceful presence.

On the morning of 29 November 1864, the Third Colorado Volunteers, under the command of Colonel John Chivington, took up position around Black Kettle's encampment. Over his tipi, he raised the American flag and a white truce flag. Nevertheless, Chivington's troops, many of whom were drunk, swept into camp, slaughtering and sexually mutilating the fleeing Indians. Black Kettle managed to escape, but about two hundred others, mostly women and children were killed.

The news of the slaughter caused a wave of condemnation. Chivington was brought before the Committee on the Conduct of the War, and was condemned, denounced, and forced to resign from the military. Meanwhile, the Cheyenne sought swift and destructive retribution; travel across the Great Plains to Denver was completely halted.

Despite this, Black Kettle still encouraged his people to remain at peace. He signed a treaty at the Medicine Lodge council in 1867 that granted reservations to the Southern Cheyenne, the Southern Arapaho, the Comanche, and the Kiowa within Indian Territory (Oklahoma). Black Kettle led his followers to the Washita River and traveled to Fort Cobb to assure the garrison there that he wanted nothing but peace. Nevertheless, U.S. officials refused to issue guns and ammunition to Southern Cheyenne men for fear that they would raid settlers or other Indian tribes. Consequently, about two hundred Cheyenne raided several settlements in Kansas and caused U.S. troops to enter the field. Major General Philip Sheridan organized three columns of troops in an offensive aimed against the recently relocated Plains Indians.

Lieutenant Colonel George Armstrong Custer learned about the presence of Black Kettle's encampment on the Washita from Osage scouts. Disregarding the fact that the camp was on the reservation and had been guaranteed safety, he and the Seventh Cavalry attacked at dawn on 27 November 1868. Black Kettle rode out with his wife in a blinding snowstorm hoping to prevent the attack by parleying with the soldiers. Both were shot dead on sight and their bodies trampled by the advancing columns. The regimental band played "Garry Owen" as Custer and his men killed another hundred Cheyenne, mostly women and children.

Ethel Blondin-Andrew (1951–)
Dene secretary of state and member of Parliament

The Honorable Ethel Blondin-Andrew was born in the northern community of Fort Norman, in the Northwest Territories, Canada. She is a member of the Dene Nation, which includes a number of different peoples who live in the Northwest Territories. In accordance with the custom of her people, Blondin-Andrew was adopted by her aunt and uncle at the age of three months and spent her early childhood living in various hunting-and-trapping communities with her extended family. As a child, she attended residential school in Inuvik, Northwest Territories and later attended a school designed to promote leadership among Native and northern Canadian youth. Blondin-Andrew received a bachelor's of education degree from the University of Alberta in Edmonton, Alberta.

From 1974 to 1984 she taught in the remote Northwest Territories communities of Tuktoyaktuk, Fort Franklin, Providence, and Yellowknife. During this time, she was the recipient of an award from a private foundation for her work in developing a Dene teaching program. In the mid-1980s, her focus shifted first to public service and then to elected office. From 1984 to 1986, she was first manager and then acting director of the Public Service Commission of Canada, the commission representing federal public servants in Ottawa, the nation's capital. Returning to the Northwest Territories, Blondin-Andrew was appointed assistant deputy minister of culture and communications in Yellowknife.

She was first elected to the Canadian Parliament in 1988, and quickly became a strong voice for aboriginal people by serving on committees relevant to indigenous affairs. In 1993, she was appointed secretary of state, training and youth. She was reappointed in 1997 to the position. Her efforts led to the creation of Youth Service Canada and Youth Employment Strategy. She is married and has three children.

George Blue Spruce Jr. (1931–)
Laguna/San Juan Pueblo dentist and health worker

George Blue Spruce Jr., is a retired public health administrator who works to increase the number of Indians in the medical profession. Born at Santa Fe, New Mexico, on 16 January 1931, Blue Spruce received a degree in dentistry from Creighton University in Omaha, Nebraska, in 1956. Upon graduation he went into private practice but soon went to work for the U.S. Public Health Service as dental officer on the reservation in Taos, New Mexico.

He later returned to school, earning a master's degree in public health from the University of California, Berkeley (1967), and then served as a public health officer in several agencies connected with the Department of Health, Education, and Welfare (HEW). He was appointed director of the Phoenix Area Indian Health Service, a division of the Department of Health and Human Services.

Over the years, Blue Spruce has received numerous honors and has written influential articles on the need for Indian medical professionals. Besides these activities, he is also an avid tennis player; he was captain of his college team and winner of the men's singles competition at the Second Annual National Indian Championships in 1977. In the early 1990s, Blue Spruce was director of Phoenix Area Indian Health Service and a member of national dental, health, and educational organizations. He publishes in the newsletter of the Association of American Indian Physicians.

Frank M. Blythe (1940–)
Cherokee motion picture and television producer

Frank Blythe is a founding member and executive director of Native American Public Telecommunications, Inc. (NAPT). Born at Pipestone, Minnesota, on 7 November 1940, Blythe received his bachelor's degree in radio and television management at Arizona State University (1962). He is also NAPT director for American Indian radio on Satellite Network, co-director for the American Indian Higher Education Consortium's Distance Education Network, and director of Vision Maker Video. NAPT maintains a media library through which Native American programs are made available for public television, Indian organizations, and other educational users. The organization also provides grants for the creation of new programs concerning Native American subjects and themes.

Among Blythe's own production credits are *I am Different from My Brother*, *American Indian Artists II*, and *Native American Calling*. Blythe served as the operations manager for KAET-TV in Phoenix from 1971 to 1977. He has been a member of several advisory boards, including the National Association of Education Broadcasters, the Nebraska Committee for the Humanities, and the Nebraska Arts Council.

Jarrett Blythe (1886–1977)
Eastern Cherokee tribal leader

Jarrett Blythe was principal chief of the Eastern Cherokee for twenty-four years over several terms. The Cherokee are a southeastern tribe, most of whom who relocated to Oklahoma during the 1830s.

Born in Cherokee, North Carolina, on 30 May 1886, Blythe was descended from a group of Cherokee who defied the government's order to relocate in Oklahoma Territory and instead took refuge in the Smoky Mountains. Finding it difficult and expensive to enforce their original order, the government finally allowed them to remain and establish a reservation there.

Blythe went to school on the reservation, then attended Hampton Institute in Virginia and Haskell Institute in Lawrence, Kansas. On completing his education, he spent four years working on a government reclamation project in Montana. Then, feeling a "hang for home," he returned to the reservation in Cherokee, North Carolina, and never left again.

Blythe was elected tribal chief in 1931 and served four consecutive terms; he was elected again in 1955 and in 1963, holding the office for a total of twenty-four years. Each of his administrations produced major economic results: most importantly, he initiated a loan fund for tribal members wishing to go into business for themselves, and he helped to arrange for the purchase of land to build a high school. He also made valuable gifts of land to young couples, which became known as Jarrett Blythe Homesteads.

In the area of cultural activities, Blythe founded the Cherokee Historical Association and also helped initiate performances of the historical drama *Unto These Hills*, which relates the story of the Cherokee removal.

Gertrude Simmons Bonnin (Zitkala-Sa) (1876–1938)
Sioux author and activist

Gertrude Simmons Bonnin, also known as Zitkala-Sa, or Red Bird, was born at the Yankton Sioux Agency in South Dakota on 22 February 1876, the third child of Ellen Simmons, a full-blood Sioux. Sioux agency land allotment applications indicate that her father was white. She was reared as Sioux until she was eight years old, at which time she left the reservation to attend a Quaker missionary school for Indians, White's Indiana Manual Labor Institute in Wabash, Indiana. She received her high school diploma and at the age of nineteen went on to Earlham College in Richmond, Indiana, where she received recognition and prizes for her oratorical skills. Following graduation Bonnin taught for two years at Carlisle Indian School in Carlisle, Pennsylvania. She then left to study at the Boston Conservatory of Music. In 1900, she accompanied the Carlisle Indian Band to the Paris Exposition where she performed as a violin soloist. During this period she also wrote three autobiographical essays, which were published in the *Atlantic Monthly* and two stories based on Indian legends for *Harper's Monthly*. Her book *Old Indian Legends* was published in 1901.

She returned to Sioux country and in 1902 married Raymond Talesfase Bonnin, a Sioux employee of the Indian Service. In 1902, they transferred to the Uintah and Ouray Reservation in Utah, where she was employed as a clerk and briefly as a teacher. She organized a brass band among the children of the reservation and undertook home demonstration work among the women. During this period, she also became a correspondent of the Society of American Indians, entering into what would become a life work in Indian reform. The society, organized at Ohio State University in 1911, was the first Indian reform organization to be managed exclusively by Indians and to require that active members be

of Indian blood. Its aims included not only governmental reforms, but also the employment of Indians in the Indian Service, the opening of the Court of Claims to all equitable claims of Indian tribes against the United States, and also the preservation of the accurate Indian history and its records. Essentially, the society's aims were assimilationist: citizenship for all Indians, abolition of the office of Indian affairs (after 1930s called the Bureau of Indian Affairs), and termination of communal property holdings.

Bonnin was elected secretary of the society in 1916 and moved to Washington, D.C., which remained her home until her death in 1938. She carried on the society's correspondence with the Office of Indian Affairs, lectured from coast to coast as its representative, and acted as editor of its periodical, the *American Indian Magazine*. After the demise of the society in 1929, Bonnin organized the National Council of American Indians. She remained its president until her death, lobbying in Washington on behalf of Indian legislation.

Bonnin's activities as author slackened after she abandoned the editorship of the *American Indian Magazine*. Her second book, *American Indian Stories* (1921), reprinted stories written at the beginning of the century. She retained her interest in music, and one of her last undertakings was the composition, with William F. Hanson, of an Indian opera, *Sun Dance*. She died in Washington, D.C., in 1938, at the age of sixty-one.

Lionel Bordeaux (1950–)
Sioux educator and administrator

Lionel Bordeaux is president of Sinte Gleska College in South Dakota. Born on the Rosebud Sioux Reservation in South Dakota on 9 February 1940, Bordeaux graduated from St. Francis Indian Mission High School in St. Francis, Minnesota (1958), then received a bachelor's degree from Black Hills State College (1964). From 1964 until 1972, he worked for the Bureau of Indian Affairs in various Indian communities as a teacher, counselor, or educational specialist. During these years he also continued his own education, completing a master's degree at the University of South Dakota and becoming a doctoral candidate in educational administration at the University of Minnesota in Minneapolis.

In 1973 he became president of Sinte Gleska College, where he helped develop the first fully accredited bachelor's and master's degree programs at a reservation-based college. He also provided leadership for congressional passage of important legislation relating to the authorization of tribal colleges. Besides these activities as an educator, Bordeaux has played a major role in tribal leadership, serving as a councilman in the

Rosebud Sioux tribal government for eight years, co-chair of the White House Conference on Indian Education, chair of the Rosebud Sioux Tribal Education Committee, and chairman of the United Sioux Tribal Education Board.

Mary Bosomworth (Coosaponakeesa) (1700–1763)
Creek tribal leader

As a young girl, Mary Bosomworth was taken from Creek country to South Carolina, where she was educated and baptized into the Church of England. Her father was English and her mother Creek. As a young woman, she returned to her tribe and married John Musgrove, a trader who lived and worked among the Creek. In 1733, Bosomworth was hired by the governor of Georgia to act as interpreter between the colonial government and the Creek. During this time she became an influential figure among the Creek and rallied their support behind the British against Spanish influence in the Southeast. The Spanish colony in Florida had tried to win the political, military, and trade alliance of the Creek as a means of opposing the expansion of the English colonies. In 1749 Mary Bosomworth married her third husband (her first two had died), Thomas Bosomworth, who, a few years later, was appointed by the Carolina colonial agent to the Creek. At the same time, Mary Bosomworth proclaimed herself empress of the Creek Nation. As such, Bosomworth and her husband laid claims to a large piece of land in South Carolina and a number of islands off the Georgia coast. The Bosomworths, who had fallen deeply into debt, demanded payment by the colonists for their diplomatic services. After marching on Savannah with a contingent of Creek warriors, they were briefly imprisoned by colonial officials. They continued to press grievances all the way to England, and in 1759 they were granted a small settlement and official title to two islands off the Georgia coast.

Elias Boudinot (1803–1839)
Cherokee editor and writer

Elias Boudinot's Cherokee name was Galgina (Buck). His parents sent him to study in Salem, North Carolina, at a school run by Moravians, an extremely strict German Protestant sect. In 1818, the New Jersey philanthropist, Elias Boudinot, sent Galgina and several other young Cherokee scholars to a mission school in Cornwall, Connecticut. Galgina adopted the name Elias Boudinot in honor of his benefactor. He studied at Cornwall for a few short years, then he and John Ridge,

another Cherokee scholar, met and courted local girls, whom they decided to marry. This caused considerable disturbance within the town and, although the marriages took place, the incident resulted in the closing of the school.

Upon returning to the Cherokee Nation, Boudinot served the Cherokee government as clerk for the national council and in 1828 was appointed editor of the *Cherokee Phoenix*, the new Cherokee national newspaper written in English and Cherokee. Along with Samuel Worcester, Presbyterian missionary to the Cherokee, Boudinot worked on a translation of the Bible into Cherokee, using the Cherokee syllabary created by Sequoyah. In 1835, Boudinot supported the Treaty of New Echota, under which a minority of economically well-off Cherokee agreed to migrate to present-day Oklahoma because they thought it not possible to preserve the Cherokee Nation from U.S. territorial and political threats. Most Cherokee opposed the treaty, and after the U.S. Army forced most of them to migrate during the winter of 1838–1839, in a march called the Trail of Tears, they became embittered against the treaty makers. In the summer of 1839, Elias Boudinot and several other treaty advocates were assassinated.

Billy Bowlegs (1810–1864)
Seminole tribal leader

Billy Bowlegs was the leader of the last group of Seminole Indians to remain in Florida against the will of the United States government. In the Seminole War of 1835–1842, following the death of Seminole leader Osceola and the surrender of other leaders, Bowlegs led two hundred Seminole warriors in an 1839 attack on a government trading post that had been opened on Seminole land, killing most of the garrison. Following the attack, Bowlegs and his band hid in the Florida Everglades for almost a year, hiding during the day and raiding during the night.

Bowlegs was a superior warrior who resisted efforts to remove his tribe. After many battles he finally made peace with the U.S. Army, and on 14 August 1842, Bowlegs surrendered and was allotted a small parcel of land. That same year Bowlegs and other Seminole chiefs visited Washington, D.C., and the U.S. government announced the end of the eight-year Seminole War, the most costly Indian war in U.S. history: 1,500 soldiers killed and $20 million spent.

In 1855, as the result of a party of army engineers and surveyors stealing crops and destroying others belonging to Bowleg's band, violence flared up in what is sometimes referred to as the Third Seminole War. Bowlegs led his warriors in a campaign of guerrilla warfare, attacking settlers, trappers, and traders in the region, then retreating into the wilds. Once again neither army regulars nor volunteers could contain them.

Finally, in 1858, negotiations between the U.S. government and Bowlegs took place and an offer of peace was made. As a result Bowlegs and members of his band agreed to emigrate to Indian Territory, in present-day Oklahoma, which they did in 1859. Bowlegs fought for the North in the Civil War in 1861.

LaNada Means Boyer (contemporary)
Shoshone/Bannock activist

LaNada Means Boyer was one of the original Indians who occupied Alcatraz Island on 20 November 1969. In addition to being an organizer and leader on the island, Boyer traveled throughout the United States giving lectures and raising support for the occupiers on Alcatraz.

Boyer moved to the San Francisco Bay Area as part of the U.S. government relocation program, which was intended to assimilate reservation Indians into urban populations. During the occupation of Alcatraz Island, she commuted daily from the island to the University of California, Berkeley, to continue her studies, and received her B.A. from Berkeley in 1972. She completed her master's degree work in public administration and in 1999 earned a doctorate of arts in political science at Idaho State University.

Beth Brant (1941–)
Mohawk writer and poet

Beth Brant, Degonwadonti, is a widely published writer and poet. Many of her works appear in *Kitchen Talk: An Anthology of Canadian Women's Prose and Poetry* (1992); *Getting Wet* (1992); *An Anthology of Native Canadian Literature in English* (1992); *Talking Leaves* (1991); and *Piece of My Heart* (1991). A variety of magazines and journals have published her stories, and "Turtle Gal" was adapted and aired by the Canadian Broadcasting Corporation in Toronto, Ontario, in 1990. Her publications include *Mohawk Trail* (1985), *A Gathering of Spirit* (1989), *Food and Spirits* (1991), *Writing as Witness* (1995), and *I'll Sing Till the Day I Die* (1996).

Brant was a lecturer at the University of British Columbia in 1989 and 1990 and has contributed to numerous writing workshops, such as the Women of Color Writing Workshop in Vancouver, British Columbia, and the Michigan Festival of Writers in East Lansing, Michigan, both in 1991.

In 1992, she participated in the Festival of North American Native Writers in Norman, Oklahoma, at the International Feminist Book Fair in Amsterdam, Holland, and at the Flight of the Mind Writing Workshop for Women in Eugene, Oregon.

In 1993 Brant was the writer-in-residence at the Kanhiote Library on the Tyendinaga Mohawk Reserve in Canada, and guest lecturer in women's studies and Native studies, at New College, University of Toronto, Ontario. She has received many grants and awards including grants from the Michigan Council for the Arts (1984 and 1986) and the Ontario Arts Council (1989), and in 1991, she received the National Endowment for the Arts Literature Fellowship. In 1992, Brant was awarded the Canada Council Award in Creative Writing.

Clare Clifton Brant (1941–1995)
Mohawk psychiatrist

Clare Clifton Brant was a psychiatrist of Mohawk descent. Born in Belleville, Ontario, on 7 July 1941, Brant received his medical degree at Queen's University in Ontario (1965) and then went on to obtain a degree in psychiatry from the University of Western Ontario (1978). He worked as a psychiatrist in private practice and, earlier in his career, was an assistant professor of psychiatry at the University of Western Ontario.

Brant has many scholarly publications to his credit, including articles entitled "Programming for Native American Mental Health" (1982) and "The Examination of the North American Indian" (1983). He served as chairs of the Native Mental Health Association of Canada and the Native Health Program of the Canadian Psychiatric Association.

Joseph Brant (Thayendanegea) (1742–1807)
Mohawk tribal leader

Joseph Brant (Thayendanegea) was a British Army officer and a Mohawk tribal leader. The Mohawk were the easternmost tribe of the Iroquois Confederacy (a group of six nations), and their native territory is located along the Hudson and Mohawk River Valleys in New York State and Canada.

He was the son of a full-blooded Mohawk chief. After the death of the father, his mother remarried a man named Brant; thus he became known as Joseph Brant among the colonists. His sister Molly married Sir William Johnson, a British official who was superintendent in charge of Indians north of the Ohio from 1755 until 1774, and the young Brant went to live in their home as a child.

He attended a Christian school in Connecticut and mastered spoken and written English. In the early 1760s and 1770s, as a translator and diplomat, he helped the English to negotiate with Iroquois tribes. When the American Revolution broke out, Brant aligned himself with the Loyalist cause and traveled to England in 1775. He was quickly commissioned a colonel in the British army and put his diplomacy skills to work enlisting Iroquois allies for the Loyalist cause.

Brant participated in a number of battles directly, and insisted on using his own military tactics and stratagems. In 1777 and 1778, the persistent raids by Indians and British soldiers against settlements in the Ohio Valley convinced General George Washington, the future U.S. President, to send an army into Iroquois country. The Americans succeeded in destroying a number of Iroquois villages, but Brant did not sanction the subsequent American-Iroquois peace treaty and continued to launch raids against American forces.

In appreciation of his military services the English gave him a retirement pension and a large tract of land along the Grand River in Ontario, Canada. Like many others, Brant was an Indian who lived between two worlds. He is credited with having translated the Bible into the Mohawk language and died near his estate near Brantford, Ontario, on 24 November 1807.

Mary (Molly) Brant (1736–1796)
Mohawk tribal leader

Mary Brant, better known as Molly Brant, was probably born in the Mohawk Valley in New York and was reportedly the daughter of a Mohawk sachem. She was a sister of Joseph Brant, a famous Mohawk leader.

Brant first attracted the attention of Sir William Johnson, one of the wealthiest and most influential men in colonial America, when she displayed her spirit and agility by vaulting to the back of a galloping horse behind a military officer. She became Johnson's consort after his first wife, Catherine Weisenberg, died. Her name first appears in Johnson's papers in 1759 when she bore him the first of nine children. In Johnson's will, he referred to them as his natural children by his housekeeper, terms implying no legal marriage.

Brant became the mistress of the Johnson home at Fort Johnson on the Mohawk River in present-day New York State and in 1763 of the new baronial mansion at Johnstown, New York, where Johnson lived a life of gentlemanly elegance in a frontier setting. Brant presided at Johnson Hall with dignity and charm, entertaining distinguished visitors and, by her influence with

Indian leaders, supplementing Johnson's diplomacy in pacifying the Indian nations.

Following Johnson's death in 1774, Brant and her children moved to a farm near Canajoharie, New York, where she engaged in trade. During the Revolutionary War, she and her relatives aided the British. Peter Johnson, a son, was credited with the capture of Ethan Allen during the fighting at Montreal. Joseph Brant, another son, led Iroquois forces against the Americans in the Mohawk Valley and elsewhere. It was Molly Brant who informed the British of the patriot movements before the battle of Oriskany, and Joseph Brant later testified that "she sent ammunition to the Loyalists and fed and assisted such as had taken refuge in the woods." When the American commander, General Nicholas Herkimer, forced Brant to leave her home, she sought refuge with relatives among the Iroquois Nation farther west, where she used her great prestige to keep the Cayuga and Seneca on the British side.

With the coming of peace in 1783, Brant went with other loyalists to Cataraqui (Kingston, Ontario), where she lived for the remainder of her life. A devout Anglican, she died in Kingston, where she was buried in the St. George's Churchyard. Brant contributed in some measure to the great influence exerted by Sir William Johnson over the Indians of the northern colonies; during the Revolution, the force of her personality, buttressed by the dominant role of women in Iroquois society, enabled her to influence the Iroquois toward alliance with the British.

Lester Jack Briggs, Jr. (1948–)
Chippewa college administrator

Lester Jack Briggs, Jr., is president of Fond du Lac Community College. Born at Duluth, Minnesota, on 18 September 1948, Briggs attended Rainy River Community College and Bemidji State College, both in Minnesota, where he completed a bachelor's degree in community service in 1980. He later went on to receive a master's in education administration from the University of Minnesota, Duluth (1990). During these years he also received special training in substance abuse and alcoholism counseling at the University of Minnesota, Duluth, and Rutgers University.

His first professional position was as American Indian student advisor and planning assistant for the Minnesota Higher Education Coordinating Board (1978–1981). He then became regional director for the Services to Indian People Program at Arrowhead Community College in Minnesota (1983–1989). Over the years, Briggs has been involved in many community activities involving education and social welfare, and was named American Indian Administrator of the Year by the Minnesota Education Association in 1986 and 1987.

Ruth M. Bronson (1897–1982)
Cherokee educator

Ruth Bronson was a teacher who devoted her career to helping Indian youth understand and appreciate their heritage. Born in Whitewater, Oklahoma, in 1897, Ruth Bronson began her career as a YMCA playground instructor for Apache children. She studied at the University of Kansas in 1922 and later received an A.B. degree from Mount Holyoke College in South Hadley, Massachusetts. She was employed at the Bureau of Indian Affairs in 1931 and in 1935 taught at Haskell Institute in Kansas.

Bronson served as the director of the Bureau of Indian Affairs scholarship and loan program from 1931 until 1943 and later became the executive secretary of the National Congress of American Indians. In 1957 she took a position as health education specialist for the San Carlos Apache Reservation in Arizona, which she held until her retirement in 1962. After retiring, Bronson worked among the Papago and Yaqui in Arizona as a representative for the Save the Children Foundation, an organization that serves needy children all over the United States. She passed away on 12 June 1982 at the age of eighty-four.

Louis R. Bruce, Jr. (1906–1989)
Oglala Sioux and Mohawk commissioner of Indian affairs

Louis R. Bruce, Jr., is an administrator and businessman of Oglala Sioux descent. Born on the Oglala Sioux Reservation at Pine Ridge, South Dakota, on 30 December 1906, Bruce grew up on the Onandaga Reservation in rural New York where his father served as Methodist pastor. He studied at Cazenovia Seminary, a Methodist school, and later graduated from Syracuse University with a degree in psychology.

During the Great Depression, Bruce proposed a plan to employ Indian youth as counselors and teachers of Indian lore in summer camps for children in New York and other New England states. This program was a huge success, creating jobs for more than six hundred Indian boys. He was soon after appointed New York State director of Indians under the National Youth Administration in 1935.

In the following years, Bruce found success in different types of business and administrative positions. He worked as manager of a large dairy farm (480 acres) that he inherited from his wife's father, as an executive for a national advertising firm, as a special assistant commissioner for the Federal Housing Administration, and as public relations director for a chain of supermarkets.

Bruce was appointed commissioner of Indian affairs in August 1969, becoming the third Indian to be chosen for this position. As commissioner he sought to increase the role of Indian people in business and management. Upon receiving an Indian Council Fire Achievement Award, Bruce said: "The way to Indian progress is involvement. . . . I want to see Indians buying cars from Indians on reservations, and buying food in Indian-owned stores, driving on Indian-planned and Indian-built roads, talking on Indian-owned telephone systems, and living in an Indian-managed economy."

Joseph Bruchac (1942–)
Abenaki writer and editor

Joseph Bruchac lives with his wife Carol in the Adirondack foothills where he was raised by his grandparents. Much of Bruchac's writing draws on that land and the Abenaki heritage from the maternal side of his

Joseph Bruchac.

family. Although his Indian heritage is only part of an ethnic background that includes Slovak and English, his Native roots are deepest and he has cultivated them the most.

Born on 16 October 1942, Bruchac received his bachelor's degree in English from Cornell University (1965), then went on to complete a master's in English from Syracuse University in 1966. From 1966 to 1969 he lived and taught in Ghana, West Africa, and on his return to the United States, founded the Greenfield Review Press. From 1972 to 1974, Bruchac completed the doctoral program at Union Institute Graduate School in Yellow Springs, Ohio. His articles, stories, and poems have appeared in more than five hundred publications and have been translated into several different languages. He has authored more than seventy books, including *Keepers of the Earth* (with Michael J. Caduto), *Tell Me a Tale, Dawn Land, The Waters Between,* and *The Heart of a Chief.*

Bruchac has won several awards for his writing over the years, including fellowships from the National Endowment for the Arts (NEA) and the Rockefeller Foundation, a PEN Syndicated Fiction Award, the Cherokee Nation Prose Award, Wordcraft Circle of Native Writers and Storytellers Writer of the Year, and the 1999 Lifetime Achievement Award from the Native Writers Circle of the Americas.

Leonard Bruguier (Tashunke Hinzi) (1944–)
Yankton Sioux historian

Leonard Bruguier is director of the Institute of American Indian Studies and assistant professor of history at the University of South Dakota. Bruguier was born in Wagner, South Dakota. He earned a bachelor's and master's degree in public administration from the University of South Dakota, and a doctorate at Oklahoma State University. Bruguier served in the U.S. Marine Corps in Vietnam from 1963 to 1970. He reached the rank of sergeant and received a Combat Action Ribbon, a Presidential Unit Citation, a Vietnam Service Medal, a Vietnam Campaign Ribbon, an Armed Forces Expeditionary Medal, and a National Defense Medal.

His research interests focus on the Pipe religion and its influence in Indian-U.S. relations. He is also conducting ongoing research into Indian men and women who served in the U.S. Armed Forces and their impact on reservation, government, and social patterns. Bruguier is a member of the Organization of American Historians and the Western Historical Association. He has received a Minority Doctoral Study Grant by the Oklahoma State Regents for Higher Education, a Towsend Memorial Minority Scholarship, and an Archie

B. Gillfillan Award for Creative Writing. His published works include *Remember Your Relatives, Conference on Reburials, The Yankton Sioux,* and *South Dakota Leaders.*

Louis (Smokey) Bruyere (1948–)
Ojibwa activist

Smokey Bruyere was raised in bush camps in northwestern Ontario. He attended school until the age of eighteen and then worked with a mining company for a year and in the lumber industry in the bush camps for more than ten years. During this time, Bruyere helped establish the Ontario Métis and Non-Status Indian Association, an organization geared to the advancement of the Métis people. The Métis are persons of mixed Indian-European heritage who forged a common identity on the plains of Western Canada in the nineteenth century; non-status Indians are aboriginal people not legally recognized by Canadian authorities as Indians. Bruyere served as president of the association for two years and was involved in constitutional reform and dealings with the provincial government of Ontario, trying to secure better housing and employment services for his people.

In 1979, Bruyere turned his attention to the Native Council of Canada, a national organization representing Métis and non-status Indians. He was subsequently elected president of the council in 1981 and served in this capacity until 1988. During this time, aboriginal issues were attracting greater attention on the national stage, and Bruyere and the council advocated stronger constitutional guarantees to protect aboriginal people. He also was at the forefront of a movement to amend federal law so that Indian women no longer were treated as non-Indians by law when they married non-Indian men. In March 1991, Bruyere was hired by the federal Department of Indian and Northern Affairs as a spokesperson for aboriginal trappers. After eight years of negotiation, Bruyere, as an Indian and Northern Affairs Canada (INAC) member of the International Humane Trapping Standards Negotiating Team agreed to scientific standards with the European Union and Russia for the humane trapping and marketing of fur bearing animals. For their work, the negotiating team was presented with an Award of Excellence by the Canadian government in 1999.

Bruyere has long been a domestic and international advocate of aboriginal people. He has traveled with the World Council of Indigenous Peoples to the United States, Central and South America, and Europe, assisted in the drafting of a United Nations Declaration of Indigenous Peoples, and lectured in many universities throughout the world on indigenous peoples and the law.

Buffalo Hump (1810–1870)
Comanche tribal leader

Born in the early 1800s, Buffalo Hump proved himself as a war chief of the Comanche in his many raids into Texas and Mexico for horses and slaves. Buffalo Hump also led Comanche attacks on the neighboring Cheyenne and Arapaho. He is most often remembered for his participation in the attacks following the Council House Affair in 1838. The Texas Rangers, who were pursuing the Comanche and had suffered heavy casualties, seized a number of chiefs who had come to San Antonio to bargain for the release of Texas prisoners held by the Comanche. Thirty-five Comanche were killed during the fight even though the Comanche were negotiating under a flag of truce. In reaction, Buffalo Hump led a war party down from the Comanche lands, north of the Red River along the Guadalupe Valley, all the way through Texas to the Gulf of Mexico, attacking villages and killing settlers as they went. The Texas Rangers ambushed the Indians on their return northward at Plum Creek, near Lockhart, and managed to kill some warriors. The breaking of the truce at the Council House had proved much more costly to Texas than to the Comanche.

Buffalo Hump became principal chief of the Penateka Band of Comanche in 1849, following the cholera epidemic that swept through the Southern Plains. In the late 1850s, Texas Rangers and army regulars launched a coordinated campaign against the Comanche. Buffalo Hump managed to evade the combined force although his band suffered a major defeat at Rush Springs, Oklahoma. Fifty-six warriors and two women died.

In October 1865, Buffalo Hump, with chiefs from other Southern Plains tribes, attended a treaty council with U.S. commissioners along the Little Arkansas River, in present-day Kansas. As a result of the treaty, the Comanche, Kiowa, Kiowa-Apache, Southern Cheyenne, and Southern Arapaho were forced to relinquish claims to territory north of the Arkansas River.

Buffalo Hump's son, who inherited his father's name, carried on the fighting under the new Comanche chief Quanah Parker.

George Burdeau (1944–)
Blackfeet producer, director, and screenwriter

George Burdeau is a screenwriter and director of Blackfeet descent. He was born on 16 November 1944. He received a bachelor's degree in communications from the University of Washington and did graduate work at the Anthropology Film Center in Santa Fe, New Mexico. He also studied at the Institute of American Indian Arts in Santa Fe.

The earliest of his works include various documentaries on Native American subjects that were produced for the Public Broadcasting System (PBS), and since the mid-1980s, Burdeau has become increasingly active as a producer and director for major network television programs. His projects include *Forest Spirits, Surviving Columbus, Colonization of the Pacific*, the Plains Indian segment of *The Native Americans* series for TBS, *The Witness, Cherry Tree*, and *Backbone of the World*. Burdeau is currently a producer/director for the Alaskan Native Heritage Association and a consulting producer for the Pequot Tribe.

Diane Burns (1957–)
Anishinaabe (Ojibwa) and Chemehuevi poet

Diane Burns is a poet of Anishinaabe (Ojibwa) and Chemehuevi descent. She studied at the Institute of American Indian Arts in Santa Fe, New Mexico, where she was awarded the Congressional Medal of Merit for academic and artistic excellence. She also attended Barnard College in New York City.

Her first book of poetry, *Riding the One-Eyed Ford* (1981), was nominated for the William Carlos Williams Award and was named one of the ten best books of the year by the St. Marks Poetry Project. Her poetry has also appeared in magazines and journals such as *The Greenfield Review, Sunbury, White Pine Journal, New York Waterways*, and *Hard Press*.

Burns is also a painter and illustrator and has been a book reviewer for the Council on Inter-Racial Books for Children. She is a member of the Poet's Overland Expeditional Troop (POET), which performs theatrical presentations of poetry in galleries and schools throughout the United States. Burns also belongs to the Third World Writers Association and the Feminist Writers Guild.

Barney Furman Bush (1945–)
Shawnee and Cayuga poet and educator

Barney Bush, Shawnee and Cayuga, is president of LifeBlood International, a corporation designed to create small businesses, whose profits will endow the new College of the Redwinds, the first indigenous peoples' institution of its kind in the world.

Born in August 1945, he studied graphic arts at the Institute of American Indian Arts in Santa Fe, New Mexico, earning a bachelor's degree in humanities at Fort Lewis College in Durango, Colorado (1972). He later completed a master's degree in English and fine arts at the University of Idaho (1978).

His books of poetry and fiction include *Longhouse of the Blackberry Moon*, *My Horse and a Jukebox*, *Petroglyphs*, *Inherit the Blood*, *By Due Process*, and *Redemption of the Serpent*, a recently completed novel. His poems are widely published, anthologized, translated into more than a dozen languages, and recorded, including *A Sense of Journey*, *Left for Dead*, *Remake of the American Dream*, *Destinations*, *Oyate*, and *By Due Process*.

Bush has served as visiting writer/artist in public schools and colleges through the arts councils of a dozen states. He has been awarded grants and fellowships from the National Endowment for the Arts, PEN, the Author's Guild, and the Newberry Library. His work has been used in international films and for public radio and television.

He has taught his artforms, Native American literature, and related subjects at the University of Wisconsin, Brunswick College, the Institute of American Indian Arts, and New Mexico Highlands University. He has three grown sons and is a member of the Four Corners Gourd Dance Society.

George Bushotter (1864–1892)
Teton Sioux ethnographer

George Bushotter lived only twenty-eight years, but during his short lifetime he crossed the boundaries between two worlds and became the first Lakota to write an account of his own people in their own language. Born in Dakota Territory in 1864, he showed many signs throughout his childhood that he would probably become a medicine man. Instead he traveled east, motivated by a curiosity about Americans and a desire to learn more about them. He entered Hampton Institute in Hampton, Virginia, in 1878 and made such excellent progress that he worked as an assistant teacher in 1881.

In 1887, Bushotter began working for the Reverend James Owen Dorsey, a Siouan scholar employed by the Bureau of Ethnology in Washington, D.C. Dorsey worked out a method by which he could work independently, writing a myth or other text phonetically in the Lakota language and then adding free translations and more detailed word-for-word translations in English. In this way, he produced some 258 separate texts and a total of 3,296 pages of Lakota ethnographic material during a period of only ten months. These texts, currently among the holdings of the National Anthropological Archives (Smithsonian Institution), are important not only because they are the earliest cultural documents obtained

from a Lakota Indian, but because Bushotter himself determined the subject matter.

Bushotter suffered periodically from various illnesses after he arrived in the East and passed away on 2 February 1892, in Hedgesville, West Virginia.

Frank Arthur Calder (1915–)
Nisga'a tribal leader

Frank Calder was the first Indian member of a Canadian legislature, serving as a member of the National Assembly of British Columbia for twenty-six years and as a provincial cabinet minister for a short time in the 1970s. His people, the Nisga'a, occupy the Nass River valley and adjacent lands of the British Columbia coastline. Calder was raised by his aunt and uncle, whose own son had died, and in accordance with Nisga'a custom, they adopted him in order to pass family rank onto a son. His adoptive mother, Louisa, was the eldest of six sisters in a leading Nisga'a family. His adoptive father, Arthur Calder, himself played a leading role in the political life of the Nisga'a Nation. Calder attended a Methodist residential school far from home that was established to inculcate Anglo-Canadian values in First Nation children. Much of his tribal cultural learning occurred during summers when, home from school, he went fishing with his father and other elders who instructed him on his future responsibilities as a Nisga'a leader.

Calder has been an important political leader of the Nisga'a Nation. He was the founder and president of the Nisga'a Tribal Council, which united four diverse clans (Eagle, Wolf, Raven, and Killer Whale) located in four communities in northwest British Columbia (Kincolith, Greenville, Canyon City, and Aiyansh). He is also widely known as a result of the landmark Supreme Court of Canada decision in *Calder v. The Queen* (1973), in which the Court held that aboriginal people located in British Columbia possessed special rights to their ancestral lands that survived the establishment of the province. He received a Lifetime Achievement Award by the National Aboriginal Achievement Foundation in 1996.

Ben Nighthorse Campbell (1933–)
Northern Cheyenne U.S. senator

Campbell is the first Native American elected as a United States senator. Born in Auburn, California, he received a bachelor's degree in physical education and fine arts from San Jose State University in 1957 and later attended Meiji University in Tokyo in 1960 as a special research student. Before entering college, Campbell served in the U.S. Air Force from 1951 to 1953, stationed in Korea, attaining the rank of Airman Second Class.

Senator Campbell's athletic career in judo was particularly outstanding, because he took the gold medal at the Pan-American Games in 1963 and won the United States championship in his weight division three times. He was also a member of the United States Olympic team in 1964 and wrote a judo manual, *Judo Drill Training* (1975).

He became the second Native American elected to the Colorado legislature, where he served from 1983 to 1986. His committee assignments included agriculture and natural affairs and business and labor. During this period he was also appointed as an advisor to the Colorado Commission on International Trade and the Arts and Humanities. He was named Outstanding Legislator of 1984 by the Colorado Bankers Association and was voted one of the Ten Best Legislators of 1986 in a survey of state legislators conducted by the Denver Post and News Center 4.

Campbell has always been a man of many talents. Campbell is also a self-employed jewelry designer, rancher, and a trainer of champion quarter horses. He was inducted into the Council of Forty-Four Chiefs by his Northern Cheyenne tribe in Lame Deer, Montana.

Senator Campbell currently belongs to four key Senate committees. He chairs the Indian Affairs Committee and the Treasury and General Government Committee. He is a member of the Interior, Foreign Operations, Transportation and Commerce, Justice, State, and Judiciary subcommittees. He is vice-chairman of the National Parks, Historic Preservation, and Recreation subcommittee. Senator Campbell also serves on the Veterans' Affairs Committee and is co-chairman of the Helsinki Commission.

Canassatego (d. 1750)
Onondaga tribal leader

This Onondaga leader was a strong supporter of the Iroquois League of Nations, the government of the Mohawk, Oneida, Onondaga, Tuscarora, Cayuga, and Seneca of present-day upstate New York. He represented the league in a number of important conferences, alliances, and agreements with English colonists. Canassatego worked to ensure that no treaties were signed by members of the league without full consent of the league's governing body.

In 1742, Canassatego, with translator Conrad Weiser, negotiated an alliance between the Iroquois League and Pennsylvania officials who were anxious to ally themselves with the Indians in order to prevent French encroachment. During these negotiations, Canassatego demonstrated a keen understanding of republican principles and urged the English colonists to respect the pledges and concepts of the league and its "league of friendship" with the colonists. A few years later in 1750 at Albany, New York, Canassatego also advised the English on issues concerning colonial unity. He recommended that the English colonies form a union like the Iroquois League, since the colonies would be stronger united than when they acted separately.

It is believed that Canassatego was killed by a fellow Iroquois allied with the French. According to English reports from this era, Canassatego was an impressive speaker with a presence that commanded attention from all persons in a room with him. This might explain why, after his death, he was "immortalized" in a British literary work that romanticized the Iroquois leader and built him into a nearly mythical figure. John Shebbeare immortalized Canassatego in his book *Lydia, or, Filial Piety* (1755), which satirized the materialism, impersonality, and inequality of British urban life as compared to the Iroquois political and social views of equality and negotiated political consensus.

Captain Jack (d. 1873)
Modoc tribal leader

Captain Jack was a famous Indian leader in the Modoc War of 1872–1873. The original territory of the Modocs was centered around lower Klamath Lake and Tule Lake in southeastern Oregon and northeastern California. Modern descendants of the tribe also live on reservations in Oklahoma.

Born somewhere along the Lost River in present-day Modoc County, California, the man whom the U.S. settlers would call Captain Jack was originally given the Modoc name Kintpuash. He became the leader of his band when his father died in 1846. Captain Jack was drawn into the Modoc Wars through a complex series of events that began in 1864, when the Modoc signed away much of their indigenous territory and were removed to the Klamath Reservation in Oregon. The living conditions on the reservation were miserable; there was much disease and not enough food to support both the Modoc and the Klamath tribe. The Modoc request for their own reservation in California was rejected.

Captain Jack and the Modoc returned to California anyway, but there were many complaints from white settlers and the federal government ordered troops to the area in 1872. A series of violent incidents ensued;

then Captain Jack and his followers escaped and worked their way south to a volcanic area with lava formations that offered excellent natural fortifications. Another Modoc group joined them so that the rebel group consisted of about two hundred people, eighty of whom were warriors. They ambushed a wagon train on December 22, thus obtaining more ammunition, and in January 1873 they successfully repulsed a force of over three hundred regular soldiers led by Lieutenant Colonel Frank Wheaton.

Shortly thereafter, General Edward Canby planned to lead another attack and gathered a force of about a thousand men. At the same time a peace plan was set in motion. The first negotiation on February 28 produced no results, and at the second meeting Captain Jack produced a hidden revolver and fatally shot General Canby. Modoc warriors Boston Charlie and Schonchin John also fired on the peace commissioners that had been sent by President Grant, and the Modoc retreated to another lava formation to the south. Throughout these months there were scattered conflicts such as the one that took place on 26 April 1873, when the warrior Scarfaced Charlie attacked a patrol of sixty-three soldiers and killed twenty-five, including all five officers.

Despite their successes, however, the Modoc were badly lacking food and water, and their forces became less and less unified. General Jefferson C. Davis finally organized a relentless pursuit of the scattered bands that remained, and Captain Jack and other leaders were finally cornered in a cave and captured on 1 June 1873. Captain Jack was executed by hanging on 3 October 1878, while two other Modoc leaders were sentenced to life imprisonment on Alcatraz, a penal facility on an island in San Francisco Bay. On the night after the hanging, Captain Jack's head was stolen by grave robbers, embalmed, and put on display in a carnival that toured cities in the eastern United States.

The Modoc War was one of the few Indian wars that ever took place in California, as tribes of the California region were not highly organized militarily. Because of this and the relatively late date of the uprising, it had a shocking effect on the public, gaining a great deal of national attention. A more detailed account of the events described here is given in Keith Murray's book *The Modocs and their War* (1969).

Douglas Joseph Cardinal (1934–)
Métis architect

Douglas Cardinal is an internationally renowned architect. Born in Red Deer, Alberta, Douglas Cardinal was the eldest son of a family of eight. His father was half Blackfoot and worked as a provincial wildlife

Douglas J. Cardinal.

warden. The Blackfoot are located on the plains of western Canada. His mother was a nurse. Cardinal enrolled in the University of British Columbia School of Architecture at the age of nineteen, but was asked to withdraw from the program in his second year because his architectural designs were considered too radical. Several years later, he enrolled at the University of Texas and graduated in 1963. He then returned to Red Deer to begin an architecture career that continues today.

Cardinal's first commission was to design the round Guloien House, a private residence, in Sylvan Lake, Alberta. He then designed St. Mary's Church in Red Deer, pioneering the use of computer-enhanced electronic drawing. St. Mary's Church is considered by many to be an architectural triumph, with its circular and semi-enclosed design. In the 1970s, he immersed himself in Native religion and numerous aboriginal causes. In 1983, Cardinal was awarded the commission to design the Canadian Museum of Civilization in Hull, Quebec. With its unique curves, the museum now stands along the banks of the Ottawa River, opposite the Parliament buildings and the Supreme Court of Canada.

His firm, a pioneer and world leader for incorporating computers in architecture, has designed and undertaken many projects, including the design commission for the National Museum of the American Indian, the Edmonton Space Science Center, the Saskatchewan Indian Federated College in Regina, Saskatchewan, and a major hotel complex and Children and Elders' Center for the Oneida Indian Nation of New York.

He is a recipient of the Order of Canada, Canada's highest honor. In 1999 he was awarded the Royal Architectural Institute of Canada Gold Medal, the highest award bestowed in the Canadian profession of architecture.

Gil Cardinal (1950–)
Cree/Métis filmmaker

Gil Cardinal is president and co-founder of Kanata Productions. A skilled director, producer, writer, and editor, Gil Cardinal has been working both in front of and behind the camera for over twenty years. He graduated in 1973 from the Radio and Television Arts Program at the Northern Alberta Institute of Technology in Edmonton, and in 1976 became the director and associate producer of *Come Alive*, a daily, live magazine-format show in Alberta. Cardinal continued to produce and direct a variety of shows, including *Shadow Puppets*, a series of seven programs adapting Cree and Blackfoot legends to electronic animation.

Cardinal began his association with Canada's National Film Board, a federally established organization devoted to the advancement of film, in 1980. His numerous projects include *Children of Alcohol* (1983), a documentary on the effects of parental alcoholism; *Discussions in Bioethics: The Courage of One's Convictions* (1985), an inquiry into medical/legal ethics; and *Fort McPherson* (1986), a look at a community's struggle with alcohol and suicide. *Foster Child* (1987), which traces Cardinal's search for his natural family and features him as a director, associate editor, and subject, has won nine film festival awards since its premier.

Cardinal's varied experience in Canadian media also includes a half-hour television drama, *Bordertown Cafe* (1988), and a one-hour documentary, *Tikinagan* (1991), for Tamarack Productions of Toronto, Ontario. His latest National Film Board documentary, *The Spirit Within* (1990), co-directed with Wil Campbell, focuses on the importance of Indian spirituality for Native inmates in Canada.

He directed numerous episodes of the Gemini award-winning CBC series *North of 60*, and episodes of CBC television's Native anthology series *Four Directions* and *The Rez*. In 1997, Cardinal received a National Aboriginal Achievement Award for his work in film and television.

Harold Cardinal (1945–)
Cree tribal leader/scholar

Harold Cardinal is a political leader and writer, active on the provincial and national level. He was born in High Prairie, Alberta, on 27 January 1945, and raised on the Sucker Creek Reserve in north-central Alberta. Cardinal attended Joussard Indian Residential School and then high school in Edmonton, Alberta. Cardinal interrupted two years of university study at St. Patrick's College in Ottawa, Ontario, where he studied sociology, to work with the Canadian Union of Students as associate secretary for Indian affairs in 1966 and 1967. That same year, Cardinal was elected president of the Canadian Indian Youth Council.

In May 1968, Cardinal returned to Alberta to take up what he thought would be a summer job with the Alberta Native Communications Society. In June 1968,

Harold Cardinal.

he was elected president of the Indian Association of Alberta, with associated membership on the board of the National Indian Brotherhood, a national organization devoted to the advancement of aboriginal rights, and worked with others to develop the Assembly of First Nations.

As president of the Indian Association of Alberta, Cardinal served nine terms in office, initiating a variety of programs to promote Native culture and economic development. He assisted in the drafting of Citizens Plus (1970), an aboriginal response to federal efforts to abolish differential treatment of aboriginal people in Canada. He authored two texts, *The Unjust Society* (1969, 1999) which describes the social and political conditions of First Nations in Canada, and *The Rebirth of Canada's Indians* (1977) affirming the importance of Indian identity and culture. In 1977, Cardinal was appointed regional director general of Indian affairs for a controversial seven-month term, after which he became a consultant to northern Alberta Indian Bands. He worked as the Prairie Treaty Alliance representative in the Constitutional Conferences with the Assembly of First Nations, federal, and provincial governments.

In 1992, Cardinal studied law at the University of Saskatchewan. He obtained his degree in law and earned a master's in law at Harvard University. He was awarded an honorary doctorate of law and an indigenous scholar-in-residence from the University of Alberta. From 1997 to 1999, he worked as a negotiator for the Treaty Eight First Nations of Alberta Bilateral Process. Cardinal is currently working with the Assembly of First Nations on traditional governance and treaty rights while completing his doctorate in law at the University of British Columbia.

Tantoo Cardinal (1950–)
Cree/Métis actress

Born in Fort McMurray and raised in Anzac, a small town 350 miles northeast of Edmonton, Alberta, Tantoo Cardinal is one of Canada's most renowned Native film actresses. Never formally trained as an actress, she began her career in the 1970s with a series of small roles in film, theater, and television. Her first feature film appearance occurred in *Marie Anne* in 1977, produced in Canada by Fraser Films and directed by Martin Walters. In 1985, Cardinal played the lead role in *Loyalties*, a feature film written, directed, and produced by Anne Wheeler, which tells the fictional story of a British man who moves to the Canadian plains to escape his past. For her stirring performance, Cardinal was nominated for the prestigious Canadian film award, the Genie, as best actress, and she received a best actress award at the American Indian Film Festival, as

well as a number of other awards. Her performance served to expand Cardinal's audience beyond the Native community in which she was well known.

She has enjoyed significant success in television, film, and theater. Her credits include *Grand Avenue, Where the Rivers Flow North, Dances With Wolves, Smoke Signals, The Education of Little Tree, Honey Mocassin, The Campbells, Street Legal,* and *Wonderworks,* as well as hosting a five-episode public television series *As Long as the Rivers Flow* and a nine-episode series entitled *Native Indians: Images of Reality.*

Edward D. Castillo (1947–)
Cahuilla and Luise–o historian, anthropologist, and professor

Edward Castillo is a university professor specializing in Native American Studies. Born at San Jacinto, California, on 25 August 1947, Castillo graduated from the University of California, Riverside, in 1969 and went on to receive his master's degree and doctorate in anthropology from the University of California, Berkeley (1977). He was a lecturer in Native American Studies at UC Berkeley from 1970 to 1971 and 1973 to 1977,

Ed Castillo.

then became associate professor of Native American Studies and director of the Native American Studies Program at UC Santa Cruz from 1977 until 1982. He was director of a Title IV Program for the Laytonville, California, Unified School District from 1985 until 1988, and since then he has been the director of the Native American Studies Program at Sonoma State University in Rohnert Park, California.

He has numerous publications in anthropology and Native American Studies, but is best known for the chapters entitled "History of the Impact of Euro-American Exploration and Settlement on the Indians of California" and "Recent Secular Movements among California Indians, 1900–1973" in the Smithsonian Institution's *Handbook of North American Indians*, Volume 8: California (1978). He also wrote a book entitled *Native American Perspectives on the Hispanic Colonization of Alta California* (1990).

John Castillo (1956–)
Chiricahua Apache social worker and community organizer

John Castillo is the former executive director of the Southern California Indian Center, Inc. (SCIC), located in Garden Grove, California. Castillo's commitment to work in the Indian community was encouraged by his parents. His father moved to Gardena, California, from Arizona. John, his three sisters, and one brother were born in Southern California. His parents emphasized the importance of working within and for the Native American community because they knew firsthand the needs of reservation and urban Indians.

Castillo attended Orange Coast College for two years and then went on to graduate with a bachelor of arts in ethnic studies from California State University, Fullerton. In 1979, he entered the University of California, Los Angeles (UCLA) in the graduate school of social welfare. In 1981, he graduated with a master's degree in social work with an emphasis on community organization and joined SCIC, becoming executive director in 1989. Castillo has worked in many capacities in the SCIC, including as a classroom trainer and coordinator. He established the SCIC's program sites in Los Angeles and Long Beach, before assuming administrative work in the main office. In October 1985, Castillo was named a Kellog National Fellow, a prestigious award. From 1985 through 1989, he conducted research on the leadership skill, styles, knowledge, and motivations of tribal leaders in the United States and abroad.

Castillo has taught American Indian studies and social work at California State University at Long Beach. He has also served as chair of the Los Angeles City/County Native American Indian Commission, the Los Angeles County Child Welfare Task Force, and the Los Angeles American Indian Mental Health Task Force. He has lectured on American Indian issues for over two hundred television and radio shows, served as guest lecturer on American Indian issues at major universities, and has published articles on job training programs.

Castillo's years of service to the urban Indian community are the result of his early vision and commitment to make a contribution to the community. In recent years he has worked for nonprofit agencies related to Indian affairs.

Duane Champagne (1951–)
Turtle Mountain Chippewa sociologist and professor

Duane Champagne is a sociologist and university professor of Chippewa descent. Most of his writings

Duane Champagne, director of the UCLA American Indian Studies Center.

focus on issues of social, cultural, and political change in American Indian societies as they adapted to European political domination, cultural interpenetration, and economic incorporation.

Champagne received his bachelor's degree in mathematics from North Dakota State University in 1973. After serving a year with Volunteer in Service to America (VISTA), a domestic peace corps program, he finished a master's degree in sociology at North Dakota State University in 1975. In 1982, he received a Ph.D. in sociology from Harvard University. In 1982 and 1983, Champagne received a postdoctoral award from the Rockefeller Foundation and, during this time, completed fieldwork trips to the Tlingit of southeast Alaska and to the Northern Cheyenne in Montana. He taught at the University of Wisconsin, Milwaukee, in 1983 and 1984 and started teaching at the University of California, Los Angeles (UCLA) in 1984, where he became full professor in 1997. In 1986, Champagne became editor of the *American Indian Culture and Research Journal*, and, in 1991, he became director of the UCLA American Indian Studies Center, which carries out research, offers a master's degree program in American Indian studies, and publishes books for academic and Indian audiences.

Champagne has published broadly in both sociology and American Indian studies. He has published two books, *American Indian Societies: Strategies and Conditions of Political and Cultural Survival* (1989), and *Social Order and Political Change: Constitutional Governments among the Cherokee, the Choctaw, the Chickasaw, and the Creek* (1992). In addition, he has published articles in various academic journals, edited many books, and contributed numerous chapters to other books. In 1999 he received Writer of the Year award for anthology/collections from the Wordcraft Circle of Native Writers and Storytellers.

Paul L. A. H. Chartrand (1943–)
Métis lawyer and professor

Paul Chartrand is a private consultant and a commissioner on the Manitoba Aboriginal Justice Implementation Commission. He was born to J. Aime Chartrand and Antoinette Bouvier in the historic Métis fishing village of Saint-Laurent, Manitoba. Until the age of seven, Chartrand lived with his family in a log cabin. His father was a fur trapper, and he would dry muskrat skins on frames in the house. His father also dug seneca root, a medicinal plant. Chartrand himself snared rabbits for food and hunted small game and waterfowl in

the nearby marshes. He attended school in the village, where missionary nuns were his teachers.

When he finished grade twelve, Chartrand moved with his family to Winnipeg, and he continued his studies with degrees from the Manitoba Teachers College and the University of Winnipeg, Manitoba. He later studied law at the Queensland University of Technology in Australia, graduating with an honors degree, and at the University of Saskatchewan, where he specialized in Native law and received a master of law degree. In 1991, he was appointed by the Canadian government to serve as a commissioner for the Royal Commission on Aboriginal Peoples, which was established to inquire into and report on a wide range of matters relating to aboriginal peoples in Canada.

He has served as head of the Department of Native Studies at the University of Manitoba and was a founding member of the Aboriginal Healing Foundation. He is a member of the Indigenous Bar Association of Canada, a member of the advisory committee for the Canadian National Judicial Institute, the author of numerous publications in law and policy, and performs consulting work in the area of domestic, comparative, and international law and policy. He lives in Victoria, British Columbia, is married, and has three children.

Dean Chavers (1941–)
Lumbee educator

Dean Chavers, a member of the Lumbee tribe, is an important figure in Native American education. Born in Pembroke, North Carolina, on 4 February 1941, Chavers attended the University of Richmond from 1960 to 1962. He then entered the United States Air Force and served with distinction as a navigator, flying 138 missions during the Vietnam Conflict. He left active duty in 1968 with the rank of captain, having won the Distinguished Flying Cross, the Air Medal, and eight other decorations. He returned to school and received a bachelor's degree in journalism from the University of California, Berkeley (1970), then went on to obtain master's degrees in communications (1973) and anthropology (1975) from Stanford University in Palo Alto, California. He later received his Ph.D. in communications at Stanford, writing a dissertation entitled "Social Structure and the Diffusion of Innovations: A Study of Teachers at Four Indian Boarding High Schools and the Effects of their Interpersonal Communication Behavior on their Adoption of New Ideas in Education" (1976).

Dean Chavers.

Even as a student, Chavers was very productive in communications and education, serving as the managing editor of *Indian Voice* magazine (1972) and as an assistant professor of Native American studies at Hayward State University (1972–74). During this period he was chair of the Higher Education Committee of the California Indian Education Association.

Between 1970 and 1978, Chavers was the president of the Native American Scholarship Fund, an organization which raised more than $300,000 for Indian college students and made 522 grants to Indian students in northern California. He served as president of Bacone College in Muskogee, Oklahoma, from 1978 to 1981, then returned to his work as an educational fundraiser and communications consultant in the position of president of his own company: Dean Chavers and Associates (1981–1988). He resumed his post as president of the Native American Scholarships Fund, now called Catching the Dream, and continues working for this important organization today.

Chavers has won awards and honors throughout his life, including the Virginia State spelling championship as a high school student in 1959. He has published five books, including *How to Write Winning Proposals*

(1983), *Funding Guide for Native Americans* (1983), *Tribal Indian Development Directory* (1985), and *The National Indian Grant Directory* (2000), and more than thirty articles.

Shirley Cheechoo (contemporary)
Cree filmmaker

Shirley Cheechoo, a member of the Cree Nation, James Bay, Quebec, is an award-winning actress, producer, director, and visual artist. She first gained national attention in 1991 with her play, *Path With No Moccasins*. She made her directorial debut with the short film *Silent Tears* (1997), which has won several film festival awards for Best Short Film. It was screened at the 1998 Sundance Film Festival and was awarded the Telefilm Canada/Television Northern Canada Award for Best Canadian Aboriginal Language Television Program.

Cheechoo is the first aboriginal woman to write, produce, direct, and act in a feature length film from Canada. In 1998, she attended the Sundance Institute's filmmaker/screenwriters lab, where she workshopped and filmed scenes of *Backroads*, a 1970s story of three sisters who suffer the consequences of racism and sexism when one of them is accused of murder. The 1999 movie was screened at the 2000 Sundance film festival. Cheechoo has also appeared on several Canadian film and television series and programs, including *The Rez*.

Her latest work is *Tracks in the Snow* (2000), a short film documenting a sixty-two-mile traditional journey into the bush during which Cree students, adults, and elders camped for four days and four nights, teaching the children the traditional way of life.

Michael Chiago (1946–)
Tohono O'Odham illustrator and dancer

Michael Chiago is an illustrator whose art reflects his experiences as a powwow dancer. Born in Kohatk Village on the Tohono O'Odham Reservation in Arizona on 6 April 1946, Chiago started dancing and drawing when he was just a boy. He attended St. John's Academy High School in Laveen, Arizona, then joined the U.S. Marines, and served in Vietnam and Okinawa.

On returning home, Chiago studied commercial art and magazine layout techniques at the Maricopa Technical School. He is best known for a style of painting that he developed by himself. He uses water color and adds a special coating or glaze to certain parts when the painting is finished, thus producing a surface of unusual depth and brilliance.

Chiago's paintings are surrealistic in character, rather than being strictly representational, and they often depict dramatically costumed Indian dancers, drawing on Chiago's personal experiences as a powwow dancer who has toured throughout Arizona, California, Nevada, and the East Coast. Chiago has been recognized as an outstanding dancer since he was a young man, and he often attends powwows to watch and learn from the techniques of other dancers. All these images find a place in his paintings, which are included in the permanent collection at the Heard Museum in Phoenix, Arizona, and are often exhibited throughout Arizona and New Mexico.

Robert Keams Chiago (1942–)
Navajo educator

Robert K. Chiago was born on 22 June 1942 in Arizona. He received a bachelor of arts degree in education from Arizona State University in Tempe in 1965. He served in Vietnam from 1967 to 1968 as an officer in the United States Marine Corps, where he attained the rank of captain. He was company commander of a marine unit near Phu Bai and Hue and served with the First Battalion Ninth Marines at Con Tien. He was logistics officer with Shore Party Battalion in Khe Sahn, Dong Ha, and in other parts of Vietnam.

After the Vietnam War, Chiago received a master's degree in education from Northern Illinois University in 1970 and his first post was as associate director at the American Indian Culture Center at UCLA. In 1971 he was the director of the Ramah Navajo School Board (now called Pine Hills School) in New Mexico and, from 1971 to 1973, he was the director of the Navajo Division of Education in the Navajo Nation (Reservation). From 1973 to 1983, Chiago was the director of Native American Studies, director of the Indian Education Program, and a visiting assistant professor of humanities at the University of Utah, Salt Lake City. He has also served as special assistant to the chairman of the Navajo Tribal Council, and deputy assistant director for intergovernmental operations in the Department of Economic Security of the state of Arizona. From 1988 to 1991, Chiago was the director of the Department of Education of the Salt River Pima-Maricopa Indian Community. During that period, with the aid of grants from the U.S. Department of Education, he established three learning centers in the reservation. In 1991, Chiago was appointed the executive director of NACIE, the National Advisory Council on Indian Education, and managing editor of NACIE's newsletter.

Chiago has published several articles including "A Review of Indian Energy Resources from a Manpower and Educational Perspective" in *Bureau of Indian Affairs Education Research Bulletin* 6, number 1 (1978) and "Making Education Work for the American Indian," published in *Theory into Practice* XX, number 1 (1981).

Chiago has been a delegate to the White House Conference on Indian Education Advisory Committee and is currently working as a BIA line education officer for schools at the Ft. Apache Agency.

Rosemary Ackley Christensen (1939–)
Mole Lake and Bad River Wisconsin Ojibwe educator

Rosemary Ackley Christensen teaches at the University of Wisconsin, Green Bay. Born on the Bad River Reservation in Wisconsin on 16 February 1939, Christensen received her master's degree in education from Harvard University (1971) and obtained her doctorate in education at the University of Minnesota (1999). Her dissertation was entitled "Anishinaabeg Medicine Wheel Leadership: The Work of David Courchene, Jr."

In addition to teaching, Christensen has ample experience as an administrator, curriculum developer, writer, researcher, and Indian education advocate. She is a founding member of the National Indian Education Association (NIEA), and in recent years she worked with the Ojibwa language, writing and producing five units for family use.

Edward P. Churchill, Sr. (1923–)
Tlingit fisherman and tribal leader

Edward P. Churchill, Sr., is a Tlingit fisherman and lobbyist for Alaska Natives and natural resources. The Tlingit are a Northwest Coast tribe occupying the southeastern Alaskan coastline from Yakutat Bay to Cape Fox.

Born at Ketchikan, Alaska, on 1 January 1923, Churchill graduated from Wrangell (Alaska) High School in 1941 and became first mate on a tugboat for the U.S. Corps of Engineers (1942–1944). He served in the U.S. Army from 1944 to 1946 and has mainly worked as a commercial fisherman since then. Since 1988, he has been the chairman of Alaska Aquaculture, a fish hatchery at Burnett Inlet, Alaska, and a member of the Southeast Alaska Native Fisheries and Native Resources Commission.

Churchill has been active as a lobbyist for Alaska Native land claims in Washington, D.C., and is the only

Rosemary Auckley Christensen.

Ward Churchill. (Photo by Leah Renae Kelly)

Indian to have been elected mayor of Wrangell, Alaska. Churchill is a member of the Alaska Native Brotherhood and he has served as secretary and treasurer of the Salmon Bay Protection Association.

Ward Churchill (1947–)

Creek/Keetoowah Cherokee Métis activist, academic, and educator

After reading one of Ward Churchill's many books, including *Fantasies of the Master Race: Literature, Cinema, and the Colonization of American Indians* (1992), *Agents of Repression: The FBI's Secret War Against the Black Panther Party and the American Indian Movement* (1988), and *Indian Are Us? Culture and Genocide in Native North America* (1994), it becomes clear that he holds important opinions not to be ignored. His work in academia and his role as an activist have bestowed upon Churchill a serious reputation for trying to create and inspire change across Native America. Specifically, Churchill's goal is to incite others to question the reality that oppressors create for subaltern peoples and to explore the power that lies in refusing to accept that reality.

The to-be academic was born and raised in and around Urbana, Illinois, to Maralyn Allen and Jack Churchill. His parents divorced early and his mother remarried, eventually providing Churchill with two half-brothers and a half-sister. Churchill graduated from Elmwood Consolidated High School and received his associate's degree from Illinois Central College.

Churchill's experiences in the Vietnam War awoke his radical sentiments. In 1968 Churchill found himself sent on missions into "Indian Country," a phrase used in Vietnam to refer to the Vietcong's territory. He then received an undergraduate degree from Sangaman State University with a major in communications. Churchill continued his education at Sangaman and received a master's degree in cross-cultural communications in 1975.

While focused on academics and activism, Churchill was also an artist. His work, which consisted mostly of painting and printmaking, was exhibited at nationally recognized museums across the United States. The art Churchill created related to his activism and academic work. In 1983, however, he decided to focus solely on these latter aspects of his life, leaving his artwork behind.

Since then Churchill has been actively amassing job titles and positions in activist organizations and academia. He was the co-director of the American Indian Movement of Colorado, the vice-chairperson of the American Anti-Defamation Council, the national spokesperson for the Leonard Peltier Defense Fund, and the associate chair of the Department of Ethnic Studies at the University of Colorado, Boulder. He is the author or editor of approximately seventeen books and is currently a full professor of ethnic studies and joint professor of communications with a specialization in American Indian Studies at the University of Colorado, Boulder.

Churchill does not draw a line between his roles as an activist and academic. Because there is no such thing as objectivity, he argues, there should never be a line between the two professional fields. His objective is to integrate his life and work, something he has done successfully for many years.

The professor is presently working on a retooling of *Indians Are Us?*, which examines the connections between American culture and genocide in Native North America. In addition, he is completing a companion book to *Native North American Studies*, a comprehensive history of FBI repression, and a book to be titled *Diversions of Justice*. He currently lives in Boulder County, Colorado, with his wife, photographer Leah Renae Kelly.

Carter Blue Clark.

Carter Blue Clark (1946–)
Muscogee (Creek) historian

Carter Blue "CB" Clark is interim director of the Native American Legal Resource Center and David Pendleton Professor of American Indian studies at Oklahoma City University. He is a member of the Muscogee (Creek) Nation, a member of the Cedar River/New Tulsa ceremonial town, and a member of Big Cussetah United Methodist Church. He received his bachelor's, master's, and Ph.D. (1976) from the University of Oklahoma at Norman. Clark wrote his dissertation on the history of the Ku Klux Klan in Oklahoma. He has taught history at a variety of colleges and universities, such as the University of California at Los Angeles, San Diego State University, Morningside College, the University of Utah, and the University of Oklahoma, and was professor of ethnic studies, U.S. History, and American Indian studies at California State University at Long Beach from 1984 to 1993, where he also served many years as director of the university's American Indian Studies Program.

He served as president of Oklahoma City University in 1997 and as provost and executive vice-president from 1992 to 1998. Professor Clark is president of the Oklahoma City Muscogee Association, chairman and co-fundraiser for the Tribal Flag Plaza at the Oklahoma State Capital, and fundraiser for the 1996 PBS documentary *Beyond Reservation Road*.

He is the editor of four books and the author of four books, sixty-one book chapters and journal articles, twenty-five book reviews, and twenty-two professional papers or commentaries. Clark published the prize-winning *Lone Wolfe v. Hitchcock: Treaty Rights and the Law at the End of the Nineteenth Century* in 1994.

Joseph J. Clark (1893–1971)
Cherokee admiral and businessperson

Joseph J. Clark was a military man and business executive. Born in Pryor, Oklahoma, on 12 November 1893, Clark graduated from the U.S. Naval Academy at Annapolis, Maryland, in June 1917. He then served in World War I and became an instructor at the Naval Academy after the war, earning the rank of naval aviator in 1925. During the years that followed and throughout World War II, Clark served in several different shore and sea assignments. He received numerous decorations, including the Navy Cross, the Distinguished Service Medal (twice), and the Legion of Merit. His last command was as commander-in-chief of the Seventh Fleet.

Clark retired from the navy in 1953 with the rank of admiral and then pursued a career as a business executive, becoming chairman of the board at Hegeman Harris, Inc., a New York stock investment firm. He died at St. Albans Naval Hospital in New York on 13 July 1971.

Frank Clarke (1921–)
Walapai and Mission physician and administrator

Frank Clarke is a retired physician and hospital administrator. Born at Blythe, California, on 11 November 1921, Clarke first went to school at Sherman Institute, a high school for Indian students in southern California, then studied at Los Angeles City College, and completed his bachelor's degree at UCLA. He later obtained an M.D. in obstetrics from St. Louis University School of Medicine.

Clarke is said to have decided on a career in medicine when he was only ten after recovering from a severe eye condition that nearly caused him to be blind. Unfortunately, his family had no funds to pay for such an education, and he had to work as a field hand and a janitor to get through the early years of college.

Clarke enlisted in the navy and served for twelve years, seeing active duty in the Solomon Islands during World War II. After seven major engagements with the enemy, he was selected for Naval Officer Training and then began his pre-medical education. When the navy college program ended, he went back to school and supported himself by working nights as a laboratory assistant.

He eventually graduated from St. Louis University School of Medicine, and after two years of private practice was named chief of medicine, and chief and president of staff at Memorial Hospital in Exeter, California, the first time that one person had held both positions. Clarke also headed the Department of Obstetrics at the same hospital. He has won numerous honors and awards over the years, and was winner of the Indian Council Fire Achievement Award in 1961.

Henry Roe Cloud (1884–1950)
Winnebago educator

Henry Roe Cloud was best known as an educator, minister, and humanitarian. He was born on 28 December 1884, in Winnebago, Nebraska, and raised in a traditional Winnebago manner, speaking only the Winnebagan language until he was ten years old. Cloud mastered English, Latin, and Greek as well by the time he turned seventeen. When he entered the government school, his name was Anglicized to Henry Cloud, after his grandfather, Yellow Cloud. He entered Yale University when he was sixteen, and earned his bachelor and master of arts degrees in anthropology.

While at Yale, Cloud was adopted by Dr. and Mrs. Walter Roe, whose last name he adopted as his own. In 1910, at Fort Sill, Oklahoma, he helped his foster father obtain the freedom of Apache, Comanche, and Kiowa children who were considered prisoners of war (see the biographies of Geronimo, Naiche, Quanah Parker, and other southern Plains chiefs). Cloud was ordained a Presbyterian minister at Auburn Theological Seminary in 1913 and received a Doctor of Divinity degree in 1932 from Emporia Kansas College.

Cloud served as vice-president of education on the board of the Society of American Indians, an Indian rights organization highly active during the 1920s. He established the American Indian Institute for boys in Wichita, Kansas, and successfully administered it for fifteen years. He turned the school over to the Presbyterian ministries when, in 1931, he accepted an appointment with the U.S. Indian Service and spent two years developing plans for the Indian Reorganization Act, which was passed in 1934 and provided for greater Indian self-government and cultural practice. In 1933, Cloud became superintendent of the famous Indian boarding school, the Haskell Institute in Lawrence, Kansas, and became its supervisor of education three years later. His final Indian Service post was superintendent of the Umatilla Indian Reservation at Pendleton, Oregon.

Elouise Cobell (1946–)
Blackfeet businesswoman and political activist

After leading a class-action suit against the Interior Department and the Bureau of Indian Affairs (BIA) for mismanagement of Indian trust accounts, Elouise Cobell made a name for herself across the United States. Before she gained national attention, however, Cobell was making business news among her people, the Blackfeet, located in northwest Montana, just east of Glacier National Park.

Born at the southern tip of the 1.5-million-acre Blackfeet Reservation, Cobell and her eight brothers and sisters attended a one-room school. The young leader often helped the teacher care for the younger students, and led field trips onto the reservation's prairies, searching for arrowheads. Because of her reservation's lack of modern conveniences, such as running water and telephones, Cobell longed for the comforts of urban life.

Once she was old enough to leave the reservation, Cobell moved to several different cities in the western half of the United States. While she enjoyed the conveniences such a lifestyle offered, she always kept one eye on home.

When her mother died in 1968 while Cobell was pursuing an undergraduate degree in business, she decided to leave college and return home to help her father run their family's ranch, despite a pleading call from the dean of the university.

Because of her training in the business arena, Cobell and her husband, Alvin "Turk" Cobell, and their son, Turk Russell, eventually took over the family ranch's business affairs. The ranch had $18,000 in debts when she took it over, and her research into the ranch's financial affairs led her on a winding and complicated path with no easy answers. She went to the BIA and to several congressional leaders to uncover the details of her family's financial matters. After twenty years of searching, Cobell was left with contradictory information and little explanation from the federal government.

During her search for answers to her family's financial troubles, Cobell served as tribal treasurer for her reservation from 1976 to 1988, responsible for a $20 million budget. During her tenure the savvy business-woman corrected past budget mismanagement and gained the trust of her tribal constituency. She also was the driving force behind the creation of the first national bank established on a reservation. When the Blackfeet National Bank opened its doors in 1987, the tribe owned 94 percent of the operation. The bank has prompted a substantial growth in business based on the Blackfeet Reservation. Most of these ventures are Indian-owned and operated. Cobell considers her work as the chair of the bank's board the most rewarding of her professional experiences.

While serving as her tribal government's treasurer, Cobell began noticing discrepancies in the BIA's reports to the tribe. When she discovered that other tribal governments were facing similar difficulties, Cobell and other tribal representatives took their complaints to Congress. In 1989, a scandal erupted that has yet to be quelled. Federal auditors calculated discrepancies of $17 million in the BIA's botched records.

Soon after this discovery, Cobell approached the Native American Rights Fund (NARF) about filing a lawsuit. With NARF's support, she and many other Indians from across the country filed a class-action lawsuit against the federal government for their failure to compensate individuals and tribes for money it was

presumably managing for them. *Cobell v. Babbitt* is still in the courts and has yet to be resolved by the U.S. government. The financial scandal, however, is said to be more complex than the savings and loan crisis of the 1980s. It seems that the Individual Indian Monies Trust has so drastically mishandled records over the years, that Cobell and others filing the suit do not know exactly how much money they are due to receive for resources, including oil and timber, that were taken from their land.

Cobell has been recognized as a great economic reformer by the national government as well as Indian Country. In 1992 she was one of fifty women invited to build an economic agenda for President-elect Bill Clinton, and she serves on the board of both the National Rural Development Finance Corporation and Women and Foundations/Corporate Philanthropy. In 1997 Cobell was awarded a MacArthur Foundation Genius Grant.

Cochise (1812–1874)
Chiricahua Apache tribal leader

In 1861, Indians in the Southwest United States began an ongoing war against the U.S. settlers and army in a series of conflicts known as the Apache Wars. From 1863 to 1872, Cochise was the leader of this resistance.

The Apache Wars began when Cochise, falsely accused of abducting a rancher's child, was imprisoned by an American lieutenant. He escaped, but the ensuing years were a cycle of attack and revenge. From his stronghold in the Dragoon Mountains (located in southern Arizona), Cochise and his ally, Mangas Coloradas, led an effective guerrilla campaign against U.S. and Mexican forces. In 1863, the United States military stepped up its campaign to pacify the Apache. Although losses and atrocities occurred on both sides and the Apache were forced to return to their mountain strongholds, no Apache band was ever conquered.

In 1871, Cochise rebuffed efforts to relocate his people to a reservation in New Mexico. A year later, however, the Apache leader agreed to abstain from attacks in exchange for reservation land in eastern Arizona. Consequently, peace did come to the region for the few short years before Cochise's death in 1874.

Karita Coffey (1947–)
Comanche ceramics artist and educator

Karita Coffey is a world-renowned ceramic artist. Born at Lawton, Oklahoma, on 10 August 1947, Coffey received her high school diploma from the Institute of

American Indian Arts in Santa Fe, New Mexico (1965). She then completed her bachelor's degree in art (ceramic design) at the University of Oklahoma (1971) and went on to graduate study in art and education at the same university. She received her teaching certificate in art in 1975 and a master's of education in 1979.

Coffey has exhibited her ceramics throughout the United States and abroad since 1964. Some of her outstanding shows have been at the Edinburgh Festival in Scotland; the Berlin Festival in Germany; the thirty-second Annual American Indian Artists Exhibition at Tulsa, Oklahoma; and an exhibit entitled "American Indian Art Now," at the Wheelwright Museum in Santa Fe, New Mexico. She also had a solo exhibit at the C. N. Gorman Museum at the University of California, Davis. Coffey has been an artist-in-residence for the Oklahoma City Public Schools System and has organized and presented workshops for Indian Education Programs in Oklahoma and at Dartmouth College in Hanover, New Hampshire.

Coffey has received many honors and awards over the years, including a scholarship from Oklahomans for Indian Opportunity (1967) and the Letzeiser Art Award (1971–1972). In 1977 and 1978, she was named a Bilingual/Bicultural Fellow by the Department of Health, Education, and Welfare. She is also included in *Who's Who in American Indian Art* (1973) and the *Dictionary of International Biography* (1973). She currently teaches at the Institute of American Indian Arts.

Mangas Coloradas (1797–1863)
Mimbreno Apache tribal leader

Mangas Coloradas was a member of the Mimbreno Apache, a tribe closely related to the Chiricahua Apache. Coloradas was a leader in the early years of the Apache Wars of the 1860s.

Coloradas fought two enemies during his lifetime. In the 1830s, there was conflict between the Apache and the Mexican government. In 1837, a number of important Mimbreno leaders were massacred by Mexican trappers who were motivated by the Mexican government's bounty on Indian scalps. Following the massacre, Coloradas united a number of tribes in present-day southern Arizona and New Mexico to rid themselves of intruding Mexican miners and trappers.

In 1846, the United States took possession of the New Mexico Territory, and Coloradas's enemy became the United States Army. In the 1850s, American miners began pouring into the region. Coloradas was captured and whipped by a group of miners, then released as a message to other Indians to stay away. Coloradas, who

was probably close to sixty years old at the time of the beating, survived and stepped up his warring against U.S. and Mexican miners. In the early 1860s, when the U.S. cavalry left the southwest region to fight in the Civil War, military protection for settlers and miners was taken on by the governor of California, who dispatched around three thousand troops to the region. In 1862, Coloradas and his Apache ally, Cochise, attacked the California troops in southern Arizona at a place now known as Apache Pass. Coloradas was wounded, but continued to press his attacks. As a result, in 1863, he was invited to a peace parley by U.S. military authorities. The peace parley was a ruse. Coloradas was murdered at Fort McLane, although U.S. authorities reported that he was killed while trying to escape. After his death, Coloradas's son, Mangus, continued his father's war to retain possession of the Apache land.

Elizabeth Cook-Lynn (1930–)
Crow Creek Sioux intellectual, writer, and professor

Elizabeth Cook-Lynn comes from a family of political leaders and scholars. Her father and grandfather served on the Crow Creek Tribal Council for years, and a great-grandfather (Gabriel Renville) was a Native linguist who helped develop early Dakota dictionaries. Cook-Lynn herself was raised on the Crow Creek Reservation and speaks Dakota.

Born on the Crow Creek Reservation in South Dakota, on 17 November 1930, Cook-Lynn received a bachelor's degree in journalism and English from South Dakota State College (1952) and later completed the master's degree in education, psychology, and counseling at the University of South Dakota (1970). She completed additional graduate work in literary criticism at the University of Nebraska, Lincoln, and at Stanford University.

Early in her career, she worked as a journalist and teacher at the secondary level, but since 1970 Cook-Lynn has been on the faculty at Eastern Washington State University and, in 1993 was professor emeritus (retired) of English and American Indian studies. She is a founding editor of *The Wicazo Sa Review*, a journal of Native American studies, and since her retirement from Eastern Washington University, has been a visiting professor and consultant in Native American Studies at University of California-Davis and Arizona State University.

She is considered by many to be a modern American Indian intellectual and author. After the age of forty, her stature as a poet grew with publication of *Then Badger Said This* and *Seek the House of Relatives*. Her short stories have appeared in journals such as *Prairie Schooner, Pembroke Magazine, South Dakota Review, Sun Tracks,* and *The Greenfield Review.* She is the author of three novellas, and her collection of essays, *Why I Can't Read Wallace Stegner and Other Essays* (1996) was awarded the Myers Center Award for the Study of Human Rights in North America in 1997. She has been writer-in-residence at several universities and lives in the Black hills of South Dakota.

Matthew Coon Come (1956–)
Cree tribal leader

Matthew Coon Come is national chief of the Assembly of First Nations, after his recent election in July 2000. A former grand chief of the Council of the Cree of Northern Quebec, he is the principal architect of the effort by the Cree to stop a hydroelectric development in northern Quebec known as James Bay II or the Great Whale project. Coon Come was born in northern Canada, and at the age of six he was forcibly removed by Canadian authorities to attend school. He then went on to study at Trent University, and spent two years studying law at McGill University. During his university studies, Coon Come kept close ties with his people.

From 1981 to 1986, Coon Come served as a board member and an executive committee member of the Grand Council of the Cree, a province-wide organization devoted to advancing the interests of Cree in Quebec. He studied law, political science, economics, and Native studies at Trent and McGill universities.

While at law school in 1987, Coon Come was asked by Cree elders to become grand chief to lead the struggle against the James Bay project, which threatened to flood much of the Cree homeland in northern Quebec. Coon Come accepted and began to chart an extremely successful campaign against hydroelectric development in the area. He quickly organized environmental, human rights, and indigenous communities on the local, national, and international levels to create a strong coalition opposing the project. Primarily targeting New York State as a likely hydroelectric consumer, Coon Come also organized a canoe trip of Cree elders from James Bay, through Lake Erie, and down the Hudson River. Under his leadership the Cree people were able to renegotiate with Quebec the terms under which hydroelectric development would occur in the north.

Coon Come has served as chairman of the James Bay Eeyou Corporation, managing over one hundred million dollars in assets. He was also chairman of James Bay Native Development Cooperation, which under his leadership assisted in starting up fifty-four businesses within the Cree communities. He was a founding director of the First Nations Bank of Canada in 1995.

He was awarded the Goldman Prize, considered the "Nobel Prize of Environmental Awards" (1994). In 1998, Trent University granted him the degree of Doctor of Laws Honoris Causa in further recognition of the significance of his work. He also received the National Aboriginal Achievement Award in 1995. He is married and is the father of five children.

Nellie Cornoyea (1940–)
Inuvialuit politician

Nellie Cornoyea is the chair and chief executive officer of the Inuvialuit Regional Corporation (IRC). The Inuvialuit Regional Corporation is a company set up to administer the Inuvialuit people's 1984 land claim settlement with the Canadian government. Before her election as chair, Cournoyea was premier of the Northwest Territories for four years beginning November 1991. Representing the Western Arctic riding of Nunakput from 1979 to November 1995, Cournoyea held a number of portfolios including Health and Social Services, Renewable Resources, and Culture and Communications.

The second of eleven children, she was born near Aklavik in the Canadian Arctic to Nels Hvatum, a Norwegian, and Maggie, a member of the Inuvialuit who live in the western Canadian Arctic. Cornoyea spent her childhood in the bush, hunting, trapping, and fishing with her family and educating herself through correspondence courses. When she turned eleven, she worked as a volunteer secretary for the local hunters' and trappers' association. At the age of eighteen, she married and had two children. The marriage broke up soon thereafter, and Cornoyea obtained work at a new Canadian Broadcasting Corporation (CBC) station in Inuvik, a town in the far northwestern corner of the Northwest Territories, in order to support her young children. Cornoyea worked for the CBC for more than nine years as an announcer and station manager, persuading many young people to take up radio as a career.

Before her election to the Northwest Territories Legislative Assembly in 1979, she was a founding member for the Committee for Original People's Entitlement (COPE), an organization devoted to the rights of the Inuvialuit of the western Arctic. She was also a land claims officer for the Inuit Tapirisat of Canada, a national agency mandated to promote Inuit culture and identity and to develop Inuit political, economic, and environmental policy. In 1984, the Inuvialuit of the western Arctic signed an agreement with the federal government in which they received title to large areas of land. Cornoyea coordinated aspects of the implementation of the agreement and served on the board of directors of the Inuvialuit Petroleum Corporation, the Inuvialuit Development Corporation, and the Enrollment Authority and Arbitration Board.

She received the Woman of the Year Award from the Northwest Territories Native Women's Association (1982) and, in 1996, she was honored with a National Aboriginal Achievement Award for her contributions and public service.

Cournoyea was the first managing director of the IRC, after being part of the land rights negotiating team. She also held the position of implementation coordinator for the Inuvialuit Final Agreement for several years, and served on the board of directors of the Inuvialuit Petroleum Corporation, the Inuvialuit Development Corporation, and the Enrollment Authority and Arbitration Board. She decided not to run in the 1995 NWT election and returned to the Beaufort-Delta where she was elected chief executive officer and chair of IRC in 1996. She was reelected for a third two-year term in 2000.

Cornplanter (d. 1836)
Seneca tribal leader

Cornplanter was a leading warrior and village leader among the Seneca, one of six nations of the Iroquois Confederacy, who lived in present upstate New York. The Iroquois Confederacy consisted of forty-nine chiefs, or sachems, whose families attended the first meeting of the Iroquois Confederacy some few hundred years before Europeans arrived in North America. Cornplanter belonged to the Seneca Turtle clan, whose sachem held the title of Handsome Lake. Cornplanter, however, was not elected sachem. He earned his role as leader largely through military command and personal influence, which attracted friends and relatives to live on his reserved lands, which by 1800 totaled 1,300 acres in northern Pennsylvania.

Cornplanter's father was a trader named John O'Bail, who, during the 1730s, lived among the Seneca and traded manufactured goods for furs and skins. O'Bail chose not to live among the Iroquois and left his Seneca wife and child in care of her clan. Cornplanter grew to be a warrior leader. He fought with the French during the French and Indian War (1755–1759) and with the British during the American Revolutionary War (1775–1783).

After the Revolutionary War, Cornplanter argued that the Iroquois would not survive unless they adopted agriculture and U.S. forms of government. He was opposed by the nationalistic Seneca leader, Red Jacket, who thought the Iroquois would lose their identity if they adopted American life-styles. Between 1799 and 1815, however, Cornplanter's half-brother, Handsome Lake, led a religious and social movement that reorganized much of Iroquois culture. Cornplanter supported this movement, which led to adoption of agriculture, small farms, and new emphases on moral and religious order within Iroquois communities. Late in life, Cornplanter emphasized the need to retain Iroquois culture and ways.

Jesse Cornplanter (1889–1957)
Seneca cultural interpreter and author

Jesse Cornplanter was an interpreter of the cultural traditions of the Seneca, whose native territory is centered south of Lake Ontario in western New York State.

Born in 1889 on the Cattaraugus Seneca Reservation in upstate New York at a place called Newton Longhouse, Cornplanter grew up in a very traditional setting. He learned Seneca as his first language and was an avid player of lacrosse, a Native American goal game in which players use a long-handled stick that has a triangular head with a loose mesh pouch for carrying and catching the ball. He also participated in religious events of the longhouse from his earliest childhood, beginning as a dancer and later becoming a singer in traditional Seneca ceremonies, such as the Great Feather Dance and the Drum Dance.

Although he thought in Seneca, Cornplanter wanted to learn English even as a child. He attended the district school and went as far as the fifth grade, after which he was largely self-taught. He worked as a touring showman during his early twenties, performing in a dramatization of "Song of Hiawatha," a poem by the American poet Henry Wadsworth Longfellow (1802–1887). He later joined the army and served in World War I, receiving the Purple Heart for injuries suffered during combat in France.

Cornplanter was thoroughly imbued with his own traditions and became a major source of current knowledge concerning songs, mythology, crafts, and other aspects of Seneca culture. Despite his limited formal education, he recorded a vast body of cultural information in letters written to anthropologists and others during the years between 1900 and 1957, and to a lesser extent in publications that appeared in his own name. Among his own published works are *Iroquois Indian Games and Dances* (1903) and *Legends of the Long House* (1938), but he also provided information that was presented in the writings of anthropologists such as William Fenton, Harold Conklin, and Frank Speck.

Like William Beynon and George Bushotter, Cornplanter was an intellectual figure who bridged the gap between two worlds and two ways of thinking.

Robert T. Coulter (1945–)
Potawatomi lawyer and activist

Robert T. Coulter, an attorney who focuses on Indian law and international human rights, is currently the executive director of the Indian Law Resource Center in Helena, Montana.

Born in Rapid City, South Dakota, on 19 September 1945, Coulter received his bachelor's degree from Williams College in Williamstown, Massachusetts, (1966) and went on to get a degree in law from Columbia University Law School (1969).

Coulter is the past chairperson of the American Bar Association Committee on Problems of American Indians, Section of Individual Rights and Responsibilities (1982–1984) and was a Ralph E. Shikes Visiting Fellow, Harvard Law School, in 1995. He has published numerous articles, essays, and books, and is also a longstanding member the American Society of International Law.

Robert T. Coulter, executive director of Indian Law Resource Center.

Bruce Cox (1934–)
Anishinabe anthropologist and professor emeritus

Bruce Cox is an environmentally conscious anthropologist and a retired university professor. He was born at Santa Rosa, California, on 29 June 1934. Cox earned his bachelor's degree in anthropology at Reed College in Oregon (1956), obtained a master's degree from the University of Oregon (1959), and a doctorate from the University of California, Berkeley (1968). Over the years, he has taught courses in anthropology at Lewis and Clark College in Idaho (1964–1965), the University of Florida (1966), the University of Alberta (1967–1969), and taught at Carleton University in Ontario, Canada, from 1969 to 1999.

Cox is mainly interested in the cultural ecology of indigenous North American peoples and understanding how these Native beliefs and institutions concerning the environment are disrupted by large-scale energy development projects such as the James Bay hydroelectric plant near Quebec (Ontario, Canada) or the coal strip-mining of Black Mesa in northern Arizona. These issues are discussed in his publications, including *Cultural Ecology of Canadian Native Peoples* (1973), *Native People, Native Lands* (1988), and *A Different Drummer: Readings in Anthropology with a Canadian Perspective* (1989).

Crazy Horse (1842–1877)
Oglala-Brule Sioux tribal leader

Crazy Horse was a war leader of the Oglala subgroup of the Teton Sioux. He was born to the east of the sacred Black Hills near present-day Rapid City. As a boy, he was called Curly. Since his mother was a Brule Sioux, he spent time in the camps of the Oglala and the Brule. By the time he was twelve, he had killed a buffalo and received his own horse. His father, a holy man, changed Curly's name to the same as his own, Crazy Horse, after watching his son's exploits in battle against another tribe. While still a young man, Crazy Horse had a vivid dream of a rider on horseback in a storm, which his father interpreted as a sign of future greatness in battle.

In the 1866 to 1868 war over the Bozeman Trail, Crazy Horse joined the Oglala chief Red Cloud in raids against U.S. settlements and forts in Wyoming. In these forays, Crazy Horse became adept in the art of decoying tactics. With the 1868 treaty at Fort Laramie, the U.S. Army agreed to abandon its posts along the Bozeman Trail. Crazy Horse became war chief of the Oglala and married a Cheyenne woman. He later took a second Oglala wife.

The Black Hills Gold Rush in 1876 brought more conflict to the region when miners and speculators began indiscriminately exploring the Sioux's sacred territory. Crazy Horse's camp became a rallying point for many warriors eager to drive the intruders away. On the upper Rosebud Creek in present-day southern Montana, in the spring of 1876, General George Crook's army of thirteen hundred attacked Crazy Horse's force of twelve hundred. Crazy Horse's feinting and assault techniques baffled Crook, who withdrew after heavy losses. Crazy Horse then moved his camp to the Bighorn River in Montana and joined Sitting Bull and Gall. U.S. Army troops, including a force led by Colonel George Armstrong Custer, set out to find and pacify the Sioux and Cheyenne, who were gathering at the Bighorn River.

On 25 June 1876, the famous Battle of the Little Bighorn commenced. In a masterful series of decoys and feints by the Sioux, aided by poor military judgment by Colonel Custer, Crazy Horse and his predominantly Cheyenne warriors attacked Custer's men from the north and west. Gall, after routing Major Marcus Reno's forces, charged Custer from the south and east. The U.S. troops were surrounded and completely annihilated.

Despite several other brilliant campaigns against U.S. troops, the Sioux were starving and weary of battle. On 6 May 1877, Crazy Horse reluctantly surrendered with eight hundred followers at Fort Robinson in northwestern Nebraska. However, the promises of a reservation for the Sioux were not kept. Crazy Horse was bayoneted at Fort Robinson during an attempt to confine him to a guardhouse on 5 September 1877. According to legend, he is buried in his homeland near Wounded Knee, South Dakota.

Roland Crowe (1943–)
Piapot Cree tribal leader

Roland Crowe is chief of the Piapot First Nation and a senator of the Federation of Saskatchewan Indian Nations (FSIN), an organization devoted to the advancement of aboriginal rights in Canada. He was born and raised on the Piapot Indian Reserve, located approximately twenty-four miles north of Regina, Saskatchewan. His father was a farmer and later a driver training instructor. His mother was a social worker with the Family Service Bureau. The oldest of six children, Crowe worked on the family farm and eventually became a farmer himself.

At the age of fifteen, Crowe worked as a page at the Saskatchewan Legislative Assembly, a job that sparked a deep and abiding interest in politics. Soon after this experience, Crowe worked as a corrections officer at a provincial corrections center. Other jobs early in his life included a stint at the federal Department of Indian Affairs and program director/executive director of the Regina Friendship Center, an institution aimed at providing support to urban Indians.

Crowe entered politics at the band level, serving as band councillor for two years and then, for six years, as chief of the Piapot Indian Reserve until his election as chief of the Federation of Saskatchewan Indian Nations. As chief, Crowe spearheaded the historic 1992 Treaty Land Entitlement Agreement, which resulted in the addition of 1.6 million acres to First Nations' land base and over $550 million for First Nations to carry out land acquisitions. He played a key role in obtaining 1,000 low-income housing units through the creation of off-reserve housing programs and securing 18 million dollars in funding for the training and employment of First Nation people in the Saskatchewan region.

He has counseled a philosophy of non-violent protest by aboriginal people in their dealings with the Canadian state and is committed to the negotiation of aboriginal self-government in Canada. Chief Crowe lives in Regina with his wife Brenda and family.

Crowfoot (circa 1830–1890)
Blackfoot Confederacy tribal leader

Crowfoot (Isapo-Muxika) was born a Blood Indian at Blackfoot Crossing near present-day Calgary, Alberta, but upon his father's death moved with his mother to the Blackfoot lodge of her new husband. Crowfoot was known as Bear Ghost (Kyi-i-staah) among his people during his youth and was only thirteen years old when he participated in the first of nineteen battles as a Blackfoot warrior. He became known to settlers when he rescued a Roman Catholic priest from Cree Indians in 1866. In 1877, Canadian authorities treated Crowfoot as head chief of the Blackfoot Confederacy, which included at the time the Blackfoot, Blood, Peigan, and Sarcee tribes, at the signing of Treaty Seven, one of the several treaties that Canada entered into with First Nations. In the same year, Crowfoot was commended by Queen Victoria of England for refusing to assist Sitting Bull of the Sioux Nation during the wars between the Plains Indians and the American Cavalry. Following the Battle of the Little Bighorn (known as Custer's Last Stand), many Sioux fled to Canada, at which time Crowfoot and Sitting Bull shared tobacco and achieved peace between the two nations.

By the summer of 1879, the Blackfoot faced starvation and were forced to follow the last buffalo herds into Montana. Two years later they crossed back into Canada and faced continued shortages of food. Eventually, the Blackfoot were forced to sell many of their possessions, including their horses, to survive. In 1885, Crowfoot's adoptive son, Poundmaker, led a Cree attack on the town of Battleford on the North Saskatchewan River, as part of a larger rebellion, known as the second Northwest Rebellion of 1885, in which Louis Riel, leader of the Métis people, sought to form a provisional government in Saskatchewan against the wishes of Canadian authorities. Crowfoot kept the Blackfoot out of the rebellion, although he encouraged his people to assist any Cree passing through their territory. Crowfoot lost most of his children to smallpox and tuberculosis.

Charles Curtis (1860–1936)
Kaw and Osage politician and vice president of the United States

Charles Curtis served as vice-president of the United States under Herbert Hoover, as well as many years in Congress. Born near the present-day town of Topeka, Kansas, in 1860, Curtis was only one-eighth Indian but was raised on the Kaw Reservation near Council Grove. He attended the Indian mission school on the reservation, then returned to Topeka when the Kaw were attacked by Cheyenne militants. As a young man, he worked as a jockey during the summer seasons and attended Topeka High School.

Curtis became a lawyer in 1881 and later entered politics as a Republican, serving eight consecutive terms in the U.S. House of Representatives from 1892 until 1906. As a legislator Curtis is best known as sponsor of the Curtis Act of 1898, which called for the dissolution of tribal governments and the institution of civil government throughout Indian Territory (Oklahoma). This was intended to hasten the assimilation of Indian peoples. The act also extended the allotment policy to all of the tribes in Indian Territory, by authorizing the Dawes Commission, a special congressional committee, to extinguish tribal title in Indian Territory and proceed to make allotments of land to Indians as individuals. These efforts toward assimilation and allotment were opposed by many Indian leaders, who felt that the United States had no right to dissolve their tribal governments and did not wish to enter U.S. society.

Curtis was later elected to the Senate and served in that body from 1907 to 1913 and 1915 to 1929. He campaigned for president and lost, then ran successfully for vice-president on the ticket with Herbert Hoover. They served one term in office, from 1929 until 1933.

Linwood Little Bear Custalow (1937–)
Mattaponi tribal leader and physician

Linwood Little Bear Custalow was born on the Mattaponi Indian Reservation in King William County, Virginia, where he lived until age thirteen. Custalow was sent by the State Board of Virginia to an Indian high school on the Cherokee Reservation in North Carolina. At his request, he was allowed to complete his high school education at Bacone High School in Muskogee, Oklahoma.

He graduated from the University of Richmond with a degree in chemistry to become the first American Indian from a tribe in Virginia to graduate from a Virginia university. He went on to earn a medical degree from the Medical College of Virginia in 1964, becoming the first American Indian to graduate from medical school in Virginia.

In 1969, Custalow set up his own medical practice in Hampton, Virginia. In 1970, he and several American Indian physicians formed the Association of American Indian Physicians, based in Oklahoma City, Oklahoma, where he served as president and remained on the executive board for ten years

Besides his medical career, Custalow is an advocate for Native American issues, with a focus on the Indians from King William County. He was instrumental in organizing the Adams Town urban group of King William County American Indians into a tribe under the name Upper Mattaponi Tribe, using the tribal name at the permission of the Mattaponi tribal chief.

He is a diplomat of the American Board of Otolaryngology and the American Board of Environmental Medicine. He is a fellow of the National Board of Medical Examiners, the American Academy of Otolaryngology-Head and Neck Surgery, and the International College of Surgeons.

Custalow is currently retired from private practice. He is actively assisting the Mattaponi Tribe and is chairman of the finance committee of the Association of American Indian Physicians.

Datsolalee (Luisa Keyser) (d. 1925)
Washo basketmaker

Datsolalee was a Washo woman who became famous for her skills as a basketmaker. The Washo are a

Hokan-speaking tribe occupying the eastern slopes of the Sierra Nevada Mountains in northern California and Nevada.

She was born near Carson City, Nevada, around 1835 and learned the refined art of traditional basketry as a girl. Basketry is particularly developed among the California tribes, and Washo styles are among the more intricate, involved designs with as many as thirty-six stitches per inch. In 1844, Datsolalee was one of the Washo who welcomed John C. Fremont, the famous early explorer of territories west of the Mississippi River, when he arrived in the Carson City area. She later married a Washo man named Assu and had two children by him. Upon Assu's death, she married another Washo man named Charlie Keyser, and thus she also became known by an English name, Louisa Keyser.

Datsolalee's historical importance is owed at least partly to the bravery she showed in a marketing conflict with the Paiute. During the 1850s, this neighboring tribe had defeated the Washo in battle, and they prohibited the Washo from selling baskets to U.S. settlers, in order to increase their own sales. Without this source of income, the Washo suffered extreme poverty. Finally, however, Datsolalee decided to defy the ban, and in 1895 she took several of her finest pieces and sold them to Abram Cohn, a merchant in Carson City. This was the beginning of a long-standing relationship, and over the years Cohn bought some 120 works from Datsolalee, who is said to have produced about 300 baskets in her lifetime.

Datsolalee worked on baskets until she died, even though she had become nearly blind long before then. Her baskets, the largest and most intricate of which took more than a year to produce, became very valuable after her death, and one of them is said to have sold for $10,000 only five years later.

Nora Dauenhauer (1927–)
Tlingit author and translator

Nora Dauenhauer is an author and translator of the language of the Tlingit, a Northwest Coast tribe occupying the southeastern Alaskan coastline. Born in Juneau, Alaska, in 1927, Dauenhauer received her bachelor's degree in anthropology from Alaska Methodist University in Anchorage (1976) and then completed a special research training program for Native Americans sponsored by the Smithsonian Institution in 1977. From 1978 until 1980, she served as a cultural coordinator for the Cook Inlet Native Association, one of the twelve Alaska Native regional associations, and in 1980 and 1981 she conducted a translation project that was supported by the National Endowment for the Humanities.

Though Dauenhauer turned to cross-cultural research relatively late in life, she has spent considerable time since 1977 collecting and translating Tlingit oral traditions. Her translation of Tlingit oratory has been published in the volume *Because We Cherish You* (1981), and she and her husband published language texts entitled *Beginning Tlingit* (1976) and *A Tlingit Spelling Book* (1984). Dauenhauer is also a creative writer whose poems and stories have been published in two anthologies entitled *Earth Power Coming: Short Fiction in Native American Literature* (1983) and *That's What She Said: Contemporary Poetry and Fiction by Native American Women* (1984). Her recent books *The Droning Shaman, Haa Shuka, Our Ancestors*, and *Haa Tuwundaagu Yis, For Healing Our Spirit*. Other writings by Dauenhauer have also appeared in *The Greenfield Review* and *Northward Journal*.

Alice Brown Davis (1852–1935)
Seminole tribal leader

Alice Brown Davis served for many years as an emissary of the Seminole Nation and the U.S. government, and was appointed chief of the Seminole in 1922. Born near Park Hill, in the Cherokee Nation in Indian Territory, present-day Oklahoma, she was the daughter of Dr. John F. Brown, a Scot, and Lucy Redbeard, a Seminole of the Tiger clan. During the Civil War Alice lived at Fort Gibson, and following the war she met and married George Davis. The young couple lived for a time in Okmulgee in the Creek Nation, Indian Territory, but returned to the Seminole Nation, Indian Territory, in 1882, where they established a trading post. Davis gave birth to eleven children and, after being widowed, raised her four sons and seven daughters while running the trading post. In 1903, Davis spent three months at Santa Rosa, Chihuahua State, Mexico, with other Seminole, as delegates to a conference on important tribal affairs. In 1905 she went to Palm Beach, Florida, to act as an interpreter for the U.S. government in a murder trial involving a prominent Seminole Indian.

In 1909, Davis was sent as an emissary from the Indians of her nation to the Seminole still living in the Florida Everglades. She remained with them for many months, living among them, preaching to them, and endeavoring to interest them in the advantages of civilization. As a result of her visit, a more friendly understanding was established, and the Oklahoma Seminole began to receive visits from Seminoles and other tribes from Florida to become better acquainted.

Davis made two trips to Mexico City in 1905 and 1910, trying to gain information regarding a vast tract of land allegedly granted to the Seminole by the Mexican government in exchange for protection from ongoing Indian attacks. The title grant was never proved, however.

In 1922, President Warren G. Harding appointed Davis chief of the Seminole Nation, to succeed her brother, John F. Brown Jr., who had served his people for thirty years. Davis proved to be an excellent choice, because she was a vigorous woman with a clear and intelligent mind, devoted to the interests of the Seminole. On 21 June 1935, the Associated Press announced the death of Chief Davis, a victim of heart disease, at the age of eighty-two years.

Frank Day (1902–1976)
Concow Maidu painter and tribal historian

Frank Day was a self-taught artist whose surreal paintings drew upon Maidu history and mythology. The Concow Maidu are a California tribe whose native territories covered a fairly large area surrounding the modern cities of Chico and Oroville in northern California. Like many other California Indian traditionalists, Frank Day remained outside the mainstream of modern American Indian culture, and there is little published information about his life. His father was a village headman, and Day inherited ceremonial knowledge and responsibilities from him upon his death in 1922. One of Day's own legacies was to help in the founding of a dance group called the Maidu Dancers; he accomplished this by teaching the younger dancers the songs, the meaning of the words in the songs, and the dance steps that should be used.

His paintings are more widely known, but Day probably did not consider himself a "professional" artist in the generally accepted sense of the word. His paintings are powerful, filled with religious significance and imagery derived from a period when the world was being created. The style is without formal training but visionary, and there are about three hundred of his paintings in existence, mainly in private collections.

Ada E. Deer (1935–)
Menominee educator and activist

Ada E. Deer is a Menominee social worker and political organizer who was involved in restoring federal recognition to her tribe in the 1970s. The Menominee

Ada E. Deer.

(whose name means Wild Rice People in Ojibwa) are located along the Menominee River in Wisconsin and Michigan.

Born at Keshena, Wisconsin, on 7 August 1935, Deer received her bachelor's degree in social work from the University of Wisconsin-Madison (1957) and went on to complete her master's degree in social work at Columbia University (1961).

In the 1970s, Deer played a major role in the social and political development of her tribe. During 1972 and 1973, she was vice-president and Washington lobbyist of an organization called National Committee to Save the Menominee People and Forest, Inc. From 1973 until 1976, she was the chair of the Menominee Restoration Committee, and the group was largely responsible for congressional action to restore Menominee to tribal status following the termination of the tribe in 1954. The Menominee were one of the major tribes whose reservation was dissolved by federal policies of the 1950s, and since 1977 several other terminated tribes have been restored to federal recognition, all following the Menominee example.

From 1977 to 1993, Deer was a faculty member in the School of Social Work and Native American Studies at the University of Wisconsin-Madison. She has won many awards and honors over the years, including honorary doctorates from Northland College in Wisconsin and the University of Wisconsin-Madison. Ada E. Deer is the first woman assistant secretary for Indian Affairs in the history of the Department of the Interior. President Clinton announced his intention to nominate Deer on 11 May 1993. She was confirmed by the United States Senate on 16 July 1993. Deer served as assistant secretary until November 1997. She then became the first woman to serve as chairperson of her tribe and is currently director of American Indian studies at the University of Wisconsin-Madison.

Deganawida (circa 1300)
Huron spiritual leader

Deganawida is the founder of the Iroquois Confederacy. Its origin is unknown, but it is generally dated before the landing of Columbus in 1492. In Iroquois history, Deganawida lived in a time when there was little peace among the Iroquois-speaking nations, of which the Huron, Deganwida's tribe then residing in present-day Ontario in southern Canada, is one. These nations were often at war with one another because there was no agreed-upon means of resolving conflict between the various nations. A murder of one man by a man of another nation led to revenge raids and war between the nations.

Deganawida had a vision from the Great Spirit that instructed him to give the Great Law, a set of rules and procedures for working out differences and settling hostilities between nations. Deganawida traveled among the Iroquois Nations in present-day New York and Ohio spreading the message of peace. Most rejected the message, but on his travels he met Hiawatha, a member of the Iroquoian-speaking Mohawk Nation living near present-day Albany, New York. Since Deganawida had a speech impediment, Hiawatha, a powerful orator, became the spokesperson for the message of Deganawida and the Great Spirit. Both Deganawida and Hiawatha traveled among the Iroquois Nations, and after some resistance among the Onondaga, convinced the Seneca, Cayuga, Onondaga, Oneida, and Mohawk to form a confederacy of forty-nine chiefs. Through ceremonies and agreements they settled their disputes peacefully at the annual gatherings of the Confederate Council, which met at Onondaga, near present-day Syracuse, New York. Decisions of the Confederate Council required unanimous consensus among all nations, thereafter called the Five Nations. The elderly clan matrons nominated and deposed the chiefs of their own lineages from office if they did not conform to the will of the lineage. The purpose of the league was to create peace and to spread the Great Law of peace to all nations in the world.

Joseph B. DeLaCruz (1937–2000)
Quinault tribal leader

For twenty-two years Joseph B. DeLaCruz was the president of the Quinault Nation, located in the northwestern part of Washington State. During this time he was involved in domestic-tribal, intertribal, state-wide, regional, national, and international issues. As a tribal leader, he provided policy guidance and instruction on Quinault Business Council directives, and he served as primary representative for the Quinault Nation in government-to-government, corporate, and intertribal relations. Among the activities he promoted to preserve Quinault Nation interests were development of the Quinault Forestry Management Program, the Quinault land restoration, and the Quinault Housing program, as well as two enterprises: the Quinault Seafood Plant and the Quinault Land and Timber Enterprises. In 1992, DeLaCruz supported a tribal ordinance that provided tribal members with a means to secure financing for home construction on reservation land.

From 1977 to 1981, DeLaCruz was president of the National Tribal Chairmen Association, an organization developed as a tribal leaders forum for instituting legislation, and monitoring and evaluating decisions in priority areas in Indian Country such as education, housing, and economic development. From 1977 to 1982, he helped organize the Conference of Tribal Governments, which provided the foundation for the state and tribal relations on a government-to-government basis. From 1985 to 1988, he mediated the negotiation among the United States, Canada, and Indian tribes in the Northwest of the Pacific Salmon Fisheries Treaty, which regulates the fishing in those waters. Beginning in 1985, he was a member of the Northwest Indian Fish Commission that serves as an intergovernmental fisheries management and technical assistance agency for tribes in western Washington. The commission was also a mechanism for developing co-management strategies for state and federal agencies and Indian tribes. DeLaCruz also served two terms as president of the National Congress of American Indians, a major national lobbying organization for Indian issues and legislation.

In 1991 and 1992, DeLaCruz was the commissioner for the National Commission on American Indian, Alaska Native, and Hawaiian Housing. The commission was composed of twelve members and conducted on-site visits to remote Native areas where housing problems still exist. The commission's duty was to submit a report to Congress and to make recommendations for housing and opportunities for development, management, and modernization of housing on reservations.

Delaware Prophet (circa 1760s)
Delaware (Lenape) spiritual leader

During the early 1760s—a time of threatened trade, military, and diplomatic domination by the English—several religious leaders emerged among the Delaware Nation living in the eastern Ohio region. In North America, the French and Indian War had just been concluded in December 1759 when Montreal in New France fell to Indian and English troops. The defeat of the French left many Indians who had fought with the French cause without allies and military support. The British threatened to gain monopoly control over the fur trade, the distribution of guns and manufactured goods, and threatened to establish military control over the Ohio and Great Lakes region by occupying the old French forts at places such as Detroit.

With their economy potentially in crisis, the Delaware responded to the rise of new leaders who attempted to reorganize their society. Although we do not have their names, the strategies of two of them are sufficiently different to distinguish them as a militant prophet and a church-building prophet.

The militant prophet had a vision that he died and visited heaven, where he was given a message for gaining the spiritual and political salvation of the Indian people. He preached that because the Indians gave up the traditions and lifestyle of their forbears and traded and accepted the goods of the Europeans, the path to heaven for the Indians was blocked. Concepts of heaven and the strong emphasis on personal salvation were ideas borrowed, probably indirectly, from the Christian religion. Pontiac, an Ottawa leader, supported the teachings of the militant prophet as a means to form a multi-tribal military alliance that would push the English out of Indian territory in the Great Lakes region. In 1763 Pontiac initiated a coordinated military attack on the British-occupied forts, but he was not able to sustain the fight or evict the English.

The church-building Delaware Prophet, unlike the militant prophet, had a religious message only for the Delaware, not for a multi-tribal coalition. This Delaware Prophet brought together elements of Delaware religion and formed a centralized Delaware national ceremonial and religious order, often called the Bighouse Religion. Previously, the Delaware were formed into about forty small bands, which were severely disrupted during the colonial period. The prophet reorganized the kinship and political organization of Delaware society and instituted a system of three phratries—often called

Turtle, Turkey, and Wolf—and each of which was subdivided into twelve smaller clans or subdivisions. This prophet created a system of chiefs for the Delaware with ceremonies of installation, and one chief, who led the Turtle phratry, was designated principal chief, although he had little authority over the other two major chiefs. The three major divisions were recognized with the Bighouse Religion ceremonies and each had complementary religious and political duties. After 1765, the Delaware prophets appear to disappear from the record.

Ella Deloria (1888–1971)
Yankton Sioux ethnologist, linguist, and novelist

Ella Deloria was an anthropologist whose work focused mainly on the language and culture of her own tribe, the Sioux (also called Dakota).

Deloria was born on the Yankton Sioux Reservation in southwestern South Dakota. She attended All Saints Boarding School in Sioux Falls, and later studied at Oberlin College in Ohio and received her bachelor's degree from Columbia University in 1915. Upon graduation, she returned to teach at All Saints and then in 1919 accepted a job with the YWCA as secretary of health education for Indian schools and reservations. In this position, she traveled widely throughout the western United States and became acquainted with many different Indian tribal groups.

Her career in anthropology began in 1929, when she accepted an offer from Franz Boas to be a linguistic informant and research associate at Columbia University. Because she was a fluent speaker of Dakota (Sioux), she gave instruction on various dialects of the language and also worked on several publications. During this period she wrote *Dakota Texts* (1932) and co-authored *A Dakota Grammar* with Boas in 1941.

After Boas's death in 1942, Deloria began working on her own and produced books that attempted to move beyond the standard anthropological point of view. *Speaking of Indians* (1944) was a non-technical but sophisticated description of Indian (especially Sioux) culture, and the first draft of her novel *Waterlily* was also written during the 1940s, although it remained unpublished until 1988. All the while, she also kept up her purely anthropological studies and became one of the leading authorities on Sioux culture in her lifetime.

Philip Sam Deloria (contemporary)
Standing Rock Sioux lawyer

Philip Sam Deloria is director of the American Indian Law Center, Inc. (AILC) in Albuquerque, New Mexico, and is a member of the Standing Rock Sioux. Deloria is responsible for policy, staff, budget, and management of the law center. One of the most important functions of the AILC is its summer program, which provides a three-month intensive course for Indian students who wish to enter the field of law.

The program provides financial support to Indian law students, as well as educational enrichment in areas of Indian law not covered in the normal curriculum of many law schools. In addition, the law center conducts research, technical assistance, and training with respect to legal issues confronting American Indians, with particular attention paid to tribal government.

The AILC also conducts research on such matters as intergovernmental relationships and the status of tribal government with the federal domestic assistance program delivery system. Deloria received a bachelor of arts degree in philosophy from Yale University in New Haven, Connecticut, and received his law degree from Yale Law School.

He is the former deputy assistant secretary for Indian affairs for the U.S. Department of the Interior, the former secretary general for the World Council for Indigenous Peoples, and originator of the Commission on State-Tribal Relations.

Vine Deloria, Jr. (1933–)
Standing Rock Sioux writer, lawyer, and professor

Through his widely published books *Custer Died for Your Sins* (1969) and *God is Red* (1973), Vine Deloria, Jr., has brought greater understanding of American Indian history and philosophy to a vast global audience. He was born in Martin, South Dakota, to an unusually distinguished family. His grandfather was a Yankton chief. His aunt (Ella Deloria) was a noted scholar of Indian ethnology and linguistics, and his father (Vine Deloria, Sr.) was an Episcopal minister. The younger Vine Deloria graduated from Iowa State University in 1958, then took a master's degree in theology (Lutheran School of Theology, 1963) and later a degree in law (University of Colorado, 1970).

While assuredly influenced by the religious teachings of his father, Deloria became known as a revolutionary thinker who spoke out against the decadence of U.S. culture and insisted that young Native Americans receive traditional teachings before exposing themselves to the philosophies of the dominant Euro-American culture. He has always held that Indian people must remain Indian, rather than assimilating into U.S. society, and that education and ideology—not violence—are the keys to achieving dignity and justice for Native Americans of all tribes.

Deloria served as the executive director of the National Congress of American Indians in Washington, D.C., from 1964 to 1967. He has also provided leadership in other organizations such as the Citizens Crusade Against Poverty, the Council on Indian Affairs, the National Office for the Rights of the Indigent, the Institute for the Development of Indian Law, and the Indian Rights Association. He was a member of several college and university faculties before taking a post as professor of political science at the University of Arizona at Tucson in 1978. In 1990, he moved to the University of Colorado, Boulder, and taught history until his retirement in 2000.

Deloria has received many awards, literary citations, and honorary degrees. Some of his other well-known books include: *We Talk You Listen* (1970), *Behind the Trail of Broken Treaties* (1974), *The Metaphysics of Modern Existence* (1979), *The Nations Within: The Past and Future of American Indian Sovereignty* (1984), *The Aggression of Civilization: Federal Indian Policy Since the 1880s* (1984), *American Indian Policy in the Twentieth Century* (1985), *Red Earth, White Lies* (1995), *Documents of American Indian Diplomacy* (1999), *Spirit and Reason* (1999), *Singing for a Spirit* (1999), and *Tribes, Treaties, and Constitutional Tribulations* (2000).

Vine Deloria, Sr. (1901–1990)
Yankton Sioux minister

Vine Deloria, Sr., was the first American Indian to be named to a national executive post in the Episcopal Church. His father, Philip Deloria, was a full-blood Sioux and served as a missionary priest at Standing Rock Sioux Reservation, converting thousands of Indians to Christianity during his career. He was even honored with a statue in the Episcopal Cathedral in Washington, D.C. As a boy, Deloria attended a military academy, where he rose to the rank of cadet colonel, and then he received a bachelor of arts degree from Bard College in New York. His first job was as a mine worker in Colorado, then later he became an advisor in an Indian school.

Only after this did he decide to join the ministry. He completed the theological course at General Theological Seminary in New York City and was subsequently ordained in his father's church, where he had been baptized and confirmed. He served in the Indian missions for thirty-seven years and for several years as assistant secretary in the Division of Domestic Missions on the national staff of the Episcopal Church in New York City. Before his retirement in 1967, Deloria was made archdeacon of the Niobrara Deaconry, a

Vine Deloria, Jr.

William G. Demmert.

position in which he worked among Indian people all over the state of South Dakota.

William Demmert (1934–)
Tlingit and Sioux professor and administrator

William Demmert is a professor of education at Western Washington University, Bellingham. Born on 9 March 1934, Demmert received his doctorate in education from Harvard University in 1973. His dissertation was entitled "Critical Issues in Indian Education" (1972–1973), and he has published prolifically in the field since then. He is co-author of the report *Characteristics of Successful Leaders* (1986) and has written several articles and essays, including "Education for Marine Resources Management" (1981), "The Process of Education: A Personal Experience" (1983), and "Indian Education Revisited: A Personal Experience."

Demmert served as a dean at the University of Alaska, Juneau, and was a visiting scholar and professor at Stanford University. He has taught at the University of Washington, and directed the American Indian Program at Harvard University early in his career. He also served as the director of Indian education for the U.S. Bureau of Indian Affairs from 1976 to 1978 and was

the first U.S. deputy commissioner of Indian Education at the U.S. Office of Education (1975–1976). In the 1980s he was commissioner of education for the state of Alaska.

The pedagogue was a member of the National Commission on Teaching and America's Future. He continues to be active in educational policy as the chairperson of an international steering committee that focuses on the education of Native peoples in the circumpolar north. He is a member of the Independent Review Panel, a congressionally created group that provides advice to Congress and the secretary of education on all federal programs administered by the U.S. Department of Education.

Lionel H. deMontigny (1935–)
Turtle Mountain Chippewa physician

Lionel deMontigny, is a retired physician and public health specialist who has served several Indian communities through his work in the U.S. Public Health Service.

Born at Belcourt, North Dakota, on 17 October 1935, he received both a bachelor of arts and bachelor of science degree from the University of North Dakota. He then graduated as a medical doctor from the University of Wisconsin Medical School and went on to complete a master's degree in public health from the University of Oklahoma.

DeMontigny joined the U.S. Public Health Service as a field officer in 1962. He was soon appointed to a three-year residency training program in preventive medicine established by the Division of Indian Health in cooperation with the University of Oklahoma School of Medicine and the Oklahoma State Health Department. After this special training, he was appointed deputy director of the Portland (Oregon) area office of the U.S. Public Health Service. While working there deMontigny initiated many tribally operated health programs and encouraged Indian youth to take up careers in medicine.

He has won many awards and honors, including a scholarship from the Division of Indian Health and a fellowship from the John Hay Whitney Foundation. He is a member of the American Public Health Association and the American Medical Association.

John Deserontyon (circa 1740–1811)
Mohawk tribal leader

John Deserontyon, popularly known as Captain John Deserontyon, was an accomplished warrior and chief of the Mohawk Nation. Before the American Revolution, he became chief of the Mohawk village at Fort Hunter in New York State. When the revolution began, Deserontyon, along with many Mohawk, sided with Britain and actively participated in raids and scouting expeditions into American territory to gather intelligence for the British. On one expedition into upper New York State in 1777, he scouted the defenses at Fort Stanwix in Rome, New York, and discovered that the fort was more secure than had been previously thought. When the British subsequently attacked the fort, Deserontyon was part of a force that defeated a group of American militia approaching to offer reinforcements in what has become known as the Battle of Oriskany.

When peace returned it became clear that the Mohawk would not be able to re-occupy ancestral lands in upstate New York. Deserontyon, together with Joseph Brant, another Mohawk chief who had sided with Britain during the revolution, negotiated with the British for a new homeland for their people. Initially, the choice was for lands bordering the Bay of Quinte, on the north shore of Lake Ontario just west of Kingston, Ontario. Brant, however, changed his mind and decided in favor of the valley of the Grand River, north of Lake Erie. Despite British pressure, Deserontyon stuck with the initial choice, with the result being that two separate Mohawk villages were established. With British assistance, he built a church and school for his people. The town of Deseronto in eastern Ontario is named after Captain John Deserontyon.

Billy Diamond (1949–)
Cree tribal leader

Billy Diamond, a spokesperson for Cree opposition to hydroelectric development that threatened Cree homelands, is the son of Malcolm Diamond, a chief of the Rupert House Cree and a trapper. He was born in a tent on the outskirts of Rupert House, Quebec, on the shore of James Bay. When he was growing up, Billy Diamond lived in the bush, helping his father with his traplines. At the age of eight, he was sent to a residential school run by Canadian authorities. Diamond went on to complete high school, but he decided to forgo university studies at the behest of his father, who urged him to return to Rupert House and work for his people. In 1971, at the young age of twenty-one, Diamond was elected chief of the Rupert House Cree, and he immediately began to develop links with other Cree in the north. In 1974, Diamond became a founding member of the Grand Council of the Cree of Quebec, a province-wide organization devoted to advancing the interests of Cree in Quebec, and he served as grand chief of the council from 1974 to 1984. Diamond galvanized the Cree in opposition to hydroelectric development in James Bay and ultimately negotiated an agreement in the 1970s with the provincial government that gave the Cree greater political control over their homelands. The agreement stands as a model to many other aboriginal communities in Canada that are seeking greater autonomy and control over their identities.

Diamond became chairman of the Cree Regional Authority, which was established in 1975 and administered the implementation of the James Bay Agreement in relation to land development and services affecting the Cree. Diamond has served as chairman of the James Bay Cree School Board, founder and president of Air Creebec, a Cree-owned regional airline, owner of Cree Commercial Construction Company Limited, and Cree Yamaha Motors.

Olive Patricia Dickason (1920–)
Métis historian

Olive Dickason is professor emeritus at the University of Alberta, and adjunct professor at the University of Ottawa. She is the author of several books and

Professor Olive Patricia Dickason.

countless articles on the history of relations between Europeans and the indigenous peoples of North America, including *Canada's First Nations: A History of Founding Peoples* (1992, 1997, 2001), which won the Sir John A. Macdonald Prize from the Canadian Historical Association in 1992.

Born in Winnipeg, Manitoba, to an English father and a Métis mother whose people were buffalo hunters in the Dakotas, Dickason and her family moved one hundred miles north of Winnipeg during the Great Depression of the 1930s, where her father had mining property. Dickason received a high school education by correspondence and then went on to study at Notre Dame College, a collegiate affiliate of the University of Ottawa located at Wilcox, Saskatchewan. After obtaining a bachelor of arts degree in philosophy and French in 1943, Dickason worked for almost thirty years as a journalist for several dailies, including the *Regina Leader-Post*, the *Winnipeg Free Press*, the *Montreal Gazette*, and the *Toronto Globe and Mail*. She also reared three girls.

During this time, Dickason became increasingly aware of her Métis heritage, a subject that was never spoken of when she was growing up. She returned to academic life, this time to study the history of relations between French settlers and indigenous people. She obtained her master of arts degree in 1972 and her doctorate from the University of Ottawa in 1977. Her Ph.D. dissertation, "The Myth of the Savage and the Beginnings of French Colonialism of the Americas," which she researched in Ottawa, Quebec City, England, and France, was subsequently published by the University of Alberta Press in 1984 and became an instant classic.

A prolific and careful scholar, Dickason was named a member of the Order of Canada in 1996, received a lifetime achievement award from the National Aboriginal Achievement Foundation in 1997, and holds eight honorary doctorate degrees. She has presented many papers at conferences in the United States and Canada, and is a member of the Métis Nation of Ontario Cultural Commission and the Women of the Métis Nation of Alberta.

Henry Chee Dodge (1860–1947)
Navajo businessperson and tribal leader

Henry Chee Dodge was a businessman and chairman of the Navajo Tribal Council. The Navajo occupy extensive parts of Arizona and New Mexico (14 million acres) and have the largest population of any tribe in the United States or Canada.

Dodge has been called the Horatio Alger of the Navajo Nation because he grew up during hard times yet succeeded against all odds. When he was only four years old, he and his family were among the thousands of Navajo who were imprisoned and forced to make "the Long Walk" from Canyon de Chelly to Fort Sumter. They were forced to march for three hundred miles at bayonet point, carrying their belongings. Many did not survive the journey, but those who did faced conditions even worse at Fort Sumter, as disease and famine were rampant there. Eventually the government acknowledged their error and allowed the Navajo to return to their own land.

Dodge lived through all of this to become a wealthy and progressive businessman. He graduated from the Indian School at Fort Defiance, Arizona, and went on to become the owner of two ranches with large herds of sheep and cattle. He was the first chairman of the Navajo Tribal Council, and he served in that capacity for eight years. His son, Thomas Dodge, became an attorney and superintendent of the Navajo Nation, while daughter, Annie Dodge Wauneka, was the first woman elected to the Navajo Tribal Council.

Donnacona (?–circa 1536)
Iroquois tribal leader

Donnacona was the headman of the St. Lawrence Iroquoian village of Stadacona near Quebec City between 1534 and 1536, when Jacques Cartier, the first French explorer to the region, voyaged to and from France and North America. Donnacona met Cartier while fishing in the mouth of the St. Lawrence River in what now is the province of Quebec and protested when Cartier raised his cross to claim French sovereignty. Donnacona was seized, but then befriended by Cartier, and he permitted Cartier to take his sons Domagaya and Taignoagy back to France. A year later, they showed Cartier the way to Stadacona.

Donnacona taught Cartier's men how to cure scurvy with a drink rich with vitamin C made from white cedar. He also spoke to Cartier of the Kingdom of Saguenay to the west, said to be rich in gold and silver and inhabited by white men. Some historians have suggested that Donnacona knew of the Spanish in Mexico, but most believe that Donnacona was embellishing facts about copper deposits around Lake Superior and possibly referring to the Huron in what is now the province of Ontario. Cartier reconsidered his plan to find a passage to the Pacific Ocean and instead established a French colony on the St. Lawrence River as a base to explore the interior of the continent. To this end, Cartier lured Donnacona and his sons onto his ship. Although initially resistant, Donnacona agreed to accompany Cartier to France, when he was promised that he would be returned within a year. Upon his arrival in France, Donnacona was presented to France's King Francis I, who was impressed by Donnacona's description of the Kingdom of Saguenay and decided to challenge Spanish claims to North America by establishing a French settlement on the St. Lawrence. Cartier did not live up to his promise that he would return Donnacona to his homeland, and Donnacona died abroad.

Marie Dorion (1786–1853)
Iowa guide and interpreter

Marie Dorion, who was from the Iowa Nation, served as guide and interpreter for several trapping expeditions in the early 1800s. The Iowa were Siouan speakers, who lived in the north central parts of the Mississippi Valley.

Dorion was born along the Red River, in present-day Arkansas. She married Pierre Dorion, a mixed French Canadian and Yankton Sioux. Her husband was a fur trader and worked a route extending from St. Louis in present-day Missouri to Mandan, a town in North Dakota.

In 1811, Marie Dorion accompanied her husband on an expedition led by Wilson Price Hunt. Hunt's reservations about bringing Dorion along were quickly dispelled. Like Sacajewea, who contributed greatly to the success of the Lewis and Clark expedition, Dorion proved to be a valuable guide, interpreter, and diplomat for Hunt's expedition. Dorion lost a child during the trip, but arrived successfully in Astoria, Oregon, in February 1812.

In that same year, Dorion set out on another expedition to the Snake River country in the Pacific Northwest. All members of the party were killed by hostile Indians, except Dorion and her two sons. They endured a harsh winter, and in the spring Dorion led her boys to Walla Walla Indian country in eastern Washington. In the years that followed, Dorion married twice more to trappers, who valued her skills. Her eldest son, Baptiste, became an interpreter for the Hudson's Bay Company, the major fur trading establishment in Canada and the Pacific Northwest. In 1841, she settled in the Willamette Valley, where she lived until her death in 1853.

Michael Dorris (1945–1997)
Modoc novelist and scholar

Michael Dorris was a novelist and anthropologist who taught Native American studies at Dartmouth College in New Hampshire.

Born in Dayton, Washington, on 30 January 1945, Dorris was raised in Washington, Idaho, Kentucky, and Montana. He studied English and classics at Georgetown University, graduating with honors in 1967. He then received a master's degree in anthropology from Yale University in 1970.

After leaving Yale, Dorris held various teaching positions and became a professor of anthropology and Native American studies at Dartmouth in 1972. He produced many scholarly publications in this area, most importantly the books *Native Americans: Five Hundred Years After* (1975) and *A Guide to Research on North American Indians* (1983), co-authored with Arlene Hirschfelder and Mary Lou Byler.

However, Dorris became better known as a novelist. His first novel *A Yellow Raft on Blue Water* was published in 1989, and he wrote a best-selling novel entitled *The Crown of Columbus* (1991) with his wife Louise Erdrich, a well-known fiction writer. Dorris and Erdrich also co-wrote *The Broken Cord: A Family's On-Going Struggle with Fetal Alcohol Syndrome* (1989); this nonfiction book describes the effects of the syndrome on the couple and their adopted son Adam. Other important works by Dorris include *Guests* and *Morning Girl,* children's books, *Paper Trail*, a collection of personal essays, and *Working Men*, a collection of short stories. His writing is praised for its sensitive and intelligent treatment of American Indian issues.

Lewis Downing (d. 1872)
Cherokee tribal leader

Lewis Downing was principal chief of the Cherokee Nation from 1867 until his death in 1872. Downing was a popular Baptist minister whose church in Delaware Town, in present-day northeast Oklahoma, was the center of the Baptist mission to the Cherokee Nation. The Delaware church was the site of large gatherings of Christian Cherokee, most of whom were converts of the Baptist ministers Evan Jones and his son John. Downing was a close religious and political associate of the Joneses. During the Civil War, the Cherokee Nation divided into southern and northern supports. The conservative Cherokee of the National Party, led by Principal Chief John Ross, eventually sided with the North, while the relatively well-to-do Cherokee slave-owners sided with the South. These differences resulted in an internal Cherokee civil war and bloodshed on both sides. During most of the Civil War, Ross resided in the East and left Lewis Downing as acting chief of the loyal Cherokee. In 1866, the Cherokee agreed to a treaty of reconciliation, and he died soon after. Ross's nephew, William P. Ross, served as acting principal chief until an election was held in 1867.

Lewis Downing, the Joneses, many members of the National party, and some selected former slaveowners formed a new party of reconciliation, and Downing won the office of principal chief over the National party candidate. Serving from 1867 to 1872, Downing emphasized postwar reconstruction, national and political unification, prohibition of U.S. railroads over Cherokee Nation land, and strong support for the rights of citizenship for Cherokee freedmen.

After his death, the political coalition that was forged in 1866 won the election for principal chief in 1875 and was named the Downing party. It was composed primarily of conservative small-holding Cherokee, but issues over preservation of Cherokee national government, and the death of Downing and the Joneses, broke the Downing coalition in the late 1870s, and most of the conservative Cherokee returned to the National party, which became the party of the conservative small farmers. The Downing party then became the party of the former slave-owners and businessmen. The Downing party gained control of the Cherokee government in the 1887 election and maintained control until dissolution of the Cherokee constitutional government in 1907.

Edward P. Dozier (1916–1971)
Santa Clara Pueblo anthropologist and linguist

On 23 April 1916, Edward Dozier was born at Santa Clara Pueblo, one of twenty-three villages of Pueblo Indians in New Mexico and Arizona.

He attended off-reservation high schools, and earned his doctorate in anthropology at the University of California at Los Angeles. He served in the air force as a staff sergeant during World War II and was married and had three children.

Dozier earned an international reputation in the field of anthropology. He was a fellow at the Center for Advanced Studies in the Behavioral Sciences at Stanford, California. He held a Senior Postdoctoral Fellowship from the National Science Foundation and was also a Guggenheim fellow. Dozier was a vice-president for the Association on American Indian Affairs (an Indian advocacy organization) and a fellow of the American Association for the Advancement of Science, the American Anthropological Association, and the American Sociological Association.

Dozier's works in linguistics include studies of Native people in the Philippines. His works on the Pueblo are particularly significant and highly reliable, since non-Indian anthropologists have always had difficulty obtaining accurate Pueblo linguistic materials. Dozier was a member of the Linguistic Society of America.

Dozier is perhaps best known for his book *The Pueblo Indians of North America*, which remains a cornerstone in the anthropological field.

Wayne Ducheneaux (1936–)
Cheyenne River Sioux tribal leader

Wayne Ducheneaux is executive director of the Cheyenne River Tribal Housing Authority. In 1968, he began serving the Cheyenne River Sioux Reservation as chairman of the reservation district surrounding Eagle Butte, South Dakota. From 1974 to 1978, he was elected chairman of the Cheyenne River Sioux tribe. During the same years, Ducheneaux was vice-chairman and then chairman of the task force on tribal-state relations of the Indian Affairs Commission, vice-chairman of the United Sioux Tribes, founder and chairman of the American Indian Agriculture Credit Consortium, and a member of the President's Commission on Indian Nutrition. He was also founder and chairman of the NCAI (National Congress of American Indians) Litigation Committee, which monitors Indian legal rights and legal claims.

As a tribal official, Ducheneaux helped make many reservation improvements. Under his administration, a main waterline from Cheyenne River to Eagle Butte was completed, as was a modern underground telephone system; a 1,200-mile rural water distribution system was built, and improvements were made to the existing hospital. Ducheneaux established a tribal computer division, a centralized accounting system, and a centralized records and microfilm system. He also developed a buffalo program on the reservation and a new criminal, juvenile, and civil code for the Cheyenne River Sioux Tribe.

From 1986 to 1990, Ducheneaux was again tribal chairman of the Cheyenne River Sioux, and chairman of the Indian Agriculture Working Group, which evolved into the Indian Agriculture Council. He was also the honorary co-chairman of the Indian AIDS Committee.

Ducheneaux served as president of the National Congress of American Indians from 1989 to 1991, and he was appointed special judge in the Cheyenne River Sioux Tribal Court. During his second term at NCAI, he obtained a resolution declaring war on drug and alcohol abuse. He also instituted alcohol-free Indian fairs, rodeos, and powwows and a drug testing program for law enforcement personnel and tribal council members. He established a legal division, strengthened the tribal court system, and established an investment policy for the tribe.

Dull Knife (1810–1883)
Northern Cheyenne tribal leader

Dull Knife and his warriors were active in the Cheyenne-Arapaho War in Colorado in 1864 and 1865, the Sioux Wars for the Northern Plains in 1866 and 1867 (including the Fetterman Fight), and the War for the Black Hills of 1876 and 1877. Many of his warriors participated in the battle of the Rosebud and the Little Bighorn in June 1876, where Colonel Custer and over two hundred soldiers met their death in present-day southern Montana.

Dull Knife and Little Wolf, another Cheyenne war chief, proved difficult to capture, even during the massive government retaliation for the Little Bighorn defeat. On 25 November 1876, General George Crook attacked Dull Knife's camp in the battle of Dull Knife on the Red Fork of the Powder River in Wyoming. The Indians suffered twenty-five deaths and 173 tipis destroyed, along with food and clothing, plus five hundred ponies captured. In May 1877, Dull Knife and his followers surrendered at Fort Robinson in Nebraska, and were relocated to a reservation in Indian Territory (present-day Oklahoma).

The Northern Cheyenne were not happy living in Indian Territory, far from their traditional lands on the Northern Plains. The government had provided few supplies, little food, and malaria was rampant. Dull Knife and Little Wolf led an escape of nearly three hundred people from the assigned reservation in September 1878. They set out for their Tongue River homeland in northern Wyoming and southern Montana.

In a six-week, 1,500-mile flight, Dull Knife and his followers eluded some ten thousand pursuing soldiers and an additional three thousand civilians until many became too sick or exhausted to continue the flight. Dull Knife's group was captured on 23 October 1878, and taken back to Fort Robinson. Upon learning that they were once again en route to Fort Robinson, Dull Knife led his followers on another breakout on 9 January 1879, in the dead of winter. Only Dull Knife, his wife, son, daughter-in-law, grandchild, and another boy escaped capture and completed the trip to Chief Red Cloud's Pine Ridge Reservation in present-day South Dakota. Dull Knife and his small party were allowed to remain at Pine Ridge until, finally, in 1884, the Northern Cheyenne were officially granted the Tongue River Reservation in Montana. Dull Knife had died the year before, however, and was buried on a high butte near the Rosebud River in present-day South Dakota.

Gabriel Dumont (circa 1837–1906)
Métis tribal leader

Gabriel Dumont was active in the second Northwest Rebellion of 1885, in which Louis Riel, another Métis leader, sought to form a provisional government in Saskatchewan. Dumont could neither read nor write, but he had a great reputation as a guide, hunter, canoeist, and warrior. Dumont first engaged in plains warfare at the age of thirteen, when he took part in the defense of a Métis encampment against a Sioux war party. At the age of twenty-four, with his father, Dumont concluded a treaty between the Sioux and the Métis, which helped bring peace to the Canadian prairie. Dumont also participated in the creation of a treaty between the Blackfoot Nation and the Métis. When he was twenty-five, Dumont was elected permanent chief of his community.

In 1884, Dumont traveled to Montana where Louis Riel was living in exile, and he obtained Riel's agreement to return to Canada to lead resistance to the settlement of what is now known as Saskatchewan. Dumont became the militant leader of approximately three hundred Métis, in what became known as the second Northwest Rebellion. They were victorious in several battles against Canadian authorities, including a violent attack on Frog Lake in what is now Alberta, where nine people were killed. While Riel subsequently surrendered to authorities, Dumont fled to the United

States. Dumont attempted to organize an escape route for Riel, which never came to pass, and Riel was executed in 1885 for treason. Dumont spent several years living with the Métis of Montana before returning to Canada in 1890. In addition to dictating two memoirs of the rebellion, Dumont continued to hunt and trade up until his death in 1906.

W. Yvon Dumont (1951–)
Métis tribal leader

Yvon Dumont is the former president of the Manitoba Métis Federation. He was born at St. Laurent, Manitoba, on 21 January 1951. His father, William Dumont, was a noted political leader with the Manitoba Métis Federation, and drew his son into political life at a young age. At the age of sixteen, Dumont was elected secretary-treasurer of the St. Laurent Local of the Manitoba Métis Federation. Five years later, he was elected vice-president of the Native Council of Canada, a national organization devoted to advancing the rights of Métis and other aboriginal people not accorded Indian status by Canadian authorities.

During this time Dumont maintained his involvement with the Manitoba Métis Federation and was elected president of the federation in 1984, having run on a platform of fiscal responsibility for the federation and a promise to recommence a complicated Métis land claims case, which had been stalled in the courts for some time. Dumont hired a new lawyer, Thomas Berger, a high-profile proponent of Native rights and a former justice of the Supreme Court of British Columbia. Berger had been successful recently in gaining several important procedural victories before the Supreme Court of Canada.

Under Dumont's leadership, the finances of the Manitoba Métis Federation have stabilized and grown, and the federation has been able to participate in the building of new housing projects and related initiatives for its people. Dumont continues to be active in advocating the Métis cause throughout Manitoba and Canada. Dumont is also a governor of the University of Manitoba and has served on the National Board of the Canadian Aboriginal Economic Development Strategy.

Sophia McGillivray Durant (circa 1760–?)
Creek interpreter

Sophia McGillivray was the daughter of Lachlan McGillivray, a Scot, and Sehoy Marchand, the daughter of a Creek woman of the Wind clan, the most powerful family in the Creek Nation. She married Benjamin Durant, of Huguenot ancestry.

While not a chieftain, Durant is described as having "an air of authority about her, equal, if not superior, to that of her brother, Alexander," the famous Creek leader. During the Revolutionary War, Alexander McGillivray became a leader among the Creek in the present-day Alabama. Durant was well acquainted with the Indian language of her people, and when her brother held councils she delivered his ideas and sentiments in a speech, to which the Creek headmen listened with attention. She was accustomed to writing letters for her brother to the Spanish governor and other officials.

In the summer of 1790 while McGillivray was in New York negotiating a treaty of peace with President George Washington, some Creek threatened to attack a U.S. settlement near the Creek country. Durant and a companion mounted horses and rode for four days to prevent the attack. When she arrived at Hickory Ground, her home village and one of the most sacred towns in the Creek Nation, she assembled the Creek chiefs and threatened them with the vengeance of her brother when he returned from the North. Her bravery put a stop to the planned murders, and the leaders were arrested. Two weeks later Durant gave birth to twin daughters.

Charles A. Eastman (1858–1939)
Wahpeton (Santee) Sioux physician and author

Charles Eastman was the first Native American physician to serve on the Pine Ridge Reservation and a prolific author of works about Indian life and culture. Born at Redwood Falls, Minnesota, in 1858, Eastman was raised in a traditional Santee Sioux setting and had little contact with American society until the age of fifteen. His mother died shortly after his birth, and he was raised by his father's extended family. His father was a Sioux warrior named Many Lightnings. Many Lightnings was taken prisoner by the army during the Minnesota Sioux uprising of 1862 and later executed. After that, Eastman was raised by a paternal grandmother and learned much about the old ways and practical things that hunters and warriors had to know.

In 1874, the family moved to Flandreau, South Dakota, and Eastman was enrolled in school, which brought him into contact with U.S. culture for the first time. He would gradually come to know American society remarkably well and became a well-known Native American intellectual. Eastman attended Dartmouth College and Boston University Medical School, receiving a degree in medicine in 1890. He then became a physician at the Pine Ridge Indian Reservation in South Dakota, the first Native American in a position of authority there. During this time he witnessed the Ghost Dance

Movement and was one of the first people to visit Wounded Knee after the massacre of 1890.

Eastman later became a prolific author whose writings dealt with Indian culture and basic philosophical differences between Native beliefs and those of U.S. society. His autobiographical work *Indian Boyhood* (1902) describes his childhood and reflects a concern with youth and the experience of growing up that would last throughout his career; he was later active in the Young Men's Christian Association and was one of the founders of the Boys Scouts of America. His autobiography was followed by a series of novels on Indian life including *Red Hunters and the Animal People* (1904), *Old Indian Days* (1907), *Wigwam Evenings: Sioux Folktales Retold* (1909), and *The Soul of the Indian* (1911).

In later writings, Eastman focused more on the conflicts between Indian and U.S. culture and the historical experiences of Native American people. A second autobiography, *From the Deep Woods to Civilization* (1916) tells of his experiences as an adult Indian person in U.S. society and is strongly critical of its values and the actions of the United States government. Other, related historical subjects are treated in *The Indian Today* (1916) and *Indian Heroes and Great Chieftains* (1918).

Attorney Walter R. Echo-Hawk.

Walter Echo-Hawk (1948–)
Pawnee attorney

Walter Echo-Hawk was born on 23 June 1948, near Pawnee, Oklahoma. He received a political science degree from Oklahoma State University in 1970 and a law degree from the University of New Mexico in 1973. He has been admitted to practice law before the U.S. Supreme Court, the Supreme Court of Colorado, and several courts of appeal.

Echo-Hawk is a senior staff attorney of the Native American Rights Fund (NARF), a national, Indian-interest legal organization headquartered in Boulder, Colorado. His legal experience includes cases involving religious freedom of American Indians, prisoner rights, water rights, treaty rights, and reburial rights. In recent years, Echo-Hawk has been active in issues concerning protection of Native American human remains and Indian graves from desecration and mistreatment. He was involved in precedent-setting Nebraska legislation that directs museums to return human remains and funerary objects to tribes of origin upon request.

In 1989, Echo-Hawk represented a number of Indian tribes in negotiating the Smithsonian Institution reburial agreement, which received national attention and was enacted into law. In 1989 and 1990, he was a national leader in the Indian campaign to obtain passage of the Native American Grave Protection and Repatriation Act, which is considered the most important human rights law for Native people ever passed by Congress. He also represented the Native American Church of North America to secure passage of the 1994 amendments to the American Indian Religious Freedom Act, protecting the religious use of peyote by Indians.

Echo-Hawk is well published in the areas of religious freedom of American Indians, prison law and rights of prisoners, water rights, treaty rights, and issues concerning protection of deceased Native Americans. In 1991, he was awarded the Civil Liberties Award from the American Civil Liberties Union of Oregon "for significant contributions to the cause of individual freedom."

John E. Echohawk (1945–)
Pawnee attorney and rights activist

John Echohawk, executive director of the Native American Rights Fund (NARF), is an attorney who has

John E. Echohawk, executive director of the Native American Rights Fund.

devoted all his attention to Native American legal questions. Born in Albuquerque, New Mexico, on 11 August 1945, Echohawk graduated from the University of New Mexico in 1967, and entered a special pre-law program at the University of New Mexico School of Law that had just been initiated for Native Americans. He then went on to take a degree in law from the University of New Mexico School of Law in 1970.

On graduating, he received the Reginald Heber Smith Community Lawyer Fellowship to work with the California Indian Legal Services program in Berkeley, California. Shortly thereafter he became a cofounder of the Native American Rights Fund (NARF), a national organization centered in Boulder, Colorado, which takes major legal cases for Indian tribes.

Echohawk has been very active in community service over the years and worked to create opportunities for Indian youth. He has served on the board of directors of groups such as the Association on American Indian Affairs, the American Indian Lawyer Training Program, and the National Committee on Responsive Philanthropy. He has received several honors for these activities, receiving the President's Indian Service Award from the National Congress of American Indians and a Distinguished Service Award from the Americans for Indian Opportunity.

Eda'nsa (c. 1810–1894)
Haida tribal leader

Eda'nsa (Melting Ice from a Glacier) was a Haida chief, born on Graham Island of the Queen Charlotte Islands off the coast of mainland British Columbia. Eda'nsa also called himself Captain Douglas, testifying in 1878 that he descended from Haida Chief Blakow-Coneehaw, who had secured a trade alliance and exchanged names with a British captain named William Douglas in 1788. Eda'nsa reportedly had an association with James Douglas, governor of the colony of Vancouver Island from 1851 and governor of British Columbia until 1864.

In 1841, Eda'nsa became Haida Eagle chief of the Sta Stas Shongalth lineage, one of three lineages that vied for control of the Eagle town of Kiusta on Graham Island. Upon becoming chief, Eda'nsa succeeded in asserting his authority over the town. It has been noted that while Eda'nsa sought to be the greatest Haida chief of all, his people were not in unanimous approval of his methods. Eda'nsa became a trader in Indian slaves, acquired by other Natives by barter or raid. White traders were certainly aware of his prominence, and he served as a useful guide through the difficult waters of the Queen Charlotte Islands. It is said that trading boats occasionally encountered raiding parties from the Haida when they were in trouble. In one instance, a neighboring Haida chief raided a vessel being piloted by Eda'nsa, took white men as prisoners, plundered the strong box, and burned the ship. It was believed by the white captain that Eda'nsa had been complicit in the raid and shared in the spoils, but this charge was never proved. Eda'nsa became a Christian in 1884 and continued to seek new trading opportunities in the Queen Charlotte Islands until his death, when his title passed to his nephew Charlie Edenshaw, a renowned Haida artist.

Charlie Edenshaw (1839–1924)
Haida artist

Charlie Edenshaw was a prosperous and renowned Haida artist, member of the Eagle clan, and chief of Yatza village on Graham Island located in the Queen Charlotte Islands of British Columbia. Named Takayren (Noise in the House) at birth, Edenshaw was schooled in Haida tradition by his uncle, Eda'nsa, who himself was a chief of the Sta Stas Eagle clan of Graham Island. It is said that upon reaching adulthood, his mother gave him a small pistol. He promptly held it to his head and pulled the trigger three times. The gun went off on the third try, wounding him slightly in the face. In celebration of his brush with death, he held a potlatch, a Haida traditional ceremony and feast involving the giving of food and goods, in which he demonstrated the episode to others. Charlie Edenshaw also became known among his people as Nngkwigetklas (They Gave Ten Potlatches for Him), perhaps in recognition of his repeated participation in potlatches. Charlie Edenshaw married and had five children. The early death of his only son, Robert (Gyinawen), profoundly affected him, and it is said that he never fully recovered from the loss.

Charlie Edenshaw demonstrated artistic talent at an early age and became a skilled carver of wood and argillite, a type of black slate. His work, noted for its flowing sculptural design, grew in popularity, and he became one of the first professional Haida carvers. Edenshaw was equally talented as a silversmith, goldsmith, and woodcarver. He frequently met with anthropologists and art collectors, and so provided others with insight into Haida culture and art. Many of his carvings, including model totem poles, as well as drawings and sketches, were collected by museums and art patrons. His work dramatically illustrates the intricacy of Northwest Coast art.

Lloyd Elm (1934–)
Onondaga educator

Lloyd Elm was born in 1934 and attended the Haskell Institute in Lawrence, Kansas, where he graduated in 1953. He served in the United States Marine Corps and was released with an honorable discharge in 1958. Elm then attended Syracuse University, where he received a bachelor of arts degree in biology and education in 1964. In 1966 and 1967, he received a National Science Foundation Grant in science education. Elm was employed first in 1970 as a classroom teacher in biology and physics, then as principal of the Onondaga Indian School in Lafayette, New York. From 1976 to 1981, Elm was education programs specialist in the Office of Indian Education at the U.S. Department of Education in Washington, D.C. In 1973 and 1974, he was elected to the board of directors of the National Education Association, and from 1972 to 1978, he served on the board of directors of the National Indian Education Association. In 1976, Elm published, in the special edition of the *New York Conservationist*, an essay entitled "The History of the Ho–Dee-Nau-Sau-Nee, the People of the

Longhouse." During the 1970s, Elm resumed his education, receiving a master's degree in educational administration from Pennsylvania State University in 1979 and a Ph.D. in educational administration from the same university in 1983. He then began serving as principal of the Native American Magnet School Number 19, in Buffalo, New York, the first American Indian magnet school in the country.

From 1987 to 1990, Elm served on the New York State Commission on Education and on the initial Native American Advisory Committee on Native American Education. From 1990 to 1991, he served on the Social Studies Syllabus Review and Development Committee, and in 1992, he was appointed by the New York State Board of Regents to serve on the New York State Curriculum and Assessment Committee for Social Studies.

Georges Erasmus (1948–)
Dene tribal leader

Georges Erasmus has been a central figure in aboriginal politics in Canada since the 1970s. He was born at Fort Rae in the Northwest Territories just after the World War II. His people, the Dene Nation, are Athabaskan Indians in the Northwest Territories. Athabaskan is a Cree term that covers all the indigenous people from the interior of Alaska to the Hudson Bay whose languages are related to one another. In their own languages, these people refer to themselves as Dene or Dinneh.

Erasmus became president of the Dene Nation in 1976, during which time he successfully led efforts to stop the construction of the Mackensie Valley Pipeline, a proposed natural gas pipeline running south from Alaska through the Northwest Territories and British Columbia. In 1985, he was successful in persuading Greenpeace, an international environmental organization, to halt a proposed anti-fur campaign, arguing that it threatened traditional ways of life of his people.

Erasmus served from 1985 to 1991 as the national chief of the Assembly of First Nations, a national organization of First Nations in Canada. In 1991, Erasmus was appointed co-chair of the Royal Commission on Aboriginal Peoples. The commission was established by the federal government to examine and report on a broad range of issues concerning aboriginal peoples in Canada, including government, treaties, economic, social and cultural issues, as well as matters relating to the administration of justice and aboriginal people. Erasmus also serves as board member for many organizations and foundations across Canada dedicated to the advancement of human rights and ecological concerns. He is the co-author of *Drumbeat: Anger and Renewal in Indian Country* (1989). He has received the Order of Canada and honorary doctorate of law degrees from seven universities.

Louise Erdrich (1954–)
Turtle Mountain Chippewa novelist, poet, and critic

The daughter of a German-American father and Chippewa mother, Louise Erdrich was born at Little Falls, Minnesota, in 1954 and raised in Wahpeton, North Dakota. She was among the first group of Native American women to be recruited and accepted to Dartmouth College shortly after they began accepting women, and graduated with a major in English and creative writing in 1976. After graduation, Erdrich returned to North Dakota and conducted poetry workshops throughout the state under the auspices of the Poetry in the Schools Program of the North Dakota Arts Council. She later returned to graduate school and completed a master's degree in creative writing from Johns Hopkins University, after which she moved to Boston and became editor of the Boston Indian Council newspaper.

Erdrich's intricately interwoven novels include *Love Medicine* (1984), *The Beet Queen* (1986), *Tracks* (1988), *The Bingo Palace* (1994), *Tales of a Burning Love* (1996), and *The Antelope Wife* (1998). Erdrich has often collaborated with her late husband, Michael Dorris, and together they co-authored a best-seller entitled *The Crown of Columbus* (1991) and a non-fiction book entitled *The Broken Cord: A Family's On-Going Struggle with Fetal Alcohol Syndrome* (1989), which describes the effects of the syndrome on the couple and their adopted son Adam. Erdrich is a prolific poet, as evidenced by her highly praised works *Jacklight* and *Baptism of Desire: Poems*.

William R. Ernisse (1949–)
Seneca corporate executive

William R. Ernisse is vice-president of sales operations and marketing for the Western Operations of Xerox Corporation. Ernisse's organization is responsible for supporting the achievement of customer satisfaction, revenue, and profits from Illinois to Texas, and from Alaska to California. It represents $3.5 billion in annual revenue.

Ernisse joined Xerox in 1970 as a financial analyst in Rochester, New York. Since then he has held a number

William Ernisse.

of key management positions, including vice-president of worldwide training and vice-president of field operations for Xerox' western area. Most recently, he served as vice-president and general manager of Xerox's Greater Los Angeles Customer Business Unit.

Ernisse is one of the select group in Xerox who has earned the company's top achievement award, the President's Award, for superior performance. In addition, he has won top awards from the American Society of Training Development and the National Society for Performance and Instruction. He has been actively involved with education issues and "stay in school" initiatives for over thirteen years; he most recently served as a business representative with Al Gore's initiative on after-school programs.

Ernisse earned his undergraduate and business degrees from the Rochester Institute of Technology. He has served on the Workforce Los Angeles Steering Committee and is a member of the Los Angeles Public Education Council, and the advisory board of the Los Angeles Business Council. Ernisse has been active in establishing the first business partnership with the Los Angeles Philharmonic. In addition, he is a board member of both the Long Beach Police Athletic League and the United Way, and a board chairman of the Center for the Improvement of Child Caring. He resides with his wife, Margarete in Mission Viejo, California, and has two grown children.

Pierre Falcon (1793–1876)
Métis poet

Pierre Falcon, a well-known poet and troubadour, was born in the Swan River Valley, in what is now east-central Saskatchewan, at a trading post of the Hudson's Bay Company, a British trading company active in the Canadian plains. Falcon's father was French, and his mother was a Missouri River Indian, possibly Mandan or Cree. Thus, Falcon was Métis, a term that refers to persons of mixed Indian-European heritage who forged a common identity on the plains of western Canada in the eighteenth and nineteenth centuries. When Falcon was five, his father took him to Quebec, where he attended school until the age of fifteen, when he obtained work with the North West Company, another trading company active in the plains of Canada. He moved back to the Swan River Valley, where he traded for the company and set up a home.

Falcon's interests soon turned political, in the face of a settlement that threatened Métis landholdings in the nearby Red River Valley. Falcon joined other Métis in a skirmish, the Battle of the Seven Oaks, that resulted in the death of the governor of the territory. In the evening following the battle, Falcon composed the famous song, "Chanson de la Grenouilliére," known to many as the Battle Hymn of the Métis.

Falcon eventually settled at White Horse Plain in the Canadian prairies and embraced agriculture and the annual buffalo hunt. For several years, he served as commander of the Métis buffalo hunt and then as a justice of the peace for White Horse Plain. Falcon authored many poems and songs commemorating the Métis. He died at the age of eighty-three.

Gary Dale Farmer (1953–)
Cayuga actor, producer, and activist

Gary Dale Farmer is an actor and producer involved with Native American projects for film, television, and radio. Born on the Six Nations Reserve in Ontario, Canada, on 12 June 1953, Farmer studied at Genesee Community College and Syracuse University (both in New York State). He also had theater training at various private studios in Toronto, Canada. Farmer's first theatrical role was in Michael Cook's *On the Rim of the Curve*, which was produced during the 1976 Olympics in Montreal.

He co-starred in *Powwow Highway* (1988), which won best film at the American Indian Film Festival and for which he took the best actor award. His performance also won him a nomination for best actor from the Independent Feature Project West in Los Angeles. He appeared in the 1992 film *The Dark Wind*, based on the novel by Tony Hillerman, and co-executive produced by Robert Redford. Other films Farmer has appeared in are *The Believers* (1987), *Police Academy*, *Dead Man* (1996), and the award-winning *Smoke Signals* (1998).

Farmer has many acting credits in television, theater, and radio dramas, and recently he has also been active as a producer of television and radio programs dealing with Native American subjects. He produced a series of television shows called *Our Native Land* for the Canadian Broadcasting Corporation, and in 1989 he produced and hosted a magazine-style radio program called *Prevailing Winds*. He also produced and hosted a series of eight thirty-minute programs called *Powwow for Multilingual Television* (MTV) in Canada.

Since 1989, Farmer has lectured on Native American issues and other related topics at Dartmouth College, Cornell University, and many other campuses in the United States and Canada. In these talks, he discusses Native media programming, the importance of literacy, protecting the environment, and the need for taking an active role in community affairs. Since then he has played in countless Native theater productions and toured throughout Canada's Northern Native communities. He has published the journal *Aboriginal Voices* since the early 1990s.

Donald Fixico (1951–)
Creek/Seminole/Sac and Fox/Shawnee historian and professor

Donald L. Fixico is professor of history and director of the Indigenous Nations Studies Program (a master's degree program) at the University of Kansas. Born in Shawnee, Oklahoma, Don is a full-blood American Indian of the Sac/Fox, Shawnee, Creek, and Seminole tribes. After earning a doctorate from the University of Oklahoma, he received postdoctoral fellowships at the University of California, Los Angeles' American Indian Studies Center and the D'Arcy McNickle Center for the History of the American Indian at the Newberry Library in Chicago. He has been a visiting lecturer at the University of California, Berkeley and Los Angeles, and visiting professor at San Diego State University and at the University of Michigan, Ann Arbor. He was an exchange professor at the University of Nottingham, England, and a visiting professor in the John F. Kennedy Institute at the Freie University in Berlin, Germany. He has been on the faculty at the University of

Donald Fixico.

Wisconsin-Milwaukee and at Western Michigan University, Kalamazoo.

Fixico has written four books, *Termination and Relocation: Federal Indian Policy, 1945–1960* (1986); *Urban Indians* (1991); *The Invasion of Indian Country in the Twentieth Century: American Capitalism and Tribal Natural Resources* (1998); and *The Urban Indian Experience in America* (2000). He has edited two books: *An Anthology of Western Great Lakes Indian History* (1988) and *Rethinking American Indian History* (1997). He is completing a new book, *The American Indian and History: Native Reality and Indigenous Ethos*. His publications include over forty articles on Indians in the nineteenth and twentieth centuries.

Harry Fonseca (1946–)
Maidu artist

Harry Fonseca grew up in Sacramento, California, and has been creating art for over forty years. He has exhibited nationally and internationally in numerous solo and group shows. While pursuing an art degree at Sacramento State College, Fonseca became interested in Indian and other Native cultures and the power of

imagery invoked by ancient mythologies. At that point, he says, he became drawn to the old myths "like a magnet" and would sit for hours listening to stories told by his uncles and cousins. He states that he did some library research then but found that the writings of anthropologists and scholars lacked the excitement and personal involvement in stories told by his own relatives.

Fonseca is probably best known for paintings and other graphics depicting Coyote, the cunning, reckless, and irresponsible trickster of Maidu mythology. In these works, Coyote is typically rendered in ultra-modern clothing or absurd situations that somehow produce satirical images of contemporary American society. One painting from the early 1980s depicts Coyote and his female counterpart, Rose, performing a ballet step in Tchaikovsky's *Swan Lake*.

Fonseca had already mastered formal painting techniques and established a reputation as an artist before becoming involved with Coyote and other subject matter based on Maidu mythology. His career took a major leap when the Coyote paintings first appeared at the Wheelwright Museum in Santa Fe, New Mexico, during the 1970s. Countless delightful manifestations have been produced in the years since then. The artist currently lives in Santa Fe, exploring new images and new techniques in painting and print-making.

Philip Fontaine (1944–)
Sagkeeng Ojibway leader

Philip Fontaine is former national chief of the Assembly of First Nations and former grand chief of the Assembly of Manitoba Chiefs. He is well-known in Canada for his work in advancing the cause of aboriginal rights. He was born at the Fort Alexander Reserve ninety miles north of Winnipeg, Manitoba, in 1944. Fontaine learned English while attending residential school. He went on to complete high school and earn a bachelor's degree in political studies from the University of Manitoba in 1981.

Fontaine served as chief of the Fort Alexander/ Sagkeeng First Nation between 1972 and 1976. During this time, he worked to introduce unique reforms, including one of the first locally controlled First Nation school programs in the country, a locally controlled child welfare agency, and the first alcohol treatment center for aboriginal people in Manitoba. As grand chief of the Assembly of Manitoba Chiefs, Fontaine was one of several aboriginal leaders who fought successfully for the demise of the Meech Lake Accord, a 1990 federal proposal to amend the Canadian Constitution to respond to demands by the province of Quebec for greater autonomy, but which ignored aboriginal concerns. Fontaine was also responsible for organizing a leadership debate on aboriginal issues during Manitoba's provincial election in 1990. In addition, he has been a leader in calling for the public disclosure of, and a federal inquiry into, Native child abuse by residential school authorities. Fontaine has worked to reunite Native children adopted early in life out of their communities with their birth mothers, sought to place authority traditionally exercised by federal authorities over such matters as education and medicine in the hands of First Nations themselves, and has been active in the politics of constitutional reform in Canada.

Jack D. Forbes (1934–)
Powhatan and Lenape author and scholar

Born in Long Beach, California, on 7 January 1934, Jack Forbes once wrote that his heritage is "the long trail of Indians from the east coast, driven little by little towards the west." He graduated from the University of Southern California in 1953 and went on to receive his master's degree (1955) and Ph.D. (1959) in anthropology from the same university. During the 1960s Forbes was an organizer of activist groups such as the Native American Movement, the Coalition of Eastern Native Americans, and the United Native Americans. He was also a founder of D-Q University in Davis, California, and worked as a volunteer instructor there. He became a professor and department chair of Native American studies at the University of California, Davis, in 1969 and continued teaching in that position until his retirement in 1998.

Forbes has guest lectured all over the world and served as a visiting Fullbright professor at the University of Warwick, England, as the Tinbergen Chair at the Erasmus University of Rotterdam, as a visiting scholar at the Institute of Social Anthropology and Linacre College of Oxford University, and as a visiting professor in literature at the University of Essex, England.

Over the years Forbes has published several important books on Indian subjects, including *Warriors of the Colorado: the Yuma of the Quechan Nation and their Neighbors* (1955), *The Indian in America's Past* (1964), *Native Americans of California and Nevada* (1969), and *Native Americans and Nixon: Presidential Politics and Minority Self-Determination* (1981). His novel *Red Blood* was published in 1997. His chapbook *What is Time?* is now in print, along with *Naming Our Land* and *El-Lay Ritos*, two collections of poetry.

Josiah Francis (Hillis Hayo) (d. 1818)
Creek and Seminole tribal leader

Josiah Francis was a leader in the Creek War of 1813 and 1814. He is also known by the name Hillis Hayo or Hillis Hadjo, which is a Muskogean religious title.

In 1811, Francis traveled with Tecumseh, helping him to spread his message of Indian confederation and unity and opposition to U.S. expansion to southeastern Indian nations. Tecumseh was trying to create an alliance of Indian nations that would block further U.S. expansion onto Indian lands. Influenced by Tecumseh, Francis helped organize the Red Stick Creek, mostly the conservative Creek villages in present-day Alabama who opposed U.S.-inspired changes in Creek government, laws, and horticulture. In the Creek War, Francis, with William Weatherford, another upper town Creek leader, led the Red Sticks against U.S. and Indian forces led by General Andrew Jackson. In 1815, Francis traveled to England in search of support for his struggle against the United States. In 1818, he was captured by U.S. forces at St. Marks, a trading post in northern Florida, after General Jackson lured him onto a gunboat flying a British flag. Jackson had Francis executed.

Francis's daughter Milly also gained notoriety during the 1800s due to an alleged incident in which she begged her father to spare the life of a Georgia militia soldier. According to the story, Francis relented and the soldier was spared, but he ordered the soldier to shave his head and join the tribe.

Lee Francis (contemporary)
Laguna Pueblo/Anishinabe and Lebanese writer/ editor and administrator

Lee Francis is associate professor of Native American studies and director of the Native American Studies Department at the University of New Mexico. He is also the national director of Wordcraft Circle of Native Writers and Storytellers.

Francis received his bachelor's degree and master's degree from San Francisco State University and a doctorate from Western Institute for Social Research in Berkeley, California. He has taught in the American studies program at The American University, in Washington, D.C., where he served as director of the Washington Internships for Native Students (WINS) program. He has also served as director of the Pre-Engineering Intensive Learning Academy for Native students at California State University, Long Beach, student affairs officer at the University of California, Santa Barbara, associate director of the Educational

Opportunity Program at San Francisco State University, and is a senior faculty member with Meta-Life Adult Professional Training Institute.

He is a member of the editorial board of Contemporary Native American Communities book series of AltaMira Press and a trustee and secretary of the board of the Laguna Pueblo Educational Foundation. Francis serves on the First Book Award (for Poetry and Prose) Selection Committee for the Native Writers' Circle of the Americas and is a member of the board of directors for the Greenfield Literary Review.

Francis has also held government appointments including Indian youth specialist with the U.S. Department of the Interior's assistant secretary for Indian Affairs Office of Alcohol and Substance Abuse Prevention, legislative assistant to United States Senator Hugh Scott, special assistant to U.S. Senator Pete V. Domenic (R-NM), and staff assistant to the Joint Committee on Congressional Operations of the U.S. Congress.

Francis is also an elected life member of the National Psychiatric Association and an active member in numerous organizations including the National Indian Education Association and the American Indian Philosophy Association.

His literary accomplishments include *Native Time: A Historical Time Line of Native America* (1996), *Reclaiming The Vision—Past, Present and Future: Native Voices for the Eighth Generation* (co-editor, 1996), and *When the Rain Sings: Poems by Young Native Americans* (editor, 1999).

Milly Francis (circa 1802–1848)
Creek recipient of Congressional Medal of Honor

Milly Francis was the daughter of Josiah Francis (Hillis Hadjo), a Creek tribal leader. In 1817, the Creek captured Captain Duncan McKrimmon of the Georgia militia, tied him to a stake, and prepared to shoot him. Milly Francis interceded and saved McKrimmon's life. McKrimmon later proposed marriage. However, Milly declined, stating that "she would have interceded for any white captive."

During the removal of the Creek to Indian Territory beyond the Mississippi River, in present-day Oklahoma, Francis relocated with the transplanted Creek Nation in present-day Muskogee, Oklahoma. Widowed and with eight children, she found it difficult to support her family. Major Ethan Allen Hitchcock reported her case to Washington, and in 1844, Congress voted her a Congressional Medal of honor and an annual pension of $96 for having saved the life of Captain McKrimmon. Four years passed, however before the U.S. agent to the Creek was instructed to notify Francis of the award.

The agent found her "in a most wretched condition," dying of tuberculosis. She died without receiving either the medal or the pension. A granite marker on the campus of Bacone College, a Baptist Indian school near Muskogee, records the main events of her life and her burial "somewhere in this vicinity."

Billy Frank, Jr. (1931–)
Nisqually activist

Billy Frank, Jr., is a grassroots political activist who for the past fifty years has fought for the land and fishing rights of Native Americans in the Pacific Northwest. Frank's own tribe, the Nisqually, live in eastern Washington State. Many Northwest Coast tribes claim the right to fish at their traditional and customary places as negotiated in treaties with the United States in the 1850s. Since then, however, many northwestern states have refused to recognize Indian treaty fishing rights. Over the past three decades Frank participated in Washington State and tribal relations as the state moved from confrontational police tactics, to litigation, and eventually to cooperation on Indian fishing rights issues.

In the 1960s, Frank was jailed frequently for his role in civil acts of disobedience, which included "fishing out of season." He opposed Washington State fishing authorities and a powerful sports fishermen's lobby. Years of resistance finally paid off. Since the 1974 *Boldt* decision that affirmed the treaty fishing rights of tribes, Frank's work has been less controversial. He is widely credited for playing a major role in turning a bitter two-decade battle between Northwest states and Indian tribes from physical and legal confrontation to negotiation.

Currently, Frank is chairman of the Northwest Indian Fisheries Commission. This organization represents twenty western Washington tribes in negotiating fisheries and habitat management plans with state and federal governments, and it makes many decisions that were once made by Frank's opponents in state government. In this role Frank has been a tireless worker on behalf of building salmon and steelhead runs for Indians and non-Indians. Celebrated nationally as a Native American leader, he was awarded the Albert Schweitzer Prize for Humanitarianism at Johns Hopkins University in Baltimore in 1991.

Gregory W. Frazier (1947–)
Crow businessperson and author

Gregory Frazier is a successful business entrepreneur who has used his expertise to help Indians in the

Northwest. Born at Richmond, Indiana, on 5 September 1947, Frazier graduated from Temple University in Philadelphia with a degree in business administration (1972), and then completed an M.B.A. (1978) and Ph.D. (1988) at the University of Puget Sound in Washington State.

Frazier has been an extremely dynamic leader in business and economic development since the early 1970s and now owns and operates several business enterprises. From 1972 until 1974, he was an instructor for the American Indian Management Institute, an educational institution for training Indian people in business; then he served as executive director of the Seattle Indian Center from 1974 to 1977. From 1977 until 1979, he was the executive director of AL-IND-ESK-A, the thirteenth regional corporation, in Seattle, Washington. As part of the Alaska Native Claims Settlement Act of 1971, the U.S. government created thirteen for-profit corporations, twelve in Alaska and one for at-large shareholders consisting of Aleut, Indian, and Eskimo people living in the lower forty-eight states. This thirteenth corporation became known by the acronym AL-IND-ESK-A.

In 1977, Frazier also became president of Absarokee Investments in Seattle and, during the 1980s, started several other private businesses including Alpine Adventure Films and Cablestar Distributing, both of Englewood, Colorado. Besides running these and other business enterprises, Frazier has remained active in organizations such as National Advisory Council on Indian Education and the National Urban Indian Council. He is the author of several books, including *While We're At It, Let's Get You a Job* (1984), *American Indian Index* (1987), and *Smoke Signals* (1989). Frazier is a professional motorcycle road racer and top desert race competitor. One of only seven Americans to complete a global motorcycle tour, Frazier is currently on an unprecedented second tour of the world.

Robert Lee Freeman (1939–)
Dakota and Luiseño graphic artist

Robert Lee Freeman was born at Valley Center on the Rincon Indian Reservation in southern California on 14 January 1939. His mother was a Dakota (Sioux) from the Crow Creek Reservation in South Dakota, and his father a Luiseño who was raised nearby. He began painting in 1961 and received an associate of arts degree from Palomar College in San Marcos, California, in 1976. Freeman works in a variety of styles ranging from cartooning to fine art painting and is adept in a variety of media including oil and watercolor painting,

etching, pen and ink drawing, bronze sculpture, airbrush painting, and lithography. He has applied his diverse abilities as a teacher of Native American art at Grossmont College in San Diego and at Palomar College in San Marcos, California.

Freeman has won more than 150 major Indian art awards and has numerous exhibitions to his credit, including shows at the Department of the Interior (Washington, D.C.), the Heard Museum (Phoenix, Arizona), and the Scottsdale National Indian Art Exhibit. He has a forty-five-foot mural installed at the Los Angeles Public Library.

Gall (Pizi) (1840–1894)
Hunkpapa Sioux tribal leader

In the 1860s and 1870s, Gall was a leader in the wars for the Bozeman Trail and the Black Hills in present-day Wyoming, Montana, and South Dakota. He was one of the principal strategists in the Battle of Little Bighorn, where in June 1876 Colonel George Custer and some two hundred U.S. soldiers were badly defeated. Gall is credited with developing the successful tactics that led to Custer's defeat.

Raised as an orphan until his adoption by Sitting Bull, a major Sioux leader, Gall proved his abilities as a warrior early in life. During the skirmishes for control of the Bozeman Trail in 1866 and 1867, Gall established and honed the guerrilla techniques and decoy tactics he used later in the struggle for control of the Black Hills. During the war for the Black Hills, he was Sitting Bull's chief military strategist. In the now-famous Battle at Little Bighorn, Gall's military prowess gained its greatest notoriety, and his tactics played a major role in the victory.

After the Indian defeats following Little Bighorn, Gall left for Canada with Sitting Bull. In 1881, he returned to the United States with about three hundred people and surrendered at the Poplar Agency in present-day eastern Montana. He was relocated on the Standing Rock Reservation in North Dakota. There, Gall became friends with Indian agent James McLaughlin and adopted a way of life more European than Indian. Gall negotiated a number of treaties that divided Sioux lands, and he did not take a stance in the Ghost Dance Uprising of 1890. His relationship with the U.S. government was not well perceived by other Indians, including those who had fought with him years earlier. In a gesture of rejection by another veteran of the Little Bighorn Battle, Kicking Bear left out Gall's portrait from a famous pictographic version of Custer's defeat.

Carol Geddes (1945–)
Tlingit filmmaker and writer

Born in the small Yukon village of Teslin, Carol Geddes received a B.A. in English and philosophy from Carleton University in Ottawa, Ontario, Canada's capital city. She later did post-graduate work in communications at Concordia University in Montreal, Quebec.

Beginning in 1983, Geddes has devoted herself to filmmaking and occasional writing. In her first documentary, *Place For Our People* (1983), Geddes introduced the successful Montreal Native Friendship Centre and called for the development of similar community institutions across the country. In 1986, Geddes wrote and compiled a report entitled *Community Profiles: The Native Community*, for the National Film Board of Canada, a federally funded organization devoted to the advancement of film. Geddes's report highlighted the needs of First Nations in Canada and evaluated existing films on Native people. From 1986 to 1990, Geddes produced twenty videos, many focusing on the traditions and art of Native people in Canada. Her first major film, *Doctor, Lawyer, and Indian Chief* (1986), documented the lives of five Native women in Canada and won an award at the 1988 National Educational Film and Video Festival in San Francisco. As a writer, Geddes received the *National Magazine*'s Silver Foundation Award in 1991 for her article, "Growing Up Native," which appeared in *Homemaker's* magazine.

In 1990, Geddes was appointed the first producer of the National Film Board's Studio One, located in Edmonton, Alberta, and devoted entirely to the production of indigenous media. Recently, she directed *No Turning Back* (1997), *Forgotten Warriors* (1997), and *Picturing a People: George Johnston, Tlingit Photographer* (1997).

Hanay Geiogamah (1945–)
Kiowa/Delaware playwright, director, and scholar

Hanay Geiogamah is professor of Theatre and American Indian studies at the University of California, Los Angeles. He was artistic director of the Native American Theater Ensemble (NATE) in New York City from 1972 to 1976. He received a bachelor's degree in theater and drama in 1980 from Indiana University in Bloomington, where he worked also as freelance director, producer, and instructor-organizer for American Indian communications and arts projects. From 1980 to 1982, he was the artistic director of Native Americans in Arts in New York City. Then in 1983, he was visiting professor of theater and Native American Studies at Colorado College in Colorado Springs. He also has been artistic director of the Native American Theater Ensemble in Los Angeles and of the American Indian Dance Theater, a national professional dance company.

Geiogamah served as director of communications and then executive director of the American Indian Registry for the Performing Arts in Los Angeles from 1984 to 1988, and in 1989, he worked as technical consultant advisor for *Dark Wind*, a feature film produced by Wildwood Production, whose executive producer was Robert Redford. In the following years, he combined his professional career with teaching experiences, as well as with writing and producing plays. From spring 1988 through January 1989, he conducted tours of the American Indian Dance Theater in the United States and Europe, with a special eight-week engagement at the Casino de Paris Theater in Paris, France. In 1989, Geiogamah co-directed and helped produce the American Indian Dance Theater's Special on *Great Performances*, *Dance in America Series*, aired nationally on the Public Broadcasting System in 1990. Also in 1990, he wrote a teleplay based on N. Scott Momaday's 1969 book *The Way To Rainy Mountain*.

Geiogamah's plays have been written for productions by American Indian Theaters and performing arts groups. Among them are *Body Indian* (1972), performed both in the United States and in Europe; *Foghorn* (1973), premiere production by the Native American Theater Ensemble in Reichskabarrett, West Berlin, Germany; and *Coon Cons Coyote* (1976). He has received various honors and awards, such as the William Randolph Hearst National Writing Award from the University of Oklahoma in 1967 and the Charles MacMahon Foundation Scholarship in Journalism in 1963, and he was guest speaker at the American Theater Association's Forty-Sixth National Convention in New York City in 1982. From 1972 to 1989, Geiogamah received numerous grants from a variety of institutions to develop and promote NATE, the American Indian Registry for Performing Arts, and for NAPAF, the American Indian Dance Theater/Native American Performing Arts Foundation.

Alexander General (Deskahe) (1889–1965)
Cayuga and Oneida tribal leader and activist

Alexander General was a tribal leader and intellectual figure of Cayuga and Oneida descent. The Cayuga and Oneida are both tribes of the Iroquois Confederacy; the Cayuga were located along the shores of Cayuga Lake in New York State, and the Oneida are also located in New York, though some now also live in Wisconsin and Ontario, Canada.

Born on the Six Nations Reserve in Ontario, Canada, in 1889, General was the youngest of eight children. His family lived in poverty as marginal subsistence farmers, a situation that worsened after the accidental death of his father when General was only ten years old.

After his father's death, General went to work to help support his mother and therefore never went beyond the fourth or fifth grade in school. He later said that he learned more English through working than in school, holding jobs on the railroad and in foundries. Through diligence and good fortune he gradually saved enough money to go into farming with his brother and became a very successful farmer by reservation standards.

Alexander belonged to a chiefly lineage of the Iroquois Confederacy and at the age of eighteen he began memorizing the ritual speeches of the Iroquois longhouse, the meeting place of confederate council. He gradually became known as the major speaker and ritualist of his community, and later, at the age of thirty-six, General was elected by his lineage to represent their views and took the chiefly title Deskahe.

Because of his cultural knowledge and his ability to explain Longhouse ceremonials and religious concepts in an intellectual manner, Deskahe became an important figure in anthropology. Frank Speck's book *The Midwinter Rites of the Cayuga Longhouse* (1949) was written as a collaboration with Deskahe and includes his name on the title page, but Speck was only one of many scholars who worked with this extraordinary leader and ritualist during the years between 1932 and 1959.

Most importantly, Deskahe was a political activist who once even traveled to England (in 1930) to argue that Canada had no jurisdiction over the Iroquois. He felt that tribal sovereignty could only be guaranteed by retaining the hereditary Iroquois council, and he also fought to re-establish the position of traditional Iroquois chiefs and to broaden their authority. He argued to anthropologists, in the news media, and to anyone who would listen, that his people had been robbed of their birthright. He also organized groups such as the Indian Defense League and the Mohawk Workers to help the Iroquois resist Canadian government authority.

Dan George (1899–1981)
Squamish actor

Dan George was an accomplished and acclaimed actor, perhaps best known for his portrayal of a Cheyenne elder named Old Lodge Skins in the film *Little Big Man*. For this role, he was awarded the New York Film Critics Award for best supporting actor in 1970. Popularly referred to as Chief Dan George, he was born on

the Burrard Indian Reserve near Vancouver, British Columbia, and began acting late in life. Until the age of sixty, he worked as a longshoreman, logger, and musician. He was chief of the Squamish band of Burrard Inlet, British Columbia, from 1951 to 1963.

Dan George was discovered as an actor in 1959, and he dedicated the rest of his life to improving the image of Indian people in film, theater, and television. He portrayed an Indian elder in Canadian television and theater, including the Canadian Broadcasting Corporation production of *Caribou Country* and the original production of *The Ecstasy of Rita Joe*, a contemporary drama about Indian people. He had roles in at least eight feature films, including *Smith* (1969), *Harry and Tonto* (1974), and *The Outlaw Josey Wales* (1975), as well as his role in *Little Big Man*. He also was the author of two books of prose-poetry, *My Heart Soars* (1974) and *My Spirit Soars* (1982). Dan George refused to endorse Indian political causes, but throughout his career he sought to change dominant images of Indian people in the media. Dan George died in Vancouver at the age of eighty-two.

Forrest J. Gerard (1925–)
Blackfeet government administrator and assistant secretary of the interior

Forrest Gerard is a public health specialist who has served as an official in various government agencies relating to Native American concerns. Born in Browning, Montana, on 15 January 1925, Gerard graduated from Montana State University and had additional training at the National Tuberculosis Association Training Institute and the American Management Association. He then served as executive secretary of the Wyoming Tuberculosis and Health Association and as a staff member of the Montana Tuberculosis Association. For six years he was the tribal relations officer for the Division of Indian Health in the U.S. Public Health Service in Washington, D.C., and then he was chief of the division for four years.

In 1965, Gerard was awarded a fellowship in Congressional Operations, which allowed him a year of intensive study in Washington focusing on the organization of Congress and the legislative process. In 1966 he was appointed legislative liaison officer for the Bureau of Indian Affairs (BIA), a position in which he worked to strengthen the Indian position in government. Later, he became director of the Office of Indian Affairs in the Department of Health, Education, and Welfare.

During the late 1970s, Gerard was appointed assistant secretary of the interior for Indian affairs. This position superseded the old position of commissioner of Indian Affairs. His administration was deeply concerned with the task of implementing the Self Determination and Educational Assistance Act of 1975 (P.L. 93–638).

Gerard opposed the dismantling of the BIA, mandated by P.L. 93–638, and fought many public battles with Senator James Abourezk, who authored the act and tried to manage its implementation.

A member of numerous boards and committees, Gerard has also won many awards and honors for his service to Indian people. He was an air force pilot during World War II and flew thirty-five combat missions.

Geronimo (Goyathlay) (1825–1909)
Chiricahua Apache tribal leader

After the death of Cochise in 1874, the Chiricahua Apache once again entered an era of nearly constant warfare. Into this conflict, a younger generation of Indian leaders rose up to take the place of older Apache leaders such as Cochise and Mangas Coloradas. One of the most feared and respected of these warriors was Goyathlay, who is generally known as Geronimo.

Like many Apache of his generation, Geronimo's early years were drenched in violence and warfare. His own wife and children were killed by Mexican soldiers. From this point onward, his life was filled with a succession of military raids, captures, escapes, and brief attempts to live on Indian reservations.

Although he was pursued relentlessly, Geronimo eluded the larger U.S. forces until 1886, when he was forced to surrender. Newspapers, presidents, and politicians called for Geronimo's execution, but, instead, he was imprisoned.

In 1894, Geronimo and many of his close Apache comrades were moved to Fort Sill, Oklahoma. In 1909, Geronimo died at Fort Sill, still a prisoner of war and, as such, never allowed to return to his homeland.

Tim Giago (Nanwica Kciji) (1934–)
Oglala Lakota publisher and author

Tim Giago is editor and publisher of the *Lakota Nation Journal*. He is also founder and former editor/publisher of *Indian Country Today/Lakota Times*, the largest, independently owned American Indian weekly newspaper. Born on the Pine Ridge Reservation on 12 July 1934, Giago attended San Jose State College and the University of Nevada at Reno. His writing career

Tim Giago.

began in 1979, when he became an Indian affairs columnist for the *Rapid City Journal* in Rapid City, South Dakota. This led to a position as a full-time reporter, and in 1981 Giago created the *Lakota Times/Indian Country Today*, which he sold in 1998.

He is the author of three books *The Aboriginal Sin* (1978), *Notes from Indian Country, Volume I* (1983), and *Notes From Indian Country, Volume II* (1999). In 1984, he founded the Native American Journalists Association and became the first American Indian to serve on the advisory board of the Freedom Forum in Arlington, Virginia.

Giago continues to write a syndicated column about contemporary Indian issues that appears in newspapers nationwide and his work has been featured in *People Magazine*, *New York Times*, and the *Denver Post*. He has appeared on the *Oprah Winfrey Show*, *NBC Nightly News with Tom Brokaw*, and many national radio programs.

He is the recipient of two doctoral degrees and has won many awards, including the Civil Rights and Human Rights Award given by the South Dakota Education Association (1988). In 1982, he was named Print Media Person of the Year at the Native American Media Convention. Giago was the first American Indian to receive a Nieman Fellowship for Journalism at Harvard University. Giago was inducted into the South Dakota Hall of Fame in 1994.

George A. Gill (1925–)
Omaha educator

Born at Sioux City, Iowa, on 25 July 1925, George Gill attended the University of Nebraska and later received his bachelor's and master's degrees in education from Arizona State University. He is the first Indian to receive a master's degree with a specialization in Indian education and was the recipient of numerous awards, including scholarships from the American Indian Foundation, the National Congress of American Indians, the Association on American Indian Affairs, and the American Missionary Association.

Early in his career, Gill served as a teacher in federal Indian schools and in public schools, and he also directed workshops for instructional aides. Later he became a faculty member in the Department of Education and director of the Indian Education Center at the University of Arizona. He has been a director of the Annual Indian Education Conference and has also served as editor of the Journal of Indian Education. In 1960, he was the Arizona Indian delegate to the White House Conference on Children and Youth.

Besides these accomplishments, Gill had a total of twenty-two years and four months in the U.S. Navy (active and inactive), serving in Europe, the Mediterranean, the Pacific, and Korea; he was awarded the Navy Good Conduct and Combat medals.

James Gladstone (1887–1971)
Blood senator

As Canada's first aboriginal senator, James Gladstone was a strong advocate of the rights of First Nations. Also known as Akay-na-muka (Many Guns), he was born at Mountain Hill, Northwest Territories, on 21 May 1887, and was raised on the Blood Reserve in Alberta. In his early twenties, Gladstone worked as a typesetter for the *Calgary Herald* and then as a scout and interpreter for the Royal Northwest Mounted Police on his reserve. During World War I, Gladstone promoted bigger production from the reserves' farms. He excelled at farming his eight hundred acres of land on the Blood Reserve, where he was the first Indian to have electricity and to own a tractor.

Gladstone was one of the initial members of the Indian Association of Alberta, which was formed in

1939, and was its president from 1948 to 1954, and again in 1956. He traveled to Ottawa on a number of occasions to represent aboriginal interests in negotiations with the federal government. Gladstone became Canada's first aboriginal senator when he was appointed to the Senate in 1958. In his first speech as a Canadian senator, Gladstone spoke in Blackfoot, "as a recognition of the first Canadians."

In 1959, Gladstone was named co-chairman of a joint Senate and House of Commons committee to study Canadian Indians. Gladstone was on the committee in 1960 when treaty Indians were given for the first time the right to vote in national elections. In 1969, Gladstone travelled to Japan as a member of the Canadian delegation to the Moral Rearmament Asian Assembly. Gladstone died in Fernie, British Columbia, on 4 September 1971.

Diane Glancy (1941–)
Cherokee writer, educator, and dramatist

Diane Glancy was born in Kansas City, Missouri, in 1941. Her mother was German and English, and her father was Cherokee. She received her B.A. in English

Diane Glancy.

from the University of Missouri in 1964, her M.A. in creative studies from the University of Central Oklahoma in 1983, and her M.F.A from the University of Iowa in 1988.

Glancy was artist-in-residence for the State Arts Council of Oklahoma from 1981 to 1988. She is now a professor at Macalester College in St. Paul, Minnesota, where she teaches Native American literature and creative writing. She was also the Edlestein-Keller Minnesota Writer of Distinction at the University of Minnesota in 1998.

She has published six volumes of poetry. The latest is *The Relief of America*. She has published four collections of short stories and edited three anthologies and a collection of nine plays. Her four novels include *Flutie* and *Pushing the Bear: The 1838 Trail of Tears*.

Among her awards are an American Book Award, the Native American Prose Award, a Minnesota Book Award, a National Endowment for the Arts, a National Endowment for the Humanities, a Minnesota State Arts Fellowship, a Pushcart Prize, and the Emily Dickinson Poetry Prize from the Poetry Society of America.

Carl Nelson Gorman (1907–1998)
Navajo artist

A distinguished artist, Carl Gorman was among the first to employ traditional Navajo motifs in producing modern works of art. He was born on the Navajo Reservation at Chinle, Arizona, on 5 October 1907. A member of the Black Sheep clan, Gorman came from a distinguished family. His parents founded the first Presbyterian mission at Chinle; his father was also a cattleman and Indian trader, while his mother focused on the arts. She was a traditional weaver and translated many religious hymns from English into Navajo. Others in the family were also tribal leaders and well-known silversmiths.

During World War II, Gorman served in the U.S. Marine Corps and became one of the famous Navajo Code Talkers, whose messages in their native language confused the Japanese military in the Pacific campaigns. On leaving the service, Gorman used the GI Bill to support formal art studies at Otis Art Institute in Los Angeles, California, and he worked as a technical illustrator for Douglas Aircraft, established his own silkscreen design company, and taught Indian art at the University of California, Davis.

Gorman's works have appeared in numerous solo and group shows and is represented in many public and private collections. His works include a variety of styles and media. Always an innovator, yet firmly grounded in

tradition, this creative figure once even originated a Navajo Gourd Rattle Dance, a new dance based on a combination of traditional elements.

R. C. Gorman (1932–)
Navajo artist

R. C. Gorman is one of the leading contemporary American Indian artists. Born on the reservation at Chinle, Arizona, on 26 July 1932, Gorman is the descendant of distinguished artists and traditionalists on both sides of his family. He was encouraged while still quite young to follow in his father's footsteps, and he once said in an interview that he could remember making his first drawings when he was three years old by tracing designs with his fingers in the sand and mud of the wash at the base of the Canyon de Chelly, a beautiful and famous Navajo landmark.

As a youth he lived in a hogan, or traditional Navajo-style dwelling, and herded sheep with his grandmother, but he soon became exposed to wider influences and developed a cosmopolitan art style of considerable range and depth. After graduating from Ganado Presbyterian High School, he went on to study art at Northern Arizona University at Flagstaff and at San Francisco State University. He later received a grant from the Navajo Tribal Council to study art at Mexico City College. This was the first time the tribe had awarded a grant for study outside the United States.

Gorman has received an extraordinary number of awards and honors and is probably the most heralded of all contemporary Indian artists. In 1973, he was the only living artist to be included in the show "Masterworks of the Museum of the American Indian," held at the Metropolitan Museum in New York, and two of his drawings were selected for the cover of the show's catalog. In 1975, he was honored by being the first artist chosen for a series of solo exhibitions of contemporary Indian art at the Museum of the American Indian in New York.

Over the years, Gorman has published several articles about some of his other interests, which include Mexican art and artists and cave paintings, or petroglyphs.

Kevin Gover (1955–)
Pawnee political leader and lawyer

As the assistant secretary of Indian Affairs, Kevin Gover heads the Bureau of Indian Affairs (BIA), a part of the U.S. government's Interior Department. His appointment by the Clinton Administration came in 1997 after former BIA head Ada Deer resigned. Prior to this appointment, Gover was one of the nation's leading lawyers, focusing on Indian rights.

Born in Lawton, Oklahoma, Gover was one of three children of a white mother, Margaret Lou Richardson, and a Pawnee father, Billy Gover. When he was fifteen, a VISTA (Volunteers in Service to America) worker noticed Gover's potential and arranged for him to attend the prestigious Saint Paul's Preparatory School in Concord, New Hampshire, from which he graduated in 1973. From there, Gover attended Princeton University and graduated in 1978 with a major in public and international affairs.

During his undergraduate work, Gover's family relocated to Albuquerque, New Mexico, and immediately after college, Gover headed to his new home to attend law school at the University of New Mexico. He received his law degree from the university in 1981. It was during this time that Gover married; he and his former wife would have two children by the end of their marriage ten years later.

Soon after law school Gover was hired as a clerk to the late U.S. District Court Judge Juan G. Burciaga, and from 1983 to 1986 he worked for the well-known Washington, D.C.-based law firm of Fried, Frank, Harris, Shriver, and Jacobsen, where he specialized in environmental and natural-resource law, as well as federal Indian law.

Upon his return home to Albuquerque, Gover formed his own law firm in 1986 with Cate Stetson and Susan Williams. The firm specializes in federal Indian, environmental, natural resource, and housing law.

In 1992 Gover stepped back into national governmental affairs as the coordinator for Bill Clinton's campaign through Indian Country. He also attended the 1996 Democratic National Convention in Chicago as the head of a nation-wide voter registration for Native peoples. In the same year, Gover and his law partners contributed $22,000 to the Democratic National Committee and congressional candidates.

In 1999 Gover was the recipient of a Distinguished Alumni Award from the University of New Mexico.

Cuthbert Grant (1793–1854)
Métis tribal leader

Cuthbert Grant was perhaps the first leader of the Métis. Grant played a large role in shaping a sense of Métis nationalism. He worked most of his life as a fur trader first for the North West Company, a group of Montreal traders formed in 1779, and later in life for the company that first capitalized on the fur trade, the Hudson's Bay Company. When he was nineteen years old, he was put in charge of a small outpost in Fort Esperance, on the Qu'Appelle River in what later became Saskatchewan.

Historians claim that Grant was chosen by his superiors to foster a sense of Métis identity partly to solidify the North West Company's trading rights in the region, as it was facing stiff competition from the Hudson's Bay Company. Grant was named "captain of the Métis" by his superior in 1814 and led efforts to persuade, through friendly and unfriendly means, recent settlers who put a strain on the community's resources to return to central Canada. In 1816, Grant also led an attack on the Hudson's Bay Company, resulting in a massacre of approximately twenty people. Although charges were brought against Grant for these and other actions, they were eventually dropped, and after the Hudson's Bay Company and the North West Company merged in 1821, Grant worked for the Hudson's Bay Company in a number of different positions. He briefly served as a special constable at Fort Garry (later known as Winnipeg) and later as warden, justice of the peace, and sheriff. He served as captain of the Métis annual buffalo hunts, and in the 1840s, Grant mediated a temporary truce between the Métis and the Sioux, who had been fighting over territory and buffalo hunting.

Rayna Diane Green (1942–)
Cherokee museum administrator and folklorist

Rayna Green is a museum administrator and folklorist who has made many contributions to our understanding of Native American achievements in the areas of science and technology and has also published books on other aspects of American folklore and on the writing and other accomplishments of Native American women.

Born in Dallas, Texas, on 18 July 1942, Green received her bachelor's degree from Southern Methodist University (1963) and went on to complete her M.A. and Ph.D. in folklore and American studies at Indiana University (1966 and 1974, respectively).

On completing her doctorate she directed a major research program on Native Americans in science under sponsorship of the American Association for the Advancement of Science (1975–1980) and later served as director of a similar program at Dartmouth College (1980–1983). From 1983 to 1985, Green helped plan the American Indian Program at the National Museum of American History, Smithsonian Institution, Washington, D.C., and she has been the director of the program ever since. In previous years she was also a visiting professor at the University of Massachusetts and at Yale University.

Green has published articles in the *Handbook of American Folklore*, the *Handbook of North American Indians*, and various other scholarly volumes and magazines. She has also written or edited her own books including *Native American Women: A Contextual Bibliography* (1982) and *That's What She Said: Contemporary Poetry and Fiction by Native American Women* (1984). Her most recent work is *The British Museum Encyclopedia of Native America (1999)*.

Graham Greene (1950–)
Oneida actor

A film actor who has found success in Canada and the United States, Graham Greene is a full-blood Oneida born on the Six Nations Reserve in southwestern Ontario in 1950. He began his career in television, film, and radio in 1976. Before becoming an actor, Greene worked at a number of different jobs, including stints as a high steel worker, a civil technologist, and a draftsman. He also worked as an audio technician for rock and roll bands and owned his own recording studio in Hamilton, Ontario. Greene also lived for a short time in Britain in the early 1980s, where he performed on stage.

Upon his return to Canada, Greene was cast in the British film, *Revolution*, starring Al Pacino and directed by Hugh Hudson. Greene is perhaps best known for his performance in *Dances with Wolves*, a 1991 film produced and directed by Kevin Costner, which won several Academy Awards, including the award for best picture. Greene has been cast in a number of television series and is known for his work in *The Campbells, Spirit Bay, Captain Power, Running Brave, Adderley,* and *Night Heat*. His film roles include *Powwow Highway, Clearcut, Medicine River, Die Hard With a Vengeance, The Education of Little Tree,* and *The Green Mile*.

Hagler (1690–1763)
Catawba tribal leader

It is believed that Hagler was born along the Catawba River in northern South Carolina and became principal chief of the Catawba about 1748. By this time the Catawba had been greatly reduced in numbers as the result of warfare with their traditional enemies, the Shawnee, Cherokee, and Iroquois, as well as from European-introduced diseases such as smallpox.

Hagler developed friendly relations with the British colonists, meeting with them on numerous occasions for negotiations, and thus helped ensure his people's survival and maintenance of their traditional ways. In 1751, he attended a peace conference in Albany, New York. In a meeting with North Carolina officials in 1754 and in a letter to the chief justice in 1756, he argued against the sale of liquor to the Catawba. In 1758, during the French and Indian War, Hagler and his warriors sided with the English in an attack on the French garrison at Fort Duquesne (present-day Pittsburgh, Pennsylvania). In 1759, Hagler assisted the English in battle against Cherokee militants. Because of his support, the English built forts along the Catawba River to prevent attacks on the Catawba by other tribes. They also granted a reservation to the Catawba in 1792, near present-day Rock Hill, South Carolina.

Hagler was killed by a party of Shawnee in 1763. In 1826, South Carolina erected a statue of Hagler at Camden, considered to be the first such memorial to an American Indian in the United States.

Janet Campbell Hale (1947–)
Coeur d'Alene novelist

Janet Campbell Hale was born in Los Angeles, California, in 1947 and raised mainly on the Yakima Indian Reservation in Washington State. She returned to California and received her bachelor's degree from the University of California, Berkeley, and her M.A. in English from the University of California, Davis. She attended law school at Berkeley and Gonzaga Law School in Spokane, Washinton.

Hale's first novel *Owl's Song* (1974) focuses on the experiences of an Indian boy who is forced to live with alcoholism and other social problems on the reservation, and then finds himself placed in an urban setting and urban schools that are unprepared to deal with Indian students. Her other major work is entitled *The Jailing of Celia Capture* (1985), which portrays an urban Indian woman trying to cope with alcoholism and to rebuild her life after being separated from her husband and children. She also wrote *Bloodlines: Odyssey of a Native Daughter* (1993) and has a forthcoming volume of short stories entitled *Women on the Run*. She currently lives in Idaho on the Coeur d'Alene reservation.

Hancock (early 1700s)
Tuscarora tribal leader

From 1711 to 1713, the Iroquoian-speaking Tuscarora, living in present-day North and South Carolina, fought a series of battles to protect their lands against English settlers. Hancock, who some colonists called "King Hancock," was a Tuscarora leader in these wars.

The open conflict between the Tuscarora and English settlers began in 1711. Swiss settler Christoph Von Graffenried forced a group of Tuscarora families off their land. When Von Graffenried refused to pay for the land he seized, Tuscarora warriors retaliated with raids against settlements between Pamilic Sound and the Neuse River. A series of attacks and counterattacks ensued. In 1712, leaders in North and South Carolina sent a large military brigade led by Colonel John Barnwell to quell the Tuscarora. The first battle took place in Cotechney, Hancock's home village. After the English attackers were repulsed, a temporary truce was struck between Hancock and Barnwell. North Carolina officials, however, ordered Barnwell back into the field. In the face of another battle, Hancock agreed to a lasting truce, which was quickly violated by Barnwell's men, who captured Tuscarora for slaves. (During the late 1600s and early 1700s, many Indians were sold to work on plantations or shipped for sale in the Caribbean Islands off the southern coast of the present-day United States.)

In 1713, the colonists amassed a final assault on the Tuscarora. Under the command of Colonel James Moore, the colonial army and 1,000 Indian allies defeated Hancock and his followers. Hundreds of Tuscarora were killed, and hundreds more sold into slavery. Many Tuscarora survivors fled northward to the New York colony.

When they arrived in New York, the Tuscarora found that they spoke a language closely related to the Iroquois of the Iroquois Confederacy, composed of the Seneca, Oneida, Mohawk, Cayuga, and Onondaga Nations. The Tuscarora were not allowed to place their leaders among the forty-nine chiefs of the Iroquois confederate council, but Tuscarora interests were represented by the Oneida chiefs. The Tuscarora took up residence near Oneida villages and have ever since maintained close alliance with the Oneida. Before the arrival of the Tuscarora in the 1710s, the Iroquois Confederacy was often called the Five Nations, but after the Tuscarora arrival the confederacy was often referred to as the Six Nations.

Handsome Lake (d. 1815)
Seneca spiritual leader

The name Handsome Lake is the sachem title of the Turtle clan from among the Seneca, the westernmost nation of the Iroquois Confederacy. The Iroquois Confederacy consisted of six nations and forty-nine sachems, or chiefs, chosen from historically privileged families. Handsome Lake obtained his title sometime before 1799 and held it until his death in 1815. A relative within the Turtle clan, reckoned only through the female line, assumed the name and leadership role after his death.

As a young man, Handsome Lake participated in the forest wars of the period: the French and Indian War (1755–1759), Pontiac's War (1763), and the American Revolutionary War (1775–1783). By the late 1790s, the once-powerful Iroquois lost most of their territory and were relegated to small reserves in upstate New York. While the Iroquois were experiencing social and cultural depression resulting from their recent losses, starting in 1799 Handsome Lake reported a series of visions and preached the *Gaiwiio* or "Good Word" to the Iroquois. He quickly obtained many followers and taught that the Iroquois must reorganize central aspects of their economic, social, and religious life. Under Handsome Lake's guidance, many Iroquois communities adopted new moral codes, men took up agriculture and constructed family farms, and many individuals adopted new religious ceremonies and beliefs. Handsome Lake's message combined elements of Quakerism, Catholicism, and traditional Iroquois beliefs. The new religion helped the Iroquois make the transition from a hunter society to a reservation agricultural community. In the 1830s, after his death, Handsome Lake's followers formalized his teachings into a church, known as the Handsome Lake Church; his teachings are still practiced today by many Iroquois.

Chitto Harjo (1846–1912)
Creek tribal leader

Chitto Harjo (Crazy Snake) was born in Indian Territory, in present-day Oklahoma, and was a member of the ancient holy town of Abihka in the Creek Nation. The sacred white towns among the Creek western or upper town villages were always centers of resistance to political and cultural change in Creek society. After Isparhecher, the leader of the conservative Creek, became principal chief in 1895 but failed to prevent the dissolution of the Creek government, Harjo assumed leadership of the Creek conservatives, who did not wish to surrender their government or their land. The Curtis Act of 1898 decreed the allotment of land and the abolishment of the governments in Indian Territory. The Creek government had little choice but to conform to the demands of the stronger U.S. government.

In a last-ditch effort to avoid allotment and abolishment of the Creek government, the conservative Creek elected Harjo leader. Between 1897 and 1901, the conservative Creek, called Snakes, formed a "snake" or underground government. Harjo was declared hereditary chief, and the government was installed at Hickory Ground, a sacred village within the Creek tradition. The Snakes held the position that the Creek Treaty of 1832 guaranteed them the right to maintain their own government. They refused to recognize that the United States had the power to abolish the Creek government. Harjo ran for principal chief in 1903 but lost handily to Pleasant Porter, who was willing to accommodate the U.S. plans for allotting Creek land and dismantling the Creek government. The Snakes under Harjo's leadership continued to disobey the Creek constitution and government, and on several occasions between 1900 and 1912, U.S. troops and marshals were called in to arrest Snake leaders, quell unrest, and break up Snake meetings. In one skirmish, Harjo was wounded and later died from his wounds. Without this strong leader, the Snake movement faded away.

Joy Harjo (1951–)
Muscogee poet and educator

Joy Harjo is associate professor of American Indian studies and English at the University of California, Los Angeles. She was born in Tulsa, Oklahoma, and is an enrolled member of the Muscogee Nation. She is a graduate of the Institute of American Indian Arts in Santa Fe, New Mexico. She received a BA from the University of New Mexico and an MFA in creative writing from the University of Iowa. She has also completed the filmmaking program at the Anthropology Film Center and a songwriting workshop at Berkelee School of Music in Boston.

She has published six books of poetry, including *The Last Song, What Moon Drove Me to This?*, *She Had Some Horses, In Mad Love and War, The Woman Who Fell From the Sky*, and her latest, *A Map to the Next World*.

Harjo was the narrator for the *Native Americans* series on the Turner Network and also narrated the Emmy award-winning show, *Navajo Codetalkers* for National Geographic.

Harjo has received several wards for her writing, including the 1998 Lila Wallace–Reader's Digest Award, the 1997 New Mexico Governor's Award for Excellence in the Arts, The Lifetime Achievement Award from the Native Writers' Circle of the Americas, the William Carlos Williams Award from the Poetry Society of America, the poetry award from the Oklahoma Center for the Arts, and the Oklahoma Book Award.

She also performs nationally and internationally alone and with her band, Joy Harjo and Poetic Justice. Their first CD, *Letter from the End of the Twentieth Century*, was released in 1997.

Suzan Shown Harjo (1945–)
Cheyenne and Muscogee activist and poet

Born in El Reno, Oklahoma, Suzan Shown Harjo has worked to reshape federal Indian policy in Washington, D.C. An energetic and effective advocate, she has helped Native peoples recover over one million acres of land and has developed the most important Native cultural laws in the modern era, including the 1996 Executive Order on Indian Sacred Sites, 1990 Native American Graves Protection and Repatriation Act, 1989 National Museum of the American Indian Act, and the 1978 American Indian Religious Freedom Act.

President of the Morning Star Institute in Washington, D.C., since 1984, she is an Artists Council founder and co-chair of Indian Art Northwest (1996–), and a founding trustee of the National Museum of the American Indian (1990–1996). A special assistant in the Carter Administration and principal author of the President's Report to Congress on American Indian Religious Freedom in 1979, she also served as executive director of the National Congress of American Indians (1984–1989).

Harjo has an extensive background in journalism in addition to her accomplishments as a widely-published

Joy Harjo.

poet and curator of numerous art shows at the House and Senate Rotundas, Peabody Essex Museum, and Eitlejorg Museum.

Elijah Harper (1949–)
Cree provincial legislator

Elijah Harper is perhaps best known in Canada for his opposition to the Meech Lake Accord, a 1990 federal proposal to amend the Canadian Constitution to respond to demands by the province of Quebec for greater autonomy. Harper became the voice of aboriginal people, who objected to the exclusion of aboriginal concerns from the accord. In June 1990, Harper blocked the accord's passage in the Manitoba legislature. The accord's demise heightened the awareness of political demands by aboriginal people in Canada and led to new talks on constitutional reform that placed aboriginal issues at the top of the agenda.

Harper was born at Red Sucker Lake, Manitoba, and attended residential school. After completing high school, he studied anthropology at the University of Manitoba in Winnipeg from 1970 to 1972. He married Elizabeth Ann Ross in the fall of 1973, and they have four children. During these years, Harper worked in a number of different community development positions and was elected chief of his home community's Red Sucker Lake Band in 1977. He held that post until his election to the Manitoba legislature in 1981, with reelections in 1986, 1988 and 1990. Harper served as legislative assistant to the minister of Northern Affairs between 1981 and 1986 and co-chaired the Native affairs committee of the provincial cabinet. In 1986, Harper was appointed minister responsible for Native affairs and in 1987 became minister of Northern Affairs.

The image of Harper standing in the Manitoba legislature, holding a single eagle feather and depriving the legislature of the necessary unanimous consent to pass the Meech Lake Accord struck a deep chord in the Canadian national psyche. Harper was awarded the 1990 Canadian press newsmaker of the year award and, in 1991, the Stanley Knowles Humanitarian Award.

LaDonna Harris (1931–)
Comanche activist

LaDonna Harris is a Comanche woman who has promoted equal opportunity for Indian people on a national level and has accomplished much in helping to strengthen self-government and economic self-sufficiency among Native Americans throughout the United States. Born in Temple, Oklahoma, on 15 February 1931, Harris was raised in a conservative household and spoke only the Comanche language before attending public school. Her work in the public eye began during the 1960s, when she was thrust onto the national political scene as the wife of Fred Harris, the Democratic Senator from Oklahoma. In 1965 she founded Oklahomans for Indian Opportunity, a nationally known Indian self-help organization, and since then she has been active as chair or board member of groups such as the Women's National Advisory Council on Poverty, the National Rural Housing Conference, the National Association of Mental Health, and the Joint Commission on Mental Health of Children. In 1970, Harris founded and served as president of Americans for Indian Opportunity, a national advocacy group dedicated to helping Indian tribal groups achieve self-determined political, economic, and social goals. In 1980 she became the vice-presidential nominee for the environmentalist Citizen's Party.

A strong activist for world peace, Harris has participated in several international conferences on peace since 1968. She has traveled in the (then) Soviet Union, Mali, Senegal, and various South American countries as a representative of the Inter-American Indigenous Institute, an agency of the Organization of American States. Harris has received many awards, including an honorary doctorate in law from Dartmouth University. LaDonna Harris lives in New Mexico, and currently serves as the president of Americans for Indian Opportunity, which manages many Indian leadership training programs including The American Indian Ambassador Program.

Ned A. Hatathli (1923–1972)
Navajo businessperson and educator

A person of many talents, Ned Hatathli contributed to the welfare of the Navajo people in various ways. Hatathli was born in a Navajo hogan in Coalmine Mesa, Arizona, on 11 October 1923, and was raised in a very traditional setting. He attended a government boarding school in Tuba City, Arizona, and got his first glimpse of the outside world when the school sponsored a field trip to industrial areas in the south. From that point on, he sought further education. He attended Haskell Institute in Lawrence, Kansas; then, after serving two years in the U.S. Navy during World War II, he attended Northern Arizona University and received his bachelor's degree. He later received a doctorate in education from the University of Colorado, Boulder.

Hatathli's service to the Navajo community began as manager of the Navajo Arts and Crafts Guild. He also played a major role as a member of the tribal council in developing the utilization of natural resources—especially coal, uranium, and timber—and is credited with helping to produce major increases in employment on the Navajo Reservation. Hatathli was a founder and the first Indian president of Navajo Community College. He once said that the college "stands for Indians controlling their own destiny"; when asked what made it different from other colleges, he said, "Well, we don't teach that Columbus discovered America."

Ira Hamilton Hayes (1923–1955)
Pima World War II hero

A full-blooded member of the Pima tribe, Ira Hayes was probably the most famous Indian soldier of World War II. Born in Sacaton, Arizona, on 23 January 1923, Hayes joined the marines in 1942 and saw action throughout the Pacific as a paratrooper. In February 1945, he landed as part of the Fifth Marine Division assault troops on Iwo Jima, a barren island considered important as a base for launching air strikes against Japan. There he took part in a forward attack on Mount Suribachi and was one of six marines who raised the United States flag on the summit of the volcanic peak in the midst of heavy enemy fire. An Associated Press photographer captured the moment on film, and it became one of the most inspiring war photographs ever taken. The famous bronze monument commemorating the battle of Iwo Jima in Washington, D.C., is based on this image.

Brought back to the United States with two other survivors of the Mount Suribachi flag-raising, Hayes was feted as a hero and indeed received extra attention because he was an Indian. However, he was confused and disturbed by the unwanted and excessive publicity. He became an alcoholic, was arrested many times, and died of exposure on 24 January 1955. He once said, "Sometimes I wished that guy had never made that picture."

King Hendrick (1680–1755)
Mohawk-Mahican tribal leader

Born among the Mahican, an Algonkian Nation living in present-day eastern Connecticut, Hendrick was adopted by the Mohawk, one of the Five Nations of the Iroquois Confederacy. He was an important leader of his people and liaison to British settlers when he made his famous trip to England in 1710. Though American Indians had visited England before 1710, the visit of Hendrick and his Iroquois colleagues was the first royal invitation. The event generated a mountain of publicity. The four Mohawk visitors were dined, feted, toured, and gawked at, much like any instant celebrity. Of the four "kings," only Hendrick could be construed in any way as an ambassador of his people. After his return to North America, Hendrick became a spokesman for the Iroquois League and was a key English ally in their battles against the French in New France, present-day Canada. In 1754, Hendrick was invited to the Albany Congress where he consulted with the colonists on their plans for unification. Hendrick also chastised the colonial government for failing to protect the "frontier" against the French and hostile enemies. Perhaps as a result of Hendrick's relationship with colonial leaders, the colonial and later U.S. government in many ways reflected the structure of the Iroquois League. In 1755 Hendrick died of wounds suffered at the battle of Lake George, during the French and Indian War (1756–1763). He had been leading a force of Mohawk warriors with British troops against French forces. Hendrick lived on, however, albeit in a rather fanciful way, in the imagination of English readers. A number of English literary works glorified and extolled Hendrick as an example of the "noble savage," a popular philosophical and literary theme of this era.

William L. Hensley (1941–)
Inuit state senator and lawyer

William L. Hensley is an Alaska state senator whose district covers more than 150,000 square miles and has a population of nearly twenty thousand people, 90 percent of whom are Eskimos like himself. The term *Eskimo* is actually an Algonquian derogation meaning "raw meat eaters," which historically has been used to identify Inuit- and Yupik-speaking peoples living along the Arctic Rim in North America and Asia. Many modern descendants feel that the word Inuit would be more correct, but this term excludes the Yupik-speakers of Alaska.

Born in Kotzebue, Alaska, in 1941, Hensley attended the University of Alaska in 1960 and 1961, then studied at George Washington University in Washington, D.C., and received his bachelor's degree from that school in 1966. He later studied law at the University of Alaska (1966), the University of New Mexico (1967), and the University of California, Los Angeles (1968).

Hensley has been active in land claims implementation and rural economic development since the late 1960s, when he served as chair of the Alaska State Rural

William L. Hensley.

Affairs Commission (1968–1972) and also directed the Land Claims Task Force (1968). In 1966 he wrote a paper "What Rights to Land Have the Alaska Natives: The Primary Issue" where as a graduate student at the University of Alaska he circulated the paper that argued the Alaska Native lands had never been sold. Also in 1966 Hensley wrote letters to all the villages in his home area and helped gather them into a unified organization called the Northwest Alaska Native Association (NANA), composed mainly of Inupiat Villages in the Kotzebue region. He was one of the founding members (1966) and president (1972) of the Alaska Federation of Natives (AFN), a state-wide organization that lobbied in Washington for resolution of Native land claims in Alaska during the 1960s. He played an active part in the passage of the Alaska Native Claims Settlement Act of 1971, which granted Alaska Natives $962 million and 44 million acres of land.

Hensley served in the Alaska House of Representatives from 1966 to 1970 and has been a member of the state senate since 1970. He has been active in many Native organizations over the years, including executive director of the Northwest Alaska Native Association in 1968. He was commissioner with Alaska Department of Commerce and Development from 1995 to 1997 and served on various state boards concerned with economic development and employment training. Since 1997 Hensley has been working for Alyeska Pipeline.

Lance David Henson (1944–)
Cheyenne poet and playwright

To date Lance Henson has seventeen books of poetry published. Of these, half are published in the United States and the others are printed in countries around the world. He has lectured and read in nine countries, and his work has been translated into twenty-five languages. Clearly, this Southern Cheyenne poet and playwright is the one of the foremost Native American writers of the late twentieth century.

Born in Washington, D.C., Henson was reared on a farm by his grandparents and their family on government-allotment land outside Calumet, Oklahoma. The poet has described his childhood as culturally centered and traditional. In fact, he is an active member of the Native American Church and has participated in the Cheyenne Sun Dance on several occasions as both a painter and a dancer. A member of the Cheyenne Dog Soldier Society, Henson served in the U.S. Marine Corps after high school and during the Vietnam War. He is a black belt in karate.

The poet remained in Oklahoma for college, receiving his bachelor's degree in English from Oklahoma College of Liberal Arts (now the University of Science and Arts of Oklahoma) in Chickasha. He then obtained his master's degree in creative writing at the University of Tulsa.

In the early 1970s, Henson published his first book of poetry, *Keeper of Arrows*, with Renaissance Press in Johnstown, Pennsylvania. The work, along with others published in that decade, including *Naming the Dark: Poems for the Cheyenne* (1976) and *Buffalo Marrow on Black* (1979), focus on Cheyenne culture, language, and history. The poems often explore the exploitation of the tribe by the encroaching white population. His more recent works, such as *Another Song for America* (1987), *Teepee* (1987, published in Italy), and *Another Distance: New and Selected Poems* (1991), broaden his subject base by bringing in his travel experiences, recent historical events, environmental issues, and human rights. Many critics contend that his newer poems expound on tribal concepts and culture.

Expanding his literary talents, Henson has become recognized as a playwright in recent years. He co-wrote two plays in the early 1990s: *Winter Man*, with Andy Tierstien, and *Coyote Road*, with Jeff Hooper. The former received a warm reception at the La MaMa Experimental Theatre Company.

For ten years following his education, Henson conducted poetry workshops for the Artist in Residence program of the State Arts Council of Oklahoma. After this, the poet began traveling throughout the United States and Europe. While Henson continues to lecture and read around the globe, he inherited his grandparents' land and considers the home there his base.

Charlotte W. Heth (1937–)
Cherokee ethnomusicologist and educator

A leading figure in research on American Indian music, Charlotte Heth is equally well known for developing innovative programs in Native American studies at the university level. Born 29 October 1937, Heth took her bachelor's and master's degrees at the University of Tulsa in Oklahoma and went on to complete a doctorate in ethno-musicology at the University of California, Los Angeles (1975). She then became a member of the faculty in ethnonomusicology at UCLA for the next thirteen years, also serving as director of the UCLA American Indian Studies Center for much of this time.

Cherokee ethnomusicologist and educator Charlotte W. Heth.

After completing a two-year visiting professorship at Cornell University (1988–1989), Heth returned to UCLA and retired in 1992.

As an ethnomusicologist, Heth is perhaps most important for bringing attention to contemporary developments in American Indian music and underlining the importance and validity of these art forms for contemporary Indian people. This marked a significant departure from earlier research, which mainly sought to characterize Indian music from an anthropological perspective. Her focus on actual Indian singers also led Heth to produce a series of eight videotapes in which Native performers talked about their music and musical techniques in their own terms. Besides these activities she produced six record albums of Native American music for New World Records and has several books and articles on the subject to her credit. Heth was the editor of a collection of essays on Indian music in the series entitled *Selected Reports in Ethnomusicology* at the University of California, Los Angeles, and wrote the introductory article, "Traditional Music of the North American Indians" (1980).

As an educator and administrator, Heth helped develop and implement an interdisciplinary master's degree program in American Indian studies at UCLA and was co-author (with Susan Guyette) of a book-length needs assessment entitled *Issues for the Future of American Indian Higher Education* (1985). She has been the recipient of numerous honors and fellowhips and served on various arts and humanities panels in California, New York, and Washington, D.C.

John Brinton Napoleon Hewitt (1859–1937)
Tuscarora anthropologist

John Hewitt was a noted anthropologist in the late 1800s and into the 1900s. His study and research of Iroquois political and social systems shed light on the nature of the Iroquois Confederacy and drew parallels with the democratic system of the United States.

Hewitt was born in western New York, of a part-Tuscarora mother and a Scottish father. He gave up his first ambition to be a doctor of medicine (like his father) to pursue anthropology. In 1880, he met Erminie A. Smith, who employed him to help her record Iroquois legends. Six years later, when Smith died, Hewitt continued his research and information collecting. By this time, Hewitt was in the employ of the Smithsonian Bureau of Ethnology. Hewitt also interviewed two future principal chiefs of the Creek Nation, Pleasant Porter and Legus Perryman, in the early 1880s. He wrote a manuscript on Creek history and society, which remained unpublished until 1939. The manuscript was edited by the famous anthropologist John Swanton and published as "Notes on the Creek Indians" *Anthropological Papers*, American Bureau of Ethnology, Bulletin 123. Hewitt provided a major source of information about the history and culture of the Creek Nation, who traditionally lived in present-day Georgia and Alabama, but most now live in Oklahoma. Many of Hewitt's ideas can be examined in his published collection of letters to Arthur C. Parker, another famous Iroquois scholar.

Hiawatha (unknown)
Iroquois tribal leader

Aiowantha, who is sometimes called Hiawatha, devoted his life to ending the bloodshed between the Five Nations—the Mohawk, Oneida, Cayuga, Seneca, and Onondaga. In conjunction with Deganawida, he established the Confederation of Five Nations or the League of the Iroquois.

The exact date is unknown but most likely before 1492, Hiawatha, together with the Huron prophet Deganawida, developed plans to end tribal feuding by establishing laws and ceremonies for peacefully settling disputes among the Five Nations. Because Deganawida had a speech impediment, Hiawatha became the principal spokesperson. His early efforts to end the violence plaguing the Iroquois Nations were thwarted by a powerful Onondaga opponent named Tadodaho, who opposed the reform movement and confederation plan. When Hiawatha's message fell upon unreceptive ears among his own people, he left his home to preach his message among the Mohawk, Oneida, and Cayuga who embraced his ideas. Eventually even the Onondaga, and Tadodaho himself, were convinced (Deganawida gave Hiawatha increased legitimacy in the eyes of the Onondaga) of the benefits offered by Hiawatha's plan. The Onondaga were persuaded to join the proposed league, and the Iroquois Confederacy, based on democratic, representative government, came into being. The Founding Fathers of the U.S. Constitution knew about and discussed the example of the Iroquois League. They borrowed a number of political concepts from the confederacy such as political equality, separation of governmental powers, checks and balances on political powers, and emphasis on preserving political freedom.

Tomson Highway (1951–)
Cree playwright

Tomson Highway was born in a tent along his father's trapline in northern Manitoba on 6 December 1951. His first language was Cree; he learned English when he was sent to a boarding school in The Pas, Manitoba, at the age of six. Highway remained at the Catholic-run school until he was fifteen, returning to his family for only two months each year. He went on to high school in Winnipeg, Manitoba, living in white foster homes and graduating in June 1970. At the University of Manitoba and later at the University of Western Ontario, Highway studied music, graduating with a bachelor of music honors in 1975. He then worked for seven years with several Native organizations, helping to develop cultural programs with Native inmates and children.

At the age of thirty, Highway decided to write his first play, hoping to bring life on "the rez" to a mainstream audience. The reaction to *The Rez Sisters* in December 1986 took Highway by surprise. It was a huge success, winning the prestigious Dora Mavor Moore award for best new play in Toronto's 1987–1988 theater season; it was runner-up for the Floyd S. Chalmers award for outstanding Canadian play of 1986. *The Rez Sisters* toured to sold-out audiences across Canada and was one of two plays representing Canada on the main stage of the Edinburgh International Festival, a festival that showcases international drama. Highway's next play, *Dry Lips Oughta Move to Kapuskasing*, won four Dora Mavor Moore awards, including best new play. The University of Toronto produced *Rose*, the third play in the Rez Cycle, in 2000.

Until June 1992, Highway was the artistic director of Native Earth Performing Arts, Inc., Toronto's only professional Native theater company. Highway has written five other plays and continues in his quest to celebrate Canada's Native people through his art. His first novel, *The Kiss of the Fur Queen* (1998), was on the Canadian Best Sellers list for seven weeks.

Charlie Hill (1951–)
Oneida-Mohawk-Cree comedian and actor

After frequent spots on *The Tonight Show* and *Late Night with David Letterman*, as well as several television bit parts, Charlie Hill has become a nationally recognized entertainer and performer. Hill believes that the tragedies of Indian history are made easier through laughter, and he strives to make people laugh with—not at—Indian life.

Born the son of Eileen and Norbert S. Hill, Sr., Hill grew up mostly in Detroit and on the Oneida Indian Reservation in Wisconsin. Throughout his elementary and high school years, Hill's teachers often reprimanded him for entertaining instead of learning. As is his style, Hill took such censure positively, a sign of his eventual break into the comedy scene.

Writer, comedian Charlie Hill.

Hill's first comedy appearance was at Catch a Rising Star in New York City. While he was somewhat comfortable onstage due to his background in theater, Hill feels that stand-up is a performer's greatest challenge, for the only person stand-up comedians have to depend on is themselves. Such challenges did not stop him, however. A few years later in Los Angeles, Hill auditioned at The Comedy Store for Richard Pryor, who gave Hill his first national television appearance. Pryor, in fact, is one of Hill's idols, alongside such comic geniuses as Lenny Bruce and Dick Gregory.

Hill's on-stage performance led to several television and screen roles, including a part on the *Bionic Woman* and on the hit show *Roseanne*. He eventually became a writer for *Roseanne*, writing jokes and creating story lines.

The Native comic emphasizes the importance of traditional comedians in Indian mythology and history. He oftentimes refers to the *heyokas*, traditional Lakota holy men, and other trickster figures who contribute to a powerful history of Indian laughter and humor.

Hill has received the American Indian Entertainer of the Year award four times, and has been voted the number one Indian comedian in America. In the fall of 2000 a documentary on Hill was released on PBS

entitled *On and Off the Rez with Charlie Hill*. In addition the comedian hosts a national comedy series on public television titled *Club Red with Charlie Hill*. He lives in Los Angeles with his wife Lenora and children Nizhone, Nasbah, Nanabah, and Nabahe.

Gwendolyn A. Hill (1952–)
Chippewa and Cree educator and administrator

Born in Fort Belknap, Montana, on 31 October 1952, Gwendolyn Hill received her bachelor's degree in education from Northern Montana College (1976) and later completed a master's degree in public administration at the University of South Dakota (1989). From 1975 to 1980, she was a teacher at Stewart Indian School near Carson City, Nevada. She later became the dean and president of Sisseton-Wahpeton Community College in Sisseton, South Dakota.

Over the years, Hill has helped to promote Indian education nationally and at the local level, working with organizations such as the American Indian Higher Education Consortium, the Native American Student Advisory Council, and the Sisseton (South Dakota) Public Schools Parent Advisory Committee.

Norbert S. Hill, Jr. (contemporary)
Oneida educator

Norbert S. Hill, Jr., is the former executive director of the American Indian Science and Engineering Society (AISES) in Boulder, Colorado, and is the founder of *Winds of Change*, a magazine devoted to developing young scientists and engineers within the Indian community. At the University of Wisconsin-Oshkosh he received a bachelor of science in sociology/anthropology in 1969 and a master of science in guidance and counseling. He is completing his Ph.D. at the University of Colorado on social foundations of education.

For more than fifteen years, Hill has actively developed and administered educational programs for American Indians. He worked as a high school guidance counselor before becoming director of the Indian Education Opportunity Program at the University of Colorado in 1977. Hill created or co-founded many successful projects and was selected as educational policy fellow by the Institute of Educational Leadership in 1980.

He served as executive director of AISES from 1983 to 1998 and transformed it from a professional society to a national resource in Indian education. He has written over a dozen articles and reports in the fields of education and Indian history and demography. Hill's honors include the National Council for Minorities in Engineering's Reginald H. Jones Distinguished Service

Norbert S. Hill, Jr.

Award and the Chancellor's Award from the University of Wisconsin-Oshkosh in 1988.

Roberta Hill (1947–)
Oneida poet, short story writer, and educator

A well-known and highly respected poet, Roberta Hill, formerly published as Roberta Hill Whiteman, is best known for her 1984 poetry collection *Star Quilt*, published by Holy Cow! Press. More recently, however, Hill published Philadelphia Flowers in 1996. Her work has been anthologized in numerous publications, including *Carriers of the Dream Wheel: Contemporary Native American Poetry* edited by Duane Niatum (1975), *Reinventing the Enemy's Language: Contemporary Native Women's Writing of North America* edited by Joy Harjo and Gloria Bird (1997), and *The Third Woman: Minority Women Writers of the United States* edited by Dexter Fisher (1980).

Professor Roberta Hill. (Photo by Timothy Francisco)

A member of the Oneida Nation of Wisconsin, Hill was born in Baraboo, Wisconsin, to parents Eleanor Smith and Charles Allen Hill. Throughout her youth, Hill and her family traveled frequently between Green Bay and Oneida. While her mother died when Hill was young, her father and grandmother played crucial roles in shaping Hill's poetic predilection. Her father was a musician and teacher, and taught Hill the importance of rhythm and language. Her grandmother often told stories, recited poetry, and read aloud to the young girl, who was already avidly writing in journals and experimenting with poetry.

Despite her natural inclination toward creative pursuits, Hill's father wanted her to become a doctor like her grandmother. Initially, Hill majored in pre-med at the University of Wisconsin; later, however, she would shift her focus to creative writing and psychology, graduating with a double major. After college, Hill continued her education, receiving an M.F.A. from the University of Montana in 1973. While in Montana, Hill worked with Richard Hugo, a student of Theodore Roethke, who taught the developing writer to make poetry her life's work.

In addition to Hugo, Hill credits many other poets—especially Native lyricists—with helping her develop a distinct poetic voice. In particular, Hill spoke and worked with Lance Henson, Leslie Marmon Silko, and James Welch throughout her early years. Before her works were published together in *Star Quilt*, her work was published in various literary magazines and anthologies in the mid-1970s. During this period, Hill worked for the Poets-in-the-Schools Program in several states, including Arizona, Wyoming, Oklahoma, South Dakota, and Minnesota. She taught on the Oneida and Rosebud reservations, and at the University of Wisconsin, Eau Claire.

In 1980 Hill married Ernest Whiteman, an Arapaho artist, with whom she had three children, Jacob, Heather, and Melissa. Many of her poems focus on her children, and on her life as a mother and a woman. In addition, her poetry often creates conceits, or elaborate metaphors, between seemingly disparate ideas or images. Her work has been noted for its focus on detail, and for its spiritual Oneida consciousness.

Hill is an advisory board member for the *Wicazo Sa Review* and is currently a professor of American Indian studies and English at the University of Wisconsin, Madison. She is working on a biography of her grandmother, Doctor L. Rosa Minoka-Hill.

Geary Hobson (1941–)
Cherokee/Quapaw writer and scholar

Geary Hobson is associate professor of English at the University of Oklahoma. He was born 12 June 1941, in Chicot County, Arkansas. His mother, Edythe, is Quapaw and his father, Gearld, was Cherokee. Hobson graduated from Desha High School in Rohwer, Arkansas, in 1959. He received a bachelor of arts degree (1968) and master's degree (1969) in English from Arizona State University. In 1986 he completed a Ph.D. in American studies at the University of New Mexico. Before beginning a college teaching career, he worked as a farm laborer, a trapper, a construction worker, and a surveyor's assistant. He also played semi-pro baseball and served in the U.S. Marine Corps.

Hobson has taught at the university level since 1970. He taught English at the University of New Mexico from 1970 to 1976 and served as coordinator for the Native American Studies Program there from 1976 to 1978. Between 1980 and 1982 he taught English at the University of Arkansas at Little Rock and at Central Arkansas University.

He is completing a two-volume work, *Indian Country: Native American Literature Since 1968*, a comprehensive study of Native American writers from the United States and Canada.

Geary Hobson.

Hobson's other writings include an anthology of Native American literature entitled *The Remembered Earth* (1979), a collection of poems, *Deer Hunting and Other Poems* (1990), and a novel, *The Last of the Ofos* (2000). He is perhaps best known for his article "The Rise of the White Shaman as a New Version of Cultural Imperialism," in *Y'Bird* 1 number 1 (1977), which objects to non-Indian poets representing themselves as true Indian writers and visionaries.

Linda Hogan (1947–)
Chickasaw writer

Linda Hogan is a writer, poet, and essayist whose work reflects ideas and images of Chickasaw life. She was born in Denver, Colorado, in 1947, but raised mainly in Oklahoma. She received a master's degree in English and creative writing from the University of Colorado at Boulder.

Hogan's poetry has appeared in several important anthologies devoted to Native American writers, including *Carriers of the Dream Wheel* (1975) and *Harper's Anthology of Twentieth Century Native American Poetry* (1988). Her own poems are featured in the collections *Eclipse* (1983) and *Seeing through the Sun* (1985).

Besides her poetry, Hogan has published a collection of short stories entitled *That Horse* (1985) and the novel *Mean Spirit* (1990), which was a finalist for the Pulitzer Prize for fiction. She received a fellowship for fiction from the National Endowment for the Arts in 1986 and has been poet-in-residence for the Oklahoma and Colorado state art councils. In 1998, she was awarded the Lifetime Achievement Award of the Native Writers' Circle of the Americas, an international Native American writers' organization.

Other works by Hogan include *Red Clay: Poems and Stories* (1991), *The Book of Medicines* (1993), *Dwellings: A Spiritual History of the Living World* (1995), *Solar Storms* (1995), *Power* (1998), and *Intimate Nature: The Bond Between Women and Animals* (1999). She teaches at the University of Colorado, Boulder.

Hole-In-The-Day (1825–1868)
Chippewa (Ojibwa) tribal leader

Hole-In-The-Day was a leader among the Chippewa, who lived near the mouth of the Mississippi River in present-day Minnesota. In 1846, Hole-In-The-Day became chief and continued the efforts of his father (who had the same name) to prevent encroachment by Sioux living west of the Mississippi. Hole-In-The-Day also negotiated a number of important treaties and agreements with the U.S. government.

Hole-In-The-Day and his father fought against the Sioux for land located between Lake Superior and the upper Mississippi River in present-day Minnesota. Armed with European-made guns, the Chippewa pushed the Sioux westward and back across the Mississippi River. Hole-In-The-Day also represented his people in their dealings with the U.S. government, making several trips to Washington, D.C., where he negotiated a number of important agreements with the federal government. During one of these trips, Hole-In-The-Day met and married an American woman. She was one of Hole-In-The-Day's eight wives.

Hole-In-The-Day's relations with the U.S. government jeopardized his standing among his own people. He was accused by tribal leaders of using his influence in Washington for personal aggrandizement. Hole-In-The-Day must have felt besieged from both sides when, in 1862, the U.S. government accused him of planning an uprising among the Chippewa. The accusation was fueled by the general unrest among Indians, such as the 1862 Sioux uprising in western Minnesota, and U.S. officials were fearful that more Indian nations would

join in the hostilities. Beginning in 1864, Hole-In-The-Day signed a series of treaties that ceded large amounts of Chippewa land in present-day Minnesota. Consequently, by 1868 most of Hole-In-the-Day's band was settled on the White Earth Reservation, a small plot of land in western Minnesota. In that same year Hole-In-The-Day was murdered, most likely for his role in negotiating treaties with the United States.

George P. Horse Capture (1937–)
Gros Ventre museum curator

George Horse Capture, a museum curator and administrator, is actively engaged in researching Indian art, history, and culture.

Born in Fort Belknap, Montana, on 20 October 1937, Horse Capture graduated from the University of California with a bachelor's degree in anthropology in 1974. He later received a master's degree in history from Montana State University (1979) while working as an assistant professor in the American Indian Studies Department. Horse Capture served as curator of the Plains Indian Museum at the Buffalo Bill Historical Center in Cody, Wyoming, from 1980 until 1990. In 1996,

George P. Horse Capture.

Montana State University awarded him an Honorary Doctorate in Letters.

Besides having curated exhibits on numerous subjects including Wounded Knee, the site of a U.S. Army massacre of Sioux Ghost Dancers in 1890, and the Indian powwow, Horse Capture has been very productive in other areas of Indian culture and history. He edited a book entitled *The Seven Visions of Bull Lodge* (1980) and was winner of the 1983 William E. Cody Motion Picture Award for his film *I'd Rather Be Powwowing*. He is, in fact, an active participant in powwows and has also conducted research on Indian artwork in museums throughout the United States, Canada, and Europe. He recently published a study on a collection of Indian robes at the Musee de l'Homme in Paris that had been obtained by the Jesuit explorer Jacques Marquette during the seventeenth century.

In 1990, the American Association for State and Local History presented Horse Capture with an Award of Merit for historical research in bridging the cultures. Since that year, he has worked for the Fort Belknap tribes and lectured at Harvard, Yale, the Smithsonian Institution, and other organizations across the country. Most important in this regard is his role as an ongoing consultant in the development of the National Museum of the American Indian in Washington, D.C., where he is employed as special assistant, cultural resources, and senior counselor to the director. He now resides in Kensington, Maryland.

Allan Houser (1914–1994)
Chiricahua Apache artist and art instructor

Allan Houser was an internationally recognized sculptor and painter whose works have a serene but powerful quality that reflects Chiricahua Apache culture. Born in Apache, Oklahoma, on 30 June 1914, he attended Santa Fe Indian School in New Mexico and later studied art at Utah State University. A muralist and painter during the late 1930s, Houser had to give up his artwork during a long period when he lived in the Los Angeles area in the 1940s and supported his family by working as a pipefitter and at various construction jobs. During this period he turned to wood carving and got a commission to create a stone monument at Haskell Institute, a junior college for Indian students in Lawrence, Kansas. The resultant work, entitled *Comrade in Mourning*, was a memorial to the Indian casualties of World War II carved from a half-ton block of marble.

In the following year (1949), Houser was awarded a fellowship from the Guggenheim Foundation and from that point his career was established. He later had many solo shows at places such as the Museum of New

Mexico in Santa Fe; the Heard Museum in Phoenix, Arizona; the Southern Plains Museum in Anadarko, Oklahoma; and the Philbrook Center in Tulsa, Oklahoma. He won many prizes during his mid-career, including the Palmes Academique, awarded to Houser by the French government in 1954.

In 1962, Houser became a teacher at the Institute of American Indian Arts in Santa Fe, New Mexico, and he remained on the faculty there until retiring as head of the sculpture department in 1975.

Ron Houston (1945–)
Pima-Maricopa educator and administrator

Ron Houston was born in Los Angeles on 18 January 1945. He received a B.A. in elementary school education in 1967 from Arizona State University in Tempe. In 1970, he earned an M.A. degree in education counseling from Northern Illinois University in De Kalb. His teaching career started in 1967, when he taught third grade at Tuba City Elementary School in Tuba City, Arizona. From 1968 to 1979, Houston was a teacher and counselor at Fremont Junior High School in Mesa, Arizona. During this time, from 1974 to 1976, he was also a community school specialist responsible for identifying the needs of the community and acquiring teachers to teach classes for the Mesa Public Schools. In 1976, he became a counselor at the Mesa Community College, in charge of personal and academic counseling with junior college students; he also taught personal resources development classes.

Houston joined the National Education Association (NEA) in 1979, and since then he has been actively involved in providing technical assistance, training, and information to local and state NEA affiliates and to American Indian members. He was the principal author of the NEA booklet *The Quest for Quality Education*, published in 1982, and coordinated the development of the NEA handbook *American Indian/Alaska Native Education: Quality in Classroom*, for teachers of American Indian and Alaska Native children. From 1989 to 1992, Houston was the vice president of the National Education Association Staff Organization in Washington, D.C.

Oscar Howe (1915–1983)
Yankton Sioux graphic artist

Born at Joe Creek, South Dakota, on the Crow Creek Reservation in 1915, Oscar Howe's Sioux name was Mazuha Koshina (Trader Boy). He graduated from

Pierre Indian School in South Dakota (1933), then studied painting at the U.S. Indian School in Santa Fe, New Mexico (1934–38), and had special training in mural techniques at the Indian Art Center in Fort Sill, Oklahoma. He later received a bachelor's degree (1952) from Dakota Wesleyan University in Mitchell, South Dakota, and a master of fine arts degree from the University of Oklahoma at Norman (1954).

Howe served as an assistant instructor during his years at Dakota Wesleyan and taught art at Pierre High School in South Dakota from 1954 to 1957. He then became a professor of fine arts and artist-in-residence at the University of South Dakota at Vermillion; he remained on the faculty there until well into the 1970s. Howe employed a modern style to depict poignant images of Indian culture in transition and once wrote, "One criterion for my painting is to present the cultural life of the Sioux Indians. It is my greatest hope that my paintings may serve to bring the best things of Indian culture into the modern way of life."

Howe's paintings have been shown in numerous solo shows and group exhibitions. He was named the Artist Laureate of South Dakota by Governor Herseth in 1960 and also received the Waite Phillips Trophy for Outstanding Contributions to American Indian Art from the Philbrook Art Center in Tulsa, Oklahoma, in 1966. He has also created distinguished murals that were commissioned for the Civic Auditorium in Mobridge, South Dakota, (1942) and for the walls of Proviso High School in Hinsdale, Illinois, (1956).

Howe contracted Parkinson's disease while in his sixties and passed away in his sleep on 7 October 1983.

George Hunt (1854–1933)
Tlingit cultural interpreter

George Hunt was an interpreter of the culture of the Tlingit, a tribe located along the southeastern Alaska coastline, and other Northwest Coast tribes. He was born at Fort Rupert, British Columbia, in 1854. His mother was a Tlingit named Mary Ebbets, and his father was British and director of the Hudson Bay Company's trade business with Indians on the coast of British Columbia. Hunt's cultural heritage was yet more complex and enriched by the fact that he was raised among the Kwakiutl Indians (another tribe of the Northwest Coast, located further south), and he married a Kwakiutl woman.

Hunt's career as a guide and cultural interpreter began in 1881, when he was hired by the Norwegian-born Johan Adrian Jacobsen to help collect ethnological artifacts for a museum in Berlin. He later worked for anthropologist Franz Boas, beginning in 1886, and provided Boas with cultural information that was later published in *Kwakiutl Texts* (1905–1906) and *The Ethnology of the Kwakiutl* (1921). In 1897 Hunt served as a guide and interpreter for the Jesup Expedition, a major collaborative research survey that sought to investigate the cultural factors connecting the Northwest Coast Indians and Alaskan Eskimos with the indigenous peoples of northeastern Asia.

Hunt helped to organize the Northwest Coast exhibit at the American Museum of Natural History in New York City in 1903, and he was instrumental in recreating Native ceremonials and other scenes shown in Edward Curtis's film *In the Land of the War Canoes*. He was eventually selected as a chief of the Kwakiutl. Hunt passed away in 1933 at the place where he was born.

Ishi (d. 1916)
Yahi/Southern Yana survivor

In 1911, this middle-aged Yahi from northern California became famous throughout the United States as "the last wild Indian." The Yahi (also called Southern Yana) originally lived along Mill Creek and Deer Creek, two eastern affluents of the Sacramento River in northern California.

In August 1911, Ishi wandered out of the mountains and found himself in the town of Oroville (Butte County). He was the last survivor of a tribe that had gone into seclusion more than forty years before. For much of this time, Ishi had been living in a band that never numbered more than a dozen for most of his adolescent and adult life. His last years before discovery were spent with just three other people: an old man and woman, probably his parents, and a middle-aged woman who was his sister. For the last several months, he had been completely alone, until finally—weaponless, pressed by hunger, and his hair still singed from mourning for his relatives—he gave up a lifetime of hiding and allowed himself to be captured.

Apparently, he expected to be killed but was instead placed in jail for a few days and soon afterwards was taken to the San Francisco Bay area, where he was studied by Alfred Kroeber and other anthropologists at the University of California until his death in 1916. The researchers marveled at the genuineness of his aboriginal condition, which was also sensationalized in the press: here, after all, was a completely unacculturated Indian who spoke no English and still practiced ancient skills such as flint shaping and bow making. A number of publications on Yahi language and culture came about because of Ishi's knowledge, but he is probably best known to most Americans because of Theodora

Kroeber's book *Ishi in Two Worlds* (1960). For most Americans, Ishi is a romantic symbol of the last unspoiled Native, but to many Native Americans in California, he represents a terrible era of genocide and cultural devastation.

Isparhecher (1829–1902)
Creek tribal leader

Isparhecher was born in the upper Creek towns of present-day Alabama. While only a small child of six or seven, he and the Creek were forced to leave their homeland in the U.S. South and migrate to Indian Territory in present-day Oklahoma. During the U.S. Civil War, the Creek Nation was evenly divided between the upper towns (the more conservative villages, who favored Union alliance) and the lower Creek towns, which contained the largest proportion of Creek slaveowners, who favored alliance to the South. Isparhecher at first fought with the Confederates, but later chose to switch sides and fight with the conservative Creek in alliance with the Union Army. He became a leader of the conservative Creek.

After the Civil War, in 1867 the Creek formed a new constitutional government, and Isparhecher was elected to the national council, but instead accepted a position as judge. In the early 1870s, however, he was impeached from the court for alleged misuse of funds. This experience embittered Isparhecher, and he joined the conservative Creek, who met at Nuyuka, a white town of refuge in the traditional Creek Nation. When in the late 1870s, the conservative Creek leader Lochar Harjo died, Isparhecher succeeded to leadership. His leadership inspired the conservatives to more actively pursue the restoration of the traditional Creek government by town chiefs, and inspired them to try to topple the progressive or constitutional party, which supported the new Creek constitutional government.

Throughout the 1870s, 1880s, and 1890s, the conservatives challenged the legitimacy of the Creek constitutional government, which was strongly supported by the U.S. government. The major outbreak occurred in 1882 and 1883, the so-called Green Peach War, in a controversy about the election procedures, which plagued Creek politics until the 1890s. In the Green Peach War, Isparhecher and the conservatives, about a third of the Creek men, were driven out of the Creek country after a series of minor skirmishes. The U.S. Army brought the conservatives back, and they agreed to pledge allegiance to the Creek government. Isparhecher continued to run for the office of Creek principal chief and was elected in 1895, on a campaign to prevent the United States from abolishing the Creek

government and allotting its land to individual Creek. During his four-year term, Isparhecher was not able to resist the forced breakup of the Creek government, and after 1899, he retired to his ranch in a state of depression and despair. In 1907, the Creek government was superseded by the state of Oklahoma.

G. Peter Jemison (1945–)
Seneca artist and arts administrator

G. Peter Jemison is director of Ganondagan (Seneca) Historic Site in New York. He is well known for his paintings and drawings and for his active participation in Indian cultural affairs. He was the administrative director for the Seneca Education Program in 1973 and 1974; project director for the North American Indian Culture Center in Buffalo, New York; director of the Seneca Nation Organization for the Visual Arts; and, starting in 1978, gallery coordinator of the Gallery of American Indian Community House in New York.

Jemison was born in 1945 in Silver Creek, New York, and received his bachelor of science degree in art education at the State University of New York's College at Buffalo and attended additional courses at both the University of Siena (Italy) and the State University of New York at Albany. His cultural interests include a wide variety of experiences, from his collection of art by Seneca children to his posts as member of the New York State Iroquois Conference and board member for the America the Beautiful Foundation in New York.

Jemison's activities are focused on preserving Seneca cultural heritage within the contemporary society, as shown by his illustrations for the controversial book about Iroquois contributions to the U.S. Constitution, *The Iroquois and the Founding of the American Nation* (1977). The cultural issues of the Mohawk, Oneida, Onondaga, Tuscarora, Seneca, and Cayuga tribes, which constitute the New York Iroquois, find expression in his works and in his promotion of cultural programs for Iroquois Indians. He is chairman of the Haudenosaunee Standing Committee on the Burial Rules and Regulations.

E. Pauline Johnson (1861–1913)
Mohawk poet

Pauline Johnson was an internationally acclaimed Mohawk poet and performer who lived and worked in the second half of the nineteenth century. A distant relative of Joseph Brant, a Mohawk chief who fought alongside the British during the American Revolution, Pauline Johnson was born to a Mohawk father, George

Johnson, and a non-Native mother, Emily Howells. The Johnsons lived in Chiefswood, across the Grand River from the Six Nations Indian Reserve located near Brantford, in southwestern Ontario. Pauline wrote poetry as soon as she learned to write, and as a young child she was a voracious reader. She was educated mostly at home until she went to college in Brantford, where she performed in plays and pageants and decided to become a poet and performer. During her teens, she wrote many poems and had several minor publishing successes with local and regional magazines.

When her father died in 1885, Pauline moved with her mother to Brantford, where she often attended recitals and theater productions. Johnson's career blossomed when she started to recite her poetry in front of audiences. As a result of her successes, she saved enough money to travel to London, England, where she gave numerous recitals and arranged publication of a book of her poems, entitled *The White Wampum*, released in 1895. Upon her return to Canada, Johnson traveled from Newfoundland to Vancouver, performing and reciting her poetry. She also toured throughout the United States.

Besides being a poet, Johnson was also one of the first Indian women to publish short fiction. Especially interesting is *The Moccasin Maker* (1913), a collection of short stories on diverse subjects but mainly focusing on the lives of Indian and non-Indian women in Canada. Some are love stories, some focus on pioneer women who established homes for their families despite great hardships, and several deal with what would become a dominant theme in American Indian literature of the twentieth century: the mixed-blood's search for his or her proper place in the modern world. One story called "A Red Girl's Reasoning" tells of a mixed-blood woman who remains true to her Indian values even when the decision forces her to leave her husband, who is critical of such ideas. Johnson also was a prolific author of essays and magazine articles. She died in 1913 after a lengthy illness.

Basil H. Johnston (1929–)
Ojibwa (Chippewa) author and educator

Basil Johnston was born 13 July 1929 on the Parry Island Reserve in Ontario, Canada. He graduated from Loyola College in Montreal in 1954 and received a secondary school teaching certificate from the Ontario College of Education in 1962. Johnston started his career as assistant manager and manager of the Toronto Board of Trade from 1957 to 1959, and he taught for the first time at Earl Haig Secondary School from 1962 to 1969. Beginning in 1969, he was a lecturer at the

Ethnology Department at the Royal Ontario Museum, and in 1974, he became an English teacher for the Ojibwa in Toronto.

Johnston has been affiliated with the Canadian Indian Center in Toronto, the Union of Ontario Indians, and the Indian Eskimo Association, for whom he was legal and executive member of the committee from 1965 to 1968. He was also a member of the Indian Hall of Fame from 1968 to 1970 and of the Ontario Geographic Names Board beginning in 1977.

Johnston has written numerous stories and essays, as well as guides to learning the Ojibwa language, including *Ojibwa Language Course Outline* (1979), *Ojibwa Language Lexicon for Beginners and Others* (1979), and *Ojibwa Heritage* (1976). Among his works of fiction are *Moose Meat and Wild Rice* (1978), and numerous short stories that appeared in *The Ontario Indian*, such as "Where's Simon?" (December 1980), "My Rope" (February 1981), and "Batman and Robin" (March 1981). *By Canoe and Moccasins* (Lakefield, ON: Waapoone Publishing and Promotion, 1986) is one of his best-known works of children's literature.

Johnston's non-fiction articles have appeared in various Canadian magazines dealing with educational issues, including "Forget Totem Poles," (March 1975) and "Indian History Must Be Taught" (March 1971), both published in *The Educational Courier*. He has written on racial and interracial issues in "Indian, Métis and Eskimos" in *Read Canadian* (1972), and "Cowboys and Indians" in *The Ontario Indian* (August 1981). Johnston has received many honors and awards, including the Centennial Medal in recognition of work on behalf of the Native community in 1967, the Samuel S. Fells Literary Award for first publication, "Zhowmin and Mandamin" in 1976, and the Order of Ontario in 1989, for services of great distinction and singular excellence, benefiting society in Ontario and elsewhere. His most recent books are *The Bear-Walker and Other Stories* (1995) and *Crazy Dave* (1995).

Ted Jojola (1951–)
Isleta Pueblo scholar and author

Ted Jojola is a professor in the master's program in Community and Regional Planning, School of Architecture and Planning at the University of New Mexico. He was director of Native American studies from 1980 to 1996.

Jojola was born in Isleta Pueblo, New Mexico, in 1951. He received a B.A. in architecture from the University of New Mexico, an M.A. in city planning from the Massachusetts Institute of Technology, and a Ph.D.

in political science from the University of Hawaii in Manoa in 1982. In 1985, he received a Certificate of International Human Rights and Law from the University of Strasbourg in France. Jojola began his career as internal planner at the National Capital Planning Commission in Washington, D.C. in 1973. In 1976 he was legal and historical researcher for the Institute for the Development of Indian Law in Washington. From 1977 to 1982, he was a visiting researcher at the Institute of Philippine Culture in Manila, visiting professor of urban planning at the University of California at Los Angeles, and assistant professor of planning at the University of New Mexico in Albuquerque.

Jojola has conducted research on a variety of topics, such as a preschool computer program in isolated American Indian communities in 1985, a 1990 project for the U.S. Census Bureau on ethnographic undercounts, and research involving the Isleta Pueblo living in New Mexico and Arizona, descendants of the ancient cliff dwellers, in cooperation with the U.S. Department of Health and Human Services in 1989.

Among Jojola's numerous grants and honors are a postdoctoral fellowship at the American Indian Studies Center at UCLA in 1984, and the Atherton Trust, a public grant in Honolulu, in 1976. Jojola has appeared in two editions of *Who's Who in the West* (Marquis, 1985) and *Who's Who Among Young Emerging Leaders* (Marquis 1987). In 1976, he published *Memoirs of an American Indian House: The Impact of a Cross-National Housing Program on Two Reservations*, and in 1988 he was the guest editor of *Wicazo sa Review*, a journal of Indian studies with emphasis on issues, literature, and culture. He was also the series editor of *Public Policy Impact on American Indian Development*, and *Pueblo Style and Regional Architecture* (1989).

Peter Jones (1802–1856)
Ojibwa minister, chief, and translator

Peter Jones was a well-known religious leader and spokesman for Native rights. He was born in Ontario in the Credit River Mississauga settlement near the west end of Lake Ontario on 1 January 1802. His father, Augustus Jones, was a Welsh surveyor and a friend of Joseph Brant, the Mohawk leader. His mother, Tuhbenahneeguay, was the daughter of the Mississauga Ojibwa chief Wahbonosay. Jones's Ojibwa name was Kahkewaquonaby (Sacred Feathers), and he lived traditionally until he was about sixteen. At sixteen, his father had him baptized into the Episcopalian faith and he was given the name Peter. As a young adult, Jones became actively involved in services at the Wesleyan

Methodist Church and became the first Native Methodist missionary to the Ojibwa in 1827.

As a Methodist missionary, Peter Jones visited several bands in western Ontario and, with his brother John, provided the first translations of the Bible from English into Ojibwa. In 1830, Jones was made a deacon of the Methodist church and in 1833 became a minister. He was elected chief of two Ojibwa bands and visited New York, London, and several other large cities on behalf of the Ojibwa. Jones was well known not simply for his religious activities, but as an articulate spokesman for the protection of Native land rights.

Jones married an Englishwoman, with whom he had four sons. One son assumed his father's name and published a local journal, *The Indian*, devoted to Native matters of the day. Jones died near his birthplace, in Brantford, Ontario, on 29 June 1856. His *Life and Journals of Kah-ke-quo-na-by (Rev. Peter Jones) and History of the Ojebway Indians* were both published posthumously. In 1857, a monument dedicated to Jones' memory was erected by the Ojibwa in Brantford.

Rosalie M. Jones "Daystar" (contemporary)
Pembina Chippewa artist, choreographer, educator

Born on the Blackfeet Reservation in Montana, Jones holds a master's degree in dance from the University of Utah (1968) and studied at the Juilliard School in New York City (1969–1970).

She began her artistic career as a solo dancer during the 1970s, touring numerous reservations where she taught and performed dance. In 1980, she founded her own dance company, Daystar: Contemporary Dance Drama of Indian America.

The Daystar Company was the first company of its kind in America. Daystar is credited with pioneering the early development of modern, Native American dance, which fuses traditional Native and Western modern dance and drama techniques.

Some of her significant choreography, deriving from tribal oral traditions, include Wolf (Anishinabe), Tales of Old Man (Blackfeet), Legend of the Black Butterfly (Maidu), and The Gift of the Pipe (Lakota).

She helped revitalize performing arts at the Institute of American Indian Arts in Santa Fe, New Mexico, while serving as chair of performing arts during the early 1990s. She was Distinguished Visiting Artist at American University in Bulgaria, and the Chancellor's Distinguished Visiting Professor in Dance at the University of California, Irvine. As a guest of Roots of Theatre in Helsinki, Finland, during the 2000 Millennium Celebration, she conducted workshops and performances. She was artist-in-residence of the School of

Rosalie M. Jones, artistic director of the Daystar Dance Company.

Arts and Performance at the SUNY College at Brockport, New York, from 1999 to 2001.

Joseph (1840–1904)
Nez Percé tribal leader

Joseph was born in the Wallowa Valley in present-day Oregon. The Nez Percé lived in the area where the present-day states of Washington, Oregon, and Idaho adjoin. The various Indian tribes in this region signed the Isaac Steven's Treaty in 1855 ceding Indian lands in the Washington Territory in exchange for reservation lands, homes, tools, and money. As more settlers and miners arrived into the region, however, the treaty was ignored. Like his father before him, Joseph originally carried out a plan of passive resistance to U.S. land encroachment and to efforts by the U.S. government to relocate his people to the Nez Percé Reservation.

A fragile peace was shattered in 1877, when U.S. settlers began moving into the Wallowa Valley. The government had recently overturned an earlier decision granting this land to the Nez Percé as a reservation, and they were given thirty days to relocate. On June 12, the inevitable fighting erupted when three young Nez Percé killed four settlers who had moved into the Wallowa Valley.

After some initial battles, in which Joseph showed remarkable military skill by defeating superior U.S.

forces, Joseph and the Nez Percé from the Wallowa Valley decided to attempt an escape into Canada. For roughly the next three months they eluded both U.S. troops and enemy Indian bands. In late September the Nez Percé group was only miles from the Canadian border when they found themselves surrounded and outnumbered by forces augmented with howitzer cannons and Gatlin guns, which were early machine guns. On 5 October 1877, Chief Joseph finally surrendered, but not before hundreds of Nez Percé escaped to Canada.

When the long odyssey was finally over, many of the Nez Percé leaders were dead or in Canada. The final surrender agreement was signed by Joseph. Subsequently, the exhausted leader is credited with giving a dramatic, often quoted, speech at the surrender. The actual text of the speech is unknown, and popular interpretations glowed in the hands of embellishing journalists. In the minds of the American public, Joseph became permanently identified with the courageous journey taken by the Nez Percé. According to historical accounts, the campaign of the Nez Percé in 1877 was characterized by restraint and relative non-violence on the part of Joseph and the tribe. Sent to Indian Territory in Oklahoma, the Nez Percé were allowed to return to Idaho in 1883 and 1884. Joseph spent the rest of his life on a number of different Indian reservations, but was allowed only a brief return to his homeland in the Wallowa Valley. He died on the Colville Indian Reservation in the state of Washington.

Betty Mae Jumper (1923–)
Seminole tribal leader

Betty Mae Jumper was born in 1927 in Indiantown, Florida. She was the first Seminole to receive a high school diploma, which she obtained in 1949 from the Cherokee Indian School in Cherokee, North Carolina. Within the Seminole community, she served first as secretary-treasurer for the tribal council, then as vice chairperson until 1967, when she became the first woman elected chair of the tribe, holding the post for four years. Jumper was also director of communications and editor-in-chief of the *Seminole Tribune*, the newspaper of the Seminole tribe in Florida.

In 1968, Jumper joined representatives of three southeastern tribes in signing a Declaration of Unity in Cherokee, North Carolina, which implemented the Inter-Tribal Council of the United Southeastern Tribes. While serving as chair of the Seminole tribe, she was appointed by President Richard Nixon one of eight Indian members of the National Congress on Indian Opportunity.

Jumper did much to improve health, education, and social conditions among the Seminole. In 1984, she published . . . *And With the Wagon Came God's Word*, published by the Seminole Print Shop. After retirement Jumper published *Legends of the Seminoles* (1994). She has been a speaker on the Seminole at schools throughout Florida, and an advisor for the Manpower Development and Training Committee for the state of Florida. She was a member of the Native American Press Association and the Florida Press Association. Jumper was chosen Woman of the Year by the Department of Florida Ladies Auxiliaries of Jewish War Veterans of the United States, for her outstanding contribution in the field of humanities.

She still lives on the Hollywood Reservation, and is the mother of three children, grandmother to ten, and great-grandmother to three.

Hattie Kauffman (contemporary)
Nez Percé national news correspondent

Hattie Kauffman has made her name as the first Native American journalist to report a national broadcast. She received her bachelor of science degree from the University of Minnesota, where she also attended the Graduate School of Journalism under a WCCO-TV Minorities in Broadcasting Scholarship. Kauffman launched her career as a journalist early by broadcasting on-air radio reports while in college.

In November 1999 Kauffman was named national correspondent for CBS News' *The Early Show*. Prior to this appointment, she served as senior consumer correspondent for *This Morning* from 1990 to 1999.

Her particular style of reporting human-interest stories has earned her acclaim throughout her successful career. She also reports on intriguing vacation ideas, as evidenced in her five-part series, "Something Wild," in which Kauffman went rock climbing, white-water rafting, and scuba-diving.

Before working for *This Morning*, Kauffman worked as a reporter for *Good Morning America* from 1987 to 1990. Early in her career she worked for KING-TV in Seattle, during which time she earned four Emmy Awards for her work.

William W. Keeler (1908–1987)
Cherokee businessperson and tribal leader

In 1949, William Keeler was appointed principal chief of the Cherokee Nation in Oklahoma. He served as appointed principal chief until 1971, and between 1971 and 1975 was the first elected principal chief since 1907. Keeler's initial appointment was made under laws that abolished the Cherokee government in 1907. Between 1907 and 1971, the Cherokee principal chief was appointed by the U.S. president and was responsible for administering the Cherokee land estate and attending to associated legal and political issues. It was thought that the Cherokee Nation would ultimately dissolve. In 1971, however, the Cherokee regained the right to elect their own leadership, and the nation continues.

Starting at age sixteen, as a part-time worker, Keeler pursued a corporate business career with Phillips Petroleum Company. In 1951, he was elected to the board of directors. In 1968, he was elected chairman of the board and vice-president of the executive department. Because of his reputation as a strong administrator, government agencies often tapped Keeler for advice on solving problems in the oil and refining industry. Keeler actively contributed his services to many public interest groups, including fraternal, veteran, civic, and business organizations.

During Keeler's administration as principal chief, he gained a reputation as an able administrator and leader. He served on two major government task forces, which investigated and reported on major issues in Indian affairs. One task force reported in 1961 with a critical review of government policies toward Indians during the 1950s, which included termination or the dissolving of tribal reservations and governments. In 1962, Keeler also served on a task force that investigated conditions of Alaska Natives and their land claims. He also helped establish the Cherokee Foundation, which endeavors to promote the welfare and culture of the Cherokee Nation and its members.

Peter Kelly (1885–1966)
Haida activist and minister

Peter Kelly was an Indian activist of Haida descent. The Haida people live in the Queen Charlotte Islands off the coast of mainland British Columbia (BC) and are recognized for their totem poles and huge communal houses made of cedar. Kelly was an ordained Methodist, and later a United Church minister. By the time he was twenty-six, Kelly became involved in various ancestral land claims brought by Indians of BC. In 1916, he organized a conference in Vancouver to address tribal rights to land. Sixteen tribal groups from across the province were represented, and the conference formed itself into the Allied Indian Tribes of British Columbia. Kelly was elected chairman of the executive committee. In 1919, after extensive consultation, the

Allied Tribes prepared a statement of Indian rights to ancestral land in British Columbia that many viewed as the authoritative statement of BC Indian claims. It also lobbied the federal and provincial governments extensively on Indian issues. In 1927, Kelly testified before a special parliamentary committee in Ottawa formed to address Indian issues. In calling for the recognition of Indian title to ancestral lands in BC, Kelly stated: "Why not keep unblemished the record of British fair dealing with Native races? Why refuse to recognize the claim of certain tribes of Indians in one corner of the British Dominions, when it has been accorded to others in another part of the same Dominion?" The committee refused to recognize aboriginal title and recommended the prohibition of any transaction designed to assist the bringing of Indian land claims to court. When the committee's recommendation became law in 1927, it was the death knell for the Allied Tribes, and Kelly devoted himself to the ministry. He re-emerged politically in the 1940s when he joined the Native Brotherhood of BC, a province-wide Indian organization formed in the wake of the Allied Tribes' demise.

Kenekuk (Kickapoo Prophet) (1785–1852)
Kickapoo tribal and spiritual leader

Kenekuk was the religious and political leader of a community of Kickapoo, which was later joined by some Potawatomi. The Kickapoo lived in Illinois, while the Potawatomi occupied parts of present-day Michigan, but a small group of them joined Kenekuk and his Kickapoo community when they were removed to Kansas after 1933. Kenekuk was influenced by the Shawnee prophet, who before the War of 1812 advocated strong and overt military resistance to U.S. settlers and territorial expansion. The War of 1812 left the Kickapoo and other northern Great Lakes Indian nations in a state of disarray and destitution. In 1819, the Kickapoo ceded half of the present-day state of Illinois to the U.S. government. Thereafter during the 1820s, some Kickapoo Bands migrated to Texas, while others sought refuge in Mexico.

Kenekuk, like the Shawnee prophet before him, claimed he had a vision, containing a message from the Great Spirit for the Indian people, but for the Kickapoo in particular. Kenekuk's vision differed from the Shawnee prophet's message in that it preached accommodation to U.S. culture and land demands. The Kickapoo prophet worked to create a new moral and religious community for his followers, one that drew on elements of Catholic, Protestant, and traditional Kickapoo religious beliefs. He advocated the taking up of agriculture, the formation of self-sufficient Indian farming communities. He banned alcohol, instructed his followers to maintain friendly relations with U.S. settlers, and developed a self-contained religious moral community, which tried to preserve its land and identity from the onslaught of U.S. settlers and the demands of the U.S. government.

In 1832, Kenekuk's community did not join with Black Hawk in his war to regain parts of Illinois. Nevertheless, he tried hard to avoid the removal of his people from Illinois to present-day Kansas. In 1833, however, he and 350 followers were required to move. In Kansas, Kenekuk continued his preaching, and he attracted some converts from among the Potawatomi. He died in 1852, but his community continues to survive until this day, and the people retain the distinct religious teachings of the Kickapoo prophet.

William Kennedy (1814–1890)
Métis explorer

William Kennedy was the son of a Cree mother and a Scottish father who worked for the Hudson's Bay Company, a trading company active in the Canadian interior. As a result, Kennedy was Métis, a term that refers to persons of mixed Indian-European heritage who forged a common identity on the plains of Western Canada in the nineteenth century. At the age of eleven, William and his brother, George, were sent to Scotland to obtain an elementary education for seven years. Upon his return to Canada, Kennedy began to work for the Hudson's Bay Company, but left, disillusioned with the company's trading practices.

His life changed dramatically in 1851, when he was chosen to lead an expedition to search for Sir John Franklin, an explorer who had gone missing while searching for a Northwest passage between the Hudson Strait and the Pacific Ocean. Kennedy returned to Scotland, where he captained a ship and a crew of seventeen and set sail for the Canadian Arctic. Seventeen months later, Kennedy and his crew returned to Scotland without having located Sir Franklin and his ship; nonetheless Kennedy was able to discover, identify, and map a great deal of territory in the Canadian north.

Kennedy eventually made what was to become the province of Manitoba his home, and he worked diligently to secure the establishment of a direct transportation and mail route between Toronto and Fort Garry in the Canadian plains. He also worked for the extension of Canada westward into the area that has now become Manitoba. Kennedy was unstinting in his support for the betterment of Native people, devoting much time to the education of young people and the establishment of colonies for Native people on productive land.

Maurice Kenny (1929–)
Mohawk poet, short story writer, and educator

Nominated for the Pulitzer Prize in 1982 for *Blackrobe: Isaac Jogues, b. March 11, 1607, d. October 18, 1646*, and in 1987 for *Between Two Rivers: Selected Poems 1956–1984*, Maurice Francis Kenny is one of the leaders of the Native American literary renaissance of the 1970s. His poetry explores the links between the human spirit and the natural world, and many of his poems speak from the perspective of natural objects.

Born to Andrew Anthony Kenny and Doris Marie Parker Herrick Kenny Welch in Watertown, New York, Kenny is of Mohawk and Seneca ancestry. His hometown is set at the foothills of the Adirondacks, and his experiences there shaped his poetic relationship with nature.

In 1956, Kenny graduated with a bachelor's degree in English from Butler University in Indianapolis, Indiana.

Maurice Kenny.

Soon after graduation, Kenny moved back to his home state, where he studied at St. Lawrence University in Canton, and at New York University in New York City. While in the city, Kenny studied with poet Louise Bogan, who helped him hone his technical expertise and his passion for poetry. His first book of poetry, *Dead Letter Sent*, was published by Troubador Press in 1958.

Kenny left New York, going on a long hiatus to Mexico and the Virgin Islands, ending his travels in Chicago where he wrote obituaries for the *Chicago Sun*. While Kenny returned to New York in 1968 a productive writer, most of his work would not be published until the following decade. The poet stayed in New York City, however, until later in life, when he moved back to Adirondack country in New York State.

I Am the Sun, a collection of poems, was released in 1973, and in the mid-1970s Kenny established the Strawberry Press, which published poetry and art by Native people. Also during this time Kenny and J. G. Gosciak began co-editing *Contact/II*, an influential magazine dedicated to the contemporary world of poetry. Kenny was also an advisory editor for *S.A.I.L.*, *Akwesasne Notes*, and *Time Capsule*.

The early 1980s brought Kenny wide recognition for his poetic and literary accomplishments. In 1984 *The Mama Poems* won the American Book Award and *Blackrobe* received the National Public Radio Award. The next year, Kenny left Brooklyn to teach at North Country Community College, where he was also poet-in-residence. In 1987 and 1988 Kenny coordinated the Robert Louis Stevenson Annual Writers Conference, and he has lectured and read throughout the country. His most recent books are *On Second Thought: A Compilation* (1995), *Backward to Forward: Prose Pieces* (1997), and *Tortured Skins, and Other Fictions* (2000). He presently lives in Saranac Lake, New York, teaching Native American literature at St. Lawrence University from which he received an honorary doctorate in literature in 1995.

Kenojuak (1927–)
Inuit artist

Kenojuak is probably the best-known Inuit artist in Canada. She was born on Baffin Island, Northwest Territories, north of the province of Quebec in the Canadian Arctic. Cape Dorset, on Baffin Island, was a community well known in artistic circles for soapstone carvings. Kenojuak was the first woman to become involved in a new printmaking shop established at Cape

Dorset in the 1950s. The shop experimented with stone-block printing, in which the design is carved on a slab of soapstone, which is then inked, and the paper is pressed onto it to create a print. Kenojuak began to draw and make prints of her drawings at that time. Her drawings were and still are primarily of birds and human beings, and they often involve intertwined figures and fantasies. Strong, colorful, richly composed and designed, Kenojuak's drawings and prints were almost immediately recognized as unique and valuable, and they continue to be sought after by national and international collectors and museums.

Although she is primarily known for her drawings and paintings, Kenojuak also carves and sculpts soapstone and other material. She was acclaimed for a mural that she and her now-deceased husband created for the 1970 World Fair in Osaka, Japan. Kenojuak has traveled widely throughout Canada and Europe and has shown her work in many exhibitions, perhaps the most famous being a thirty-year retrospective of her art at the McMichael Canadian Collection Gallery in Kleinburg, Ontario, just outside of Toronto, in 1986. Kenojuak has been featured in a film about her work produced by the National Film Board of Canada in 1962 and in a limited edition book published in 1981. In 1992 Kenojuak was awarded honorary degrees from Queens University and the University of Toronto. In 1995, she received the Lifetime Aboriginal Achievement Award.

Keokuk (1783–1848)
Sac (Sauk) tribal leader

Keokuk was born around 1783 in the village of Saukenuk in present-day Illinois. He obtained a position of power among his people by demonstrating bravery against the Sioux, although he was not a hereditary chief.

By the early 1800s, the official policy of the U.S. government had become one of forced treaties and acquisition of Indian land. Keokuk, though not recognized as a chief among his own people, was selected by the U.S. government as the official representative of the Sauk because of his refusal to support the British in 1812 and his friendly overtures to the United States. During this era, the government used bribery to bring Keokuk into line with federal land policies. Keokuk signed a number of treaties that included an exchange of Sauk land in the Rock River country for a tract located westward and an annual cash compensation, which was to be administered by Keokuk.

In the 1830s, Keokuk redeemed himself in the eyes of some Sauk by his skillful defense of Sauk land interests

Keokuk.

against Sioux territorial claims in Washington, D.C. In 1845, Keokuk ceded Iowa lands in exchange for a reservation in Kansas. He died three years later, amid reports that followers of Black Hawk had killed him. Though it is believed Keokuk actually died of dysentery, the rumors of murder were not surprising since in the eyes of many, Keokuk, unlike his peer Black Hawk, did not represent his people in the most loyal fashion.

K. Kirke Kickingbird (1944–)
Kiowa lawyer

Kirke Kickingbird is former director of the Native American Legal Resource Center at the Oklahoma City University School of Law, a position he filled since the center opened in July, 1988. He was appointed by Governor Henry Bellmon to serve on the Oklahoma Constitutional Revision Commission (1988–1991) and by Governor David Walters to serve on the governor's Health and Human Services Cabinet Review Team in

1991. Kickingbird was co-curator of "Moving the Fire: The Removal of the Indian Nations to Oklahoma," an International Monetary Fund Visitor's Center Exhibit in Washington, D.C., presented 21 January through 15 April 1993, coinciding with the United Nations resolution to declare 1993 the International Year of the World's Indigenous Peoples. He was appointed on 24 August 1992 by orders of Chief Justice Marian P. Opala to serve as a member of the Oklahoma Supreme Court Committee to recommend standards for granting full faith and credit to the judicial proceedings of the Indian tribes, nations, and bands.

Before joining the faculty at Oklahoma City University Law School, he founded and directed a private nonprofit Indian legal research center (1971–1985), the Institute for the Development of Indian Law, in Washington, D.C., where he worked with tribes throughout the United States and Canada. From 1976 to 1977, he served as general counsel of the U.S. Congress American Indian Policy Review Commission, which made a special two-year study of U.S. Indian policy.

In 1988 and 1989, Kickingbird was a member of the U.S. delegation to the International Labor Organization (ILO) annual conference, a United Nations agency, which revised the only modern treaty addressing the rights of indigenous peoples. In 1980 he lectured at universities in northern Europe as part of a U.S. International Communications Agency program. In 1977, he was member of the U.S. delegation to the United Nations International Conference on Discrimination Against Indigenous Populations in the Americas. The Australian Constitutional Centenary Foundation invited him to present a paper at Canberra, Australia, on 3–4 June 1993 at a conference on the Position of Indigenous Peoples in National Constitutions. The International Conference on the Law of Indigenous Peoples asked him to present a paper in Moscow on September 24–26 on "Indigenous Peoples Rights: Legislation and Implementation in the United States."

His first book on Indian land issues, *100 Million Acres*, was published by Macmillan in 1973. Kickingbird has written numerous books and articles on Indian affairs and Indian law. His latest, *Indians and the U.S. Constitution: A Forgotten Legacy*, won an award in 1988 from the U.S. Commission on the Bicentennial of the Constitution.

Kickingbird was appointed in 1995 by the governor of Oklahoma as special counsel on Indian affairs. Kickingbird is a past chair of the Oklahoma Indian Affairs Commission and Chief Justice of the Supreme Court of the Cheyenne and Arapaho Tribes of Oklahoma. From 1996 to 1999 he was a member of the Board of Governors of the American Bar Association (ABA).

He was the first Native American to serve on the ABA Board of Governors in the history of the association.

Clara Sue Kidwell (1941–)
White Earth Chippewa-Choctaw historian and professor

Clara Sue Kidwell is director of Native American Studies at the University of Oklahoma. She was born on 8 July 1941, in Tahlequah, Oklahoma. She received her diploma from Muskogee Central High School in Muskogee, Oklahoma, in 1959 and continued her academic studies at the University of Oklahoma at Norman where she received both a master of arts (1966) and a Ph.D. (1970) in the history of science.

Since 1966, Kidwell has taught history at various institutions, including Everett Junior College in Everett, Washington, and the Kansas City Art Institute in Kansas City, Missouri. In 1970, she became coordinator of publications at the Experimental Education Unit at the University of Washington, Seattle. From 1970 to 1972, she worked as an instructor in social sciences and chair of the Social Sciences Division at the Haskell Indian Junior College in Lawrence, Kansas. From 1974 to 1993, Kidwell taught in the Native American studies program at the University of California, Berkeley.

Kidwell published her first article, "The Apiarium: An Early Example of Microscopic Study," in *Proceedings of the Oklahoma Academy of Sciences XLVI* in 1966, and since has published twenty-four essays and numerous book reviews. In 1980, she authored *The Choctaws: A Critical Bibliography*, a bibliographic guide to the study of the Choctaw. In 1995, she published *Choctaws and Missionaries in Mississippi*.

Her Indian background shapes most of Kidwell's research and studies, which are focused on various aspects of American Indian culture. She is interested in American Indian women's issues, as shown in the essay "The Status of Native American Women in Higher Education" in *Proceedings of a Conference on the Educational and Occupational Needs of Native American Women* (1980), as well as in historical events of the Indians of South America, as seen in "Aztec and European Medicine in the New World, 1521–1600," published in *Anthropology of Medicine* (1982).

Throughout her active academic life, Kidwell has received numerous fellowships: the National Defense Education Act Title IV Fellowship, 1962–1965; the John Hay Whitney Foundation Opportunity Fellowship, 1965–1966; and the Rockefeller Foundation Humanities Fellowship, 1977–1978. More recently, she was awarded the University of California Humanities Fellowship, the Newberry Library Summer Fellowship, and in 1984, the Smithsonian Institution Fellowship.

Gary Kimble (1943–)
Gros Ventre lawyer and educator

Gary Kimble is head of the Native American Program at the Office of Child Support Enforcement in Washington, D.C. He is a member of the Gros Ventre tribe and was raised on the Fort Belknap Reservation in northern Montana, near the Canadian border. Kimble received a bachelor's degree in journalism from the University of Montana in 1966 and a law degree from the same university in 1972. In 1972, he was elected to the Montana House of Representatives and served for three terms, specializing in environmental policy and labor law. During the years 1974 and 1979, he was assistant professor of American Indian studies and Indian law at the University of Montana. In 1979, he was chief counsel for his tribe at the U.S. Senate Select Committee on Indian Affairs in Washington, D.C.

In 1978, Kimble was the first American Indian to run for the U.S. House of Representatives in more than twenty years. In 1980, he was appointed to direct the Columbia River Inter-Tribal Fish Commission in Portland, Oregon, a federal tribal advocacy organization for the inter-tribal fishery in the Columbia River basin. Kimble returned to Montana in 1982 and organized Kimble and Associates, a management and legal consulting firm, in Missoula. His chief clients were the governor's office in Montana, American Training and Technical Assistance in Albuquerque, and numerous tribal governments and groups in Montana and the Northwest.

In 1986, Kimble moved his business to Portland, Oregon, and began teaching federal Indian law at the Northwestern School of Law at Lewis and Clark College. In 1989, he became executive director of the Association on American Indian Affairs in New York and a member of the Aboriginal Public Policy Institute, a northern California organization that provides networking and technical assistance to aboriginal people worldwide. From 1994 to 2000, he served as commissioner of the Administration for Native Americans (Children and Families).

Thomas King (1943–)
Cherokee/Greek writer/photographer and scholar

Thomas King, an award-winning novelist, short story writer, scriptwriter, and photographer of Cherokee and Greek ancestry, is associate professor of English at the

University of Guelph (Canada). He was born in Sacramento, California, in 1943, and obtained his Ph.D. from the University of Utah (1986).

His first novel, *Medicine River* (1990), won several awards, including the runner-up for the 1991 Commonwealth Writers prize. King adapted the novel into a television movie in 1992, which won the Best Film award at the 1993 American Indian Film Festival in San Francisco, California.

He has also written two acclaimed children's books, *A Coyote Columbus Story* (1992) and *Coyote Sings to the Moon* (1998). His highly praised collection of short stories, *One Good Story, That One* (1993), was a Canadian bestseller.

Other works by King include *All My Relations: An Anthology of Contemporary Canadian Native Literature* (ed., 1990), *Green Grass, Running Water* (1993), which won the Canadian Authors Award for fiction, and *Truth and Bright Water* (2000).

King is also creator of CBC Radio One's *Dead Dog Café Comedy Hour*. He is currently working on a photography exhibition and *Warriors*, a television movie.

Rosemarie Kuptana (contemporary)
Inuit journalist and tribal leader

Rosemarie Kuptana was born in Sachs Harbour, a community of just over a hundred Inuit people on Banks Island, in Canada's Northwest Territories. She went to school in Inuvik, a village in the Northwest Territories, and first became involved with Inuit organizations in 1975. In 1979, she joined the northern service branch of the Canadian Broadcasting Corporation (CBC), hosting the morning and noon radio shows on CBC Western Arctic. Her programs focused on the cultural, social, and political issues of the day, including the Inuvialuit land claim, where Inuits sought province-like self-government within the Canadian government, and oil and gas explorations in the Beaufort Sea, located off the north shore of eastern Alaska and the western Northwest Territories.

After a period of work with community organizations in Sachs Harbour, Kuptana joined the Inuit Broadcasting Corporation (IBC). IBC's programs, which are in the Inuit Native language of Inuktitut, are a mixture of current affairs and contemporary and traditional Inuit culture of the Arctic, Alaska, and Northern Canada. She began as assistant production coordinator in

1982 and was promoted to network production coordinator; she was elected IBC president in December 1983. As president from 1983 to 1988, Kuptana supervised IBC's programming and managed a staff of fifty located in six widely dispersed production centers. She initiated many of the IBC's existing systems, such as its administrative policy, training programs for production staff, journalistic policy, as well as a children's educational television programs in Inuktitut language.

In recent years, Kuptana has researched and published a book about child sexual abuse in Inuit communities, promoted Inuit interests at the 1991 Canada-USSR Cooperation Conference held in Moscow and Leningrad, and continued her interests in journalism as vice-chair of Television of Northern Canada.

She also co-chaired the International Arctic Council, a project that would have eight circumpolar governments cooperate on a wide range of issues with special attention to the concerns of circumpolar Native peoples. Kuptana has also served as president and as the Canadian vice-chair of the Inuit Circumpolar Conference (ICC). The ICC is the international political organization representing Inuit from Canada, Alaska, Greenland, and the former Soviet Union.

From April 1991 to June 1996, Kuptana was elected president of the Inuit Tapirisat of Canada, the national political voice of Canadian Inuit. In this capacity Kuptana was engaged in a series of constitutional negotiations involving aboriginal leaders, territorial, provincial, and federal first ministers. In the last round of negotiations she obtained the recognition in principle of the inherent right of aboriginal self-government, as third order of government, by all the Canadian governments. In 1994, she was awarded the National Aboriginal Achievement Award for public service.

Richard Vance La Course (1938–)
Yakima journalist

Richard Vance La Course is a journalist who has worked extensively for the mainstream press and for the American Indian press. He was born in Toppenish, Washington, and studied at Portland State University, Oregon, and the University of Washington, Seattle. From 1969 to 1971, La Course was news editor and correspondent for the *Seattle Post-Intelligencer*. He was managing editor of the *Confederated Umatilla Journal* in Pendleton, Oregon, from 1971 to 1974; and of the *Yakima Nation Review* in Toppenish, Washington, from 1975 to 1978. In 1977, he founded and became managing editor of the *Manatabla Messenger*, published by the Colorado River Tribes in Parker, Arizona.

Since 1983, La Course has managed his own company, La Course Communications Corporation, in Washington, D.C. The corporation is an Indian-owned media firm that provides services in publication research and development, graphic design, publication of directories, market analysis, and specialized mailing lists related to American Indian concerns. La Course hopes eventually to publish a full-size weekly newspaper.

La Course is a co-founder and board member of Native American Press Association and co-founder of the Northwest Indian News Association. He is a member of the Nation Congress of American Indians, a national Indian political interest organization, and Americans for Indian Opportunity. In 1978, La Course was the keynote speaker and honoree at the Second Annual Indian Media Conference and American Indian Film Festival in San Francisco, California. In 1980, he was the recipient of the Indian Media Man of the Year Award at the Nation Indian Media Conference held in Anaheim, California. In 1984, he received a National Recognition Award of Accomplishment given by the Americans for Indian Opportunity, Washington, D.C.

La Course is the author and editor of *The Schooling of Native America: Native American Teachers Corps and Northwest Tribal Profiles*.

Winona LaDuke (1959–)
Ojibwa (Chippewa) Anishinaabe political and environmental activist, journalist, and author

An enrolled member of the Mississippi band from the White Earth Reservation in Minnesota, Winona LaDuke is one of the most respected women in American Indian politics. Among her many interests, LaDuke is best known for her strong environmental stances and for her work in favor of American Indian land restoration. She protested the uranium mines on the Navajo Reservation, resisted Hydro-Quebec's construction sites built at James Bay, and demonstrated against the toxic waste sites on Native Canadian and Alaskan lands bordering the Arctic Ocean.

The daughter of activists Vincent (Sun Bear), a Chippewa writer, and Betty, a Jewish painter, LaDuke was reared in a politically charged environment. Because of her father's occupation as an extra in Hollywood Westerns, she was born in Los Angeles. When she was five, however, her parents divorced and LaDuke and

Activist Winona LaDuke.

her mother moved to Ashland, Oregon. LaDuke maintained her Native ties, however, frequenting her father's home on the White Earth Reservation throughout her youth.

LaDuke received her bachelor's degree in economic development from Harvard University in 1982. While there she met Jimmy Durham, a well-known Cherokee activist, who helped her formulate ideas of activism and grassroots organization. When she was just eighteen, LaDuke spoke to the United Nations about environmental exploitation issues occurring throughout Indian Country.

After her undergraduate work, LaDuke moved to the White Earth Reservation and began to protest environmental racism and work for Ojibway land recovery. In the late 1980s, the activist graduated from Antioch University with a master's degree in rural development.

LaDuke received the first Reebok Human Rights Award, which recognizes activists under the age of thirty, in 1989. With the $20,000 grant she received with the award, LaDuke founded the White Earth Land Recovery Project (WELRP), an organization formed to raise funds to regain original White Earth land holdings. If people do not manage their own land, LaDuke argues, they do not control their future. WELRP has regained more than 1,000 acres of land for the White Earth people and LaDuke hopes to bring approximately 30,000 acres of land under Ojibway control by 2010.

In addition to WELRP, LaDuke also co-founded the Indigenous Women's Network (IWN), an organization helping Indian women achieve change in their own communities. In addition, LaDuke and the Indigo Girls, along with other activists, formed Honor the Earth, which has raised over $500,000 for Native environmental issues to date.

LaDuke has testified at many government hearings and has published numerous articles in books, newspapers, journals, and magazines throughout the United States. Some of her numerous articles may be found in *Ecocide of Native American: Environmental Destruction of Indian Lands and Peoples* (1995) edited by Donald A. Grinde and Bruce E. Johansen; *A Gathering of Spirit: A Collection by North American Indian Women* (1988) edited by Beth Brant; the feminist magazine *off our backs* (February 1981); and the politically focused *Utne Reader* (January/February 1990). Her most recent book, *All Our Relations: Native Struggles for Land and Life* (1999), is dedicated to Native environmentalism.

While most of LaDuke's writing is non-fiction, she has published a novel entitled *Last Standing Woman* (1997), a story of three generations of women named Ishkwegaabawiikwe, or Last Standing Woman. Interwoven into this plot is the history of the White Earth Reservation and the Anishinabe community at large from 1860 to the present. The work addresses many of those issues LaDuke considers important in her life, including the social, economic, and racial injustices the Anishinabe faced and continue to face after contact with American colonists.

LaDuke was named one of the fifty most promising future leaders by *Time* in 1995 and ran for vice president of the United States with Ralph Nader for the Green Party in 1996 and 2000. She presently lives on the White Earth Reservation with her two children and continues her work.

Francis La Flesche (1857–1932)
Omaha anthropologist

Francis La Flesche was the first American Indian to become a professional anthropologist. Born on the Omaha Reservation in Nebraska in 1857, La Flesche grew up in a family of distinguished individuals. His father, Joseph La Flesche (Iron Eye), was half-French but became a head chief and a force for change among the Omaha. (Because of his support for adopting Christianity and other European customs, his village became known as "Place of the Make Believe White Men.") One of Francis's sisters, Susan, became the first Indian physician and an activist for social reform. Another, Susette (Bright Eyes), became well known as a lecturer, writer, and painter.

Francis himself was raised on the Omaha Reservation near Bellevue and learned the traditional customs of his tribe, participating in buffalo hunts and ceremonials. He began lecturing and interpreting for other Native speakers during the late 1870s and became an advisor and interpreter for the Bureau of Indian Affairs in 1881.

While living in Washington, D.C., La Flesche became acquainted with Alice Cunningham Fletcher and together they wrote the classic studies *A Study of Omaha Music* (1893) and *The Omaha Tribe* (1911). La Flesche also wrote an autobiographical book describing his life as a student in a Presbyterian mission school in northeastern Nebraska during the Civil War titled *The Middle Five* (1900). He also wrote *A Dictionary of the Osage Language* (1932).

Susan La Flesche (1865–1915)
Omaha physician and tribal leader

Susan La Flesche has been labeled the first female Indian physician, although this label reflects a rather narrow, Western definition of medicine. In the late 1800s, La Flesche practiced medicine among the Omaha Indians, a Siouan-speaking nation living in Nebraska. She was also a political liaison for her people with the federal government and was active in the temperance movement. She is the sister of Susette La Flesche, a well-known activist.

La Flesche was the daughter of the Omaha chief Joseph La Flesche. Her mother, Mary Gale, was part Iowa, a tribe of Siouan-speaking Indians who were then living in Kansas. As a child, La Flesche studied with Christian missionaries. After attending the Elizabeth Institute for Young Ladies in New Jersey and the Hampton Institute in Virginia, she went on to receive her degree in medicine from the Women's Medical College of Pennsylvania in 1889.

In the years following, La Flesche practiced medicine on the Omaha Reservation, often traveling by buggy or on foot to reach patients unwilling or unable to come to her office. Besides her work doctoring for the Omaha, La Flesche was a temperance speaker and worked for the Women's National Indian Association. She married in 1894 and established a private practice in Bancroft, Nebraska, where she treated both Indian and non-Indian patients. After the death of her husband in 1905, La Flesche worked as a missionary at the

Blackbird Hills Presbyterian Church and continued to practice medicine. In her later years, La Flesche became a political advocate for her people and traveled to Washington, D.C., in 1910 to lobby the federal government for tribal land rights.

Susette La Flesche (1854–1903)
Omaha activist

Susette La Flesche devoted much of her life to working for women's and Indian rights. Her father was Chief Joseph La Flesche, and she was a stepsister of Francis La Flesche, the famous Omaha anthropologist. La Flesche was also known by her translated Omaha name, Bright Eyes (Inshata Theumba).

Like her sister, Susan La Flesche, Susette was educated by Christian missionaries and later studied art at the University of Nebraska. From 1877 to 1879 she was a teacher and conducted a Sunday school for Omaha children. During that time La Flesche became involved in the plight of the Ponca and the controversy over their removal. In 1877, the Ponca were forced by the U.S. government to leave northern Nebraska and move to Indian Territory, present-day Oklahoma, and settle on a 101,000-acre reservation. The Ponca were greatly dissatisfied with the forced removal and petitioned Congress for permission to return to their homeland in Nebraska. They were eventually granted a 10,000-acre reservation in Nebraska, but lost their Oklahoma lands to U.S. settlers. In 1879 and 1880, La Flesche made a speaking tour of the eastern United States, with her brother Francis and Ponca chief Standing Bear on behalf of the Ponca. La Flesche was called "Bright Eyes" on the tour. The purpose of the tour was to publicize the conditions and plight of Standing Bear and his people. La Flesche continued to tour the United States speaking on Indian affairs. In 1881, she met and married philanthropist and journalist Thomas H. Tibbles. Throughout the late 1880s, La Flesche and her husband made numerous public appearances, including trips to England and Scotland, where they made pleas for improving the condition of the Omaha and Ponca. In 1894, La Flesche and her husband were supervising editors of *The Weekly Independent*, a Populist newspaper in Lincoln, Nebraska. With Standing Bear, La Flesche co-authored *Ploughed Under: The Story of an Indian Chief*.

Moscelyne Larkin (1925–)
Shawnee/Peoria ballerina

Moscelyne Larkin is an internationally renowned ballerina of Russian and Shawnee/Peoria descent. Born in Miami, Oklahoma, on 14 January 1925, Larkin first studied ballet with her mother, Eva Matlagova, and later continued her studies in New York City. At the age of fifteen Larkin joined the Original Ballet Russe and became first soloist and then ballerina. She toured South America, the United States, Canada, and Europe as a member of the Original Ballet Russe, and in 1947 London critics described her as "the first ray of sunshine" after World War II.

Larkin then became a protege of Alexandra Danilova in the Ballet Russe de Monte Carlo and toured the world with Danilova's Great Moments of Ballet. In 1956, Larkin and her husband, Roman Jasinski, also an outstanding performer in the Ballet Russe, founded the Tulsa Civic Ballet, which evolved into the Tulsa Ballet Theatre, a nationally acclaimed ballet company of thirty-two dancers, with an extensive national touring schedule.

Larkin and her late husband have received several important awards and honors, including the prestigious *Dance Magazine* Award, which had previously been given to legendary dance artists such as Mikhail Baryshnikov, Rudolph Nureyev, and Fred Astaire. The couple were awarded honorary doctorates of fine arts from the University of Tulsa in 1991. Other honors bestowed on Larkin individually include the Governor's Arts Award, the Harweldin Award, and memberships in the Oklahoma Hall of Fame and the Tulsa County Historical Society Hall of Fame.

Stella Leach (contemporary)
Oglala Sioux/Colville activist

Stella Leach was a central participant in the 1969 Indian occupation of Alcatraz Island in San Francisco Bay. The occupation was an attempt by urban Indians to attract national attention to the failure of U.S. government policy toward American Indians and was a symbolic cry for self-determination following the official government policy of termination of federal responsibility for Indian tribes.

Before the Alcatraz occupation Leach worked in the all-Indian Well Baby Clinic in Oakland, California, a clinic she had helped organize in 1963. In 1969, she took a three month leave of absence and went to join the Indian protesters on Alcatraz Island where she set up a health clinic for the Indian occupiers and their families. Because of her dedication to the occupation and the continuing need for a clinic, she received an additional three-month leave of absence from the Well Baby Clinic. Leach was elected to the Island Council, the elected governing body of Indian occupiers on Alcatraz Island. She was a recognized leader when the negotiations between the Indian occupiers and the federal government reached an impasse in 1970. When questioned about what she would like to see take place on the island she stated "to see the dreams of all of these young people who took this island come true. If a University is what they want then I am all for it. Whatever pleases our young people, because to me this is the greatest thing that has occurred in my generation. To see our Indian youth take their place in society and once again become warriors in our society." Leach's four sons, Mike, Gary, Leo, and David, three of whom were Vietnam veterans, accompanied Stella on the island and served as members of the island's security police.

Greenwood LeFlore (1800–1865)
Choctaw tribal leader

By the middle 1820s, Greenwood LeFlore was one of the biggest owners of black slaves and one of the wealthiest men among the Choctaw. Of the three Choctaw political districts, he resided in the northwestern or Okla Falaya (The Long People) district. In 1826, LeFlore gained enough political support to replace the northwestern district chief, Robert Cole, on the grounds of lack of education and inability to resist U.S. land demands. LeFlore and other young chiefs wrote a constitution and advocated adoption of agriculture, education, and Christianity as ways to strengthen Choctaw resistance to U.S. territorial demands.

In January 1830, two district chiefs resigned and delegated their authority to LeFlore, who became principal chief. They argued that the traditional government of three equal chiefs inhibited government decision making and uniform law enforcement. By 1830, LeFlore was convinced that resistance to U.S. territorial expansion was not possible. He negotiated a treaty to cede Choctaw lands and migrate west, but it failed ratification by the U.S. Senate, which thought the treaty too generous. Meanwhile, Moshulatubee and Nitakechi, traditional leaders in the northeastern and southern districts, challenged LeFlore's authority as principal chief. LeFlore failed to suppress the rebellion and was forced to recognize the two district chiefs. Later in 1830, at the Treaty of Dancing Rabbit Creek, Choctaw leaders agreed to migrate to present-day Oklahoma. The Choctaw reacted by deposing the chiefs, but the United States refused to recognize any chiefs but those who signed the treaty. LeFlore did not migrate west, but remained on his plantation in the state of Mississippi, later serving in the state legislature.

Left Hand (Nawat) (1840–1890s)
Southern Arapaho tribal leader

As one of the principal chiefs of the Southern Cheyenne, Left Hand tread the delicate line between advocating peace and defending against U.S. encroachment. He also represented his people in negotiations with the federal government in the early 1890s.

In 1864, Colonel John Chivington, a U.S. officer commanding some seven hundred soldiers, attacked the Southern Cheyenne and Southern Arapaho in order to open their hunting grounds for U.S. settlers. Left Hand tried to keep his people out of the conflict. He and his warriors were present with the Southern Cheyenne leader Black Kettle at the Battle of Sand Creek in November 1864, when about two hundred Cheyenne men, women, and children were indiscriminately killed by Chivington's troops. The incident was considered one of the most grievous of the Civil War. Left Hand was wounded during the shooting, but he refused to take up arms and return fire against Chivington's forces. His pacifist stance met with skepticism from some of his warriors, and a number of them adopted a more militant posture.

Left Hand became the principal chief of the Southern Arapaho in 1889, upon the death of Little Raven. In 1890, he agreed to allotment of Southern Cheyenne land in present-day Oklahoma, despite opposition from most Southern Cheyenne who preferred traditional sharing and collective ownership of land. Allotment settlements allowed the U.S. government to divide Indian land and distribute them to individual Indians for farms, usually about 160 acres for a head of household. Any surplus land available after allotment usually was sold to U.S. settlers. The allotment of land left most Indians in Oklahoma with a greatly reduced land base.

David Lester (1941–)
Creek economic development administrator

David Lester has been active in government and private organizations that promote economic development in the Indian community. He was born in Claremore, Oklahoma, on 25 September 1941. In 1967 he received a bachelor's degree in political science and public administration from Brigham Young University in Provo, Utah. In Denver, Colorado, Lester became executive director of the Council of Energy Resource Tribes (CERT), a coalition of energy resource-rich Indian tribes that consults with and helps tribes negotiate more favorable contracts for the sale of minerals and energy resources like oil, gas, uranium, and coal. For two years, Lester served as vice-chairman of the

American Indian Scholarships, Inc., in Taos, New Mexico, an organization that provides grants to Indian college and graduate students. For eight years, he was president of the United Indian Development Association in Los Angeles, an organization that seeks to strengthen Indian business enterprise, usually in urban areas. Lester also served as commissioner to the Administration for Native Americans (ANA) at the U.S. Department of Health and Human Services in Washington, D.C. ANA provides federal administrative assistance and funds to tribal governments and urban Indian organizations in order to enhance their greater administrative capacities. Along with his interests in Indian economic development, Lester served as a member of the board of directors for the American Indian National Bank in Washington, a federally funded bank that provides economic development loans to reservation Indian businesses. Since 1992, he has been member of the board of trustees of the Institute of the American Indian Arts in Santa Fe, New Mexico, a member of the board of directors of the National Center for American Indian Enterprise Development in Mesa, Arizona, and also member of the Secretary of Energy's Advisory Board Task Force on Radioactive Waste Management.

Among his community activities, Lester has served as presidential appointee to the National Advisory Council on Minority Enterprise, which advised cabinet-level officials on strategies to stimulate minority business ownership, and he was human relations commissioner and chairman of the Los Angeles American Indian Commission. He is currently a trustee of the Institute of American Indian Arts.

Among Lester's honors and awards are the Americans for Indian Opportunity's Distinguished Services Peace Pipe Award, a proclamation of David Lester Day by the governor of Oklahoma, and the White Buffalo Council of American Indians' National Award for outstanding service to American Indians.

Jane Lind (contemporary)
Aleut actress, director, playwright, and choreographer

Jane Lind was one of seven children born on her father's trapping grounds in Humpback Bay, near the village of Perryville on the Alaska Peninsula. She is of Aleut, Russian, and Swedish descent, and she was raised in the Russian Orthodox Church.

Lind began her professional career while a high school student at the Institute of American Indian Arts in Santa Fe, New Mexico. Her performances there led her to a variety of roles in famous theaters. In the early 1970s, she helped found the Native American Theater

Jane Lind.

Ensemble and performed in various productions, such as Hanay Geiogamah's *Body Indian*, John Vaccaro's *Night Club*, and Andrei Serban's *Fragments of a Greek Trilogy*. After appearing in *The Taming of the Shrew* at the Alaska Repertory Company in 1982, Lind helped teach drama in rural communities in Alaska as a way to help children improve their educational skills and self-esteem.

During the ensuing years, she has sung, acted, and directed in various productions across the United States and Europe, including a stage performance with Robert Redford. In numerous off-Broadway productions, she has played in Peter Brook's *The Birds*, Ellen Stewart's *Another Phaedra Via Hercules*, Dave Hunsaker's *The Summer Face Woman*, and Jack Gelber's *The Independence of Eddi Rose*. Lind has worked also for television productions such as *Footprints in Blood*, *Days Of Our Lives*, and *Ryan's Hope*.

In 1991, Lind appeared in the movie *Salmonberries*, directed by Percy Adlon, which won first place in a Canadian film festival. She played the Eskimo wife opposite Chuck Connors. In 1992, Lind was the female lead and choreographer for Robert Jonanson's production of *Black Elk Speaks*, a new version of Christopher Sergel's play, originally presented at the Folger Theater in Washington, D.C., and based on the book of the same name.

In 1993, she played the role of Many Tears in the mini-series *Return to Lonesome Dove*. In 1994, she won an award for best choreographer for the Denver Center Theater production of *Black Elk Speaks*. The next year, she received the First Americans in the Arts award for best actress for her performance in the production.

She also appeared in the TNT production of *Crazy Horse* (1996). In 1998, she wrote, directed, and choreographed *So They Say* at Seward, Alaska. In 2000, she directed Hanay Geiogamah's play *Grandma* at Sinte Gleska University.

Marigold Linton (1936–)
Cahuilla and Cupeno psychologist and educator

Born on the Morongo Indian Reservation in southern California on 30 September 1936, Marigold Linton received a bachelor's degree in experimental psychology from the University of California, Riverside, in 1958. She then did graduate work at the University of Iowa from 1958 to 1960 and completed her doctorate in experimental psychology at the University of California, Los Angeles, in 1964.

Linton is an internationally recognized expert in the area of long-term memory and has published more than twenty research papers in this area, including "Transformations of Memory in Everyday Life" (1982) and "Memory as Chimera: the Changing Face of Memory" (1990). She is also co-author of a text entitled *The Practical Statistician: A Simplified Handbook of Statistics* (1975), which has sold more than 75,000 copies.

Linton was professor of psychology at San Diego State University (1964–1974) and at the University of Utah (1974–1986). She was director of the Office of Educational Services in the College of Education at Arizona State University (1986–1994) and director of American Indian Programs (1994–1998).

She has been director of American Indian Outreach at the University of Kansas since 1998 and was cofounder of the National Indian Education Association, served on the board of directors of SACNAS (Society for the Advancement of Chicanos and Native Americans in Science).

Little Crow (1810–1863)
Santee Sioux tribal leader

Little Crow was a Santee Sioux and son of a chief of the Kaposia Band of Mdewakanton Santee, who live in western Minnesota. Upon his father's death in 1834,

Little Crow became the fifth hereditary chief to lead his people. He lived at the present site of south St. Paul, Minnesota, and had six wives and twenty-two children during the course of his life. Through much of his chieftaincy, Little Crow maintained good relations with the United States.

In 1851, Little Crow signed the Treaty of Mendota in 1851, which transferred much of the Santee land to the United States in exchange for a reservation on the upper Minnesota River, plus annuities in an annual payment. In 1858, Little Crow was part of a Sioux delegation that traveled to Washington, D.C., for further treaty negotiations with the U.S. government. His participation in the signing of the Treaty of Mendota angered many members of his tribe, and he was not nominated as a tribal representative to the general council.

In August 1862, the Santee Sioux rose up against the settlers of Minnesota when the government annuity, guaranteed by the treaty of 1851, was delayed. The Sioux were hungry and impatient, while U.S. government agents stole and delayed distribution of necessary food to the Santee Sioux. Little Crow opposed the uprising at first, but eventually joined it and led several successful skirmishes. The Santee opened their war with raids on trading posts and settlements. As many as four hundred Minnesotans died the first day. Little Crow led an assault on Fort Ridgely where he lost approximately a hundred warriors before calling off the siege.

After a protracted battle at Birch Coulee, thirteen miles from Fort Ridgely, many of the surviving Santee withdrew to Dakota Territory or Canada, Little Crow among them. He died in July 1863 on a horse-stealing expedition out of Canada to Minnesota, shot by settlers who were paid bounties for Sioux scalps.

Little Turtle Michikinikwa (1752–1812)
Miami-Mahican tribal leader

Little Turtle was the leader of a Miami Band located near present-day Fort Wayne, Indiana. He was principal war chief of his people during the 1780s and 1790s.

After the American Revolution, a number of wars broke out in the Old Northwest between the Indians living in this region and the growing number of white settlers. Between 1783 and 1790 ongoing skirmishes and attacks made the region a flash point for Indian relations. In 1790, President George Washington ordered federal troops into the region to quell the attacks. Their staunchest opponent was Little Turtle, principal war chief of the regional tribes. During his initial encounters with the federal troops, Little Turtle perfected military tactics, making the best use of concealment, and quick, short attacks. The methods were devastatingly effective in two major encounters against Generals Josiah Harmar and Arthur St. Clair. On 3 November 1791, Little Turtle and his forces surprised St. Clair leaving behind over 600 dead, and almost 300 wounded. It was the worst defeat suffered by U.S. forces against Indians.

Washington's response was to field a third army, this time under the leadership of a seasoned revolutionary war veteran, General Anthony Wayne. Wayne planned his attack carefully and cautiously. Little Turtle's warriors, with the encouragement of British officials, were confident of victory. Little Turtle himself, however, counseled peace in the face of Wayne's well-organized campaign. The attack came in an area known as Fallen Timbers. Wayne's forces took so long to get to the battle that many of Little Turtle's troops had left the battle site. Though the Battle of Fallen Timbers was short, with only a few casualties, it was a disheartening defeat for Little Turtle and his followers, who realized that their British supporters were not going to come to their aid. After the battle, Wayne proceeded to destroy Indian villages and farmlands.

The defeat changed Little Turtle's outlook. A year later Wayne dictated the terms of the Treaty of Greenville, in which Little Turtle ceded large sections of Ohio and parts of Indiana. Little Turtle also signed a number of treaties in Fort Wayne in 1803 and 1809, and put his signature on the Treaty of Vincennes in 1805. Little Turtle spent the later part of his life traveling to eastern cities, where he met some of his former adversaries, including George Washington. The former U.S. adversary was granted an annual pension by the government and returned to his homeland on the Maumee River. Even the pleas of Tecumseh to join his cause could not persuade Little Turtle to take up arms again. The former war chief was committed to peace, and encouraged his people to take up farming and abstain from alcohol. He died in 1812 while at Fort Wayne.

Little Wolf (circa 1820–1904)
Northern Cheyenne tribal leader

Little Wolf was a chief of the Cheyenne military society known as the Bowstring Soldiers and, along with Dull Knife, was a war leader of the Northern Cheyenne. Little Wolf established his reputation as a war chief in his battles against the Comanche and Kiowa.

During the 1866–1868 war for the Bozeman Trail, Little Wolf fought alongside the Sioux leaders Crazy Horse and Gall in an attempt to protect Sioux lands in present-day Montana and Wyoming. In May 1868, Little

Wolf was one of the signers of the Fort Laramie Treaty, which obligated the U.S. government to vacate the forts along the Bozeman Trail. In July 1868, after the Indians had driven the soldiers from the Powder River country, Little Wolf and his followers occupied Fort Phil Kearny (one of the Bozeman Trail forts in present-day northern Wyoming), abandoning and burning it one month later.

When the Southern Cheyenne surrendered in 1875, however, the government concentrated on uniting the two Indian tribes onto one Indian reservation, primarily because gold was discovered in the Northern Cheyenne area of the Black Hills in present-day South Dakota. Little Wolf was one of the most active war chiefs in the War for the Black Hills of 1876–1877. He was shot seven times during the Battle of Dull Knife (in present day Wyoming) in November 1876 but survived the wounds.

The Northern Cheyenne were not willing to live in Indian Territory (Oklahoma) and repeatedly tried to return to their homeland in present-day Wyoming and Montana. Little Wolf joined Dull Knife, the Cheyenne chief, in the flight of the Northern Cheyenne from their assigned reservation in Indian Territory and proved difficult to capture. Dull Knife surrendered in October 1878, but Little Wolf successfully evaded government troops until March 1879, when he surrendered. The soldiers forced Little Crow and his remaining warriors to march from North Dakota south to Indian Territory. Though Little Wolf and Dull Knife escaped during the forced march, they finally surrendered in 1879.

Little Wolf became an army scout for General Nelson Miles and was allowed to remain in the Tongue River country of Montana. In 1880, he killed a fellow Cheyenne and lost his standing as chief. As was the Cheyenne tradition, he went into voluntary exile until his death in 1904.

J. Wilton Littlechild (1944–)
Cree legislator and athlete

Willie Littlechild was first elected to the Canadian House of Commons in 1988 after a landslide victory in Wetaskiwin, Alberta, a constituency on the outskirts of Edmonton. Littlechild was born on the Ermineskin Indian Reserve in Hobbema, Alberta, where he attended grade school. He then went to St. Anthony's College and subsequently to the University of Alberta, both located in Edmonton. At the University of Alberta, Littlechild obtained bachelor's and master's degrees in physical education before entering law school and graduating with a bachelor of law degree in 1976.

Before his election to the House of Commons, Littlechild ran his own law office and was involved in a number of different business ventures. He also devoted much of his time attempting to foster a sense of physical and mental well-being among his people through sports and physical exercise. He assisted in the organization and development of the Indian Sports Olympics, which helped to create sports and recreation programs on Indian reserves. He has been active in a host of organizations devoted to sports among aboriginal people, including the Native Golf Association, the Indian Hockey Council, the Native Summer Games, the National Indian Activities Association, and the National Indian Sport Council. He has coached basketball, football, hockey, and a swim team. The Willie Littlechild Award, presented by the Indian Association of Alberta in his honor, rewards Native students in Alberta for outstanding contributions to their communities as well as for athletic and academic excellence.

In his elected capacity, Littlechild has sat on a range of parliamentary committees, including aboriginal affairs and justice and the solicitor general committees. Littlechild is married and has three children, all of whom share their father's enthusiasm for athletics.

He has been inducted into three Sports Halls of Fame and the University of Alberta Wall of Honour. He recently became the first two-time F'ete Excellence Laurette winner for sports at the United Nations in Geneva to go with two Tom Longboat Trophies as the most outstanding Indian Athlete of the Year in Canada. In 1999, he received the highest Canadian civilian award, the Order of Canada.

Kevin Locke (1954–)
Lakota/Anishinabe musician and dancer

Kevin Locke is a performer and teacher interested in preserving Indian, especially Lakota, artistic traditions. Born in 1954 on the Standing Rock Reservation in South Dakota, Locke is a member of the Lakota tribe. Fluent in Lakota (a subgroup of the Sioux) languages and a preeminent traditional flute player and hoop dancer, he received master's degrees in educational administration and community education from the University of South Dakota.

Locke is also a popular performer and storyteller, working to ensure that his cultural heritage survives and prospers. He has traveled throughout the world, performing and lecturing in more than seventy countries, his goal being to show people, through the Lakota hoop dance, that humanity can be unified through an appreciation of diversity. Locke uses twenty-eight hoops to tell a story, depicting such things as flowers, butterflies, stars, the sun, and an eagle. The hoops represent

Actor Kevin Locke.

unity, and their colors—black, red, yellow, and white—represent the four directions, the four winds, the four seasons, and the four complexions of people's skin.

In 1982, Locke performed in the play *In Deo* and in *The Night of the First Americans* at the Kennedy Center in Washington, D.C. In his performances, he uses a traditional flute, which for the Lakota/Dakota Nations is the essence of the wind. The flute gives voice to the beauty of the land, and its sound is the sound of the wind rustling grass and leaves. The instrument consists of seven notes; four represent the directions, one represents the heavens, another the earth, and the last one represents the place where the six come together—the heart of the people listening to it.

Locke also organizes children's interactive and participatory workshops involving games, music, dancing, and storytelling, as well as lectures on American Indian issues, value and belief systems, social structure, and education. In the early 1990s, he participated in various festivals and programs such as the Hunter Mountain Festival in Hunter Mountain, New York; the Frontier Folklife Festival in St. Louis, Missouri; and the First Annual Storytelling Festival in Reno, Nevada. In 1992, he was appointed a delegate for Earth Summit 1992, an international environmental conference held in Rio De

Janeiro, Brazil. Locke was a featured performer at the 1996 United Nations Habitat II Conference in Turkey.

In 1990, Locke was awarded a National Heritage Fellowship by the National Endowment for the Arts for his contributions to the preservation of his cultural heritage and for his efforts to make it known and appreciated around the world.

Arlinda Faye Locklear (1951–)
Lumbee lawyer

Arlinda Locklear is an attorney with wide experience in federal Indian law and in complex federal litigation at all levels, including two successful appearances before the United States Supreme Court. Locklear is an enrolled member of the Lumbee tribe of North Carolina, a tribe living mostly in North and South Carolina. In 1973, she received a B.A. degree with high honors in political science from the College of Charleston in South Carolina, and in 1976 a law degree from Duke University School of Law in Durham, North Carolina. In 1990, she was awarded the Doctor of Humane Letters from New York State University.

In 1975 and 1976, Locklear was the winner of the Moot Court Competition at the New York City Bar Association. This competition is a reproduction of a trial based on an actual case, in which students from different law schools confront one another; the most outstanding among them eventually reach the national competition and confront real judges.

Since the beginning of her career, Locklear has worked in the area of federal Indian law. From 1976 to 1987, she was employed as a staff attorney with NARF, the Native American Rights Fund, where she had primary responsibility for major litigation on behalf of tribes located in Arizona, Florida, Nebraska, New York, South Dakota, Wisconsin, and Virginia.

Locklear was the first Indian woman to argue a case before the United States Supreme Court. In 1983, she argued *Solem v. Bartlett*, which challenged the jurisdiction of the state of South Dakota to prosecute a member of the Cheyenne River Sioux tribe for on-reservation conduct. She won the case unanimously. In 1985, she argued her second case in the Supreme Court, *Oneida Indian Nation v. County of Oneida*, in which the Oneida of New York sought to reclaim lands from control of the local county government. In this case, she formulated a theory under federal common law that allows tribes to claim title to their homelands whenever Indian land was taken without the consent of the United States government. Because of her successes in these cases, Locklear is recognized as the leading authority on tribal land claims.

Locklear has published several articles on legal claims: "The Oneida Claims: A Legal Overview," in *Iroquois Land Claims* (Syracuse University Press, 1988); "The Historic Quality of Nation-to-Nation Relationship," in *Northeast Indian Quarterly* (1988); and "The Allotment of the Oneida Reservation and Its Legal Ramifications," in *The Oneida Indian Experience: Two Perspectives* (1988).

Frederick Olgilve Loft (1862–1934)
Mohawk activist and soldier

Fred Loft was known for his vision of a unified organization speaking for Indian people from coast to coast in Canada. Born in Grand River in Mohawk territory in southwestern Ontario, Loft was largely self-educated and served as an officer for the Canadian army during World War I. In addition to enlisting himself (by claiming to be ten years younger than he was at the time), Loft brought with him a number of other Ontario. They were assigned to the forestry corps, and Loft was commissioned lieutenant for the duration of the war. During his months in service in France, Loft met other enlisted Indian men from Canada and discovered that, despite their differences, they shared similar difficulties when dealing with Canadian authorities. Before returning home, he met King George V of England and spent some time talking to him in private.

Loft began to realize his vision of a unified Indian organization as soon as he returned home. He created the League of Indians of Canada and was elected president-chief in 1919. He spent several years writing to Indian people across the country informing them of the aims of the league, which were to protect Indian rights to ancestral lands and to seek a greater voice in governmental decisions. Canadian authorities did not take kindly to Loft's organizational efforts, and they unsuccessfully sought to persuade Loft to renounce his heritage in return for the right to vote and own property. In the early 1920s, Loft traveled to Saskatchewan and Alberta to meet with Plains Indians about the league. His wife of many years, Affa Northcote Gears, fell ill in 1923, and they moved to her hometown of Chicago so she could recuperate. Loft tried to run the league from Chicago, but his advancing years, lack of resources, and continued harassment by Canadian authorities made it almost impossible to continue.

John Logan (Tachnechdorus) (1725–1780)
Mingo (Cayuga) tribal leader

John Logan was a Mingo leader during the Lord Dunmore's War of 1774, when the Mingo and Shawnee

Nations tried to block Virginia settlers from crossing the line set by the Proclamation of 1763, which forbade colonial settlement beyond the crest of the Appalachian mountains. Despite the proclamation, settlers and merchants continued to swarm into the Mississippi and Ohio Valleys. During this era a number of Shawnee and Mingo allies attempted to withstand the onrush. The Mingo were a group of Iroquois who moved to live and trap in the Ohio Valley and left their homeland in present-day upstate New York.

Logan (Tachnechdorus) was the leader of the bands of Iroquois-speaking Mingo who lived near the headwaters of the Ohio River in western Pennsylvania. He was born a Cayuga, an Iroquois nation, near the Susquehanna River. Over the years Tachnechdorus was given the name Mingo or The Great Mingo. Mingo is the tribal name given to Iroquois living in Pennsylvania and Ohio. After moving to the Ohio region, Logan became a strong supporter of peaceful relations with the colonists. However, when members of his family were massacred for no apparent reason by settlers in 1774, Logan adopted a militant stance and began a series of raids against settlers throughout the trans-Appalachian region. His actions were abetted by British allies and the Shawnee leader, Cornstalk. Logan and Cornstalk fought together in what is known as Lord Dunmore's War. After their defeat in 1774, at the Battle of Point Pleasant, Pennsylvania, Logan refused to attend a peace conference at Scioto, Ohio. It is believed (though some doubt its authenticity) that he delivered an eloquent letter much admired at the time and later cited by Thomas Jefferson. Logan continued his attacks during the American War for Independence. He was killed while returning from Detroit in 1780.

Charles Loloma (1921–1991)
Hopi artist

Charles Loloma's jewelry is among the most distinctive in the world. The originality of his designs stems from the combination of non-traditional materials, like gold and diamonds, with typical Indian materials like turquoise. He received great recognition as a potter, silversmith, and designer.

Loloma was born in Hotevilla, Arizona, in 1921. He grew up and was educated on the Hopi Reservation in northern Arizona; he attended the Hopi High School in Oraibi and the Phoenix Indian High School in Phoenix. In 1939, Loloma painted the murals for the Federal Building on Treasure Island in San Francisco Bay, as part of the Golden Gate International Exposition. The following year, he was commissioned by the Indian Arts and Crafts Board to paint the murals for the Museum of Modern Art in New York. Also in 1940, Loloma was drafted into the army, where he spent four years working as a camouflage expert in the Aleutian Islands off the Alaskan coast. After his discharge, he attended the School for American Craftsman at Alfred University in New York, a well-known center for ceramic arts. This was an unprecedented move on Loloma's part, since ceramics was traditionally a woman's art among the Hopi, but it was also indicative of his future course.

In 1949, Loloma received a Whitney Foundation Fellowship to study the clays of the Hopi area. After that, he and his wife set up a shop in the newly opened Kiva Craft Center in Scottsdale, Arizona, which was intended to become a center for high-quality arts and crafts. From 1954 to 1958, he taught pottery during the summers at Arizona State University, and in 1962 he became head of the plastic arts and sales departments at the newly established Institute of American Indian Arts in Santa Fe, New Mexico.

In 1963, Loloma exhibited his work in a private showing in Paris and then returned to the institute in Santa Fe until 1965, when he moved back to the Hopi Reservation in northern Arizona. By this time, his reputation as a jeweler was well established, and his pieces were winning first prizes in Indian arts competitions. By the mid-1970s, his jewelry was exhibited throughout the country and in Europe. Loloma spent the rest of his years on the Hopi Reservation, where he continued working and teaching his art to several apprentices. He was one of the first prominent Indian craftsmen who worked outside the traditional Indian influence; a variety of influences resulted in his unique personal style, which has been widely imitated among Indian artisans.

Linda Lomahaftewa (1947–)
Hopi-Choctaw painter and educator

Linda Lomahaftewa, a painter whose works highlight the culture of the Plains Indians, is professor of painting and drawing at the Institute of American Indian Arts (IAIA), in Santa Fe, New Mexico. She was born on 3 July 1947 in Phoenix, Arizona. In 1962, she entered IAIA, where, in 1965, she received her diploma in art. She also received a bachelor of fine arts degree and a master of fine arts degree (1971) at the San Francisco Art Institute.

Since 1970, Lomahaftewa has been an art educator, first as a teaching assistant at the San Francisco Art Institute and, from 1971 to 1973, as assistant professor of Native American art at California State College in

Linda Lomahaftewa.

Tsianina Lomawaima.

Sonoma. From 1974 to 1976, she was an instructor of painting and drawing in the Native American Studies Program at the University of California in Berkeley.

During the 1970s, Lomahaftewa's paintings were shown in more than forty exhibitions, including "New Directions," an Institute of American Indian Arts alumni traveling exhibition, and "Contemporary Native American Artists" at the Alternative Center for International Arts in New York City in 1977. In 1977, her works were also presented in the exhibition "Eleven Women Artists" at the Elaine Horwitch Gallery in Santa Fe, New Mexico.

Lomahaftewa's paintings were featured in a solo show in 1978 at the C. N. Gorman Museum at the University of California at Davis. Her work was exhibited in the "Pintura Amerindia Contemporanea" tour, organized by the United States Communication Agency in 1979. In 1980, she exhibited her paintings at the special exhibition organized by the Indian Arts and Crafts Board's Southern Plains Indian Museum and Crafts Center in Anadarko, Oklahoma. Lomahaftewa was listed among other prominent figures of the contemporary Native American artistic scene in two editions of *Who's Who in American Indian Arts*, in 1976 and in 1978.

K. Tsianina Lomawaima (1955–)
Creek anthropologist

K. Tsianina Lomawaima is professor of American Indian studies at the University of Arizona. She received a bachelor's degree in anthropology in 1976 from the University of Arizona, earned a master of arts degree in 1979, and a doctorate in anthropology from Stanford University in 1987. From 1979 to 1980, she was the curriculum developer on the Northern Cheyenne Reservation at Lame Deer Public School in Lame Deer, Montana, and then was a lecturer in Native American studies at the University of California at Berkeley. From 1988 to 1994, Lomawaima taught anthropology and American Indian studies at the University of Washington in Seattle.

Professor Lomawaima's publications appear mainly in the *American Indian Quarterly*, where she has published "Oral Histories from Chilocco Indian Agricultural School, 1920 to 1940" (1987), as well as several book reviews and review essays. Her first book, *They Called It Prairie Light: The Story of Chilocco Indian School* (1993), won the 1993 North American Indian Prose Award, and 1995 Critic's Choice Award of the American Educational Association.

Lomawaima has received numerous fellowships, honors, and grants, such as the Phillips Fund research grant from the American Philosophical Society in 1983, the Summer Research Grant from the College of Arts and Sciences of the University of Washington, Seattle, in 1989, and a Distinguished Teaching Award from the University of Washington in 1991. In 1992 she earned a grant from the Institute for Ethnic Studies for a study entitled "Southwest Pueblos and the Atchinson Topeka and Santa Fe Railway."

Lone Wolf (Guipago) (1820–1879)
Kiowa tribal leader

During the 1860s and 1870s, Lone Wolf became one of his tribe's most respected band chiefs and warriors. He was one of the signers of the Medicine Lodge Treaty of 1867 and later fought a series of military campaigns against U.S. forces.

During the first part of his life, Lone Wolf came to negotiate with U.S. agents in a spirit of peace and hope for close, friendly ties. In 1863, he visited President Abraham Lincoln as part of a delegation of southern Plains Indian leaders. In 1866, he became principal chief of the Kiowa. The election of Lone Wolf was a compromise between the militant Satanta and the pacifist Kicking Bird. As chief, Lone Wolf signed the Medicine Lodge Treaty of 1867, which established the boundaries of the combined Kiowa and Comanche Reservation in present-day Oklahoma. When members of his tribe refused to comply with the treaty, Lone Wolf was taken hostage by U.S. authorities.

Although Lone Wolf traveled to Washington, D.C., in 1872 to negotiate a peace settlement, the death of his son at the hands of federal soldiers in 1873 pushed him into war. For the next two years, he and other tribal leaders of the Southern Plains met federal and state troops in a number of consequential engagements. Lone Wolf participated in the Red River War (1874–1875) fighting alongside Quanah Parker, the Comanche leader. During the middle 1870s, the Kiowa and Comanche feared that the wholesale slaughter of buffalo by U.S. hunters would destroy their economic base and way of life. The Kiowa and Comanche started the Red River War to discourage buffalo hunters from killing the buffalo herds. After the battle at Palo Duro Canyon in September 1874, however, Lone Wolf's supply of horses and tipis was devastated. He was forced to surrender at Fort Sill in the Indian Territory in 1875. Lone Wolf, along with Mamanti, a Kiowa spiritual leader, was sent to Fort Marion in Florida. (The exiles had been handpicked by Kicking Bird, whom U.S. officials had appointed Kiowa chief.) Lone Wolf returned to his homeland in 1878 and died one year later of malaria.

Buffalo Child Long Lance (Sylvester Long) (1891–1932)
Catawba/Cherokee actor

Buffalo Child Long Lance was an author, newspaper reporter, and movie actor of the 1920s and 1930s. He was born Sylvester Long in Winston, North Carolina, in 1891. His father, Joe Long, was part Catawba Indian and part Black. Long Lance attended a school for Blacks until the age of twelve, at which time he joined a Wild West show. At the age of eighteen, he applied for admission to Carlisle Indian School in Pennsylvania, enrolling as a Cherokee.

In 1915, Long Lance was a candidate to West Point, but instead he went north to join the Canadian army, as that country was already at war with Germany. Long Lance served overseas with the Canadian Expeditionary Force and rose to the rank of staff sergeant. He was wounded twice in action. After discharge, he became a reporter for the *Calgary Daily Herald*, traveling across western Canada and writing numerous articles on the Native peoples. During this time, he became a friend of Archdeacon S. H. Middleton, the Anglican missionary on the Blood Reserve in western Canada, who accepted Long Lance completely as a Cherokee Indian and introduced him to many Indian elders. In 1922, Middleton arranged for Long Lance to be inducted as an honorary chief of the Blood tribe. An article in the 14 February 1922 *Calgary Herald* was entitled "Cherokee Given a High Honor by Blood Indians."

In 1928, Long Lance published his autobiography, *Long Lance: The Autobiography of a Blackfoot Indian Chief* (Cosmopolitan Book Corporation of New York). As a result of the ensuing publicity, Long Lance was invited to star in the film, *The Silent Enemy*, which was sponsored by the American Museum of Natural History and released by Paramount Pictures. Following *The Silent Enemy*, Long Lance was invited to star in a talking film dealing with the exploits of an Indian flying ace during the Great War. He died in 1932 in California, while preparing for his Hollywood debut.

Looking Glass (1823–1877)
Nez Percé tribal leader

Looking Glass was the son of Apash Wyakaikt, who was also called Looking Glass because of the small trade mirror he wore as a pendant. The pendant was passed on to Looking Glass the younger. Looking Glass the elder participated with Old Joseph in the Walla Walla Council of 1855 as one of the chiefs who refused to sign the treaty proposed by Governor Isaac Stevens of the Washington Territory.

Looking Glass the younger, leader of the Asotian Band of the Nez Percé, refused to sign a second treaty in 1863 that would have further reduced the tribe's land. While Looking Glass had been appointed Nez Percé tribal war chief in 1848, he hoped to avoid war with the United States. He turned militant on 1 July 1877, when a combined force of army regulars and volunteer militia attacked his camp near the forks of the Clearwater Creek in present-day Idaho.

Looking Glass's band joined with the band of Nez Percé leader Joseph, who had also been attacked on June 17. United, they fought General Oliver Howard at the Battle of the Clearwater on 11 July 1877. The Nez Percé now counted seven hundred among their ranks, but at least five hundred of these were women, children, or men too old to fight. Still, the Nez Percé warriors outfought and outflanked the larger Howard force.

Following the Battle of Clearwater, the majority of the Nez Percé chose to head east through the Bitterroot Mountains to seek a military alliance with the Crow. Looking Glass was given overall command of the journey. To his dismay, he learned that some Crow were scouting for the U.S. Army. Counseling with other leaders, Looking Glass decided to lead his band northward through Montana Territory to Canada. They now planned to seek the assistance of Sitting Bull, the famous Sioux leader, who had escaped across the border that same year. During the next two weeks, the trail- and battle-weary Nez Percé outmaneuvered and outfought the army while they wound their way through the Montana wilderness toward the Canadian border. Finally, army troops led by Colonel Nelson Miles caught up to Looking Glass and the Nez Percé near the Bear Paw Mountains, where they laid siege to the Indian camp. Howard's troops arrived on the scene on October 5, forcing an ultimate surrender by the Nez Percé. Looking Glass, who refused to surrender, was struck by a stray bullet and killed.

Phil Lucas (contemporary)
Choctaw producer and director

Phil Lucas is the owner of Phil Lucas Productions, Inc., an independent film production company that develops projects for motion picture and television productions. In 1970, he received a bachelor's degree in science and visual communication from Western Washington University in Bellingham, Washington. From 1979 to 1981, he was the co-producer, writer, and co-director of a five-part Public Broadcasting Corporation series, *Images of Indians*, which explored the problem of Indian stereotypes as portrayed and perpetuated by

Hollywood Western movies. The series won a Special Achievement Award in Documentary Film in 1980 from the American Indian Film Institute and the Prix Italia Award in 1981.

His productions deal with accurate portraits of Indians, as in *Nez Percé: Portrait of People* (1982), a twenty-three-minute color film on the culture and history of the Nez Percé tribe. His commitment to spreading information about issues affecting the Indian community has been strengthened in recent years through the production of documentaries on the AIDS virus, and drug and alcohol prevention, such as *Circle of Warriors* (1989) and *Lookin' Good* (1988). Alcoholism is treated also in *Where We've Been And Where We're Going* (1983), a two-part series produced for the University of Lethbridge in Alberta, Canada. In *I'm Not Afraid of Me* (1990), Lucas presents the story of a Native woman and her daughter, both of whom have AIDS.

His international television credits include two documentary series, *The Native Americans* for TBS in 1994 and *Storytellers of the Pacific* in 1996. Lucas also produced *The Broken Chain*, a 1995 TBS movie about the Iroquois Confederacy. The movie starred Wes Studi, Pierce Brosnan, and Buffy Saint-Marie.

Lucas lives in Issaquah, Washington, with his wife Nancy and five children. He is currently developing a major PBS series about Native Americans in the twenty-first century.

Phillip Lujan (contemporary)
Kiowa-Taos Pueblo lawyer

Phillip Doren Lujan grew up in the Rainy Mountain area of Kiowa country in western Oklahoma. In 1970, Lujan graduated from Washington University with a degree in sociology, and in 1974 he graduated from the New Mexico University School of Law in Albuquerque, New Mexico. After graduation, Lujan worked as a staff attorney for the Native American Legal Defense and Education Fund in Albuquerque, New Mexico, and from 1974 to 1976, he was a staff attorney for the American Indian Law Center at the University of New Mexico Law School. In 1976 and 1977, he was director of the Special Scholarship Program in Law at the New Mexico University Law School.

Lujan has served numerous tribal communities throughout his career as chief prosecutor for the Oklahoma Indian Affairs Commission for the Court of Indian Offenses of Western Oklahoma for the Anadarko (Oklahoma) area (1979–1981), as magistrate for the Court of Indian Offenses at the Concho Agency (1984–1986), and magistrate for the Court of Indian Offenses at the Shawnee Agency (1984–1985).

He has served as chief judge for the Court of Indian Claims for Western Oklahoma (1986–1992), chief judge for the Potowatomi tribe (1986–1993), and was chief judge for the Sac and Fox tribe (1987–1993). He currently balances tribal judicial duties and an associate professorship of communications at the University of Oklahoma.

Oren Lyons (1930–)
Onondaga tribal leader and scholar

Oren Lyons (Joagquisho) is a member of the Onondaga Nation Council of Chiefs of the Six Nations of the Iroquois Confederacy, a traditional Faithkeeper of the Turtle Clan, and professor of Indigenous studies (American studies) at the State University of New York at Buffalo.

Born in 1930 and raised on the Seneca and Onondaga reservations, Chief Lyons attended Syracuse University, earning All-American honors in lacrosse, and obtained a bachelor of fine arts in 1958.

Chief Lyons serves on the executive committee of the Global Forum of Spiritual and Parliamentary Leaders on Human Survival, is a notable member of the Traditional Circle of Indian Elders, and helped establish the United Nations' Working Group on Indigenous Populations.

He has authored numerous books including *Exiled in the Land of the Democracy, Indian Nations, and the U.S. Constitution* & as well as *Voice of Indigenous Peoples* (1992) and *Native People Address the United Nations* (1994).

His honors and awards include the Ellis Island Congressional Medal of Honor, National Audubon Award for the Environment, and the First International Earth Day Award.

Mark Andrew Macarro (1963–)
Luiseño tribal leader and gaming spokesperson

Being chairman of the Pechanga Band of Luiseño Indians' Tribal Council at the turn of the century is not easy. Not only is Mark Macarro asked to make crucial decisions for his Southern California tribe, but he was also the acting spokesman for California Indian gaming rights. Propositions 5 and 1A, the state's Indian casino initiatives, passed in 1998 and 2000, respectively, showing Macarro's well-honed and influential political abilities. These initiatives ensure that California Indian

Mark Macarro.

tribes may operate casinos on their lands without state interference.

Born in Colton, California, located in San Bernadino County, Macarro is one of four children of working-class parents, Martha and Leslie. His father worked as a landscape laborer, a barber, and a correctional peace officer for a state youth authority in Chino, California. In the late 1980s, Leslie was killed while chasing a prisoner who was trying to flee. It is through his father that Macarro traces his indigenous roots.

After graduating from high school in 1981, Macarro attended San Bernadino Valley College and later the University of California, Santa Barbara, from which he graduated with a bachelor's degree in political science. Shortly after graduation, Macarro was accepted into the Naval Aviation Officer Candidate School in Florida. After just a few days in Florida, however, Macarro was physically disqualified from the school because his "butt-to-knee length" was too short. The future tribal leader returned home and taught for a year as a middle- and high-school substitute teacher.

In the mid-1980s, Macarro was hired as the federal grants administrator for the Pechanga Indian Reservation near Temecula, California. Soon after he ran the Soboba tribe's reservation school, and became library and museum manager at the Rincon Indian Reservation in San Diego County.

Then, in 1995, Macarro was chosen to replace a Pechanga tribal chair who had left his post mid-term. The same year Pechanga opened their entertainment center, Macarro was elected tribal chair. During this time, Macarro also married wife Elizabeth in 1991. They have since had two children, David and Rebecca.

In addition to remaining active in the Native political realm, Macarro maintains ties to more traditional practices. Among other activities, he sings Nukwaanish songs in Luiseño at important ceremonial events.

Now that Native gaming rights are ensured in California, Macarro is trying to protect traditional tribal customs during this period of economic growth. Macarro hopes to use gaming at Pechanga to develop other forms of economic development and to enhance tribal institutions that may need improvement.

Peter MacDonald (1928–)
Navajo tribal leader and businessperson

Peter MacDonald is probably best known for his tenacious and imaginative defense of Navajo land and energy resource rights. The Navajo occupy extensive parts of Arizona and New Mexico (14 million acres) and have the largest population of any tribe in the United States or Canada.

He was born on the Navajo Reservation at a place called Teec Nos Pos, and Navajo was his first language. His father died when he was only two, and MacDonald was forced to leave school after the seventh grade to herd sheep and work. Later, during World War II, he served in the marines and became one of the highly esteemed Navajo Code Talkers, whose messages in the Native language confused the Japanese military cryptographers during the Pacific campaigns. On being discharged, MacDonald resumed his education, getting a bachelor's degree from Bacone Junior College in Muskogee, Oklahoma, and earning a degree in electrical engineering from the University of Oklahoma in 1957.

In 1963, MacDonald returned to the Navajo Reservation, first to serve on the New Mexico Economic Development Advisory Board and later to become director of the Office of Navajo Economic Opportunity (ONEO). His aggressive management brought in more than $20 million in federal grants between the years 1965 and 1968. These successes led to his election as tribal chairman in 1970, and during his three terms in office, he fought to renegotiate the leases through which outside industrial interests gained access to minerals on Navajo land and sought a more favorable policy for controlling Colorado River water rights. MacDonald also worked to keep industrial development under tribal control and tried to expand Navajo influence by encouraging the people to participate in elections.

MacDonald has received numerous honorary awards and served on many advisory boards, both in his capacity as a political leader and as an engineer.

Over the years, MacDonald has been an outspoken critic of the Bureau of Indian Affairs. His administrations faced serious issues, such as the land dispute between the Navajo and Hopi, and were subject to charges of fraud and favoritism. But his achievements in energy use management and Navajo self-determination are hard to question.

He is currently in the seventh year of a fourteen-year sentence for conspiracy to overthrow the Navajo Nation government and bribery. He was convicted of profiting from a deal in which real estate agents sold a ranch near Seligman, Arizona, to business associates of his for $26.2 million. The next day, they sold it to the Navajo Nation for $33.4 million, and he was paid a small sum of the profits. MacDonald, now seventy, was pardoned by the Navajo Nation Council in 1995 and is seeking a medical release from prison due to health concerns.

Edna Ahgeak MacLean (contemporary)
Iñupiaq administrator and scholar

Edna Ahgeak MacLean is president of Ilisagvik College, in Barrow, Alaska. She earned her master's in bilingual education from the University of Washington and received her doctorate in education from Stanford University. MacLean also did graduate study in Greenlandic Eskimo at Aarhus University and received her teaching credentials from University of California, Berkeley.

While at the University of Alaska, Fairbanks, MacLean was awarded tenure and promoted to associate professor of Iñupiaq Eskimo. For several years, she was the special assistant for Rural and Alaska Native Education to the State of Alaska Commissioner of Education.

A Native speaker of Iñupiaq, Edna MacLean has developed many documents used extensively as references and guides to the Iñupiaq language and is well-known for her numerous presentations and workshops at conferences and seminars.

MacLean received the Alaska Federation of Natives Higher Education Award (1995), and has been elected as a fellow of the Arctic Institute of North America. In

1999, she received the Educator of the Year Award from the Alaska Native Education Council.

Wilma P. Mankiller (1945–)
Cherokee tribal leader

Chief Wilma Mankiller's roots are planted deep in the rural, Rocky Mountain community in Adair County, Oklahoma. She was born at the Indian hospital in Tahlequah, Oklahoma, and grew up with few amenities. When she was eleven, her family moved to California as part of the Bureau of Indian Affairs Relocation program.

She experienced an awakening, or call to action, during the occupation of Alcatraz Island, and performed volunteer work among Native Americans in California before returning to Oklahoma with her two children.

Her initial work for the Cherokee Nation included the recruitment of young Native Americans for university training in environmental science. In 1979, she earned a bachelor's degree in social work, and then began commuting to the University of Arkansas for graduate study. En route to school, she was in a near fatal head-on automobile collision. She implemented

Wilma Mankiller.

what Cherokees call "being of good mind," in order to recover from her extensive injuries.

As the founding director of the Cherokee Nation Community Development Department (1980–1983), she persistently pursued proposals to improve housing, education, and health care projects for Cherokee people.

In 1983, she was the first woman elected deputy chief of the Cherokee Nation. When the Cherokee principal chief resigned in December 1985, she succeeded him. In the historic 1987 tribal election, Mankiller became the first woman elected principal chief of the Cherokee Nation, with 56 percent of the vote.

She was reelected, in 1991, receiving nearly 83 percent of the vote. During her tenure as principal chief, the annual budget doubled, tribal membership tripled in size, and health services and programs benefiting children were significantly expanded.

Chief Mankiller, who left office in 1995, is the recipient of honorary doctorate degrees from thirteen colleges and universities, and served as a Montgomery Fellow at Dartmouth College during the 1996 winter term. She also co-authored *Mankiller: A Chief and Her People* (1993), authored *Keeping Pace With the Rest of the World* (1997), and co-edited the *Reader's Companion to the History of Women in the United States* (1998).

She has been inducted into the Oklahoma Women's Hall of Fame (1986), the International Women's Forum Hall of Fame (1992), the National Women's Hall of Fame (1993), San Francisco State University Hall of Fame (1995), and the Oklahoma Hall of Fame (1995).

Her honors and awards include *Ms.* Magazine's Woman of the Year (1987); the Henry G. Bennett Distinguished Service Award, Oklahoma State University (1990); The Freedom Forum, Free Speech, Free Spirit Award (1994); The National Education Association Leadership Award (1995); The Chubb Fellowship, Timothy Dwight College, Yale University (1995); Who's Who in America, One of the Fifty Most Important People in the U.S. (1996); The Elizabeth Blackwell Award (1996); the Dorothy Height Lifetime Achievement Award (1997); The Presidential Medal of Freedom (1998); and "One of the 50 Most Influential People of the Century," in the State of Oklahoma (2000).

Chief Mankiller is a trustee for the Freedom Forum, First Amendment Center, and the Ford Foundation. She is on the advisory boards of the Native American Preparatory School and Cornell University Indian Publishing and a board member of the Leadership Academy, University of Maryland, and the Buffalo Trust.

She is married to Charlie L. Soap, has two daughters, three sons, and seven grandchildren. She lives in the Rocky Mountain community of Adair County, Oklahoma, on the Mankiller land allotment.

Henrietta Mann.

Henrietta Mann (contemporary)
Cheyenne tribal leader and educator

Henrietta (Whiteman) Mann, "The Woman Who Comes to Offer Prayer," has made important contributions in promoting understanding of Cheyenne culture.

The great-granddaughter of White Buffalo Woman, a Cheyenne medicine woman, she earned a master of arts degree from Oklahoma State University and a doctoral degree in American Studies from the University of New Mexico in 1982.

Mann is the first individual to occupy the Endowed Chair in Native American Studies at Montana State University, Bozeman. Prior to becoming the Endowed Chair at Montana State, she was on the Native American Studies faculty at the University of Montana, Missoula, for twenty-eight years. She served a two-year Interpersonnel Assignment to Haskell Indian Nations University as visiting professor in Indian Studies and interim dean of instruction.

On both state and national levels, Mann served two terms on the board of the National Indian Education Association and a two-year term as a commissioner for the National Commission on Head Start Fellowships of the Head Start Bureau, Administration on Children, Youth and families, U.S. Department of Health and Human Services.

Mann serves as secretary of the Native Lands Institute in Albuquerque, New Mexico, and she is on the board of Native Action, a contemporary Cheyenne women's society, located on the Northern Cheyenne Reservation. She is also the secretary for the Montana Advisory Committee for House Bill 412, which is in the process of changing the names of seventy-four Montana sites that have a pejorative Indian word as a name. She is also in her second term as a board member of the Smithsonian's National Museum of the American Indian.

In 1998, the University of Colorado Press published her book, *Cheyenne-Arapaho Education, 1871–1982*. She has been an interviewee, consultant, and technical advisor for television and movie productions, including the American Experience's *In the White Man's Image* & Discovery Channel's *How the West Was Lost* & Home Box Office's *Paha Sapa : The Struggle for the Black Hills* & and PBS's documentary *The West*. She was the Cheyenne consultant and a language coach for the film, *Last of the Dogmen*.

Mann presented a workshop, served as a panelist, and delivered a keynote address at the closing general assembly of the 1999 World Indigenous Peoples' Conference on Education in Hilo, Hawaii. She has lectured extensively throughout the United States, as well as in Mexico, Canada, Germany, Italy, and New Zealand.

George Manuel (1921–1989)
Shuswap tribal leader

George Manuel was born in the Shuswap village of Neskainlith, on the South Thompson River, about thirty miles east of Kamloops, in south-central British Columbia. The Shuswap people are one of four groups that comprise the Interior Salish people, the others being the Lillooet, Thompson, and Okanagan peoples. Salmon fishing is one of the major activities of the Interior Salish, and the Shuswap would spend summers and falls in mobile bands intercepting the spawning runs in numerous canyons that slice through the interior of the province. During the winter, they would form relatively permanent villages, living on stored food and engaging in major social and ceremonial activities. There they would live in pithouses, subterranean structures that protected them from the cold.

During his early years, Manuel was raised more by his grandparents than by his parents. He spent some time in a Kamloops residential school. He fell ill with tuberculosis, however, and was transferred to a hospital for children in Coqualeetza in the Lower Fraser

Valley. There he was able to improve his reading and writing skills. His formal education was never resumed.

Manuel became chief of his people in the late 1940s. He began to organize the Interior Salish people and launched an organization in 1958 called the Aboriginal Native Rights Committee of the Interior Tribes of British Columbia, which in 1960 reconstituted itself as the North American Indian Brotherhood. Manuel was elected president of the brotherhood that year, and shortly thereafter he presented a lengthy brief to a parliamentary committee in Ottawa detailing his people's claims to land.

In 1966, Manuel was hired by the federal government to be a community development worker with the Cowichan Band on southern Vancouver island. His stint there was highly successful, although a subsequent assignment with the Nuu-chah-nulth on the western coast of the island was not, as the Nuu-chah-nulth were resistant to outside advisors. During this time, Manuel remained active in pressing the claims of aboriginal people in British Columbia with federal authorities. He was active in the formation of the Union of British Columbia Indian Chiefs in 1969, a province-wide organization devoted to the advancement of Aboriginal claims, and was elected president of the National Indian Brotherhood in 1970, a national organization of Indian groups. Manuel was also a major figure in the World Council of Indigenous Peoples, an international organization of indigenous peoples.

Manuelito (1818–1894)
Navajo tribal leader

Manuelito was a Navajo leader during the Navajo War of 1863 to 1866. Born in southeastern Utah, he became a powerful warrior in raids against the Mexicans, Hopi, and Zuni, and rose to prominence within his band. Unlike the peaceful Navajo leader, Ganado Mucho, Manuelito carried out a number of attacks and maintained resistance against U.S. Army troops.

Manuelito succeeded Zarcillas Largas as the head of his band in the 1850s when the latter resigned over failure to control his warriors' reprisals against U.S. soldiers. Although a major peace treaty had been ratified in 1849 by both sides, there were continuing clashes and depredations between the United States and the Navajo. The area around Fort Defiance in present-day Arizona was a major point of contention; both sides wanted the pasture land for their livestock to graze on, and both shot or stole the other's horses.

Troops destroyed Manuelito's home, crops, and livestock in 1859. The next year, he and the headman of another band led a contingent of warriors in an attack on the fort and nearly succeeded in capturing it. Colonel E. R. S. Canby (who later campaigned against the Modoc, a California Indian tribe, and was killed by the Modoc leader Captain Jack) pursued Manuelito and his followers into the Chuska Mountains near the present-day Arizona and New Mexico border. In early 1861, both sides met at Fort Fauntleroy, later renamed Fort Wingate in present-day western New Mexico, and at the council agreed to work toward a peaceful resolution. But in September 1861, hostilities again erupted after a horse race at the fort in which the Navajo claimed that Manuelito had been cheated. Artillery was fired into the crowd of Navajo to quell the ensuing riot, and ten Indians were killed. Warfare resumed between both sides.

Troops and Ute scouts and allies under Colonel Kit Carson began a scorched-earth policy culminating in the Navajo War. Carson's orders were clear: kill all hostiles and relocate all prisoners to Bosque Redondo near Fort Sumner in present-day eastern New Mexico. Of all the resistant Navajo bands, Manuelito's held out the longest. Faced with army pursuit and starvation, Manuelito led his remaining warriors back to Fort Fauntleroy and surrendered. He joined other Navajo held in captivity at Bosque Redondo.

Along with headmen of other bands, Manuelito traveled to Washington, D.C., to petition for the return of the Navajo homelands. A peace treaty was ratified by both sides in 1868. Manuelito returned to serve as principal Navajo chief and chief of tribal police. He again traveled to Washington and met President Ulysses Grant before his death at the age of seventy-six.

Leonard Stephen Marchand (1933–)
Okanagan Canadian senator

Len Marchand has been a pioneer in the field of government. He was born in Vernon, British Columbia, on 16 November 1933. He attended residential school and then became the first Native person to graduate from his hometown's high school. Marchand went on to earn a bachelor of science degree in agriculture in 1959 from the University of British Columbia and a master's degree in forestry from the University of Idaho in 1964. During this time, Marchand became active in the North American Indian Brotherhood, a national organization devoted to advancing the rights of aboriginal people in Canada, working to obtain the federal vote, self-government, and improved education for aboriginal people.

In 1965, Marchand was the first Indian appointed as special assistant to a cabinet minister, and in 1968 he was the first Indian to be elected to the Canadian House of Commons. Marchand was reelected in 1972 and again in 1974. In 1977, Marchand was named minister of state for small business and became minister of state for the environment in 1977. Upon the defeat of the Liberal government in 1979, Marchand returned to British Columbia to work for four years as an administrator for the Nicola Valley Indian Bands, an organization representing Indian bands located in the Nicola Valley in south-central British Columbia. At this time, Marchand also became a director of the Western Indian Agricultural Corporation, a company designed to encourage the use of advanced agricultural techniques and production among Native people. Marchand also acted as a consultant on a variety of projects, among which was the Round Lake Treatment Centre, the first Native drug and alcohol treatment center located near Vernon, his place of birth. Marchand was appointed to the Canadian Senate in June 1984 and has remained active on agricultural and aboriginal committees. Marchand resigned from the Canadian Senate in 1998. He has been named honorary chief of the Okanagans, a people who live in south-central British Columbia.

Marin (d. 1834)
Miwok tribal leader

This Coast Miwok chief is known through fairly obscure historical sources. He played an important role in the early history of the San Francisco Bay area. The territory of the Coast Miwok included most of modern Marin County in northern California.

Marin led his people in several successful battles against the Spanish during the years between 1815 and 1824, but despite these victories he was subsequently captured and imprisoned. Later he escaped on a balsa raft and took refuge on a small island in San Francisco Bay. After he was recaptured by the Spaniards, Marin was nearly executed, but priests from the nearby mission at San Rafael intervened on his behalf. He was later converted to Catholicism and lived close to the mission until he died there in 1834. The island where he took refuge, the adjacent peninsula, and county were named after him.

In 2000, the federal recognition status of the Coast Miwok tribe was restored, granting the tribe access to land and tribal benefits.

Peter Martin (1841–1907)
Mohawk physician

Peter Martin, perhaps the first Mohawk licensed by Canadian authorities to practice medicine, was born in 1841 in the Grand River valley in southwestern Ontario.

Mohawks had moved to the Grand River valley after the American Revolution, when they had sided with the British against the American revolutionaries. Peter Martin's Mohawk name was Oronhyatekha (Burning Cloud). He first attended a small school near his home and then was sent to the Wesleyan Academy at Wilbraham, Massachusetts, where, in his final year, he was first in his class. Martin returned to his hometown for a year to teach in a local school and to raise funds for further schooling. He attended Kenyon College at Gambier, Ohio, for three years and then spent one year at the University of Toronto in Ontario, for preparatory courses in medicine.

At the young age of twenty, Martin had the occasion to greet, on behalf of his people, the Prince of Wales, later to be King Edward VII, on a visit by the prince to Canada. Their encounter led to an invitation from the prince to attend Oxford University to study medicine. After three years of study, Martin returned to the University of Toronto for a final year of study necessary to obtain his degree in medicine and to marry Ellen Hill, a Mohawk woman from the Bay of Quinte on Lake Ontario in eastern Ontario.

Martin and his new wife moved a number of times early in their marriage, as Martin practiced medicine in several small towns in southern Ontario, including Frankfort, Stratford, Napanee, and Deseronto, eventually moving to London, Ontario, in 1873. His practice in London was very successful, and he eventually became involved in a number of fraternal organizations, including the Good Templars, the Orange Order, and the Royal Order of Foresters. His wife, Ellen, died in 1901. Peter Martin lived for another six years.

Phillip Martin (1926–)
Choctaw political leader and chief of the Mississippi Choctaw Nation

In Philip Martin's forty-year tenure as Mississippi Choctaw leader, the tribe's economy has brought thousands of jobs to the reservation and to the east-central Mississippi area in which the reservation is located. Born in Tucker, Mississippi, located in the heart of the Mississippi Choctaw Reservation, Martin was the middle of six children. Unlike many living on the reservation at the time, Martin's father was regularly employed by the Bureau of Indian Affairs (BIA) office in Philadelphia, Mississippi, where he acted as both a janitor and as a Choctaw interpreter.

In 1937, when Martin was only eleven, his father died suddenly in a car accident. Immediately following this traumatic loss, a BIA superintendent began coaxing Martin to attend a BIA-run boarding school. The school catered largely to Cherokee students and was located in North Carolina, far away from his family and tribe. Because Martin did not want to leave his home, he told the superintendent that he was not interested in attending school. However, the BIA employee persevered and eventually drove Martin to the boarding school, promising to buy the boy new clothes upon arrival. When the representative did not fulfill his promise, Martin knew that he could not trust any U.S. government official.

Martin stayed at the far-off school for six years, visiting home only once during that time. Before graduation in 1945, the young man left the school to join the Air Force. Like his two brothers, Raymond and Edmund, he planned to become a part of the World War II effort. While Martin arrived in France in January 1946, just after the end of the war, his brother Raymond fought at Normandy Beach in 1944 and was later killed in battle just before the war's close.

After spending several years in Europe, as well as in places such as San Francisco and Okinawa, Martin was discharged from the Air Force in 1955. He moved home to his reservation, bringing with him his new wife, Bonnie Kate Bell. The couple raised two daughters, Debbie and Patricia, who later provided them with six grandchildren and one great-grandchild.

Martin did not expect to stay on his reservation for a long time, for he felt that there were no economic opportunities on or around his people's land. His wife liked living on the reservation, however, and landed a job as a secretary at the BIA agency in Philadelphia, Mississippi. Because of his wife's success, Martin decided to stay with the Choctaws. Bonnie continues to work at the agency today, and has become the education program administrator.

Working odd jobs for six years, Martin was not as lucky as his wife in finding a regularly paying job. He worked as an electrician and a plumber for a time, and eventually was hired by the Meridian-based Naval Air Academy in 1961 to work in the maintenance department.

During the time that Martin was not regularly employed, he attended tribal council meetings with his wife, who was acting as an interpreter for the BIA superintendent, for the meetings were conducted largely in the Choctaw language. Because of his dissatisfaction with the way politics were handled on the reservation, Martin ran for tribal council in 1957 and won. In 1959 he was reelected and was appointed chairman of the tribal council by the other tribal representatives.

While the appointment was an important one, Martin knew that the economic prospects of his people were bleak at best. The tribe had neither money nor governmental space—they were meeting at four-month intervals in a demonstration kitchen at the BIA agency

office. In addition, the councilpersons were paid nothing for their governmental work, and were thus concentrating on their other jobs to pay the bills and feed their families. With such prospects, Martin realized early that the tribe could no longer depend on the federal U.S. government. If they wanted more than the bare essentials, Martin said, the Mississippi Choctaw would have to find their own economic support system.

In order for the tribe to become economically self-sufficient, Martin knew that he and his fellow council members had to develop a reservation-based economy. Because of their large workforce, spacious land-base, and eastern-U.S. location, the Mississippi Choctaw could offer economic opportunity to private companies that were heading overseas to Third World countries to find similar opportunities. In addition, federal Indian reservations are exempt from state and local taxes, making economic development all the more alluring to private enterprise.

Since Chief Martin's appointment, the tribe's economy has boomed. He has restructured the government and drawn many businesses into the area that now employ many tribal members. He has also managed to save enough tribal funds not only to pay government employees, but also to fund many tribal resource efforts, including the Choctaw Housing Authority, the Chata Development Company, which constructs most buildings on the reservation, and the Choctaw Health Center. Choctaw factories today assemble components for clients as various as Ford, Xerox, AT;T, Harley-Davidson, General Motors, and Boeing.

Massasoit (1580–1661)
Wampanoag tribal leader

Massasoit was a principal leader of the Wampanoag people in the early 1600s who encouraged friendship with English settlers. As leader of the Wampanoag, Massasoit exercised control over a number of Indian groups that occupied lands from Narragansett Bay to Cape Cod in present-day Massachusetts. Massasoit negotiated friendly relations with the recently arrived Puritan settlers. As early as 1621, with the aid of Squanto, a Wampanoag who spoke English, Massasoit opened communications with the pilgrims at their Plymouth settlement. He established trading relationships with the settlers, exchanging food for firearms, tools, and other sought-after European products.

Massasoit helped the Puritan settlers in a number of ways including donations of land and advice on farming and hunting. Massasoit also offered the settlers important council on how to protect themselves from other tribes. In 1623, he warned them of an impending attack by hostile Indians. Massasoit's alliance with the settlers created divisions among the region's Indian nations and problems for the Wampanoag who were loyal to Massasoit. Consequently, Massasoit's warriors were forced to wage frequent attacks against hostile Indian groups less inclined to welcome the English settlers.

The Wampanoag chief became close friends with the progressive-minded theologian, Roger Williams, and according to many accounts influenced Williams's relative understanding and favorable view of New England Indians' lives and right to territory. In 1636, when Williams was threatened with imprisonment for heresy by the Massachusetts colonial government, he fled to Massasoit's home. Despite the efforts of Williams to maintain peace, Massasoit eventually came to resent the growing encroachment of English settlers. It would be his son Philip, however, who would turn this resentment into war in 1675 and 1676.

Though the exact details of the event have become clouded in secular mythology, it is believed that Massasoit participated in what has come to be called the first Thanksgiving. Around 1621, Massasoit traveled to Plymouth with a number of followers where they took part in a meal with the colonists. Judging by the inability of the colonists to provide for themselves at this time, it is most likely that Massasoit and his people provided the food for the "historic" meal.

Susan Masten (1952–)
Yurok tribal leader

Susan Masten is president of the National Congress of American Indians and Yurok tribal chairperson. She received a bachelor of science degree in 1975 from Oregon State University. In 1976, she became the secretary of the California Press Women, and is a board member of the American Indian Film Festival, emceeing the annual event in San Francisco, California.

From 1980 to 1981, Masten was the California Indian representative in the Salmon Advisory Subpanel to the Pacific Fishery Management Council, and in 1987 and 1988 her appointment was renewed. In 1988, she chaired the Del Norte County (California) Democratic Central Committee and served as a delegate to the Democratic National Convention in 1980 and 1988. Among her numerous appointments and offices are president of the Humboldt Bay Business and Professional Women in 1988, membership on the national Commission on the Status of Women, and president of the Klamath Chamber of Commerce in Klamath, California. Since 1992, Masten has been one of the organizers of a Yurok women's support group. From 1986 to 1992 she served as co-chair of "To Have A Heart Salmon and Steelhead Fishing Tournament," proceeds from which benefit the American Heart Association.

Prior to her presidency, she served as the first vice-president of the National Congress of American Indians (1994–1996), the Sacramento area vice-president (1992–1994), and the marketing and promotion specialist for United Indian Development Association.

Masten was appointed by the secretary of the interior to serve as a Yurok Transition Team member, to implement the Hoopa-Yurok Settlement Act (1988–1991). She served on the Intertribal Monitoring Association on Indian Trust Funds (1991–1999), became chair of the Klamath River Traditional Indian Fishers Committee, and has won numerous awards, including Outstanding Young Woman of America, Humboldt County's Outstanding Citizen award, and Del Norte County's Young Woman of the Year.

Matonabbee (1736–1782)
Chipewyan guide and translator

Matonabbee lived in the Hudson Bay region of Northern Canada in the mid-1700s and was brought up in both European and Indian cultures. His ability to move easily between the two worlds made him a valuable liaison for European traders and explorers in the region.

Matonabbee was born near Fort Prince of Wales, located at the mouth of the Churchill River. When Matonabbee's father died, Richard Norton, a Hudson Bay Company manager, adopted and educated him. When Norton returned to England, Matonabbee returned to live among the Chipewyan people, Athapascan speakers who lived mainly by hunting large game animals and gathering wild plants. For the next few years Matonabbee learned Chipewyan ways and traveled about much of present-day northern Manitoba, northern Saskatchewan, and the eastern Northwest Territories.

When he was sixteen years old, Matonabbee returned to Fort Prince of Wales and took employment with the British as a hunter. Matonabbee's valuable background was soon noticed by the British, who asked Matonabbee to perform other duties as well, such as negotiating with Indian tribes and translating. While accompanying the British on southern trading trips, Matonabbee learned the Algonkian language of the Cree Indians. Matonabbee's prestige rose among his own people as a result of his growing stature among the British, and he soon became a respected leader.

In the 1760s, Englishman Samuel Hearne made two failed expeditions for the Hudson Bay Company to find the Northwest Passage and copper deposits. Many explorers sought a way across northern Canada because such a route promised efficient shipping and trade routes from Europe to China and Japan. Many sea captains and explorers tried to find a Northwest Passage, but there never was an easy route to find, since the Arctic Ocean freezes over much of the year and blocks any easy shipping lanes. During his second expedition, Hearne and his company were in danger of perishing from hunger, when Matonabbee, whom Hearne had met at Fort Prince of Wales, walked into his camp and helped him return safely to the English settlements. The two became friends, and in 1771 they planned a third expedition to search for the Northwest Passage. Matonabbee provided Hearne with guides for the trip. Chipewyan bands followed the expedition and provided protection from enemies and provided food by hunting. In 1772 the expedition reached the Arctic Ocean, but Hearne was dismayed to find no passage. The return trip was brutal for the expedition and several Chipewyan died from starvation.

Lisa Mayo (contemporary)
Kuna/Rappahannock performance artist

Lisa Mayo, of Kuna and Rappahannock ancestry, was born and raised in Brooklyn, New York. Mayo and her sisters, Muriel and Gloria Miguel, founded the Spiderwoman Theater group in 1975.

Her career activities also include founding Off the Beaten Path, a Native American performing arts group, performing as a member of Masterwork Laboratory Theater of New York and training as a mezzo-soprano at the New York School of Music.

Mayo also received a CAPS Fellowship and a grant from the New York State Council of the Arts for the development of *The Pause That Refreshes*, a work she both created and directed

Mayo and fellow Spiderwoman Theater founder Gloria Miguel also received a Rockefeller grant and funding from the Jerome Foundation to create *Nis Bundor: Daughters from the Stars.*

In 1997, she received an honorary doctorate of fine art from Miami University in Ohio. Mayo has performed worldwide with Spiderwoman Theatre and she currently serves on the board of directors of the Native American Actor's Showcase at the American Indian Community House.

Published plays by the Spiderwoman Theater include *Sun, Moon, and Feather*, in *Contemporary Plays by Women of Color: An Anthology* (1996), and also published in *Stories of Our Way: An Anthology of American Indian Plays* (1999), and *Power Pipes*, in *Seventh Generation: An Anthology of Native American Plays* (1999).

David P. McAllester (1916–)
Naragansett ethnomusicologist

David McAllester has been a prolific scholar and a key figure in the history of research on Native American music. He was born in Everett, Massachusetts, in 1916 and graduated from Harvard University in 1938. During the 1940s he studied under George Herzog at Columbia University. Herzog was best known for comparative studies that attempted to define and classify various forms of ethnic music in "scientific" terms, and McAllester's dissertation, "Peyote Music" (1949) approaches its subject from this viewpoint. While studying at Columbia, however, McAllester was also influenced by Margaret Mead and became increasingly intrigued with the problem of describing Native music as a reflection of the culture from which it springs. He was also influenced in this direction by Robert Linton and Abraham Kardiner, two exponents of the culture and personality school of anthropology.

McAllester is probably best known for his research on Navajo and Apache music, but he has also conducted research on music of the Zuni, Passamaquoddy, Penobscot, Comanche, and Hopi. His mature writing mainly attempts to describe Indian music from a culture-bearer's perspective, and his work has influenced many other ethnomusicologists in this direction. Some of his other important publications include *Enemy Way Music* (1954), *Myth and Prayers of the Great Star Chant* (1956), *Indian Music of the Southwest* (1961), *Reader in Ethnomusicology* (1971), *Navajo Blessing-way Singer* (with Charlotte Frisbie, 1978), and *Hogans: Navajo Houses and House Songs* (with Susan McAllester, 1980). A book dedicated to his work *Essays in Ethnomusicology: Essays in Honor of David P. McAllester* was published in 1986. McAllester is currently emeritus professor of music and anthropology at Wesleyan University.

Alexander McGillivray (1759–1793)
Creek tribal leader

Alexander McGillivray's father was a Scottish trader who married a woman of Creek and French ancestry and who belonged to the prominent Creek Wind clan. McGillivray was born near the upper town village, Little Talisee, which was a "daughter village" or related village to Coosa, a traditional leading white, or peace, village among the upper Creek towns, located in present-day Alabama. He was sent to school in Charleston, in present-day South Carolina, and received additional private tutoring from a relative. The American Revolutionary War disrupted his studies, and he returned to the Creek Nation, where the upper towns generally favored British alliance. In late 1778, the upper town chief, Emisteseguo, also chief of Little Talisee, transferred political leadership to McGillivray, who was then only about eighteen years old. Emisteseguo, who belonged to a lowly ranked clan, feared assassination from pro-American villages and told McGillivray that his membership in the sacred Wind clan would protect him. This plan seemed to work as McGillivray was not troubled with assassination. The choice of McGillivray as upper town principal chief was unusual, since Creek leaders were generally older men who had acquired considerable training in ritual and religious knowledge. McGillivray, however, spoke English and knew colonial institutions, which were great advantages in treaty and diplomatic negotiations.

After the war, McGillivray entered into a business partnership with the British trading firm, Panton, Leslie and Company. He worked a plantation at Hickory Ground, a sacred white village in the upper town region. As chief, McGillivray tried to protect Creek lands from U.S. settlers, and tried to reorganize the Creek national council by replacing the elderly town chiefs with the village head warriors. In 1790, he negotiated a treaty with George Washington in New York City.

William McIntosh (1775–1825)
Creek tribal leader

William McIntosh, a mixed blood, became a successful entrepreneur, owning an inn, two plantations, and slaves. In addition, he rose to political influence as head warrior of Coweta. Coweta was the central red or war village among the Creek lower towns, located in present-day western Georgia. McIntosh came to prominence during the Red Stick War (1813–1814), when mainly upper town Creek villages—those in present-day Alabama—rebelled against U.S. influence over the leaders of the Creek Council. During the war, McIntosh zealously led the lower towns and cooperated with U.S. forces to secure the Red Stick defeat in 1814. In 1814 at Fort Jackson, present-day Jackson, Mississippi, General Andrew Jackson (future U.S. president) demanded 22 million acres of Creek national territory. The Creek, staggered at the demand, thereafter resolved not to cede land again to the United States, and to punish with death any persons who sold land without national council authorization.

Nevertheless, in 1818 and 1821, McIntosh led Creek delegations that ceded more land to the United States. After the second treaty, McIntosh was warned by the council that further unauthorized treaty cessions would result in his trial for treason. In the Treaty of Indian Springs of 1825, McIntosh and a dozen other chiefs ceded the last Creek holdings in western Georgia. For this act, McIntosh was condemned and executed by the Creek council. While McIntosh gained private advantages from the treaty negotiations, he argued that the Creek could not remain in their homeland in present-day Georgia and Alabama because of U.S. settler expansion. Thus, he argued, it was better to sell the land and migrate west of the Mississippi River. Most of the Creek, however, disagreed and preferred to remain in their sacred homeland by resisting land cessions.

Hilliard McNab (1916–1990)
Cree elder and tribal leader

Hilliard McNab, the youngest son of eight children of Samuel and Harriet (Pratt) McNab, was born and raised on the Gordon Indian Reserve, a small community located about seventy-five miles northeast of Regina, Saskatchewan. A prominent member of the Saskatchewan Indian community, McNab was a founding member and then a senator of the organization now known as the Federation of Saskatchewan Indian Nations, a province-wide organization devoted to the advancement of aboriginal rights in Canada.

As a child, McNab attended Gordon's Residential School before working as a farmer on the reserve. His interest in helping his people began early. During the Great Depression, he actively helped people in need on the reserve in innumerable ways. McNab served as chief of the Gordon Reserve for nine consecutive terms. He also served as a member of the Saskatchewan Human Rights Commission from its inception in 1972 until 1982 and as a member of the education council to the provincial Ministry of Education. In 1984, he received the Order of Canada, a medal conferred by the governor general of Canada to select Canadians in recognition of exemplary merit and achievement. McNab's people conferred on him the ceremonial name of Opamihow, meaning "One Flying Above." McNab's legacy to his people was a profound one. Known for his ability to mold consensus while not surrendering principle, McNab was a powerful and persuasive political leader and elder of the Saskatchewan Cree.

D'Arcy McNickle (1904–1977)
Cree and Flathead writer and government administrator

Author of several books, both fiction and non-fiction, D'Arcy McNickle also held several posts at the

Bureau of Indian Affairs and was one of the founders of the National Congress of American Indians. Born in St. Ignatius, Montana, McNickle was a mixed-blood of Cree ancestry on his mother's side and of Scotch ancestry on his father's. As a child, however, he and all his siblings, along with his mother, were adopted into the Flathead tribe.

McNickle was one of the most highly educated Indian people of his generation, having attended the University of Montana, Oxford University in England, and the University of Grenoble in France. He worked as a writer in New York City from 1925 to 1935 and then became involved in the Federal Writers Project in 1935 and 1936. This was one of four programs begun in the United States in 1935 by the Works Progress Administration as a relief to artists impoverished by the Depression. From 1936 until 1952, McNickle worked for the Bureau of Indian Affairs, first as director of tribal relations and later as executive director of American Indian development.

His novel *The Surrounded* (1936) was a masterpiece of Native American literature in its time. It describes the disintegration of a tribe as a result of the loss of Indian lands to the U.S. government and settlers and the destruction of tribal religion and values. Other important books by McNickle include *They Came Here First: The Epic of the American Indian* (1949), *Runner in the Sun: A Story of Indian Maize* (1954), *Indians and Other Americans: Two Ways of Life Meet* (with Harold Fey, 1959), *Indian Tribes of the United States: Ethnic and Cultural Survival* (1962), and *Indian Man: A Life of Oliver La Farge* (1971).

McNickle won several literary awards, including the distinguished Guggenheim Fellowship (1963–1964), and the D'Arcy McNickle Center at the Newberry Library in Chicago has become one of the leading institutions for Native American historiography.

Russell Means (1940–)
Oglala-Yankton Sioux activist

Russell Means led the American Indian Movement (AIM) in a 1973 armed seizure of Wounded Knee, South Dakota, site of the previous massacre of Sioux by Seventh U.S. Cavalry troops on 29 December 1890. AIM held off hundreds of federal agents on the Pine Ridge Reservation for seventy-one days before their surrender.

Means was born at Porcupine, South Dakota, on the Pine Ridge Reservation, but was raised around the Oakland, California, area. His father was part Oglala, part Irish, and his mother was Yankton Sioux. He was a rodeo rider, Indian dancer, ballroom dance instructor, and public accountant before returning to South Dakota

Russell Means.

to work in the Rosebud Agency's tribal office. He moved to Cleveland, Ohio, and became director of the Cleveland Indian Center, which later changed its name to Cleveland AIM.

In February 1972, an Oglala man, Raymond Yellow Thunder, died after being beaten, publicly humiliated, and locked in a car trunk in Gordon, Nebraska. AIM led a caravan of two hundred cars filled with supporters across the state line to demand the arrest of the two brothers who perpetrated the crime. Means and others were successful in dismissing the local Gordon police chief and initiating dialogue regarding racial grievances between Indians and local Nebraskans.

In January 1973, a subsequent altercation between AIM and police at the Custer, South Dakota, courthouse exploded into a riot after Wesley Bad Bull Heart was killed by a South Dakota businessman. Thirty people were arrested, and this incident prompted the Federal Bureau of Investigation (FBI) to assign sixty-five U.S. marshals to Pine Ridge to enforce security, protect mining interests, and conduct surveillance. Fed up with government intervention, Means, along with several hundred people, traveled to the small community of Wounded Knee and demanded recognition as a sovereign nation on 28 February 1973. They were quickly surrounded by the FBI and other government agents. What began as a two-day protest became a prolonged siege. When it was over, two Indians were dead and a federal marshal was permanently paralyzed. Means and Dennis Banks were prominent within the international media as spokesmen for the Sioux. Both were arraigned on ten felony counts in a trial that lasted eight months. The federal judge, Frederick Nichol, finally threw the case out of court on the grounds of prosecutorial misconduct.

In February 1974, in a hotly contested and rigged election, Dick Wilson barely defeated Means as tribal chairman. AIM was pitted against non-AIM factions. Tensions increased dramatically when Wilson's supporters ordered all those who voted for Means off the reservation and terrorized AIM members. Means was shot in the kidney by a Bureau of Indian Affairs officer and, along with six other pending charges against him, arraigned for assault.

Between 1973 and 1980, Means was tried in four separate cases, spent one year in state prison in Sioux Falls, South Dakota, was stabbed there, and survived four other shootings. In April 1981, Means and a caravan of twenty cars journeyed to Victoria Creek Canyon in the Black Hills and established Camp Yellow Thunder, with the intent to build eighty permanent structures. Claims against the U.S. Forest Service were filed for 800 acres of surrounding forest, and the issue became embroiled in legal proceedings.

Means has traveled extensively and adopted many causes, including the investigation of the oppression of the Miskito Indians in Nicaragua. In 1987, he became the first American Indian to run for president of the United States, seeking the nomination of the Libertarian party.

He has appeared in many films and documentaries, including *The Last of the Mohicans* (1992), *Windrunner* (1992), *Natural Born Killers* (1993), *Paha Sapa* (1993), and *Thomas and the Magic Railroad* (2000). He coauthored his autobiography, *Where White Men Fear to Tread*, with Marvin J. Wolf, in 1995. Means lives in Santa Fe, New Mexico.

Beatrice Medicine (1924–)
Dakota (Sioux) anthropologist

Beatrice Medicine is a recognized expert in the field of anthropology. Much of her work has focused on the study of tribal traditions among the Dakota Indians.

Medicine was born and raised on the Standing Rock Sioux Reservation in northern South Dakota. She came from a family that stressed the maintenance of her cultural identity and encouraged her to pursue her interest in researching Native American culture. Medicine has taught at a number of universities, including the University of Washington, Stanford University, Dartmouth College, Michigan State University, and the University of South Dakota, before retiring as professor of anthropology at California State University, Northridge.

In addition to work at the university level, Medicine has been involved in research with aboriginal people in New Zealand, Australia, and Canada. She has also done extensive research work in the field of mental health with a focus on issues facing Native Americans, including alcohol and drug abuse. Medicine has been an advocate for Indian leadership and has worked to establish a network of Indian social service centers in urban areas.

Medicine served as coordinator of research for the Canadian Royal Commission of Aboriginal Affairs. She is a member of the American Anthropological Association, the National Congress of American Indians, North American Indian Women's Association, and a number of other professional research associations.

She has contributed to a number of publications, including *Native American Women: A Perspective* (1978). She has written a number of articles including, "The Role of Elders in Native Education," *Indian Education in Canada II*; "Understanding the Native Community," *Multicultural Education;* and "Contemporary Cultural Revitalization: Bilingual and Bicultural Education," *Wicazo Sa Review*, Spring 1986. She has received numerous awards, including the Distinguished Service Award from the American Anthropological Association.

Menawa (1765–1865)
Creek tribal leader

Menawa, also called Hothlepoya, was war chief of the Upper Towns Creek, who were located in present-day Alabama. Born along the Talapoosa River in Alabama, he established his reputation as a daring warrior through numerous raids for horses on settlements in Tennessee. Menawa joined William Weatherford against troops under Andrew Jackson in the Creek War of 1813–1814.

Menawa earned the title Crazy War Hunter for his exploits in battle, including his bravery at the battle of Horseshoe Bend in 1814. During the battle, Menawa was shot seven times and left for dead. He crawled off to a hidden camp in the swamps where he later recovered and surrendered, losing all his land and possessions to the United States.

Menawa was one of the Creek leaders opposed to removal of the Creek to land west of the Mississippi, and he led a raiding party that killed William McIntosh in 1825. McIntosh had been sentenced to death by the Creek Council after having signed the Treaty of Indian Springs in 1825, ceding twenty-five million acres of Creek land. The selling of land without Creek Council consent was unlawful under Creek law and was punishable by death.

The death of McIntosh did not stop settlers' incursion onto Creek land, however, and Menawa himself was forced to accommodate U.S. territorial demands. He traveled to Washington, D.C., in 1826. In exchange for promises of peace, the Creek were to be allowed to retain their lands in present-day Alabama, but gave up their lands within the charter limits of Georgia. As a show of friendship, Menawa led warriors in support of federal troops early in the Seminole War of 1835–1842. Despite his assistance, and before the Seminole War was over, Menawa was forced to relocate to the Indian Territory (Oklahoma) in 1836.

Ovide William Mercredi (1945–)
Cree tribal leader

Ovide Mercredi, former national chief of the Assembly of First Nations (1991–1997), began his role as a political advocate in the late 1960s when he observed first-hand the social upheaval resulting from a massive hydroelectric development project in his home community of Grand Rapids, Manitoba. He obtained a law degree from the University of Manitoba in 1977 and practiced criminal law in The Pas, Manitoba, for several years. In the 1980s, Mercredi turned his mind to constitutional reform, and ever since he has been actively involved in efforts by first nations to amend the constitution of Canada to recognize aboriginal rights to land and government. Mercredi was one of several aboriginal leaders to speak out against a constitutional reform package known as the Meech Lake Accord. Negotiated with a view to placating nationalistic concerns of the province of Quebec, the accord did not address first nations' concerns. Mercredi provided key advice to Elijah Harper, an elected member of the Manitoba legislature who succeeded in blocking the accord's passage. In 1992, as national chief, Mercredi entered into successful negotiations with the federal government on constitutional reform.

Before his election as national chief, Mercredi represented and served his people in a number of different ways. He represented the Assembly of First Nations in Geneva in 1989 in seeking improvements to the International Convention on the Rights of the Child and acted as the assembly spokesperson for the United Nations Indigenous Peoples Working Group. He served as a

Commissioner for the Manitoba Human Rights Commission. He is the recipient of numerous awards, including Honorary Doctorates of Law from St. Mary's University (1992), Bishop's University (1994), and the University of Lethbridge (1999). He was presented the Thakore Foundation Award (1993) and is a three-time nominee by the Mahatma Gandhi Foundation for World Peace, for the Gandhi Prize.

He is the subject of two Canadian film documentaries, *Our Home and Native Land* and *Half a World Apart and a Lifetime Away*. Mercredi lives with his wife, Shelley, and daughter, Danielle, in Orleans, Ontario.

Cheryl Metoyer (1947–)
Cherokee educator and administrator

Born in Los Angeles, California, in 1947, Cheryl Metoyer received a bachelor's degree in English (1968) and a master's degree in library science (1969) from Immaculate Heart College in Los Angeles, California, and then went on to complete her doctorate in library science at Indiana University (1976). On completing her education, she went on to do important work planning and developing Indian library services both in

Cheryl A. Metoyer.

urban settings and on reservations. She was a Native American delegate to the 1979 White House Conference on Library and Information Science and has also worked for the Bureau of Indian Affairs as a consultant on library, media, and information services.

Metoyer is the director of information resources at the Mashantucket Pequot Museum and Research Center in Mashantucket, Connecticut. Her research areas include the information-seeking behavior of culturally diverse groups and the design and evaluation of information services provided by institutions to American Indians. From 1973 to 1979, she held the Rupert Costo Chair in American Indian history at the University of California, Riverside. Metoyer has published in major research journals. Her book, *Gatekeepers in Ethnolinguistic Communities*, was honored by the Association of College and Research Libraries. Her current research project, based at the UCLA American Indian Studies Center, is the development of a thesaurus of American Indian terminology.

Gloria Miguel (contemporary)
Kuna/Rappahannock performance artist

Miguel, of Kuna and Rappahannock ancestry, was born and raised in Brooklyn, New York. She and her sisters Muriel Miguel and Lisa Mayo founded the Spiderwoman Theater group in 1975. Her activities have also included studying drama at Oberlin College and appearing in numerous film, television and stage productions.

Her stage credits include performing in *Grandma*, a one-woman show written by Kiowa/Delaware playwright and producer Hanay Geiogamah, touring Canada as Peliajia Patchnose in the original Native Earth production of Cree playwright and novelist Tomson Highway's *The Rez Sisters*, and performing in *Bootlegger's Blues*, *Jessica*, and *Son on Ayash* in Canada.

Miguel has also been a visiting professor and drama consultant at Brandon University (Canada), a drama consultant for the Minnesota American Indian Youth AIDS Task Force, performer at the fourth World Women's Conference, in China, and, along with Lisa Mayo, a Rockefeller grant recipient. In 1997, she received an honorary doctorate of fine arts from Miami University (Ohio).

Muriel Miguel (contemporary)
Kuna/Rappahannock performance artist

Muriel Miguel is a founding member and artistic director of Spiderwoman Theatre, the longest-running Native American women's theatre group in North America. Miguel, of Kuna and Rappahannock ancestry, was born and raised in Brooklyn, New York.

During the 1960s, as an original member of Joseph Chaikan's Open Theatre, Miguel performed in shows as Vietrock, Handcuffs and Sidewinder. She also taught drama at Bard College for four years.

She toured Canada, playing the role of Philomena Moosetail in the award-winning work by Cree playwright and novelist Tomson Highway, *The Rez Sisters*. She teaches extensively, having worked at the Centre for Indigenous Theatre in Toronto and the Working Classroom in New Mexico, where she has been instrumental in the training of Native youth in theatre and dance. Muriel developed her latest one-woman show, *Trail of the Otter*, at the Banff Centre for the Arts during the Aboriginal arts program's Winter Village 1996.

In 1997, Muriel was selected for the Bread and Roses International Native Women of Hope poster. Also in 1997, Miguel and her sisters were awarded honorary doctorates in fine arts from Miami University (Ohio), the site of the newly founded Native Women's Playwrights' Archives. Muriel's original dance/theatre work, *Throw Away Kids*, was selected for full production during the 1999 Chinook Winds Aboriginal Dance program and was also performed at the Mashantucket Pequot Museum and Research Centre in Connecticut.

Devon A. Mihesuah (1957–)
Choctaw professor and editor

Devon Mihesuah is the editor-in-chief of the *American Indian Quarterly*, an academically focused journal of American Indian studies. She received her doctorate degree in 1989 from Texas Christian University and holds a doctorate in education.

Mihesuah is the author or editor of various articles and books, most notably *Repatriation: Social and Political Dialogues, American Indian: Stereotypes and Realities* (1996), *Cultivating the Rosebuds: The Education of Women at the Cherokee Female Seminary, 1851–1909* (1993), *Natives and Academics: Researching and Writing about American Indians* (1998), *Repatriation Reader: Who Owns American Indian Remains?* (2000), and *The Roads of My Relations: Stories* (2000).

She is a professor of history and applied indigenous studies at Northern Arizona University and has received numerous awards and honors, including the 1989 Phi Alpha Theta and Westerners International Award for Best Dissertation in Western History; the 1992 Northern Arizona University Outstanding Faculty Woman of the Year Award; the 1994 Native American

Students United Award for Outstanding Faculty; the 1995 Critics' Choice Award of the American Educational Studies Association for *Cultivating the Rosebuds* and the 1996 Ford Foundation Postdoctoral Fellowship.

Billy Mills (1938–)
Oglala Sioux athlete

On 14 October 1964, against overwhelming odds, Billy Mills won the 10,000 meter run at the Olympic games in Tokyo, Japan. He set a world record that day, and it was the first time an American had ever won a distance race in the Olympic games. His victory is still hailed as one of the greatest athletic upsets of all time.

The story of Mills's life is an inspiring comeback tale. (The real-life drama of the event was not lost on Hollywood—a movie called *Running Brave* has been made about his boyhood and Olympic victory.) He was born on the Pine Ridge Reservation in South Dakota. He attended government schools through high school and was offered a full athletic scholarship to the University of Kansas when he graduated. Though Mills was a member of his collegiate track team that won the national track championships two years in a row, and was the Big Eight cross-country champion, he did not gain much prominence. In his final year at the university, Mills tried out for the Olympic team, but did not qualify. He quit college track.

Mills graduated and accepted an officer commission in the marine corps. He married his college sweetheart along the way and had no plans to resume running. During this time, a fellow marine officer who knew of Mills's past track victories prodded him into running again. After his victory in the inter-service 10,000-meter run, the marine corps sent Mills to the Olympic trials. He was truly a dark horse in the Olympic competition. Just minutes before the race, the U.S. track coach came into the locker room Mills was sharing with Gerry Lindgren, the star U.S. runner, to discuss the ten runners he believed stood between Lindgren and the gold medal. Mills's name was never mentioned. Moments after Mills won the race, the Japanese Olympic officials had to ask him his name—he was a complete unknown, even to some of the runners.

Mills returned to the United States a hero. He raced again and set another record for the six-mile. He was eliminated from the 1968 Olympic team due to a formality in his application form. Other athletes threatened to protest if officials did not overlook the formality, but Mills was not allowed on the team. Mills put the disappointment behind him. He is now a successful businessman in Sacramento, California, active in Native American social, political, and athletic causes. An empowering public speaker, Mills travels across the United States lecturing to students, corporations, and community organizations

Olympic gold medalist Billy Mills.

Lillie Rosa Minoka-Hill (1876–1952)
Mohawk physician

Lillie Rosa Minoka was born on the St. Regis Reservation in New York State. Her Mohawk mother died shortly after giving birth to her. She then resided with her Mohawk relatives until she was old enough to attend school, at which time her father, Joshua Allen, a Quaker physician, brought her to Philadelphia. Allen taught her about her tribal heritage and sent her to the Grahame Institute, a boarding school from which she graduated in 1895.

She planned on entering nursing, but her family deemed medical school more appropriate for an educated woman. Before beginning her medical education, her father sent her to study French in Quebec where she lived in a convent and converted to Catholicism. Upon returning to Philadelphia, she entered the Woman's Medical College of Pennsylvania, graduating in 1899.

Following her internship at the Woman's Hospital in Philadelphia, she attended indigent, immigrant women at a dispensary connected with the Woman's Medical College and established a private practice with a fellow graduate student. Later, while working at a government boarding school for Native Americans, she met Charles Hill, an Oneida graduate of Carlisle Institute. They were married in 1905 and moved to the Oneida Reservation in Wisconsin, where Minoka-Hill talked with Oneida medicine men and women, adding their herbal remedies to her medical school knowledge. Neighbors who distrusted the sole physician in Oneida began to seek her services. Local physicians, including her family doctor, encouraged her to treat them, although she did not hold a Wisconsin medical license.

Minoka-Hill had six children in nine years. Charles Hill died in 1916, leaving his wife only a mortgaged farm and a few farm animals. She established a "kitchen-clinic" stocked with herbs and medicines supplied by physicians from nearby Green Bay, Wisconsin, and by her friends. Patients appeared at her door anytime from seven in the morning to ten at night; in exchange for her services, they gave her food or worked on her farm. A dedicated healer, Minoka-Hill traveled long distances to deliver babies or treat patients, many of them suffering from malnutrition and tuberculosis. Encouraged by Green Bay physicians who loaned her the $100 application fee, Minoka-Hill took the two-day examination and received her Wisconsin medical license in 1934, thirty-five years after she had graduated from medical school.

Minoka-Hill practiced medicine on the Oneida Reservation for the remainder of her life. She adjusted her fees for services and medicines to a patient's ability to pay. In 1931 she received fifteen dollars to deliver a baby; two chickens were payment for another, and nine dollars for a third.

Named outstanding American Indian of the Year in 1947 by the Indian Council Fire in Chicago, Minoka-Hill received many other honors as well. The Oneida tribe adopted her with the name You-da-gent (She Who Serves). The State Medical Society of Wisconsin granted her an honorary lifetime membership and also financed a trip to the American Medical Association national convention in 1949 and to her fiftieth college reunion. Minoka-Hill died in 1952 of a heart attack in Fond du Lac, Wisconsin.

N. Scott Momaday (1934–)
Kiowa Pulitzer Prize-winning novelist and poet

N. Scott Momaday, one of the premier writers in the United States, is regents professor of the humanities at the University of Arizona. Born in Lawton, Oklahoma,

he graduated from the University of New Mexico (B.A. 1958) and Stanford University (M.A. 1960, Ph.D. 1963). He has held tenured appointments at the University of California-Santa Barbara, the University of California-Berkeley, and Stanford University, He has been a visiting professor at Columbia and Princeton, and was the first professor to teach American literature at the University of Moscow, in Russia.

Momaday was awarded the 1969 Pulitzer Prize for his first novel, *House Made of Dawn* (1968). He is also the author of several books including *The Way to Rainy Mountain* (1969); *Angle of Geese and Other Poems* (1974); *The Gourd Dancer* (1976); *The Names* (1976), an autobiographical memoir; *The Ancient Child* (1989); *In the Presence of the Sun* (1992); *The Man Made of Words* (1997); *In the Bear's House* (1999); and *Circle of Wonder: A Native American Christmas Story* (1999).

His drawings, prints, and paintings have been exhibited in the United States and other countries. In 1992 and 1993, a one-man, twenty-year retrospective was mounted at the Wheelwright Museum in Santa Fe, New Mexico.

In 1994, his play, *The Indolent Boys*, was given its world premiere at the Syracuse Stage, and, in 1997, *Children of the Sun*, a children's play, opened at the Kennedy Center.

Momaday is a fellow of the American Academy of Arts and Sciences and president of the American Indian Hall of Fame. He sits on the boards of the Grand Canyon Trust, the Wheelwright Museum, First Nations Development Institute, and the School of American Research.

Momaday is founder and chairman of the Buffalo Trust, a nonprofit foundation for the preservation and restoration of Native American culture and heritage. He has lectured and given readings in many countries around the world, and holds twelve honorary degrees from American colleges and universities, including Yale University, the University of Wisconsin, and the University of Massachusetts.

Carlos Montezuma (1867–1923)
Yavapai physician and journalist

Carlos Montezuma was a successful physician who advocated the abolition of the Bureau of Indian Affairs. In 1915, he wrote the pamphlet "Let My People Go," and in 1916, he founded the Indian magazine *Wassaja: Freedom's Signal for the Indian*, which remained in press from 1916 to 1922.

Montezuma was born among the Yavapai Indians in Arizona, but as a boy was captured by the Pima Indians who sold him to Carlos Gentile, a white photographer, who named him Carlos Montezuma. After Gentile's death, Montezuma was shuttled between a number of non-Indian benefactors. In 1884 he graduated from the University of Illinois with a bachelor of science degree, and in 1889 graduated from the Chicago Medical College. After an attempt at private medical practice, Montezuma was appointed physician-surgeon by the Indian Service at the Fort Stevenson Indian School in North Dakota. Montezuma practiced medicine at a number of reservations until his frustration with conditions led him to take a position at Carlisle Indian School in Pennsylvania. In 1896, Montezuma opened a private practice in Chicago, specializing in stomach and intestinal diseases. The practice was successful, and Montezuma turned his attention to activist work on Indian rights.

Montezuma's experiences working in the reservation health system made him an advocate for the abolition of the Bureau of Indian Affairs and the reservation system. His criticisms were acknowledged by government officials. Presidents Theodore Roosevelt and Woodrow Wilson asked him to become the Commissioner of Indian Affairs. Montezuma refused and continued his calls for the abolition of the BIA. He wrote essays against the institutions and people he believed exploited and suppressed Indian people.

For the rest of his life, Montezuma urged citizenship and equal rights for Native Americans, though not at the cost of sublimating cultural identity. Montezuma continually stressed the importance of maintaining "Indianness" in Native American society. He died in 1923 of tuberculosis at the Fort Dowell Reservation in Arizona, where he was born.

Norval Morrisseau (1932–)
Ojibwa artist

Norval Morrisseau is a renowned, self-taught Ojibwa artist, perhaps the first Indian to break through the barriers of the non-indigenous professional art world in Canada. His unique style of painting, which combines European easel painting with the pictography of indigenous rock paintings, has been described as "x-ray art" or "legend art." With his bold and brilliant use of color and lines, he shows simultaneously the interiors and exteriors of figures—animals and humans—often using figures within figures. Morrisseau's style has given rise to a genre called "Woodlands art," which younger artists have embraced with enthusiasm and which has received international acclaim.

Morrisseau, whose Ojibwa name means "Copper Thunderbird," was born at the Sand Point Reserve near Lake Nipigon, Ontario, north of Lake Superior. His Ojibwa heritage was instilled in him at an early age by his maternal grandfather, Moses Nanakonagos. The initial inspiration for his art came from the legends of his people and from Ojibwa images on birch bark scrolls and rock paintings. Early on in his career, he came into conflict with his elders because some of his work broke a taboo against depicting legendary figures outside of Ojibwa spiritual rituals. Morrisseau was first noticed by the broader Canadian art community in 1962, when he displayed his work at the Pollack Gallery in Toronto, Ontario. His work demonstrates a deep commitment to religious and spiritual values, and Morrisseau continues to study Ojibwa shamanistic practices, which he believes assist him in his creative work. In 1978, he was awarded the Order of Canada and elected to the Royal Academy of Arts. He gave a one-man show at the 1989 Bicentennial of the French Revolution in France. Morrisseau lives in British Columbia.

Ganado Mucho (1809–1893)
Navajo-Hopi tribal leader

Culturally and linguistically similar to the Apache, their Athapaskan neighbors, the Navajo often raided other tribes throughout the Southwest for horses, livestock, and possessions. During the eighteenth and nineteenth centuries, the Navajo acquired large amounts of land for their increasing herds of sheep and cattle. Ganado Mucho was the son of a Navajo mother and Hopi father. He grew up to be a successful rancher, band headman, and peacemaker in northeastern Arizona.

Ganado Mucho was a young man when the Navajo carried out particularly vehement strikes on Mexican troops in the 1830s. From 1846 to 1849, United States troops sent five expeditions in attempts to control the marauding Navajo. It seems that Ganado Mucho did not participate in any of this warfare. However, because of his large herds, in the 1850s he was accused of cattle theft, but he successfully denied the charges. In 1858, he signed an agreement with other peaceful Navajo ranchers to report any thefts of livestock and return any livestock found. Mucho became the head of his band, but since the Navajo comprised many small bands, he possessed no authority outside his own local band group, which among the Navajo was usually composed of close relatives and in-laws.

Despite the ratification of a peace treaty between some Navajo bands and the United States, other Navajo bands continued their raids and clashes with U.S. Army troops. These forays led to the outbreak of the Navajo War of 1863. Backed by Ute Indian scouts and allies,

Colonel Kit Carson led U.S. forces through the heart of Navajo country on a search-and-destroy operation. Ganado Mucho and his followers hid from Carson, all the while encouraging peace between both sides. During the war, Mucho lost two daughters and a son to raids by the Ute and Mexicans. His band surrendered, and he led them along with others on the brutal "long walk" from Fort Defiance in Arizona to Fort Sumner at Bosque Redondo in New Mexico.

The Navajo were held as prisoners until a peace treaty was signed by Ganado Mucho and others in 1868. Until his death at age eighty-four, he lived on the Navajo Reservation, rebuilt his ranch, and continued to work for peace between the United States and the Navajo.

James Murie (1862–1921)
Pawnee ethnographer

James Murie was born in Grand Island, present-day Nebraska, in 1862. His mother, Anna Murie, was a full-blood Pawnee, a member of the Skiri Band. His father, James Murie, was a Scot who later commanded a battalion of Pawnee scouts.

Murie spent his young life in Nebraska where he lived as a traditional Pawnee. Before leaving Nebraska for Indian Territory (present-day Oklahoma) in 1874, he attended a day school at the agency in Genoa, Nebraska, for four months. After moving to the new Pawnee Reservation in Indian Territory, he attended day school for a year and spent one year at the boarding school at the agency. Murie soon learned English and served as an interpreter for the Indian agent at the reservation.

Murie entered the Hampton Normal and Agricultural Institute in Virginia in October 1879, at age sixteen. School records credit him with one year of prior schooling and the ability to speak some English. Four years later, Murie left, having received a diploma in the Normal (Teaching) Department. He returned home, the first student from an Eastern boarding school to do so.

Murie's anthropological career began in the 1890s when Alice Fletcher came to Pawnee to begin a study of Pawnee ceremonialism. Murie assisted Fletcher as a collaborator in her work and accompanied her to ceremonies and to the homes of informants to whom he introduced her. He also transcribed and translated songs and other textual material, and assisted her in various other ways. Murie continued to work with Fletcher after her return to Washington, D.C. They corresponded extensively over a five-year period from 1898 to 1902, as he answered questions and provided her with additional material. Additionally, he made several trips to Washington on tribal business with older Pawnee, and visited with Fletcher and provided her other information. In 1902 Murie ended his work with Fletcher and began full-time work for George A. Dorsey, curator of anthropology at the Field Museum of Natural History in Chicago. He worked with Dorsey until 1909 during which time he completed extensive, minutely detailed descriptions of three major Pawnee ceremonies.

Beginning in 1912, Murie began working with Clark Wissler, curator of anthropology at the American Museum of Natural History (Washington, D.C.), editing a series of descriptive papers on Pawnee warrior societies, religious and social groups for young men who acted as a police force and assisted the chiefs. Murie sought out Pawnee elders who were knowledgeable about each society and interviewed them, and subsequently wrote out what they had told him. The histories were published in 1914 as *Pawnee Indian Societies*. Murie continued to work with Wissler, and in 1921 the manuscript of "Ceremonies of the Pawnee" was completed. It was never published and remains in the archives of the Bureau of American Ethnology (now the National Anthropological Archives) in Washington, D.C.

Throughout his adult life in Oklahoma Murie was active in both tribal and community affairs. He accompanied Pawnee delegations to Washington on tribal business, and in 1915, he was elected president of the Indian Farmers' Institute in Pawnee.

Murie's unpublished work is extensive and includes the collection of ethnographic notes at the Field Museum and the Smithsonian's "Ceremonies" manuscript. These unpublished notes on Pawnee religion and ethnography constitute a rich source for further work.

R. Carlos Nakai (1946–)
Navajo-Ute musician

R. Carlos Nakai is a composer and musician. His instrument of choice is the Native flute, and in many regards, he has kept its tradition alive by defining both its presence and its haunting sound throughout his recordings. Nakai was born in Flagstaff, Arizona, and raised on the Navajo Reservation.

Nakai began playing trumpet in the 1960s, but switched to Native flute in 1972 after failing to be accepted at the Juilliard School of Music, the prominent New York City music school. He blames this rejection on evidently "being the wrong color."

In 1982, he met the founder of Canyon Records, Ray Boley, and made his first record, *Changes*. Since then, he has released a number of recordings on the Canyon label, including *Winter Dreams* and *Carry the Gift* with guitarist William Eaton; *Spirit Horses*, a concerto for Native American flute and chamber orchestra; and *Natives* and *Migrations* with pianist Peter Kater.

Nakai is a certified secondary teacher in graphic communications, and he worked as a science teacher at several schools on the Navajo Reservation. He has been a folk and visual artist in the artist-in-education program for the Arizona Commission on the Arts. In 1985, he performed at the Magic Flute Festival in St. Paul, Minnesota, with flutists from around the world. He has worked with the San Diego, California, Flute Guild of the National Flute Association in the study of theory and application of flute music in Native culture. In 1994, he was a Grammy Award finalist for "Best Traditional Folk Album." Also in 1994, Nakai released *Island of Bows*, recorded with a Japanese group using traditional Japanese instruments. In 1995, he released an album entitled *Feather, Stone & Light* and in fall 1996, he released a jazz album, *Kokopelli's Cafe*. Nakai has produced twenty-seven commercial albums and has worldwide sales of over 2 million.

Raymond Nakai (1918–)
Navajo tribal leader

Raymond Nakai is a former Navajo tribal chairman (1963–1970), and, under his leadership, the reservation made great strides toward a more technologically progressive community.

Born in Lukachukai, Arizona, and educated at Fort Wingate and Shiprock Indian schools, Nakai served in the navy in the South Pacific during World War II. Returning home, he became a radio announcer and disc jockey. In 1963, he became tribal council chairman and began a series of administrative and cultural programs designed to enhance the quality of life and produce income for the reservation. Traditional crafts such as weaving and silversmithing were fostered by the Arts and Crafts Guild. His administration encouraged the installation of irrigation systems, a hotel-motel-restaurant complex, and Navajo Community College.

However, the Nakai council also promoted the controversial production of uranium, coal, gas, oil, and timber resources on the reservation and allowed many outside plants and factories to be constructed. The industrialization resulted in increased pollution and land erosion, and such labor problems as lack of fair jobs and royalty payments. Navajo women were hired for the factories but had to relocate to dormitories far from their homes for up to two weeks at a time, leaving their husbands to care for the children.

The successes and failures of the Nakai Administration point out valuable lessons to tribal councils interested in developing their ancestral lands. Careful economic policy implementation should produce tribal self-determination without impacting social structures and natural resources.

Nampeyo (circa 1860–1942)
Hopi-Tewa potter

Nampeyo is a world-recognized potter who, besides developing her own style, was instrumental in bringing about a revival of traditional Native American ceramics.

Nampeyo was born at Hano Pueblo in Arizona. In the 1890s, Nampeyo took an interest in pottery and concluded that the ceramic work being done by the artisans of her time was inferior to that of ancient potters. Her husband, who was working with an archaeologist at the time, helped her to find shards of ancient pottery. Using these pieces as a model, Nampeyo developed her own style based on these traditional designs. Nampeyo and her husband often traveled to Chicago to display her work. Nampeyo's beautiful designs evoked images of an era long past, and were quickly embraced by the art world. The Smithsonian Institution purchased her pottery and soon it was sought after by collectors from around the world. For years, her work was sold at the Grand Canyon Lodge of the Fred Harvey Company.

Nampeyo has been credited with bringing about a renaissance of pottery-making among her people. Furthermore, it was her ideas and inspiration that elevated pottery among her people to an art form, as it had been centuries ago.

Nana (Nanay) (1810–1895)
Chiricahua Apache tribal leader

Nanay was the oldest of all the 1880s Apache resistance leaders, including Naiche, Loco, Taza, Chihuahua, Victorio, and Geronimo. Younger than Mangas Coloradas and older than Cochise, he became war leader of the Eastern Chiricahua, or Warm Springs Apache, in present-day Arizona after the death of Victorio in 1880.

The Apache intensely disliked the San Carlos Reservation in present-day Arizona, where they had been forcibly relocated in May 1877. After the murder of a number of soldiers and an Apache medicine man at Cibecue (Arizona), the Warm Springs Apache under Nanay fled the reservation. Nanay was probably in his seventies, half-blind, crippled with rheumatism, and aching from a number of wounds he had suffered during his lifetime. Nevertheless, he led forty Apache over a thousand miles of southern Arizona, New Mexico, and Mexico in raids on settlements and pack trains. They fought and won at least ten separate skirmishes while being pursued by over a thousand soldiers and civilians; they stole two hundred horses and mules along with supplies, and finally retreated to the Sierra Madre mountains with only the loss of several men.

General George Crook set about hiring two hundred Apache scouts from rival White Mountain and Pinal bands to hunt down the Chiricahua. Nanay, with Naiche and Geronimo, surrendered to Crook after the scouts traced them to their Sierra Madre stronghold. He took his followers back to the San Carlos Reservation, while Naiche and Geronimo stayed in Mexico to round up some missing Apache men. Nanay's band was moved by the Indian Service to Turkey Creek in present-day Arizona, a location they found much more to their liking.

However, the Indian Service tried to turn the Apache into farmers, and this plan was met with considerable Apache resistance and resentment. In May 1885, once again Nanay and other Apache leaders fled the reservation. They raided both sides of the U.S.-Mexican border for the next ten months. Crook again tracked them down, and Nanay and Chihuahua agreed to surrender their weapons and return to the reservation. They and their followers were immediately shipped off to Florida on a train. From there, Nanay and many Apache were transported to Mount Vernon Barracks in Alabama, then to Fort Sill in Indian Territory (Oklahoma). Nanay died shortly thereafter.

Natchez (Naiche) (1857–1921)
Chiricahua Apache tribal leader

Naiche was the younger son of the great Chiricahua Apache leader Cochise. When Cochise died and was secretly buried in the Dragoon Mountains of Arizona in 1874, Naiche assumed leadership of the Chiricahua. Never claiming to be equal to his father, Naiche guided the Chiricahua through their transition and surrender to General Oliver O. Howard in 1876.

The Chiricahua were moved north to the San Carlos Reservation in Arizona. In summer 1881, a White Mountain Apache brought news of the first Ghost Dance to the Chiricahua Apache by telling them Cochise and spirits of the great chiefs would reappear soon thereafter. At Cibecue (Arizona) in August, a number of soldiers and the Apache medicine man were murdered. When word of this spread hundreds of U.S. troops poured into Arizona to quell what was perceived to be a Chiricahua uprising. In September 1881 Naiche and his followers fled the hot, dusty San Carlos Reservation because of the Cibecue incident.

In retaliation for the soldiers' murder, two Apache scouts were sent to Fort Alcatraz in San Francisco Bay and three others were later hanged at Camp Grant, near Bonita, Arizona, the site of the 1871 massacre of nearly one hundred Apache men, women, and children. This incident marked the beginning of four more years of bloody warfare. Naiche and the Chiricahua conducted many raids along both sides of the U.S.-Mexican border.

Naiche and his group surrendered after General Crook and his Indian scouts traced them to their Sierra Madre stronghold. They returned to the San Carlos Reservation, and in May 1884 were removed to Turkey Creek in present-day Arizona. This region was more to the Apache's liking and provided cooler temperatures and more wooded terrain. It was proposed that they be given cattle and sheep to raise, but the Indian Bureau decided that the Apache should become farmers instead. Unhappy with the situation and with additional restrictions imposed upon them, Naiche, Geronimo, Nanay, and their followers again fled the reservation for Mexico in May 1885. They again raided both sides of the border for the next ten months.

Crook again met up with Naiche, Geronimo, and Nanay, and after two days of negotiation, they agreed to surrender and move to the East for a period of not longer than two years. A whisky peddler sneaked into camp that night and sold liquor to the Apache. By morning, Naiche and Geronimo and their followers were again off to the mountains. As a result of this incident, General Nelson A. Miles replaced Crook. Telegraph wires, which could easily be cut down by the Chiricahua, were replaced by the heliograph, which used the sun to send Morse code messages. Five thousand troops, nearly five hundred Apache scouts, and hundreds of Mexican troops chased the small band to no avail, so Miles reduced his forces to a contingent of scouts and sent several of them to contact Naiche and Geronimo. They agreed to surrender for the final time.

By 8 September 1886, Naiche, Geronimo, and their followers were on a train bound for Florida. From there they were transferred to Mount Vernon Barracks in Alabama. The collective group of Apache were still assimilating this move when they were transferred again to Fort Sill, Indian Territory (Oklahoma). Naiche welcomed this move because the terrain was more similar to Arizona. His family built a house, and he became a government scout. However, an attempt was made to seize even this land from them. They appealed and were finally allotted the Mescalero Reservation east of the Rio Grande in central New Mexico. Naiche and his family moved there in April 1913, and he spent the remainder of his days at peace.

Lloyd Kiva New (1916–)
Cherokee artist and art educator

Lloyd Kiva New has established himself as an important artist and designer in leather, fabrics, and fashion. He was born in Fairland, Oklahoma, and educated at Oklahoma State University. Later, he studied at the Art Institute of Chicago, where in 1938, he became the first Native American to obtain a degree in arts education. After moving back to Arizona in 1950, New turned some farmland into "Fifth Avenue," a center of shops that specialized in local and Indian arts and crafts. Using his name, New developed the Kiva Craft Center, which championed handcrafted leathers and Indian and hand-painted fabrics.

In 1959, New received a grant from the Rockefeller Foundation to develop a program in art education for Indian students at the University of Arizona. In 1961, he played a prominent role in the founding of the Institute of American Indian Arts (IAIA) in Santa Fe, New Mexico. New served as art director and, in 1967 he became president.

Lloyd Kiva New has also served on a number of committees, including the Indian Arts and Crafts Board and the National Council of the Museum of the American Indian. In 1990, he was named president emeritus of the IAIA and was honored as a Living Treasure of Santa Fe, New Mexico.

In 2000, he was awarded an honorary doctorate from his alma mater, the School of the Art Institute of Chicago. He continues to be an active contributor to Native American art education and he lives in Santa Fe with his wife, Aysen.

Duane Niatum (1938–)
Klallam poet

Duane Niatum was born in Seattle, Washington, and is a member of the Klallam tribe. As a young man, he changed his name from McGinnes to Niatum—a family name given to him by an older relative. He received his bachelor's degree in English at the University of Washington, his master's degree in Creative Writing from

Duane Niatum.

Johns Hopkins University, and his doctorate in American Cultural Studies from the University of Michigan.

He has published more than 300 poems and his work has appeared in over sixty anthologies and 1,000 American, British, and European magazines. His first book, *After the Death of an Elder Klallam*, was published in 1970 under the name Duane McGinnes. Later works include *Digging out the Roots* (1977) and *Ascending Red Cedar Moon* (1974). A 1981 collection from the University of Washington Press, *Songs for the Harvester of Dreams*, received the National Book Award from the Before Columbus Foundation in 1982. From 1973 to 1974, Niatum was the editor of the Native American authors series at Harper and Row. In 1975, he was the editor of *Carriers of the Dream Wheel*, one of the most widely read books on contemporary Native American poetry. In 1988, he edited a second anthology entitled *Harper's Anthology of Twentieth Century Native American Poetry*. His latest book, *Crooked Beak of Love*, was published in 2000.

Niatum has taught courses in poetry, fiction, and American Indian literature at several schools, including Western Washington University, Pacific Lutheran University, and the University of Washington. He currently lives in Bellingham, Washington.

Twylah Nitsch (1912–)
Seneca historian

Twylah Nitsch is the founder of the Seneca Indian Historical Society. She is credited with the preservation and advancement of the Seneca Nation history and culture.

Nitsch was born on 5 December 1912 in Irving, New York. She received her education at Empire State College and the State University of New York at Buffalo. Nitsch has been a teacher, lecturer, and historian, the focus of her work being the Seneca Nation and its history. She has presented a number of programs and lectures on the knowledge and culture of the Seneca Nation and how this information continues to be relevant to present-day society. Besides lecturing in the United States, Nitsch has presented her program in Scotland, Ireland, England, Italy, Canada, and Mexico.

Nitsch is also the founder, director, and president of the Seneca Indian Historical Society, an organization devoted to the preservation and dissemination of Seneca history and culture. Nitsch's published works include *Entering Into the Silence—the Seneca Way* (1976), *Wisdom of the Senecas* (1979), *Language of the Stones* (1980), *Language of the Trees* (1982), and *Nature Changes and Dances* (1984), all published by the Seneca Indian Historical Society. In 1991 Nitsch published *Creature Totems* and in 1997 she published *Creature Teachers: A Guide to the Spirit Animals of the Native American Tradition.*

Grayson Noley (1943–)
Choctaw educator

Grayson Noley has made important contributions in the field of educational research, school administrator preparation, and Native American education.

Noley was raised in Wilburton, Oklahoma. He received his bachelor's degree in 1969 from Southeastern Oklahoma State University, and his master of education degree and doctorate from Pennsylvania State University in 1975 and 1979, respectively. He served as assistant professor, director of the American Indian Leadership Program, and director of the American Indian Education Policy Center at Pennsylvania State University for nine years. Noley was director of the Cherokee Nation's Education Department for four years. In 1993 he was interim associate dean for personnel

Grayson Noley.

and student services at the Arizona State University College of Educational Leadership. He is currently department chair and associate professor of educational leadership and policy studies in the College of Education at the University of Oklahoma.

He has worked to promote the needs of his community through service on a number of local and national boards and committees including the Graduate Record Examination Board's Minority Graduate Minority Education Committee. He is a member of the American Educational Research Association, the Comparative and International Education Society, and the National Indian Education Association.

Noley is the author of many journal articles and book chapters on the status of American Indian education. His research has focused on teenage alcohol abuse, life in Bureau of Indian Affairs' off-reservation boarding schools, the need for more American Indian school administrators, teachers, and professors, and early-nineteenth century American Indian education policy development. Named as a fellow by the Kellogg Foundation's National Fellowship Program in 1984, Noley also was honored as a distinguished scholar by a standing committee of the American Educational Research Association in 1989.

John Norquay (1841–1889)
Métis politician

John Norquay was a Métis politician who served as the premier of Manitoba from 1878 to 1887. He was born in 1841 to Métis parents, persons of mixed Indian-European heritage. Norquay's mother died when he was only two years old, and he was left in the care of his grandmother. He excelled at school, attending a parish school during his childhood. With the help of a scholarship, he attended St. John's Academy. He then turned to teaching, first at the parish school that he attended as a child and later at a school known as Park's Creek, where he met, courted, and in 1862 married Elizabeth Setter. After the wedding, Norquay took up farming in High Bluff, and for four years he worked the land. His interests quickly turned to political matters, however, and he was elected by acclamation to Manitoba's first legislature in 1870. He quickly moved up through the political ranks, becoming the minister of public works and then minister of agriculture. When the premier of Manitoba resigned in 1878, the lieutenant-governor of the province called upon Norquay to form a new government and serve as premier. During his nine-year tenure, he faced difficult and divisive political issues dealing with French representation in the government, among other matters. His government eventually collapsed on the issue of extending the railway through the province. In an effort to force the hand of the federal government, Norquay proposed the construction of a railway to the United States. His plan backfired, however, and he was forced to resign shortly thereafter. Norquay died soon after leaving office, in 1889.

nila northSun (1951–)
Shoshoni and Chippewa poet

Nila northSun's poetry is considered part of the Native American Renaissance, the title given to American Indian literature that emerged during the Civil Rights period, or the late 1960s and early 1970s. In addition to her own books, including *diet pepsi & nacho cheese* (1977) and *a snake in her mouth* (1997), northSun's writing is anthologized in such works as *Reinventing the Enemy's Language: Contemporary Native Women's Writings of North America* (1997), edited by Joy Harjo; *The Remembered Earth: An Anthology of Contemporary Native American Literature* (1980), edited by Geary Hobson; and the German-published *Turpentine on the Rocks* (1978), edited by Charles Bukowski and Carl Weisner.

Similar to most Native American poetry, northSun's work depends on both traditional poetic forms and specific tribal sources for its inventiveness. In northSun's

nila northSun.

case, her poetry is informed by Shoshoni culture and tradition, as well as by such literary influences as Raymond Carver and Charles Bukowski.

Although she was born in Schurze, Nevada, northSun spent most of her early years in and around San Francisco, a city hosting one of the largest urban Indian populations in the United States. When northSun was a teen, she witnessed the American Indian Movement's 1969 occupation of Alcatraz Island, located off the coast of San Francisco, and the rise of American Indian activism throughout not only the Bay Area, but also the entire United States.

While California was bustling with activity in the late 1960s and early 1970s, northSun did not stay in-state for college. The to-be poet studied at the University of Montana, from which she received her bachelor's degree. It was in Missoula that northSun started delving into poetry. Once she graduated, she and then-husband Kirk Robertson founded Duck Down Press in Fallon, Nevada, part of the Fallon Paiute-Shoshoni Reservation. Her first publication, *diet pepsi & nacho cheese*, was issued in 1977 as a limited edition by their press. In addition, Duck Down Press also published two other chapbooks, or small books containing poetry by northSun: *coffee, dust devils & old radio*, co-authored by Robertson, and *small bones, little eyes*, co-authored by Jim Sagel.

Her most recent book, *a snake in her mouth*, published by West End Press, includes poetry printed in her previous books as well as more recent inventions. NorthSun now writes and works in Fallon. She is the director of a teen crisis center.

Richard Oakes (1942–1972)
Mohawk activist

Richard Oakes was born on the St. Regis Reservation in New York, near the Canadian border. He attended school until he was sixteen years old and quit during the eleventh grade because he felt the U.S. school system "never offered me anything." Oakes then began a brief career in the iron work industry, working both on and off reservation. The early years of his life were spent in New York, Massachusetts, and Rhode Island before he moved to California. During that time, he attended Adirondack Community College in Glen Falls, New York, and Syracuse University. While traveling cross-country to San Francisco, California, Oakes visited several Indian reservations and became aware of their political and economic situations.

Oakes worked at several jobs in San Francisco until he had an opportunity to enroll in San Francisco State College in February 1969. During this time, he married Annie Marufo, a Kashia Pomo Indian from northern California, and adopted her five children.

Oakes was a leader in the November 1969 occupation of Alcatraz Island, an event that became the catalyst for the emerging Indian activism that continued into the 1970s. The occupation of Alcatraz Island was an attempt by urban Indians to attract national attention to the failure of U.S. government policy toward American Indians. The press and many of the Indian occupiers recognized Oakes as the "Indian leader" at Alcatraz. He left Alcatraz Island in January 1970 after his step-daughter, Yvonne Oakes, died from a head injury after falling down a stairwell. After leaving Alcatraz Island, Oakes remained active in Indian social issues and was particularly instrumental in the Pit River Indian movement to regain ancestral lands in northern California.

On 21 September 1972, Oakes was shot and killed by a YMCA camp employee in Sonoma County, California. He had gone to the camp to find a youth who was staying with the Oakes family. The camp employee was charged with involuntary manslaughter, but charges were later dropped on the grounds that Oakes had come "menacingly toward" him.

Richard Oakes still lives in the memory of thousands of Indian people who remember the rise of Indian activism and the effort to regain traditional Indian lands in the Bay Area. Most particularly, Oakes is remembered for his leadership during the Alcatraz Island occupation.

Alanis Obomsawin (1932–)
Abenaki writer/director and producer

Alanis Obomsawin, a successful speaker, teacher, and filmmaker, was born in New Hampshire, and lived on the Odanak reservation northeast of Montreal until the age of nine. In 1970, she appeared in the Canadian film, *Eliza's Horoscope*, before becoming one of the country's leading documentary filmmakers. Her first film, *Christmas at Moose Factory* (1971), reveals Cree lifestyle as seen through the drawings and paintings of its children. Obomsawin's early films celebrate the richness and diversity of Indian culture. *Mother of Many Children* (1977) highlights the language and storytelling of traditional women, and *Amisk* (1977) explores the beauty of Indian dance and music.

Later films reveal Obomsawin's deep commitment to Canada's struggling Native people. *Incident at Restigouche* (1984) documents the brutal Quebec Provincial Police raid on the Restigouche Reserve over fishing rights, and *Richard Cardinal: Cry from a Diary of a Métis Child* (1986) is a heartbreaking story of a young Cree adolescent whose abuse and neglect by the child welfare system leads to his suicide. *Poundmaker's Lodge: A Healing Place* (1987) examines an Indian drug and alcohol center, and *No Address* (1988) focuses on Montreal's homeless aboriginal people. She also released an album in 1988, *Bush Lady*, which featured traditional Abenaki songs and original compositions.

In 1993, she wrote, directed and co-produced *Kanehsatake: 270 Years of Resistance*, a feature-length film documenting the 1990 Mohawk uprising in Kanehsatake and Oka. To date, the film has won eighteen awards and received international recognition.

Obomsawin is the former chair of the board of the directors for the Native Women's Shelter of Montreal, and was once a member of the Canadian Council First Peoples Advisory Board. She is a board member of Studio 1, the Aboriginal Studio, and a former advisor to the New Initiatives in Film, a program for women of color and women of the First Nations.

She has been honored with many awards, including the Order of Canada, the Toronto Women in Film and Television's Outstanding Achievement Award in Direction, the Canadian Native Arts Foundation National Aboriginal Achievement Award, and she was the first non-sociologist/non-anthropologist to earn the Outstanding Contributions Award from the Canadian Sociology and Anthropology Association.

Obomsawin also received a fellowship from the Ontario College of Art, an honorary doctorate of letters from York University, an honorary doctorate of laws degree from Concordia University, an honorary doctorate of law from Queen's University, an honorary doctorate of laws from Trent University, an honorary doctorate of literature from Carleton University, and a Lifetime Achievement Award from the Aboriginal Film Festival and the Taos Talking Picture Film Festival.

Her more recent films are *My Name is Kahentiiosta* (1995), *Spudwrench—Kahnawake Man* (1997), and *Rocks at Whisky Trench* (2000).

Samson Occum (1723–1792)
Mohegan minister

Occum became a Christian convert at the age of eighteen. As a minister and educator he devoted his life to teaching and converting Indians to Christianity. He was the first Indian to preach in England.

Occum was born in New London, Connecticut. He was the first student of Eleazor Wheelock, a Christian missionary who had been teaching Indians since about 1743 in his church-sponsored Indian Charity School. Wheelock's goal was to train his students to become Christian ministers. When Occum finished his studies, he became a school teacher for a short while at which time he married Mary Montauk. In 1759, he was ordained by the Presbyterian Church. Occum's parish was among the Montauk Indians, and among his duties was the recruitment of Indian youths for Wheelock's school.

In 1765, Occum traveled to England as Wheelock's representative. He stayed in England for two years, preaching and fund raising. It was during this trip that Occum obtained the funds to establish a new school for Indian children. While Occum was in England, Wheelock's Indian school was moved to New Hampshire and, in 1769, became Dartmouth College.

When he returned to New England, Occum left Wheelock's organization over differences on the emphasis and focus of their mission. Wheelock was interested mainly in training non-Indian missionaries. Occum wanted to teach and minister to the Indians directly. As a result, Occum became a minister and teacher in an Algonkian-speaking community of Indian people in eastern New York called Brotherton. Brotherton was composed of several Indian tribes that accepted Christianity, and Occum welcomed them all to his church and school. Because of encroachment by New York settlers, Occum spent many of his later years working to relocate his followers further west on Oneida territory in central New York. The Oneida, one nation of the Iroquois Confederacy, welcomed the Brotherton community and allowed them to live on their land. The resettlement to Oneida territory was completed in 1786 with the establishment of a town named New Stockbridge. Occum died six years later.

Oconostota (1710–1785)
Cherokee tribal leader

By the time he was twenty years old, Oconostota had been to England to meet King George II. He and Attakullakulla, also in the delegation, returned to South Carolina and, thirty years later, participated in the 1760 war against King George and his son, George III. Attakullakulla was the Cherokee peace chief and Oconostota their war chief. The Cherokee fought on the side of the British during the French and Indian War (1756–60) and assisted in the capture of Fort Duquesne, in present-day Pittsburgh, Pennsylvania.

Peace reigned between British and Cherokee until increasing numbers of colonists began entering Indian territory in the 1750s. In 1759, Oconostota headed a delegation of thirty-two chiefs to discuss peace at Charleston, South Carolina. The Carolina colonists demanded that the warriors, who had earlier killed several Virginia settlers, be turned over to Carolina authorities. The Cherokee delegation refused, and South Carolina governor William Littleton ordered the Cherokee arrested. Attakullakulla, however, negotiated a release that surrendered one man to Carolina authorities and released the rest of the Cherokee delegation. After this incident, however, there was little chance for negotiated peace.

Two armies were necessary to defeat Oconostota and his guerrilla warfare tactics. Fifteen hundred Scottish Highlanders under the command of Colonel Archibald Montgomery were routed by the Cherokee. However, in 1761, an army of Royal Scots, British Light Infantry, and Carolina Rangers led by Colonel James Grant adopted a scorched earth policy. Along with crops, any Cherokee town Grant encountered was burned to the ground. Many villages in the Cherokee country were destroyed.

Oconostota and the Cherokee continued to fight from their mountain retreats, but were finally forced to accept defeat and signed a peace settlement on 22 December 1761. The treaty terms were quite favorable to the colonials, and they gained large portions of Cherokee land in the bargain.

Oconostota sided with the British during the Revolutionary War, during which the Cherokee again saw many of their crops and towns destroyed by colonial troops. Oconostota relinquished his position as war chief to his son Tuksi; he died at the close of the war.

Daphne Odjig (1910–)
Odawa artist

Daphne Odjig, a well-known and influential artist, was born on the Wikwemikong Indian Reserve on Manitoulin Island in Lake Huron, Ontario, in 1910. Her father and grandfather were both artists in their own right, and they encouraged young Odjig to explore artistic activities as she grew up.

Odjig lived, painted, and worked on the reserve until 1938, when she moved to British Columbia. Her move did not signal a change in career, however, as she was subsequently elected to the British Columbia Federation of Artists. Odjig has also lived in Manitoba, where, in 1970, she opened a museum in Winnipeg devoted to indigenous art and formed an association of Native artists, including the renowned Norval Morrisseau. This had a powerful effect on her work, which combines Western techniques and styles with an emphasis on Native modes of artistic statement. Many younger Native artists owe a debt to Odjig's style, which continues to be influential in the Native artistic community.

Odjig has exhibited in Europe, Israel, and Japan, as well as in numerous cities in Canada. The National Arts Centre in Ottawa, Ontario, is home to a magnificent mural by Odjig, entitled *The Indian in Transition*. Odjig has received a number of honorary degrees from universities in Canada, and in 1987, she was made a member of the Order of Canada, an award conferred by the governor general of Canada to select Canadians in recognition of exemplary merit and achievement. In the 1990s she experimented with colored pencil art, and introduced a series of silkscreen prints entitled "Love Suite" in 1992.

V. Paul Ojibwa (1950–)
Ojibwa Catholic priest

V. Paul Ojibwa professed final vows in 1976 and was ordained into the priesthood in 1978 in Richmond, British Columbia. He earned his bachelor of arts degree in psychology at St. Mary's College of California and a pontifical degree in systematic theology from Catholic University of America in 1977, with further study in theology at Fordham and Boston universities and the Jesuit School of Theology (Berkeley). Additional studies included depth psychology and psychotherapy at the Human Relations Institute at Santa Barbara and the C. G. Jung Institute in both San Francisco and New York.

Ojibwa has been involved in parish ministry, diocesan and national leadership in Young Adult Ministry, Campus Ministry, and has been chaplain for the Ports of Los Angeles and Long Beach. He contributed to *The People: Reflections of Native Peoples on the Catholic Experience in North America*, and served as editor for several publications and published articles in professional, religious, and popular media.

Ojibwa is former liaison to the American Indian community for the Archdiocese of Los Angeles, past director of American Indian Ministry for the Archdiocese, and was director of American Indian programs at Loyola-Marymount University in Los Angeles. He is a member of the Urban Ministry Board, National Tekakwitha Conference; former commissioner for the Los Angeles County and City Native American Indian Commission; and was chair of the Gathering Table, an ecumenical collaboration of seven churches with outreach to the Native American community in Southern California. He has also served as chair of the programming committee and American Indian and religious community representative on the community advisory board for Public Broadcasting Service (PBS) affiliate KCET/Channel 28 in Los Angeles.

Since the middle 1990s, Father Ojibwa has worked in Washington D.C. as lobbyist and advisor for the Interfaith Impact For Justice and Peace.

Old Briton (d. 1752)
Miami tribal leader

In the early 1700s, Old Briton was an important trading ally of the British. The Miami leader helped to establish the trading center at Pickawillany, near present-day Piqua, Ohio. Old Briton also repulsed a number of French military attacks to maintain his control of the Miami territory in present-day Indiana.

Old Briton was a member of the Piankashaw band of Miami. He originally lived in what is now northwestern Indiana. Though the Piankashaw had traditionally traded with the French, sometime in the first half of the 1700s, Old Briton began developing a trading relationship with the British. There were two reasons for the change. First, Old Briton had become convinced of the superiority of British trading goods. Secondly, Old Briton hoped to use British influence and resources to gain stature and power among his own people. In 1748, a treaty between Old Briton and the British formalized the trading partnership. To better accommodate his new trading partners, Old Briton moved his people eastward to the village of Pickawillany.

Pickawillany eventually grew into an important trading center for the region's many Indian groups. French power in the region, however, was threatened by Pickawillany. The French made numerous attempts to destroy the trading center. In 1749, a French force was repelled when Old Briton pretended to lead his followers back to Indiana. In 1752, after an unsuccessful French attack, Old Briton executed three French soldiers in a general attempt to organize an uprising of the area tribes. The French, under command of Charles Langlade, responded with a substantial force that included a number of Ottawa, Ojibwa, and Potawatomi warriors. The force attacked Pickawillany while most of its warriors were away on a summer hunt. Old Briton was killed in the attack, while vainly hoping for military support from Pennsylvanian Colony. After Old Briton's death, his followers returned to the Wabash River in present-day Indiana.

Barney Old Coyote (1923–)
Crow administrator

Barney Old Coyote has worked extensively as a government official for the Bureau of Indian Affairs (BIA), a writer, and university professor.

Born in 1923 on the Crow Reservation in Montana, Old Coyote is the great-grandson of Mountain Sheep, a noted Crow chief. He is a highly decorated WWII veteran. An Ace in the Army Air Corps, Old Coyote flew in the lead ship with General Jimmy Doolittle on a mission over France. By speaking in the Crow language, he and his brother were able to safely break air silence to communicate important information to the next wave of American bombers.

Old Coyote has worked with the National Park Service on the Crow Agency, and for the BIA on the Standing Rock Sioux Reservation in Fort Yates, North Dakota, and the Crow Agency in Montana. From 1964 to 1969, Old Coyote was a special assistant to the secretary of the Department of the Interior. In 1970 he became the assistant area director of the BIA area office in Sacramento, California. His duties included administering to the needs and interests of the California Indian tribes. Old Coyote has taught at Montana State University, Bozeman, Montana, and was the director of the American Indian Studies program.

In 1968, Old Coyote received an honorary doctorate of humane letters from Montana State University and a distinguished service award from the U.S. Department of the Interior. He is a past president and past chairman of the board for the National Federation of Federal Employees Credit Union, which provides low cost banking services to federal workers. Old Coyote has also written on a variety of topics, including the education and general participation of American Indians in U.S. society.

Old Hop (d. 1757–1758)
Cherokee tribal leader

During the 1750s, Old Hop was the headman of the village of Chota when the village asserted leadership of the Cherokee Nation over rival villages from other regions. Old Hop was a member of the Wolf clan, the clan from which Chota selected its headman and second leader of the village. As a young man, Old Hop was a warrior, and he was not a member of a hereditary priestly lineage within Cherokee society. He was knowledgeable about Cherokee ceremony and political culture, but he was a relatively secular leader of his village.

During the 1730s and 1740s, colonial officials in Carolina had tried to establish a central authority among the Cherokee by appointing a "Cherokee Emperor." For some years the emperor was located at the village of Tellico, a leading village of the Valley Towns region within the Cherokee Nation. During this time, however, Chota was generally ignored by colonial officials, although it claimed to be "Mother Town of the Nation." During the early 1750s, the leaders of Tellico faltered when an embargo was imposed on the Cherokee Nation by the English colonies for the killing of an English trader during a battle between the Creek and Cherokee. Around the same time the Creek defeated and destroyed several Cherokee villages. The trade embargo and military defeat gave Chota, led by Old Hop, who was by this time an old man with a limp, a chance to assert leadership. Chota gained the allegiance of most Cherokee villages, and after 1752, Chota was delegated the task of managing trade and diplomatic relations with the English and French colonies. From 1752 until Old Hop's death around 1758, Chota consolidated its leadership by holding annual national councils and ceremonies during the late summer and early fall. Chota maintained leadership of the Cherokee Nation until 1788, when U.S. militia overran and destroyed it.

Old John (1850s)
Takelma/Tututni tribal leader

John, or Old John, was a chief of the Takelma and Tututni Indians living in southwestern Oregon and along the California border. These Indian tribes were commonly known as Rogue River Indians because of their repeated attacks on travelers along the Siskiyou Trail. A river in their traditional homeland became known as the Rogue River, and the 1855–1856 hostilities between the Indians and U.S. settlers were called the Rogue River War.

Old John armed his followers by having them prospect for gold in order to trade for guns and ammunition. In the spring of 1853, Rogue River warriors attacked and killed a party of miners at Cow Creek and later ambushed others at Applegate and Galice creeks.

In 1855, with tensions growing between the Takelma/Tututni Indians and the Yakima Indians and U.S. miners east of the Cascade Mountains, the commander of Fort Lane, Andrew Jackson Smith, opened up the fort for the protection of the Native population. En route to the fort, however, Oregon volunteers attacked and killed twenty-three Rogue River women, children, and old men.

In retaliation for the murder of their families, warriors raided a settlement in the Rogue Valley, killing twenty-seven settlers and setting off a renewed cycle of violence. Throughout the winter of 1855–1856, the warring parties attacked and counterattacked. Hostilities continued until the resolution of the war in 1856. General John Wool was dispatched to the Rogue River Valley after completing a campaign against the Yakima. The Rogue River chiefs, Old John, Limpy, and John, sent word to Captain Smith that they were willing to surrender at Big Meadows. Old John made plans, however, for an ambush. The ambush was foiled by advance warning, and the soldiers held out against overwhelming numbers and heavy casualties. The Indians became trapped between two forces in a pincer operation; the army regulars attacked from the rear while militiamen charged from the hilltop.

During the next weeks, many of the Indians warriors surrendered. Old John and the last of the hold-outs eventually surrendered as well. Most were relocated to the Siletz Reservation in present-day Oregon. Old John and his son, Adam, were imprisoned on Alcatraz Island in San Francisco Bay. Released several years later, it is believed that Old John spent his last days alone in the hills overlooking the Rogue River.

Earl Old Person (1929–)
Blackfeet tribal leader

Earl Old Person is chairman of the Blackfeet Tribal Business Council and former president of the National Congress of American Indians (1969–1971). He was born in Browning, Montana, on 13 April 1929, to Juniper and Molly (Bear Medicine) Old Person, who were from prominent families on the Blackfeet Reservation in northern Montana. Old Person was raised on the Blackfeet Reservation in the community of Starr School, where he attended grade school, and later graduated from Browning (Montana) High School.

By the time Old Person was seven, he had started his long career of representing Native Americans, presenting Blackfeet culture in songs and dances at statewide events. In 1954, at the age of twenty-five, he became the youngest member of the Blackfeet Tribal Business Council. He was elected as its chairman ten years later in 1964, and, except for two years, has held that position ever since. Under his guidance, a major recreational complex, an industrial park, a museum and research center, housing developments, and a community center were constructed.

Old Person also served as president of the Affiliated Tribes of the Northwest from 1967 to 1972 and was chosen in 1971 as a member of the board of the National Indian Banking Committee. In 1977, he was appointed task force chairman of the Bureau of Indian Affairs (BIA) Reorganization, which was assigned the task of recommending to the secretary of the interior changes in BIA policy that were in accordance with Indian leaders. He won the prestigious Indian Council Fire Award in 1977 and has traveled extensively and met with many dignitaries and celebrities. In 1986, President Ronald Reagan appointed Old Person to the advisory council to the congressional delegation. In 1990 he was elected vice-president of the National Congress of American Indians (NCAI), a national political interest group that lobbies on behalf of U.S. tribes. His interests have long focused on educational and business opportunities for Indians.

One of the most highly esteemed and honored individuals in the state of Montana as well as the nation, Old Person, through his gentle demeanor and sincere desire to help others, has done much to promote the ideals of Native Americans in this country and further positive relations between Indian communities and U.S. society. His involvement in national, state, and local advisory committees and organizations has been for the betterment of all people in this country.

Chief Old Person is one of the most highly esteemed and honored tribal leaders in Montana and the nation, having met with and been acknowledged by all U.S. Presidents from Eisenhower to Clinton, the English Royal Family and Canadian Prime Ministers. He became chief of the Blackfeet Nation, a lifetime appointment, in 1978. In 1998, the American Civil Liberties Union of Montana honored Chief Earl Old Person with its most prestigious award, The Jeannette Rankin Civil Liberties Award, for his efforts toward advancing civil liberties in the state of Montana.

Bernard Ominayak (1950–)
Lubicon Cree tribal leader

Bernard Ominayak is chief of the Lubicon Lake Nation. The son of a trapper, he was born in a cabin on the eastern shore of Lubicon Lake, 220 miles northwest of Edmonton, Alberta. He spent his early years living on the shores of the lake during the summers, hunting duck and small game with his father and friends, and riding horses in nearby meadows. He spent winters in a cabin on his father's trapline, where he and his family trapped by dog team and snowshoe. At the age of eight, Ominayak was sent to a residential school five miles from home in Little Buffalo, Alberta. His family joined him in Little Buffalo shortly thereafter, when it became apparent that Ominayak was unhappy being far from home. He went on to study at a nearby vocational school and returned to Lubicon Lake to marry and raise a family.

Ominayak was elected a band councilor and subsequently chief of the Lubicon Lake band at the age of twenty-eight. He soon became embroiled in a famous lawsuit against the federal government, stemming from the government's refusal to provide reserve land to the band. Legally, the Lubicon people were squatters on land they viewed as their ancestral homeland, and oil companies began to drill for oil and disturb their traditional lifestyle. Ominayak battled the federal government and several oil companies in the courts and the media for a decade, making appeals to the United Nations, the World Council of Churches, and the World Council of Indigenous Peoples. Eventually he and his people set up a peaceful blockade on their land, leading to twenty-six arrests, but resulting in a settlement in which the Lubicon Lake band obtained certain mineral rights to their homeland.

Opechancanough (1545–1644)
Powhatan tribal leader

As the brother of and advisor to Chief Powhatan, leader of the Powhatan Confederacy then living in present-day Virginia, and later in his role as de-facto leader of the confederacy, Opechancanough remained a fierce opponent to English settlement in Tidewater, Virginia. In 1622 and again in 1644, Opechancanough led the Powhatan Confederacy in war against the Virginia settlers.

More militant than his brother Wahunsonacock (Powhatan), Opechancanough early on recognized the territorial and political dangers that English settlers posed for the Powhatan people. When his brother died in 1618, Opechancanough turned away from appeasement and conciliation. The popularity of tobacco growing in Virginia had intensified English desire for Powhatan land. Opechancanough organized a surprise attack against the settlers. On 22 March 1622, over three hundred men, women, and children were killed in the English settlements. In what would become a common cycle, instead of subduing the settlers, the Powhatan attack provoked an equally violent response from the English colonists. A peace treaty signed in 1632 was broken by a second Powhatan attack on 18 April 1644. Though nearly five hundred colonists were killed, the English settlers responded with counterattacks. During one of these raids Opechancanough was captured and shot. After his death, the political and military power of the Powhatan Confederacy dissipated.

Opothleyoholo (d. 1862)
Creek tribal leader

In the early 1820s, Opothleyoholo was speaker for Tuckabatchee, the leading red town among the Creek upper towns, located in present-day Alabama; the lower towns were located in present-day western Georgia. The Creek were divided into red and white towns; white towns led during times of peace and red towns led during times of war. Between 1810 and 1862, Tuckabatchee, with U.S. political support, led the upper towns. Talisee (present Tulsa), the leading white upper town, led the opposition and favored British alliance between 1790 and 1820. In the Red Stick War or Creek War (1813–1814), most upper town Creek villages rebelled against the U.S.-supported villages, which consisted mostly of lower towns, with some exceptions like Tuckabatchee. The Red Sticks lost the war in 1814.

Opothleyoholo played an increasingly important role in Creek leadership. By the middle 1830s, he was the leading upper town chief. He led delegations to negotiate the treaty of 1826, which ceded most of western Georgia, and the treaty of 1832, which provided the Creek villages with small reservations within the state of Alabama. By 1836, the Creek reservations were overrun by settlers. A brief insurgency by several lower town villages was put down by U.S. and upper town forces. Creek leaders felt compelled to migrate west to present-day Oklahoma. While retaining upper town leadership, Opothleyoholo emphasized retention of Creek culture and political institutions, but favored adoption of agriculture. The U.S. Civil War split the Creek Nation, largely between upper and lower town factions. In 1862, while Opothleyoholo led his people north toward Union alliance and protection, he was killed by Confederate forces.

A. Paul Ortega (contemporary)
Mescalero Apache composer

A. Paul Ortega has been hailed as one of America's most renowned Native American composers and singers. His 1971 album *Two Worlds* is considered to be an important landmark in the development of contemporary Native American music.

Ortega, a member of the Mescalero Apache tribe, lives in Albuquerque, New Mexico. Ortega's music and compositions take many of their themes from traditional American Indian music. *Two Worlds* was considered a milestone in developing and spreading knowledge of this genre; then he released *Three Worlds*, which was received equally well. He has also taught music and the history and use of traditional Native American instruments at the Institute of American Indian Arts in Santa Fe, New Mexico. Ortega is a champion Apache dancer, and practices and teaches traditional Apache medicine ways. He recently released an album with Joanne Shenandoah entitled *Loving Ways*.

Alfonso Ortiz (1939–1997)
San Juan Pueblo anthropologist

Alfonso Ortiz made momentous contributions in the field of anthropology and in public service as an advocate for Native Americans. He authored *The Tewa World: Space, Time, Being, and Becoming in a Pueblo Society* (1969), a classic work in anthropology.

Ortiz was born and grew up at the San Juan Pueblo in New Mexico. He has degrees from the University of New Mexico (A.B. Sociology, 1961) and the University of Chicago (M.A. Anthropology, 1963, Ph.D. Anthropology, 1967). At the time of his death, he was professor of anthropology at the University of New Mexico. He also taught at Claremont College in California, the University of California at Los Angeles, Rutgers University, Princeton University, and Colorado College.

Much of Ortiz's work and writing as a social anthropologist focused on the Southwest Indian tribes. His first book, *The Tewa World*, is considered an exemplar in anthropological writing. He was the editor of volumes 9 and 10 (Southwest Indians) of the *Handbook of North American Indians* (Smithsonian, 1980).

Besides his accomplishments in the academic field, Ortiz is a vigorous advocate for his community. He founded University of New Mexico's Kiva Club, the first American Indian organization on campus. He also founded and headed the San Juan Indian Youth Council. He was elected to the board of the Association on American Indian Affairs in 1967 and later served as president from 1973–1988.

The Association on American Indian Affairs is credited with contributing to a number of achievements, including the Taos Pueblos community's regaining ownership of their sacred Blue Lake; the Alaska Native Claims Settlement Act of 1971, which secured 44 million acres of land for Alaska Natives; and the American Indian Child Welfare Act of 1978, which helps ensure that orphaned Indian children are placed in Indian foster homes.

Ortiz was also a member of the board of trustees of the National Museum of the American Indian from 1989–1990, and a member of the National Advisory Council on the National Indian Youth Council from 1972 to 1990.

Over his lifetime, he was awarded numerous honors, including the Roy D. Albert Prize from the University of Chicago (1964); a postdoctoral fellowship from the the the John Simon Guggenheim Memorial Foundation (1976); and a postdoctoral fellowship from the Center for Advanced Study in Behavioral Sciences in Stanford (1977–1978).

The Department of Anthropology and the Maxwell Museum of Anthropology at the University of New Mexico have recently established the Alfonso Ortiz Center for Intercultural Studies to promote the efforts of current and future community scholars, artists, healers, and writers.

Simon Ortiz (1941–)
Acoma Pueblo poet

Simon Ortiz is one of the most respected and widely read Native American poets. His work is characterized by a strong voice that resounds with and recalls Native American storytelling traditions.

Ortiz was born in Albuquerque, New Mexico, and raised on the Acoma Pueblo reservation located in western New Mexico. He attended the Bureau of Indian Affairs (BIA) school at McCartys on the Acoma Reservation, went to St. Catherine's Indian School, Albuquerque Indian School, and graduated from Grants High School.

Originally going to Fort Lewis College in 1961 with the goal of becoming a chemist, he eventually quit and joined the army, serving for three years. In 1966, he

Singer, songwriter A. Paul Ortega.

enrolled at the University of New Mexico and his poems and short fiction stories were published in a number of small magazines. In 1968, Ortiz received a fellowship to the International Writing Program at the University of Iowa.

Although he never received a college degree, Ortiz began teaching in the 1970s. Over the years, he has taught creative writing and Native American literature at San Diego State University, the Institute of American Indian Arts, Navajo Community College (now known as Dine College), College of Marin, the University of New Mexico, Sinte Gleska College (now Sinte Gleska University), Colorado College, and Lewis and Clark College.

His career has also included work as a journalist, public relations director, and literary editor. He also served as First Lieutenant Governor and Interpreter at Acoma Pueblo in the late 1980s.

In 1969, he received a Discovery Award from the National Endowment for the Arts followed by a fellowship award in 1980. Other awards, prizes, and recognition include the White House Salute to American Poetry

and Poet Honoree (1980), the Pushcart Prize for selected poems (*From Sand Creek*) in 1981, the Humanitarian Award in Literature from the New Mexico Humanities Council (1989), the Lifetime Achievement Award for Literature (1993), the Lila Wallace-Reader's Digest Writer's Award (1997–1999), the Lifetime Achievement Award from Western States Arts Federation (2000), the Lannan Foundation Writing Residency (2000), and the New Mexico Governor's Award for Excellence in the Arts (2000).

Ortiz's work is a reflection of his Native American heritage and oral tradition. He states that the social, political, and cultural movements of the 1960s were major influences on his work. During this era, Ortiz presented a contemporary tribal voice that had been absent in previous works of Native literature.

Published works by Simon Ortiz include *Naked in the Wind* (1971), *Going for the Rain* (1976), *Howbah Indians* (1976), *A Good Journey* (1977, 1985), *Song, Poetry, and Language* (1978), *Fight Back: For the Sake of the People, For the Sake of the Land* (1980), *From Sand Creek* (1981, 2000), *A Poem Is a Journey* (1983),

Earth Power Coming (Ed.,1983), *Blue and Red* (1984), *The Importance of Childhood* (1984), *Fightin': New & Collected Stories* (1984), *Willkommen Indianer* (1991), *Woven Stone* (1992), *After and Before the Lightning* (1994), *Speaking for the Generations* (Ed., 1998), *Resistere* (1999), and *Men on the Moon* (2000).

Sandra Osawa (1942–)
Makah producer and writer

Sandra Osawa, a successful, independent television producer and writer, was born in Port Angeles, Washington. In 1975, she became the first Native American to produce an informational series on Native Americans for commercial television. In 1980, she received an Emmy nomination for *I Know Who I Am*, a television program on Native American cultural affairs, made for KSTW-TV in Seattle, Washington.

A majority of Osawa's work explores modern Native American cultural, social, and political issues. She has produced more than forty videos for non-broadcast use and her video work has been featured at domestic and international venues, including the Sundance Film Festival, the Amiens Film Festival, the Vienna Film Festival, the Munich International Film Festival, and the Margaret Mead Film Festival.

She received her bachelor of arts degree from Lewis and Clark University and attended graduate school for one year at UCLA, studying creative writing and filmmaking. Over the years, Osawa has served as co-director for the Washington State Fishing Rights project, director of the Head Start program for the Makah tribe, and taught at the Clyde Warrior Institute.

A member of the Writers Guild of America, her production credits are *Lighting the Seventh Fire, In the Heart of Big Mountain*, and, more recently, *Pepper's Powwow*. Osawa and her husband currently own their own production company, Upstream Productions, in Seattle, Washington.

Osceola (1803–1842)
Seminole tribal leader

In the 1830s, Osceola led a resistance movement to prevent the relocation of his people from their homeland in Florida to Indian reservations west of the Mississippi in present-day Oklahoma.

It is believed that Osceola was born near the Talapoosa River along the border between present-day Georgia and Alabama. As a boy, he and his mother moved to Florida, where they first settled along the Apalachicola River and in 1815 moved to St. Marks, a trading post in northern Florida. During this time, the Seminole Indians were caught up in the general removal of Indians from the Southwest United States that affected, among others, the Cherokee and Creek. When he was still a teenager, Osceola fought in the First Seminole War of 1817–1818. Seven years later, Osceola would fight in a Second Seminole War for his people, but this time in the role of leader.

A number of agreements and laws in the 1820s and 1830s led to the Third Seminole War. In 1823, an agreement at Camp Moultrie, Florida, was signed by a single tribe of Seminole in which they agreed to live on a reservation in exchange for annual payments of food and money. Passed by the U.S. Congress in 1830, the Indian Removal Act authorized the removal of all Indians in Florida within three years. In 1832, a treaty signed by a minority of Seminole at Payne's Landing required them to move to lands west of the Mississippi in exchange for food and money. By 1835, many Seminole had not complied with the removal treaty. Osceola traveled from band to band, urging his people to remain in their homelands. On 28 December 1835, Osceola led a party that ambushed Wiley Thompson, an Indian agent who was working to gain Seminole compliance with the removal treaty. (This marked the beginning of the Third Seminole War, within which fighting continued long after its recorded ending date of 1842.) Three days after the ambush of Thompson, Osceola and his warriors met and defeated General Duncan Clinch and a force of eight hundred troops.

For the next two years, Osceola spearheaded a relocation resistance movement. The Seminole warriors made good use of the Florida Everglades, a swampy region, to wage a successful hit-and-run campaign. Although many of the Indian chiefs fighting with Osceola surrendered during the war, Osceola continued to fight until his capture in 1842 by General T. S. Jesup, who captured him by deceiving him into attending a "peace council." As Osceola met with Jesup's envoy several miles outside of St. Augustine, Florida, troops secretly surrounded the Seminole leader, eventually swooping in to take him and his followers prisoner. The U.S. military often used such deception to capture and control Indian leaders. Osceola died in prison three months after his capture.

The capture of Osceola marked the official end of the Third Seminole War, although many Seminole continued to resist U.S. removal efforts by retreating to the isolated swampy regions of Florida. It is estimated that the war resulted in the deaths of fifteen hundred American troops and cost the U.S. government $20 million. Although many of the Seminole eventually relocated to Indian Territory in present-day Oklahoma, a number remained behind, clinging to their strongholds in the Everglades. To this day, their descendants can be found in southern Florida, where they live on state and federally recognized reservations.

Ouray (circa 1820–1880)
Ute tribal leader

Ouray was born in what became Taos, New Mexico, and became a leader of the Ute, a nomadic tribe living in present-day Colorado. As a young man, Ouray was revered as a cunning and dangerous warrior, but his career shifted as he came to realize that white settlement in his tribe's territory was inevitable. With the growth of the mining frontier in western Colorado, the Ute had been forced by whites to cede more and more of their territory.

In 1863, Ouray helped negotiate a treaty with the federal government at Conejos, Colorado, in which the Ute ceded all lands east of the Continental Divide. In 1867, Ouray assisted Kit Carson, a U.S. Army officer, in suppressing a Ute uprising. In 1868, he accompanied Carson to Washington, D.C., and acted as spokesman for seven bands of Ute. In the subsequent negotiations, the Ute retained sixteen million acres of land.

The growth of the Colorado mining frontier continued, and more miners trespassed on Ute lands. In 1872, Ouray and eight other Ute again visited Washington, D.C., in an attempt to stress conciliation over warfare. As a result, the Ute were pressured into ceding four million acres for an annual payment of $25,000. For his services, Ouray received an additional annuity of $1,000.

Ouray encouraged his fellow tribesmen to increase their efforts at farming in an attempt to protect their claims to land. The Ute did not have a farming tradition, however, and many among them resisted, preferring their ancient hunting and gathering subsistence ways. Nathan Meeker, a new Indian agent who attempted to force farming upon the Ute, was evicted from the reservation. This resulted in a military confrontation that left twenty-three Ute and fourteen U.S. soldiers dead, and forty-three wounded. Ouray secured the release of Meeker's wife and daughter who were captured during the battle.

Ouray traveled to Washington, D.C., again in 1880, where he signed the treaty by which the White River Ute were to be relocated to the Unitah Reservation in Utah. Soon after his return from Washington, Ouray died while on a trip to Ignacio, Colorado, where the Southern Ute Agency had been relocated. He was buried at the Southern Ute Agency; however, his remains were later returned to Montrose, Colorado, for reburial.

Louis Owens.

Louis Owens (1948–)
Choctaw/Cherokee/Irish critic, novelist, and educator

Both novelist and critic, Louis Owens has published extensively on both mainstream American literature as well as Native American writing. His novels, including *Dark River* (1999), *Nightland* (1996), *Bone Game* (1994), *The Sharpest Sight* (1992), and *Wolfsong* (1991), are well-read and widely studied contributions to the American and Native American literary canons.

Born in Lompoc, California, to Hoey Louis and Ida Brown Owens, the young boy of mixed heritage spent his early years between California and Mississippi, his father's homeland. After his father's discharge from the army in the early 1950s, his parents made ends meet working as laborers on California farms and ranches. His family eventually grew to include nine children, with Owens the third oldest. Owens's first job came at nine years old when he was hired to hoe weeds in a bean field.

After graduating from high school Owens worked in a can factory in the San Francisco Bay Area before friends convinced him to enroll in junior college in San Luis Obispo, California. After two years there, where he became editor of the student newspaper, with strong encouragement from his journalism advisor Owens reluctantly applied to the University of California at Santa Barbara (UCSB) as an English major. Shortly after enrolling at UCSB Owens met the Kiowa author N. Scott Momaday, a meeting that spurred Owens's own study of Native American literature outside of the traditional university classroom where, at that time, such literature was seldom included. It was also during his time at UCSB that Owens met his wife Polly, whom he married in 1975. In addition, while at UCSB Owens began a ten-year career as a seasonal worker for the U.S. Forest Service.

After receiving his B.A. and M.A. in English from UCSB, and taking time out from school to work as wilderness ranger and firefighter in Washington and Arizona, Owens returned to school to complete a Ph.D. from the University of California at Davis. Since that time, his impressive and influential work on John Steinbeck's writings, including the 1985 *John Steinbeck's Re-Vision of America* and the 1989 *The Grapes of Wrath: Trouble in the Promised Land*, have become well-known in academia. The first fruits of his long interest in Native American writing appeared also in 1985 with *American Indian Novelists*, a work co-authored with Tom Colonnese. A few years later, his criticism and exploration of American Indian literary efforts resulted in *Other Destinies: Understanding the American Indian Novel* (1992), a book used in many introductory courses across the United States and Canada. In 1998, Owens added *Mixedblood Messages: Literature, Film, Family, Place*, a book combining critical essays and personal narratives in examinations of mixed-blood identity.

Since beginning his career in 1982 at California State University, Northridge, Owens has taught at the University of New Mexico and the University of California at Santa Cruz before joining the University of California at Davis as professor of English and Native American Studies. In 1981 he taught as a Fulbright lecturer at the University of Pisa in Italy, and since that time has received numerous awards including the American Book Award for *Nightland*, France's Roman Noir Prize for *The Sharpest Sight*, and the Writer of the Year Award from the Wordcraft Circle of Native Writers and Storytellers for *Mixedblood Messages*. His work is anthologized in many collections and appears regularly in academic journals and periodicals.

Bastonnais Pangman (circa 1778–?)
Métis political leader

Bastonnais Pangman was one of the first leaders of the Métis, a term that refers to persons of mixed Indian-European heritage who forged a common identity on the plains of western Canada in the eighteenth and nineteenth centuries. His Dutch father, Peter, was well-known in the fur trade, battling established companies for an independent share of the fur business in the Canadian prairies. His mother was Cree. Peter left his Métis family and moved to Montreal when Bastonnais was fifteen. Being a skilled hunter, Bastonnais was sought after by the North West Company to work as a fur trader, but, like his father, he valued his independence. He lived and hunted buffalo on the plains, supplying badly need buffalo meat to the newly founded colony of Selkirk. When leaders of the colony attempted to regulate the free sale and movement of buffalo meat, however, they incurred the wrath of the local Métis people. Matters came to a head in 1814, when one of the first persons to be arrested for violating the regulation was Bastonnais Pangman, who had been so helpful to the settlers in the past. Pangman and others began to lead raids on the settlement in an effort to force settlers to leave the area. One such raid, the Battle at Seven Oaks in 1816, resulted in the death of the governor of the area and twenty of his men. Although there was no evidence to suggest that Pangman was an actual participant in the incident, he was arrested by colonial authorities in 1818. Eventually Pangman was acquitted of all charges brought against him.

Elizabeth Anne Parent (1941–)
Athabaskan and Yupik educator

Elizabeth Parent is professor of American Indian studies at San Francisco State University. Born in Bethel, Alaska, she attended the Harvard Graduate School of Education from 1972 to 1974, where she received a master of education degree and a certificate of advanced study. She received a master's and doctoral degree from Stanford University. She wrote her dissertation on the relations of Moravian missionaries to the Yupik people in the Bethel Alaska area.

She has served on the board of directors of the Eskimo, Indian, and Aleut Publishing Company, as director of the Greater Fairbanks Head Start Association, and on the Fairbanks Native Association Education Committee.

Parent's research interests lie in American Indian education, history, and politics. Her work has also focused on educational psychology, women's issues, and child development. She is a member of the Society for Values in Higher Education, the American Association for Higher Education, and the National Indian Education Association. Parent has been honored with a postdoctoral fellowship from the UCLA American Indian Studies Center, and has been a Ford Fellow (1975) and a Danforth Fellow (1975–1980).

Arthur C. Parker (1881–1955)
Seneca scholar and author

Arthur C. Parker was an acclaimed expert in the field of ethnology. In his later years, Parker devoted himself to the cause of pan-Indianism and was a leader of the Society of American Indians.

Parker was born of mixed ancestry on the Cattaraugus Seneca Reservation. As a young man he studied Iroquois archaeology and folklore. He later did professional work in archaeology for the New York State Museum. He published a number of important works on Iroquois culture such as *The History of the Seneca Indians* (1926), and *Red Jacket, Last of the Seneca* (1952). A selection of Parker's work is reproduced in *Parker on the Iroquois*, edited by William Fenton (1968).

Parker also became an influential figure in the pan-Indian movement, dedicated to unifying all Indian groups. His hope was to instill a race consciousness among all American Indians to preserve their culture and people. Parker was active in the Society of American Indians, a group dedicated to pan-Indianism. He also founded and edited the society's journal, *American Indian Magazine*. In his later years, Parker devoted himself to museums and writing. Parker is the author of over two hundred books, ranging from scientific works to children's books. Parker's great uncle was General Ely S. Parker, commissioner of Indian affairs under President Ulysses S. Grant.

Ely S. Parker (1828–1895)
Seneca tribal leader, commissioner of Indian affairs, and engineer

Ely S. Parker was the first Indian commissioner of Indian affairs. During the Civil War, Parker, a close friend and colleague of General Ulysses S. Grant, served the Union cause and penned the final copy of the Confederate army's surrender terms at the Appomattox Courthouse in 1865.

Ely Parker was educated at Yates Academy in Yates, New York, and Cayuga Academy in Aurora, New York. In 1852, he became a chief among the Seneca Indians and helped the Tonawanda Seneca secure land rights to their reservation in western New York State. Parker hoped to become a lawyer, but because he was an Indian, he was denied entry to the bar. Undaunted, Parker studied engineering at Rensselaer Polytechnic Institute instead.

With the outbreak of the Civil War, Parker tried to serve the Union by enlisting in the Army Corps of Engineers but was refused again because of racial prejudice. He eventually received a commission in May

Ely Samuel Parker, first Indian commissioner of Indian Affairs.

1863 as captain of engineers in the Seventh Corps. This was due in part to his friendship with General Ulysses S. Grant, whom he had met by chance before the war and with whom he later served during the Vicksburg campaign. When Grant became president in 1868, he appointed Parker his commissioner of Indian affairs. It was the first time an Indian had held the post. As commissioner, Parker worked to rid the bureau of corruption and fraud. He was an advocate for western Indian tribes and gained a reputation for fairness and progressive thinking. In 1871, Parker was falsely accused of fraud. Although he was acquitted of all charges, Parker resigned and moved to New York City, where he lived and worked until his death in 1895.

Quanah Parker (1845–1911)
Comanche tribal and spiritual leader

In the decades following the American Civil War, the American military turned its attention to pacifying and destroying American Indian groups, including those in the southern Plains. At the Medicine Lodge Council of 1867, several Comanche leaders agreed to move onto reservations. Indian groups who refused to relocate

Quanah Parker, Comanche tribal and spiritual leader.

became outlaws. One of the most fearless and powerful of these "renegade" groups was led by Quanah Parker.

Parker was the son of Peta Nocona, chief of the Kwahadi band in Texas, a subgroup within the Comanche nation, and Cynthia Parker, a non-Comanche captive. Throughout the 1860s, Parker led numerous attacks against U.S. soldiers. He and his band escaped capture longer than most of the Comanche bands in their final days living freely on the Plains. In the 1870s, however, new high-powered rifles and increasing numbers of U.S. hunters were systematically killing buffalo and destroying the way of life for the Plains Indians. In 1875, after years of battle and their buffalo nearly gone, Parker and his warriors turned themselves in, defeated by hunters with repeating rifles. The Comanche were among the last American Indians to roam freely over the southern Plains.

Parker quickly adapted to reservation life in present-day Oklahoma. In a few short years he became a successful cattle rancher. He counseled his people to adapt to the reservation without surrendering their Comanche customs and heritage. Parker adopted the peyote religion, which offered a modified world view, different in many ways from traditional religions, but offering many Indians a new form of religious belief that provided moral and spiritual support in the reservation setting. Parker helped spread the peyote religion to the Indian peoples of the Plains when they were desperately depressed and disoriented from the early reservation captivity of the 1880s and 1890s.

Parker became an appointed judge and served in the court of Indian affairs from 1886 to 1898. By 1890, he was the chief representative for the Comanche people in the allotment of tribal lands, which divided up tribal domains into small individual plots of 160 acres or less, while government officials made the surplus available to U.S. settlers. Parker also negotiated for the release of Geronimo by offering refuge to Apache warriors on the Comanche Reservation.

Rain Parrish (1944–)
Navajo author and museum curator

Rain Parrish is the author of a number of books on Navajo arts and has served as the former curator of the Wheelwright Museum of the American Indian in Santa Fe, New Mexico.

Parrish was born in Tuba City, Arizona, and received a bachelor's degree in anthropology from the University of Arizona in 1967. In 1979, she became the curator of the Wheelwright Museum of the American Indian where she has applied her extraordinary knowledge of American Indian art. Parrish has done extensive research on Native American art, which she has applied to the exhibits in the museum. Parrish is an artist and jeweler herself. She is the co-owner of Rainon Productions, which produces filmstrips for children on Native American culture. She has also served as Navajo curriculum specialist at Rough Rock School on the Navajo Reservation.

Parrish is the author of the following publications: *The Stylistic Development of Navajo Jewelry* (Minneapolis Institute of the Arts, 1982); *Women Holy People* (Wheelwright Museum, 1983); and *The Pottery of Margaret Tafoya* (Wheelwright Museum, 1984). She is a member of the New Mexico Museum Association and was honored in 1985 as Navajo Woman of the Year in the Arts.

William Lewis Paul, Sr. (1885–1977)
Tlingit lawyer and activist

William Lewis Paul was born in southeast Alaska, and as a young man was sent to the Carlisle Boarding

William Paul, c. 1943. (Photo by William Paul, Jr. Courtesy of Frances Paul DeGermain and Sealaska Heritage)

School in Pennsylvania. He went on to complete a law degree, which he used to campaign against discrimination and to fight for labor rights and Tlingit land rights. The Tlingit are a Northwest Coast people, organized into Raven and Eagle moieties (half divisions), which are further subdivided into clans and houses.

After finishing his education, Paul became an active leader within the Alaska Native Brotherhood (ANB), which was formed in 1912 by one Tsimpshian and eleven Tlingit Indians, as an organization to fight for Tlingit and, more generally, Indian civil rights and economic development. During the 1920s and 1930s, Paul became one of the main leaders of the ANB, and the organization made considerable progress in increasing membership and in pursuing its organizational goals. From 1923 to 1932, Paul edited *The Alaska Fisherman*, a newspaper devoted to Indian issues and especially fishing rights issues. In *The Alaska Fisherman*, Paul criticized non-Indian use of fish nets that took too much fish and threatened to destroy the salmon supplies. He also took on civil rights issues and advocated the boycotting of theaters that forced Natives to sit in special sections of the theater. Paul used his legal background to gain the right of Natives to vote in

Alaska Territory elections, for Native children to attend public schools, and to form a union for Alaska Natives who worked in the cannery industry.

Paul was a central figure in the Tlingit and Haida land claim case between 1929 and 1965. The Haida are another Northwest Coast people who live at the southern tip of the Alaska panhandle and are organized by moieties and clans like the Tlingit. In 1929, the ANB initiated a land claim suit against the United States for the loss of most of the land in the panhandle of Alaska, which the U.S. government in 1912 made into the Tongass National Forest. After gaining a waiver from the U.S. government in the 1930s, the Tlingit and Haida were allowed to sue for their lost land. Nevertheless, the Tlingit and Haida claim was not settled until the late 1950s, and in 1965 Tlingit and Haida Indians were paid $7.5 million. Paul devoted much of his time to seeing through the successful resolution of the Tlingit and Haida land claims case.

For his work for and dedication to the Indian community, the Tlingit and Haida people greatly revere Paul's name and memory. His papers (1915–1970) are deposited at the University of Washington archive in Seattle.

Andrew Paull (1892–1959)
Squamish activist

Andrew Paull was born at the Mission Reserve of the Squamish Nation in southwestern British Columbia. He worked as a longshoreman until the age of twenty-one, when he quit his job to become an interpreter for the McKenna-McBride Commission, established by the federal and British Columbia governments to address issues surrounding Indian reserves in the province. Paull interpreted and translated the Salish language, the language of the Squamish people and other aboriginal groups in southwestern British Columbia. His participation brought him prominence and introduced him to many different indigenous peoples of the province.

In June 1916, Paull, with Peter Kelly of the Haida Nation, organized a conference in Vancouver to address tribal rights to land. Sixteen tribal groups from across the province were represented, and the conference formed itself into the Allied Indian Tribes of British Columbia. In 1919, the Allied Tribes, after extensive consultation, prepared a statement of Indian rights to ancestral land in British Columbia that many viewed as the authoritative statement of British Columbia Indian claims. In 1927, Paull advocated the recognition of Indian lands before a special parliamentary committee struck in Ottawa to address Indian issues. The committee refused to recognize aboriginal rights to land and recommended the prohibition of any transaction designed to assist the bringing of Indian land claims to court. When the committee's recommendation became law, the Allied Tribes ceased to exist, and Paull turned to other activities. He became a sportswriter for a Vancouver daily and promoted Indian social events ranging from lacrosse games to beauty pageants. He re-entered political life in 1944 when he served as president of the North American Indian Brotherhood for three years before quitting amid charges of financial mismanagement. Paull then spent the next decade as a spokesperson for Salish people in the British Columbia interior.

Daniel Peaches (1940–)
Navajo legislator and tribal administrator

Daniel Peaches is a Navajo tribal administrator in Arizona. He was also elected to the Arizona State Legislature and served there from 1974 to 1985.

Peaches was born 2 September 1940, in Kayenta (Navajo Country), Arizona. In 1967, he received a bachelor's degree from Northern Arizona University and, from 1968 to 1969, studied Indian Law at the University of New Mexico. He also completed an internship at the American University in 1969.

Although the main focus of Peaches's career has been his role as Navajo tribal administrator, he has served the community in a number of ways. He is a member of the board of regents at Northland Pioneer College in Holbrook, Arizona, and is the president of Navajo Community College in Tsaile, Arizona. He is also a member of the Arizona Townhall Council and has served on the National Indian Education Advisory Council.

Peaches served on the Navajo Environmental Protection Commission (1976–1985) and was a member of the Governor's Commission on Arizona Indian Affairs (1974). He has won numerous awards, including an appointment by President Nixon in 1972 to the National Indian Education Advisory Council. From 1974 to 1985, he was an elected member of the Arizona State Legislature from District 3. Peaches has been profiled in *Newsweek* (1981), *Arizona Republic, Sunday* (1982), and *Time* (1984).

In 1998, he was elected to the Navajo Nation Council, the governing body of the Navajo Nation, where he serves on the Ethics and Rules Committee, setting agenda for the quarterly meetings of the council and the annual budget session.

His articles and letters have appeared in the *Navajo Times*, *The Arizona Republic*, the *Boston Globe*, and the *San Francisco Examiner*. Peaches is also a traditional leader and a member of the Navajo Medicine Men Association.

Ethel (Wilson) Pearson (1912–2000)
Kwawkgewlth tribal leader

Ethel (Wilson) Pearson was born in 1912 in Kingcome Inlet on the coast of British Columbia. Her people, the Kwawkgewlth, are known for their potlatch system, a series of ceremonies marking special occasions such as the birth of a new heir or the completion of a carved totem pole. Prominent features of a potlatch ceremony include the distribution of gifts to guests, the giving of speeches in which speakers from the host group recount their history and hereditary rights, and elaborate dances by masked performers re-enacting ancestral encounters with spirits. Pearson was the eldest of seven children and was specifically raised to take her father's place as a leader of her people. According to traditional ways, she was married at fourteen in an arranged marriage to Alfred Coon, a man she did not know. The marriage lasted only a short time, and Pearson married Charlie Wilson and moved to the town of Comox on Vancouver Island, so their children could attend public school. After the death of her husband, Ethel married a non-Native man, Fred Pearson, and lost her Indian status under Canadian law. Loss of status resulted in the forfeiture of special benefits provided by the federal government to Indian people. Pearson, along with countless other aboriginal women, fought for repeal of the law, and eventually it was amended in June 1985.

Maria Pearson (1932–)
Yankton Sioux activist

Maria Pearson has been at the forefront of the movement to protect Indian burials. She has also been active in establishing substance abuse programs for Native Americans in Nebraska.

Pearson was born in Springfield, South Dakota. She went to school at the Marty Indian School in Marty, South Dakota, and attended Iowa Western Community College in Council Bluffs. In her career as a consultant on Indian affairs, Pearson has spearheaded the crusade for the protection of Indian burials and the reburial of remains that have been placed in museums, universities, and private collections. Pearson is credited with a major contribution toward gaining the first significant law passed on the repatriation or restoration of Indian human remains and sacred objects. Pearson's repatriation activities came to fruition in

1989 when the Nebraska legislature passed a major Indian repatriation law.

Pearson has also been an advocate for substance abuse treatment for Indians in Omaha, Nebraska, and founded one of the first programs of this kind in her area. Her efforts led to the funding of national programs for substance abuse on Indian reservations and in other cities through the Indian Health Service. Pearson has been an important advisor to the Iowa government on matters of this nature and has lectured repeatedly both locally and nationally. A number of publications have profiled Pearson and her work, including *Newsweek*, *Time*, and *The Wall Street Journal*.

Leonard Peltier (1944–)
Anishinabe-Lakota activist

Leonard Peltier is considered by many to be a political prisoner serving two consecutive life sentences for the murders of two Federal Bureau of Investigation (FBI) agents.

Born on 12 September 1944, in Grand Forks, North Dakota, Peltier spent a difficult childhood moving with his family from copper mines to logging camps. When his parents separated, he was placed in Wahpeton

Leonard Peltier.

Indian School in North Dakota, where he encountered strict disciplinary treatment. He returned to live with his mother in Grand Forks, but at fourteen, he left home to find work, and by the age of twenty, he was part owner of an auto body shop in Seattle, Washington.

Peltier first became involved with the American Indian Movement (AIM) in 1970 and was soon a member of AIM's inner circle, traveling with Dennis Banks, a major AIM leader, to raise financial support for the group. Peltier participated in many AIM activities, including the takeover of the Bureau of Indian Affairs offices in the early 1970s. In October 1973, Peltier returned to Seattle but spent the next year-and-a-half traveling about the country. In the summer of 1975, he was living on the Pine Ridge Reservation in South Dakota.

There are many conflicting stories regarding the events of 26 June 1975, which ultimately led to Peltier's conviction and jail sentence. Nevertheless, this much is clear: FBI agents Jack Coler and Ronald Williams and Pine Ridge resident Joe Killsright were killed in a shootout near Oglala, South Dakota, on the Pine Ridge Reservation. Leonard Peltier was among a group of Lakota engaged in a shooting exchange with the FBI agents. FBI and Indian police reinforcements soon arrived and returned fire, killing Killsright. Peltier and others hid out in homes of relatives or friends in Pine Ridge; Peltier then slipped into Canada, where he was arrested in early 1976.

In a controversial and disputed trial at Fargo, North Dakota, from which 80 percent of the defense testimony was excluded, Peltier was convicted of the murder of the two FBI agents. Peltier was sentenced to two consecutive life terms in prison and transferred to the high-security penitentiary at Marion, Illinois. After a brief transfer to a prison in California, Peltier was returned to the Marion prison.

He is currently seeking executive clemency from the President of the United States. Among his millions of supporters are Archbishop Desmond Tutu, the Dalai Lama, Amnesty International, the European Parliament, the Italian Parliament, the Belgium Parliament, the Green Party, fifty members of the U.S. Congress, Robert Redford, the National Congress of American Indians, and Reverend Jesse Jackson.

Leonard Peltier has continued to advocate for the human rights of Indigenous peoples and in doing so has won numerous human rights awards. He was recently declared an official Human Rights Defender at the Human Rights Defenders Summit in Paris, which commemorated the fiftieth anniversary of the Universal Declaration of Human Rights. He has also established himself as a talented artist, poet, and author, and he has worked toward establishing access to the practice of traditional Native American religions in prison.

Macaki Peshewa (1941–)
Shawnee spiritual leader

Macaki Peshewa is a roadman or spiritual leader in the Native American Church in Knoxville, Tennessee. He was born in Spartanburg, Tennessee, and received a bachelor of arts degree from Wofford College (1968), a master of science degree from the University of Tennessee (1974), and a doctorate in human development from the Native Americas University (1975).

Peshewa has served as regional coordinator of the Catawba Labor Program, chairman of the Tennessee Indian Council and the Indian Historical Society of the Americas, and founder and chairman of Native Americans in Media Corporation. His archival material was published in *Longest Walk for Survival* (1981), and he produced the film *Amonita Sequoyah* (1982).

Among Peshewa's honors and awards are notary-at-large and a Key-to-the-City Certificate of Appreciation from Knoxville, Tennessee. His interests include memoirs of living elders, existential philosophy, herbal medicine, yoga, and parapsychology.

Helen Peterson (1915–2000)
Cheyenne activist

As a young child, Helen Peterson was enveloped and surrounded with the culture of the Oglala Sioux, although she is a Cheyenne by blood. She began her education intending to be a teacher. While working in the Colorado State College education department, however, Peterson became acquainted with other fields including minority group relations. This would become the focus of much of her life's work.

She served in Nelson Rockefeller's national office of Inter-American Affairs as director of the Rocky Mountain Council on Inter-American Affairs at the University of Denver Social Science Foundation. This provided a springboard for her career in human relations. In 1949, Peterson was sent to the Second Inter-American Indian Conference in Peru, where she presented a resolution on Indian education that was adopted by the body. In 1953, Peterson was appointed executive director of the National Congress of American Indians, a national organization that works on behalf of Indian issues. Under her leadership the congress became involved in international conferences and issues. In 1961, the Chicago Conference of Indians was held at the University of Chicago. This was one of the largest gatherings of Indians activists ever held and resulted in a document outlining Indian issues and the viewpoints of the Congress of American Indians on them.

When her tenure with the National Congress of American Indians was finished, Peterson returned to Colorado and became the director of the Denver Commission on Community Relations and head of the Organization on American Indian Development.

In her work, Peterson remained a staunch advocate of maintaining tribal identity and culture. According to Peterson, an understanding of tribal identities and sovereignty is important for Indian unity and for maintaining an effective relationship with the federal government, which recognizes the tribal governments and laws.

Philip (Metacom) (1639–1676)
Wampanoag tribal leader

From 1675 to 1676, Philip planned and carried out an unsuccessful attempt to oust English settlers from New England. The conflict has come to be known as King Philip's War. It was one of the most destructive Indian wars in New England's history.

Like his father Massasoit, Philip (among the English colonists, he was called King Philip) was the grand sachem of the Wampanoag Confederacy, an alliance of Algonkian-speaking peoples living in present-day New England. Unlike his father, however, Philip found peace with the New England colonists impossible, and he led a revolt against them. The seeds of revolt were laid before Philip became grand sachem. Although Massasoit had worked successfully with the progressive-minded New England minister, Roger Williams, to maintain peaceful relations between Indians and the English, when Philip came to power the mood of his people was more militant. There were several reasons for the change: colonists now outnumbered Indians in the region two to one, and English farms, animals, and villages were overtaking Indian land. Puritans subjected Philip's people to unfair laws, taxes, and jurisdictions. Alcohol and disease were also taking their toll. It was against this back-drop that Philip planned for war against the English.

Fighting erupted in 1675 at the frontier settlement of Swansea on June 16. The conflict quickly escalated across southern New England, involving the colonies of Plymouth, Massachusetts, Connecticut, and, to a limited extent, Rhode Island. Some tribes, including the Narragansett and Nipmuck, supported Philip; others gave valuable assistance to the English. Losses on both sides were brutal. (Puritans recorded with relish the massacre of noncombatants.) Villages, farms, and animals were destroyed. The colonists had underrated

Philip's talents as a military strategist and leader. Wampanoag and Narragansett warriors fought with a deep courage fostered by equal doses of optimism and desperation. Although for the first few months of the war the outcome was in doubt, the English eventually were victorious. On 19 December 1675, a decisive battle in southern Rhode Island resulted in the deaths of as many as six hundred Indians with four hundred captured. In August 1676, Philip was killed after being betrayed by his own warriors. His body was mutilated and displayed publicly.

Archie Phinney (1903–1949)
Nez Percé anthropologist and activist

Archie Phinney was a scholar, anthropologist, and ethnographer. He grew up in a traditional Nez Percé home cherishing Indian customs and was an outstanding student. He won the Idaho State Spelling Tournament at the age of fourteen and was the first Indian to receive his bachelor of arts degree from the University of Kansas (1926). He continued in postgraduate work at George Washington University and New York University, and specialized in the study of Indian reservation life at Columbia University in New York. He was the recipient of an honorary degree from the Academy of Science in Leningrad, a high academic honor from the former Soviet Union, now Russia. He authored two anthropology books and several journal articles. His best known anthropological work is *Nez Percé Texts* (1934), which contained Nez Percé stories and legends, written in the tribe's native tongue.

Phinney worked for the Bureau of Indian Affairs (BIA) as superintendent of the Northern Idaho Agency, a local office within the BIA organization that serves a reservation Indian community. Superintendents are usually the highest administrative officer of the BIA on a reservation, and the BIA offices compose the agency. Phinney was also active in national Indian issues and became a central figure of the National Congress of American Indians, an active organization created in the late 1940s to lobby in Congress and pursue favorable Indian legislation. He received the prestigious Indian Council Fire Award in 1946, three years before his untimely death at the age of forty-six.

Piapot (circa 1816–1908)
Cree tribal leader

Also known as Payepot (One Who Knows the Secrets of the Sioux), Piapot was a respected leader and warrior during a time of many conflicts for the Cree. He was raised by his grandmother after his parents were killed by a smallpox epidemic introduced by settlers. Piapot and his grandmother were captured by the Sioux and lived among the Sioux people for fourteen years until a Cree raiding party freed them. After his rescue, Piapot became an important source of information to the Cree, due to his knowledge of the ways of the Sioux. Following his selection as chief of his community in Manitoba, Piapot led a number of successful raids against the Sioux and the Blackfoot. In 1870, he took approximately seven hundred warriors into Blackfoot territory and destroyed several lodges. The Blackfoot, with the assistance of their kindred allies, the Peigan, counterattacked, killing at least half of Piapot's warriors. According to historians, the counterattack led to a significant adjustment of power between the Cree and the Blackfoot on the Canadian plains.

Piapot was also known for his resistance to white settlement of the western Plains and, in 1874, he refused to sign a treaty with Canadian authorities that would have resulted in his people moving to a reserve. He reluctantly signed a year later but he continued to resist the containment that its terms imposed. Piapot moved his people westward into Saskatchewan and disrupted the building of the Canadian Pacific Railroad by pulling up surveyor stakes and erecting tipis in the path of crews laying track. The Mounties responded by dismantling the tipis, and Piapot again moved his people to a nearby stretch of barren reserve land. Approximately one quarter of Piapot's people died before they relocated to the more fertile valley near Regina, Saskatchewan. Piapot was eventually "deposed" as chief by white authorities after his people held a forbidden "Sun Dance," an annual tribal renewal ceremony. The Cree remained loyal to Piapot until his death in 1908.

Anthony R. Pico (1945–)
Kumeyaay tribal leader and gaming advocate

As chairman of the Viejas Band of Kumeyaay Indians, Anthony R. Pico is one of California's most outspoken advocates of Native self-sufficiency. His tribe owns and operates the Viejas Casino and Turf Club near San Diego and, according to Pico, the gaming establishment has raised the 270-member band out of economic poverty and into self-determination. Casino profits have brought revitalization in such forms as housing, jobs, loans, and scholarships.

In 1966 Pico was sent to Vietnam with the 101st airborne. He later transferred to the 25th infantry, located in Cu Chi, twenty-five miles north of Saigon. While there, Pico witnessed many men die, and saw his closest friend killed by a grenade. A year later Pico joined the 82nd airborne and was shipped back to the United States.

In the early 1980s Pico ran an adult education program for Viejas and other nearby reservations. Also, in an attempt to better understand his people's past, Pico brought an elder to a recording studio where the man performed bird songs, or ancient Kumeyaay cycle songs. Using the recordings, Pico and two of his cousins learned the songs, began using them in ceremonies, and encouraged others to train to become Bird Singers.

Soon after his teaching experiences, Pico became involved in tribal politics. In 1982 Pico was elected tribal chairperson. For years Pico struggled to find a business to serve as his reservation's economic foundation. Until gaming came along in 1991, however, nothing worked to pull Viejas Reservation out of its economic depression. The Viejas gaming establishment now provides each adult tribal member with a monthly per capita, jobs, health care, and many other government benefits. Children receive their accumulated per capita, held in trust, when they reach eighteen years.

Pico was one of the leaders of the successful and historic Yes on Propositions 5 and 1A campaigns in California (gaming initiatives) and was the driving force behind initiatives ensuring that gaming proceeds be split among all California tribes. Viejas is one of the tribal forerunners in economic diversification projects. The tribe is majority stockholder in a bank that was purchased in 1996. Also that year, the band opened the Viejas Retail Outlet Center, the only one of its kind on an Indian reservation in the United States.

During the Summer Olympics that same year, Chairman Pico was selected as one of 5,500 Community Hero Torchbearers and helped transport the Olympic Flame across the United States. Pico has been honored time and again for his political efforts and successes. In September 1998 he received the prestigious Jay Silverheels Achievement Award from the National Center for American Enterprise Development for outstanding leadership and contributions that improve the quality of life of Native Americans. In 1997 Pico was named the National Indian Gaming Association's Man of the Year and received that organization's 1999 Award for Outstanding Spokesperson for Indian Gaming. Pico was the first Native American named one of San Diego's upcoming leaders in *San Diego Magazine's* 1995 People to Watch Awards, and was one of *East County's Home Town Heroes*, a book published in 1999. Pico was also the first Native American to be honored by the American Jewish Committee, receiving the Humanitarian Award from the San Diego Chapter of the forty-four-chapter national human relations organization. He presently resides on his reservation with his son.

F. Browning Pipestem (1943–1999)
Otoe-Missouri/Osage lawyer

F. Browning Pipestem was a member of the Coordination Council on Resources to Resolve State Tribal Civil Justice Issues of the National Center for State Courts. Since 1972, Browning managed a successful general law practice in Norman, Oklahoma, where he pursued justice, recognition of tribal sovereignty, and confirmation of the rights of Indian tribes and individuals through the judicial and legislative processes. He also served as general counsel and attorney general for several Indian tribes and organizations in Oklahoma and other states, as well as being appellate judge for several tribes.

Pipestem earned his bachelor of arts degree from Northwestern Oklahoma State College and a law degree from the University of Oklahoma School of Law, and he did graduate work in law at George Washington Law School in Washington, D.C. His legal career has paralleled the development of Indian law and jurisprudence in Oklahoma, and his significant cases include *Oklahoma State v. Littlechief, CMG v. Oklahoma State*, and *Ashbrook v. Kiowa Housing Authority*. After *Littlechief*, Pipestem was the first chief magistrate for the Court of Indian Offenses in western Oklahoma since statehood (1907). He has published extensively, including *Court Rules: Court of Indian Offenses, Anadarko Area Office Jurisdiction*, and *The Mythology of the Oklahoma Indian: A Survey of the Legal Status of Indian Tribes in Oklahoma*.

Browning took great pleasure in being a member of the adjunct faculty at the University of Oklahoma School of Law where he taught tribal law. In recent years, the Indian law program at Oklahoma University Law School had become a favorite topic for Browning. He believed that the University of Oklahoma was the logical place for a premier Indian law program and had worked with the law school and the American Indian Alumni Society of the University of Oklahoma.

To honor his legacy, the F. Browning Pipestem Memorial Scholarship Fund has been established at the University of Oklahoma School of Law.

Peter Pitseolak (1902–1973)
Inuk photographer

Peter Pitseolak took up photography in his early thirties when he realized that traditional Inuit life was disappearing due to Southern and European influences. He was born on Nottingham Island in the Northwest Territories in 1902 and became an Inuit camp leader.

His first photograph was of a polar bear, taken on behalf of a non-Native man who lacked the courage to take it himself. Ten years later, Pitseolak was able to obtain a camera from a Catholic missionary while working for fur traders in Cape Dorset, and he quickly became proficient in the medium. He first developed his own photographs in a hunting igloo with the assistance of a flashlight covered with a red cloth. Pitseolak spent the next twenty years photographing Inuit camp and hunting life, and he left more than fifteen hundred negatives of traditional Inuit life for museum and public consumption.

Pitseolak was also well known as a painter of watercolors. In addition, he authored an autobiography of his early life *People from Our Side* (published posthumously in 1975), which he wrote in Inuit syllabics. Another posthumously published book is an account of near death on the Arctic ice, entitled *Peter Pitseolak's Escape From Death* (1977). Pitseolak's photographic legacy is a profound one; many of the activities and scenes he captured on film would have gone unnoticed, forgotten in the march of time, had he not served as a recorder of his people.

Mardell Plainfeather (1945–)
Crow historian

Mardell Plainfeather is a former park ranger and Plains Indian historian. Her research and work at the Little Big Horn Battlefield National Monument have extensively educated the general public about the culture and history of the Plains Indians.

Born in Billings, Montana, she attended Maricopa County Junior College in Phoenix, Arizona, and has a bachelor's degree in history from Rocky Mountain College in Billings, Montana. Plainfeather has worked at the Little Big Horn Battlefield National Monument on the Crow Reservation in eastern Montana. She was also a part-time instructor of U.S. history and Montana state history at the Crow Tribal Junior College and Little Big Horn College on the Crow Agency in Montana. Plainfeather's interests are in the cultural history of the Plains Indians from prehistory to the 1880s. She strives to be sure that history is told correctly and includes the American Indian perspective. Plainfeather is also interested in oral history and the preservation of Native American sacred sites.

She has served on the boards of the Fort Phil Kearny/ Bozeman Trail History Association and the Crow Tribal Archives. She is a member of the Little Big Horn Battlefield Historical and Museum Association, the Montana State Oral History Association, and the Montana Committee for the Humanities. In 1982 Plainfeather received a Performance Achievement Award from Custer Battlefield National Monument, and in 1987 she was honored by the St. Augustine Preservation of Indian Culture in Chicago, Illinois.

Plainfeather is the author of *A Personal Look at Curly after the Little Big Horn* and *The Apsaalooke: Warrior of the Big Horns*. She is currently the extension agent at Little Big Horn College, Crow Agency, Montana, and serves on the board of directors for the International Traditional Games Society.

Pocahontas (1595–1617)
Powhatan cultural mediator

Pocahontas was the daughter of Powhatan and the niece of Opechancanough, both leaders of the Powhatan Confederacy that occupied much of the present-day state of Virginia. She married John Rolfe, an English settler in Virginia. She is credited with helping early English settlers maintain peaceful relations with the Powhatan.

Although the actual events are undocumented, it is widely believed that Pocahontas intervened to prevent the execution of John Smith, the Jamestown (Virginia) leader who was being held captive by Powhatan allies because he was thought to have commanded raids on several Indian villages. Her actions did not guarantee her own safekeeping, however, for in 1612, Pocahontas was abducted by English settlers and held hostage. During this time Pocahontas learned English and converted to Christianity. One year later, she married John Rolfe, one of the colony's leading citizens. The good relations between the English and Indians that followed the marriage allowed Rolfe to learn about tobacco planting, thereby setting the future course of the colony, which excelled in the production and export of tobacco.

In 1616, Pocahontas and her husband made a widely publicized trip to England. For the Virginia colonists, Pocahontas was good publicity. She was offered as proof that the struggling colony could survive and maintain good Indian relations. For Pocahontas, however, the trip proved deadly; she died a year later of a European disease. The life of Pocahontas soon became popularized in fiction, often clouding the historical accuracy of what is actually known about her life.

Pocatello (1815–1884)
Shoshone tribal leader

Born in the early 1800s, Pocatello became headman of the northwestern band of the Shoshone Indians in

1847. This band was blamed for much of the violence along the California Trail, Salt Lake Road, and Oregon Trail as westward expansion and the California gold rush brought more and more settlers onto traditional Shoshone lands in the northwestern corner of present-day Utah.

Pocatello was captured and imprisoned in 1859, but worked to maintain a delicate neutrality among the different Indian bands, Mormons, miners, ranchers, and missionaries who came into the Idaho region. In 1863, he signed the Treaty of Box Elder. From 1867 to 1869, he traveled and hunted with the Washakie's Wild River Shoshone. By 1872, Pocatello's band was forced to relocate to the Fort Hall Indian Reservation in Idaho when the Union Pacific and Central Pacific railroads connected and brought further U.S. settlement into the region.

In order to be allowed to live on an off-reservation farm, Pocatello converted to Mormonism, a religion whose followers had settled at Salt Lake City, Utah. Ultimately, the local inhabitants requested federal troops to force Pocatello and other Shoshone Indians to return to Fort Hall. Pocatello then rejected Mormonism and lived the remainder of his life at Fort Hall. He became known as General Pocatello to distinguish him from other members of his family. The town of Pocatello, Idaho, is named after this Indian leader.

Pontiac (1720–1769)
Ottawa tribal leader

It is believed that Pontiac was born along the Maumee River, in present-day northern Ohio. By 1755, he was chief and probably participated in the French and Indian War of 1754–1763 as a French ally. Pontiac had built up a profitable trading partnership with the French, so it was with dismay that he watched the British gradually gain control of French land and trade relationships. Besides the less-favorable trading policies of the British, Pontiac also was apprehensive over the British propensity for settling on Indian lands. For these reasons, in 1763, Pontiac led a military campaign against the British, who were occupying the old French forts such as Detroit in the Great Lakes region.

Pontiac's plan was founded on the belief that he could unite diverse Indian nations against the British and that the French would follow through on their promises of support. Pontiac's efforts to forge an anti-British alliance were fairly successful. The Ottawa leader was a skillful orator, and he spread his message of resistance effectively throughout the Old Northwest tribes of the Great Lakes area. He was aided in this cause by the Delaware prophet, whose anti-British teachings and spiritual visions provided Pontiac's crusade with a spiritual foundation. Though Pontiac and the Delaware Prophet disagreed on the use of guns (Pontiac advocated their use), the two leaders were a potent organizing force that united many diverse Indian nations.

Traders in the region spread the news of Pontiac's alliance and eventually alerted the British, who sent reinforcements into the Detroit region. In April 1763, Pontiac made final plans for a coordinated siege carried out by separate Indian bands throughout the Great Lakes region. On May 5, he visited Fort Detroit probably for reconnaissance purposes. The fort's leader, Major Henry Gladwin, knew of the planned surprise attack and prevented Pontiac from bringing in any large numbers of his warriors. Finally on May 9, Pontiac, under pressure from restless warriors, attacked the fort. Simultaneously, he ordered a siege of the entire region, by alerting his network of sympathetic bands.

Many tribes answered Pontiac's call for attack, including Chippewa, Delaware, Huron, Illinois, Kickapoo, Miami, Potawatomi, Seneca, and Shawnee. In the ensuing attacks, about two thousand settlers were killed and a number of British posts and forts fell. In October 1763, the British government issued a Royal proclamation that forbade English settlement on land west of the Appalachians. Pontiac, meanwhile, persisted in his siege of Fort Detroit. When French support failed to materialize, however, Pontiac's warriors began to question the wisdom of continuing the siege with winter approaching and food supplies dwindling. A letter from a French commander finally persuaded Pontiac to call off the siege. Although he continued to believe in his resistance movement, he signed a peace pact in 1765 and a peace treaty in 1766. He was pardoned by the British and returned to his village on the Maumee River.

Despite the 1763 proclamation forbidding it, English settlers continued to settle on Indian lands west of the Appalachians. However, Pontiac counseled peace. In 1769, the Ottawa leader was killed by an Indian who had probably been paid by the British. The alliances that Pontiac forged among diverse Indian groups set a precedent for future resistance efforts among Indian leaders of this region, who like Pontiac, sought ways to halt settler encroachment on their lands.

Horace Poolaw (1909–1984)
Kiowa photographer

Horace Poolaw was one of the most prolific Indian photographers of his generation. His photographs captured the tumultuous period of Kiowa history, including the arrival of U.S. settlers to Oklahoma and the allotment of tribal lands. The Kiowa are a southern Plains Nation who took up the Plains culture of the horse, buffalo hunting, bundles of sacred objects given by the Great Spirit, and annual summer gatherings for ceremonial purposes. In the late 1870s, the U.S. government forced the Kiowa to settle on a reservation in present-day Oklahoma.

Poolaw was born on the Kiowa Indian Agency in Anadarko, Oklahoma. At age seventeen, he was apprenticed to landscape photographer George Long. Under Long's tutelage, and that of his successor, John Coyle, Poolaw learned the art and technique of photography. During the mid-1920s, Poolaw began to develop his own collection of photographs by taking pictures of Kiowa daily life. In 1929, the American Indian exposition opened in Anadarko (where it remains to this day). Poolaw was the official photographer of the exposition. When World War II broke out, Poolaw enlisted and served three years in the army air corps, training soldiers to take aerial photographs. A number of Poolaw's Kiowa contemporaries served with him. After the war, Poolaw returned to Oklahoma, where he raised cattle and farmed, all the while taking many photographs. In 1978, failing eyesight finally forced Poolaw to put down his camera. Poolaw's photographs were printed, cataloged, and exhibited for the first time in 1990. His work is considered one of the best sources of information about Kiowa life in the early twentieth century.

Popé (d. 1690)
Tewa Pueblo tribal leader

Popé was an important spiritual and military leader of his people. In the 1680s, he led a successful rebellion against the Spanish in the upper Rio Grande region by uniting a number of pueblo villages. After the rebellion, for nearly a decade, Popé was a central leader among the temporarily free pueblo villages.

The Spanish founded the colony of New Mexico on Indian land in 1598. The Europeans soon were using their soldiers to collect taxes and promote the Catholic religion among the Indians living in the region. Under the *repartimiento* system, Indians were forced to pay the Spanish taxes in the form of labor, crops, and cloth. Unlike British settlers in the east who chose to drive the Indians from their land, the Spanish conquerors preferred to rule over the Native inhabitants in a feudal economy. The Catholic Church in its zeal to convert Indians called for the expurgation of Indian religious beliefs and rituals. These efforts were enforced by the ever-present Spanish military. The Indians living under Spanish jurisdiction were forced to practice their beliefs in hiding. Among the pueblo villages along the Rio Grande, religious ceremonies took place in semi-subterranean ceremonial chambers known as *kivas*. Many Indians gave lip service to Christian beliefs in public, but clung to their own faith in private.

Popé was an important medicine man of the San Juan Pueblo, who had resisted repeated attempts to convert him. He was captured and flogged by Spanish authorities on at least three occasions. His beatings became a symbol of resistance to his people and enhanced his efforts to gain recruits for a hoped-for uprising. In 1675, Spanish authorities arrested Popé and a number of other Pueblo medicine men. The prisoners were taken to Santa Fe where they were jailed and beaten. An Indian delegation won their release after threatening the Spanish with violence. Upon his release, Popé went to the Taos Pueblo where he began organizing a rebellion and covertly enlisting recruits. He preached that the *kachinas*, or ancestral spirits, had ordered him to restore the traditional way of life for his people. A number of towns pledged allegiance to Popé's cause, and on 10 August 1675, he ordered an attack. Resistance fighters from numerous pueblos in the region moved against the Spanish. After a number of successful smaller engagements, a large Indian force moved on to Santa Fe in present-day New Mexico. A week of fighting and four hundred deaths later, the Spanish retreated south to El Paso, in present-day western Texas. About 250 Indians died in the uprising.

For the next twelve years, the pueblos held control of their homeland. Popé oversaw the destruction of all Spanish property and cultural institutions. Indians who had been baptized by Catholic priests were washed with suds from the Yucca plant to "cleanse" their spirits. Popé chose to live in Santa Fe and used the carriage left behind by the Spanish governor. By the time of his death in 1690, the alliance of the region's Indians had dissolved in the face of drought and attacks by Apache and Ute bands. By 1692, Santa Fe was once again under Spanish control.

Alexander Posey (1873–1908)
Creek journalist and poet

Alexander Posey was a well-known Creek poet and journalist. His skillful satirization of U.S. culture provided his people with an important source of identity during a time when their lands and culture were being stripped from them.

Alexander Posey's father was Scotch-Irish and his mother was Creek. He was raised in Creek culture by his mother near Eufaula, Oklahoma. He mastered English as a teenager while going to Bacone Indian University in Tahlequah, Oklahoma. At the university, Posey learned to set type and began writing.

Some of Posey's most direct work was done in the *Indian Journal,* a Native Oklahoma newspaper, in which he regularly satirized U.S. society. He especially liked to point out American fondness for material possessions, including Indian land. Posey cleverly mixed pidgin English, puns, and inside jokes with a recurring cast of characters who dealt with attempts to change Indian ways through new names, haircuts, and slogans. One of Posey's most beloved characters was Hotgun, a droll, seasoned veteran of the conflict between Indian cultures and U.S. culture. Hotgun's humorous comments helped Indians maintain a sense of belonging and identity. Posey's humor was a much-needed witty tonic for Indians whose way of life and lands were under siege in the late 1900s.

Posey was also directly active in tribal affairs and was superintendent of public instruction of the Creek Nation. In 1905, he helped draft a revised Creek constitution.

Poundmaker (circa 1842–1886)
Cree tribal leader

A trader who met Poundmaker in the 1860s described him as "just an ordinary Indian, [an] ordinary man as other Indians." Poundmaker's life changed several years later, however, when, during a truce between the Cree and the Blackfoot, he was noticed by a wife of the Blackfoot chief Crowfoot. The two were struck by Poundmaker's resemblance to a son who had been killed by Cree warriors before the truce. Crowfoot immediately adopted Poundmaker as his son and gave him a Blackfoot name, Makoyi-koh-kin (Wolf Thin Legs). Poundmaker's stature increased when he returned to his people in central Saskatchewan and was chosen to be one of several spokespersons for the Plains Cree in negotiations over a treaty with Canadian authorities in 1876. During negotiations, Poundmaker pressed for better terms, including education and assistance, stating that once the buffalo were gone, he and his people would have to learn how to farm and survive in a new world. His pleas fell on deaf ears, however, and he eventually signed the treaty and agreed to a reserve for his people in central Saskatchewan.

Poundmaker and his followers participated in the second Northwest Rebellion of 1885, in which Louis Riel, leader of the Métis people, sought to form a provisional government in Saskatchewan against the

wishes of Canadian authorities. Poundmaker's followers ransacked the abandoned village of Battleford in what now is central Saskatchewan. A military force of some three hundred men were sent in retaliation. When they attacked Poundmaker's camp, however, they suffered heavy casualties. When he learned of Louis Riel's surrender in 1885, Poundmaker also surrendered to Canadian authorities. He was convicted of treason and after serving a year of his three-year sentence, Poundmaker fell ill and was released. He died four months later.

Powhatan (1550?–1618)
Powhatan tribal leader

In the late 1500s and early 1600s, the Indian chief Wahunsonacock presided over the Powhatan Confederacy, an alliance of Indian tribes and villages stretching from the Potomac River to the Tidewater region of present-day Virginia. The English called Wahunsonacock Powhatan (Falls of the River), after the village where the Indian leader dwelled. (Today this village is Richmond, Virginia.) As ruler of this region, Powhatan played a pivotal role in relations with early English colonists in Virginia. One colonist described Powhatan as regal and majestic: "No king, but a kingly figure." Powhatan's daughter, Pocahontas, married John Rolfe, the Englishman who developed tobacco farming in Virginia. Powhatan's brother, Opechancanough, led the Powhatan uprisings against English settlers in 1622 and 1644.

Powhatan inherited from his father a confederacy of six tribes, but the ambitious leader quickly expanded his domain. Estimates of the Powhatan Confederacy range from 128 to 200 villages consisting of eight to nine thousand inhabitants and encompassing up to thirty different tribes. It is believed that Powhatan built the confederacy using a combination of incentives and coercion.

Communities under Powhatan's jurisdiction received military protection and adhered to the confederacy's well-organized system of hunting and trading boundaries. In return, subjects paid a tax to Powhatan in the form of food, pelts, copper, and pearls. Europeans who visited Powhatan in the 1600s have described a large structure filled with "treasures," probably Powhatan's storehouse and revenue collection center.

Powhatan was an important figure in the opening stages of English efforts to settle in the Tidewater region, in particular the Jamestown expedition of 1607. Setting foot on the shores of Powhatan's domain the

English were unaware that they were trespassing on a land ruled by a shrewd and well-organized head of state. Powhatan, approximately sixty years old at the time, could easily have demolished the faltering community, but instead chose to tolerate the English for a time—one reason being his desire to develop trade with them. Metal tools and weaponry were of special interest to Powhatan. Despite a mutual desire for trade, relations between Powhatan and the Virginia settlers were rocky; attacks and counterattacks were common.

The English government in the early 1600s knew that maintaining friendly relations with the Powhatan people was a key to establishing a foothold in the region. For this reason, Powhatan was courted by several colonial leaders. In 1609, he was offered a crown from the King of England and reluctantly agreed to have it placed ceremoniously on his head. In return, Powhatan sent the King of England his old moccasins and a mantle.

In 1614, a degree of harmony was eventually achieved after the marriage of Pocahontas (who, in 1613, was kidnapped by the Virginia settlers) to John Rolfe, a leading citizen of Jamestown Colony. After the marriage of his daughter, Powhatan negotiated a peace settlement that produced generally friendly relations with the English until a few years after Powhatan's death in 1618.

Janine Pease Pretty On Top (1949–)
Crow educator

Janine Pease Pretty On Top, president of Little Big Horn College, is a noted educator and career services specialist. She was born in Nespelem, Washington, though her tribal affiliation is with the Crow, who have a reservation in southeastern Montana. The educator received her bachelor of arts degree from Central Washington University in Ellensburg, Washington. She has worked as a counselor at Navajo Community College, women's basketball coach at Big Bend Community College, and career services director at Eastern Montana College. During her career in education, she has served on the Washington State Youth Commission (1971) and the Montana State Advisory Committee on Vocational Education (1977), co-chaired the Native American Telecommunication Demonstration (1978), and was chair of the Crow/Shell Scholarship Committee (1981).

Her honors include being nominated for Outstanding Woman of the Year in Washington (1972) and the same award in Montana (1976). Among her interests are women's rights and Native American educational issues.

Puccaiunla (Hanging Grapes) (circa 1760–1838)
Chickasaw tribal leader

Puccaiunla was the wife of Ish-te-ho-to-pah, the last hereditary principal chief of the Chickasaw (1820–1850). In 1856, the Chickasaw adopted a constitutional government, and thereafter until 1906, the U.S. government abolished the Chickasaw government. Although the extent of her authority is not known, it is known that Puccaiunla was deeply loved by her people. It is believed that the wife of the principal chief was without any authority and was regarded only as other Chickasaw women were. Before the Chickasaw removal to Indian Territory in present-day Oklahoma in 1838, however, they donated fifty dollars a year to Puccaiunla, a financial bonanza at that time. The Chickasaws felt grateful to their old leaders for long and faithful service and believed it a duty to keep them from want in their old age. A Chickasaw government bill on the Chickasaw national treasury stated, "Queen Puccaiunla is now very old and very poor. Justice, says the Nation, ought not to let her suffer in her old age; it is therefore determined to give her, out of the National funds, fifty dollars a year during her life, the money to be put in the hands of the agent to be paid out for her support, under his direction, with the advice of the chiefs."

During Chickasaw removal to Indian Territory in the early 1840s, smallpox and lack of provisions interfered with efforts to move the tribe. Puccaiunla was among those who died during the removal period.

Pushmataha (1764–1824)
Choctaw tribal leader

Choctaw legend says that Pushmataha was an orphan, and he himself maintained that he was born of a splinter from an oak tree. Such a story was unusual in Choctaw society where everyone was conscious of their Native iksa (local matrilineal family). At a young age, Pushmataha was recognized as a great warrior and hunter. He participated in many Choctaw hunting forays across the Mississippi River into the Osage and Caddo country, since by the early 1800s, fur-bearing animals suitable for trade were already significantly depleted in Choctaw country. These hunting trips led to war with the Caddo and Osage, who protected their land from the Choctaw intruders.

In 1805, Pushmataha was elected chief of the southern or Six Towns district of the Choctaw Nation. The Choctaw government was divided into three politically independent districts, each with a chief and council. From 1805 to 1824, Pushmataha led the southern district, which was the most conservative district, and, before 1760, allied to the French Louisiana Colony.

In the early 1800s, Pushmataha owned a small farm, had two wives—which was possible under Choctaw custom—and owned several slaves. Pushmataha favored friendly relations with the United States, siding with the United States against the British, and Tecumseh, the Shawnee war leader, and the Red Stick Creek during the War of 1812. For his services, he earned the rank of U.S. brigadier general. The Choctaw, including Pushmataha, signed treaties of land cession in 1805, 1816, and 1820. In 1824, Pushmataha died from an infection while in Washington negotiating yet another treaty. He was buried with full U.S. military honors.

Al Qoyawayma (1938–)
Hopi engineer and artist

Al Qoyawayma, a prominent engineer and noted ceramicist, was one of the founders of the American Indian Science and Engineering Society (AISES) and was its first chairman.

Born in Los Angeles, California, unlike many Hopi who are born on the reservation, he succeeded in maintaining his Hopi roots while prospering in the non-Hopi world.

Qoyawayma earned a bachelor of science degree in mechanical engineering at California Polytechnical State University in San Luis Obispo in 1961 and a master of science degree from the University of California in 1966. He began working in 1961 for Litton Systems, Inc., in the development of high technology systems and products, including inertial guidance systems and airborne star tracking devices, and holds several domestic and foreign patents. In 1971, as a means of providing greater assistance to Arizona Indian tribes, he became manager of environmental services for the Salt River Project in central Arizona. Among other duties, he is in charge of preparing environmental statements, recommending corporate policy, and providing computer and technical support.

Qoyawayma has become famous for his exquisite ceramics. On vacation visits to see and study with his aunt, Polingaysi Qoyawayma, he perfected various pottery techniques and currently turns out approximately thirty individual pieces per year. He uses traditional methods in personally collecting his clays and pigments, and he grinds them by hand. He then applies his engineering talents in molding and stretching the clay into art forms. His work has been displayed at the Smithsonian Institute of Natural History, the American Craft Museum, and the Kennedy Art Center in Washington, D.C.

He was a member of the dean's advisory council at California Polytechnic State University's School of Engineering in San Luis Obispo (1994–1996); a Fulbright Fellow with the Maori and South Pacific Arts/Te Waka Toi (1991); commissioner for the Arizona Commission on the Arts (1991–1992); a member of the board of directors at the Heard Museum in Phoenix (1990–1992); vice-chairman for the board of trustees at the Institute of American Indian Arts in Santa Fe, New Mexico (1988–1994); a member of the board of directors for the National Action Committee on Minorities in Engineering (1984–1986); and co-founder and chairman emeritus of the American Indian Science and Engineering Society (1977–present).

He received the Popovi Da Memorial Award from the Scottsdale National Arts Exhibition in 1976, was awarded an honorary doctorate of humane letters from the University of Colorado in 1986, and accepted the Ely S. Parker Award from the American Indian Science and Engineering Society in 1986. He also holds U.S. and international patents on Inertial Guidance Systems (IMU), 747, F-15, and other commercial and military aircraft and applications.

Rain-in-the-Face (Iromagaja) (1835–1905)
Hunkpapa Lakota tribal leader

Rain-in-the-Face was a leading Sioux war chief who participated in the defense of Sioux land in the 1860s and 1870s. He was one of several Indian chiefs who joined together to defeat Custer's Seventh Cavalry at the Battle of the Little Bighorn in June 1876.

Rain-in-the-Face was born in present-day North Dakota at the forks of the Cheyenne River. It is believed that he received his name from two episodes, one in which blood streamed down his face during a boyhood fight and a second when his warpaint became smeared during a fight with the Gros Ventre. He became a chief through meritorious deeds in battle.

Rain-in-the-Face participated in several important battles during the 1860s and 1870s for control of the Sioux lands. In 1866, he fought alongside fellow Hunkpapa leaders such as Gall, and the Oglala chief, Crazy Horse, during Red Cloud's War to prevent settlement along the Bozeman Trail in present-day Wyoming and Montana. In 1868, he led a raid on Fort Totten in North Dakota. In 1873, Rain-in-the-Face was finally arrested for murder at Fort Abraham Lincoln, near present-day Bismarck, North Dakota, but he escaped to join Sitting Bull in the fight for the Black Hills in 1876. Rain-in-the-Face was a major leader in the defeat of Colonel George Custer and about two hundred men at the 1876 Little Bighorn Battle in southern Montana.

For a time, it was believed that Rain-in-the-Face dealt the fatal blow to Custer, but this has never been substantiated.

In 1880, Rain-in-the-Face surrendered at Fort Keogh, Montana. He spent his remaining years living on the Standing Rock Reservation in North Dakota.

Ramona (1865–1924)
Cahuilla (Kawia) basketmaker

Ramona was a Cahuilla Indian who lived in present-day San Diego County, California. She became something of a celebrity in the late 1880s, due to the fictional story *Ramona* by the famous historical novelist Helen Hunt Jackson.

The central character in the novel is a romantic figure who bears little resemblance to the real-life Ramona. Jackson came to California in 1881 as an investigative reporter for *Century* magazine. While gathering information, she became entranced with the picturesque Roman Catholic past of southern California and wrote a sympathetic portrayal of the context and purposes of Spanish Catholicism and colonization in California. In contrast, *Ramona* was a work of social protest that underscored the plight of California Indians, often called Mission Indians, who were forced to live and work in the Catholic missions. In her investigative reporting, Jackson recorded the grave population decline of California Mission Indians and the role of the Spanish in this decline. Jackson became determined to write a work that would bring the plight of the Mission Indians to the American public's eye. *Ramona* was first serialized in 1884 by *Christian Union* magazine.

The real-life Ramona, a Cahuilla Indian living in present-day Temecula, California, had been married to Juan Diego, who was murdered in dramatic fashion by a local villain named Sam Temple. The novel, which incorporated a fictionalized romance, became an instant success and spawned a movie in the early 1900s, and the real-life Ramona became something of a celebrity, selling baskets and photographs of herself to eager tourists at a souvenir stand. Today, the myth of Ramona continues to live in numerous reenactments and festivals celebrating her life and character.

Elaine A. Ramos (contemporary)
Tlingit performing artist, educator, and nurse

Elaine Ramos is a nurse, educator, and the founder of a traditional Tlingit performing ensemble. She was raised by her parents to speak Tlingit and learned tribal history, legends, and culture.

After graduating from nursing school at Sage Memorial Hospital in Arizona, Ramos worked among the Navajo during a diphtheria outbreak and delivered babies in hogans. She eventually missed her Tlingit homeland and returned to Yakutat, Alaska, one of the northernmost villages of the Tlingit Indians, who live along the southern panhandle of Alaska. The northern Tlingit are well known for their strong sense of preserving traditional Tlingit culture and especially for their keeping of potlatches, a giveaway ceremony of large amounts of goods and money in honor of the clan ancestors. With the nearest hospital three hundred miles away in Juneau, the state capital, Ramos continued with her nursing as the only person in Yakutat with any knowledge of medicine. She also became active in local efforts to consolidate educational services.

Ramos enrolled at Sheldon Jackson College in Sitka, Alaska, in 1966 and was salutatorian of her graduating class. She became an assistant dean of students and was appointed vice-president of the college in 1972. In the late 1960s, she founded the Raven Dancers to promote Tlingit storytelling, singing, and costuming. The ensemble has performed across Alaska and venues in the continental United States. In 1973, Ramos received the prestigious Indian Council Fire Award.

James Ransom (1958–)
Mohawk environmentalist

James Ransom is the first director of the environmental program on the St. Regis Indian Reservation, located on the New York-Canadian border. In this capacity, he is leading a campaign to clean the region of environmental pollutants. The Mohawk are an Iroquoian-speaking people, and one of the nations of the Iroquois Confederacy (see the biographies of Deganawidah and Handsome Lake).

Ransom graduated from Clarkson University in Potsdam, New York, with a civil engineering degree in 1988; in the same year, he became the first director of St. Regis Mohawk Education and Community Fund, a program to clean up the environmental waste choking the St. Regis Indian Reservation. Pollutants are an acute problem in the area, which is a favorite dumping ground for nearby industries. The soil and water near the reservation are saturated with toxic wastes and heavy metals. In 1989, on behalf of his tribe, Ransom sued Reynolds Metals, General Motors Central Foundry Division, and major aluminum manufacturer ALCOA for environmental damage to the St. Lawrence River.

Ransom's environmental advocacy propelled him into an elected position as sub-chief of the St. Regis Mohawk tribe. Ransom's long-term goals include the creation of a consulting group that would seek out other communities and help them deal with environmental issues. Ransom believes the St. Lawrence River region can be restored as a prime fishing and recreational area once the pollution problem is addressed and remedied.

Red Cloud (1822–1909)
Oglala Sioux tribal leader

Red Cloud was a war chief and leader of the Oglala subdivision of the Teton Sioux. He was born in present-day north-central Nebraska near the forks of the Platte River. His father was Lone Man and his mother was Walks as She Thinks. Lone Man died soon after the birth of his son, and Red Cloud was raised by an Oglala headman, Smoke, his mother's uncle. Red Cloud quickly gained a reputation for bravery and cunning in raids against the Pawnee and Crow. When he was about nineteen, Red Cloud shot his uncle's rival, the most powerful Oglala chief, Bull Bear, at Fort Laramie, located in present-day eastern Wyoming. Because of these exploits, he was chosen to be leader of the Iteshicha (Bad Face) band over Man Afraid of His Horses, the hereditary leader.

Tensions dramatically increased between the Plains tribes and the United States with the advent of the Bozeman Trail, which passed through the present-day states of Wyoming and Montana, and its connection to the Oregon Trail, which provided passage to the Northwest Coast. Immigrants, miners, wagon trains, and U.S. troops began entering the area that was a prime resource to the Indians for bison hunting. The Oglala and Hunkpapa Sioux, Northern Cheyenne, and Northern Arapaho were enraged by these transgressions. Revenge for the murders of several hundred Cheyenne people at the 1864 Sand Creek Massacre in present-day Colorado may also have played a role. At Fort Laramie in 1866 Red Cloud, along with Man Afraid of His Horses, refused to sign a non-aggression treaty and declared war on all non-Indians entering the region.

Red Cloud was the architect of a number of attacks against U.S. settlers and miners who were traveling the Bozeman and Oregon trails. The Sioux employed guerrilla-like tactics to harry soldiers and would-be settlers. In December 1866, Captain William Fetterman led a relief party of eighty-one men to their deaths after supposedly boasting, "Give me eighty men and I'll ride through the whole Sioux nation." Subsequent battles, including the Wagon Box Fight and the Hayfield Fight, led the army to evacuate the region in 1868 and then agree in the Treaty of Fort Laramie to relinquish the Bozeman Trail in exchange for the cessation of further

Indian raids. The Sioux celebrated this announcement by burning down every abandoned fort along the trail.

In 1870, Red Cloud traveled to Washington, D.C., to meet with President Ulysses Grant and then went on to New York City, where he gave a public speech. A Sioux agency bearing his name was established in present-day southern South Dakota, and Red Cloud spent the remainder of his life seeking to mediate peaceful relations between the Sioux and the United States. After government officials accused him of secretly aiding the Sioux and Cheyenne bands that defeated Colonel George Custer at the Battle of Little Bighorn in June 1876, the Red Cloud Reservation was renamed Pine Ridge, which name the reservation still bears.

Few on either side trusted Red Cloud's willingness to compromise, although he maintained that he supported peace, even during the Ghost Dance Uprising in 1890, when many Sioux sought religious solutions to reservation poverty and political confinement. During his later years, Red Cloud lost his sight, and he was baptized in the Catholic Church. He died in his home on the Pine Ridge Reservation.

Red Crow (circa 1830–1900)
Blood tribal leader

Also known as Mekaisto, Red Crow was born and raised in what is currently Alberta in the Canadian Plains. Descended from a long line of Blood chiefs, including his father, Black Bear, Red Crow continued the family tradition. The Blood people, together with the Blackfoot and Peigan nations, were part of the powerful Blackfoot Confederacy that lived on the Canadian Plains. Red Crow became a warrior in his teens, and over his lifetime participated in at least thirty-three raids against the Crow, Plains Cree, Nez Percé, Assiniboine, and Shoshoni peoples. He was known for his remarkable ability to remain unscathed and late in life boasted, "I was never struck by an enemy in my life, with bullet, arrow, axe, spear or knife."

Red Crow became leader of his people, the Fish Eaters band, when smallpox claimed the life of his father in 1869. He forged alliances with the Northwest Mounted Police and Plains Indian leaders and became the leading chief of the Blood people. During the 1870s, the buffalo were virtually destroyed by American hunters in Montana Territory, and Red Crow realized that his people would have to change their ways in order to survive. In 1880, he selected a reserve for his people and organized the construction of log shanties. He and his people turned to agriculture and cattle raising. Unlike many other Plains Indian communities, Red

Crow's people did not participate in the 1885 Northwest Rebellions, in which Louis Riel, leader of the Métis people, sought to form a provisional government in Saskatchewan against the wishes of Canadian authorities. In fact, Red Crow joined a delegation of Blackfoot chiefs on a tour of eastern Canada provided as a gesture of thanks from Canadian authorities for not participating in the rebellions. After visiting the Mohawk Institute in Brantford, Ontario, a school for Mohawk students, Red Crow became a strong supporter of education and encouraged the schooling provided by various missionaries on the reserve. Red Crow died quietly in 1900 on the banks of the river that ran through his reserve.

Valerie Red-Horse (contemporary)
Cherokee-Sioux actor, director, screenwriter, and producer

With the 1998 release of the movie *Naturally Native*, Valerie Rochelle Littlestar Red-Horse Mohl and her production company, Red-Horse Native Productions, have opened doors for aspiring Native actors, writers, producers, and directors. Not only was the movie the first to be produced by the Mashantucket Pequot Tribal

Valerie Red-Horse.

Nation, but it also starred and employed almost entirely Native Americans. *Naturally Native* explores the lives of three urban Indian women who are searching for their roots. Through this search the women start their own business, making cosmetic products from traditional Native California herbs and plants.

Valerie Red-Horse grew up in Fresno, Califorina, the daughter of an English mother and a Cherokee and Sioux father, Joseph Red-Horse. Her father was seventy when Red-Horse was born and he left when she was three years old. While Red-Horse saw her father only sporadically after that, her mother encouraged her to be proud of her heritage and raised her conscious of her background.

The to-be actress and businesswoman graduated at the top of her high school class and attended the University of California, Los Angeles (UCLA). She graduated cum laude with a major in theater. She later studied at the Lee Strasberg Theater Institute as well.

While in college she met her husband, Curt Mohl, an offensive lineman for the UCLA football team and later an NFL football player. They have worked together on several business projects, including a successful advertising specialty business and the herbal cosmetic line, recently launched on the Internet and inspired by *Naturally Native*. The couple has three children, Courtney, Derek, and Chelsea.

Red-Horse's acting career started slowly. She spent her first twenty years in the business being told she was either too ethnic for mainstream or was not ethnic enough to play Native roles. She did break into the business, however, with lead roles on *Santa Barbara, The Dennis Miller Show, Anything But Love*, and *Babylon Five*. Fed up with the opportunities provided Native Americans in film and television, Red-Horse started her own production company in the early 1990s to create films that accurately portray the Native experience. Her first screenplay, *Lozen*, based on the life of the Apache woman warrior, was selected for the Sundance Institute's Writer's Lab. In 1995 Red-Horse created the story for the Emmy-award winning CBS Special *My Indian Summer*. The next year she produced an American Film Institute project entitled *Looks Into the Night*, which won Best Live Action Short at the American Indian Film Festival.

In addition to her film-related achievements, Red-Horse organizes and funds Hollywood Access Program for Natives, a nonprofit organization that provides film production internships for students from reservations. In the last three years, the program has sponsored over a dozen students. Red-Horse also heads a liturgical dance company and was the live model promoting the

Pocahontas doll. She is an active member of the Presbyterian Church and is involved with outreach ministries and youth workshops at reservations nationwide.

While an aspiring artist, Red-Horse worked for the investment banking and high-yield bond departments of the highly successful brokerage firm Drexel, Burnham & Lambert. During this time she realized a lack of American Indian presence in the financial industry and vowed to someday change that. In 1998 she formed the first American Indian-owned stock brokerage on Wall Street, Native Nations Securities, Incorporated, and is principal owner. Besides their normal business activities, the brokerage offers a complex training program for Indian youth, providing internships and preparation for their own licensing exams.

In her years of working, Red-Horse has received many awards and honors. She was awarded the Eagle Spirit and Producer of the Year awards by the American Indian Film Festival. In addition, she was a 1997 Girls, Inc. honoree and 1998 Changing Images in America honoree. In 1999 Red-Horse received a Cherokee Medal of Honor. In 2000 Red-Horse received awards from the First Americans in the Arts for outstanding achievement in directing, writing, and producing *Naturally Native*.

Red-Horse Native Productions just signed on to executive produce *Whisper the Wind*, an upcoming studio blockbuster about the Navajo Codetalkers. This feature will be coupled by *True Whispers*, a documentary about the same subject to be directed by Red-Horse. The artist presently lives with her husband and children in the Los Angeles area.

Red Jacket (1758–1830)
Seneca tribal leader

Red Jacket supported the British during the American Revolution (1777–1783) and later became a spokesman for his people in negotiations with the U.S. government. Red Jacket was also a staunch opponent of Christianity and worked to prevent Iroquois conversions to Christianity.

Although Red Jacket eventually allied himself with other Indian nations in support of the British during the American Revolution, he was originally hesitant about the affiliation. This ambivalence perhaps explains why he did little fighting during the conflict. According to a number of accounts, Red Jacket's reluctance to fight was perceived as cowardice by some Iroquois war leaders such as Cornplanter and Joseph Brant.

After the war, Red Jacket became a principal spokesman for the Seneca people. He was present at treaty negotiations in 1794 and 1797 in which major portions of Seneca land in upstate New York were ceded or partitioned into smaller reservations. During this era, Red Jacket also became an outspoken opponent of Christianity and an advocate for preserving traditional Iroquois beliefs. His efforts to protect traditional beliefs culminated in the temporary expulsion of all Christian missionaries from Seneca territory in 1824. Red Jacket and the so-called Pagan Party were undermined in the ensuing years, however, by accusations of witchcraft and Red Jacket's own problems with alcohol. In 1827, Red Jacket was deposed as a Seneca chief. He died three years later, after his own family had converted to Christianity.

Red Jacket is immortalized in a now-famous painting by Charles Bird King. In this historical painting, Red Jacket is depicted with a large, silver medal that was given to him in 1792 by President George Washington during a diplomatic visit to the then-U.S. capital at New York City.

Kevin Red Star (1942–)
Crow-Northern Plains artist

Kevin Red Star is a Crow Indian born on the Crow Reservation in Lodge Grass, Montana. His father had an

Kevin Red Star.

abiding interest in music, and his mother is a skilled craftswoman. In this nurturing environment, Red Star developed an early artistic capability. He studied at the Institute of American Indian Art (IAIA) in Santa Fe, New Mexico, from 1962 to 1964, then at the San Francisco Art Institute, and, later, at Montana State University.

In 1965, Red Star won a scholarship to the San Francisco Art Institute. As a freshman there, he was awarded the governor's trophy and the Al and Helen Baker Award from the Scottsdale National Indian Arts Exhibition. Red Star's first one-person exhibition was in 1971 at the Museum of the Plains Indian in Browning, Montana, where he drew heavily upon his Plains Indian culture, using Crow art and design concepts to inspire his own interpretation of the life force that exists beyond the surface of decorated objects. In 1974, after having worked as an assistant art instructor at his alma mater, Lodge Grass High School, Red Star was invited to return to IAIA to participate in the artist-in-residence program and became the first graduate of IAIA to return as an artist-in-residence. While in Santa Fe, he expanded his art to include lithography, serigraphs, and etchings and was selected as Artist of the Year by *Sante Fean* magazine in 1976 and 1977.

Red Star returned to his own community to teach art and served as Crow tribal art consultant, helping to form the Crow-Cheyenne Fine-Arts Alliance to organize art exhibitions. Redstar has emerged as one of the premier Northern Plains fine artists. His latest works include exciting use of color and refined graphic design. Red Star continues to work daily, primarily in oils. With galleries all over the country, he is free to live where he chooses. Red Star's goal is to move to his native Pryor area to create a studio for monotypes and ceramics and to focus on art and music. Red Star has been recognized as being among the masters of Indian artists.

William Ronald "Bill" Reid (1920–1998)
Haida sculptor

Bill Reid was a renowned Haida sculptor, known around the world for his monumental sculptures of Haida life. He was born in Vancouver, British Columbia, in 1920 to a Haida mother and a Scottish-American father and was unaware of his indigenous background until he was a teenager. It was only in the 1950s, after studying jewelry and engraving in Toronto and working as a broadcaster for the Canadian Broadcasting Company, that Reid began to explore Haida art and sculpture in earnest. He continued with his artistic education, studying at the Central School of Art and Design in London, England. He eventually returned to British Columbia where he quickly became known as an accomplished expert on Haida art, while simultaneously transforming the tradition to include his work. Perhaps his best known piece is a four-and-a-half ton cedar sculpture on display in the University of British Columbia School of Anthropology entitled *Raven and the First Humans*. It depicts an enormous raven perched on top of a half-open seashell from which human beings are peering out at the world. Other noteworthy works include a bronze killer-whale sculpture entitled *The Chief of the Undersea World* on display at the Vancouver Aquarium. Reid is accomplished in a number of media and has illustrated and collaborated on a number of books. He was awarded an honorary doctorate from the University of British Columbia in 1976. Prior to his death in 1998, Reid was involved in efforts to preserve South Moresby Island, located in the Queen Charlotte Islands off the coast of British Columbia, from economic development and the logging industry.

Ben Reifel (1906–1990)
Dakota-Brule U.S. congressman

Ben Reifel's mother was a Sioux, and his father a German-American. As a young man, Reifel had to fight for his education; his father wanted him to remain on the family farm. Reifel left his family and eventually received a high school diploma. He went on to earn a bachelor's degree and a master of science degree from South Dakota State College. He later became one of the first Native Americans to obtain a doctorate degree from Harvard University. Reifel entered public service after active duty in the U.S. Army during World War II where he was commissioned a second lieutenant. After the war Reifel entered the Indian Service where he worked to establish and organize Indian businesses as legislated by the Indian Reorganization Act of 1932. From that post, Reifel was promoted to superintendent of the Pine Ridge Reservation in southern South Dakota. He was the first Sioux Indian to hold that position, the highest Bureau of Indian Affairs administrative post on an Indian reservation.

In 1960, Reifel was elected to the U.S. House of Representatives and was reelected for five consecutive terms in races that demonstrated a growing popularity with voters. As a representative, Reifel served on the Appropriations Committee, Interior and Related Agencies Subcommittee, Legislative Subcommittee, and was a ranking minority member. Reifel's effectiveness as a legislator was certainly aided by his own research and data collection on the land and people living in the Plains area.

Carter Revard.

Carter Revard (1931–)
Osage writer

Carter Revard is a nationally acclaimed writer whose works, drawn from traditional images of Native American culture, is combined with contemporary issues. Osage on his father's side, he was born in Pawhuska, Oklahoma. When he was two, his mother remarried and he grew up with an Osage stepfather, Addison Jump, six brothers and sisters, his Ponca aunt, Jewell McDonald, and her children, in the Buck Creek community.

The Osage people may earlier have been connected with the Cahokia Mound people of the Mississippian culture, who flourished from 800 to 1400 C.E. Before 1835, Osages dominated the Ozark region of Missouri, south of the Missouri River, but then were forced onto a reservation in southern Kansas until 1872, when they moved to present-day northeastern Oklahoma.

After graduating from Buck Creek School, he completed high school in Bartlesville, Oklahoma. He then won a radio-quiz scholarship to the University of Tulsa, graduating in 1952. The same year, he was given his Osage name by tribal elders, and with the help of a Rhodes Scholarship, he took a degree from Oxford University in 1954, and in 1959, a Ph.D. from Yale University.

After teaching at Amherst College until 1961, Revard moved to Washington University, in St. Louis, Missouri, where he taught medieval English and contemporary Native American literature until his retirement in 1997. He has also served as member, secretary, and president of the American Indian Center of Mid-America.

Revard is a Gourd Dancer, a sacred traditional dance among the southern Plains Indians (originating among Kiowa and Comanche people).

Revard's books of poetry and prose include *War Dancers: An Eagle Nation*, which won an Oklahoma Book Award in 1984, and *Winning the Dust Bowl*. Revard's writings have also been published in several anthologies of Native American writing, including *Earth Power Coming, The Remembered Earth, Voices of the Rainbow, Voices of Wahkontah, Native American Literature, Returning the Gift, Norton Anthology of Poetry,* and *Nothing But The Truth: An Anthology of Native American Literatures.*

Everett B. Rhoades (1931–)
Kiowa physician

Everett Rhoades was the first Kiowa to obtain a medical degree and complete medical training. Though his life's work is in medicine, he is also an active member of the Kiowa Tribal Council and an advocate for his people in political and social issues.

Rhoades attended the University of Oklahoma and became chief resident in medicine at the university's medical center. After five years of active duty in the U.S. Air Force, Rhoades accepted an appointment at the University of Oklahoma Medical Center as chief of infectious diseases at the Veterans Administration Hospital and as assistant professor of medicine and microbiology. In 1970, Rhoades went to South Vietnam on a special assignment for the American Medical Association and the Agency for International Development, where he acted as consultant to the University of Saigon Medical School.

Throughout his career, Rhoades has studied Indian health issues, including the rates of infectious diseases and infant mortality among Indian people. In his addresses to Indian groups, Rhoades has been critical of welfare-providing agencies in the Indian community, and he argues that Indian communities must assume responsibility for their health.

Rhoades is a member of the National Congress of American Indians health committee and an advisor on long-range planning for the Indian Health Service. Rhoades is currently clinical professor and associate dean for community affairs in the Department of Medicine at Oklahoma University Health Science Center in Oklahoma City.

John Rollin Ridge (1827–1867)
Cherokee journalist and author

John Rollin Ridge was the son of John Ridge (1803–1839) and the grandson of Major Ridge (1771–1839), both Cherokee leaders who favored Cherokee removal from Georgia in the 1830s. Both Ridges were assassinated in 1839, in part because they led the Treaty Party, a group of economically well-off Cherokee slaveholders, merchants, and plantation owners who agreed to migrate west to present-day Oklahoma by signing the Treaty of New Echota in 1835. Most Cherokee were not in favor of removal to the West, and many conservative Cherokee blamed the elder Ridges and other Treaty Party leaders for the deaths of their relatives during the Trail of Tears (1838–1839), when the U.S. Army forced most Cherokee to migrate from the East to present-day Oklahoma.

John Rollin Ridge grew up in the ensuing internal political disturbances among the Cherokee. In 1849, he killed a member of the conservative anti-Treaty Party and was forced to flee for his life. He traveled to California and worked as a newspaper editor and author. Ridge often wrote in defense of the political rights of the Cherokee, Creek, and Choctaw. Although California Indians of his day were suffering greatly from political oppression and even genocide, Ridge did not take up a consistent defense of the California tribes. In 1854, he published *The Life and Times of Joaquin Murieta, the Celebrated Californian Bandit*, which was a romantic and probably fictitious story about a Spanish-American bandit who raided the American gold fields. The book on Murieta became his most famous work and is well known in Mexican and Chilean literature. Ridge lived a lively but short life, and left a legacy of writings in politics, fiction, and poetry.

Major Ridge (1771–1839)
Cherokee tribal leader

In his younger days, Major Ridge went by his Cherokee name, Nunna Hidihi (He Who Stands on the Mountaintop and Sees Clearly), a name of great respect for a man who showed wisdom and understanding in the Cherokee councils. As a young man, Ridge fought as a warrior in the numerous border wars with U.S. settlers until the peace emerged about 1795. Thereafter, Ridge and a small group of Cherokee leaders

decided that agriculture and political change were the only means of ensuring Cherokee national survival from U.S. pressures for land cessions. Between 1797 and 1810, Ridge was a leading advocate for abolishment of the law of blood, the rule that clans exacted a death for a death in cases of murder. During the Creek War of 1813–1814, many Cherokee fought with the U.S. Army and lower town Creek villages. Ridge rose to the rank of major, and thereafter was called Major Ridge.

Between 1810 and 1828, the Cherokee incrementally formed a constitutional government, modeled after the U.S. government. The new Cherokee government instigated strong efforts by surrounding state governments to resettle the Cherokee west of the Mississippi River, because they feared the Cherokee might remain permanently in their eastern homeland. In 1835, Ridge and a minority group of Cherokee planters signed the Treaty of New Echota, thereby agreeing to migrate to present-day Oklahoma. The treaty signers feared that remaining in the east was impossible because American settlers were confiscating Cherokee property and the Cherokee government was outlawed. Many conservative Cherokee considered Major Ridge and the others traitors for signing the treaty and were embittered by the significant loss of life during the ensuing forced removal, the Trail of Tears, during the winter of 1838–1839. Major Ridge and several others were assassinated in 1839.

Louis David Riel Jr. (1844–1885)
Métis leader

Louis Riel was a leader of the Métis people. He led what have become known as the Northwest Rebellions of 1870 and 1885. Riel was born to a French-Ojibwa father, Louis Riel Sr., a political leader in his own right, and a French mother, Julie Lagimodiere, in the Red River Settlement in what is now Manitoba. He began his education in St. Boniface, Manitoba, and went on to study languages, philosophy, mathematics, and the sciences in a Montreal seminary, and then went on to study law.

After traveling throughout the United States, he returned to the Red River in 1868 and became involved in the first Northwest Rebellion, in which he and his followers drove away federal surveyors planning to section off the territory into townships contrary to Métis patterns of landholding that divided the land into strips extending out from the river. A group of Canadians responded with an attempt to organize a militia, but Riel formed his own "Comité National des Métis," peacefully seized Fort Garry in Winnipeg, took numerous prisoners, and declared a provisional government in 1869. After declaring an amnesty of all prisoners, his government re-arrested one William Scott, who had plotted an attack on Fort Garry. Scott was found guilty and sentenced to death. When Riel supported the verdict, sentiment against him in the rest of Canada hardened. Riel fled to the United States shortly after his government reached an agreement with Canada to create the province of Manitoba. Riel was elected twice in absentia to the Canadian Parliament, returning once to claim his seat only to be evicted by a motion of the House of Commons. Shortly thereafter he suffered a nervous breakdown and was admitted for a short time to a mental institution. Released in 1878, Riel moved to Montana where he became an American citizen, married, and worked as a schoolteacher. He returned to Canada to help lead Métis resistance to the settlement of Saskatchewan in 1884, seizing a local church and again establishing a provisional government. He surrendered two months later, and was convicted of treason and executed in Regina, Saskatchewan, in 1885.

Lynn Riggs (1899–1954)
Cherokee playwright and poet

Lynn Riggs was born on 31 August 1899 in Indian Territory, near present-day Claremore, Oklahoma. Following the death of his mother, Rosa Ella Duncan Riggs, when he was two, Riggs lived with his father and stepmother before spending the majority of his youth with his aunt, Mary Riggs Brice.

In 1917, he graduated from Eastern University Preparatory School in Claremore, Oklahoma, and moved to Chicago and later New York, where he worked as a movie extra and began his interest in theatre. He also lived in Tulsa, Oklahoma, and Los Angeles, California, before returning to Oklahoma. Riggs attended the University of Oklahoma from 1920 to 1923, serving as poetry editor of the *University of Oklahoma Magazine*.

He authored more than twenty plays and numerous poems. His first play, *Cukoo*, was produced at the University of Oklahoma, in 1922. His play, *Green Grow the Lilacs*, was produced by the Theatre Guild and, in 1931, was a success in New York. Rodgers and Hammerstein later adapted the play for the classic musical, *Oklahoma!*

Other works by Riggs include *The Cherokee Night*, *Knives from Syria*, *Sump'n Like Wings*, *Big Lake*, *All the Way Home*, *Roadside*, *Out of Dust*, *A Lantern to See By*, *Russet Mantle*, and *The Cream in the Well*. *The Cherokee Night*, which addresses early-twentieth century Cherokee identity, is still considered a groundbreaking play in the field of Native American drama.

He worked as a writer throughout the rest of his life, living mostly in Santa Fe, New Mexico, and New York, and was inducted into the Oklahoma Hall of Fame in 1948.

Rebecca Robbins (1951–)
Standing Rock Sioux educator

Rebecca Robbins is president of Robbins Enterprises, Inc., and a specialist in the field of Native American education. She is also an assessment team member for the Ford Foundation's Rural Community College Initiative, a cluster evaluation team member (ORBIS Associates) for W. K. Kellogg Foundation's Native American Higher Education Initiative, and, in 1999, an evaluation team member for the David and Lucile Packard Foundation's Tribal Scholars Program.

She earned her B.A. in elementary education/library science at Arizona State University (1975), her master of education in educational administration at Pennsylvania State University (1978), and her doctorate in education theory and policy/speech communication at Pennsylvania State University (1983).

She has held academic positions in the Pennsylvania State Native American Graduate Program, was director

Rebecca Robbins.

of the National Indian Education Association (NIEA) education research projects, and taught and served as director of the American Indian Leadership Program at Arizona State University. Robbins served on the ERIC/CRESS All-Indian Task Force from 1976 to 1981, and the ERIC/CRESS National Advisory Board from 1976 to 1980. ERIC/CRESS is an organization that provides a national information service to teachers and researchers about issues in educational research and practice. Robbins has also served as an advisor and participant on many special education commissions and committees for the state of Minnesota and for the federal government, such as the National Conference for Inclusion of Minority Women and the Commission on Status of Women, which meets in Washington, D.C.

In addition to publishing numerous essays and articles, Robbins has edited eight semi-annual issues of the National Education Association's refereed journal of higher education, *Thought and Action*; written and edited forty-six issues of the National Education Association's newsletter, *The NEA Advocate for Higher Education*; and edited five issues of the National Education Association's annual *NEA Almanac of Higher Education*.

Rose Robinson (1932–1995)
Hopi journalist

Rose Robinson made vital contributions in the areas of Indian communications and journalism. A member of the Butterfly Clan, Robinson was born in Winslow, Arizona, and earned degrees from the Haskell Institute and the American University (journalism studies). She was a founding board member and former executive director of the American Indian Press Association, which is currently known as the Native American Journalist Association.

Robinson served as a member of the Indian Arts and Crafts Board of the U.S. Department of the Interior (1963–1968); information officer in the Office of Public Instruction, Bureau of Indian Affairs (1972–1975); assistant director, Bicentennial Program, Bureau of Indian Affairs (1975–1976); vice president and director, American Indian Program, Phelps-Stokes Fund, Washington, D.C. (1976–1986); and director of the Commission for Multicultural Ministries, Native American Program in Chicago (1987).

Robinson has also taken leadership roles with the National Congress of American Indians, the North American Indian Womens' Association, and was the BIA liaison for coordinating the first Indian women's conference in 1970. She also oversaw the publication of periodicals for the Native American-Philanthropic News Service, which issues publications such as the quarterly magazine *The Exchange, The Roundup*, and *D.C. Directory of Native American Federal and Private Programs*.

She was named Indian Media Woman of the Year in 1981 and served on numerous boards, including the National Indian Lutheran Board, the National Indian Education Association, the American Indian Graduate Program, and the National Committee on Indian Work for the Episcopal Church, U.S.A., and its subcommittee on economics and justice.

Viola Marie Robinson (1936–)
Micmaq tribal leader

Viola Robinson has been a strong advocate for the rights of indigenous peoples, especially non-status Indians. The daughter of Micmaq herbal apothecary Frank Cope, she attended elementary school at the Micmaq Indian Day School on the Micmaq Indian Reserve in Shubenacadie, Nova Scotia. She went on to study at Sacred Heart Academy, a convent in Meteghan near Digby, Nova Scotia. When she was thirteen, Robinson's mother died suddenly, and she went to live with her grandfather. She then studied commercial secretarial courses at the Maritime Business College in Halifax, Nova Scotia—courses that helped her to become self-sufficient in her working life.

Robinson married early, at the age of sixteen, and had four of her six children by the time she was twenty-two years old. Although full Micmaqs, she and her husband were not recognized as "Indians" by the federal law and thus lived off the reserves. In early November 1974, Robinson was visited by a Micmaq woman named Catherine Brown who was organizing a grassroots effort to change the law governing Indian status in Canada. Robinson decided to attend a meeting on the subject convened by a group of similarly situated Indian people, where she spoke out on discrimination that she had faced as a "non-status" Indian. The meeting became the founding meeting of the Non-Status Indian and Métis Association of Nova Scotia, an organization that later changed its name to the Native Council of Nova Scotia. Robinson subsequently served as president of the council for fifteen years. Throughout this period she was synonymous with advocacy for the rights of non-status Indian people in Nova Scotia and across Canada. Over the years, she has initiated countless community-based efforts at improving the social and economic conditions of indigenous people in Canada. In 1991, Robinson was appointed commissioner of the Royal Commission on Aboriginal Peoples, which was established by the Canadian government to inquire into and report on all aspects of the lives of aboriginal peoples. She has also served as president of the Congress of Aboriginal Peoples and president of the Native Council of Canada.

Howard Rock (1911–1976)
Inupiat activist and editor

Howard was born at the Inupiat (Eskimo) village of Point Hope in northeastern Alaska. As a boy he attended Bureau of Indian Affairs boarding schools, often traveling long distances from home. In the mid-1930s, he attended the University of Washington, Seattle. During the 1940s and 1950s, he worked as an artist, producing work with Inuit cultural themes, much of his work was bought by tourists. Rock was not happy with his life or work as an artist. In the early 1960s he returned to Point Hope, in search of some direction to his life within traditional Inuit culture.

In the late 1950s and early 1960s, the U.S. government was planning to use an atomic bomb to create a harbor near Point Hope. This project was billed as a peace time use of atomic energy. The Inuit people in the area, however, hunted sea mammals like whales and seals, which would be exposed to serious radiation from exploding an atomic device. Since Rock had some writing skills, the village elders of Point Hope commandeered him to join in the protest movement called Inupiat Paitot, or The People's Heritage. In order to publicize the issue and to gather Native Alaskan and other supporters, the Inupiat Paitot created a newsletter and Rock became the editor. This newsletter became the means of publicizing Inuit and other Native issues and in 1962, it became the Native newspaper *The Tundra Times*. At first *The Tundra Times* was published at Fairbanks, Alaska, but it soon moved to Anchorage, the largest urban center in Alaska. Rock was the first editor and served from 1962 until his death in 1976.

After successfully preventing the use of atomic explosives at Point Hope, the Alaska Natives were confronted with a series of other issues such as protection of their right to hunt game and the prevention of the Rampart Dam, which threatened to flood large areas of Athabaskan hunting land in central Alaska. Perhaps the most important issue was the claim of the state of Alaska of about ninety million acres of Native land. Between 1961 and 1965, Alaska Natives tried to mobilize and protect their land. Through *The Tundra Times*, Howard Rock wrote editorials, printed articles, actively brought Native issues to the press, and helped Native villages and regional organizations form protests. In 1965, he helped organize the first Alaska Federated Natives (AFN) meeting in Anchorage. The

AFN was a state-wide Native organization that represented the land, political, and social welfare issues of Alaska Natives. From 1965 to 1971, the AFN lobbied Congress for a solution to Native land issues in Alaska, and in 1971 helped gain passage of the Alaska Native Claims Settlement Act (ANCSA), which provided 44 million acres of land and $962.5 million to the Alaska Natives in return for surrendering claims to about 250 million acres.

Rock published articles on Native culture, history, Native land claims, and social and welfare issues, and wrote many commentaries about the events leading up to passage of the ANCSA. *The Tundra Times* became revered as a representative of the Alaska Native communities, and Rock was honored throughout Alaska for his tireless and selfless contributions toward solving Native issues.

Paul Albert Roessler (1920–)
Navajo economist

Paul Roessler in an international economic consultant who has done extensive work for the U.S. government.

He was born in Buckman, New Mexico, earned a bachelor of arts degree in foreign service from Georgetown University, and did post-graduate work at the University of Maryland. During his military service in World War II (1941–1945), Roessler was awarded a Purple Heart with cluster, a Philippine Defense Medal, a Philippine Liberation Medal, and a Philippine Presidential Unit Citation with two clusters. Roessler served in some of the most significant military campaigns against Japan in the Pacific theater.

From 1949 to 1951, he worked as a field representative for the War Claims Commission in Washington, D.C., and from 1951 to 1952 he was a legislative analyst for the Foreign Claims Settlement Commission. He worked in the Foreign Service as Philippine Liaison officer in 1952 and as assistant atomic energy attaché to Japan from 1957 to 1961. From 1963 to 1965, Roessler was the associate program director of the National Science Foundation (NSF) in Washington, D.C. The NSF is a major backer of scientific projects in the United States. Roessler worked for the U.S. Army as an international economist from 1965 to 1975, then he was appointed chief of the Division of Economic Development in the Office of Policy Planning. In 1980, Roessler began working for the Bureau of Indian Affairs (BIA) and also became president of American Economic Consultants, Inc. He is a member of the National Economists Club, the Society of Government Economists, and the American Political Science Association.

William Rogers (1879–1935)
Cherokee entertainer

Will Penn Adair Rogers was a cowboy, writer, actor, entertainer, and unique humorist who became widely famous during the Great Depression of the 1930s for his witty, homespun commentaries. He was born near Oolagah, Indian Territory (now Claremore, Oklahoma) on 4 November 1879 of parents who were prominent mixed-blood Cherokee ranchers.

Rogers grew up in the saddle, enjoying the freedom of roping and riding on the range. He attended four schools on the Cherokee Reservation but was never more than an average student. He was a cowboy in Texas in 1898 and went to Argentina to work as a gaucho at the age of twenty-three. Several months later, he joined his first traveling company in South Africa, Texas Jack's Wild West Show, and toured Australia, New Zealand, and the United States as "The Cherokee Kid." Between his trick riding stunts, he developed the witty, engaging patter with audiences that became the hallmark of his performances.

Rogers's popularity increased when he attracted media attention in the 1920s. He published widely read books, including *The Peace Conference* and *Rogerisms—the Cowboy Philosopher on Prohibition* (1919), *Illiterate Digest* (1924), and the posthumous *Autobiography* (1949). He participated in lecture tours, radio broadcasts, and at least fifteen motion pictures. He wrote nearly three thousand "daily telegrams," over one thousand newspaper articles, fifty-eight magazine pieces, and published hundreds of various other items. He also raised a great deal of money for victims of a hurricane in Florida, floods in Mississippi, a drought in the Southwest, and an earthquake in Nicaragua, among other numerous benefits.

Rogers was killed along with pilot Wiley Post in a plane crash near Point Barrow, Alaska, on 15 August 1935. His family ranch in Oklahoma and his own ranch near Santa Monica, California, were both designated state parks in his honor.

Roman Nose (1830–1868)
Southern Cheyenne tribal leader

Roman Nose was a leader of Indian warriors and a member of the Crooked Lance Society of the Cheyenne Indian tribe. During the wars of the 1860s, he became a prominent warrior and because of his bravery in battle earned the respect of a war chief.

Roman Nose fought in the Battle of the Platte Bridge in July 1865 during the Bozeman Trail dispute in present-day Wyoming and Montana. In 1866, Roman Nose fought alongside the Southern Cheyenne Dog Soldiers military society. In 1867, he was present at the Fort Larned Council with General Winfield Scott Hancock. Roman Nose declared to members of the Dog Soldiers that he intended to kill Hancock, but was prevented from doing so by Tall Bull and Bull Bear.

Roman Nose attended the preliminary meetings preparing for the Medicine Lodge Council of October 1867 but did not participate in the council itself or the signing of the Medicine Lodge Treaty. During 1867, he and the Dog Soldiers carried out numerous raids along the Kansas frontier, focusing on wagon trains and railroad work parties. In August 1867, he and his warriors defeated the U.S. Cavalry at the battle of Prairie Dog Creek in Kansas.

Roman Nose was killed in September 1868 in an engagement known by non-Indians as the Battle of Beecher's Island in present-day Kansas and to Indian people as the Fight When Roman Nose Was Killed. Major George Forsyth and his troops had prepared for battle by digging themselves in on Beecher's Island, and during an afternoon charge, Roman Nose was shot. He died later that day. According to Cheyenne tradition, Roman Nose's "medicine" had been broken either when his feathered war bonnet was touched by a woman or when he ate food prepared with metal utensils.

Juan de Jesus Romero (Deer Bird) (1874–1978)
Taos tribal and spiritual leader

If there was one cause in life for which Juan de Jesus Romero fought, it was the return of the sacred Blue Lake (Maxolo) to the Taos Pueblo. He was hereditary *cacique* or headman of Taos Pueblo as well as its spiritual leader.

As early as 1906, Romero began a personal campaign for the return of the ancestral lands surrounding Blue Lake that the U.S. government had expropriated from the Taos Indians. Romero met with little success in this endeavor, but vowed to keep up pressure on the government. The Taos believe that Blue Lake, in present-day eastern New Mexico, is a sacred site where the world was created and, therefore, has great religious and symbolic significance in Taos Pueblo culture. Ceremonies acknowledging the creation of the world and of man were annually celebrated by the Taos community at Blue Lake. Forty-five years passed before the tribe filed a lawsuit against the government for the area including the lake and the land. In 1965, the Taos were awarded cash compensation in lieu of their claims, but this was rejected by them in favor of their original claim.

Romero was adamant that the lake be returned, and he traveled to Washington, D.C., in 1970 to plead his case before President Richard M. Nixon. A motion was put before the U.S. Senate and passed, with seventy senators for and twelve against the return of Blue Lake to the Taos along with 48,000 acres of surrounding land. Nixon signed the bill in 1971, and Blue Lake was again within the Taos domain. For his lifelong efforts in the fight for Blue Lake, Romero won the prestigious Indian Council Fire Award in 1974.

Wendy Rose (1948–)
Hopi and Miwok poet

Wendy Rose is the coordinator of American Indian Studies at Fresno City College, where she is also a full-time instructor. Rose is a poet whose work explores the conditions of Native Americans in modern urban society. Several collections of her poetry are published, and she teaches at the Fresno City College where she is also affiliated with the American Indian Studies Program.

Rose was born in Oakland, California, and descends from Hopi and Miwok parentage. She studied at Contra Costa College and the University of California at Berkeley. Growing up in a large city influenced her later writings, which focus on the experiences of urban Indians in America. Rose also confronts in her writing the "hybrid" nature of her heritage and culture. She states: "The poetry, too, is hybrid—like me, there are elements of Indian-ness, of English-ness, of mythology, and of horse-ness." Besides writing and teaching, Rose has been active in a number of Indian organizations, and served as editor for the *American Indian Quarterly*, a scholarly journal in Indian studies.

Published works by Rose include *Hopi Roadrunner Dancing* (1973); *Long Division: A Tribal History* (1976); *Academic Squaw: Reports to the World from the Ivory Tower* (1977); *Builder Kachina: A Home-Going Cycle* (1979); *Lost Copper* (1980); *What Happened When the Hopi Hit New York* (1982); *The Halfbreed Chronicles and Other Poems* (1985); *Going to War With All My Relations* (1993); *Now Poof She Is Gone* (1994); and *Bone Dance: New and Selected Poems, 1965–1992* (1994).

John Ross (1790–1866)
Cherokee tribal leader

John Ross was probably only one-eighth Cherokee and spoke halting Cherokee, yet he led the Cherokee Nation as principal chief from 1828 to 1866. His father was a Scottish trader, who married a part-Cherokee woman. For his early education, Ross's parents hired private teachers, and he later attended school in Kingston, Tennessee. While a young man, Ross became

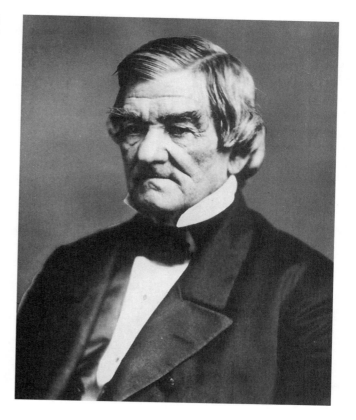

John Ross.

a successful merchant and plantation-slave owner. He strongly advocated agricultural and political change for the Cherokee as a means to preserve the nation from U.S. demands for cessions of land and for Cherokee migration west of the Mississippi River. In 1811 he was appointed to the standing committee, which met to transact Cherokee government business while the national council, composed of about fifty village headmen, was not in session.

During the 1820s, the Cherokee incrementally adopted a constitutional government and became an agricultural nation. During much of the 1820s, Ross served as secretary to the Cherokee principal chief, Path Killer, who was greatly influential among the conservatives, who constituted a large majority within the nation. Most conservatives preferred to remain in their eastern homeland and declined U.S. pressures to migrate west. After Path Killer's death in 1827 Ross inherited his great influence among the conservatives. In 1828 he served as chairman of the Cherokee Constitutional Convention and was elected principal chief by the Cherokee National Council. Between 1828 and 1866, Ross led the Cherokee conservatives, who formed the National party. The conservative majority consistently reelected Ross as principal chief, and in return he worked to preserve

Cherokee national and territorial independence from U.S. encroachments.

Mary G. Ross (1908–)
Cherokee engineer

Mary Ross is an important aeronautical engineer, philanthropist, and philologist of Cherokee culture and history. She was born in Oklahoma, and her great-great grandfather, John Ross, was principal chief of the Cherokee Nation between 1828 and 1866. Ross graduated from high school at the age of sixteen, received a bachelor of arts degree from Northeastern State Teachers College in Tahlequah, Oklahoma (1928), and a master's degree in mathematics from Colorado State University (1938).

Ross taught science and mathematics for eight years and was girls' advisor at a Pueblo and Navajo coed school becoming a researcher for Lockheed, a large aerospace company, in 1942. At first, she worked under a mathematician solving differential motion equations for fighter and transport aircraft. Supervisors decided that she should become an engineer, and she took further classes in mechanical and aeronautical engineering from UCLA. In 1949, Ross became a registered professional engineer. From then until 1953, she worked on payloads, stress analysis, and computations involving vehicles breaking through the sound barrier.

When the company formed what would be known as the Lockheed Missiles and Space Company, Ross was chosen to be one of the first forty employees and the only female engineer in the group. She worked for five years on feasibility, performance, and evaluation research of defense and ballistic missile systems, and she also studied ocean wave pressure distribution and velocities affecting ships. She became a research specialist in 1958 and focused her attention on satellite orbital calculations and on the Agena rocket series that boosted every Apollo mission and took astronauts to the moon and back. Ross graduated to advanced systems engineer and, among other projects, worked on the Polaris reentry vehicle and engineering systems for manned space flights. She appeared on the television show *What's My Line?* and stumped the panel with her esoteric occupation. Ross retired from Lockheed in 1973, closing out her career in the field of planetary engineering of flyby space vehicles designed to explore the surfaces of Venus and Mars.

Ross's achievements in engineering were exemplary. She was a charter member of the Los Angeles section of the Society of Women Engineers (1953), and served as its national treasurer (1969–1971), national audit committee chairman (1977–1978), and as a member of the Fellowship Selection Committee (1983–1984). *The San Francisco Examiner* nominated her Peninsula Woman of the Year (1961).

Ross is also a respected historian of Cherokee legacy, and her home is filled with a collection of Native American carvings, rugs, and pottery as a remembrance of her heritage. The Mary G. Ross Award is named in her honor, and is given to outstanding Native Americans who make significant contributions to American society. Now retired, Ross promotes educational opportunities for American Indian youth.

Sacajawea (1784?–1812)
Shoshone guide

In the early 1800s, Sacajawea accompanied Meriwether Lewis and William Clark on their historical expedition from St. Louis, Missouri, to the Pacific Ocean. Sacajawea is responsible in large part for the success of the expedition, due to her navigational, diplomatic, and translating skills.

Although Sacajawea's exact date of birth is unknown, the best estimates are 1784 or 1787. She was born among the Lemhi Shoshone who lived in present-day Idaho. When she was only ten years old, a group of Hidatsa Indians kidnapped her during a raid and took her to a village near present-day Mandan, North Dakota. In 1804, she was purchased, or won, by French-Canadian fur trader Toussaint Charbonneau. When Charbonneau was hired by Lewis and Clark in 1804, he insisted that Sacajawea accompany the expedition. Sacajawea herself entertained hopes that she would be reunited with the Shoshone Nation during the trip.

Sacajawea proved to be a valuable liaison for the U.S. explorers, since she spoke a number of languages, including Shoshone and Siouan. Sacajawea translated Shoshone into Hidatsa for her husband, who would then translate again into English for the leaders of the expedition. When language barriers were insurmountable, Sacajawea communicated with others by sign language. During the expedition Sacajawea revealed to Lewis and Clark important passageways through the wilderness. She also provided the expedition with valuable information about edible plants. Besides these duties, Sacajawea performed countless services during the trip, like the time she saved the expedition's records when her boat capsized. One of the most amazing incidents during the trip was the almost miraculous reunion of Sacajawea with her brother Cameahwait in

August 1805. They met at the Three Forks of the Missouri River in present-day Montana. Cameahwait was then chief of his band. He gave the expedition horses and the use of an elderly Shoshone guide. The expedition reached the Pacific Ocean in 1805.

The strength and endurance of this amazing woman cannot be exaggerated. Just two months before the expedition left Mandan in 1805, Sacajawea gave birth to Charbonneau's child. The journals of the trip show there was no hesitation over a teenage Sacajawea carrying an infant on her back at least as far as the Rocky Mountains. Throughout the trip she carried the infant (known as Little Pomp to those on the expedition) in a cradleboard strapped to her back. Sacajawea continued to travel despite a debilitating illness that struck her midway through the trip. Besides her duties as guide and interpreter, Sacajawea was responsible for housekeeping and food preparation. However, Lewis and Clark only paid her husband.

Buffy Sainte-Marie (1942–)
Cree singer and composer

Buffy Sainte-Marie is a well-known folk singer and Academy Award-winning songwriter. Throughout her career as a recording artist, she has remained an advocate for Indian rights.

Sainte-Marie was orphaned as an infant and was raised in Massachusetts by a Micmaq couple. In college, she studied Oriental philosophy. Sainte-Marie has been playing guitar and writing songs since she was sixteen years old. In the 1960s, spurred on by the positive reaction to her singing, Sainte-Marie went to New York City, where she began singing in the numerous folk clubs in the Greenwich Village section of the city. In a short time, she was offered a recording contract with Vanguard Records.

Her song "Up Where We Belong," recorded by Joe Cocker and Jennifer Warnes for the film *An Officer and A Gentleman*, won an Academy Award in 1982.

Over the years, she had numerous hit singles, including "Universal Soldier" and "Until It's Time for You to Go." Her 1993 recording entitled *Confidence and Likely Stories*, marked a departure for the artist. The new songs included lush strings and multi-rhythmic textures that set them apart from her earlier pop and folk recordings.

Sainte-Marie has infused both her recording career and her general life with a sense of purpose relating to Indian culture and concerns, both past and present. She has contributed writings to *The Native Voice*, *Thunderbird, American Indian Horizons*, and *Boston Broadside* in the field of North American Indian music and Indian affairs. Sainte-Marie is the author of *Nokosis and the Magic Hat* (1986), a children's adventure book set on an Indian reservation.

In February 1996, Sainte-Marie released *Up Where We Belong*, a collection of new songs with new recordings of her best songs. She was also awarded the Award for Lifetime Musical Achievement by the First Americans in the Arts. She has taught at York University, Indian Federated College in Saskatchewan, Evergreen State College in Washington State, and the Institute for American Indian Arts in Santa Fe, New Mexico. Buffy Sainte-Marie is president of the Cradleboard Teaching Project, which promotes multicultural education programs to grade schools around North America.

Velma S. Salabiye (1948–1996)
Navajo librarian

Velma (Vee) Salabiye was born, raised, and educated in Arizona. She is originally from Lower Greasewood, Navajo Nation. Her education extended from kindergarten at Bellemont Hogan School, a school especially for children of parents employed at the Navajo Army Depot, to the University of Arizona, Tucson, where she earned a bachelor's degree in elementary education in 1971 and a master's degree in library science in 1974. Having earned provisional certification in special education from Northern Arizona University in 1971, she taught developmentally handicapped and emotionally disturbed Navajo children at St. Michael's School for Special Education. This school was the first of its kind established on an Indian reservation. As a librarian, Salabiye began the first planning and industrial development library for the Navajo Nation in 1975. She was a recipient of a D'Arcy McNickle fellowship from the Newberry Library Center for the History of the American Indian in 1979 and is a founding member of the American Indian Library Association, an affiliate of the American Library Association. She is acknowledged in various scholarly publications.

Salabiye served on the advisory committee for *Native Press Journal* and was an assistant editor for the *American Indian Culture and Research Journal*. Her work as a consultant included a 1991 video *The Land Is for the People*. She also was a book purchasing consultant for the UCLA bookstore. Among her published works are *American Indian Library Resources at UCLA* (1980), "Library and Information Resources" in *A Guide to Library-Based Research* (1981), and "Selection of Materials for Culturally Diverse Communities" in *Developing Library Collections for California's Emerging Majority: A Manual of Resources for Ethnic Collection Development* (1991). The 1993 edition of *Indi'n Humor: Bicultural Play in Native America* by Kenneth Lincoln includes her "Humor and Joking of the American Indian: A Bibliography." Salabiye was also a contributor to the first edition of this volume.

Lilly Salvador (1944–)
Acoma Pueblo potter

Lilly Salvador is a nationally acclaimed potter and founder of the first pottery gallery at the Acoma Pueblo, New Mexico, which she hopes to develop and expand into a major southwestern art center. There are nineteen Pueblo villages in eastern New Mexico, all of which continue to adhere closely to their religious and cultural traditions. Salvador's pottery is displayed in numerous museums throughout the United States.

Salvador was educated at New Mexico State University. She has traveled extensively throughout the Southwest and Northwest regions of the United States to exhibit her traditional handcrafted and hand painted Acoma Pueblo pottery and figurines. Her work is displayed at museums in Boston (Boston Museum of Fine Arts), Phoenix (Heard Museum), San Diego (Museum of Man), Los Angeles (Natural History Museum), and Boulder (Whitehorse Gallery).

Salvador has won numerous awards for her work, including first, second, and third prizes from the Southwest American Indian Arts Association and first prize from the Gallup (New Mexico) Intertribal Indian Ceremonial. She is an active member within the Acoma Pueblo community and is a member of the Southwest American Indian Arts Association, the National Indian Arts and Crafts Association, and the Smithsonian Institution.

Samoset (1590–1653)
Pemaquid tribal leader

Samoset was a sachem of the Pemaquid band of Abnakis, living on Monhegan Island off the coast of present-day Maine. He greeted the Pilgrims, at Plymouth, in present-day Massachusetts, in English (which he had learned from contact with traders) and became an instrumental liaison between the Pilgrims and the Indians.

Samoset and Squanto, the Wampanoag Indian who had been taken to England as a slave arranged a meeting between the colonists and Massasoit, grand sachem of the Wampanoag Confederacy, an alliance of Algonkian-speaking Indians in present-day New England. Squanto, who had returned to North America in 1619, also spoke English, and he and Samoset helped negotiate the first peace treaty with the Wampanoag chief Massasoit in 1621.

In 1625, Samoset signed the first land deed in America, ceding close to twelve thousand acres of Pemaquid lands to John Brown of New Harbor, Maine. In 1653, he sold an additional one-thousand acres to the Englishmen William Parnell, Thomas Way, and William England. Samoset died later that same year.

Will Sampson (1934–1987)
Creek actor and artist

Will Sampson was a widely known American Indian actor when he died in 1987. He received high acclaim for his portrayal of an Indian chief feigning muteness in the film, *One Flew over the Cuckoo's Nest* (1975, directed by Jan Kadar).

Sampson was born and raised in Oklahoma. He came to acting late in life. After stints as a cowboy, forest ranger, and professional artist, he received an opportunity that would change his life. A friend of Sampson who was a rodeo announcer had been asked by a member of producer Michael Douglas's staff to keep his eye out for a "large" Indian. Sampson, who was six feet seven inches tall, was found and subsequently hired for the part in *One Flew over the Cuckoo's Nest*. The film, based on a novel by Ken Kesey, won five Academy Awards and critical praise for Sampson's portrayal of Chief Bromden. Sampson was nominated for an Academy Award as best supporting actor, and his acting career was launched.

Sampson went on to act in a number of films, including *The Outlaw Josey Wales*, *White Buffalo*, *Buffalo Bill and the Indians*, *Old Fish Hawk* (in which he had the title role), *Orca*, and *Fighting Back*. In 1982, he was awarded best narration honors by the Alberta, Canada, film commission for his work on *Spirit of the Hunt*, a major Canadian film. Sampson also joined the American Indian Theater Company of Oklahoma and took on the role of Red Cloud in the production of *Black Elk Speaks*.

Sampson said that he studied acting the way he prepared for his paintings of cowboys, Indians, and western landscapes. "I research thoroughly," said Sampson, who did not accept the *Cuckoo's Nest* role until he had read the book. "I've done paintings of the all the great Indian chiefs and I studied everything about them." His art work has been featured in numerous shows, exhibitions, and galleries.

Joe S. Sando (1923–)
Jemez Pueblo educator

Educator Joe Sando is director of the Institute for Pueblo Indian Studies and Research at the Indian Pueblo Cultural Center, in Albuquerque, New Mexico. He was born at Jemez Pueblo, New Mexico, on 1 August 1923, educated at Santa Fe Indian School, received a bachelor of arts degree from Eastern New Mexico University, and studied audiology as a graduate student at Vanderbilt University.

As a young man, Sando was too small to play football and basketball, games he dearly loved. His English was limited, and this drawback motivated him to devote his life to education. He enlisted in the navy at the onset of World War II (1941–1945) and took part in the invasion of the Gilbert and Marianas islands in the Pacific campaign against the Japanese Empire. He worked as a counselor in government Indian schools before becoming an audiologist and speech pathologist in Albuquerque, New Mexico. While there, he worked with many air force test pilots and future astronauts. He also traveled to New Zealand, in 1969, under an exchange program funded by the Ford Foundation.

Joe Sando inaugurated the first All-Indian Track Meet at Jemez Pueblo. He is former chairman of the All-Indian Pueblo Housing Authority, past chairman of the New Mexico Judicial Council, and once chaired the Educational Committee of the All-Indian Pueblo Council. He has served on the boards of Americans for Indian Opportunity and the Northern New Mexico Economic Development District.

He has taught at the Institute of American Indian Arts, International Universities, and he has lectured in West Germany, Spain, Italy, and Brazil. His publications include *Pueblo Indian Biographies*, *The Pueblo Indians*, and *Popé*.

Greg Sarris (contemporary)
Miwok-Pomo-Filipino-Jewish author, professor, and chief of the Coast Miwok Nation

A full professor of English at the University of California, Los Angeles, Greg Sarris is the author of several fiction and non-fiction books, all pertaining to modern and traditional Native American life. His first

novel, *Watermelon Nights*, was published in 1998 and received acclaim across Native and non-Native North America.

Born and raised in Santa Rosa, California, Sarris's father was of Native American and Filipino decent, while his mother was Jewish. Sarris, adopted at birth, was brought up in both white and American Indian households. After attending Santa Rosa Junior College, Sarris matriculated at and graduated from the University of California, Los Angeles. He later received his Ph.D. from Stanford University in 1989.

His first book, *Keeping Slug Woman Alive: A Holistic Approach to American Indian Texts*, was published in 1993 by the University of California Press. The book is a collection of critical essays that deals with cross-cultural interpretation. Mabel McKay, a Cache Creek Pomo medicine woman, helped raise the to-be academic and artist, and in 1994 *Mabel McKay: Weaving the Dream*, the story of McKay's life, was released. Sarris describes the lauded work as a bi-autobiography in that the text also describes Sarris's life and experiences with McKay.

While both the above titles are non-fiction, Sarris has received substantial recognition for his two fictional works. *Grand Avenue*, a collection of short stories, was published in 1994, and was adapted by Sarris for an Home Box Office (HBO) mini-series, for which Sarris was executive producer (along with Robert Redford) and screenwriter. The HBO adaptation received many awards, including Best Picture and Best Screenplay from the First Americans in the Arts and Best Picture from the American Indian Film Festival. His second work of fiction, *Watermelon Nights*, continues the family saga introduced in *Grand Avenue*. In addition to these works, Sarris edited *The Sound of Rattles and Clappers: An Anthology of New California Indian Writing*, released from the University of Arizona Press in 1994. Sarris draws on the stories of his people to inform his work. He is also strongly influenced by American writers such as William Faulkner and Herman Melville.

The writer plans to expand his creative repertoire in the near future. He has been commissioned to write plays, teleplays, and a musical, all due out in the next two years. He just completed a three-hour miniseries for Showtime about a Mexican-American family in Los Angeles to be directed by Alfonso Arau, who directed *Like Water for Chocolate*. Sarris is writing a pilot and three episodes for a weekly one-hour HBO series entitled *Casino*. In addition, he is developing a musical (commissioned by Jeffrey Sellers) called *Homesong*. Other titles to look out for in the next few years include *Land of Dreams* (teleplay), *Laguna Beach Indians* (play), *The Life and Times of Latina Turner* (play), and *Seagulls* (play).

While creative work demands much of Sarris's time, he also is the chief of the Federated Coast Miwok Tribe of northern California. In July 1998 Sarris co-authored and introduced a bill to Congress that would restore his tribe's land to trust status. In 2000 the tribe was recognized by the federal government.

Sassacus (1560–1637)
Pequot tribal leader

In the 1630s, Sassacus was grand sachem of the Pequot Nation, which was located in present-day Connecticut. He led the Pequot against English colonists in the Pequot War that took place in 1636 and 1637.

When English settlers first arrived in New England, the Pequot Indians were consolidating and conquering their weaker Indian neighbors under the strong and ambitious leadership of Sassacus, who became grand sachem in 1632. Under Sassacus's leadership the Pequot domain had grown to include most of present-day Connecticut and Long Island. For a while, Sassacus skillfully played English and Dutch traders against one another, but eventually the Pequot's power became too much of a threat to the growing settler population.

The Pequot Indians living in the Connecticut River Valley were among the first of the New England tribes to resist the growing English presence on their lands. In 1936, English soldiers attacked the Pequot Nation in retaliation for the murders of two traders, John Stone and John Oldham, although it is not clear that the perpetrators were Pequot. For two years after Stone's death in 1633, a precarious peace had been maintained in the area. The death of Oldham, however, in 1636 resulted in a coordinated offensive on the behalf of the settlers against the Pequot. Acting at the behest of Massachusetts Bay officials, Captain John Endecott, with a force of about ninety men, attacked a number of Indian villages on Block Island, which was located off the southern coast of present-day Rhode Island. Although the villages there belonged to the Narragansett Nation, who were not connected with the killings of English traders, this seemed not to matter to the English forces sent there. Endecott then marched to the Connecticut mainland seeking out Pequot to demand reparations. After a minor encounter in which one Indian was killed, Endecott returned to Boston, leaving the Connecticut settlers to contend with the Pequot. Sassacus laid plans for war and attacked several English settlements, including those at Fort Saybrook, located at the mouth of the Connecticut River. In 1637, a retaliatory brigade of English colonists, Narragansett warriors, and seventy Mohegan, another Algonkian nation living in present-day Connecticut, attacked a major Pequot town on the Mystic River. Sassacus and his warriors managed to repel the assault behind their well-fortified palisades until the colonists set the town on fire. It is estimated that six hundred to a thousand Pequot perished in the flames. The Plymouth governor called it a "sweet sacrifice."

Sassacus managed to escape and sought sanctuary among the Mohawk, a trade rival and enemy nation to the Mohegan. Fearful of English reprisals, the Mohawk put Sassacus to death. At the end of the so-called Pequot War, the people of the Pequot Nation dispersed. Many who were captured faced enslavement or subjugation under old enemies, but some migrated to the Ohio valley and joined the Shawnee Nation.

Satank (Sitting Bear) (1810–1871)
Kiowa tribal leader

Satank was born in the Black Hills and became a prominent war chief among the Kiowa and a leader among the Principal Dogs military society. Satank was instrumental in establishing the peace between the Kiowa and Cheyenne, thus producing a formable fighting force against the U.S. settlers on Indian lands in the southern Plains. Though respected by his tribe, his vengeful personality bred fear among even his own people.

In 1867, Satank was one of the principle spokesmen for the Kiowa at the Medicine Lodge Council. This council had been called by advocates of President Ulysses Grant's peace policy and cited the Sand Creek massacre as an example of heavy-handed military tactics. The resulting Medicine Lodge Treaty of 1867 assigned the Kiowa to a combined reservation (with the Arapaho) in Indian Territory in present-day Oklahoma. Raiding for the Kiowa was a way of life, however, and would persist, despite U.S. attempts at acculturation, Christianizing, and pacifying the Indians. Satank continued to lead these raids.

In May 1871, Satank joined Satanta and Kicking Bird, two other Kiowa leaders, in an attack on an army wagon train traveling along the Butterfield Southern Stage Route in Young County, Texas. In the ensuing battle, the Kiowa killed eight of the twelve defenders, routed the rest, and plundered the wagons.

Lured into a council by General William Tecumseh Sherman, Satank and Satanta were later arrested. En route to Fort Richardson, Texas, for trial for the wagon train murders, Satank attempted an escape from the army guards and was shot and killed. He was buried in the Fort Sill military cemetery.

Satanta (1830–1878)
Kiowa tribal leader

In the 1860s and 1870s, the Kiowa Indians waged an ongoing battle to protect their land and way of life from U.S. encroachment. Satanta, also known as White Bear, was a major Kiowa leader in favor of resistance. Besides his prowess as a warrior, Satanta was also a famed orator, attested to by his American-given nickname the Orator of the Plains.

Satanta was born on the northern Plains, but later migrated to the southern Plains with his people. His father, Red Tipi, was keeper of the tribal medicine bundles or Tai-me. Much of Satanta's adult life was spent fighting U.S. settlers and military. He participated in raids along the Santa Fe Trail in the early 1860s, and in 1866 became the leader of the Kiowa who favored military resistance against U.S. military forces. In 1867, he spoke at the Kiowa Medicine Lodge Council, an annual ceremonial gathering, where, because of his eloquent speech, U.S. observers gave him his nickname. At the council, Satanta signed a peace treaty that obligated the Kiowa to resettle on a reservation in present-day Oklahoma. Shortly thereafter, however, he was taken hostage by U.S. officials who used his imprisonment to coerce more Kiowa into resettling on their assigned reservation.

For the next couple of years, Satanta participated in a number of raids in Texas where cattle ranchers and buffalo hunters were steadily pushing Kiowa and Comanche Indians onto reservations. It was one of these raids that eventually led to Satanta's capture. In May 1871, Satanta planned an ambush along the Butterfield Stage Route on the Salt Creek Prairie. After allowing a smaller medical wagon train to pass, Satanta and his warriors attacked and confiscated the contents of a larger train of ten army freight wagons. Unfortunately for Satanta, the train he had allowed to pass was carrying General William Tecumseh Sherman, the famous Civil War general, then commander of the U.S. Army. Sherman took the attack as a sign that a more militant and coordinated offense was needed to subdue the Kiowa and Comanche, who were unwilling to settle permanently onto reservations. A short time later Satanta was lured into a peace council and then arrested and was sentenced to death. Humanitarian groups and Indian leaders protested the harsh sentence. In 1873,

Satanta was paroled on the condition he remain on the Kiowa Reservation.

In 1874, during the Comanche and United States conflict called the Red River War, Satanta presented himself to U.S. officials to prove that he was not taking part in the hostilities. His demonstration of loyalty was rewarded with imprisonment. Four years later, an ill Satanta was informed that he would never be released. He jumped to his death from the second story of a prison hospital.

Helen Maynor Scheirbeck (1935–)
Lumbee educator

Scheirbeck has devoted much of her life to children's welfare, serving on a number of human resource agencies, including the Office of Education and the Department of Health, Education, and Welfare.

Born in Lamberton, North Carolina, she was educated at Berea College in Berea, Kentucky. She went on to receive a doctorate from the Virginia Polytechnic Institute and State University in 1980, for which she wrote her dissertation, "Public Policy and Contemporary Education of the American Indian."

Scheirbeck has served on a number of important government agencies and chaired the Indian Education Task Force of the American Indian Policy Review Commission. Other positions include director of the Congressional Office of Indian Affairs; staff member of the U.S. Office of Education, within the Department of Housing, Education, and Welfare; and member of the U.S. Senate Subcommittee on Constitutional Rights. Scheirbeck also served with the Save the Children Federation in Westport, Connecticut.

Author of such works as *The History of Federal Indian Education Policy*, "Indian Education: Tool for Cultural Politics," "The First Americans," and "A Study of Three Selected Laws and Their Impact on American Indian Education," Scheirbeck has been honored with the John Hay Whitney Foundation Opportunity Award, the Outstanding Lumbee Award, and an Outstanding Indian Award. She currently works in the U.S. Department of Health and Human Services, Head Start Program, American Indian Branch, in Washington, D.C.

Fritz Scholder (1937–)
Luiseño artist

Fritz Scholder is recognized as a leading modern artist in the United States. His work often deals with themes relating to the Native American experience.

Scholder was born in Breckenridge, Minnesota. His grandmother was a member of the Luiseño tribe, although Scholder describes himself as "a non-Indian Indian." He earned his master of fine arts degree from the University of Arizona in 1964. For five years, Scholder was instructor of advanced painting and art history at the Institute of American Indian Arts.

Although Scholder's upbringing was not acutely focused on his Native American heritage, his art awakened in him a desire to explore this background. Scholder's work often combines surrealist pop imagery and Native American mysticism. The artist has frequently addressed issues facing American Indians, including alcoholism, assimilation into mainstream U.S. society, and the degradation of Native American culture. In some ways, Scholder has been controversial. His critics complain that he has not taken Native American problems seriously enough and that his pop art has reduced their culture to kitsch—popularized art with little aesthetic value. Some would like to see Scholder use his high profile as a popular artist to advance Native American causes. Scholder himself prefers to communicate through his work. He states, "I'm not at all militant. I have a way out: I can put something down on canvas or do a lithograph."

In 1980, Scholder made a promise to himself to no longer paint "Indians." The decision was based entirely on artistic grounds. In 1992, he broke that rule, for a lithograph titled *Indian Contemplating Columbus*. The forty-by-sixty-inch work is the largest ever made by Scholder. "I'm very divided about Columbus," Scholder states, "because I grew up thinking of him as a hero. When I was a boy, I didn't think about my being part-Indian. . . . But now, I can understand the other side, and now, after much more reading as an adult, I realize that Columbus's trip was the beginning of the end for many cultures." The lithograph portrays a silhouetted figure sitting in a chair, facing the corner. A brightly colored moccasin on his foot is the only clue that the figure is Indian.

Bert D. Seabourn (1931–)
Cherokee-Chickasaw painter

Bert D. Seabourn is an internationally known painter who has exhibited his works both in the United States and abroad.

Seabourn was born in Iraan, Texas. He earned a master of fine arts degree from Oklahoma City University and also attended Central State University in Edmond, Oklahoma, and the University of Oklahoma. He served in the U.S. Navy from 1951 to 1955.

Seabourn works mainly in watercolor, oil, graphics, acrylics, and drawings, and has also done some sculpture. His works are exhibited at the Heard Museum in Phoenix, Arizona; the Five Civilized Tribes Museum in Muskogee, Oklahoma; the Oklahoma Art Center in Oklahoma City, Oklahoma; Red Cloud Indian School, Pine Ridge, South Dakota; the Vatican Museum of Modern Religious Art, Rome, Italy; and the Inter-Tribal Indian Ceremonial Association, Gallup, New Mexico.

Seabourn has received many honors and awards for his work, including Best of Show award at the Oklahoma Art Guild Annual, Oklahoma City, 1966; Grand Award in acrylics at Five Civilized Tribes Museum, Muskogee, 1973; Best of Show award in watercolors at Red Cloud National Indian Art Exhibition, Pine Ridge, 1974; Governor's Award, presented by Governor George Nigh at Oklahoma state capitol, Oklahoma City, 1981; sculpture commissioned by Southwestern Bell Corporate Headquarters, Oklahoma City, 1986; and Best of Show award for Master Artist Show at Five Civilized Tribes Museum, 1988. Seabourn has also shown his work internationally in such places as Taiwan, Singapore, and Germany. He lives in Oklahoma City, Oklahoma.

Seattle (Sealth) (1788–1866)
Duwamish-Suquamish tribal leader

In the early 1800s, U.S. settlers poured into the Pacific Northwest region, leading to inevitable conflict with the Indians living there. During the first half of the nineteenth century, Sealth, a principal chief of the Duwamish people, encouraged friendship and commerce with the newcomers and avoided being drawn into the ongoing regional conflicts between settlers and Indians that were permeating the Northwest during this time.

Sealth had already witnessed the growing number of U.S. settlers moving into his homeland as a youth. In the 1830s, he was influenced by French missionaries and converted to Catholicism. Throughout the Gold Rush era of the 1850s, he maintained peace, despite the influx of miners and settlers. Sealth fostered trading relationships with the newcomers. By 1855, tensions between settlers and the other Indians in the area were mounting, and the breaking of treaty terms finally led to the Yakima War of 1855–56. Sealth chose not to fight and signed the Fort Elliot Treaty, in which he agreed to relocate his people to a reservation. Chief Sealth and his people remained allied with American forces and withstood an attack by the neighboring Nisqually Indians. He and his people later relocated to the Port Madison Reservation, near present-day Bremerton,

Washington. The city of Seattle, Washington, was named after the Duwamish chief Sealth in 1852.

Thomas Segundo (1921–1971)
Papago (Tohono O'Odham) tribal leader

When he was elected chairman of the Papago (now called Tohono O'Odham) Indian Tribal Council in 1951, Thomas Segundo became the youngest Indian chief in the United States. During his tenure, he was a staunch advocate for his people and strengthened the tribe's economic and political institutions.

Segundo was born on the Papago Reservation in southern Arizona. As a young man, the future tribal chairman left his traditional culture behind and settled in California, earning a living in the shipbuilding industry, eventually being promoted to a supervisory position. Originally, Segundo planned to continue his career in shipbuilding by obtaining a degree in engineering. In 1946, however, he returned for a vacation to his homeland on the Papago Reservation. The poverty and desolation that he found there changed the direction of his life. The Papago asked Segundo to help them improve the economic conditions on the reservation. He never returned to his job in the shipbuilding industry.

Segundo's initial efforts on the reservation were on a small scale, helping the Papago to feed their livestock more economically and developing athletic activities for Papago youth. Segundo was amazed at the range of needs demanding his attention. The Papago took notice of him and persuaded him to run for tribal chairman. He won the 1951 election by a large percentage.

Segundo worked to revive the tribal government. By taxing traders who had previously taken advantage of reservation resources, Segundo dramatically increased tribal revenue. Segundo himself was able to serve as tribal leader full time. Papago who previously had gone to U.S. government officials for help turned to Segundo. He codified Papago laws and organized a large voter registration drive on the reservation. After seven terms as tribal chairman, Segundo went to the University of Chicago for courses in law and social science. He returned to his home with hopes of implementing a long-range development plan, which had a multi-pronged focus. Acknowledging the limited potential of the arid Papago land, Segundo proposed conservation measures to increase range land for cattle ranchers and implemented irrigation programs for farmers. He believed that no matter how productive the reservation land could be made, however, one-third of the Papago people would have to find livelihoods off the reservation. He hoped to provide the training and education they needed for these careers on the "outside." Segundo also proposed the construction of boarding schools for children and expanded public health facilities. Segundo's plan was the result of a long process of evaluation that included input from the Papago people. As a result, it was endorsed nearly unanimously.

Sadly, Segundo was killed in 1971 in a plane accident. His contributions to the Papago people, however, continue to impact the Papago community.

Eugene Sekaquaptewa (1925–)
Hopi educator

Eugene Sekaquaptewa is best known for his work in the field of education. He was born on 7 July 1925 in Hotevilla, Arizona, on the Hopi Reservation. Hotevilla is the Hopi village where many of the most conservative Hopi people live. Many conservative Hopi try to preserve their ancient customs, religion, and way of government. He received his bachelor of science and master of arts degrees from Arizona State University.

Sekaquaptewa enlisted in the marines during World War II (1941–45), and survived the early morning beach assault of Iwo Jima, a volcanic island in the Pacific Ocean, within air attack distance of the Japanese mainland. He and several other U.S. marines rescued a wounded soldier from enemy fire. Besides Iwo Jima, he took part in the invasion of Saipan, Tinian, and the Marshall Islands, all of strategic significance for the U.S. war effort against Japan. After discharge from the armed forces, he served as a captain in the U.S. Air Force Reserves.

Sekaquaptewa was a Hopi Tribal Council representative, a training specialist for the Arizona State University (ASU) Indian Community Action Project and has taught education courses at ASU. He also taught at the Sherman Institute, an Indian boarding school, and was recreation director on the Navajo Reservation. Sekaquaptewa has written a number of professional papers on Hopi education and curriculum and is the author of *Coyote & the Winnowing Birds: A Traditional Hopi Tale* (1994).

Sequoyah (1770–1843)
Cherokee linguist

Sequoyah is justly celebrated for his development of the Cherokee syllabary, which is a set of symbols for each syllable sound in the language, rather than an alphabet in which symbols represent fewer but shorter sounds. Sequoyah's syllabary served the Cherokee people admirably for many decades and was the genesis of several Cherokee publications.

Sequoyah was born in Taskigi near present-day Vonore, Tennessee. His mother was Cherokee and his father a U.S. trader. Sequoyah's early life was varied. He was a skilled farmer, hunter, and trader. He also served under General Andrew Jackson in the Creek War of 1813–1814.

The Cherokee language is still spoken by approximately ten thousand Cherokee whose families were deported to Oklahoma in the 1830s and the thousand or so who remain in North Carolina. In 1809, while living in present-day Arkansas, Sequoyah began working on a written version of the Cherokee language. He recognized the importance of a written constitution and official records, and this was originally his main purpose in developing a written Cherokee language. At first he developed a pictographic version of the Cherokee language, but soon abandoned this approach in favor of syllabary of eighty-six characters representing the different syllable sounds. It took twelve years for Sequoyah to finish the project. It was a historic achievement in many ways. Despite limited proficiency in English and little in the way of formal education in writing, Sequoyah produced a workable syllabary of Cherokee characters, one of the few people in world history to singlehandedly create an entire syllabary.

Sequoyah's achievement was initially met with some skepticism by his fellow Cherokee, but after a demonstration of how the system could be used to carry messages from an Indian family in Arkansas to relatives living in the east, it was adopted with enthusiasm. The Cherokee Council sanctioned the syllabary, and in a few short months, thousands of Cherokee were reading and writing. Christian missionaries, inspired by the translation of the Bible into Cherokee, helped obtain a printing press with a Cherokee syllabary font. In 1828, the *Cherokee Phoenix*, the first Cherokee newspaper was published in both English and Cherokee. Also in 1828, the Cherokee constitution was ratified and written down. Sequoyah was invited to Washington, D.C., by the U.S. government, and his achievement was celebrated.

In subsequent years, Sequoyah continued to play an active role in politics and linguistics. In the late 1830s, as president of the Western Cherokee he sponsored the Cherokee Act of Union, which united eastern and western parts of the Cherokee nation. Before 1838, some Cherokee had migrated west as part of U.S. removal policies that encouraged eastern Indian tribes to exchange their land for territory in present-day Kansas or Oklahoma. The plan was designed to free more eastern Indian land for U.S. settlement. Most

Cherokee refused to migrate west, but in 1838–39, most were forced on the "Trail of Tears" to migrate west. For several years the late Cherokee arrivals, who were the majority, and the earlier migrants, the "Old Settlers," could not agree on a shared government. The Act of Union in July 1839 helped provide a basis for a united government.

In 1842, Sequoyah set out on an expedition to locate a lost band of Cherokee who had migrated westward during the American Revolution. He hoped to locate them by cross-referencing languages. When he failed to return from the expedition, a fellow Cherokee named Oonoleh went searching for him. Sadly, Sequoyah had died during his quest for the lost band. In perhaps the most eloquent testimony to his lifetime achievement, the news of Sequoyah's death reached his people in the form of a letter written in the syllabary he had created. Sequoyah has been honored in many ways, including the naming of a distinct genus of giant redwood trees, sequoia, found along the northern California coast.

Bill Shakespeare (1901–1975)
Northern Arapaho tribal leader

Bill Shakespeare was born in May 1901 on the Wind River Reservation in Wyoming. His father, War Bonnet, had attended Carlisle Indian Industrial School and was a strong influence on his son; he encouraged Bill to learn both Arapaho and English. As a result, Shakespeare emerged bilingual under the tutelage of his father. He was acknowledged as one of the few Arapaho who spoke "old time" Arapaho and could communicate fluently and eloquently in the Arapaho language.

Shakespeare's early school days were spent at St. Stephen's Indian Mission operated by Jesuits on the Wind River Reservation, attending intermittently from 1908–1917. In October 1917, he enrolled under the name Nestor Whiting at Haskell Institute Boarding School in Lawrence, Kansas, but attended for only two months. Shakespeare next enrolled at Genoa Boarding School in Genoa, Nebraska, in September 1918, where he attended until April 1919, at which time he left to enlist in the army.

Shakespeare returned to the reservation and throughout the next three decades made sporadic attempts to construct a role for himself in the reservation community. On the reservation he was able to use his bilingual skills as interpreter and secretary for tribal meetings. He married and at various times worked as a policeman, government herder, and interpreter. He served on the council of Arapaho leaders and frequently spoke for his tribe in dealings with federal agents, on one occasion writing to the secretary of the interior to request an investigation of financial irregularities on the part of the Indian agent assigned to the Wind River Reservation. Shakespeare was an important intermediary, serving as a communication link between tribe and agent in the days when few Arapaho spoke English.

Shakespeare was a Hollywood actor and a world traveler, and in later years he worked as an informant for anthropologists studying Arapaho language and culture. Toward the end of his life, he spoke on Indian culture and history in many schools around the country.

Joanne Shenandoah (contemporary)
Oneida actress, singer, and songwriter

Joanne Shenandoah is a woman whose art focuses sharply on issues vital to Native Americans. Her music has garnered her an international reputation as an artist with a unique vision that reflects her Oneida roots.

A wolf clan member of the Iroquois Confederacy's Oneida Nation, Shenandoah's musical roots can be traced to her parents. Both lovers of music, they insisted on providing their children (Shenandoah is one of four children) with formal music training. In fact, her father, the late Clifford Shenandoah, was an Onondaga chief and jazz guitarist. Her mother, Maisie, was a singer.

Shenandoah worked as a computer programmer in Washington, D.C. for fourteen years before devoting herself to music full time. She attributes this dramatic career change to her rediscovery of the stories and songs of her people. Since her decision to change her career's direction, she has sung with musical greats such as Willie Nelson, Robbie Robertson, and Neil Young. Her first album was released in 1989.

Many of her songs deal with vital issues in Indian Country, including the desecration of Native American graves and the treatment of American Indian leaders and activists throughout the history of colonization. In fact, she contributed to *In the Spirit of Crazy Horse*, a compilation album dedicated to the plight of activist Leonard Peltier, who was imprisoned for allegedly contributing to the murder of two FBI agents. She has recorded her music for several national and international companies, including NATO Records in France, EYE-Q Records in Germany, and Featherwind Productions, Silver Wave Records, and Canyon Records in the United States.

The singer performs tirelessly throughout the world, especially in the United States, Canada, and Europe. Recently she performed in Capetown, South Africa, at the Parliament on World Religions, and at the White House for First Lady Hillary Clinton and Tipper Gore in 1999. In addition, Shenandoah has composed and contributed to several film soundtracks, including songs from "Naturally Native," "Indian in the Cupboard," and "Dance Me Outside."

The singer's hard work has brought her multiple awards, including several Native American Music Awards, including 1998 and 1999 Best Female Artist of the Year awards. Some of her most popular albums include *Matriarch: Iroquois Women's Songs*, *Once in a Red Moon*, and *All Spirits Sing*, a children's album.

Peacemaker's Journey, released in March 2000, is an artistic journey recounting Iroquois history and myth. She lives with her husband, Doug George, and her daughter, Leah, in Oneida, New York.

Leslie Marmon Silko (1948–)
Laguna Pueblo novelist and poet

Leslie Marmon Silko is an acclaimed novelist. She is the author of the highly praised novels *Ceremony* (1977) and *Almanac of the Dead* (1991).

Silko was born in Albuquerque, New Mexico, although she spent her childhood at the Laguna Pueblo in eastern New Mexico, where she was surrounded with the culture and lore of the Laguna and Keres people. It was during these years that she learned about the traditions of Native American storytelling, principally through her grandmother and aunt. Silko received a bachelor's degree in English from the University of New Mexico, at which time she wrote her first short story, "The Man to Send Rain Clouds." Published in 1969, the story, based on an incident that had occurred at Laguna, gained Silko a National Endowment for the Humanities Discovery Grant.

Silko temporarily considered a law degree but, after three semesters, left law school to pursue a career in writing. In 1974, *Laguna Woman*, a book of poetry, was published. In 1977, *Storyteller*, a collection of short stories, and *Ceremony*, a novel, were published. *Ceremony*, the story of an inner journey that takes a young Indian back to his roots, established Silko's reputation as a leading U.S. author. This novel had crossover appeal for the larger audience of serious readers. Largely on the basis of *Ceremony*, Silko received one of twenty-one "genius" fellowships awarded by the MacArthur Foundation, which granted her a five-year annual stipend of $33,600 to pursue her writing.

In 1991, *Almanac of the Dead* was published. The seven-hundred-page novel was called by one reviewer, "the most ambitious literary undertaking of the past quarter century." The novel interweaves an apocalyptic depiction of declining Western society with sacred traditions of the Native American people. Underlying the entire work is the tragedy and anger Silko feels for the violation and humiliation Native Americans have suffered since the 1500s.

Silko believes that "our identity is formed by the stories we hear when we're growing up. Literature helps us locate ourselves in the family, the community and the whole universe." Consequently, Silko's work has the "feel" of traditional Native American storytelling, interweaving tales that she has remembered and imagined. Silko's recent writings include *Yellow Woman and a Beauty of the Spirit* (1996) and *Gardens in the Dunes* (1999).

In addition to writing, Silko has taught at the University of New Mexico, Navajo Community College, and the University of Arizona. In 1994, she was awarded the Lifetime Achievement Award of the Native Writers' Circle of the Americas, an international Native American writers' organization.

Mary Sillett (1953–)
Inuit tribal leader

Mary Sillett was born in the small town of Hopedale, Labrador. Labrador is mainland Newfoundland, on the northeastern border of the province of Quebec. Her parents, Ester and Jerry Sillett, both of Inuit ancestry, raised a large family, of which Mary was the oldest girl. She attended elementary and high school in Labrador, and then went on to receive a bachelor of social work degree from Memorial University in St. John's, Newfoundland, in 1976.

She has been involved with aboriginal issues at the regional, provincial, national, and international levels. Her career began with the Labrador Resources Advisory Council, a body created to advise the province on the impact of economic development on the Inuit.

Sillett has served numerous organizations in many capacities, including executive assistant to the president of the Labrador Inuit Association; a senior policy analyst with the Aboriginal programs of Heritage Canada; the president and executive director of the Inuit Women's Association of Canada; a commissioner on the Royal Commission of Aboriginal Peoples; and the vice-president and president of the Inuit Tapirisat of Canada (the national Inuit political organization). In 1997 Sillette was a member of the jury for the National Aboriginal Achievement Awards (NAAA).

She is currently the district social worker in Hopedale, the mother of two sons, Matthew and Martin Lougheed, and a foster parent and guardian.

Jay Silverheels (1912–1980)
Mohawk actor

Jay Silverheels is probably best known for his role as Tonto, the Lone Ranger's Indian partner, in the popular 1950s television series of the same name.

Silverheels, whose real name was Harold J. Smith, was born in Canada and came to the United States as a member of Canada's national lacrosse team in 1938. A short time later he began acting in films. His first role was as the Indian prince in *The Captain from Castille*. In 1950, he portrayed Geronimo in the movie *Broken Arrow*, which has been hailed as the first film to portray Indians in a sympathetic light. Silverheels gained his greatest notoriety, however, playing Tonto. He was actually the second actor to play the role of the Lone Ranger's sage companion. The popular series ran for eight years. Two film features were also made based on the television series, and Silverheels appeared in both.

In the middle 1960s, Silverheels founded the Indian Actors Workshop in Hollywood. He was the original director of this organization. During the same period, he worked extensively with public service projects focusing on substance abuse and the elderly. In 1979, he became the first Native American awarded a star on Hollywood's "Walk of Fame."

Konrad Haskan Sioui (1953–)
Huron tribal leader

Konrad Sioui is the chief negotiator and political advisor for the Montagnais-Innu Council of Septiles, Quebec, as well as First Nations specialist for the Senate of Canada. He was born in Wendake, a Huron village in the province of Quebec, on 16 April 1953. The fifth of seven children of Georges and Eléonore Sioui, he was raised in traditional ways by the mothers of the Sioui clan and was taught by the elders of his people. He also attended elementary school on the reserve before going on to obtain a bachelor's degree in sociology and a master's degree in administration.

Sioui served two terms as the vice-grand chief of the Huron-Wyandotte First Nation and three terms as the grand chief of the Quebec and Labrador Assembly of First Nations. When the Innu people of Labrador protested low-level flying, Sioui personally took up their cause and joined their fight for government recognition of their rights. He invited the Innu to join the Quebec Assembly of First Nations, creating a new organization in the process. Nationally, he has served as senior analyst and special advisor with the Royal Commission on Aboriginal Peoples. He was also director of international affairs for the Assembly of First Nations, and he has worked with the 1992 Nobel Peace Prize recipient Rigoberta Menchu Tum to foster ties between North and South American First Nations and to improve conditions for aboriginal people in Guatamala and Columbia.

He is perhaps best known for successfully asserting, together with three of his brothers, a treaty entered into by the British Crown and the Huron Nation in 1760 against provincial laws that curtailed the exercise of religious practices of the Huron people. In 1990, the Supreme Court of Canada held that the Huron Nation was entitled to rely on the treaty to engage in a number of protected practices. The Court's ruling supported their claim that Huron people can carry on their traditional activities on Crown Land. In 2000, Sioui received the National Aboriginal Achievement Award for public service.

Sitting Bull (1831–1890)
Hunkpapa Sioux tribal leader

Sitting Bull was a major military, spiritual, and political leader of his people in the 1800s. He was an important figure in the war for the Black Hills from 1876 to 1877 and helped to engineer the Indian victory at Little Bighorn.

Sitting Bull's military and leadership abilities became evident at an early age. At age twenty-two, he was leader of a warrior society known as the "Strong Hearts." It was probably not a coincidence that a warrior society would come into existence in the 1850s. It was during this time that U.S. settlers were sowing the seeds for a larger conflict that would force Sioux warriors like Sitting Bull into a major military confrontation.

The Hunkpapa Sioux were able to avoid the early confrontations in the 1860s. However, when Red Cloud, a major Hunkpapa Sioux leader, negotiated the Fort Laramie Treaty of 1868, Sitting Bull chose not to abide by its territorial provisions, which would have restricted his ability to hunt and travel. Sitting Bull's adherence to traditional ways of life had made him a spiritual as well as military leader among his people. In 1874, gold was discovered in the Black Hills, and the subsequent illegal incursions by U.S. miners created tension with Sitting

Bull and the Sioux bands. After a number of limited skirmishes with the U.S. military, matters came to a head in 1876. It was in this year that the U.S. government ordered all hunting bands to report to U.S. government agencies attached to reservations. It was an impossible situation for Sitting Bull who now prepared for all-out battle with U.S. forces. As it turned out, the confrontation would be a historical one.

To enforce the U.S. order to have all Indian bands report to agencies by the January 1876 deadline, a number of military divisions were sent. A three-pronged military attack had been planned by U.S. forces to pin down the Indians in the Bighorn Valley in present-day eastern Montana. Unbeknownst to U.S. forces, one of the largest concentrations of Plains Indians ever assembled had gathered in response to the U.S. presence. Due in large part to Sitting Bull's influence, a village of between twelve and fifteen thousand Indians gathered along the Little Bighorn River. Sitting Bull engaged forces under General George Crook in the Battle of the Rosebud on June 17 and sent the U.S. Army into retreat. Eight days later, the U.S. troops led by Colonel George A. Custer attacked several points along the Indian encampment and were soundly defeated. Custer's forces were annihilated. The Battle of Little Bighorn is recorded as a signal Indian victory.

The Indian successes at Rosebud and at Little Bighorn were the last major Indian victories of the campaign. As was the custom, the large Indian encampment dispersed into small bands, since there was not enough food and grazing land to sustain such a large population for long at one place. The U.S. increased its military presence and forced many of the Sioux into surrender. Instead of capitulation, Sitting Bull and a number of his followers escaped to Canada. The Canadian government, however, offered no refuge, and the emigrant Sioux led by Sitting Bull were near starvation. Sitting Bull and most of his camp surrendered to U.S. authorities on 19 July 1881, at Fort Buford, North Dakota. For nearly two years, Sitting Bull was held prisoner; in 1883, he was allowed to settle on the Standing Rock Reservation, which straddles the border of present-day North and South Dakota.

From 1885 to 1886, Sitting Bull joined William Cody's Wild West Show, a traveling exhibition of "Indian fighters" and "Indian War Chiefs." In 1886, Sitting Bull left the Wild West Show and returned to Standing Rock Reservation.

In his remaining years, he continued to oppose assimilation into U.S. culture and the seemingly inevitable breakup of Sioux land. Sitting Bull was killed by government-paid Indian police in October 1890 over a dispute that erupted during a Ghost Dance ceremony at Standing Rock. Government officials were extremely nervous about Sioux participation in the Ghost Dance, because they thought it might lead to the organization of militant resistance to U.S. authority.

Allogan Slagle (1951–)
Cherokee lawyer

Allogan Slagle has been a professor of Native American studies at Berkeley, California, and an attorney advocating for the rights of Native healers and Indian inmates to practice Indian religion in prisons. He is staff attorney with the Association on American Indian Affairs, a New York-based activist organization working for Indian civil rights and legislation.

Slagle has served as assistant director for advocacy in the Lutheran Office for Governmental Affairs in Washington, D.C.; attorney-trustee member/chair of California Legal Services; and assistant librarian at the University of California Research Library, Serials Department, in Los Angeles. He co-authored *The Good Red Road: Passages into Native America* (1987) with Kenneth Lincoln and has written or reviewed over forty articles. His current activities include acting as a consultant to tribes, scholars, organizations, tribally run schools, and California minority-oriented treatment

Allogan Slagle.

programs. He is a member of the board of directors of Urban Indian Health Clinics.

Much of Slagle's energy since the mid–1980s has focused on providing legal and research assistance to Indian communities seeking recognition from the federal government. As many as 150 Indian communities that usually do not have treaty or administrative relations with the U.S. federal government are seeking to gain federal recognition under a congressional act passed in 1978. Slagle's primary focus has been on the national legislation of the recognition process, and he has been active in preserving the federal recognition status of the Keetoowah Band of Cherokee in Oklahoma and many of the numerous California Indian tribes. Allogan Slagle has represented the United Keetoowah Band (UKB) of Cherokee Canadian District since 1992, and serves as Chair of the Membership Committee, and on the Law Reform Committee and the Gaming Commission. He represented the UKB in their effort to regain federal recognition. His work has been supported by the Association of American Indian Affairs since 1989.

John Slocum (d. 1896–1898)
Coast Salish spiritual leader

John Slocum was a member of the Squaxin Band of Southern Coast Salish Indians and achieved importance as the founder the Indian Shaker Church. Slocum was born near Puget Sound, Washington, during the early 1830s, but there was nothing particularly remarkable about his life until the fall of 1881, when he became sick and apparently died. Friends had been summoned and preparations were being made for the funeral when he suddenly revived. He then announced that he had been to visit the judgment place of God and received instructions about certain ways in which Indian people needed to change their lives if they wanted to achieve salvation. This visionary experience became the basis of Tschaddam or the Indian Shaker Church as it is known in English.

This religion is exclusive to Indians and has no connection to millenarian Shakerism as practiced by ascetic Protestant communities in New England. Indian Shakerism incorporates Christian beliefs concerning God, heaven, hell, and the relationship between sinfulness and damnation, but in this religion these ideas are combined with Native concepts, particularly beliefs relating to sickness as a penalty for spiritual offenses.

The "shake" element developed out of a later incident. About a year after his "resurrection," Slocum became ill again and was expected to die. Faced with the impending catastrophe of his death, his wife Mary became hysterical; she approached his prostrate body praying, sobbing, and trembling uncontrollably. When her convulsion had passed, it was observed that Slocum had recovered slightly. This was attributed to her seizure, which was understood as a manifestation of divine power. Thus, curing through "the shake" and laying on of hands became a basic element in Shaker services which continues to this day.

The Indian Shaker religion still flourishes among coastal Indians of British Columbia, Washington, Oregon, and northwestern California. John Slocum died between 1896 and 1898, and the religion has undergone many changes since its inception in 1881.

Nelson Small Legs (1932–1993)
Peigan tribal leader

Nelson Small Legs, chief of the Peigan Indian Reserve from 1976 to 1991, was known to many Canadians because of his and his people's aggressive stance against the construction of a dam on the Oldman River in Alberta. The Peigan Nation, together with the Blackfoot and Blood Indians, formed part of the once-powerful Blackfoot Confederacy on the North American Plains. Small Legs held a variety of jobs before being elected as chief, including working as a farm laborer and miner in Washington and Idaho during his teens and early twenties. He also worked as a ranch hand for several farmers in the Brocket area of southern Alberta before becoming an operator of heavy oilfield equipment in 1966. After failing health forced him to resign his position on the oilfields, Small Legs took a job with the Native Counselling Services of Alberta.

His work counseling Native people led Small Legs to develop an interest in Native politics. Following his election as chief of the reserve, which is located about ninety-five miles west of Lethbridge, Alberta, Small Legs led his band in 1978 in a three-week blockade of the dam site in disobedience of a court-ordered injunction. He eventually reached a highly publicized settlement worth approximately $3.5 million with the government of Alberta permitting development but granting access rights to the Peigan people. Small Legs, with his wife, Florence, raised a large family of eleven children.

Redbird Smith (1850–1918)
Cherokee tribal leader and activist

Redbird Smith was an advocate for the restoration of cultural traditions among his people and led a resistance movement against policies of the U.S. government to redistribute Indian lands. He and a number of colleagues revived the Keetoowah Society to protect Indian sovereignty.

Redbird Smith was born near Fort Smith, Arkansas. His father was Cherokee and his mother part-Cherokee. By the late 1890s, the U.S. government's land allotment policies were finally reaching the so-called Five Civilized Tribes in present-day Oklahoma. The Choctaw, Chickasaw, Cherokee, Creek, and Seminole were called the Five Civilized Tribes because they had formed constitutional governments, many had accepted Christianity, and they had organized school systems. For most Indians, allotment was tantamount to cultural and political extinction. In 1898, Congress passed the Curtis Act, which abolished most operations of the governments among the Five Civilized Tribes. For land to be allotted, however, the government still sought some degree of Indian acceptance. This approval was usually obtained through rather unscrupulous methods. In response to these events, some members of the Cherokee Nation revived the Nighthawk Keetoowah society, an old religious group with a strong interest in perpetuating Cherokee culture and religion. Redbird Smith was one of the primary leaders in the revival movement.

The Nighthawk Keetoowah was a conservative wing of the original Keetoowah society that had been reorganized in the late 1850s before the U.S. Civil War in order to promote political unity among the Cherokee. Smith and the Nighthawks claimed that their society was a religious organization and refused to recognize the right of the U.S. government to disperse tribal lands. Smith led a passive resistance movement that used civil disobedience tactics to disrupt enrollments for distribution of allotted land, which was usually about 160 acres for a male head of household. In 1902, Smith was arrested by federal marshals and forced to sign the enrollment. Under unrelenting federal pressure, the allotment agreements were eventually signed.

In 1907, the Indian Territory became the state of Oklahoma. Smith himself was elected principal chief of the Cherokee in 1908. His activism did not end, however. In 1912, he co-founded the Four Mothers Society, dedicated to preserving and advocating for the political and legal rights of Indian tribes. The Keetoowah society continues to exist today, including the Nighthawk segment revived by Smith's activities in the mid–1890s.

H. A. (Butch) Smitheram (1918–1982)
Okanagan tribal leader

Butch Smitheram is best known for his political activities with non-status Indians in British Columbia. He was born in Penticton, in the interior of British Columbia. His mother was Okanagan and his father was English; at the time of their marriage, an Indian woman who married a non-Indian man lost her status as Indian under Canadian law. After starting but not finishing high school, Butch Smitheram held a variety of jobs before he began to work for the federal Department of Indian Affairs in 1950. Several years later, he decided to go back to school, passed the provincial high school equivalency examinations, and studied English literature at the University of British Columbia.

Smitheran was a founder of the British Columbia Association of Non-Status Indians, which sought to include not only non-status Indians but Métis in British Columbia, the latter being non-status Indians whose mixed Indian-European origin can be traced to the settlement of the prairies and the Northwest Territories but not to the settlement of British Columbia. Smitheram saw that non-status Indians and the Métis people shared similar disadvantages, which could be overcome through unity and shared purpose. He fought hard for improvements in education, as he believed that the education of the young was critical to improve the conditions of his people: "Children are the wealth of our nation—give them the opportunity and the inspiration and they will build on the foundations that you have laid for them." Smitheram was also instrumental in the establishment of the Native Council of Canada, a national organization of non-status Indians in Canada.

Smohalla (1815–1907)
Wanapam spiritual leader

Smohalla was a member of the Wanapam Indian tribe, which lived along the upper Columbia River in present-day eastern Washington State. He left this area around 1850 after a dispute with a local chief. Smohalla traveled for several years. Despite being influenced by Catholic missionaries, Smohalla became a warrior. He was wounded and left for dead during an encounter with a Salish war party. When he returned to his homeland he claimed to have visited the Spirit World during this near-death ordeal. He brought back a message which, to the Wanapam, had the ring of authenticity due to his death-and-resurrection experience.

Smohalla's preaching was a combination of nativist sentiment, cultural purity, and resistance to the U.S. government and Christianity. His popularity came at a time when the Indian population of the region was declining due to diseases and land losses to U.S. settlers. According to Smohalla, religious truths came to him in dreams, thus the name of his religion: "Dreamer Religion." Among Smohalla's teachings was the repudiation of U.S. culture, including alcohol and agricultural practices. Smohalla has been credited with the oft-mentioned quotation, "You ask me to plow the

ground. Shall I take a knife and tear my mother's bosom? You ask me to cut grass and make hay and sell it and be rich like white men. But dare I cut off my mother's hair?" Smohalla also prophesied that Indians would be resurrected and banish whites from their lands. He taught that Indians would be saved though divine intervention, but did not advocate violence. His teachings and sermons were often accompanied by ceremonial music and dance.

Smohalla spread his message throughout the region and had many converts, including Old Joseph, a former Christian. His teachings got him into trouble with U.S. authorities and Smohalla was often jailed. Smohalla's teachings influenced a number of later prophets who also preached a message of resistance and cultural identity.

Reuben A. Snake Jr. (1937–1993)
Winnebago tribal and spiritual leader

Reuben Snake was a founding trustee and the spiritual advisor for the American Indian Ritual Object Repatriation Foundation. He was born in Winnebago, Nebraska, and was educated at the University of Nebraska (1964–1965) and Peru State College (1968–1969).

Snake was a legislative aide to Senator Robert Kerrey of Nebraska and worked with numerous national Native American organizations, serving as national chairman of the American Indian Movement (1972), national president of the National Congress of American Indians (1985–1987), and council to the Americans for Indian Opportunity, Washington, D.C.

He was chairman of the Winnebago Tribal Council from 1975 to 1988, and his other professional posts include college instructor and conflict management specialist. Among his awards are the 1986 Citizenship Award from the Nebraska Indian Commission, 1986 Distinguished Nebraskan, and 1986 Certificate of Recognition by the U.S. Secretary of the Interior.

David Sohappy, Sr. (1925–1991)
Yakima fisherman and activist

After he was laid off from a sawmill in the 1960s, David Sohappy returned to the traditional Indian way of life, settling in a self-made wooden house on the Columbia River. From there he undertook a campaign for Indian treaty fishing rights along the rivers in Washington state. For Sohappy, there was no compromising his belief that Indians have the right to fish when and where they want guaranteed by the Yakima Nation's Treaty of 1855. In a long-standing battle to assert tribal fishing rights, Sohappy was arrested numerous times and had 230 fishing nets confiscated over twenty years because of his insistence on fishing out of season on the Columbia River to assert his tribal right to take fish in the usual and accustomed places and times. The 1968 case *Sohappy v. Washington State* started a series of legal rulings and investigations resulting in the 1974 Boldt Decision by U.S. District Court judge George Boldt, who held that treaties negotiated in the 1850s gave many western Washington State Indian nations the right to catch half the harvestable salmon in Washington waters. The Boldt Decision was considered a great victory for Indian fishing rights and cleared the path for a resurgence of commercial and subsistence fishing activity by the western Washington State Indians.

In 1983, Sohappy was convicted of selling 317 fish out of season to undercover agents taking part in a federal sting operation. When he was sent to prison, he served eighteen months and was released in poor health in 1988. He died at a nursing home in Hood River, Oregon, at the age of sixty-six. He is considered a major figure and activist within the Northwest Coast Indian fishing rights campaign, a major economic issue in the region that continues to require legal and legislative attention.

Cora Nicolasa Solomon (1933–)
Winnebago health worker

Cora Solomon is an important leader in developing health care delivery systems within Native American communities. She is also a community leader of the Winnebago Indians of Nebraska.

She was born in 1933 in Winnebago, Nebraska, and has served as director of the National Community Health Representatives (CHR) Program. The program, which is part of the Indian Health Service (IHS), is a community-based health delivery system using indigenous paraprofessionals.

She has been the director of the Winnebago Tribe of Nebraska Health Department and secretary of the Winnebago Tribal Council. She has also served on the Winnebago public school board and the Nebraska Indian Commission. Solomon is also a member of the Nebraska Indian Inter-Tribal Development Corporation, the Goldenrod Hills Community Action Agency, the Seven States Indian Health Association, and the American Indian Human Resource Center Board, which administers an alcohol abuse program.

Solomon is a member of the National Association of Community Health Representatives and the National Congress of American Indians (NCAI), a major national Indian lobbying organization that looks after Indian interests in Congress. She has received numerous honors and awards, including the Woman Pioneer Award given to her by the governor of Nebraska.

Towana Spivey (1943–)
Chickasaw historian, archaeologist, and curator

Towana Spivey has spent his professional career preserving and interpreting the prehistory/history of the Trans Mississippi West with a particular interest in the Oklahoma area.

Born in Madill, Oklahoma, he is a descendent of several generations of Chickasaw who came to Indian Territory, now Oklahoma, in 1842 from northern Mississippi. He received an undergraduate degree in history/natural science and did graduate work in museum studies and anthropology. A recognized authority in the restoration and interpretation of nineteenth century structures, he has conducted archaeological investigations at nineteenth-century military posts such as Fort Washita, Fort Sill, and Fort Towson.

Towana Spivey.

Spivey has served on advisory committees and boards for the Oklahoma Archaeological Survey, the governor's review committee for the Oklahoma State Preservation Office, Oklahoma's Museum Association, and the Southwestern Oklahoma Historical Society. He worked as historic archaeologist for the Oklahoma Anthropological Society, curator of anthropology at the Museum of the Great Plains, and director/curator of the Fort Sill Museum.

He has authored several books and articles and has served as a primary or featured consultant in at least thirty-five television documentaries. In 1984, he recorded several hours of tape on Native American and frontier history for the *Voice of America*, broadcast in the Soviet Union.

Spivey has regularly been involved with preserving the history, language, and material culture of many Oklahoma tribes, including the Comanche, Kiowa, Chiracahua and Warm Springs Apache, Apache Tribe of Oklahoma and others. He has also testified as an expert witness in state and federal courts on Native American issues.

He was director of the Fort Sill Museum (1982–2000) in Fort Sill, Oklahoma, where he incorporated major cultural programs, designed and implemented Native American sculptures, and utilized bilingual exhibit labels.

Chris Spotted Eagle.

Chris Spotted Eagle (contemporary)
Houma film producer and director

Chris Spotted Eagle is a member of the Muskogean-speaking Houma people, who live in Louisiana. He is an independent film producer and director from Minneapolis, Minnesota. He has worked as a photojournalist, advertising photographer, project manager, and field producer at Twin Cities Public Television, KTCA, in Minneapolis. Spotted Eagle is a veteran of the U.S. Army and Air Force and his interests include cultural work, art, and social activism toward peace and justice.

He has produced such films as *Our Sacred Land* (1984) and *The Great Spirit Within the Hole* (1983), balancing his livelihood with commercial endeavors. His personal work emphasizes the expression of Indian views on land and legal issues that affect Indian peoples in the twentieth century.

Spotted Eagle's major films are designed to give non-Indian audiences access to the thoughts and political positions that American Indians have on land issues

and insights to their world views, especially creation histories and views of the sacred found within various Indian nations.

He has served as a staff director for the American Indian Center in Minneapolis and as a board member of numerous civic and community organizations, including the Minnesota Humanities Commission, Minnesota Civil Liberties Union, and the Twin Cities Chapter of the National Lawyers Guild. Spotted Eagle remains active in the Minneapolis Indian community making videos and continues to have a strong interest in Native spiritualism.

Spotted Tail (1833–1881)
Brule Sioux tribal leader

Spotted Tail was born in the 1830s, either along the White River in South Dakota or near Fort Laramie in Wyoming. His adult name, Spotted Tail, is associated with a raccoon and was given to him by a trapper. Spotted Tail and Little Thunder, another Brule chief, sought revenge for the 1854 killing of the Sioux chief

Brave Bear during a battle with army forces near Fort Laramie. In August 1855, at Ash Hollow, Nebraska, troops under William S. Harney overtook the Brule Sioux and on October 18, Spotted Tail and his companions surrendered. Following his release from prison, Spotted Tail took a more diplomatic line with U.S. settlers, though he continued to struggle for Sioux land rights.

Although famed as a warrior, he generally advised peace to his fellow Sioux. During the War for the Bozeman Trail of 1866–1868, under Red Cloud, he counseled accommodation with U.S. intruders. He was one of the signers of the Fort Laramie Treaty of 1868, establishing the Great Sioux Reservation in present-day North and South Dakota.

In 1870, Spotted Tail traveled to Washington, D.C., and met with President Ulysses S. Grant and his Seneca Commissioner of Indian Affairs, Ely Parker. Spotted Tail made subsequent trips to Washington and proved to be a skillful negotiator. In 1873, agencies bearing his name and that of Red Cloud were established in Nebraska. In his largest negotiating role, the government offered the Sioux $6 million for the Black Hills following the discovery of gold; Spotted Tail demanded $60 million, which the U.S. government rejected.

The influx of miners into the Black Hills led to new wars in 1876 and 1877, led by the Sioux leaders Sitting Bull, Crazy Horse, and Gall. Following the Indian victory at Little Bighorn in 1876, Spotted Tail was appointed chief of the Sioux at the Spotted Tail and Red Cloud agencies. After the Little Bighorn battle, Spotted Tail negotiated the surrender of Sioux militants in 1877. Following the surrender, the government relocated the Sioux from the Spotted Tail and Red Cloud agencies into the Great Sioux Reservation. In 1878, the two agencies were renamed the Rosebud and Pine Ridge agencies, respectively.

Though respected by many of his people, some of the Sioux never forgave Spotted Tail for negotiating the surrender of the militants and for the death of Crazy Horse, which soon followed. Spotted Tail was killed by a fellow Sioux, Crow Dog, in 1881 at Rosebud. An ensuing U.S. Supreme Court decision, *Ex Parte Crow Dog*, based on the killing of Spotted Tail by Crow Dog, resulted in a landmark court decision, which stated that federal courts did not have criminal jurisdiction for major crimes in Indian Country. This ruling incensed Congress, which in 1881 passed the Major Crimes Act, giving federal government jurisdiction over major crimes such as murder and kidnapping in Indian Country. The act curtailed the rights of tribal governments to manage crimes among their own people.

Squanto (Tasquantum) (1580–1622)
Wampanoag interpreter and cultural mediator

In 1605, Tasquantum, also known as Squanto, was abducted in present-day Massachusetts by Europeans and sold into slavery in Malaga, an island off the Mediterranean coast of Spain. He eventually escaped to England where he enlisted in the Newfoundland Company. After sailing to America and back again, Squanto finally returned to his homeland in 1619 to find his people wiped out by disease. Squanto took up life with the Pilgrims at Plymouth and provided invaluable instruction on farming, hunting, fishing, and geography. According to one colonial historian: "He directed them how to set their corne, when to take fish, and to procure other commodities, and was also their pilott to bring them to unknowne places for their profitt." It is also believed that Squanto helped the Pilgrims maintain friendly relations with neighboring tribes.

In 1622, Squanto died of disease while helping the Pilgrims negotiate trade agreements with the Narragansett Indians. In recent history the story of Squanto and the Pilgrims has become an oft-repeated, frequently distorted tale for young people as an example of friendly relations between Indians and the early colonists.

Steven L. A. Stallings (1951–)
San Lusieno corporate executive

Steven Stallings, a member of the Rincon Band of San Lusieno Mission Indians, is senior vice-president and director of Native American Banking Services for Wells Fargo.

He was born and raised in San Diego, California, and attended San Diego High School. Raised in a single parent family, he is the oldest of two sisters and four brothers. As a young boy, he began working in his grandfather's small construction company, fueling his interest in business.

As a business school graduate of California State University, Long Beach, and the University of Southern California, he went to work for the United Indian Development Association (UIDA), a California-based business assistance program for American Indians.

He became president, taking the organization to a national-level and changing its name to the National Center for American Indian Enterprise Development (NCAIED), and opened offices in Phoenix, Arizona; Seattle, Washington; and Los Angeles, California. Under Stallings's leadership, it raised over $800 million in capital and sales contracts for tribal and Indian companies.

Steve Stallings.

In 1995, he joined Wells Fargo, where he is responsible for the delivery of commercial credit and treasury management products to Native American communities and enterprises throughout Wells Fargo's twenty-three-state region. In 2000, Stallings was awarded the Annie G. Ross Award, which is presented to an outstanding American Indian whose life and career have made contributions to American society and bring honor to all American people.

Stallings is currently vice-president of Wells Fargo Bank, a board member of the American Indian Graduate Center (a scholarship fund located in Albuquerque, New Mexico), and a member of Atlatl, a national Native American Arts organization. He resides in Chandler, Arizona, with his wife Peggy (Navajo), and his two daughters, Stefanie and Celena.

Stand Watie (1806–1871)

Cherokee tribal leader

Stand Watie was a Cherokee tribal leader and Confederate general. He was a leading member of the Treaty Party favoring Cherokee removal west in the 1830s.

Born near present-day Rome, Georgia, Stand Watie received his education in mission schools, then returned to his homeland to work with his brother, Elias Boudinot, on the *Cherokee Phoenix* newspaper. During this time Stand Watie became a pro-removal supporter and embraced the Treaty of New Echota in 1835, which forced the Cherokee to leave their homeland in present-day western Georgia, eastern Tennessee, western Carolina, and eastern Alabama. Together with his cousins John and Major Ridge, Stand Watie and Boudinot led a pro-removal group known as the "Treaty Party." The inevitable tension with anti-removal forces almost cost Stand Watie his life in 1839 when embittered anti-removal Cherokee killed Boudinot and the two Ridges.

From 1845 to 1861, Stand Watie built and maintained a successful plantation in Indian Territory (present-day Oklahoma) using black slave labor. During this time, Stand Watie served on the Cherokee Council, including stints as speaker of the lower Cherokee legislative house.

When the Civil War broke out in 1861, Stand Watie, now a well-to-do landowner, joined the Confederate forces and organized a cavalry regiment. He was commissioned colonel in the First Cherokee Mounted Rifles in October 1861. Stand Watie had major roles in several battles. In the 1862 Battle of Pea Ridge, Arkansas, Stand Watie's troops captured Union artillery positions that had been a major obstacle to Confederate strategy. As the war progressed, a number of Indian Confederate leaders withdrew from the conflict. Stand Watie, however, continued the fight, and was promoted to brigadier general. Under his command two regiments of Mounted Rifles and three battalions of Cherokee, Seminole, and Osage infantry fought throughout Indian Territory, Arkansas, Missouri, Kansas, and Texas, and won a number of significant battles. It is believed Stand Watie's unit fought more battles west of the Mississippi River than any other Confederate unit.

In 1865, Stand Watie surrendered to Union forces, the last general in the Confederate Army to do so. After the war, he acted in his new capacity as principal chief of the southern Cherokee, rebuilding tribal assets (including his own diminished holdings) during Reconstruction. Stand Watie and his nephew, Elias C. Boudinot, entered the tobacco processing business in 1868. He and his nephew were temporarily arrested over a legal dispute on Cherokee tax exemptions. Subsequently, the U.S. Supreme Court ruled in 1870 that Cherokee enterprises were not exempt from federal tax laws. Stand Watie was married to Betsy Bell, with whom he had five children.

Standing Bear (Mochunozhi) (1829–1908)
Ponca tribal leader

Standing Bear was a Ponca principal chief who won a U.S. federal case to bury his son in the Ponca homelands of Nebraska. Traditional enemies of the Sioux, the Ponca negotiated a treaty in 1858 that established boundaries between the two tribal groups. The treaty was abrogated when the government included Ponca lands within the Great Sioux Reservation in the Fort Laramie Treaty of 1868. In 1876, Congress passed a law to remove the Ponca from their homeland in present-day northern Kansas and forcibly relocate them to Indian Territory (Oklahoma).

One-third of the tribe perished from disease and hunger once they arrived. Two of Standing Bear's children died, and he set out to return his son's body to the old Ponca homeland. Accompanied by thirty warriors, the party set off on the journey. They were spotted by settlers, and, fearing an uprising, General George Crook ordered cavalry officers to arrest them. They were taken to Omaha, where they were interviewed by journalist Thomas H. Tibbles.

After the nature of the Ponca trip was understood, General Crook and others were sympathetic to Standing Bear's mission. However, federal attorneys argued that the Indians were not legally persons under the U.S. Constitution and therefore had no rights. Federal judge Elmer Dundy ruled against the attorneys, and Standing Bear's party was allowed to continue. He buried his son in northeastern Nebraska. Sympathy grew for the Ponca, and Standing Bear went on a lecture tour of the East. Congress formed a commission to study the Ponca case and granted Standing Bear and his party land in Nebraska in 1880. He lived until he was about eighty years old and was buried on the original Ponca homeland (see also the biography of Sarah Winnemucca).

Dorothy Stanley (1924–1990)
Miwok basketmaker

Dorothy Stanley was a basketmaker and cultural spokeswoman among the Northern Miwok, a group of tribes whose native territory was centered in the Sierra Nevada mountains of eastern California.

Born in Los Angeles, California, on 14 July 1924, Stanley was descended from families of hereditary leaders among the Northern Miwok in the areas of West Point and Railroad Flat, California. Her early life was difficult, as she was raised in many different households, often far from home, but she still managed to absorb much traditional Miwok knowledge and passed these teachings on to many other people, both Indian and white, during her lifetime.

Stanley was educated at Stewart Indian School in Stewart, Nevada, and worked at the nearby Wai-Pai-Shone Trading Post until she graduated from Stewart in 1942. Over the following decades, she held many types of jobs in various places in California and Nevada, but finally returned home in the early 1970s. Remembering the teachings she received from her relatives, she then became very active in promoting, defending, and teaching her culture. She worked as a Native American liaison for the Department of the Interior, as tribal chair for the Tuolumne Mewuk Tribal Council, as director of a tribal health project, and as supervisor of the Indian Cultural Program at Yosemite National Park.

A warm and outspoken person, she was known as much for her teaching as for her basketry, which was very fine, and she gave cultural demonstrations of basketmaking and other Native crafts for festivals and classes from Los Angeles to Washington, D.C. Stanley valued the past and fought against the loss of Miwok culture by younger Miwok whom she saw embracing the trappings of pan-Indian culture rather than their own distinctive culture.

Emmet Starr (1870–1930)
Cherokee historian

Emmet Starr was born in the Going Snake District, Cherokee Nation, Indian Territory (present-day Oklahoma), on 12 December 1870. He was educated in the Cherokee Nation public schools, graduated from the Cherokee National Male Seminary in 1888, and received a degree in medicine from Barnes Medical College at St. Louis in 1891.

According to tradition, Starr dreamed of becoming the "Herodotus of the Cherokees." Herodotus is a famous Greek historian who wrote during the fifth century. Starr practiced medicine for five years and began gathering materials for his *History of the Cherokee* about 1891, but in 1896, he began to devote himself full time to studying Cherokee history. In 1899, he issued a prospectus for his book *Gazeteer of the Cherokee Nation, Indian Territory*. The book, however, never appeared. Starr also served one term in the Cherokee National Council as a representative of the Cooweescoowee District and as a delegate to the Indian Territory statehood meeting known as the Sequoyah Convention in 1905. The Sequoyah convention was trying to hold off the U.S. abolition of the Indian Territory governments, but was unsuccessful since by 1907 Oklahoma had become a state.

After Oklahoma statehood, Starr continued the preparation of his Cherokee histories. He published four books: *The History of the Cherokee Indians* (1922), *Early History of the Cherokees* (1917), *Cherokees West* (1910), and *Encyclopedia of Oklahoma* (1912). While working on his histories, Starr was associated with the Cherokee National Seminaries and the Normal School which became Northeastern State University in Tahlequah, Oklahoma. In 1958, a bronze plaque was placed on the wall of the Northeastern State College Library honoring him as a former college librarian.

Undoubtedly, the most popular sections of Starr's *The History of the Cherokee Indians* were the chapters and charts entitled "Old Families and Their Genealogy." Starr's genealogical notes were used as evidence by the Dawes Commission in establishing eligibility for Cherokee settlements and for listing on the official tribal rolls.

Emmet Starr is recognized as a major Cherokee historian. Nevertheless, he died in St. Louis, Missouri, in 1930, suffering a self-imposed exile, convinced that he had failed his people in a mission to "perpetuate the facts relative to the Cherokee tribe."

Henry Bird Steinhauer (circa 1818–1884)
Ojibwa missionary

It is believed that Henry Bird Steinhauer was originally known as Sowengisik (Southern Skies). He was born in 1818 to Ojibwa parents on the Rama Indian settlement at Lake Simcoe just north of Toronto, Ontario. When he was ten years old, he was given the name Henry Bird Steinhauer after an American benefactor who agreed to finance the education of an Indian boy if the child adopted his name. Steinhauer attended school in Ontario from 1829 to 1832 and then attended a seminary in Cazenovia, just east of Syracuse, New York, until 1835.

Steinhauer was sent by the Wesleyan Methodist Church to teach at the Credit River Mission on Lake Ontario in 1835 and later was enrolled at the Upper Canada Academy in Cobourg, Ontario. After interrupting his studies briefly to teach, Steinhauer graduated from the academy at the top of his class. Several years later, he was sent west to northern Ontario and Manitoba to assist in the translation of the Bible and hymns into Cree, as it was thought that his knowledge of Ojibwa would be of assistance since the two languages share the same language group. Steinhauer married in 1846 and eventually was the father to five children. He was ordained in 1855 and immediately sent to Lac La Biche in what is now Alberta. Steinhauer moved his mission several times, eventually settling in an area called Whitefish Lake. Steinhauer is known in later life for a letter written to the Missionary Society of the Wesleyan Methodist Church in Canada in which he stated that "there is always a distrust on the part of a native to the foreigner, from the fact that the native has been so long down-trodden by the white man."

Ralph Garvin Steinhauer (1905–1987)
Métis politician

Ralph Steinhauer, the first Native person to serve as lieutenant-governor of a Canadian province, was born in 1905 in Morley, a small town in east-central Alberta. His great-grandfather, Henry Bird Steinhauer, was a distinguished Ojibwa missionary. Ralph attended the Brandon Indian Residential School. Until the age of twenty-three, he also worked on his father's farm in Saddle Lake during the summer and at a local store during the winter. In 1927, Steinhauer met Isabel Davidson, who had recently moved from the eastern United States to Alberta with her widowed mother. They were married the following year and moved to the Saddle Lake Indian Reserve in east-central Alberta to farm in earnest. The Steinhauer farm grew steadily, and he became an enormously successful farmer, teaching others to use the reserve system to maximize agricultural opportunities.

Steinhauer began to develop an interest in politics, serving as chief of the Saddle Lake Reserve for three years. In 1963, he was nominated by the Liberal party to run for election to the federal House of Commons, although he did not get elected. However, his successes were many. He was a founder of the Indian Association of Alberta, a province-wide organization devoted to the advancement of aboriginal rights. In 1974, Steinhauer was sworn in as the lieutenant-governor of Alberta, a position he held until 1979. In light of his contribution to his community, Steinhauer was named a Companion of the Order of Canada, an award conferred by the governor general of Canada to select Canadians in recognition of exemplary merit and achievement. He also received honorary doctoral degrees from the Universities of Alberta and Calgary.

Rennard James Strickland (1940–)
Osage-Cherokee lawyer

Rennard Strickland is dean and Philip H. Knight Professor of Law at the University of Oregon. He was born in St. Louis, Missouri, and earned a bachelor of

Rennard Strickland.

arts degree from Northeastern State College in 1962 and two law degrees from the University of Virginia, in 1965 and 1970, respectively.

Strickland is the first person to have served as both president of the Association of American Law Schools and chair of the Law School Admission Council. He was also editor-in-chief for the third edition revision of *Cohen's Handbook of Federal Indian Law* for the U.S. Department of the Interior (1975–1982) and was appointed by the Federal District Court for the Northern District of Oklahoma as chair and arbitrator for the Osage Constitutional Commission (1992–1995).

He has been dean of the College of Law at Oklahoma City University (1996–1998), dean of the College of Law at Southern Illinois University (1985–1988), and acting dean at the University of Tulsa (1974–1975). Strickland has also been director of the American Indian Law Center, and professor of law at the University of Oklahoma School of Law (1990–1996) and the University of Wisconsin at Madison (1988–1990). He served as director of the Indian Heritage Association of Muskogee, Oklahoma (1966–1984), and chairman of the Indian Advisory Board of the Philbrook Art Center (1979–1983).

Among Strickland's honors and awards are the Spirit of Excellence Award of the American Bar Association

Commission on Minorities in the Profession (1997), the SALT Award for legal reform from the Society of American Law Teachers (1980), the Sacred Sash of the Creeks for Preservation of Tribal History (1970–1971), Fellow of the Doris Duke Foundation (1970–1973), Award of Merit from the Association for State and Local History (1981), and Distinguished Service Citation from the American Indian Coalition (1985).

He has published numerous books including *Tonto's Revenge* (1998), *Masterworks of American Indian Art* (1983), *The Indians in Oklahoma* (1980), *Fire and Spirit* (1975), and *Cherokee Spirit Tales* (1969).

His interests include law, culture, and ethnohistory of American Indians, contemporary American Indian art and painting, and the development of traditional legal systems among tribes.

Diosa Summers-Fitzgerald (1945–1992)
Mississippi Choctaw artist

Diosa Summers-Fitzgerald was an educator and artist who worked with Native American art forms, and she developed and designed art programs to teach Native American art and traditions.

Born in New York City she earned a bachelor of arts from State University College at Buffalo (1977), and a master of education degree from Harvard University (1983). The focus of her work and studies was Native American art. She was both an artist herself and a teacher of Native American art traditions. In the classroom, Summers-Fitzgerald worked to foster a clearer understanding of the roots of Native American tradition through art.

From 1975 to 1977, Summers-Fitzgerald was the director of education of the History and Continuing Education Department at the State University College of New York College at Buffalo, and an instructor at Haffenreffer Museum of Anthropology in Bristol, Rhode Island, from 1979 to 1980, at which time she was also acting tribal coordinator of the Narragansett Tribal Education Project. From 1982 to 1985, she was artist-in-residence at the Folk Arts Program in Rhode Island State Council on the Arts in Providence, Rhode Island, and also an artist working with the Native American Art Forms Nishnabeykwa Production in Charlestown, Rhode Island. Beginning in 1985, she served as the education director of the Jamaica Arts Center in Jamaica, New York.

Summers-Fitzgerald authored several Indian museum brochures including "Native American Food," "Finger-weaving," "Narrative and Instruction," and "Ash Sapling Basketry."

Sun Bear (1929–1992)
Chippewa spiritual leader

Sun Bear became best known as president of the Bear Tribe Medicine Society in Spokane, Washington, and the editor and publisher of *Many Smokes* magazine.

Born on the White Earth Reservation in eastern Minnesota, Sun Bear was an actor and technical director for *Wagon Train, Bonanza,* and *Wild, Wild West* television shows from 1955 to 1965. He founded the Bear Tribe Medicine Society to spread Native American culture, and he taught, lectured, and toured extensively for the cause. His international tours include Europe, Australia, and India. In the 1980s, his ideas on self-sufficiency and living with the earth were embraced by a number of environmental and holistic living groups.

Sun Bear is a member of the Midiwiwin Society, a Chippewa association of spiritual leaders and healers, and the National Congress of American Indians, a national organization that lobbies in Congress for Indian political interests. Books written by Sun Bear include *At Home in the Wilderness, Buffalo Hearts, Walk in Balance, The Bear Tribe's Self-Reliance Book, The Medicine Wheel Book,* and *Sun Bear: The Path of Power.*

Sweet Grass (?–1877)
Cree tribal leader

Sweet Grass, also known as Wikaskokiseyin, was born in Cree territory to a Crow mother who had been kidnapped during a war between her people and the Cree. As a young man, he was called Le Petit Chef or Apistchikoimas, and was supposedly renamed Sweet Grass when, during his youth, he entered into enemy Blackfoot territory by himself, killed a Blackfoot warrior, and stole more than forty horses. Upon his return home amid cheers of victory, it is said that he held up a fistful of grass dipped in the blood of his victim and thereafter became known as Sweet Grass.

In 1870, Sweet Grass converted to Roman Catholicism and was baptized as Abraham. He had already become the principal chief of many of the Plains Cree, and in the same year he wrote to Canadian authorities protesting the effects of European settlement, hunting, and fishing. In relation to the acquisition by Canada of land that soon became Manitoba, Saskatchewan, and Alberta, Sweet Grass wrote, "We heard our lands were sold and we do not like it; we do not want to sell our lands; it is our property, and no one has a right to sell them." He sought assistance in the form of a treaty: "Our country is getting ruined of the fur-bearing animals, hitherto our sole support, and now we are poor and want help—we want you to pity us. We want cattle, tools, agricultural implements, and assistance in everything when we come to settle—our country is no longer able to support us." Six years later, Sweet Grass signed a treaty with Canadian authorities on behalf of his people. He died a few months later, but his name is memorialized in the Sweet Grass Reserve established for his people near Battleford in central Saskatchewan.

Ross O. Swimmer (1943–)
Cherokee tribal leader

Ross Swimmer is president of the Cherokee Group, L.L.C., and a former assistant secretary of Indian affairs with the U.S. Department of the Interior. He was born in Oklahoma and received a bachelor of science degree and a law degree from the University of Oklahoma.

Swimmer has been general counsel and principal chief of the Cherokee Nation (1972–1985) and president of the First National Bank of Tahlequah, Oklahoma (1975–1985). He has served as co-chairman of the Presidential Commission on Indian Reservation Economies (1983–1984), executive committee member of the Eastern Oklahoma Boy Scouts of America, former chairman of the Tahlequah Planning and Zoning Commission, and past president of the Cherokee National Historical Society.

From 1986 to 1989, Swimmer was assistant secretary of Indian affairs within the Department of the Interior. This is the highest ranking U.S. government administrative position and oversees the Bureau of Indian Affairs, the major government agency concerned with U.S. Indian issues. Swimmer, appointed by President Ronald Reagan, worked to carry out the business and self-sufficiency goals of the Reagan Administration, promoting economic development and encouraging tribal governments to take more leadership and financial responsibility for their tribal communities.

He returned to Tulsa, Oklahoma, in 1989, and joined the law firm of Hall, Estill, Hardwick, Gable, Golden and Nelson, P.C., to begin the practice of tribal law. The firm has offices in Tulsa, Oklahoma City, Fayetteville, and Washington, D.C.

Swimmer is president of the Simon Estes Educational Foundation, Incirca, a Tulsa-based scholarship granting organization; a member of the Philbrook Museum board of trustees; a trustee for the University of Tulsa; and a board member of the Cowboy Hall of Fame and Western Heritage Center in Oklahoma City, Oklahoma.

Swimmer has been awarded the Distinguished Service Award from the University of Oklahoma, an honorary doctorate from Phillips University, and the Crystal

Crown Award from Birmingham, Alabama, for his work with American Indians.

Gerald Tailfeathers (1925–1975)
Blackfoot artist

Gerald Tailfeathers, one of the first Native Canadian artists to pursue a professional artistic career, was born in 1925 at Stand Off, Alberta. His talent was apparent to others early in his life; in his teens, he received a scholarship from the Anglican Church to study art and was not yet twenty when he had his first exhibition. He trained in art at the School of Fine Arts in Banff, a small resort town in the Rocky Mountains in Alberta, and at the Provincial School of Technology and Art in Calgary, Alberta. Tailfeathers's career began to flourish while he was in his twenties; apart from a stint as a technical draftsman for a petroleum company, he worked as a full-time artist.

Tailfeathers's painting style was pictorial and nostalgic. His paintings often depicted his people, the Blackfoot and Blood Indians, as they lived in the nineteenth century, hunting buffalo, setting up camp, and engaging in ceremonial practices. He was influenced by other Indian painters of his generation, as he traveled often to view the work of others. He spent a summer studying at the Summer Art School in Glacier National Park in Montana, for example, with several portrait painters, including Winold Reiss and Carl Linck from New York. Later in his career, after a visit to the Arizona studio of the sculptor George Phippin, Tailfeathers began to experiment with bronze sculpture depicting life on the Plains.

Maria Tallchief (1925–)
Osage ballerina

Maria Tallchief is a world-renowned ballerina and one of the premiere American ballerinas of all time. She was the first American to dance at the Paris Opera and has danced with the Paris Opera Ballet, the Ballet Russe, and later with the Balanchine Ballet Society (New York City Ballet).

Tallchief was raised in a wealthy family. Her grandfather had helped negotiate the Osage treaty, which created the Osage Reservation in Oklahoma and later yielded a bonanza in oil revenues for some Osage people. Tallchief began dance and music lessons at age four. By age eight, she and her sister had exhausted the training resources in Oklahoma, and the family moved to Beverly Hills, California. By age twelve, Tallchief

was studying under Madame Nijinska (sister of the great Nijinsky) and David Lichine, a student of the renowned Russian ballerina Pavlova. At age fifteen at the Hollywood Bowl, Tallchief danced her first solo performance in a number choreographed by Nijinska. Following high school, it was apparent that ballet would be Tallchief's life. Instead of college, she joined the Ballet Russe, a highly acclaimed Russian ballet troupe. Tallchief was initially treated with skepticism—the Russian troupe was unwilling to recognize the Native American's greatness. When choreographer George Balanchine took control of the company, however, he recognized Tallchief's talent and selected her for the understudy role in The Song of Norway. Under Balanchine, Tallchief's reputation grew, and she was eventually given the title of ballerina. During this time, Tallchief married Balanchine, and when he moved to Paris, she went with him.

As with the Ballet Russe, Tallchief was initially treated with condescension in Paris. Her debut at the Paris Opera was the first ever for any American ballerina, and Tallchief's talent quickly won French audiences over. She later became the first American to dance with the Paris Opera Ballet at the Bolshoi Theatre in Moscow. She quickly became the ranking soloist and, soon after, joined the Balanchine Ballet Society, now the New York City Ballet. At the New York City Ballet, Tallchief became recognized as one of the greatest dancers in the world. When she became the prima ballerina, she was the first American dancer to achieve this title. In 1949, Tallchief danced what was perhaps her greatest role in the Balanchine-choreographed version of *The Firebird*. Balanchine had choreographed the role for Tallchief, and her dazzling blend of physical control and mysticism enchanted audiences.

Mary TallMountain (1918–1994)
Athabaskan poet

Mary TallMountain was a widely respected Athabaskan author and poet. She was born in 1918 in Nulato, a village along the Yukon River in Alaska, of Athabaskan-Russian and Scots-Irish parents. At age six, because her mother was sick with tuberculosis, she was adopted by a non-Indian couple. Although her adoptive parents could teach her little about her culture, she retained vivid memories of her early childhood, and much of her poetry captures a delighted child's view of village life among the Athabaskan of central Alaska.

As an adult, TallMountain moved to San Francisco, where she worked as a legal secretary and began to write poetry, which was featured in dozens of anthologies and periodicals, such as *Earth Power Coming, The*

Remembered Earth, The Language of Life, The Harper's Anthology of Twentieth Century Native American Poetry, The Alaska Quarterly, Animals Agenda, and *That's What She Said.* In 1960, she came under the tutelage of Pueblo poet and author Paula Gunn Allen. TallMountain has published several collections of poems, including *The Light on the Tent Wall* (1990), *A Quick Brush of Wings* (1991), and a posthumous collection *Listen To the Night* (1995). The Rasmussen Library at the University of Alaska in Fairbanks houses an archival collection of TallMountain's published and unpublished works.

Mary TallMountain had a close association with the Tenderloin Reflection and Education Center (TREC), a community-based nonprofit spiritual and cultural center in her San Francisco neighborhood. She was a poet-in-residence there in 1991 and 1992 and participated in many of TREC's workshops and performances.

The TallMountain Circle was established as a project of TREC and each year the advisory board selects Mary TallMountain Awards for Creative Writing and Community Service to benefit low-income writers, particularly Native Americans and writers living in San Francisco's Tenderloin District.

Luci Tapahonso (1951–)
Navajo poet

Luci Tapahonso, a member of the Salt Water clan of the Navajo Nation, teaches in the American Indian Studies and English departments at the University of Arizona.

She is the author of collections of poetry, short stories, and children's books, including *Songs of Shiprock Fair* (1999), *Blue Horses Rush In* (1997), *Naanii Dhatall: The Women Are Singing* (1993), *A Breeze Swept Through* (1989), and *Seasonal Woman* (1982).

Tapahonso has also taught at the University of New Mexico and the University of Kansas. Her awards include the New Mexico Eminent Scholar award from the New Mexico Commission of Higher Education (1989), Woman of Distinction from the National Association of Women in Education (1998), and the Mountains and Plains Booksellers Award for her poetry (1998).

She has served on the board of directors at the Phoenix Indian Center, was a member of the New Mexico Arts Commission Literature Panel, steering committee of Returning the Gift Writers Festival, Kansas Arts Commission Literature Panel, Phoenix Arts Commission, Telluride Institute Writers Forum advisory board, and commissioner of the Kansas Arts Commission. She is a member of the Modern Language

Association, Poets and Writers, Inc., Association of American Indian and Alaska Native Professors, and the New Mexico Endowment for the Humanities.

Drew Hayden Taylor (1962–)
Ojibwa playwright, scriptwriter, director, short story writer, and journalist

One of Canada's most prominent writers, Drew Hayden Taylor, an Ojibway from the Curve Lake First Nations, works in a variety of genres to describe and satirize modern Native North American life. Known for his use of humor in depicting Native responses to public opinion and government decisions, Taylor is a frequent columnist for *The Globe and Mail* and *The Toronto Star* and is often featured as a commentator on the Canadian Broadcasting Corporation's *Newsworld.* He is a regular columnist for three Canadian newspapers.

Perhaps best known for his plays, Taylor is one of the former artistic directors of Native Earth Performing Arts, a Toronto-based company that provides a home for Native writers, actors, artists, and technicians. *Someday* (1993), one of his more popular plays, was adapted from one of Taylor's short stories, the only piece of fiction ever printed on the front page of *The Globe and*

Drew Hayden Taylor.

Mail. Some of his other plays include *Only Drunks and Children Tell the Truth* (1996), *A Contemporary Gothic Indian Vampire Story* (1992), *The Bootlegger Blues* (1990), and *Toronto at Dreamer's Rock* (1989). Two of his most recent plays, *alterNATIVES, TDR.com* and *400 Kilometres*, are often performed throughout Canada and the United States, and in the fall of 2000 his eleventh book, which contains two one-act plays for youth titled *The Boy in the Treehouse* and *Girl Who Loved Her Horses*, was released. The writer's drama is studied not only throughout North America, but also in countries such as Italy, Germany, and New Zealand.

These plays have brought him substantial literary recognition. He won the Canadian Authors' Association Literary Award for Best Drama and the Floyd S. Chalmers Canadian Play Award in 1992, the Dora Mavor Moore Award for Outstanding New Play in the Small Theatre Division and the University of Alaska Anchorage Native Playwriting Award in 1996, and the James Buller Award for Playwright of the Year in 1997.

Screenwriting and directing are yet other genres in which Taylor explores the issues of Native North American life. His forays into screenwriting include not only scripts for some of Canada's most popular television shows, including *Street Legal* and *North of 60*, but also an independently produced short entitled *The Strange Case of Bunny Weequod*. In August 2000 the National Film Board of Canada launched a documentary Taylor directed on Native humor called *Redskins, Tricksters, and Puppy Stew*. He is also in development with the Canadian Broadcasting Corporation for a Native sketch comedy series. The working show's title is *Seeing Red*.

Taylor has published two books of essays entitled *Funny You Don't Look Like One: Observations of a Blue-Eyed Ojibway* (1998) and *Funny You Don't Look Like One Two: A Second Collection From a Blue-Eyed Ojibway* (1999). He has also released a collection of short stories, *Fearless Warriors* (1998).

Tecumseh (1768–1813)
Shawnee tribal leader

In the early 1800s, Tecumseh and his brother Tenskwatawa organized Indian resistance to U.S. territorial expansion along the Mississippi Valley. Tecumseh was born in a Shawnee settlement known as Old Piqua (near the present-day city of Springfield, Ohio) in the Ohio Valley. Tecumseh, (which means "goes through one place to another"), learned warfare early in life. In his early teens Tecumseh took part in the American Revolution on the side of the British.

After the revolution, the Shawnee regularly took up arms to defend their Ohio land against U.S. settlers. In 1795, many of the Indian leaders living in the Ohio region gathered at Greenville, Ohio, to negotiate sale of land to the United States. When the land exchange was formalized in the Treaty of Greenville, Tecumseh refused to recognize it. Upon hearing of U.S. intentions to buy Indian land, Tecumseh is said to have replied, "Sell the land? Why not sell the air, the clouds, the great sea?" This belief in an Indian land with no tribal borders would become the foundation for Tecumseh's Indian confederation in the years to follow.

Tecumseh soon emerged as a spokesman for the Midwest Indians. He attended councils, studied treaties, and learned all that he could about the historical and legal status of American Indians. It was during this time that Tecumseh conceived a new mission for his life, a destiny linked to the growing restlessness among the Indians of the Old Northwest Territory (present-day Great Lakes area). This restlessness was caused in part by the preachings of a new Indian leader spreading a message of religious rebirth and resistance. Tecumseh knew this emerging leader very well for he was Laulewasika, his younger brother who had changed his name to Tenskwatawa (which means "open door") but was generally known as the Shawnee Prophet.

The two brothers united to forge an intertribal confederacy, which they hoped would contain U.S. territorial expansion into Indian lands. Tecumseh and his brother urged their people to forgo the sale of Indian land, to reject European ways, and to renew Indian traditions. In particular, the brothers warned against the use of alcohol, which was devastating many Indian communities.

Within a few years, the brothers had assembled a growing community of believers in Prophetstown, located at the junction of the Wabash River and Tippecanoe Creek in present-day Indiana. Tensions between the growing Indian community and the U.S. government were high, however, because of Indian resentment over recent treaties ceding about 110 million acres to the United States. At the Battle of Tippecanoe in November 1811, the Prophet and his followers fought U.S. Army units. The Prophet proclaimed that his spiritual power would protect the Indians from army bullets, but when the Indians suffered significant casualties in the battle, the Prophet lost prestige and his followers abandoned him. Many members of Tecumseh's alliance dispersed, and Tenskwatawa himself fled to Canada.

Tecumseh joined the British to fight against the Americans in the War of 1812. He played a decisive role in the British capture of Detroit. In the months to follow, Tecumseh rallied other Indians to the British effort and continued to lead them into battle. On 5 October 1813, however, he was killed at the Battle of the Thames, in southern Ontario.

Kateri Tekakwitha (1656–1680)
Mohawk Catholic nun

Kateri Tekakwitha, whom many Catholics call Lily of the Mohawks, converted to Christianity in the 1670s and became a nun. She was a person of uncommon religious conviction and is currently a candidate for canonization by the Roman Catholic Church.

Tekakwitha was born near present-day Auriesville, New York. Her father was a Mohawk chief and her mother an Algonquin who had been captured by the Mohawk. Tekakwitha's mother was a Christian convert. Her parents died when she was four years old, and she grew up with her uncle in the village of Caughnawaga, near present-day Fonda, New York.

Jesuits visited Tekakwitha's village in the 1670s, and she was baptized at the age of twenty by Jacques de Lamberville, a Jesuit missionary. Her uncle, also a Mohawk chief, opposed her conversion, and her religion caused her ridicule and made her an outcast among her people. In 1677, Tekakwitha fled her village with some visiting Christianized Oneida Indians. She settled near a Christian Mohawk community outside of present-day Montreal. Tekakwitha hoped to establish a convent on Heron Island. Church authorities rejected her plan, but did accept her into an order of nuns. Tekakwitha's religious fervor never wavered, and her almost fanatical devotion and commitment to helping others were well known among her people. Many stories have grown around Tekakwitha, including the account that when she died in 1680, scars from a childhood case of smallpox disappeared.

Tekakwitha became a candidate for sainthood in the Roman Catholic Church in 1884. In 1943, the Church declared her venerable, and in 1980 blessed. These are the first two steps toward sainthood.

Tenskwatawa (Open Door) (1778–1837)
Shawnee spiritual leader

Tenskwatawa, better known as the Shawnee Prophet, was the brother of Tecumseh, the famous Indian leader who tried to rally Indian forces against U.S. expansion before and during the War of 1812. Tenskwatawa was born at Piqua near present-day Springfield, Ohio, of a Shawnee war chief and his Cherokee-Creek wife. As a result of their defeat at the Battle of Fallen Timbers in 1794 and the Treaty of Greenville the next year, the Shawnee were left leaderless and demoralized throughout Tenskwatawa's childhood. He became an alcoholic and lost the sight in his left eye in a hunting accident. In 1806, while living in the Delaware villages in present-day Indiana stretching from Indianapolis to Munsee, Tenskwatawa was influenced by the cultural and ceremonial revival created by the Munsee prophetess, who in 1804 and 1805 reformed the Delaware Big House religion, the main religious ceremony of the Delaware people. Since 1675, many Shawnee had lived with the Algonkian-speaking Delaware, or Lenape, and some groups within both nations became very closely tied. In February 1806, Tenskwatawa had an out-of-body experience and a vision that he died and went to heaven to see the Great Spirit, and brought back a message to the Indian people.

Tenskwatawa began to preach a return to traditional Shawnee customs, condemned intermarriage with Europeans, and rejected contact with them. He promoted claims that he could cure sickness and prevent death. The brothers Tenskwatawa and Tecumseh envisioned a vast Indian confederacy strong enough to keep the colonists from expanding any further west. Tenskwatawa's influence began to grow with other Indians, and he and Tecumseh traveled extensively among tribes from Wisconsin to Florida spreading the message. Indiana governor William Henry Harrison challenged him to "cause the sun to stand still" and "the moon to change its course." Tenskwatawa promptly did as much in accurately predicting the total eclipse of the sun on 16 June 1806. Thousands of Indians quickly became believers and hastened to join the new religion.

Tecumseh and Tenskwatawa founded Prophet's Town along the confluence of the Wabash River and Tippecanoe Creek in Indiana, and many Indians came to live there. Tecumseh began to exert a larger presence than his brother in the organization of the town and its operations. When he left on a trip in 1811, leaving Tenskwatawa in charge, Tecumseh cautioned his brother to avoid any confrontation with Harrison's troops. Perhaps seeking to regain preeminence, Tenskwatawa was drawn into attacking Harrison at the Battle of Tippecanoe in November 1811. During the battle, he stayed at the rear using magic to drive the U.S. soldiers into retreat. Tenskwatawa had no power that day, and the Indians were soundly defeated at Tippecanoe. After the battle, the prophet was left without influence and could no longer command believers.

As a result, upon his return, the enraged Tecumseh broke with his brother. Tenskwatawa fled to Canada, returning fifteen years later in 1826 and eventually settling in Wyandotte County, Kansas. George Catlin painted Tenskwatawa in 1830. The oil-on-canvas portrays a pensive old man wearing a nose ring. Holding his once-powerful firestick wand in his right hand, and in the left, a sacred string of beads given to him during the long-ago vision, his portrait seems to contemplate what once was to be.

Louis Tewanima (d. 1969)
Hopi athlete

Louis Tewanima was teammate of the famous Indian athlete Jim Thorpe, and world-class athlete in his own right. He was born at Shongopovi, Second Mesa, New Mexico, on the Hopi Indian Reservation. The Hopi are a Pueblo people who live in villages and practice elaborate seasonal dances and religious rituals. As a boy, Tewanima would chase jackrabbits. When he arrived at the famous Carlisle School in Pennsylvania, Tewanima weighed only 110 pounds. He approached the legendary coach Glenn "Pop" Warner for a position on the track team, and when Warner saw him run, he compared Tewanima to a deer in flight.

Tewanima established world records in long-distance running. He competed in the 1908 Olympics in the marathon and placed ninth. At one track meet, Tewanima, Jim Thorpe, and Frank Mount Pleasant of Carlisle beat twenty athletes from Lafayette College. Tewanima and Thorpe were selected for the U.S. Olympic team without having to undergo trials, which was a rare honor. They sailed from New York to Stockholm on Flag Day, 14 June 1912; they returned as U.S. heroes. Thorpe had been proclaimed "the greatest athlete in the world" by the king of Sweden. Tewanima won a silver medal in the 10,000-meter race, and his performance set a time record that lasted for fifty-two years until Billy Mills, the Sioux distance runner, surpassed it in the 1964 Tokyo Olympics. Tewanima was the first athlete from Arizona to win a medal in the Olympics.

Tewanima returned home to Second Mesa and decided to do what he enjoyed the best—tending his sheep and raising his crops. Just for fun, to watch the trains go by, he would run to Winslow, Arizona, eighty miles away. In 1954, he went back to New York to be named to the All-Time United States Olympic Track and Field Team. In 1957, he was the first person inducted, to a standing ovation, into the Arizona Sports Hall of Fame at a dinner given in his honor.

Into his nineties, Tewanima remained active and happy. A traditional religious man, he participated in Hopi kiva ceremonies throughout his life.

Russell Thornton (1942–)
Cherokee sociologist and author

Russell Thornton is professor of anthropology at the University of California, Los Angeles. He is a well-known sociologist who graduated from the University of Florida with a doctorate in demography, the study of human population growth and decline. Thornton has become one of the leading experts in the study of Native American demography, with population studies of U.S. Indians in a book named *American Indian Holocaust and Survival: A Population History Since 1492* (1987), and a more specific demographic study of the Cherokee in *The Cherokees: A Population History* (1990). Recently, he edited *Studying Native America: Problems and Prospects* (1998).

In addition, Thornton has published articles and a book on the demographic conditions of Plains Indians during the 1870s and 1890s and their influence on the rise of the first (1870) and second (1890) Ghost Dance Movements. The Ghost Dances were a reaction of the California, Plains, and other Indians to the harsh political and economic conditions of the early reservation period in the latter part of the 1800s. Many Indians sought a spiritual solution to their problems by means of the new Ghost Dance religion, which promised a quick return of dead relatives and ancestors, the return and restoration of the buffalo and other depleted animals, and restoration of the old Indian life, free from the reservations and suppression of the United States.

His book *We Shall Live Again: The 1870 and 1890 Ghost Dance Movements* (1982) provides an argument that the rapid declines in population among the Indians during the latter part of the 1800s helped trigger the eruption of the Ghost Dances and also contributed to the Ghost Dance emphasis on the return of dead relatives. In addition, Thornton co-edited with Mary Grasmick an annotated bibliography on urban Indians entitled *Sociology of American Indians: A Critical Bibliography* (1980). This volume provides a listing of major references on issues of Native American urbanization and urban life. In addition, he is the author of numerous academic and other articles on Indian history, demography, and higher education.

Professor Thornton has taught at numerous universities and colleges, including the University of Minnesota, the University of California at Berkeley, and Dartmouth College.

Professor Thornton has served as chair of the Smithsonian Institution's Native American Repatriation Review Committee and is a member of the Native American Studies Advisory Panel for the Social Science

Research Council and the North American Committee of the Human Genome Diversity Project. He has published articles in the *American Indian Quarterly*, *Ethnohistory*, the *American Sociological Review*, and the *American Journal of Physical Anthropology*.

Grace F. Thorpe (1921—)
Sauk and Fox political and environmental activist

Born in Yale, Oklahoma, Grace F. Thorpe, or No-ten-o-quah (Wind Woman), has dedicated her life to improving the conditions of her people as well as American Indians across the nation. She belongs to the Thunder Clan and received her great-grandmother's name—No-ten-o-quah—through a naming ceremony conducted when she was young. Both she and her father, Jim Thorpe, a renowned football player and the first American Indian Olympic gold medalist, received degrees from the Carlisle Indian School in Pennsylvania and the Haskell Institute in Kansas.

Thorpe's career as an activist began around her fiftieth birthday in the 1960's. Before that time, she served two years in New Guinea as a member of the Women's Army Corps during World War II. After being appointed to General Douglas McArthur's staff in Japan,

Grace Thorpe (No-ten-o-quah or Wind Woman).

Thorpe met and married Fred Seeley. The couple gave birth to a son, Thorpe, and a daughter, Dagmar, but later decided to end their marriage.

Around 1950, after selling the Yellow Pages in New York suburbs, Thorpe sold her house, and moved to Washington, D.C., where she worked for the National Congress of American Indians (NCAI), a pan-Indian lobbying organization, for a year. In 1966, Thorpe helped secure land for an educational institution geared toward the needs of American Indian and Chicano students, D-Q University.

While active in the political realm, Thorpe's career as an activist was earmarked by the American Indian occupation of Alcatraz Island in 1969 and 1970. She and her daughter lived on Alcatraz during the first months of 1970, and Thorpe acted as a liaison between the protesters and the media and various governmental agencies. Through her astute negotiations, Thorpe acquired an emergency generator for the island, which helped to prolong the occupation.

After her experiences at Alcatraz, Thorpe and several other activists began demonstrating to reacquire land for American Indians. In June 1970, for example, Thorpe joined a group of Pit River Indians to combat Pacific Gas and Electric's attempts to destroy a 52,000-acre sacred site in Big Bend, California. Although Thorpe was arrested for trespassing, the demonstration was a success. Her later attempts to bring awareness of and change to Native Americans' lives, however, would employ less direct action and more educational and congressional lobbying efforts.

Through the 1970s, Thorpe earned a bachelor degree from the University of Tennessee and pursued postgraduate training in urban studies at the Massachusetts Institute of Technology. In addition, she worked for the American Indian Policy Review Commission and served as a legislative assistant to the U.S. Senate Subcommittee on Indian Affairs. On a more local level, Thorpe taught a seminar on surplus land acquisitions at D-Q University when it opened its doors in 1971 and helped form Return Surplus Lands to Indian People Committees, organized to facilitate the return of unused government lands to Indians.

Thorpe's Oklahoma retirement through the 1980s did not last when she learned in 1992 that her tribe's government was considering nuclear-waste storage in an effort to develop the tribe's economy. The U.S. Department of Energy (DOE) was offering $100,000 to any entity willing to store such wastes. Because of Thorpe's concerted efforts to educate her people about the ill effects of nuclear power and waste, however, tribal members ultimately rejected DOE's offer. After learning that NCAI was holding seminars to promote nuclear-waste storage, she initiated a campaign to ensure that all Indian reservations are nuclear-free, and now 75 tribal communities are nuclear-free zones. She continues to educate Indian peoples about nuclear hazards, participating in such organizations as the National Environmental Coalition of Native Americans and the Nuclear Information and Research Service, and in 1999, she received the Nuclear Free Future Resistance Award in Los Alamos, New Mexico.

She also organized a successful campaign to have her father, Jim Thorpe, declared ABC's *Wide World of Sports*' Athlete of the Century, which was proclaimed prior to Super Bowl XXXIV, on 30 January 2000. Thorpe lives with her daughter, Dagmar, and granddaughter, Tena, in Prague, Oklahoma.

James Francis Thorpe (1887–1953)
Sac and Fox athlete

King Gustav of Sweden described Jim Thorpe as "the greatest athlete in the world." The young man from Prague, Oklahoma, had just won gold medals in the pentathlon and the decathlon in the 1912 Stockholm Olympics and was on top of the sporting world. Seven months later, however, he was stripped of the medals, and his records were expunged from the official Olympic record book. A newspaper reporter learned that he had played semi-professional baseball for fifteen dollars a week. By the Olympic rules in effect in 1912, acceptance of payment for athletic performance disqualified Thorpe from further amateur sports and from eligibility for participation in the Olympic games.

Jim Thorpe excelled in athletics at Carlisle College in Pennsylvania. He held world records in track and field and was a college All-American in lacrosse, basketball, and football. He was coached in football by the legendary Glenn "Pop" Warner and scored fifty touchdowns in forty-four games. In a memorable game against Harvard, he scored a touchdown and kicked four field goals as Carlisle won by a score of 18–15.

After the Olympics, Thorpe played professional baseball from 1913 to 1919 with a career batting average of .252. He went on to play professional football, became the first president of the American Professional Football Association, an organization that would evolve into the modern National Football League.

He was named to both college and professional football halls of fame. The Associated Press voted him the greatest athlete of the first half of the century in 1950. Also in 1950, a feature film starring Burt Lancaster and directed by Michael Curtiz was made about his life.

Jim Thorpe died three years later on his sixty-fifth birthday at his home in Lomita, California. In 1954, a town in Pennsylvania was renamed in his honor. Many Americans from all walks of life began a campaign to have his Olympic medals restored. A rule was found stating that all complaints against athletes had to be filed within thirty days after the conclusion of events; it was not until seven months had gone by that the grievances against Thorpe had been brought up. Twenty years after his death and seventy years after the Stockholm Olympiad, replicas of his medals were returned to his children Charlotte, Gail, Grace, Carl, Bill, and Jack, during the 1984 Olympics in Los Angeles.

On 30 January 2000, ABC's *Wide World of Sports* proclaimed Thorpe Athlete of the Century. He is still the only athlete in history to win both the pentathlon and decathlon in Olympic competition.

John W. Tippeconnic III (1943–)
Comanche-Cherokee educator

John Tippeconnic is professor of education and director of the American Indian Leadership Program at Pennsylvania State University. He previously served as director of Indian education programs with the Department of Education in Washington, D.C. As director, he

John W. Tippeconnic, III.

supervised most of the national Indian education programs that are not delivered by the education division within the Bureau of Indian Affairs. He is also the former director of the Center for Indian Education at Arizona State University, a major research organization focusing on Indian education issues.

He was born in Oklahoma and received a bachelor of arts degree in secondary education from Oklahoma State University and a doctorate from Pennsylvania State University (1975).

Tippeconnic has been a teacher at the Tuba City Boarding School, vice-president of Navajo Community College, and associate professor at Arizona State. He has published twelve articles including "The Place of Bilingual Education in the Education of American Indians" (1982) and "Public School Administration on Indian Reservations" (1984). In 1999, he co-authored with Karen Gayton Swisher, *Next Steps: Research and Practice to Advance Indian Education.*

He has served on the editorial board of the National Association for Bilingual Education, the advisory board of the Urban Indian Law Project, and as consultant at the Native American Research and Training Center at the University of Arizona. His service includes two terms as president of the National Indian Education Association, chair of the American Education Research Association American Indian Education Special Interest Group, and membership on the National Family Literacy Board.

Tippeconnic has served as a consultant to numerous organizations, such as the Native American Rights Fund, National Science Foundation, and the W. K. Kellogg Foundation. His interests include studies in educational policy, Indian control of education, and leadership.

Tomochichi (circa 1650–1739)
Creek tribal leader

Tomochichi was born in the mid-1600s and lived at the Creek village of Apalachukla, along the Chattahoochee River in present-day Alabama. Tomochichi moved to present-day Georgia in the early 1700s when the new English colony was rapidly being settled with the active assistance of Creek leaders like Tomochichi. The Creek tribe was the most cooperative with the English settlers in the Georgia colony.

In 1733, Tomochichi was visited by a party of English colonists led by James Oglethorpe, the founder of the Georgia colony, at which time he signed a peace treaty on behalf of the Creek Nation. In return for massive land grants, the Creek were accorded privileges, such as protection under English law and liberal trading rights.

Tomochichi was praised for his peacemaking efforts and, in 1734, headed a Creek delegation to England with Oglethorpe, where he and his family were presented to King George II and Queen Caroline. The artist Cornelis Verelst painted a famous portrait of the chief and his nephew, Toonahowi, which is on display at the Smithsonian Institution in Washington, D.C.

Tomochichi's friendship with the English led to a long-term Creek-British trade relationship, and he remained a friend to the English for the remainder of his life.

John Baptiste Tootoosis, Jr. (1899–1989)
Cree activist

The grandson of Poundmaker, the famous Cree chief who fought for better treaty terms from Canadian authorities for his people, John Tootoosis was an important political organizer and leader of the Plains Cree people, a tribe that had moved west from central Canada to the Canadian plains with the expansion of the fur trade in the seventeenth century. He was born on his grandfather's reserve, the Poundmaker Indian Reserve in Saskatchewan, and was one of eleven children. When he was young, Tootoosis tended to his father's sheep. At the urging of Canadian authorities, he was sent by his parents to a residential school. At the age of sixteen, John worked for a farmer in Saskatchewan to contribute to the family expenses. In his late teens, he nearly died of an unknown disease, and while he was ill, he vowed that he would devote his life to his people if he were to recover.

Upon his recovery, Tootoosis was chosen chief of his people at the tender age of twenty, only to be informed by Canadian authorities that Canadian law prohibited the selection of a chief under twenty-one years of age. In the same year, Tootoosis demonstrated his rebellious and proud nature by fencing in land on his reserve to prevent Canadian authorities from leasing it to third parties against his people's will. Tootoosis spoke out often against the failure of Canadian authorities to permit Indian people to participate in decisions that affect their lives. He fought for better health care and educational facilities for his people. Tootoosis was instrumental in organizing Native people throughout the province of Saskatchewan and indeed across the country. He was a founding member of the League of Indians of Canada in 1919, the National American Indian Brotherhood in 1943, and the Union of Saskatchewan Indians in 1946. Later in life, Tootoosis worked as a teacher and an authority on the Cree language.

Sheila M. Tousey (contemporary)
Menominee performer

Born in Keshena, Wisconsin, Tousey was raised on both the Menominee and Stockbridge-Munsee reservations in Wisconsin. She began dancing as a small child but did not perform on stage until she attended the University of New Mexico at Albuquerque. At first, she enrolled in the University of New Mexico's Indian Law Program, because she was interested in a career in Indian law, with specialization in federal contracts and Indian-federal legal relations. Later, Tousey changed her major from pre-law to English and studied theater arts.

After completing her undergraduate degree, Tousey attended the graduate acting program at the New York University (NYU) Tisch School of Arts, where she received a master of fine arts degree in 1989. While at NYU, she performed in numerous plays such as *Yerma, The American Dream, The Bald Soprano, The Normal Heart, Children of the Sun, As You Like It,* and *Endgame.*

In 1989, Tousey began performing with the American Indian Dance Theatre, an internationally acclaimed dance troupe based in New York City. As an actress, she has appeared at the Vortex Theatre in Albuquerque, New Mexico, where she had parts in plays such as *Baby with the Bath Water* and *And a Nightingale Sang.*

She made her motion picture debut in *Thunderheart* (1992), and she soon delivered award-winning performances in *The Silent Tongue* (1993), *Medicine River* (1993), and *Grand Avenue* (1996). Her film credits also include *Slaughter of the Innocents* (1994), *Lord of Illusions* (1995), *Ravenous* (1999), *Wildflowers* (2000), and *Backroads* (2000).

Toypurina (fl. 1780s)
Gabrielino tribal leader

Toypurina was a religious and political leader, who, in the 1780s, led a short-lived rebellion against the Spanish at the San Gabriel Mission near present-day Los Angeles, California.

Like many Indians of this region in the late 1700s, Toypurina's people were struggling with the institutions of Spanish settlement and rule. Many Gabrielino Indians believed that Toypurina had spiritual powers that would help them to overcome their Spanish overlords. In 1785, Toypurina planned an uprising against the San Gabriel Mission. She was aided by her apprentice, Nicolas Jose. Together they convinced the Indians of six villages to unite against the Spanish. The recruits were convinced that Toypurina had slain the inhabitants of the mission with her powers. On October 25,

the war parties moved on the mission. The priests and soldiers in the mission had learned of the uprising, however, and arrested the Indian forces.

During their trial Toypurina and Nicolas Jose spoke out against the Spanish. Toypurina decried the taking of Indian land by the Spanish and the suppression of Indian culture and traditional ceremonies. The accusations fell on unsympathetic ears. Participants in the raid were flogged. Nicolas Jose was imprisoned in the presidio at San Diego. Toypurina was exiled from her people to the San Carlos Mission in present-day Carmel, California.

Clifford Trafzer (1949–)
Wyandotte historian

Clifford Trafzer is a distinguished professor of American Indian history and culture at the University of California, Riverside. He is also director of Native American Studies and Public History, and he serves as curator of history at the Western Center.

He was born in Mansfield, Ohio, was raised in Arizona, received his bachelor and master degrees in history from Northern Arizona University, and earned his doctorate in 1973 from Oklahoma State University.

Trafzer has won the Governor's Book Award for *The Renegade Tribe* (1986), the Penn Oakland Award for *Earth Song, Sky Spirit* (1993), and a Wordcraft Circle of Native American Writers Award for *Death Stalks the Yakima* (1999).

He has published over twenty-five books, including *As Long As the Grass Shall Grow and Rivers Flow* (2000), *Exterminate Them!* (1999), and *Chemehuevi People of the Coachella Valley* (1997). He is completing a biography of Wyandot-Huron elder Eleanore Sioui, a new study of Chemehuevi people, and a book on tuberculosis among southern California Indians.

Trafzer has been a museum curator for the Arizona Historical Society, archivist of Special Collections at Northern Arizona University, and tribal consultant for the Colville Confederated Tribe, Shoalwater Bay Tribe, and Twenty-Nine Palms Band.

Mark N. Trahant (1957–)
Shoshone-Bannock publisher, editor, and journalist

Mark Trahant is chairman and chief executive officer at the Robert C. Maynard Institute for Journalism Education in Oakland, California. A member of the Shoshone-Bannock Tribe of Idaho, Trahant was born in Fort Hall, Idaho. He attended Pasadena City College and Idaho State University.

His successful career includes work as a columnist for the *Seattle Times*, editor and publisher of the *Moscow-Pullman Daily News* in Idaho, and syndicated columnist of "Letter from Moscow."

Trahant was also executive news editor at the *Salt Lake City Tribune* & editor-in-chief for the *Sho-Ban News* & a reporter at the *Arizona Republic* & publisher of the tribal weekly *Navajo Times Today* & and the founder, editor, and publisher of *Navajo Nation Today.*

In 1983, he converted the *Navajo Times* into the *Navajo Times Today*, making it the first daily newspaper published for a Navajo audience. As editor and later as publisher, he raised the daily circulation from 2,000 to nearly 12,000. In 1995, he received the National Press Foundation's Editor of the Year citation.

He also was the national desk reporter for *The Arizona Republic*, where he was a finalist for the Pulitzer Prize in 1989 for co-authoring "Fraud in Indian Country." Trahant is also the recipient of the Elias Boudinot Award for Lifetime Contributions to Journalism, the Paul Tobenkin Memorial Prize from Columbia University, the Heywood Broun Award, and the George Polk Award for National Reporting.

In 1995, Trahant was a visiting professional scholar at the Freedom Forum's First Amendment Center at Vanderbilt University. He is the author of *Pictures of Our Nobler Selves* (1995), a historical survey of American Indian contributions to journalism.

He is a trustee of the Freedom Forum and serves on a number of advisory boards, including the D'Arcy McNickle Center for American Indian History at the Newberry Library in Chicago. Trahant is past president and a current member of the Native American Journalists Association. He is married to LeNora Begay Trahant, and they have two sons, Marvin and Elias.

John Trudell (1947–)
Santee Sioux activist and musician

John Trudell was an active leader in many Native American protests of the 1960s and 1970s.

He participated in the 1969 occupation of Alcatraz Island by Indians of All Tribes, Inc., an organization that symbolized participation of all American Indians. He joined the Alcatraz occupation ten days after the 20 November 1969 landing and remained on the island until U.S. officials removed the last fifteen occupiers on 11 June 1971. The occupation of Alcatraz Island was an attempt by urban Indians to attract national attention to the failure of U.S. government policy toward American Indians. Trudell became the occupation's voice through Radio Free Alcatraz, a radio station set up on the island which broadcast from Berkeley, Los Angeles,

John Trudell.

and New York City, thus bringing the occupation and the concerns of Indian people before a national audience. During the occupation period, Trudell traveled throughout the nation, speaking to Indian and non-Indian groups regarding the occupation and raising support for the return of Alcatraz Island to Indian people. Alcatraz Island, however, later became a national park. The occupation of Alcatraz Island is seen by many as an early catalyst to the rising Red Power movement which continued into the mid-1970s.

Trudell joined the American Indian Movement (AIM) in the spring of 1970 and became a national spokesman for AIM soon thereafter. Although much of its inspiration derived from Indian fishing-rights battles during the 1960s and 1970s in the states of Washington and Oregon, AIM's initial concerns were jobs, housing, education, and the protection of Indians from police abuse and violence. In 1970, AIM started a program to assist juvenile offenders as an alternative to reform school.

Trudell participated in the 1972 Trail of Broken Treaties, a national car-caravan bringing together urban and reservation Indians from across the nation designed to culminate in the presentation of a formal list of demands on the federal government by Indian people. Lack of communication between leaders of the caravan and federal officials resulted in an impasse and a seventy-one hour occupation of the Bureau of Indian Affairs office in Washington, D.C., where thousands of dollars worth of damage to the building and office equipment occurred.

Trudell was elected co-chair of AIM in 1973, and he participated in the 1973 armed seizure of Wounded Knee, a small town in the heart of the Pine Ridge Sioux Reservation in South Dakota. Wounded Knee is the site of the 1890 massacre by the Seventh Cavalry of Sioux Chief Big Foot and two hundred or more Sioux men, women, and children.

In 1976, he coordinated the AIM support for the defense of Leonard Peltier, who was convicted of murdering two FBI agents in June 1975 on the Pine Ridge Reservation. Trudell's wife Tina, her mother, and the three Trudell children were burned to death in a mysterious fire on 11 February 1979, twelve hours after Trudell, during a demonstration in support of Leonard Peltier, burned an upside-down American flag on the steps of the FBI building in Washington, D.C.

Devastated by the loss of his family, Trudell began writing poetry as a form of therapy. In 1981, Trudell published a book of poetry, *Living in Reality*, and soon decided he wanted to combine his poetry with music.

In 1985, he met Jesse Ed Davis, a Kiowa guitarist from Oklahoma. A year later, Davis provided the music on Trudell's debut album, *AKA Grafitti Man*. Released on Trudell's own label, Peace Company, in cassette-only format, the album gained critical attention despite its limited distribution. Trudell and Davis released a second album, *Heart Jump Bouquet*, together and recorded in the Tribal Voice series, *...But This Isn't El Salvador*, in 1987.

Following the death of Davis in 1988, a tour as the opening act for the popular and highly politicized Australian band, Midnight Oil, brought Trudell and the Grafitti Band mainstream exposure. In 1991, Trudell recorded a third album, *Fables and Realities*. In 1992, Trudell produced a third in the Tribal Voice series titled *Child's Voice: Children of the Earth*. The same year, he signed with Rykodisc and with a remake of his original *AKA Grafitti Man*, produced by Jackson Browne, his music reached worldwide distribution. *Johnny Damas and Me*, his second album with Rykodisc, was released in 1994.

Trudell has also appeared in numerous films and documentaries, including *Powwow Highway* (1989), *Incident at Oglala* (1992), *Thunderheart* (1992), *On Deadly Ground* (1994), *Extreme Measures* (1996), *Smoke Signals* (1998), and *Alcatraz Is Not an Island* (2000).

He tours worldwide with his band, lives in Los Angeles, California, and is currently completing *Permanent Paranoia*, an autobiographical play.

Roger Tsabetsye (1941–)
Zuni Pueblo artist

Roger Tsabetsye was born in Zuni, New Mexico. The Zuni Pueblo is one of nineteen villages in eastern New Mexico known for their strong ties to their traditional religion, ceremonies, and culture. Tsabetsye was educated at the Institute of American Indian Arts, the government-operated Indian art school in Santa Fe, New Mexico, and also studied at the School for American Craftsmen, where he majored in silver and metal processing, and the Rochester Institute of Technology.

He is one of the first people, along with Fritz Scholder, the famous California Indian artist, to actively express their combined traditional and modern artistic training gained from the arts program at the Institute of American Indian Arts. Tsabetsye taught art at the institute and helped develop the school's curriculum and philosophy.

Working principally in three different media—painting, ceramics, and silver—Tsabetsye has exhibited at the Heard Museum in Phoenix, the Scottsdale (Arizona) Indian National Art Show, the Museum of Santa Fe, the New York American Indian Art Center, and numerous other exhibitions. His work has received many awards and honors, and in 1968 he was asked by President Lyndon Johnson to create a squash blossom for the president of Costa Rica. During this time, Tsabetsye was an Indian representative at several conferences in Washington, D.C., to help initiate President Johnson's War on Poverty.

Tsabetsye is also the founder and owner of Tsabetsye Enterprises, a company specializing in the merchandising (retail and wholesale) of Zuni jewelry. The company illustrates Tsabetsye's personal philosophy that American Indians should be partners with the rest of U.S. society.

Richard Van Camp (1971–)
Dogrib author

A recipient of the 1997 Canadian Authors Association Air Canada Award for "most promising Canadian author under 30," Richard Van Camp is a member of the Dogrib Nation from Fort Smith, Northwest Territory (NWT), Canada. He is the author of a novel, *The Lesser Blessed*, and two children's books: *A Man Called Raven* and *What's the Most Beautiful Thing You Know About Horses?*, illustrated by Cree artist George Littlechild.

Besides receiving his bachelor of fine arts in creative writing from the University of Victoria and two certificates—one from the En'owkin International School of Writing (Certificate in Native Creative Writing) and the other from Aurora College (Certificate in Native Management Studies)—he has studied land claims in Yellowknife, NWT, Reiki in Bella Bella, British Columbia, and acupuncture in Hangzhou, China.

Van Camp was a script and cultural consultant for CBC Television's *North of 60* television series for four seasons. He has been published in numerous anthologies including *Crisp Blue Edges: Indigenous Creative Non-Fiction, A Shade of Spring, Blue Dawn, Red Earth, Gatherings,* and *Descant* (Summer 1993); *Inner Harbour Review,* and *Whetstone* (Fall 1994); and *Steal My Rage.* He was also commissioned to write a radio drama in 1998 for CBC's Festival of Fiction. "Mermaids" was broadcast nationally several times and was narrated by Cree actor Ben Cardinal. "Mermaids" was later published in the *International Indigenous Anthology: Skins.*

His awards include the 1992 Bessie Silcox Scholarship Award from the Dene National Office; the 1992 En'owkin International School of Writing's William Armstrong Award for Poetry; the 1993 Yellowknife Rotary Club's Donald J. Cardinal Memorial Award; the 1993 NWT Literacy Council's Norman Macpherson Award; the 1995 University of Victoria Scholarship's Millen Undergraduate Award; the 1996 University of Victoria Scholarship's The Hazel Partridge-Smith Bursary in Creative Writing; and the 1999 Canadian Children's Centre's Our Choice Award for *What's The Most Beautiful Thing You Know About Horses?*

Van Camp has toured internationally with visits from coast to coast Canada to Jamaica, Australia, and the United States. *The Lesser Blessed* was recently translated into German by Ravensberger. Van Camp is currently working on a graphic novel titled *Gift.*

Joseph Vasquez (1917–)
Sioux-Apache activist

Joseph Vasquez has been an advocate for Native American causes throughout his life, on both national and local levels. Among his many posts and positions, he has served as a Los Angeles city commissioner (1968–1970) and president and chairman of the Los Angeles Indian Center from 1958 to 1970.

Vasquez was born in Primero, Colorado. He was educated at the U.S. Armed Forces Institute and later attended classes at the University of California, Los Angeles. He served in the U.S. Army Air Corps from 1943 to 1945 as a pilot and flight engineer. From 1947 to 1968, Vasquez worked for Hughes Aircraft as a small business coordinator and minority group representative. From 1970 to 1972, he worked for the National Council on Indian Opportunity in Washington, D.C. From 1972 to 1980, Vasquez worked for U.S. Department of Commerce, Office of Minority Business Enterprise. Vasquez held a number of other positions, including officer of the National Congress of American Indians, a national organization for mobilizing Indian communities on congressional legislative issues. He also founded and promoted the National Business Development Organization for Native Americans. Vasquez has served on advisory committees for the mayor of Los Angeles and the California attorney general's office. Vasquez retired by 1980.

Pablita Velarde (1918–)
Santa Clara Pueblo painter

Pablita Velarde is an acclaimed Native American painter whose works reflect the culture and heritage of her people.

Velarde was born in the Santa Clara Pueblo of New Mexico and educated at the Santa Fe Indian School. Her love for art and talent as an artist has been traced to a childhood eye disease that temporarily restricted her sight. According to one biographer, when Velarde's sight was regained, it gave her a new appreciation of visual perception. Velarde studied art under Dorothy Dunn, a pioneer among Indian artists. In 1938 Velarde built a studio for her work in Santa Clara and began her career in earnest.

One of Velarde's first works is still her most renowned—a series of painted murals containing composite pictures depicting the day-to-day life and culture of the Rio Grande Pueblos. In 1954 she was decorated by the French government in appreciation of her art. During the middle 1950s, Velarde developed a unique painting technique that employs colored rocks that are ground and mixed to create a pliable, textured painting material. With this material, Velarde has produced works that recall the art of her ancestors and that make effective use of traditional designs and pictographs in her work. Another of Velarde's paintings that has received widespread acclaim is *Old Father, the Story Teller* (1960). With a unique and insightful composition, the painting links traditional Native American legends and universal human beliefs. Velarde is also the author and illustrator of *Old Father, the Story Teller* (1989), in which the painting of the same name appears. Her work is shown in the Museum of New York's Hall of Ethnology, the De Young Museum of San Francisco, many southwestern galleries, and held in numerous private collections.

Wilma Victor (1919–)
Choctaw educator

Wilma Victor is a distinguished educator who is now retired. Born in Idabel, Oklahoma, she was educated at Haskell Institute, an Indian boarding school, and at the University of Kansas. She received a bachelor of sciences degree in education from the University of Wisconsin, then earned a master of school administration degree from the University of Oklahoma in 1952 and a doctorate from Utah State University.

Victor grew up listening to tales of the Choctaw Trail of Tears to Indian Territory (present-day Oklahoma), and she decided at an early age to complete school and pursue the field of education. It was rare in those days for an Indian woman to aspire to higher education. After receiving her bachelor's degree, she worked for the Bureau of Indian Affairs (BIA) in Shiprock, New Mexico, on the Navajo Reservation. During World War II, she enlisted in the Women's Army Corps (WACs) from 1943 to 1946. Then Victor resumed work for the BIA, where she steadily rose through the ranks and worked in several important positions, including deputy area director for its Phoenix, Arizona, office, and for the Institute of American Indian Arts in Santa Fe, New Mexico.

Other duties Victor has had include superintendent of the Intermountain School District, director of women's programs for the U.S. Department of the Interior, acting director of Indian Education, and special assistant to Secretary of the Interior Rogers C. B. Morton. Her honors include Indian Council Fire National Achievement Award, the Anadarko Indian Exposition's Indian of the Year Award (1971), Distinguished Alumnus Award from the University of Wisconsin (1972), and Distinguished Service Award from the Department of the Interior (1975), the department housing the BIA which is responsible for managing Indian affairs. Her interests feature women's advocacy issues and Indian self-determination.

Victorio (Beduiat) (1825–1880)
Mimbreno Apache tribal leader

As a young man, Victorio fought with Mangas Coloradas, a leader in the early Apache war of the 1860s. Upon Coloradas's death in 1863, Victorio assumed control of his followers. The fighting group consisting of warriors from many tribes collectively came to be known as Ojo Caliente (Warm Springs), since their agency was located near Ojo Caliente in present-day southwest New Mexico.

Throughout the 1870s, Victorio and his followers alternated between sporadic raiding and confinement to reservation lands. In 1877 Victorio agreed to end the fighting if he and his followers were allowed to settle at Warm Springs. When these negotiations broke down, Victorio and his followers were moved to the San Carlos Reservation in present-day Arizona. They found reservation life unbearable, however, and on 2 September 1877, Victorio and about three hundred followers escaped the reservation. Though the majority of the Apache gave themselves up a month later, Victorio and about eighty warriors remained in mountain hideouts where they continued to wage a war of resistance for several years. His strategically placed encampments forced U.S. soldiers to fight in small numbers, allowing Victorio's forces to make good use of their limited numbers.

In 1879, Victorio tried once again to settle at Warm Springs, then later at the Mescalero Reservation at Tularosa, New Mexico. When U.S. authorities threatened to try him for murder, however, Victorio escaped. Joined by a large force of Mescalero, Victorio continued to wage strikes in Texas, New Mexico, and Arizona. For several months, Victorio confounded U.S. forces by keeping them off balance and forcing them to disperse their troops over wide areas, thereby diminishing their effectiveness. Finally, in October 1880, he was surprised by Mexican forces on the plains of Chihuahua in Mexico. He fought until his ammunition was gone, then killed himself.

Gerald Robert Vizenor (1934–)
Chippewa author and teacher

Gerald Vizenor, professor of American studies at the University of California, Berkeley, is a teacher, novelist, and poet. He was born in Minneapolis, Minnesota, and spent a difficult childhood as a consequence of his family's poverty and his father's death. Both of these elements have been incorporated as metaphors in a number of his works.

Vizenor was educated at New York University, received a bachelor of arts from the University of Minnesota, and later studied at Harvard University. He has been a social worker, civil rights organizer, journalist, and community advocate for tribal people living in urban centers. He organized an Indian Studies program at Bemidji State University in Minnesota, and has previously taught tribal literature at Lake Forest College, the

University of Oklahoma, and the University of California, Santa Cruz.

Vizenor has been recognized as a multifaceted writer, and his published works include novels such as *Darkness in Saint Louis/Bearheart* (1978), *Griever: An American Monkey King in China* (1987), which won the American Book Award, and *The Trickster of Liberty* (1988). He has created volumes of haiku, a Japanese form of writing poetry, some of which are published in *Raising the Moon Vines* and *Seventeen Chirps* (1964) and *Empty Swings* (1967). Narratives and traditional tales and songs are published in *The Everlasting Sky: New Voices from the People Named Chippewa* (1972), *Wordarrows: Indians and Whites in the New Fur Trade* (1978), and *Summer in the Spring* (1981).

His most recent publications include critical studies, *Manifest Manners: Narratives on Post-Indian Survivance* (1999), and *Fugitive Poses: Native American Scenes of Absence and Presence* (1998); novels, *The Heirs of Columbus* (1991), *Dead Voices* (1992), *Hotline Healers: An Almost Browne Novel* (1997), and *Shadow Distance: A Gerald Vizenor Reader* (1994); autobiographical works, *Interior Landscapes: Autobiographical Myths and Metaphors* (1990), and *Post-Indian Conversations* (1999).

Wabaunsee (1780–1848)
Potawatomi tribal leader

Wabaunsee was a renowned Potawatomi war chief who lived on the Kankakee River in present-day Illinois, forty miles southwest of Lake Michigan. During the War of 1812, Wabaunsee fought on the side of the British, helping take Fort Dearborn in present-day Michigan. After the battle, however, he protected U.S. captives from execution.

Wabaunsee participated in the Greenville Council in July 1814, in which he and several other tribes agreed to ally themselves with the United States against Britain. In 1816, he signed the Treaty of Wabash in Indiana, selling tribal lands to the U.S. government. In 1826, Wabaunsee signed the second Treaty of the Wabash, ceding even more Potawatomi lands. This selling of Indian lands led to internal strife among the Potawatomi, and Wabaunsee was attacked and stabbed. Indian agent Thomas Tipton intervened and saved his life.

In 1832, during the Black Hawk War, Wabaunsee joined the Illinois militia and fought against the Sac and Fox. In 1835, he traveled to Washington, D.C., and signed a treaty ceding the remainder of Potawatomi lands in Illinois and Indiana in exchange for territory west of the Mississippi River in present-day Kansas.

Wabaunsee settled on the Missouri River near Council Bluffs, Iowa.

Walkara (Walker) (1801–1855)
Ute tribal leader

Between 1830 and 1855, Walkara was probably the most powerful and renowned Native American leader in the Great Basin area, largely western Nevada. His daring bravery and cunning sagacity earned him nicknames such as Hawk of the Mountains, Iron-Twister, and Napoleon of the Desert. Walkara's sheer prowess, physical strength, and agility allowed him to gain enough influence to eventually surmount tribal feuds between the Ute, Paiute, and Shoshone, and organize a corps of raiders who terrorized an area from the Mexican border almost to Canada and from California to New Mexico.

A fierce opportunist, Walkara at various times collaborated with Indians, mountainmen, and Mormons, a religious sect that settled around Salt Lake in present-day Utah. In the winter of 1839, he and several companions stole more than three thousand horses in a daring night raid on the wealthiest Los Angeles rancheros. This escapade earned him the title Greatest Horse Thief in History. For over a decade, he and his followers raided villages for slaves and demanded goods and supplies from travelers on the Old Spanish Trail, which passed through much of present-day Nevada. He became wealthy, kept a number of wives, and wore both Indian and American finery.

Accepting of the Mormons at first, Walkara even converted to their religion under the persistence of Brigham Young, an early founding leader of Mormonism. However, their ubiquitous population of Ute tribal territories soon frustrated him. Overgrazing of land, coupled with a measles epidemic, and an Indian-Mormon confrontation at Springville, Utah, led him to fight and lose the bitter "Walker War" in 1853. His power all but gone and his land now in the possession of the Mormons, Walkara died two years later. Fifteen horses were killed in his honor at his funeral.

Kateri Walker (contemporary)
Ojibwa actress

Kateri Walker, whose full name is Mary Margaret Kateri Tekakwitha Walker, has acted in many films and plays, including the 1994 and 1995 theater production of *Black Elk Speaks*, the 1998 film *Outside Ozona*, the 1999 Ojibway language film *The Strange Case of Bunny Weequod*, and the HBO television series *Arliss*. While these are some of the actress' personal favorites, she

Kateri Walker.

also appeared in the 1995 film version of Nathaniel Hawthorne's *The Scarlet Letter*, and on the popular soap opera *As the World Turns*.

Walker was born in Michigan, the fifth of six children to Mary Anne Julienne (DeLeary) Walker (Chippewa of the Thames First Nations) and James Raymond Walker (Saginaw Chippewa). Although her early years were spent on the reservation, she attended a government-run Catholic boarding school for Indian children, where she officially performed for the first time. When she was six, Walker and her best friend performed at a school assembly. The nuns, however, did not support their creative efforts and told the girls that acting was an unethical profession not worth pursuing.

When Walker was in second grade, her mother moved the family off the reservation to give them a better life. Despite conflicts with her high school counselor, who told her that her SAT scores were too low and that she had little chance of becoming successful, Walker graduated with honors and entered Michigan Technological University, the only school to which she applied. While there, Walker studied chemical engineering. Before graduation, however, the to-be actress decided to follow her dreams; she transferred to the University of Michigan, where she received her degree in theater and drama.

Walker feels that the performance industry needs more Native voices and perspectives: "Unless we continue to grow as writers, producers, directors, and actors, our concerns will lay dormant. We won't be able to address our concerns regarding ourselves until we tell our stories." She argues that Native actors continue to be cast in a romantic light. Native American performers must take an active role in changing and expanding their career options.

In addition to her acting, Walker is a jingle-dress dancer on the powwow circuit. She also spends a lot of time speaking to people about American Indian issues and cultures. Walker believes that education is the key to understanding and overcoming differences.

The actress has received several awards for her performances. In 1999, she accepted a Horizon Award for Rising Talent at the San Francisco Film Institute's American Indian Motion Picture Awards for her lead roles in *Home*, a film short, and *The Strange Case of Bunny Weequod*. The same year, Walker was presented with the Outstanding Performance by an Actress in Film Award at the First Americans in the Arts, held in Beverly Hills, California, for her role in *Outside Ozona*.

Walker now resides in the Los Angeles area and is a devoted aunt to her fifteen nephews and three nieces.

Nancy Ward (circa 1740–1822)
Cherokee tribal leader

Nancy Ward was a descendant of Osconostota, the Great Warrior of the Cherokee Nation. While some authorities argue that she was a full-blood, others state that her father was a British officer named Ward. Nancy Ward was of the Wolf clan and was the niece of Old Hop, emperor of the nation in the 1750s, and sister to Attakullaculla, the Wise Councillor of the Cherokee, also active in the 1750s.

Ward received her title Ghighau, "Beloved Woman," from the Cherokee as the result of her bravery during the battle of Taliwa in 1755. While still a teenager, she came to the battlefield at Taliwa (near the present Canton, Georgia) with a five-hundred-man attack party led by Osconostota, the Great Warrior of the Cherokee. Fighting bravely, Ward stood fast in the battle against the Creek, enemies of the Cherokee. As a result of the battle, the Creek abandoned their Georgia and Alabama towns and opened that land to the Cherokee, who gradually occupied the area.

As a reward for her participation in the battle, Ward received a Negro slave and became the first Cherokee slaveholder. She then rejoined her two children at

Chota, the Cherokee capital in present-day Monroe County, Tennessee, and took her place of leadership in the Cherokee Nation. She married Brian Ward, a trader who had fought in the French and Indian War.

In the years following the Battle of Taliwa, Ward intervened on numerous occasions to save the lives of non-Indian captives of the Cherokee, a supreme right available only to the Ghighau (denied even to chiefs), and during the outbreaks of 1780, she helped many colonial prisoners escape, thus earning the respect of the American troops encroaching on Cherokee lands. Ward accompanied Old Tassell, chief of the Cherokee, to Hopewell on the Keowee River in South Carolina for a council with the Americans. Ward spoke for the Cherokee people at the peace conference and, following her speech, gave two strings of wampum, a pipe, and some tobacco to the U.S. commissioners. Following the treaty, Ward and her people entered into a more peaceful era. Her last recorded official act was a warning to the Cherokee people against further treaties and land cessions. The document was a premonition of the treaties that ultimately took Cherokee lands and forced them onto the infamous Trail of Tears and relocation to Indian Territory in present-day Oklahoma.

Ward's counsel, according to her people, bordered on the supreme. A granite statue of Ward now stands in Arnwine Cemetery, Granger County, Tennessee, a lasting tribute to a Beloved Woman.

Washakie (Gambler's Gourd) (1804–1900)
Flathead-Shoshone tribal leader

Few Indians were as helpful to the westward passage of immigrants as Washakie. He was probably born in Montana's Bitterroot Mountains. When his father died, Washakie went to live with his mother's eastern Shoshone family in the Wind River mountain chain of Wyoming. He was evidently a brave fighter as a young man against the Blackfeet and Crow. The Shoshone in this area maintained friendships with mountain men and trappers. During the 1820s through the 1830s, Washakie met and became friends with Jim Bridger, the famous mountain man, and Christopher "Kit" Carson, the U.S. commander who rounded up the Navajo in the 1860s.

Washakie became the principal head of his band in the 1840s. The Shoshone became known for their hospitable relations with the United States. Washakie went as far as providing regular patrols of his men to guard and assist immigrants along that region of the Oregon Trail. During this time, he became friends with Brigham Young and spent part of one winter at the Mormon leader's home.

Washakie's band settled on the Wind River Reservation in present-day Wyoming. The Treaty of Fort Bridger in 1863 guaranteed safe passage for U.S. travelers in exchange for a twenty-year annuity paid to Washakie. The same year, he signed a second treaty giving the Union Pacific Railroad Company right-of-way to lay track in the region. The Shoshone served as scouts for the military against the Arapaho, Cheyenne, Sioux, and Ute in 1869, when Camp Brown was constructed in present-day Wyoming. In 1876, Washakie and two hundred warriors joined forces too late to help General Crook against the Sioux at the Battle of the Rosebud in southern Montana, but harassed and pursued Crazy Horse's warriors to the Powder River region in present-day eastern Montana.

In honor of his help to the U.S. military, Camp Brown was renamed Fort Washakie in 1878. President Ulysses S. Grant gave him a silver saddle the same year, and President Chester A. Arthur visited him in 1883 on a trip to Yellowstone Park. In 1897 Washakie became a Christian and was baptized as an Episcopalian. He died three years later and was buried with full military honors at the fort bearing his name.

Lucille J. Watahomigie (1945–)
Hualapai educator

Lucille Watahomigie is an educator and has extensive skills in Indian education, health, program development, and employment. She was born in Valentine, Arizona, and received a master of science degree specializing in education from the University of Arizona (1973). Watahomigie is a member of the Hualapai tribe of Arizona, a people who lived near the Grand Canyon and whose economy was based on hunting and gathering in the desert and river terrain.

Watahomigie worked as a curriculum specialist for San Diego State University (1978–1980). She has served as a member of the Hualapai Tribal Council (1978–1981) and as chair of the Hualapai Tribal Education Committee (1980–1981). She has published extensively about Hualapai studies. Her written work includes *Spirit Mountain: An Yuman Anthology of Stories and Songs* (1984), co-edited with Leanne Hinton, an anthropologist, and *Hualapai Reference Grammar* (1982), co-edited with Jorigine Bender and Akira Y. Yomaota. Watahomigie's honors include the Phoenix High School Hall of Fame (1977) and she was designated an Outstanding Young Woman of America (1980). She remains active publishing papers on language and literacy among American Indians and with a focus on the

Hualapai language. In 1998 she published "The Native Language is a Gift: A Hualapai Language Autobiography" in *The International Journal of the Sociology of Language* 132. Among her interests are women's advocacy activities centered on child-care programs.

Charlie Watt (1944–)
Inuit senator

Charlie Watt was born in Fort Chimo, a small settlement destined to become the administrative center of the Inuit community in northern Quebec, as well as its largest population center. Watt learned the Inuit skills necessary to become a respected hunter and fisherman. He entered a training program sponsored by Canadian authorities and later found employment with the federal Department of Indian Affairs and Northern Development. During this period, Watt became increasingly critical of the department's policies regarding the Inuit people, and he concluded that the Inuit needed to organize in order to speak for themselves. He was soon conducting a tour of all the Inuit communities in northern Quebec to promote an Inuit association. His work and travels paid off when, in 1972, he became the founding president of the Northern Quebec Inuit Association.

Charlie Watt soon occupied the national spotlight when Quebec announced plans to construct a massive hydroelectric project, known as James Bay I, in the north of the province. Watt and his association, in alliance with the Cree people, fought the project and later participated in the negotiation of a land claims agreement with the Quebec government. The agreement created numerous Inuit governmental agencies, including the Makivik Corporation, an exclusively Inuit organization mandated to represent and promote Inuit interests. Watt became the founding president of the Makivik Corporation in 1978.

Watt also was one of several aboriginal leaders to negotiate with the federal government in the 1980s on matters relating to constitutional reform and aboriginal people. In recognition of his contribution to Canada, Watt was appointed to the Canadian Senate in 1983. As senator he has been active in many Native and Inuit issues. At a meeting of the Inuit Circumpolar Conference in 1998, Senator Watt proposed formation of an economic union among the Inuit peoples of the circumpolar region, which spans the United States, Canada, Russia, and Greenland. He has consistently promoted economic development for his people, and he has been involved in numerous successful business ventures, including a commercial fishery and the first aboriginal-owned airline in the country. In 1994, he was awarded

the Order of Quebec, and in 1997, he received a National Aboriginal Achievement Award.

George Watts (1945–)
Nuu-chah-nulth tribal leader

George Watts's people, the Nuu-chah-nulth, are located on the western coast of Vancouver Island, British Columbia. They are famed canoe builders, known for carving oceangoing canoes out of huge cedar trees. Watts was born and raised in Port Alberni, British Columbia, in a large family and spent his childhood picking wild berries and vegetables in the mountains. His father worked six days a week and Watts sold fish at a local market to buy clothes for school. He attended elementary and high school in his hometown until 1963, and then moved to Vancouver to attend Vancouver City College and then the University of British Columbia to study chemical engineering and education. During his university years, he worked in a local paper mill to help finance his studies.

Watts has served as president of the Nuu-chah-nulth Tribal Council, formed in 1958 to advance the rights and interests of the Nuu-chah-nulth Nation, comprised of otherwise disparate and dispersed communities. The tribal council has been extraordinarily successful in this regard; it has shaped aboriginal politics in the province and produced aboriginal leaders of significance. For a relatively brief period in the 1970s, Watts also was a member of the executive committee of the Union of British Columbia Indian Chiefs, a province-wide organization devoted to aboriginal rights, at a time when the union placed great emphasis on grassroots organizing and economic and political self-sufficiency for aboriginal people in the province.

In more recent years, Watts was instrumental in directing and organizing a challenge to clear-cut logging on Meares Island, British Columbia, and in 1985, he and his people succeeded in obtaining an injunction against further logging activity. The court's reasons had major, positive ramifications for similar claims made by other aboriginal groups in the province. Watts has participated in a number of federal and provincial committees and boards addressing matters of economic development and education. He is a board member of Forest Renewal, British Columbia, and the owner of a consulting firm. As a chief of the Nuu-chah-nulth Tribal Council, representing twelve First Nations, Watts participated in negotiations for a modern treaty with British Columbia. After six years of negotiation, in December 2000 British Columbia made a formal treaty offer to return land, funds, and economic and cultural rights to the Nuu-chah-nulth Tribal Council. The offer is under negotiation.

Annie Dodge Wauneka (1910–1997)
Navajo tribal leader

Annie Dodge Wauneka, the daughter of Henry Chee Dodge, was a strong advocate for the Navajo people in politics, economics, and health. She was the first woman to be elected to the Navajo Tribal Council and in 1964 was the first Native American to receive the Presidential Medal of Freedom.

Wauneka's passion for Native American advocacy can be traced, in part, to the influence of her father Henry Chee Dodge, who was an important figure in the Navajo community. His ideas and actions became a model for many Navajo in the early twentieth century. Annie Dodge was born in a hogan in Old Sawmill, Arizona, and attended the Albuquerque Indian School. Perhaps her principal education, however, came at the side of her father, as he traveled the Navajo Reservation tending to the needs of his people. The poverty and sickness she witnessed as a young child became the focus of her life's work.

Wauneka concentrated her efforts on reducing death and illness from tuberculosis on the reservation. After studying with the U.S. Public Health Service, she sought to implement a health education program in her own community. Four years after her father's death, Wauneka was elected to the tribal council.

As a member of the tribal council, Wauneka focused on Navajo health issues and was appointed chair of the council's Health and Welfare Committee. In this role she campaigned for and won funds for water sanitation and home improvements. Wauneka also established a radio program that focused on health information and an open discussion of social concerns. Wauneka's efforts paid off; during her years as health director the incidence of tuberculosis among her people was greatly reduced.

Wauneka was equally adamant about obtaining better education for her people. She believed that poor education was a major factor inhibiting a better life for the Navajo. Wauneka was also an outspoken advocate against alcohol abuse and combined her health and education programs with alcohol awareness and treatment.

Wauneka received numerous awards and honors throughout her lifetime, including Arizona's Woman of the Year Achievement Award, given by the Arizona Women's Press Association, the Josephine B. Hughes Memorial Award, and the Indian Achievement Award. She continued to advise the Navajo tribal council and

her people on numerous issues until her death on 10 November 1997, at the age of eighty-seven.

James Welch (1940–)
Blackfeet-Gros Ventre novelist

James Welch is a critically acclaimed novelist whose works have dealt with realistic portrayals of life on and off the Blackfeet Indian Reservation in Montana. He was born in Browning, Montana, and attended the University of Minnesota, Northern Montana College, and received a bachelor of arts degree from the University of Montana. He has been a laborer, forest service employee, firefighter, and counselor for Upward Bound. He served on the literature panel of the National Endowment for the Arts and on the Montana State Board of Pardons. He has taught American Indian literature and creative writing at the University of Washington, Cornell University, and Colorado College.

His novel *Fools Crow* (1986) received an American Book Award, the *Los Angeles Times* Book Prize, and the Pacific Northwest Bookseller's Award. Welch's other novels include *Winter in the Blood* (1975), *The Death of Jim Loney* (1979), *The Indian Lawyer* (1990), and *The Heartsong of Charging Elk* (2000). Other works include a collection of poetry, *Riding the Earthboy 40* (1971), and a non-fiction book with Paul Steckler, *Killing Custer* (1994).

W. Richard West (1943–)
Cheyenne/Arapaho museum director and lawyer

Before becoming director of the Smithsonian Institution's National Museum of the American Indian, W. Richard West was a legal partner in the Washington, D.C., legal office of Fried, Frank, Harris, Shriver, and Jacobson, and later in the Indian-owned Albuquerque office of Gover, Stetson, Williams, and West, P.C. While working in this capacity, West represented numerous Indian people, tribes, and organizations before federal, state, and tribal courts, various executive departments of the federal government, and Congress. He devoted much of his personal time to working with American Indians on cultural, legal, and governmental issues.

As director of the National Museum of the American Indian, West is responsible for guiding the successful opening of the three facilities that will comprise the entire museum's holdings and facilities. He oversaw the completion of the George Gustav Heye Center, the museum's exhibition that opened in October 1994 in New York City. He is presently supervising the overall planning of the museum's Cultural Resource Center in

Painter W. Richard West.

Suitland, Maryland, which will house the museum's 800,000-object collection. The Mall Museum, the last to be added to the National Mall in Washington, D.C., is scheduled to open in 2002.

West is a member of the Ford Foundation, the American Indian Research Institute, the National Trust for Historic Preservation, the Bush Foundation, and the National Support Committee of the Native American Rights Fund. He is the former chair (1998–2000) of the board of directors of the American Association of Museums, the nation's only national membership organization representing all types of museums and museum professionals.

West grew up in Musckogee, Oklahoma, and was born in San Bernardino, California, to Walter Richard West, Sr., and Maribelle McCrea West. He earned a bachelor of arts degree in history from the University of Redlands in California in 1965. He received his master's degree in American history from Harvard University in 1968. West graduated from Stanford University School of Law in 1971, where he was the recipient of the

Hilmer Oehlmann, Jr., Prize for excellence in legal writing.

West is married to Mary Beth Braden West, who is an attorney and an ambassador with the Department of State in Washington, D.C. The couple is rearing two children, Amy and Ben.

Wetamoo (1650–1676)
Wampanoag tribal leader

Wetamoo was a sachem of the Pocasset band of Wampanoag in 1675 when King Philip's War broke out. She provided important military support to Philip during the conflict.

Wetamoo was raised in the area around Tiverton, Rhode Island, not far from the outskirts of Plymouth Colony. Her father was a sachem of the Wampanoag Confederacy, which was an alliance of Algonkian-speaking Indians living in present-day New England. When Wetamoo's second husband died, Wetamoo succeeded him as a sachem of the Pocasset band of Wampanoag, making her a representative in the Wampanoag Confederacy. Wetamoo's third husband was King Philip's brother, Alexander, who died in 1661. Wetamoo and Philip believed that the colonists had poisoned Alexander. Upon Alexander's death, Philip became grand sachem of the Wampanoag Confederacy in 1662.

In 1675, when King Philip's War erupted, Wetamoo was married to Petononowit, who expressed his intention to align himself with the colonists. Wetamoo, however, left him and threw her forces into the fray on Philip's behalf. She provided Philip with valuable military support during the war. One of the war's first major conflicts took place near Wetamoo's village in Pocasset Swamp in July 1675. Wetamoo sent her warriors into the battle. The battle, however, turned out badly for the Wampanoag, and Wetamoo took refuge with the Narragansett leader Canonchet, who refused to give her over to the English. It is believed that Wetamoo helped construct rafts and canoes that were used during the Great Swamp Battle in December 1675. In 1676, however, English forces surrounded Wetamoo's village. When she tried to escape by canoe, soldiers fired upon her and she drowned.

Cornelia Wieman (contemporary)
Six Nations psychiatrist

Cornelia Wieman, a member of the Little Grand Rapids band in Northern Manitoba, is the first and only practicing aboriginal female psychiatrist in Canada.

A 1993 graduate of McMaster University, Wieman was elected president of the Resident's Association at

McMaster University in 1996, and she was instrumental in developing the chief resident position in emergency psychiatry at McMaster University. She also was elected the chair of the Native Mental Health Section of the Canadian Psychiatric Association.

During her residency, she played an important role in developing the Six Nations Mental Health Services in Ohsweken, Ontario, and was awarded the Medical Services Branch Indian/Inuit Health Careers Scholarship and the Medical Research Council of Canada Farquharson Scholarship.

In 1998, she was the recipient of a National Aboriginal Achievement Award, presented by the National Aboriginal Achievement Foundation, in recognition of her career achievements as an aboriginal professional. Wieman is currently a psychiatric emergency consultant and the Native students health sciences coordinator at McMaster University.

Robert A. Williams, Jr. (1955–)
Lumbee lawyer and educator

Robert A. Williams, Jr., is the E. Thomas Sullivan Professor of Law and American Indian Studies at the

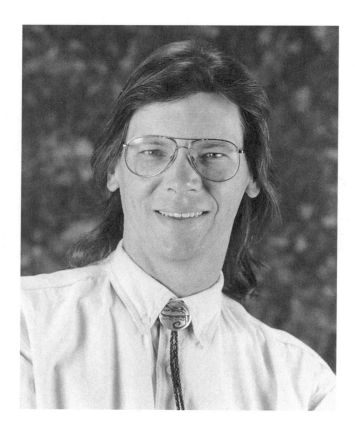

Robert Williams, Jr.

University of Arizona. He is a noted legal scholar and teacher in the fields of federal Indian law and indigenous human rights. He received his education from Loyola College with a bachelor of arts degree (1977) and obtained a law degree from Harvard University (1980).

His teaching posts have included associate professor of law at the University of Wisconsin, visiting professor of law at the University of Washington, and the Bennett Boskey Visiting Lecturer and Professor of Law at Harvard University.

He is director of the Indigenous Peoples Law and Policy Program at the University of Arizona. He is also chief justice of the Court of Appeals of the Pascua Yaqui Indian tribe and serves as legal counsel and advisor to Indian tribes and indigenous peoples organizations in the United States, Canada, Australia, and Latin America.

Williams is the author of *Federal Indian Law: Cases and Materials* (Fourth edition, with D. Getches and C. Wilkinson), *The American Indian in Western Legal Thought: The Discourses of Conquest*, and *Linking Arms Together: American Indian Treaty Visions of Law and Peace, 1600–1800*.

Susan M. Williams (1955–)
Sisseton-Wahpeton Sioux lawyer

Susan M. Williams is a member of the Albuquerque, New Mexico, law firm of Williams, Janov, and Cooney, P.C., which focuses on Indian and environmental law. She was born in Klamath Falls, Oregon, on 8 May 1955, and received her education from Radcliffe College, earning a bachelor of arts degree in 1977 and a law degree from Harvard University in 1981. She was subsequently admitted to the bar in the District of Columbia and in New Mexico in 1988. Admission to the bar means that the person has passed a test that measures knowledge about the law, and passage of the tests grants the individual the right to practice law.

She has served as chairperson of the Navajo Tax Commission (1983), a board member of the Conservation Foundation/World Wildlife Fund (1986), the University of Colorado Natural Resources Law Center (1988), and the Grand Canyon Trust (1999). In 2000 Williams was elected to the board of directors of the Harvard University Alumni Association.

Williams's interests focus specifically on taxation laws as applied to the Navajo, to non-Indian corporations, and to reservation lands in Colorado and New Mexico and water laws. Among her published writings

Susan M. Williams.

are *Mineral Development in Indian Land* (1989), "Multiple Taxation of Mineral Extraction in Indian Country: State and Indian Tribal Jurisdiction," "State and Indian Tribal Taxation on Tribal Reservations: Is It Too Taxing?" (1989), and "Tribal Jurisdiction Over Reservation Water Quality and Quantity" (1998).

Elvin Willie, Jr. (1953–)
Pomo/Paiute tribal leader

Elvin Willie is a public health administrator and a member of the Pomo and Paiute tribes. Born on the Walker River Paiute Reservation in Schurz, Nevada, on 15 September 1953, Willie received a bachelor's degree in political science at the University of California, Berkeley, in 1976, and later returned to complete a master's degree in health policy and administration in 1989.

In the interim he held various positions for the Walker River Paiute tribe. He worked in education in 1976 and 1977, developing an Indian-oriented curriculum and a resource center library for elementary school students; then, from 1977 to 1979, he managed a tribal retail store. From 1979 to 1986, Willie served as the

tribal chairman, supervising a staff of forty persons and managing all phases of tribal government operations.

Since then, Willie has been particularly active in the area of public health as related to rural Indian communities, publishing articles in the *Journal of Rural Community Psychology* (1988) and the *Alcohol Treatment Quarterly* (1989). His article "Suicide Contagion among American Indians" appeared in *Handbook on Suicide among Indians,* edited by Eduardo Duran (1989), a publication of the U.S. Indian Health Service. Willie is currently an officer of the U.S. Indian Health Service and works between the Walker River Paiute Reservation and the agency office in Phoenix, Arizona.

Bill Wilson (1944–)
Kwawkgewlth tribal leader

Bill Wilson is well-known in Canada for advancing the rights of aboriginal people. Born in 1944 to Charles William Wilson and Ethel Johnson, Wilson is a Kwawkgewlth Indian. The Kwawkgewlth live on the northern coast of Vancouver Island and the nearby coast of British Columbia. Wilson began to work for his father when he was twelve at a fish purchasing plant in Comox, British Columbia, on Vancouver Island while attending grade school and high school. Although he wanted to quit school when he turned fifteen, his parents persuaded him to continue, and Wilson went on to obtain a bachelor of arts degree from the University of Victoria on Vancouver Island in 1970 and a bachelor of law from the University of British Columbia in 1973. During his summer vacations and weekends, he worked at numerous jobs, including stints as a taxi driver, fisherman, logger, laborer, pulp-mill worker, bartender, and car salesman.

Wilson became involved at an early age in Indian political activities. At fourteen, he joined the Native Brotherhood of British Columbia, a province-wide organization devoted to advancing the cause of Indian rights. His early involvement with the Native Brotherhood of British Columbia developed into a full-time commitment to aboriginal politics that has spanned more than three decades, during which time he has actively participated in countless aboriginal organizations.

While in law school, Wilson was instrumental in the creation of the Union of British Columbia Indian Chiefs, an organization representing Indian bands across the province. In 1976, Wilson was the founding president of the United Native Nations, an association designed to represent aboriginal people by tribe instead of according to bands defined by Canadian authorities. In 1990 and 1991, Wilson was a vice-chief of the Assembly of First Nations, a national organization representing Indian bands across the country, and in 1991 he became the political secretary of the Assembly of First Nations. As the chairman of the First Nations Congress, Wilson succeeded in commencing negotiations on land claims in the province for the first time with the government of British Columbia.

He was recently elected to the Task Group of the British Columbia First Nations Summit, which represents 90 percent of the aboriginal people in British Columbia. Since 1997 he has been chief negotiator for the Lheidli T'enneh Band within the British Columbia treaty making process. Most British Columbia bands are negotiating modern treaties with the province of British Columbia and the government of Canada. He is now one of the two senior Indian leaders in British Columbia. Wilson has two daughters and a son, and currently lives in Vancouver.

Winema (1836–1920)
Modoc cultural mediator

Winema was a peacemaker and negotiator during the Modoc War of 1872–1873. She was born among the Modoc Indians in northern California, in a village located along the Link River. Among her people she was well respected for her bravery. According to one story, at the age of fourteen, she rallied the warriors of her village to victory during a surprise attack by another California tribe. However, she tested her people's patience a year later when, at age fifteen, she married a Kentucky miner named Frank Riddle. She and her husband settled on a ranch, and Winema became known as Toby Riddle. Initially, Winema's own people refused to sanction the marriage. Eventually, however, she became a valuable interpreter for the Modoc in their negotiations with U.S. settlers. Over time, Winema developed a reputation as a peacemaker and diplomat— two skills that would be sorely needed in the Modoc War.

In the mid-1860s, a group of Modoc Indians who had settled in the Klamath Reservation in Oregon returned to their homelands along the Link River. Foreseeing the likelihood of conflict with the growing settler population, Winema tried to convince some of her relatives to return to Oregon and petition for a separate Modoc Reservation. Captain Jack, a Modoc leader, accused Winema of over-friendliness to settlers. In the years to follow, a number of battles between the Modoc and settlers ensued. Winema and her husband served as negotiators, interpreters, and intermediaries for the opposing sides. In February 1873, a peace council was held on neutral ground. During the parley, Captain Jack and another Modoc killed two U.S. military officers. A third U.S. officer, Alfred Meacham, was saved when Winema threw herself between him and a gun. After the ordeal, Winema nursed the wounded Meacham back to health.

Winema's actions made her a celebrity in the U.S. national media. She was escorted to Washington, D.C., for a special visit with President Ulysses S. Grant. For the next seven years she toured eastern cities with Meacham and family members in dramatic re-enactments of Indian history and issues. Winema spent her remaining years in Oregon. Her son, Jeff Riddle, published *The Indian History of the Modoc War*, which was based largely on Winema's recollections.

Winnebago Prophet (Wabokieshek) (1794–1841)
Winnebago spiritual leader

Wabokieshek (White Cloud) was an important supporter of Black Hawk, the Sac and Fox leader, during the final conflicts for the old Northwest Territory in the 1830s. Due to his prophetic visions, he has also been called the Winnebago Prophet. The Winnebago are a Siouan-speaking people who currently live in Nebraska and Wisconsin.

Wabokieshek was born in the heart of what was to become the final battleground for control of the old Northwest Territory, now known as the Great Lakes region. His homeland was situated near the present-day site of Prophetstown, Indiana, at the junction between the Tippecanoe and Mississippi rivers. Although Wabokieshek had long preached for resistance to U.S. encroachment and culture, he had advocated peace with the United States during the Winnebago uprising of 1827. Five years later, however, he agreed to take up arms in support of Black Hawk in the so-called Black Hawk's War of 1832.

Wabokieshek came to Black Hawk in 1832, when the Sac and Fox leader was gathering forces for his return to Saukenuk, a major Sac village in present-day Illinois. Wabokieshek told Black Hawk of his visions, in which the Great Spirit would help defeat their enemies. He promised that with the aid of certain ceremonies, he could create an army of spirit warriors who would aid Black Hawk in defeating the U.S. Army. Thereafter, the Indians could reclaim their homelands that were occupied by the United States. Prophecies of this sort were not uncommon. Both the Delaware Prophet (1760–1763) and Tenskwatawa, the Shawnee Prophet (1806–1811), had made similar prophecies in their people's conflicts with European colonists and U.S. settlers. Wabokieshek's alliance with Black Hawk resulted in the enlistment of a number of Sac and Winnebago warriors to Black Hawk's cause. Wabokieshek remained with Black Hawk throughout the conflict and was at his side when the Indian leader surrendered at Prairie du Chien in present-day Wisconsin. Wabokieshek was imprisoned with Black Hawk and traveled with him as a kind of war trophy in the eastern United States. After his release, Wabokieshek lived for a number of years in relative obscurity, first with the Sac and later with the Winnebago.

Sarah Winnemucca (1844–1891)
Northern Paiute activist and educator

Sarah Winnemucca was active as a peacemaker, teacher, and defender of her people's rights. She was born near the Humboldt River in western Nevada, the fourth of nine children. When she was ten, she and her family moved to where her grandfather, Truckee, lived near San Jose, California. When she was fourteen, she moved in with the family of a stagecoach agent, Major William Ormsby, where she learned English. She returned to San Jose in 1860 at her grandfather's dying request. Winnemucca was able to study at a convent school only one month before several non-Indian parents objected to the presence of Paiute girls. Thereafter, she found work as a servant and spent much of her salary on books.

The Paiute War began in 1860 and was led by Winnemucca's cousin, Numaga. She and many non-hostile Paiute were moved to a reservation near Reno, Nevada. During the Snake War in 1866, the military requested that she and her brother, Naches, act as intermediaries. Winnemucca became the official interpreter in the military's negotiations with the Paiute and Shoshone. She was convinced that the army could be trusted more than the Indian agents, and she voiced her concerns to U.S. Senator John Jones about mistreatment of Indians by Indian service employees.

Some northern Paiute, including Winnemucca, were relocated to the Malheur Reservation in Oregon in 1872. While there, she met and became friends with reservation agent Samuel Parrish. She assisted with his agricultural program, served as interpreter, and taught school. Agent William Rinehart replaced Parrish, and his failure to pay the Paiute for their agricultural labors led to the Bannock War of 1878. General Oliver Howard used Winnemucca as a peacemaker and interpreter. The Paiute were forced to leave the Malheur Reservation and relocate to the Yakima Reservation in present-day Washington State.

Winnemucca went to San Francisco and Sacramento in 1879; in lectures to sympathetic audiences, she discussed the treatment of Indians by Indian service employees. Despite widespread public support for the Paiute's right to return to Malheur, no funding was raised for the project. Winnemucca commenced a lecture tour of the East in 1883 and 1884 and dressed as an Indian princess to draw crowds. While there, she met with many important sympathizers of Indian rights and published *Life among the Paiutes, Their Wrongs and Claims*. Winnemucca returned to Nevada and founded a school for Indians with the money she had saved and from private donations. The school operated for three years until funding ran out and Sarah's health faltered. She died of tuberculosis at the age of forty-seven.

Shirley Hill Witt (1940–)
Mohawk anthropologist

Shirley Witt is an anthropologist who has done extensive research in the area of civil rights. In 1981, she became the director of the Rocky Mountain Regional Office of the U.S. Commission on Civil Rights. She is also an author and co-editor of numerous publications.

At age twenty-two, Witt had her second child. That same year, she enrolled at the University of Michigan and went on to obtain her doctorate in anthropology from the University of New Mexico. Witt distanced herself from an overly specialized focus early on and developed a multi-disciplinary approach to her work. Her thesis research was on migration into the San Juan pueblo. She went on to teach at the University of North Carolina and Colorado College.

Witt's career led her to an interest in the employment problems of women, including discrimination against women by male department heads. When the U.S. Commission on Civil Rights offered her a job, Witt accepted. The position offered her a chance to apply her anthropological skills to day-to-day problems. Her work entails directing a research unit made up of social scientists, attorneys, and writers who investigate civil rights violations in a six-state region. Her research resulted in written recommendations to the president and Congress. Although Witt's work encompasses the challenges faced by Native Americans, the research addresses all cultural groups in the United States. Since the early 1990s, Witt has been a foreign service officer working for American embassies on overseas assignments. Eventually, she hopes to return to the academic field and participate in a multi-disciplinary program to apply anthropological theory to social problems.

Witt was the co-editor of *The Way: An Anthology of American Indian Language and Literature* (1972) and

The Tuscaroras (1972). She has written numerous articles including "Pressure Point in Growing Up Indian" in *The Indian Reader* I, number 2 (Summer/Fall 1986); and "Punto Final," "Seboyeta Chapel," and "La Mujer de Valor" in *That's What She Said: Contemporary Fiction and Poetry of Native American Women*, ed. Rayna Green (1983).

Laura Waterman Wittstock (1937–)
Seneca and Stockbridge Munsee journalist and author

Laura Waterman Wittstock is president of MIGIZI Communications, a nonprofit media corporation located in Minneapolis, Minnesota, that provides information to the Indian public, educates elementary, secondary, and adult students in a communications-related setting, and commits resources to address problems which threaten the stability of the Indian community.

She has made significant contributions in the field of media communications with a focus on issues relating to Native Americans. She has been recognized for her commitment to developing a free tribal press. Wittstock has also helped establish alcoholism abuse and education programs in the Indian community.

Wittstock was born on the Cattaraugus Indian Reservation in New York and was educated at the University of Minnesota. Much of her life's work has been in media communications. In 1975 she was the executive director of the American Indian Press Association. She was also the editor of a monthly report on legislation affecting Native Americans. She has worked abroad with indigenous people and with the International American Treaty Council, a non-government organization working for international recognition of Indian treaty and political rights.

Her recent publications are a children's book, *Ininatig's Gift of Sugar: Traditional Native Sugarmaking* (1993) and *Changing Communities, Changing Foundations: The Story of the Diversity Efforts of Twenty Community Foundations*.

She continues to serve on numerous boards, including the Minneapolis Foundation, Intermedia Arts, the Community Solutions Fund, and the Institute for Research and Education (HealthSystem Minnesota). She is treasurer of the Minnesota Partnership for Action Against Tobacco (MPAAT), and vice-chair of the Minnesota Minority Health Advisory Committee.

Wittstock received the 1992 Minnesota Advocates for Human Rights Award for twenty years of work in free expression and alternative media coverage of American Indians, and she is currently a St. Paul Companies

LIN grant recipient, conducting research on Dakota reconciliation.

Rosita Worl (contemporary)
Tlingit tribal leader and educator

Rosita Worl has made important contributions in developing public awareness of Tlingit culture and Alaska Native subsistence cultures.

A member of the Thunderbird Clan and House Lowered from the Sun of Klukwan, Alaska, and a Child of the Sockeye Clan, Worl earned a master of science degree and a doctoral degree in anthropology from Harvard University in 1998.

Worl holds a joint appointment as assistant professor of anthropology at the University of Alaska Southeast and president of the Sealaska Heritage Foundation. The foundation is dedicated to preserving and maintaining the Tlingit, Haida, and Tsimshian cultures and languages.

Rosita Worl.

In the late 1980s, she was elected to the board of the Sealaska Corporation, which owns the land base of the Southeast Alaska Indians and is the major economic institution in contemporary Tlingit society and in southeast Alaska.

On both state and national levels, Worl serves on the boards of the Alaska Native Heritage Center and the subsistence committee for the Alaska Native Federation of Natives.

She served as the first chair of the Alaska Native Education Association, and, in 1977 she was chairperson of the first Alaska Native Women's Statewide Caucus and Alaska State delegate to the International Women's Year Houston Conference. Worl was also a founding member of the Smithsonian's National Museum of the American Indian and was appointed to President Bill Clinton's Northwest Coast Sustainable Development Commission.

Worl has done extensive research throughout the Alaska and circumpolar Arctic and has served on the National Science Foundation Arctic Program Committee, the National Science Committee overseeing the social scientific studies of the Exxon Valdez oil spill, the Scientific Committee of the Arctic Eskimo Whaling Commission, and the International Whaling Commission (1979).

She has written a number of landmark studies and reports published by foundations, universities, federal organizations, and Alaska Native organizations on bowhead whale and seal hunting, impacts of industrial development on Native communities, repatriation, and Tlingit real and property laws. Worl was elected to the board of directors of Sealaska Corporation (1987–2000), is executive director for the Sealaska Foundation, works with the Alaska Native Federation, and teaches at the University of Alaska-Southeast.

Wovoka (Jack Wilson) (circa 1856–1932)
Paiute spiritual leader

The Ghost Dance religion of 1890 originated with this Paiute visionary and prophet, who grew up in the area of Mason Valley, Nevada, near the present Walker Lake Reservation. His proper name, Wovoka, means "The Cutter" in Paiute. On the death of his father he was taken into the family of a white farmer named David Wilson and was given the name Jack Wilson, by which he was known among local American settlers.

During the late 1880s, Wovoka became ill with a severe fever at a time that happened to coincide with a solar eclipse. In his feverish state, Wovoka received a vision, and an account of this experience as told in Wovoka's own words was documented by James

Mooney in his book *The Ghost Dance Religion and the Sioux Outbreak of 1890*: "'When the sun died,' Wovoka said, "I went up to heaven and saw God and all the people who had died a long time ago. God told me to come back and tell my people they must be good and love one another, and not fight, or steal, or lie. He gave me this dance to give to my people.'" This vision became the basis of the Ghost Dance religion, which was based upon the belief that there would be a time when all Indian people—the living and those who had died—would be reunited on an earth that was spiritually regenerated and forever free from death, disease, and all the other miseries that had recently been experienced by Indians. Word of the new religion spread quickly among Indian peoples of the Great Basin and Plains regions, but it is said that Wovoka himself never traveled far from his birthplace. A complex figure, he was revered by Indians while being denounced as an impostor and a lunatic by the local settlers throughout his entire life.

Allen Wright (Kiliahote) (circa 1825–1885)
Choctaw principal chief, minister, and translator

Allen Wright was born along the Yaknukni River in Mississippi, the son of mixed-blood Choctaw parents. Wright was removed to Indian Territory with his father and sister in 1832 during the government relocation era.

Kiliahote received his name, Allen Wright, from a Presbyterian missionary, Cyrus Kingsburn, who took an interest in the boy and provided him with an education at local missionary schools. Wright continued his education in New York, graduating from Union College in 1852 and from Union Theological Seminary in 1855. In 1856, Wright was ordained into the Presbyterian Church after which he began work among the Choctaw. He became involved in tribal affairs and was elected to the Choctaw House of Representatives and the senate, and served as the tribe's treasurer. During the Civil War, Wright served in the Confederacy.

Following the war, Wright was elected principal chief of the Choctaw Nation and served two terms, from 1866 to 1870. Wright is given credit for first suggesting the name Oklahoma, meaning "red people's land" in the Muskogean language, for the new Indian Territory. Following the Removal Act, part of the land which is now Oklahoma was designated Indian Territory comprising the Choctaw and Cherokee Nations, and later the Chickasaw Nation. Following the Civil War, the U.S. government began to consider the idea of merging all the tribal governments in the territory, at which point Wright suggested they rename it Oklahoma. The reorganization did not take place until 1890, in an act that was passed by Congress, and Oklahoma became the official name of the state in 1907.

During the 1870s and 1880s, Wright translated numerous works, including the Chickasaw constitution and codes of law into English. In 1880, his Choctaw dictionary was published.

Ray A. Young Bear (1950–)
Mesquakie poet and novelist

Author of the highly acclaimed works *Winter of the Salamander* (1980), *The Invisible Musician* (1989), *Black Eagle Child: The Facepaint Narratives* (1992), and *Remnants of the First Earth* (1997), Ray A. Young Bear has made a name for himself among Native and non-Native literati. Born in Marshalltown, Iowa, and raised on the Mesquakie Tribal Settlement, Young Bear's first language is Mesquakie. The author draws on the language's complex oratory style to shape his English writing. His maternal grandmother, Ada Kapayou Old Bear, influenced his appreciation of the lyrical, and his wife, Stella L. Young Bear, continues to support his literary endeavors.

Young Bear attended Claremont College, the University of Iowa, Grinnell College, Northern Iowa University, and Iowa State University. The writer began writing poetry in the late 1960s, and his first poem was published in 1968, although his formal introduction as a tribal poet came later when he was published in the *South Dakota Review*. Young Bear performs readings throughout the country and conducts workshops with young poets. He has held visiting faculty positions at several universities, including the University of Iowa and Eastern Washington University.

In 1983 Young Bear and his wife Stella formed the Woodland Song and Dance Troupe, also referred to as Black Eagle Child. The performing arts group brings together Mesquakie artists who perform traditional Mesquakie song and dance styles for Native and non-Native audiences. Young Bear often begins these performances with readings of his own works, as well as Mesquaki songs.

Young Bear's poetry draws extensively from his people's oral tradition. His writing is a reflection of old-time storytelling and events and modern-day speech patterns and actions. When referring to or describing his work, Young Bear often uses the third-person plural (the pronoun we), because his work is the product of many minds and lives. The cover of Young Bear's books are decorated with his wife's elaborate bandolier-style beadwork. He presently lives on his tribe's settlement with his wife and nephew, Jesse.

James Young Deer (fl. 1900–1920)
Winnebago actor, producer, and director

Little is known about the talented Young Deer, who produced, directed, and acted in many notable Indian-themed Western movies during the silent film era, before the 1920s. Born in Dakota City, Nebraska, he performed in circuses and Wild West shows as a child and, about 1900, entered the moving picture industry. Young Deer and his wife, Princess Redwing, performed in Cecil B. DeMille's *The Squaw Man* (1914), served as technical advisors for film pioneer D. W. Griffith, and gained roles in *The Mended Flute* (1909) and *Little Dove's Romance* (1911). Young Deer's expertise behind the camera led to his position as chief of the West Coast division of Pathé Fréres Studios, a French film company in Orange County, California. In 1912, Young Deer produced and directed dozens of short western movies, many of them highly successful and featuring Indian stories such as *The Cheyenne Brave*, *Red Deer's Devotion*, *Squaw Man's Revenge*, and *The Yaqui Girl*.

By 1913, however, the Pathé Fréres Company left its Orange County studio location and transferred Young Deer to its studios in France. According to some film historians, while in France, Young Deer directed several films and returned to the United States after World War I. For a short time, Young Deer operated an acting school in Hollywood, California, and then resumed production of low-budget films.

Peterson Zah (1928–)
Navajo tribal leader

Peterson Zah is the former chairman and president of the Navajo Nation, which occupies extensive parts of Arizona and New Mexico (14 million acres) and has the largest population of any tribe in the United States or Canada.

As a youth, teachers at the Phoenix Indian School discouraged Zah from entering college; nevertheless, he attended college on a basketball scholarship and graduated from Arizona State University with a bachelor's degree in education in 1963. On completing his education, Zah returned to Window Rock, Arizona, on the Navajo Reservation, to teach carpentry as part of a pilot program intended to develop employment skills among Navajo adults. He then served as a field coordinator at the Volunteers in Service to America (VISTA) Training Center at Arizona State University. VISTA was a federally sponsored domestic peace corps, and Zah was involved in cultural sensitivity training for VISTA volunteers in preparation for their service on Indian reservations throughout the United States.

In 1967, Zah joined DNA-People's Legal Services, Inc., a nonprofit organization chartered by the state of Arizona to help indigent and other economically disadvantaged Indian people. DNA had nine offices on the Navajo, Hopi, and Apache reservations, and in San Juan County, New Mexico. Zah later became executive director of this organization, a position he held for ten years. In this capacity he supervised thirty-three tribal court advocates, thirty-four attorneys, and a total of 120 employees. Under his direction, DNA lawyers took several landmark cases to the U.S. Supreme Court, winning cases that helped establish the rights of individual Native Americans and the sovereignty of Indian nations.

In 1982, Zah was elected chairman of the Navajo Tribal Council; in this capacity, he presided over the tribal council and served as chief executive officer of the Navajo Nation government. In 1987, he became chief fundraiser for the Navajo Education and Scholarship Foundation, a nonprofit organization that solicited funds from the private sector and provided scholarships to needy and worthy Navajo students. In 1988, he founded Native American Consulting Services, a private firm which provided educational services to school districts on and off the reservation. As sole proprietor of the company, he developed curriculum materials on Navajo culture and history and worked with Congress on efforts to secure funds for new school construction on the Navajo and San Carlos Apache reservations.

Zah was elected president of the Navajo Nation in 1991, a new position created by the Navajo Nation Council in a reorganization of the Navajo Nation governmental structure. As such, Zah became the only Navajo leader to be elected as chairman and president, and the first elected president in the history of the Navajo Nation. In recent years, Zah acts as a special consultant to the president at Arizona State University. He continues to work on national boards, national political issues, and Indian education issues.

Ofelia Zepeda (1954–)
Tohono O'odham linguist, poet, and educator

Ofelia Zepeda's scholarly achievements distinguish her as one of the leading scholars in Native American language study, or linguistics. Her 1983 book *A Papago Grammar*, the first grammar of the Tohono O'odham language, remains one of the most highly regarded books in its field.

The first member of her family to graduate from high school, Zepeda was born in Stanfield, Arizona, a rural community near the Tohono O'odham and Pima reservations. Zepeda, along with her eight siblings and parents, traveled to Mexico during the summers to visit relatives and participate in tribal ceremonies. While Zepeda and her family may have traveled to their homeland during her childhood, her community in Arizona was tight and tribal traditions and history remained distinct, despite the borders separating the Tohono O'odham from their home base.

Zepeda began her higher education at Central Arizona College, but later transferred to the University of Arizona, where she initially studied sociology. After delving into her tribe's language as part of an outside project, however, the academic's focus moved to a more linguistic level. Her passion for scholarship is clear through her quick academic achievements: Zepeda received her bachelor's degree in 1980, her master's degree in 1981, and her doctorate in linguistics in 1984.

In 1986, Zepeda was appointed director of the American Indian Studies Program at the University of Arizona and continues to be associated with the department. She is a professor of linguistics, and the former president of the American Indian Alumni Association.

Zepeda is currently co-director of the American Indian Language Development Institute (AILDI), an internationally recognized summer program sponsored by the University of Arizona for American Indian educators in the fields of language education, promotion, and revitalization. The organization, which emerged when several academics and parents expressed interest in studying aspects of their Native languages, assists educators and practitioners throughout Native America, Canada, and parts of Mexico develop and promote Native-language learning. She often works as a consultant in Native language curriculum development with the Tohono O'odham and other tribes. Zepeda also is an executive board member of the Institute for the Preservation of the Original Languages of the Americas (IPOLA), and is also an executive board member for the National Museum of the American Indian, a branch of the Smithsonian Institute.

In addition to these achievements, Zepeda is currently the series editor of Sun Tracks American Indian Literary series published by the University of Arizona Press. In 1995, she authored a book of poetry entitled *Ocean Power: Poems from the Desert* and co-edited *Home Places: Contemporary Native American Writing* with Larry Evers. Her work has been anthologized in numerous collections.

In 1996, Zepeda accepted the Tanner Award from the University of Arizona's American Indian Alumni Association for her significant contribution to the American Indian community, and in 1997 she received a grant from the Endangered Language Fund in order to continue work on the Tohono O'odham dictionary project. Most recently, Zepeda was awarded a 1999 MacArthur Fellowship for her work as a linguist, poet, editor, and community leader.

Glossary

A

aboriginal The first people or native people of an area. The Native Americans are the aboriginal people of North America. Under the Canadian Constitution Act of 1982, an aboriginal person is defined as being an Indian, Inuit, or Métis. Aboriginal is often used interchangeably with the terms *native* and *indigenous*.

aboriginal rights Rights enjoyed by a people by virtue of the fact that their ancestors inhabited an area from time immemorial before the first Europeans came. These rights include ownership of land and resources, cultural rights, and political self-determination. There are widely divergent views on the validity of these rights. On one end of the spectrum, some deny the existence of aboriginal rights; on the other end, some claim that aboriginal rights give natives the inherent right to govern themselves and their lands.

aboriginal title The earliest discussion of aboriginal title in Canada came in a nineteenth-century lawsuit involving Indian lands in Ontario. At that point, aboriginal (then "Indian") title was understood to be of a usufructuary nature, that is, to give Indians a temporary right to use their lands for subsistence purposes. Indian title was not understood to equal "fee simple" ownership. A century later, however, the doctrine of aboriginal title has been expanded to include in practical terms much broader rights. *See* fee-simple ownership *and* usufructuary.

abrogation The termination of an international agreement or treaty, for example, when Congress enacts a law completely abolishing a treaty and breaking all the U.S. promises to an Indian nation.

acculturation The transference of culture from one group to another, usually from a more dominant group to a less dominant one, which thereby loses its previous culture.

age grades A series of social and ceremonial associations based on age. Members enter the first grade at the appropriate age and then proceed through the set.

agriculturalists Indian peoples who depended to a significant extent on crops which they planted themselves.

Alaska Native Claims Settlement Act (ANCSA) A 1971 congressional act that extinguished Alaska Natives' claims to land. In compensation, the Alaska Natives retained 44 million acres and received $962.5 million.

Algonkians A group of Indian peoples who speak an Algonkian language. This is the largest language group in Canada. It includes many peoples with very different cultures, from the Atlantic coast to the western prairies.

alienate Transfer of an ownership interest, for example, when tribal land is sold to nontribal members.

alkaloid Any of a number of colorless, crystalline, bitter organic substances, such as caffeine, morphine, quinine, and strychnine, having alkaline properties and containing nitrogen. Alkaloids are found in plants and, sometimes, in animals and can have a strong toxic effect on the human or animal system.

allotment The policy, peaking in the 1880s and 1890s, of subdividing Indian reservations into individual, privately owned ("patented" or "fee patent") parcels of land. The division of communally held lands on many Indian reservations into individually owned parcels, thereby nearly eliminating communal ownership of land and resources, which was a defining element of tribal life. The allotment policy was ended in 1934, but it left a legacy of "checkerboard" land ownership on reservations, where often, the tribe, non-Indians, and Indian allottees own small and scattered segments of land. *See* General Allotment Act of 1887.

Amargosa complex   A series of artifacts linked to the ancient hunting and gathering peoples of the Mohave Desert in the southwest, dated from 1600 B.C.E. to C.E. 1000.

American Indian Movement (AIM)   An Indian activist organization originating in Minneapolis, Minnesota, in the 1960s. AIM was originally organized to protect urban Indians from police harassment and to assist Indian children in obtaining culturally sensitive education. In the 1970s, AIM expanded its activities to include more traditional issues, such as assertion of treaty rights, tribal sovereignty, and international recognition of Indian nations.

Anasazi   An early pueblo culture that flourished between C.E. 900 and 1200. The present-day Hopi Indians are believed to be descendants of the Anasazi, which in Hopi means *ancient ones*.

annuities   In the United States, annuities are annual payments for land in accordance with Indian treaties. Instead of paying for Indian land in one large sum, the U.S. government usually spread the expense by paying smaller sums over a number of years. In Canada, annuities were small annual payments made to bands, which surrendered lands to the Crown, or English monarch, who formally claimed public land in Canada.

archaeology   The study of past cultures through an analysis of their physical remains, such as tools or pottery. From such remains, archaeologists piece together an idea of what ancient cultures may have been like.

Archaic period   The time between eight thousand and two thousand years ago defined in most areas by cultures dependent on hunting and gathering.

Articles of Confederation   The original agreement among the thirteen original U.S. colonies to form a new, independent country. The articles were adopted on November 15, 1777, ratified by the thirteen colonies in 1781, and remained in force until 1789, when the present constitution was ratified.

artifacts   Any products of human cultural activity, such as tools, weapons, or artworks, found in archaeological contexts.

Assembly of First Nations (AFN)   The successor organization to the National Indian Brotherhood (NIB) as the national political body representing first nations of Canada at the national political level, such as at the First Ministers' Conferences, where the Canadian prime minister and provincial leaders met to discuss provisions of a new Canadian constitution. The chiefs of each Indian first nation represent their bands at the national assemblies of chiefs, which constitutes the AFN.

assimilation   The idea that one group of people, usually a minority, are becoming like another and are being absorbed by a majority society. For example, for many years it was believed that U.S. Indians were assimilating into the dominant culture, but that idea no longer holds much credence.

associated funerary objects   Objects believed to have been placed with individual human remains at the time of death or later as a part of the death rite or ceremony of a culture and which, along with the human remains, are currently in the possession or control of a federal agency or museum. Items exclusively made for burial purposes or to contain human remains are also considered associated funerary objects.

Athapaskan   A group of Indian peoples who speak an Athapaskan language. These languages dominate in northwestern Canada south of the tree line.

B

band   (1) A small, loosely organized social group composed of several families. (2) In Canada, originally a social and economic unit of nomadic hunting peoples, but, since confederation, a community of Indians registered under the Indian Act. Registered Indians are called "status Indians." Each band has its own governing band council, usually consisting of one or more chiefs and several councillors. Today, many bands prefer to be known as First Nations. *See* status Indians.

band council   In Canada, the local form of native government consisting of a chief and councillors, who are elected for two- or three-year terms to carry on band business. Community members choose the chief and councillors by election, or sometimes through traditional custom. The actual duties and responsibilities of band councils are specified in the Indian Act. *See* Indian Act.

band council resolution   The method by which Canadian band councils pass motions or record decisions. Band council resolutions are statements outlining a decision of the band council. The minister of Indian and Northern Affairs Canada, or senior officials of that department, must approve band council resolutions whenever they involve band lands or monies.

Berengia   During the last glacial age, before fifteen thousand years ago, a land mass between Asia and Alaska in the Bering Sea that served as a land bridge for the first migrations to the continents of the western hemisphere.

bicultural/bilingual education   An education system that combines the languages, values, and beliefs of two cultures in its curriculum to give students the skills to live and function in both cultures.

bilateral kinship   A system of descent and inheritance that recognizes relationship to both a person's mother's and father's kin.

Bill C-31   The pre-legislation name of the 1985 *Act to Amend the Indian Act* of the Canadian Parliament that restored legal status to aboriginal women and their children who had lost status through marriage to non-Indians. The bill corrected a section of the Indian Act that revoked status for women married to non-Indians while permitting Indian men to confer Indian status upon non-Indian wives. While aboriginal women's groups welcomed this change, many Indian communities opposed the bill as an intrusion into their jurisdiction over band membership. Bill C-31 enabled people affected by the discriminatory provisions of the old *Indian Act* to apply to have their Indian status restored. Since 1985, over 100,000 individuals have successfully regained their status.

bill of rights   A statement of fundamental rights guaranteed to members of a nation. The U.S. Bill of Rights consists of the first ten amendments to the Constitution and were adopted in the late 1780s. Canada adopted its first bill of rights in 1960. The fundamental purpose of the Canadian Bill of Rights was to ensure equality of rights, and, as a consequence, Canada's native people were allowed to vote in Canadian federal elections.

boarding school   A school run by the government or a religious or private organization, in which the children live. Boarding schools designed to educate native children took them away from the influence of their family and culture.

"booming"   Forceful nineteenth-century advocacy of the desirability of seizing most of the remaining land of Native Americans.

Bosque Redondo   The Navajo reservation in present-day eastern New Mexico where for four years (1864–1868), the Navajo were forced to live after being rounded up and concentrated together.

branch   In linguistics, a subdivision of a language grouping (either a phylum or a family of languages).

Branch of Acknowledgement and Research (B.A.R.)   Established in 1978 by an act of Congress, a Bureau of Indian Affairs department, and at that time called the Federal Acknowledgement Project (F.A.P.), that established procedures to extend federal recognition to previously unrecognized Indian tribes and communities. About 150 Indian communities have applied to the U.S. government for certification as Indian tribes. *See* federal recognition.

British North America Act (1867)   The legislation passed by the British Parliament in 1867 that created the country of Canada. The British North America Act was renamed the Constitution Act, 1867. The act outlines in section 91 the areas of federal (Canadian national government) jurisdiction, and sub-section 24 of section 91 gives the Canadian Parliament exclusive powers to pass legislation concerning "Indians, and lands reserved for the Indians."

Bureau of Indian Affairs (BIA)   A federal agency charged with the trust responsibility for tribal land, education, and water rights.

C

Cadastral   Mapping property boundaries and other details of realty, as well as of territory, hence reservations, and keeping such records in a cadastre (map office).

California Missions   The twenty-one individual Catholic missions founded between 1769 and 1823, containing a church, a dormitory for Native Americans, and successful farm and cattle operations based on forced Indian labor.

camas   A plant (Camassia quamash), the bulbs of which were an important source of food for the native people of the Northwest Coast and the Columbia Plateau. The bulbs were gathered in the late summer and baked to prepare for eating or storage.

Campbell tradition   Archaeological remains of a group of California cultures dated from 3000 B.C.E. to C.E. 1500 and later. The remains are believed to be ancestral to the present-day Chumash from the Santa Barbara area.

Canada   Originally this designation referred only to part of France's possessions in Canada (roughly corresponding to today's southern Quebec). After 1791 it came to refer to the two Canadas, Lower Canada (southern Quebec) and Upper Canada (southern Ontario). With confederation by the British North American Act in 1867, it came to refer to all the provinces and territories collectively.

Canadian Aboriginal Economic Development Strategy (CAEDS)   Launched in 1989, a program that seeks to promote economic development among native people. The program coordinates funding services of several federal agencies to focus on aboriginal economic development problems. Participating federal agencies include the Indian and Northern Affairs Canada (INAC), the Department of Employment and Immigration Canada (EIC), and the Department of Industry, Science and Technology. The program emphasizes long-term planning and is geared toward business ventures and entrepreneurship.

Canadian Charter of Rights and Freedoms   This section of the Canadian Constitution Act, 1982, combines protection of individual rights, such as freedom of conscience and religion, with group rights involving issues such as language. Judicial decisions involving the charter are having a profound impact on Canadian society. In the 1982 Constitution, aboriginal and treaty rights were not included in the charter itself but in a separate part of the text. A provision of the Canadian charter that differentiates it from the U.S. Bill of Rights allows governments to "opt out" of charter requirements through legislative fiat.

Canadian test of basic skills   A test of a student's reading, writing, and mathematical skills commonly used in Canada.

castor gras   A French term meaning *greasy beaver*, which referred to beaver pelts that had been used as clothing long enough for the long guard hairs to fall out and for the shorter barbed hairs to absorb body oils and perspiration. Especially during the early fur trade, Europeans sought castor gras because of its value for making felt.

cautery   The act of cauterizing, which is to burn with a hot iron or needle, or with a caustic substance, so as to destroy dead or unwanted tissue in order to prevent the spread of infection.

caveat   Meaning "caution." A legal action by which a person or party claims ownership of, or interest in, land registered in the name of another party.

cession   Giving up of Indian land, often in exchange for a reservation or grant of land set aside for the Indians' permanent and exclusive use and occupancy.

Charlottetown Accord (1992)   An attempt at constitutional reform in Canada, named after the Prince Edward Island city where it was reached. It would have entrenched the inherent right to aboriginal self-government in the Constitution, as well as decentralizing many aspects of Canadian government. In the process of drafting this accord, national aboriginal leaders were included as quasi-equal participants for the first time. However, in a national referendum in October 1992, both aboriginal and other Canadians rejected the Charlottetown Accord, and aboriginal political aspirations were again forced to seek out non-constitutional forums.

chiki   A Seminole word for their open-sided, thatched-roof shelter, which evolved in Florida from the Creek cabin of their ancestors.

cimarrone   A Spanish term for wild or untamed. Cimarrone was applied to the Lower Creek Indians who migrated into Florida in the latter part of the eighteenth century and later became the Seminole Indians.

circle sentencing   A way of dealing with community members who have broken the law, that is most frequently practiced in Canada and several communities in Minnesota. Based on traditional practices, the process emphasizes peacemaking, consensus decision making, and taking the interests of the offender, the victim(s), and the community as a whole into account as the offender accepts responsibility for the crime. The participants sit in a circle, speaking in turn as a "talking piece" comes to them, and express themselves concerning the matter at hand and their support for all concerned. Each participant must agree on the outcomes that emerge from the discussion. These outcomes are the sentence.

"citizens plus"   In Canada, the concept that Indians are a distinct class of persons with special rights by virtue of their aboriginal title and treaty rights, which non-Indian citizens do not enjoy.

civil law   The body of law developed from Roman law that is codified into a single comprehensive body of laws, as opposed to developed from case law or custom. Civil law is the legal system used in most non-English speaking jurisdictions. It is also used in the state of Louisiana and the province of Quebec in Canada. The term "civil law" is also used within the common law system to refer to all non-criminal laws.

civil service reform   Late nineteenth-century movement in the United States to reform government service. The policy separated politics from government office holding, which meant in the Indian Service that elected officials were prevented from directly appointing political friends to well-paying positions. Appointment to and retention of government administrative positions became based on competence and the possession of formal qualifications of individual applicants and job holders.

"civilization" or forced acculturation   A major U.S. Indian policy from 1887 to 1934 that included pacification of Indians, their conversion to Christianity, and their adoption of a "civilized" occupation such as farming. *See* acculturation *and* assimilation.

clan   The basic social and political organization of many, but not all, Indian societies, which consists of a number of related house groups and families. In some cases, persons claim to be related and share a common symbol or totem, often an animal, such as the bear or the turtle.

Clovis points   Ancient spearheads made in a style of polished, tapered, and cylindrical shape, which first appeared among North American peoples about 10,000 B.C.E. These peoples practiced a hunting and gathering way of life that depended on many now-extinct species such as woolly mammoth and dire wolf.

Cochise culture   The name that refers to groups of hunters and gatherers who lived in present-day southeastern Arizona and southwestern New Mexico from about 13,000 to 500 B.C.E. This cultural period is named in honor of the Apache leader, Cochise, who in the late 1800s resisted U.S. troops in the same area.

common law   The body of law that is based on principles developed by judges in case law as opposed to statute. First developed in England, this system of law forms the legal foundation in English speaking jurisdictions including the United States (except Louisiana) and Canada (except Quebec). The term "common law" is also used to refer to the legal principles created within the royal courts of England in contrast to those principles coming from the courts of equity.

Community Health Representatives (CHR) Program   A Medical Services Branch (MSB) program to train Indian and Inuit people at the community level in elementary public health, so that they can provide a link between their community and the health facility in that community.

Compact of 1802   Agreement between the state of Georgia and the U.S. federal government in which the latter retained rights to negotiate land treaties with Indians in present-day Mississippi, Georgia, and Alabama, while Georgia was restricted to its present-day boundaries and given assurance that the federal government would peaceably remove any Indian nations from within Georgia's chartered limits.

comprehensive claim   According to the Canadian government's land-claims policy, an aboriginal claim, based on aboriginal rights, to land not covered by treaty.

concentration   A major U.S. government Indian policy of the mid-nineteenth century involving concentration of Indian tribes on reservations west of the Mississippi River. *See* Removal Act.

Concordat   In Roman Catholic Church law ("canon law" or sacred law), a treaty made by the Vatican (or "Holy See" or the Pope).

confederacy   An alliance of friendship among several tribes or bands in which they agree to regulate some of their activities under common rules and obligations. This could mean the obligation to give military aid if attacked or the right to seek redress for personal or group injuries suffered from other alliance members before the body of the confederacy. The latter was the case within the Iroquois Confederacy of upstate New York.

consensus   Universal agreement. Indian political or social decisionmaking usually required that all interested groups agree to a proposition before it was binding. Majority rule was not sufficient for a decision, but rather all groups (bands, clans, lineages, villages, or triblets) had to agree, otherwise each group acted the way it thought proper or best.

conservatives   Members of an Indian nation who followed traditional ways of living, often claiming the native American way as preferred. Conservatives often represent a cultural and political segment of an Indian nation and usually live differently. They have political and cultural goals of preserving Indian culture and identity that other members of the nation might be willing to give up.

constituencies Groups of individuals, where each group forms a district for purposes of representation.

constitution The written form of a country's governing structure, which establishes the basic functions and division of powers between different levels of government, such as federal and provincial governments in Canada, or federal, state, and city governments in the United States. In the United States, the Constitution was adopted in 1789, but since then several amendments or changes have modified the original document. The Canadian constitution is set forth in the Constitution Act 1867, 1930, and 1982. *See* British North America Act.

Contract Health Service (CHS) The purchase of health care by the Indian Health Service (IHS) through contractual arrangements with hospitals, private physicians, and clinic groups, and dentists and providers of ancillary health services to supplement and complement other health care resources available to American Indians and Alaska Natives.

Council on Energy Resource Tribes (CERT) An organization formed by U.S. Indian tribes who have substantial marketable natural resources on their reservation lands. CERT provides its member tribes with expertise for marketing and managing their resources.

Crown The formal head of state, symbolized by the king or queen of England. In Canada, the Crown is divided between the federal government, "the Crown in right of Canada," and the provincial governments, as "the Crown in right of (name of province)."

crown lands Land under the sovereign ownership or protection of the Canadian federal government or the provincial governments. The treaties recognized the Indians' right to hunt and fish on "unoccupied Crown lands," which has been greatly diminished by privatization of land, designation of national parks or wilderness parks, or reservation by legislation (i.e., "occupied") by any purpose.

cultural patrimony Refers to any object having ongoing historical, traditional, or cultural importance central to the Native American group or culture itself, rather than property owned by an individual Native American. It therefore cannot be alienated, appropriated, or conveyed by any individual regardless of whether the individual is a member of the tribe. Any such object is considered inalienable, not for sale, by such Native American group at the time the object was separated from the group.

culture The nonbiological and socially transmitted system of concepts, institutions, behavior, and materials by which a society adapts to its effective natural and human environment.

culture area A device anthropologists have used to discuss large numbers of people in a contiguous geographical area. Generally, it is assumed that the various peoples in a culture area are similar in lifeways.

D

Dawes Act *See* General Allotment Act of 1887.

demography The statistical study of populations, including migration, birth, death, health, and marriage data.

dependence (1) In nineteenth-century international law and federal Indian law, the relationship between a weak country and a strong country that agrees to protect it. In 1831, the Supreme Court labeled Indian tribes as "domestic nations," because the United States had agreed, by treaty, to protect them from others. (2) The situation by which Indians came to depend on trade of animal furs for European manufactured goods, especially metal goods like hoes, guns, and hatchets. Indians stopped producing their own stone tools and came to depend on trade to supply some necessary economic goods.

diminutive In linguistics, a grammatical construction conveying a meaning of smallness.

discouraged workers Unemployed workers who have abandoned their search for a new job.

diuretic An agent that increases the amount of urine.

domestic dependent nation The expression was used by U.S. Supreme Court Justice John Marshall in the case *Cherokee Nation v. Georgia* in 1831, which denied the Cherokee Nation, and all Indian nations, status as independent foreign nations. Instead, Justice Marshall described the relation of the Indian governments to the United States as more akin to "domestic dependent nations."

Dorset culture An Inuit (Eskimo) cultural tradition dated from 1000 B.C.E. to C.E. 1000. They were adapted to the harsh environments of the Canadian Arctic, relying heavily on fishing and hunting sea mammals.

E

Economic Opportunity Act of 1964   A congressional act that provided funding to local Community Action Programs (C.A.P.) and authorized Indian tribes to designate themselves as C.A.P. agencies for the purposes of the act.

economy   The sphere of society in which individuals and the community organize to satisfy subsistence needs with production of food, clothing, shelter, and, in some societies, personal wealth.

edema   An abnormal accumulation of fluid in cells, tissues, or cavities of the body, resulting in swelling.

egalitarianism   The view that people are equal, especially politically or socially.

EIR or EIS   The first is an Environmental Impact Report and the second is an Environmental Impact Statement. The former is usually employed by states and local governments while the latter by the federal government.

Encinitas tradition   Archaeological remains of a group of cultures derived from Paleo-Indian ancestors. The Encinitas people depended heavily on fishing and collecting shellfish along the California coast. The Encinitas tradition dates from 5500 to 3000 B.C.E.

encomienda   A practice by which the Spanish king rewarded public service with grants of land and rights to demand work from the local population. Encomiendas were granted in the Southwest and throughout Latin and South America. Local Indians were forced to work for the landlords, who in turn tried to convert the Indians to Christianity.

encroach   The illegal and sometimes forcible entry of an individual or group on the land or property of another. For example, during much of the 1800s, Indian nations often complained that U.S. settlers established farms on Indian lands without permission and in violation of treaties with the U.S. government.

enema   A liquid injected into the colon through the anus, as a purgative or for medicinal purposes.

enfranchisement   In Canada's Indian Act, a process by which an aboriginal Canadian gives up legal status as an Indian and assumes all the rights of a citizen of Canada. Until 1960, this was the only procedure for a Canadian Indian to gain the right to vote or to purchase alcohol. Few native people chose enfranchisement because they would lose their treaty rights, they would have to accept their share of band trust funds, and they would surrender all rights to reserve lands or participation in band elections or community affairs.

Equal Protection Clause   Part of the Fourteenth Amendment to the U.S. Constitution, adopted in the wake of the Civil War, which requires the equal treatment of all citizens—except "Indians not taxed" (tribal Indians).

ergative   In linguistics, a grammatical construction in which the subjects of some verb forms are treated similarly to the objects of other verb forms.

ethnography   A descriptive account of a particular culture. Ethnographies generally discuss the economic, political, social, and religious life of a people.

ethnopoetics   The study of traditional oral literature, concerned with how linguistic features are used for artistic effect.

etiology   The causes of a specific disease.

evidential   In linguistics, a construction indicating the source of validity of the information in a sentence.

exclusive   In linguistics, referring to a first-person plural pronoun, which excludes the person spoken to, "I and someone else, but not you."

extended family   A family unit consisting of three or more generations.

extinguished   The act of giving up claims to land in exchange for compensation such as money, parcels of land, and goods and services.

extradition   The process by which a person who has escaped from the country where he or she is accused of a crime is demanded by and then returned forcibly to that country to stand trial. Extradition is usually governed by treaties between the countries concerned. There is no general principle in international law that requires governments to return fugitives.

F

family   In linguistics, a group of languages clearly descended from a single "parent" language.

Federal Acknowledgment Project (F.A.P.) *See* Branch of Acknowledgment and Research. *See also* federal recognition.

federal agency Any department, agency, or instrumentality of the United States.

federal lands Any land, other than tribal lands, that are controlled or owned by the United States.

federal recognition Acknowledgment by the U.S. government of government-to-government relationships with certain Indian tribes. Federal recognition can be obtained by satisfying the criteria of the Federal Acknowledgment Process administered through the U.S. Department of the Interior, by federal statute enacted by Congress, or by court decree. *See* Federal Acknowledgement Process *and* federally recognized tribes.

federally recognized tribes Those Indian tribes with which the U.S. government maintains official relations, as established by treaty, executive order, or act of Congress.

Federation of Saskatchewan Indian Nations (FSIN) An association organized along with the Indian Association of Alberta in the 1940s, which has a mandate and objective to serve the political interest of the native bands with federal treaties within the province of Saskatchewan. *See* Indian Association of Alberta.

fee-simple ownership A form of individual ownership of property, usually land, where the owner has the sole right to sell the land to any buyers, and no other parties have significant claims to the land.

fiduciary A relationship founded in trust and responsibility for looking after the best interests of a group, organization, or committee.

Fifth Amendment Part of the Bill of Rights of the U.S. Constitution, which forbids any taking of "private property" without "due process of law" and compensation. Indian treaties and reservation lands are now recognized as being "property" within the meaning of this provision.

First Ministers' Conference (FMC) A recently developed Canadian political tradition, the FMC is a gathering of Canada's "first ministers"—the ten provincial premiers and the national prime minister. In the 1990s, leaders of the Canadian territories have been included on occasion along with aboriginal leaders. At first, FMCs were oriented toward specific issues and problems; however, increasingly the FMC is supplanting traditional parliamentary politics as the primary decision-making forum in Canada.

first nations A term that came into common usage in the 1970s to replace the word "Indian" which many people found offensive. The term distinguishes and gives recognition to Canada's Indian nations as the original peoples on the North American continent. Although the term First Nation is widely used, no legal definition of it exists. Among its uses, the term "First Nations peoples" refers to the Indian people in Canada, both status and non-status Indians and treaty Indians.

Five Civilized Tribes A name given to the Cherokee, Choctaw, Chickasaw, Creek, and Seminole tribes during the second half of the 1900s because they adopted democratic constitutional governments and schools.

Folsom points Ancient flaked and grooved pieces of flint that were used as spearheads by paleo-Indians, or Stone Age Indians, before 10,000 B.C.E.

foraging economy An economic system based on obtaining foods from naturally occurring sources, hunting, fishing, and gathering plants.

Formative period A term used to describe the period of early settlement of Indians into villages. In the Southwest, the settlement of villages, with some dependence on farming, occurred between C.E. 200 and 900.

freedmen Former slaves who were freed after the Civil War and by the Thirteenth Amendment to the U.S. Constitution. The Cherokee, Choctaw, Chickasaw, Creek, and Seminole all held slaves and, after the Civil War, in one way or another included their freedmen into their national institutions.

fricative In linguistics, a consonant produced by letting the air pass through the mouth with audible noise, as contrasted with a stop, when the air is abruptly held in the mouth.

G

General Allotment Act of 1887 A law that applied the principle of allotting in severalty tribal reservation lands to individual resident tribesmen. Generally, a tract of 160 acres for a head of household, 80 acres for single people, and 40 acres per child was received in trust status for a period of twenty-five years; thereafter, the allottee owned the land in fee simple. The General

Allotment Act was designed to divide Indian reservations into small, privately owned plots and release the surplus lands to U.S. settlers. Under the General Allotment Act, between 1887 and 1934, over 90 million acres of Indian land were sold to U.S. citizens. This law is often referred to as the Dawes Act, named for the law's principle author, U.S. Senator Henry Dawes of Massachusetts.

General Revenue Sharing Program (1972–1986) A federal program to share federal tax revenues with state and local governments in the United States, including states, counties, cities, towns, and Indian tribes and Alaska Native villages, "which perform substantial governmental functions."

genetic relationship In linguistics, the relationship between "sister" languages descended from a single parent language.

Ghost Dance Part of a largely religious movement in the 1870s and into the late 1880s and early 1890s. The movement hoped to restore the buffalo herds to the Plains and restore the old Indian Plains life. It was believed that many of the people lost in epidemics and warfare would be returned to life if certain ritual and religious precautions were observed. *See* the biography of Wovoka and information on the Great Basin and Plains in the 1870s to 1890s.

glottal stop In linguistics, a consonant produced by closing and opening the vocal cords, interrupting the flow of air.

glottalization In linguistics, a closure and re-opening of the vocal cords simultaneously with the production of a sound in the mouth.

government-to-government relationship The official relation between the U.S. federal government and the tribal governments of Indian tribes, which is defined by the mention of Indian tribes in the U.S. Constitution and through legal rulings. In this relation, the U.S. government recognizes inherent rights of Indian tribes to self-government and to the ownership of land.

Great Basin Elevated region covering a great deal of several western U.S. states (Nevada, eastern California, western Colorado, Utah, eastern Oregon, and western Wyoming), which contains no drainage for water outside the region. Consequently, water must drain toward the center, hence the name Great Basin.

Great Society Name given to domestic policy during the administration of President Lyndon B. Johnson (1963–1969), especially anti-poverty and social welfare measures.

H

habeas corpus Literally, from Latin "you have the body." A claim presented to a court stating that a person is being held in custody or jail in violation of law. In Indian country, normally this writ of habeas corpus is available only to criminal defendants who have been convicted in tribal courts and who claim that their convictions were obtained without adherence to the Indian Civil Rights Act (for example, evidence was improperly seized or the criminal statute used as the basis for conviction violated rights of free speech).

Haudenosaunee The name of the people often called the Iroquois or Five Nations, or Six Nations after 1717. Literally, it means "The People of the Long House," referring to the extended multifamily houses in which the Iroquois lived.

Health and Welfare Canada The department of the Canadian federal government responsible for the health of all Canadians. It is divided into several branches; the Medical Services Branch serves the health needs of Inuit and Indians.

health status A measurement of the state of health of a given population, usually reported in numbers per 1,000 population and utilizing such indicators as morbidity, mortality, and infant death rates.

heathens Anyone of another religion with different fundamental views of religion. Indians were considered heathens by the early Catholic Spanish explorers and by the Puritans in New England. Indians considered Europeans also to have little understanding of religion or culture. For example, the Choctaw regarded early English traders as untutored and nonspiritual beings because they did not understand Choctaw religious views and did not practice correct religious rituals and social etiquette.

hierarchical Structured by class or rank.

Home Guard Indians In Canada, bands of Indians who lived near fur trade posts and had a relatively more intense trading relationship with traders than most Indian bands. Home Guard bands and traders exchanged various goods and services, and also tended to develop kinship ties.

homestead With reference to the federal lands (public domain), a homestead is a parcel of land—usually 80 to 160 acres—acquired by an adult who had to develop a portion of the land and build a minimal home on the site. The Homestead Act of 1862 was the initial law that made homesteading possible on public lands.

hunters Indians who depended on hunting, fishing, or gathering, as opposed to farming, for their food. Most aboriginal groups in Canada were hunting peoples.

I

IHS Service Population Those American Indians, Eskimos, and Aleuts (as identified by the census) who reside in the geographic areas in which the Indian Health Service (IHS) has responsibilities. These areas are the thirty-two reservation states (including California), and the geographic areas are defined as on or near reservations or within a contract health service delivery area (CHSDA).

Immersion schools Canadian schools where the language used is different from the students' first language. For example, Indian children who spoke their native language were often sent to schools where only English was spoken. This was a method of getting them to speak English and learn Canadian culture.

in situ "In place." A term applied to archaeological remains found in their original, undisturbed location or position.

inalienable In linguistics, referring to a noun for which a possessor must always be specified, especially kin terms and body parts.

inclusive In linguistics, referring to a first-person plural pronoun that includes the person spoken to, "I and you."

incorporation In linguistics, refers to the object of a noun being part of a verb form.

Indian (1) In Canada, according to the Indian Act first passed in 1876 and revised in 1985, a term that describes all the Aboriginal people in Canada who are not Inuit or Métis. Indian peoples are one of three groups of people recognized as Aboriginal in the *Constitution Act*, 1982. The act specifies that Aboriginal people in Canada consist of Indians, Inuit and Métis people. In addition, there are three legal definitions that apply to Indians in Canada: status Indians, non-status Indians and treaty Indians. (2) In the United States, any individual who self-identifies as an American Indian or Alaska Native and who is determined by his tribe to be a fully enrolled tribal member.

Indian Act In Canada, the overriding legislation that sets forth the policies of the federal government towards native people. This legislation passed by the Canadian government defines the legal status of Indians. First passed by the Canadian Parliament in 1876, the act was revised in 1951 and subsequently amended in 1985. Essentially, the Indian Act had four major objectives. First, it defined status Indians. Second, it established the reserve system. Third, it created legal entities known as bands with governments to administer reserve communities. And fourth, it created a national administrative structure, now known as Indian and Northern Affairs Canada, to administer the act. Under the Indian Act, the head of this administrative structure holds ministerial and trust responsibility for "status Indians" recognized by the Canadian federal government. The minister's responsibilities include managing certain monies belonging to First Nations and Indian lands, and approving or disallowing First Nations by-laws. *See* band, band council, British North America Act, *and* status Indians.

Indian agents In Canada, government agents appointed to Indian regions to increase contact between the Crown and Indian nations. Their presence marked the replacement of traditional Indian governments by elected governments, largely controlled by these agents.

Indian and Northern Affairs Canada (INAC) The Canadian government department (formerly known as the Department of Indian Affairs and Northern Development) that administers the *Indian Act* and delivers authorized federal funds and programs, often through provincial governments, to those Aboriginal people who qualify to receive them.

Indian Association of Alberta (IAA). Officially incorporated in 1944, IAA serves as an organization representing the political interests of the treaty Indians of the province of Alberta. The IAA promotes unity and spiritual strength of Indian nations in the protection of their lands, rights, and cultures. The organization receives its mandates from the chiefs, councillors, and members of the Alberta first nations, the member native bands of Alberta.

Indian country Land where Indian government and custom rule. In more recent times, Indian country refers to Indian reservations where Indian tribal governments are regulated by federal law and the Bureau of Indian Affairs.

Indian Delegation Act of 1946 (Public Law 687)
A congressional act that authorized substantial delegations of formal authority from the secretary of the interior to the commissioner of Indian affairs and from the commissioner to his subordinates, the twelve area directors who work on a day-to-day basis with local BIA agency offices and tribal governments on Indian reservations.

Indian Education Act (1972)   A congressional act that provided education financial assistance to communities with Indian students in their schools.

Indian Health Care Improvement Act (Public Law 94–437)   Through a program of increased funding levels in the Indian Health Service budget, the act was intended to improve the health status of American Indians and Alaska Natives up to a level equal to the general U.S. population. Funding was directed to urban populations and funds were used to expand health services, and build and renovate medical and sanitation facilities. It also established programs designed to increase the number of Indian health professionals and to improve care access for Indian people living in urban areas.

Indian Health Service (IHS)   The seventh agency within the U.S. Public Health Service, this federal agency's mission is to upgrade the health status of American Indians to the highest level possible. The IHS is composed of eleven regional administrative units called area offices. Within these units, the IHS operates 45 hospitals, 65 health centers, 6 school health centers, and 201 other treatment programs. In 1987, the state of California was designated an area office, the latest addition to the IHS. There are no IHS facilities in California, only Indian-operated and -managed clinics.

Indian New Deal   Legislation enacted in the early 1930s during the Roosevelt administration promoting tribal government and economic recovery programs for reservations.

Indian Removal   The United States government policy, beginning in the 1820s and lasting through the 1850s, of moving all Indian tribes west of the Mississippi River, to make room for U.S. settlement of the lands in the east. By 1860, this policy resulted in the removal of most eastern Indian nations to locations in present-day Kansas and Oklahoma.

Indian Reorganization Act of 1934 (IRA)   A congressional act providing reservation communities the opportunity to re-organize their tribal governments and adopt a new tribal constitution and tribal charter, and organize tribal business corporations. It also provided a revolving loan fund and other support services to participating tribes.

Indian Self-Determination and Education Assistance Act of 1975 (Public Law 93–638)   This act enabled tribes to contract, at their own option, to provide any service currently being provided by either the Bureau of Indian Affairs or the Indian Health Service. If the tribes change their policies about contracting government services, they have the right to return the administration of a contracted service to the relevant federal agency. The Self-Determination Act was designed to give Indian tribes and organizations more direct control over federal programs that operated within reservation communities.

Indian status   In Canada, an individual's legal status as an Indian, as defined by the *Indian Act*.

Indian Territory   The area west of the Mississippi River, primarily present-day Kansas and Oklahoma, to which the United States once planned to move all of the eastern Indians. Indian Territory was the home of nearly one-third of all U.S. Indians in 1880. Parts of Indian Territory were opened to U.S. settlers, over Indian objections, in 1889. By 1907, the last remnants of Indian Territory were admitted to the Union as the state of Oklahoma, as non-Indians had become an overwhelming majority of the population.

Indian tribe   Any tribe, band, nation, or other organized group or community of Indians recognized as being eligible for special programs and services provided by the United States because of its status. *See* federally recognized tribes.

indigenous   Native to the area.

industry   A term used in a classification system of economic activity in which firms that produce similar goods or services are grouped together into distinct categories.

infant death rate   A ratio of infant deaths within the first year of life to the total live births in a particular time period, usually five or ten years.

injunction   A court order prohibiting a person or legal entity from carrying out a given action, or ordering a person or organization to carry out a specific task. For example, in 1832, the U.S. Supreme Court in the case *Worcester v. Georgia* ruled that the Georgia government had no legal right to abolish the Cherokee government, which had its capital in territory claimed by Georgia. The Court, however, did not issue an injunction to the state of Georgia to prohibit it from extending its laws over the Cherokee nation.

inpatient A patient admitted to a bed in a hospital to have treatment and stay overnight at least one night.

intransitive In linguistics, characterizing verbs that have subjects but not direct objects, opposite of transitive.

Inuit Formerly known as Eskimos, Inuit are members of one of several peoples who traditionally inhabited areas north of the treeline in northern Alaska, northern Canada, and Greenland. They all speak dialects of the same language. In Canada, Inuit have the same legal status as Indians. The word Inuit means *people* in the Inuit language– Inuktitut. The singular of Inuit is Inuk. Forming a majority in the new Canadian territory of Nunavut, they are in effect self-governing since the turn of the twenty-first century.

Inuk The singular of Inuit.

Iroquoian Indian peoples who speak an Iroquoian language, such as the Huron, Mohawk, and Onondaga.

Iroquoian League The Iroquois Confederacy, an alliance of government and cultural and legal unity, which was formed before European colonization by the Mohawk, Cayuga, Onondaga, Oneida, and Seneca nations of present-day upstate New York. Also called the Five Nations and, after being joined by the Tuscarora in the early 1700s, the Six Nations.

isolate (language isolate) A language without close historical relationships to other languages.

J

Jim Crow Legislation After 1890, laws passed by many southern states designed to segregate the U.S. population by race. Many native people were automatically classified as black.

Johnson-O'Malley Act of 1934 Permitted the Indian Office to contract with the states to provide education, health, and welfare services to Indians on reservations within their borders. For example, the act allowed Indian children to attend public schools at the expense of the Indian Office.

jurisdiction The empowerment of a governing body to oversee regulations and laws within an assigned area. The extent of legal power of a government, legislature, or of a court over its people and territory. Jurisdiction is defined in terms of persons, subject matter, and geography. For example, Alabama courts have jurisdiction in cases involving people, property, or activities only in the state of Alabama.

K

Kachina A deity or group of benevolent spirit beings among the Pueblo.

kiva Among the Pueblo cultures, an underground ceremonial chamber formed in the shape of a circle. A cycle of often-secret annual rituals takes place in the kivas. Leaders gather in the kivas to discuss religious and other important issues concerning the pueblo community.

L

labiovelar In linguistics, characterizing consonants produced with the rear part of the tongue, with simultaneous rounding of the lips.

labor force participation An individual who is working or looking for work is considered to be participating in the labor force. Anyone who does not have a job and is not looking for work is not in the labor force.

land cession treaty A treaty in which a group of people surrender certain rights to land in exchange for other rights, usually hunting rights or an annual payment.

land claim, comprehensive In the 1970s, the Canadian government agreed to negotiate comprehensive land claims with aboriginal groups whose ancestors had not ceded their land rights by signing a land surrender treaty. Claims negotiations involve a lengthy process, which, when successful, leads to cash settlements, land title, and devolution of authority. When settled, comprehensive claims agreements acquire the constitutional status of treaties.

land claim, specific Specific land claims are made against the Canadian state where it is argued that treaty commitments have not been met. The meaning of treaty rights themselves has expanded considerably over the years, allowing ever more specific claims to be made on treaty grounds. But usually specific land claims refer to as-yet unallocated lands.

land tenure   Land tenure has to do with how land is held—by communities, tribes, nations, individuals—and how it functions in terms of utilization, devisement, etc. In Indian affairs, land tenure is basically dichotomous; tribal and individual (allotment), but reservations may include non-Indian allotments, federal public lands, and even state lands.

language area   A geographical region in which languages of different families have become similar due to borrowing.

law   A measure or set of rules passed by a governing body to regulate the actions of the people in the interest of the majority of the nation.

legend   A folktale that deals with the experiences of individuals or happenings of a distant past.

libertarian   A person who places great value on individual consent and personal freedom.

life expectancy   The average number of years remaining to a person at a particular age, based on a given set of age-specific death rates, generally the mortality (death rate) conditions existing in the period mentioned.

line   A unit in the structure of a literary composition, defined in terms of its parallelism of structure with an adjacent line.

lineage   A group of people who can trace actual descent from a common ancestor.

lingua franca (trade language)   A mixed language used for communication between people of different native languages.

linguistics   The study of language. Usually the sounds, structure, and meaning of a language are analyzed and compared with other languages.

litigation   The use of courts or a legal process to achieve an end or contest an issue. For example, when in the early 1830s, the state of Georgia extended its laws over the Cherokee nation, the Cherokee appealed to the U.S. Supreme Court to resolve their differences with the Georgians.

location ticket   In Canada, the right granted by the government to an Indian to use part of reserve land as if it were private property. Location tickets were part of the Canadian government's attempts to encourage Indians to accept private property rather than hold land in common.

Long Walk   The 300-mile forced walk in 1864 from the Navajo's home in the west to an assigned reservation, Bosque Redondo, near Fort Sumner, 180 miles southeast of Santa Fe, New Mexico. During the 1970s and early 1980s, several long walks by Indians traveling across the country were organized to protest treaty and Native issues. Often the long walks started at Alcatraz Island, or on the West coast, and ended in Washington, D.C. In 1972, one such long walk ended in the pillaging of the BIA offices in Washington D.C. Sacred runs continue to be organized.

longhouse   In the Northwest Coast, a longhouse is a dwelling in which several nuclear families share the structure. Usually, the families are related to one another. The Iroquois or Six Nations of upstate New York also had a similar tradition of living in longhouses with related extended families.

loyalists   An expression used during the Revolutionary War (1775–83) for persons who chose the side of the British and attempted to help the British cause.

M

Magna Carta   An agreement of fundamental rights, also known as the Great Charter of England, signed in 1215 C.E. by King John and his English noblemen. Many of our modern ideas on government and democracy have developed from this fundamental constitutional document, empowering freedom and justice. *See* Proclamation of 1763.

maize   Also known as corn, an important crop plant, initially domesticated in Mexico over six thousand years ago.

Manifest Destiny   During the 1900s, a broadly held belief among the U.S. population that it was inevitable that the U.S. nation would expand across the North American continent from the Atlantic to the Pacific Ocean. Belief in Manifest Destiny served as a rationalization for the seizure of Indian land, and, in 1846, to justify war with Mexico, which led to the annexation of Texas, New Mexico, Arizona, and California.

materialism   The belief that economic well-being or wealth are of central human concern, while spiritual or cultural understandings or comforts are of secondary concern or relatively meaningless.

Matrilineal descent   A kinship system in which relationships are traced through women. Children belong to their mother's kin group. Inheritance of names, wealth, or other property transfer through the mother's family and/or clan.

matrilocal residence   A pattern of residence where a married couple lives with or near the wife's family.

Medical Services Branch (MSB)   The branch of the Department of National Health and Welfare of the Canadian federal government responsible for Indian and Inuit health.

Medicine Chest Clause   A clause in Treaty No. 6 (1876) between the Canadian government and the Indian tribes in Northern Alberta on which is based the claim that Indian people in Canada have a perpetual right to free health care provided by the Canadian federal government.

mega-fauna   The large animals, such as woolly mammoth, ground sloth, and saber-toothed tiger, which died off about 8,000 B.C.E. after the last glacier receded far north.

Meriam Report of 1928   An exhaustive investigation of Indian administration and a major criticism of Indian policies and administration since passage of the General Allotment Act of 1887. The report had a major influence on Indian affairs during the administrations of Presidents Herbert Hoover (1929–1933) and Franklin D. Roosevelt (1933–1945). It helped formulate the policies of the Indian New Deal, which originated with passage of the Indian Reorganization Act of 1934, and allowed Indians greater self-government and the right to retain cultural ceremonies and events. Produced by the Brookings Institution's Institute for Government Research, the actual title of the report is *The Problem of Indian Administration*.

mescaline   A white, crystalline alkaloid, psychedelic drug obtained from the cactus *Lophophora williamsi* (peyote).

metate   A stone with a slightly hollow center that is used for grinding corn.

Métis   French for "mixed-blood." This term has been used in several different ways. Usually it refers to mixed-blood people in western Canada who are conscious of belonging to a distinct community. The Canadian Constitution recognizes Métis as aboriginal peoples. The term is also used to refer to any person of mixed Indian-European descent, and more specifically to a descendant of a native parent, usually Cree or Ojibway, and a non-native parent, usually French, but also some English, who settled in the Red River area of

what is now the province of Manitoba during the days of the fur trade, which lasted from the 1700s to the late 1800s.

Mississippian period   The period between C.E. 900 and 1500 when in the eastern United States there arose complex chiefdom societies and maize-farming communities. The Mississippian tradition is associated with the building of flat-topped earthen mounds, which were religious and political centers. Many of the Mississippian towns, sometimes holding as many as thirty thousand people, were fortified with palisades. One of the largest Mississippian societies was located at Cahokia, near present-day St. Louis, Missouri.

moiety   A French expression which means divided into two halves. For anthropologists, the term refers to a society divided into two major clusters of clans. For example, among the Tlingit, there are Eagle and Raven moieties, which divide the society into two groups of about twenty-five clans. Among the Tlingit, moiety relations govern marriage rules, since Raven moiety members must marry an Eagle and vice-versa.

morphology   In linguistics, the formation of words by combinations of stems, prefixes, and suffixes, as contrasted with syntax.

mortality   The proportion of deaths to population.

moxa   A soft, downy material, burned on the skin as a cauterizing agent or counter-irritant.

Muskogean   A family of related languages spoken by many Indian nations of the southeast including the Choctaw, Chickasaw, Creek, Seminole, and Natchez.

myth   A narrative tale concerned with the Creator, spirits, and the nature and meaning of the universe and humans.

N

Nation   A community of people who share the right to political self-rule, and/or who share a common identity, and who usually share a similar culture, the same language, the same economy, and a mutually recognized territory.

National Indian Brotherhood (NIB)   Founded in 1968, a Canadian national Indian political organization. The NIB now serves as the legal executive office for the Assembly of First Nations. *See* Assembly of First Nations.

Native American Of or relating to a tribe, people, or culture indigenous to the United States.

need An estimate of the amount of medical care required to provide adequate services to a population in terms of the amount of disease present or preventable, often contrasted to demand.

New Deal Name given to domestic policy during the administration of President Franklin D. Roosevelt (1933–1945).

New Frontier Name given to domestic policy during the administration of President John F. Kennedy (1961–1963).

non-IHS-service population Those Indians who do not reside in the geographic areas in which Indian Health Service has responsibility.

non-recognized tribe Indian communities that do not have official government-to-government relations with the U.S. government because they did not sign a treaty with the United States, lost their recognized status by termination, or have no executive orders or agreements that require the U.S. government to provide services or to protect their land and resources in a trust relationship.

non-status Indians People in Canada who consider themselves to be Indians but whom the Canadian government does not recognize as Indians under the Indian Act because they have failed to establish or have lost or abandoned their Indian status rights.

non-treaty Indians Canadian Indian people whose relationship with the government is not affected by any treaties. Non-treaty Indians can be either status or non-status Indians.

Northwest Passage As late as the 1790s, Europeans believed there was a short ocean passage in the northern latitudes connecting the Atlantic and Pacific Oceans. Many of the earliest European explorations in northern North America were prompted by this myth.

Northwest Territories (NWT) Today this term refers to the western central portion of Canadian territory (capital city, Yellowknife) north of the 60th parallel. The territory of Nunavut was formed in 1999 from the province of Northwest Territories as constituted at that time. Originally (1870), the Northwest Territories referred to most of Canada west of Ontario except

British Columbia, including present-day Alberta and Saskatchewan and most of Manitoba.

numeral classifier In linguistics, a grammatical element used in counting, indicating the form or shape of the objects counted.

Nunavut As of 1 April 1999, a new territory (previously part of the Northwest Territories), which covers the majority of Canada north of the tree line. Inuit are the majority of the region's population. The establishment of Nunavut was part an aboriginal land claim.

O

occupation A term used in a classification system of economic activity in which jobs that require similar activities are grouped together into distinct categories.

Oklahoma "Runs" Spectacular one-day chances to legally acquire former Indian land in present-day Oklahoma. Most of the "runs" occurred in the 1890s.

"On or near" The federal regulation that Contract Health Service can be provided only to American Indians residing on a reservation or in a county that borders a reservation.

Oolichan (Eulachon) A small fish (Thaleichthys pacificus) captured in freshwater streams by the Northwest Coast people. Oolichan were especially important as a source of oil.

oral history A historical research method that investigates the past by speaking to people rather than relying on the written word.

outpatient A patient who receives diagnosis or treatment in a clinic or dispensary connected with a hospital but is not admitted as a bed patient. (Sometimes used as a synonym for ambulatory.)

P

Paleo-Arctic tradition A term used to describe the tools left behind by the first Native Americans, who lived in the arctic regions of Alaska and Canada. The Paleo-arctic tradition began between 9000 and 8000 B.C.E. and continued as late as 5000 B.C.E.

paleo-Indians The ancestors of contemporary Native Americans and the first people to come to North America over fourteen thousand years ago.

Paleo-Plateau tradition   A term used to describe the various Archaic period cultures of the Columbia-Fraser Plateau of Washington state and British Columbia. The Paleo-Plateau tradition lasted from 8,000 to 3,000 B.C.E.

Papal Bull   A decree made by a Catholic Pope. Bulls used to have the force of law within the Roman Catholic Church, but today are considered to be statements of policy only.

patriarchy   A social system in which men have exclusive control over power and wealth in the society.

patrilineal descent   A kinship system in which relationships are traced through men. Children belong to their father's kin group.

patrilocal residence   A pattern of residence where a married couple lives with or near the husband's family.

patronage   Providing jobs in exchange for political services. For example, before 1890 most jobs with the U.S. Indian administration were jobs gained through patronage relations with congressmen and other high government officials.

Penner Report   A report prepared in 1983 by a special committee of the House of Commons on Indian self-government in Canada. The report is named after committee chairman, Keith Penner, a member of Parliament for the Liberal party.

per capita   A Latin term meaning by or for each person, equally to each individual. It is one way used for distributing funds to every adult member of a tribe.

peyote   A bitter stimulant obtained from the button-like structures of the mescal cactus plant, which some Indian groups use as part of their religious practices. The peyote buttons are taken during ceremonies of the Native American Church, which was officially established in 1918, but began on the Plains as early as the 1860s.

phoneme   In linguistics, one of the set of contrasting sound units in a language.

phylum   Plural phyla. In linguistics, a group of language families hypothesized to be descended from a single parent language.

pictograph   A simplified pictorial representation of an historical occurrence.

Piedmont   A region in the southeast United States marked by rolling hills and open valleys located between the relatively flat coastal plain and the more rugged Appalachian Mountains.

Pinto Basin tradition   A term describing a series of archaeological hunting and gathering cultures from the Great Basin, dating over the period of 5000 to 1500 B.C.E.

plenary power   The exclusive authority of Congress (as opposed to the states of the Union) to make laws concerning Indian tribes. This special power can be traced to Article I, Section 8 (the "Indian Commerce Clause") of the Constitution. Plenary means full or complete.

policy   A statement that outlines the means and philosophy by which a group or government will try to fulfill one or more of its major goals or interests.

polyandry   A marriage involving one woman and two or more men.

polygamy   Having more than one spouse at the same time.

polygyny   A marriage involving one man and two or more women.

polysynthetic language   In linguistics, a type of language marked by long word forms with complex morphologies, which may often function as complete sentences.

potlatch   A feast in recognition of important life events, e.g., birth, death, marriage. The giving of a potlatch conferred value, prestige, and honor to all those involved. During a potlatch, or "giveaway," the hosts gave food, clothes, songs, and culturally significant gifts, such as copper engraved valuables, to the guests. The potlatch ceremony was practiced by tribes in the Pacific Northwest. "Giveaways" are similar events held in other regions of North America.

poultice   A hot, soft, moist mass, as of flour, herbs, mustard, etc., sometimes spread on cloth, applied to a sore or inflamed part of the body.

preemption   The power of the federal government to override state law in fields such as Indian affairs. This power comes from Article VI, Section 2 of the U.S. Constitution (the "Supremacy Clause"), which says federal laws and treaties are "the supreme Law of the Land."

presidio Spanish military post in the American Southwest.

Privy Council (Judicial Committee of the Privy Council) In the British Empire, the Privy Council in London was the final court of appeal from the colonial governors and courts. It was a committee of Peers (titled noblemen) chosen by the Crown (the reigning King or Queen). Until 1949, the Privy Council, in London, England, was the highest court of appeal in Canada and was therefore somewhat analogous to the U.S. Supreme Court.

Proclamation of 1763 The document signed by King George III issued as a declaration of policy by the British government to address the unauthorized settlement of Indian land. The Proclamation was never fully implemented, in part due to the outbreak of the American Revolution. The commitments contained within were, however, often renewed to obtain alliances with most Indian nations in fighting against the rebels. In areas that later became part of the United States, the policy reserved the land west of the Appalachian Mountains for Indian use, and restricted English settlements to land east of the divide, or central ridge, of the Appalachians. In Canada, the Proclamation provides the basis of English recognition of Indian rights to use and live on their territory, but only at the pleasure of the British Crown, which by this act claimed ownership of all Indian lands. It remains part of the Canadian Constitution.

proto-language The prehistoric parent language from which several historical languages are descended.

Public Law 280 (1953) 67 Stat. 588 A congressional act that transferred criminal and civil jurisdiction in Indian country from the federal government to the states of California, Minnesota, Nebraska, Oregon, and Wisconsin (and after 1959 to Alaska). Other states were given the option to assume jurisdiction by legislation. In 1968, P.L. 280 was amended to require tribal consent to the transfer of jurisdiction.

pueblo A Spanish word for the multi-storied stone or adobe Indian villages of the American Southwest. Also a name used for the Indians who inhabited such communal buildings.

R

radiocarbon dating A technique that measures the natural radioactive content of organic materials, such as charcoal, in order to measure the approximate age of the materials or objects found in archaeological sites.

rancheria A Spanish word applied to the numerous, small Indian reservations of California.

range condition The annual health of browsable vegetation that supports domesticated animals—e.g., cattle, sheep, etc. The determination of a range condition will decide how many head will be permitted to graze given areas in a given year or season.

ratification The confirmation of a treaty by the national legislature—in the United States, by the Senate. In most countries, a treaty must be ratified before it becomes law.

recognized *See* federally recognized, state recognized, *and* nonrecognized tribes.

recognized & original title Recognized title lands refer to those ceded by treaties or statutes and original title lands are those that have had to be reconstructed on the basis of ethnographic and historic research, including information provided by Indian informants.

red power A term applied to an Indian social movement and a series of protest activities during the 1960s and 1970s.

reduplication In linguistics, repetition of part of a stem, often used to indicate plurality or habitual action.

referenda Referring measures passed upon or proposed by the legislature to the voters for approval or rejection. In some states a referenda can be placed on the ballot by petition of registered voters.

registered Indians *See* status Indians.

relocation In 1951, the federal government established the Direct Employment Assistance program to encourage reservation Indians to move to urban areas such as Los Angeles, Chicago, Minneapolis, and Denver. This and subsequent programs came to be known as "relocation" programs.

Removal Act A congressional act passed in 1830 which authorized and funded the peaceful exchange of lands and removal of Indians to Indian Territory, west of the Mississippi River.

repatriation Through court cases and legislative lobbying, tribes have demanded the return of museum-

and university-held skeletal remains of Indians and funerary objects for reburial or other appropriate disposition.

reservation/rancheria Lands set aside by U.S. government authority for use and occupation by a group of Indians.

reservation state An area within which the Indian Health Service has responsibilities for providing health care to American Indians or Alaska Natives.

reserve In Canada, land set aside for specific Indian bands. "Indian reserve lands" as defined by the Indian Act. Essentially the same meaning as the U.S. term "reservation." In Canada, legal title is held in trust by the federal Crown in the right of Canada and may not be leased or sold until "surrendered" to the Crown by a referendum by band members.

reserved-rights doctrine A legal theory that Indian communities and governments maintain all rights to self-government, exercise of cultural rights, religious freedom, land, water, and other resources, unless Congress expressly takes those rights away.

residential schools Schools administered by the Canadian government and religious organizations that housed and educated many Indian and Inuit children in the 19th and 20th centuries. The use of such schools was intended to achieve the goal of complete assimilation of Indians into Canadian society by way of isolating children from their families and communities. Many instances of physical and sexual abuse took place at such schools and the Canadian government as well as the churches involved are facing lawsuits as a result.

residual resource The final or remaining course of action for patients seeking medical care from a provider.

restitution Transfer of property or payment of money to prevent an unjust loss from the acts of another.

retrocession A bureaucratic procedure of the Bureau of Indian Affairs that allows Indian communities within Public Law 280 states (California, Alaska, Wisconsin, Oregon, Nebraska, and Minnesota) to petition the federal government to bar state government regulation of courts and law enforcement on the reservation.

revitalization A social movement carried out by a group, usually in response to major changes in its society, such as pressures to assimilate. Revitalization attempts to create new culture with beliefs, values, and attitudes that blend some aspects of the old culture with the new living conditions.

Robinson Superior Treaty of 1850 On 7 September 1850, at Sault Ste. Marie, Ontario, the Honorable William B. Robinson of Toronto, Ontario, acting on behalf of the British Crown, met with three chiefs and five principal men representing Michipicoten, Fort William, and Gull River bands of Ojibwa Indians to sign a document referred to as the Robinson Superior Treaty, the first modern Indian treaty in Canada.

According to the treaty, the Ojibwa people surrendered considerable land, and were paid two thousand pounds in English money and allotted three reserves. A similar agreement, referred to as the Robinson Huron Treaty of 1850, removed Indian land claims from the north shore of Lake Huron.

Rose Spring phase A term given by archaeologists to a time period (1500 B.C.E. to C.E. 500) when hunter and gatherer cultures occupied the region of the Owens Valley of present-day eastern California.

Royal Commission on Aboriginal Peoples This Commission was appointed in 1991 by the federal government of Prime Minister Brian Mulroney "to examine the economic, social and cultural situation of the Aboriginal Peoples of Canada." Seven commissioners visited 96 communities, held 178 days of hearings, heard briefs from 2,067 people and accumulated more than 76,000 pages of testimony. The five-volume report constitutes the most in-depth analysis ever undertaken on Aboriginal people in Canada. Highly controversial due to its recommendations and its cost, the current government has yet to implement any of its proposals.

royal prerogative The rights and privileges of a sovereign over subjects independent of both statutes and the courts.

rural Indian An Indian residing in a non-urban area, generally on or near a reservation.

S

sacred objects Specific ceremonial objects needed by Native American religious leaders for the practice of traditional Native American religions.

San Dieguito tradition A distinctive artifact tradition known from present-day California and Nevada and dating to about 8000 to 6000 B.C.E. The tools of the

San Dieguito people show a heavy reliance on hunting, but with some evidence of gathering of wild plants.

scrip A document given to Métis people during the late nineteenth century in order to extinguish aboriginal title. Scrip could be exchanged for money or land.

secular A word referring to the mundane or ordinary and nonreligious aspects or times of everyday life.

sedentary A term that refers to permanent settlement, where the people usually engage in farming for a livelihood and, for the most part, have abandoned hunting or nomadic herding as the mainstay of their economy.

self-determination Indians exercising their right to govern and make decisions affecting their own lives and affairs on their own land. In international law, the right of every "people" to choose its own form of government and control its own future. Since the 1970s, Congress has used this word to describe programs designed to give Indian tribes greater control over the schools, health facilities, and social services on reservations. *See* Indian Self-Determination and Education Assistance Act.

seminars Roman Catholic schools that teach religion and other subjects.

settlement acts The term refers to laws enacted by Congress that finally end conflict and litigation over designated tribal land claims. Many of these acts carry the term within their title—e.g., The Saddleback Mountain Settlement Act of 1995.

severance tax A tax assessed by a government on mining or petroleum companies when they remove minerals or natural resources from the ground.

Shaker Religion A religious movement that began with the prophet John Slocum, whose death and re-birth in the 1880s started a movement among the native people of Puget Sound. The movement combined many elements of traditional Coast Salish religion with Christianity. It soon spread through the northwest United States.

shaman/shamanism An individual versed in supernatural matters who performed in rituals and was expected to cure the sick, envision the future, and help with hunting and other economic activities. Often, a shaman is a healer who uses spiritual encounters or contacts to enact a cure on the patient. Many shamans deal with ailments that are spiritual rather than physical.

Siouan A large language family that includes Siouan-related languages such as Lakota, Nakota, Dakota, and Crow.

site In archaeology, a location of past cultural activity of defined space with more or less continuous archaeological evidence.

smallpox A highly contagious disease which left survivors with badly scarred skin. Native Americans often died by the thousands because their ancestors had not developed resistance to the infection, which was introduced to North America by Europeans.

smoke shop An Indian-owned store on a reservation that sells cigarettes at a relatively cheap price because state sales tax need not be included.

Snyder Act of 1921 Provided permanent funding authorization for "the general support and civilization of the Indians." To carry out these objectives, the act authorized the Indian Office to provide educational, health, and welfare services to Indian people, to irrigate and make other improvements on Indian lands, and to employ personnel to support these objectives. The Snyder Act signaled a change toward a permanent Indian-federal government relationship.

socialize A process by which an individual learns to adjust to the group by acquiring social behaviors of which the group approves.

Sooner Frontiersmen who illegally squatted on Indian land before the U.S. government had extinguished Indian land claims and title.

sovereignty Deriving from *sovereign*, which means a ruler or king. In international law, being completely independent and not subject to any other ruler or government. The inherent right of a nation to exercise complete and absolute governance over its people and its affairs. In U.S. federal Indian law, sovereignty means having a distinct, but not completely independent government.

specific claim According to Canadian government land claims policy since 1973, an aboriginal claim based on rights set out in treaties, Indian acts, or other legislation.

Spirit Dance In the Northwest Coast, a song and dance performed by an individual who has had a guardian spirit encounter. The Spirit Dances are held in the winter months.

squatter   A person who occupies land without having title to it.

state-recognized tribes   Those Indian communities whose governments and land are officially recognized by their surrounding state government, but are not usually recognized by the federal government as an Indian reservation.

status Indians   In Canada, if a person meets the definitional requirements of the Indian Act, they are entitled to be registered on the Indian Register (or Band Membership List) kept by Indian and Northern Affairs Canada in Ottawa. The guidelines for determining status are complex. The criteria is legal rather than based on racial characteristics or blood quantum. All treaty Indians are status Indians, but not all status Indians are treaty Indians. In 1985, Parliament passed an amendment to the Indian Act that allows each native band to adopt its own rules for determining band membership. Many of the new band codes for determining Indian status vary among themselves and with the old rules of the Indian Act.

statute   A law enacted by the highest legislature in the nation or state.

statutory   Refers to those provisions enacted by law by a legislative body.

stop   In linguistics, a consonant produced by shutting off the flow of air momentarily.

Strait of Georgia tradition   An archaeological cultural tradition from the western coastal area of Canada believed to be ancestral to the Coast Salish and other present-day Native American groups of the area. The Strait of Georgia tradition dated from 3,000 to 200 B.C.E.

subsistence   A term that describes a small and localized economy oriented to the production of goods and services primarily for household use, and bound by rules of kinship, sharing, and reciprocity.

sui generis   So unique that it constitutes a class of its own. A term that is used to explain the status of aboriginal title in Canada. It is unique and is therefore inalienable to anyone but the Crown.

Sun Dance   An annual world renewal and purification ceremony performed with some variation among many of the northern Plains Indian nations such as the Cheyenne and the Sioux. One striking aspect of the ceremony was the personal sacrifice that some men made by self-torture in order to gain a vision that might provide spiritual insight and knowledge beneficial to the community.

sweat lodge   A sacred Indian ceremony involving construction of a lodge made of willow saplings bent to form a dome and covered with animal skins, blankets or canvas tarp. A hole is dug in the middle of the lodge in which hot rocks are placed and water poured over them, often by a medicine man, in a ceremonial way often accompanied by praying and singing. The ceremony can have many purposes including spiritual cleansing and healing.

sweetgrass ceremony   A ceremony in which braided sweetgrass is burned and participants "smudge" themselves with the smoke, similar to incense in other religions.

syllabary   A type of writing system in which the basic unit represents a sequence of consonant plus vowel, constituting a syllable. In comparison, alphabets have either a consonant, a letter, or a vowel (in English—a, e, i, o, u), which compose the basic unit of the writing system, as in English or Latin. The famous Cherokee writing system invented by Sequoia is a syllabary and not an alphabet.

syncretic movements   A religious belief system that combines symbols and beliefs from two or more religions. In native North America, there are many native religions that combine elements of traditional religion with Christianity. Some such Indian religious movements are the Delaware Prophet movement of the early 1760s, the Handsome Lake movement beginning in 1799, the Ghost Dances of the 1870s and early 1890s, the ongoing Shaker movement of the Pacific Northwest, and the Native American Church or Peyote cult.

syntax   In linguistics, the combination of words into sentences, as contrasted with morphology, the formation of words by combinations of stems, prefixes, and suffixes.

T

termination   The policy of Congress in the 1950s and 1960s to withdraw federal trust status from Indian bands, communities and tribes. Those tribes that were "terminated" by an act of Congress no longer functioned as governments that made their own laws, but instead were placed under state laws.

theocracy   A government or society led by religious leaders.

Thule tradition   The archaeological culture, dated from C.E. 100 to 1500 and later, defined as the direct ancestral culture of the present-day Inuit throughout the Arctic. The Thule people were hunters skilled at exploiting sea mammals.

trade language (lingua franca)   A mixed language used for communication between people of different native languages.

traditional ecological knowledge   The knowledge of Indigenous Peoples including worldviews, values, processes and factual information.

Trail of Tears   In the 1830s, a series of forced emigrations by groups of Cherokee, Creek, Seminole, and perhaps some Choctaw, from the Southeast to Indian Territory, present-day Oklahoma, caused by the removal policy.

transitive   In linguistics, a characterizing verb that has both subject and direct object, opposite of intransitive.

treaties   Agreements negotiated between two parties, which set out the benefits both sides will receive as a result of one side giving up their title to a territory of land. In Canada, commonly referred to as Modern Treaties or Numbered Treaties. After Canada gained its own constitution under confederation in 1867, the new federal government of Canada signed a series of modern treaties numbered 1 through 11 between 1871 and 1921. Also included as "modern " treaties are the Robinson-Superior and Robinson-Huron treaties of 1850 with the Ojibway of Ontario occupying the north shores of Lake Huron and Lake Superior. The government negotiator, the Honorable William B. Robinson of Toronto is recognized for establishing the "treaty method" of obtaining Indian "title surrenders" to land in return for "treaty rights." The Chippewa and Missassauga Agreements of 1923 were the last formally negotiated Indian treaties in Canada. *See* treaty.

treaty   (1) In Canada, an agreement between Indian peoples and the Canadian government. Some maintain that these treaties are comparable to treaties between independent nations, while others claim they are merely contracts between the government and some of its subjects. Between 1871 and 1923, the Canadian government made twelve numbered treaties with native bands. Since 1923, the Canadian government has stopped using this term in its agreements with aboriginal peoples. (2) A formal agreement between two or more sovereign nations on issues of war, peace, trade, and other relations. Before 1871, the U.S. government ratified about 270 treaties with Indian nations. After 1871, the U.S. government stopped making treaties with Indians. *See* treaties.

treaty Indian   In Canada, descendants of Indians entitled to benefits under the treaties signed by the Crown and specific Indian bands between 1725 and 1921. Those who "took treaty" and surrendered their land rights for specific benefits.

tribal corporation   An enterprise owned and operated by a tribe under articles of incorporation, thereby protecting tribal assets not held by the corporation from lawsuits. While providing economic opportunities for tribal members, tribal corporations often employ many non-members as well.

tribal groups   A term, especially in British Columbia, for various language and culture groups that reject centralized bureaucracies, whether attached to government or native organizations.

tribal sovereignty   The powers of self-government held by Indian communities.

tribe   A group of natives sharing a common ancestry, language, culture, and name.

tripartite   A term meaning divide into or composed of three parts or parties. A reference to the three distinct governments within Indian Country: federal, tribal, and state.

trust   Property that is protected from being taxed or sold by the federal government for a period of time and is held in benefit of a trustee. In U.S. Indian affairs, the government holds trust of Indian lands and resources.

trust responsibility   The responsibility of the federal government to protect Indian lives and property; to compensate Indians for any loss due to government mismanagement; and, generally, to act in the best interests of Indians. Originally called "guardianship" and sometimes described by lawyers as a "fiduciary duty."

trust status   A legal relationship of an Indian person or tribe with the United States, within which the U.S. government has final and broad authority over the actions of individual Indians or over tribal governments.

U

unemployment rate   A statistic published by the federal Bureau of Labor Statistics. It is the percent of the labor force without employment. Unemployed persons who have given up their search for work are not counted in this statistic because they are not considered part of the labor force.

unilaterally   "On its own," often referring to U.S. government policy when it abandoned a treaty promise without agreement or compensation to an Indian nation.

unilineal descent   A system of kinship relations and inheritance where descent is traced through only women (matrilineal) or men (patrilineal).

urban Indian   An Indian residing in urban metropolitan areas or cities.

usufructuary   (1) In Canada, the inherent right to use and enjoy the natural products of lands (e.g., game, fish, plants, fruits) of which the underlying title belongs to another, usually the Crown. (2) A way of using land, common among Indian farmers and hunters, where land belongs to an individual, clan, or village as long as that group has a history of continual usage of the land, hunting area, or fishing site. Usufruct rights are recognized by others and are lost whenever a group discontinues use.

uvular   In linguistics, a feature of a consonant sound made with the back of the tongue and the rear of the soft palate or uvula.

V

values   The generally agreed upon goals, purposes, and issues of importance in a community.

variety   In linguistics, a local language variant, referring either to languages of the same family or to dialects of the same language.

velar   In linguistics, characterizing consonants produced with the rear part of the tongue. *See* labiovelar.

vision quest   A sacred Indian ceremony that involves an individual, often a teenage boy, going to a secluded place to fast (go without food or water) for a period of time (usually a few days) to learn about the spiritual side of himself and possibly have a vision of his spiritual helper, a spirit being who will give him guidance and strength.

voiced   In linguistics, a sound pronounced with vibration of the vocal cords.

voiceless   In linguistics, a sound pronounced without vibration of the vocal cords.

vowel harmony   In linguistics, a process in which vowels change to resemble vowels in nearby grammatical environments.

W

wampum   Small, cylindrical, blue and white beads cut from the shell of the quahog, a large Atlantic coast clam. Long strings of wampum were used as trade exchange, while broad, woven "belts" of wampum were used to record treaties among the tribes and, later, with Europeans.

Wapato   A plant (Sagittaria latifolia) that grows in shallow lakes and marshy areas. The root was an important source of food for many groups in the Northwest Coast.

wardship   According to some legal theories, the relationship between the U.S. government and Indians, where the government has trust responsibility over the affairs and resources of the Indians.

weir   A fishing device that operates by blocking off a portion of a stream with a fence-like structure. Migrating fish are then forced to find openings in the weir where the people then capture them.

Westward movement   Name given the displacement of Native American peoples by the movement of Americans from the eastern shoreline in the seventeenth century to the West Coast in the nineteenth century.

Woodland period   A major time period usually dating from 500 B.C.E. to C.E. 900. During this period, Native American cultures developed complex ceremonial centers that included construction of large mounds. The Woodland period cultures were the first to practice farming in northeastern North America.

world view   The unconscious philosophical outlook held by the members of a society.

General Bibliography

◆ General Studies ◆ Anthropology ◆ Architecture ◆ Art ◆ Atlases
◆ Autobiography ◆ Demography ◆ History ◆ Image/Stereotype ◆ Land
◆ Legal Status/Law ◆ Literature and Poetry ◆ Oral Tradition ◆ Policy ◆ Prehistory
◆ Religion ◆ Sociology ◆ Urbanization ◆ Women ◆ Canada

◆ GENERAL STUDIES

Armstrong, Virginia Irving. *I Have Spoken: American History Through the Voices of the Indians.* Athens, Ohio: Swallow Press, 1971.

Bierhorst, John. *The Mythology of North America.* New York: Morrow, 1985.

Boas, Franz. *Race, Language and Culture.* New York: Macmillan, 1940.

Bowden, Henry Warner. *American Indians and Christian Missions: Studies in Cultural Conflict.* Chicago: University of Chicago Press, 1981.

Boxberger, Daniel L., ed. *Native North Americans: An Ethnohistorical Approach.* Dubuque, Iowa: Kendall/Hunt, 1990.

Champagne, Duane. *American Indian Societies: Some Strategies and Conditions of Political and Cultural Survival.* Cambridge, Mass.: Cultural Survival, 1989.

Davis, Mary B., ed. *Native America in the Twentieth Century: An Encyclopedia.* New York: Garland Pub., 1994.

Edmunds, R. David. *American Indian Leaders: Studies in Diversity.* Lincoln: University of Nebraska Press, 1980.

Feest, Christian F. *Indians and Europe: An Interdisciplinary Collection of Essays.* Lincoln: University of Nebraska Press, 1999.

Hamilton, Charles. *Cry of the Thunderbird: The American Indian's Own Story.* Norman: University of Oklahoma Press, 1972.

Hoxie, Frederick E., ed. *Encyclopedia of North American Indians.* Boston: Houghton Mifflin Company, 1996.

Hoxie, Frederick E., and Harvey Markowitz. *Native Americans: An Annotated Bibliography.* Pasadena, Calif.: Salem Press, 1991.

Leitch, Barbara A. *A Concise Dictionary of Indian Tribes of North America.* Algonac, Mich.: Reference Publications, 1979.

Malinowski, Sharon, ed. *The Gale Encyclopedia of Native American Tribes.* Detroit: Gale, 1998.

Mihesuah, Devon A., ed. *Natives and Academics: Researching and Writing about American Indians.* Lincoln: University of Nebraska Press, 1998.

Moerman, Daniel E. *Native American Ethnobotany.* Portland, Oreg.: Timber Press, 1998.

Swisher, Karen Gayton, and AnCita Benally. *Native North American Firsts.* Detroit: Gale, 1998.

Thornton, Russell, ed. *Studying Native America: Problems and Prospects.* Madison, Wis.: University of Wisconsin Press, 1998.

Weeks, Philip. *The American Indian Experience: A Profile, 1524 to the Present.* Arlington Heights, Ill.: Forum Press, 1988.

White, Phillip M. *American Indian Studies: A Bibliographic Guide.* Englewood, Colo.: Libraries Unlimited, 1995.

♦ ANTHROPOLOGY

Bean, Lowell John. *Mukat's People: The Cahuilla Indians of Southern California.* Berkeley and Los Angeles: University of California Press, 1972.

Biolsi, Thomas. *Organizing the Lakota: The Political Economy of the New Deal on the Pine Ridge and Rosebud Reservations.* Tucson: University of Arizona Press, 1992.

Biolsi, Thomas, and Larry J. Zimmerman. *Indians and Anthropologists: Vine Deloria, Jr., and the Critique of Anthropology.* Tucson: University of Arizona Press, 1997.

Deloria, Vine, Jr. *Red Earth, White Lies: Native Americans and the Myth of Scientific Fact.* New York: Scribner, 1995.

———. *We Talk, You Listen: New Tribes, New Turf.* New York: Macmillan, 1970.

Eggan, Fred. *Social Anthropology of North American Tribes.* 2nd enlarged ed. Chicago: University of Chicago Press, 1970.

Ewers, John Canfield. *Plains Indian History and Culture: Essays on Continuity and Change.* Norman: University of Oklahoma Press, 1997.

Fowler, Loretta. *Shared Symbols, Contested Meanings: Gros Ventre Culture and History, 1778–1984.* Ithaca: Cornell University Press, 1987.

Lowie, Robert. *Indians of the Plains.* 1954. Reprint. Lincoln: University of Nebraska Press, 1982.

Miller, Jay. *Tsimshian Culture: A Light Through the Ages.* Lincoln: University of Nebraska Press, 1997.

Nabokov, Peter, ed. *Native American Testimony: A Chronicle of Indian-White Relations From Prophecy to the Present, 1492–2000.* Rev. ed. New York: Penguin, 1999.

Ortiz, Alfonso. *The Tewa World: Space, Time, Being, and Becoming in a Pueblo Society.* Chicago: University of Chicago Press, 1969.

Parker, Arthur C. *Parker on the Iroquois.* Edited by William N. Fenton. Syracuse, N.Y.: Syracuse University Press, 1968.

Sando, Joe S. *Nee Hemish, a History of Jemez Pueblo.* Albuquerque: University of New Mexico Press, 1982.

———. *Pueblo Nations: Eight Centuries of Pueblo Indian History.* Santa Fe, N.Mex.: Clear Light, 1992.

Stands In Timber, John. *Cheyenne Memories.* 1967. Reprints. Lincoln: University of Nebraska Press, 1972; New Haven, Conn.: Yale University Press, 1998.

Sturtevant, Willam C., ed. *Handbook of North American Indians.* 11 vols. to date. Washington, D.C.: Smithsonian Institution, 1978–.

Swanton, John R. *The Indian Tribes of North America.* 1952. Reprint. Washington, D.C.: Smithsonian Institution Press, 1968.

———. *The Indians of the Southeastern United States.* 1946. Reprint. Grosse Pointe, Mich.: Scholarly Press, 1969.

Swindler, Nina, et al., eds. *Native Americans and Archaeologists: Stepping Stones to Common Ground.* Walnut Creek: AltaMira Press, 1997.

Watkins, Joe. *Indigenous Archaeology: American Indian Values and Scientific Practice.* Walnut Creek, Calif.: AltaMira Press, 2001.

♦ ARCHITECTURE

Krinsky, Carol H. *Contemporary Native American Architecture: Cultural Regeneration and Creativity.* New York: Oxford University Press, 1997.

Morgan, William N. *Precolumbian Architecture in Eastern North America.* Gainesville, Fla.: University Press of Florida, 1999.

Nabokov, Peter, and Robert Easton. *Native American Architecture.* New York: Oxford University Press, 1989.

♦ ART

Berlo, Janet C., ed. *The Early Years of Native American Art History: The Politics of Scholarship and Collecting.* Seattle: University of Washington Press; Vancouver: UBC Press, 1992.

————. *Plains Indian Drawings, 1865–1935: Pages From a Visual History.* New York: Harry N. Abrams in association with the American Federation of Arts and the Drawing Center, 1996.

Berlo, Janet C. and Ruth B. Phillips. *Native North American Art.* Oxford and New York: Oxford University Press, 1998.

Brody, J. J. *Anasazi and Pueblo Painting.* Albuquerque: University of New Mexico Press, 1991.

————. *Indian Painters & White Patrons.* Albuquerque: University of New Mexico Press, 1971.

Dockstader, Frederick J. *Indian Art in America: The Arts and Crafts of the North American Indian.* Greenwich, Conn.: New York Graphic Society, 1966.

Feder, Norman. *Two Hundred Years of North American Indian Art.* New York: Praeger, 1972.

Feest, Christian F. *Native Arts of North America.* London: Thames and Hudson; New York: Oxford University Press, 1980.

Grant, Campbell. *Rock Art of the American Indian.* New York: Crowell, 1967.

Heth, Charlotte, ed. *Native American Dance: Ceremonies and Social Traditions.* Washington, D.C.: Smithsonian, 1992.

Lester, Patrick D. *The Biographical Directory of Native American Painters.* Tulsa, Okla.: SIR Publications; distributed by University of Oklahoma Press, 1995.

Mathews, Zena Pearlstone, and Aldona Jonaitis. *Native North American Art History: Selected Readings.* Palo Alto, Calif.: Peek Publications, 1982.

Matuz, Roger, ed. *St. James Guide to Native North American Artists.* Detroit: St. James Press, 1998.

National Museum of the American Indian. *The Changing Presentation of the American Indian: Museums and Native Cultures.* Washington, D.C.: National Museum of the American Indian; Seattle: University of Washington Press, 2000.

Penney, David W. *Art of the American Indian Frontier: The Chandler-Pohrt Collection.* Detroit: Detroit Institute of Arts; Seattle: University of Washington Press, 1992.

Porter, Frank W., III. *The Art of Native American Basketry: A Living Legacy.* New York: Greenwood Press, 1990.

Rushing, W. Jackson, III, ed. *Native American Art in the Twentieth Century.* London and New York: Routledge, 1999.

Wade, Edwin L., ed. *The Arts of the North American Indian: Native Traditions in Evolution.* New York: Hudson Hills Press; Tulsa: Philbrook Art Center, 1986.

Wyckoff, Lydia J. *Visions and Voices: Native American Painting From the Philbrook Museum of Art.* Tulsa: Philbrook Museum of Art; Albuquerque, N.Mex.: Distributed by the University of New Mexico Press, 1996.

◆ ATLASES

Coe, Michael D., Dean Snow, and Elizabeth Benson. *Atlas of Ancient America.* New York: Facts on File, 1986.

Ferguson, Thomas J. *A Zuni Atlas.* Norman: University of Oklahoma Press, 1985.

Goodman, James M. *The Navajo Atlas: Environments, Resources, People, and History of the Dine Bikeyah.* Norman: University of Oklahoma Press, 1982.

Prucha, Francis P. *Atlas of American Indian Affairs.* Lincoln: University of Nebraska Press, 1990.

Sturtevant, William C. *Early Indian Tribes, Culture Areas, and Linguistic Stocks.* Reston, Va.: Dept. of Interior, U.S. Geological Survey, 1991.

Tanner, Helen Hornbeck, et al., eds. *Atlas of Great Lakes Indian History.* Norman: Published for the Newberry Library by the University of Oklahoma Press, 1987.

Waldman, Carl. *Atlas of the North American Indian.* Rev. ed. New York: Facts On File, 2000.

◆ AUTOBIOGRAPHY

Allen, Elsie C. *Pomo Basketmaking: A Supreme Art for the Weaver.* Rev. ed. Happy Camp, Calif.: Naturegraph, 1972.

Bennett, Kay. *Kaibah: Recollection of a Navajo Girlhood.* Los Angeles: Westernlore Press, 1964.

Bettelyoun, Susan Bordeaux. *With My Own Eyes: A Lakota Woman Tells Her People's History.* Lincoln: University of Nebraska Press, 1998.

Blackman, Margaret B. *During My Time: Florence Edenshaw Davidson, A Haida Woman.* Seattle: University of Washington Press, 1982.

———. *Sadie Brower Neakok, An Inupiaq Woman.* Seattle: University of Washington Press, 1989.

Blaine, Martha Royce. *Some Things Are Not Forgotten: A Pawnee Family Remembers.* Lincoln: University of Nebraska Press, 1997.

Blowsnake, Sam. *Crashing Thunder: The Autobiography of an American Indian.* 1926. Reprint. Lincoln: University of Nebraska Press, 1983.

Brave Bird, Mary. *Lakota Woman.* New York: Grove Weidenfeld, 1990.

Brumble, H. David. *American Indian Autobiography.* Berkeley and Los Angeles: University of California Press, 1988.

———. *An Annotated Bibliography of American Indian and Eskimo Autobiographies.* Lincoln: University of Nebraska Press, 1981.

Campbell, Maria. *Halfbreed.* 1973. Reprint. Lincoln: University of Nebraska Press, 1982.

Cruikshank, Julie. *Life Lived Like a Story: Life Stories of Three Yukon Native Elders.* Lincoln: University of Nebraska Press, 1990.

Cuero, Delfina. *The Autobiography of Delfina Cuero, a Diegueno Indian.* 1968. Reprints. Banning, Calif: Malki Museum Press, 1970; Menlo Park, Calif.: Ballena Press, 1991.

Dauenhauer, Nora. *Life Woven with Song.* Tucson: University of Arizona Press, 2000.

Eastman, Charles Alexander. *From the Deep Woods to Civilization.* 1916. Reprint. Lincoln: University of Nebraska Press, 1977.

———. *Indian Boyhood.* 1902. Reprint. New York: Dover, 1971.

Fools Crow. *Fools Crow.* Lincoln: University of Nebraska Press, 1990.

Giago, Tim A. *The Aboriginal Sin: Reflections on the Holy Rosary Indian Mission School.* San Francisco: Indian Historian Press, 1978.

Greene, Alma. *Forbidden Voice: Reflections of a Mohawk Indian.* 1971. Reprint. Toronto: Green Dragon Press, 1997.

Hale, Janet Campbell. *Bloodlines: Odyssey of a Native Daughter.* New York: Random House, 1993.

Harris, LaDonna. *LaDonna Harris: A Comanche Life.* Lincoln: University of Nebraska Press, 2000.

Hopkins, Sarah Winnemucca. *Life Among the Piutes: Their Wrongs and Claims.* 1882. Reprint. Reno: University of Nevada Press, 1994.

Horne, Esther Burnett. *Essie's Story: The Life and Legacy of a Shoshone Teacher.* Lincoln: University of Nebraska Press, 1998.

Johnson, Broderick H. *Stories of Traditional Navajo Life and Culture.* Tsaile, Navajo Nation, Ariz.: Navajo Community College Press, 1977.

Kakianak, Nathan. *Eskimo Boyhood: An Autobiography in Psychosocial Perspective.* Lexington: University Press of Kentucky, 1974.

Krupat, Arnold. *For Those Who Come After: A Study of Native American Autobiography.* Berkeley and Los Angeles: University of California Press, 1985.

La Flesche, Francis. *The Middle Five: Indian Schoolboys of the Omaha Tribe.* Madison: University of Wisconsin Press, 1963.

Lame Deer, John (Fire). *Lame Deer, Seeker of Visions.* New York: Simon and Schuster, 1972.

Left Handed. *Left Handed, Son of Old Man Hat: A Navajo Autobiography.* 1938. Reprint. Lincoln: University of Nebraska Press, 1996.

Little Coyote, Bertha. *Leaving Everything Behind: The Songs and Memories of a Cheyenne Woman.* Norman: University of Oklahoma Press, 1997.

Lurie, Nancy Oestreich, ed. *Mountain Wolf Woman, Sister of Crashing Thunder: The Autobiography of a Winnebago Indian.* Ann Arbor: University of Michigan Press, 1966.

Mankiller, Wilma, and Michael Wallis. *Mankiller: A Chief of Her People.* New York: St. Martin's Griffin, 2000.

Mitchell, Frank. *Navajo Blessingway Singer: The Autobiography of Frank Mitchell: 1881–1967.* Tucson: University of Arizona Press, 1978.

Modesto, Ruby, and Guy Mount. *Not for Innocent Ears: Spiritual Traditions of a Desert Cahuilla Medicine Woman.* Angelus Oaks, Calif.: Sweetlight Books, 1980.

Mohatt, Gerald V., and Joseph Eagle Elk. *The Price of a Gift: A Lakota Healer's Story.* Lincoln: University of Nebraska Press, 2000.

Mourning Dove. *Mourning Dove: A Salishan Autobiography.* Lincoln: University of Nebraska Press, 1990.

Scott, Lalla. *Karnee: A Paiute Narrative.* Reno: University of Nevada Press, 1966.

Snell, Alma Hogan. *Grandmother's Grandchild: My Crow Indian Life.* Lincoln: University of Nebraska Press, 2000.

Two Leggings. *Two Leggings: The Making of a Crow Warrior.* 1967. Reprint. Lincoln: University of Nebraska Press, 1982.

Underhill, Ruth Murray. *Papago Woman.* New York: Holt, Rinehart and Winston, 1979.

Waheenee. *Waheenee: An Indian Girl's Story, Told by Herself to Gilbert L. Wilson.* Lincoln: University of Nebraska Press, 1981.

Yava, Albert. *Big Falling Snow: A Tewa-Hopi Indian's Life and Times and the History and Traditions of His People.* New York: Crown Publishers, 1978.

Yellowtail, Thomas. *Yellowtail, Crow Medicine Man and Sun Dance Chief: An Autobiography.* Norman: University of Oklahoma Press, 1991.

Zitkala-Sa. *American Indian Stories.* 1921. Reprint. Lincoln: University of Nebraska Press, 1985.

◆ DEMOGRAPHY

Cook, Sherburne F. *The Conflict Between the California Indian and White Civilization.* Berkeley and Los Angeles: University of California Press, 1976.

Crosby, Alfred W., Jr. *The Columbian Exchange: Biological and Cultural Consequences of 1492.* Westport, Conn.: Greenwood Publishing Company, 1972.

Dobyns, Henry F. *Their Number Become Thinned: Native American Population Dynamics in Eastern North America.* Knoxville: University of Tennessee Press in cooperation with the Newberry Library Center for the History of the American Indian, 1983.

Duffy, John. *Epidemics in Colonial America.* Baton Rouge, Louisiana State University Press, 1953.

Reddy, Marlita A., ed. *Statistical Record of Native North Americans.* 2nd ed. Detroit: Gale Research, 1995.

Shoemaker, Nancy. *American Indian Population Recovery in the Twentieth Century.* Albuquerque: University of New Mexico Press, 1999.

Snipp, C. Matthew. *American Indians: The First of This Land.* New York: Russell Sage Foundation, 1989.

Stearn, Esther W. *The Effect of Smallpox on the Destiny of the Amerindian.* Boston: Bruce Humphries, Inc., 1945.

Stuart, Paul. *Nations Within a Nation: Historical Statistics of American Indians.* New York: Greenwood Press, 1987.

Thornton, Russell. *American Indian Holocaust and Survival: A Population History Since 1492.* Norman: University of Oklahoma Press, 1987.

Verano, John, and Douglas H. Ubelaker, eds. *Disease and Demography in the Americas.* Washington: Smithsonian Institution Press, 1992.

◆ HISTORY

Calloway, Colin G. *First Peoples: A Documentary Survey of American Indian History.* Boston: Bedford/St. Martin's, 1999.

———., ed. *New Directions in American Indian History.* Norman: University of Oklahoma Press, 1988.

———. *Our Hearts Fell to the Ground: Plains Indian Views of How the West Was Lost.* Boston: Bedford Books of St. Martin's Press, 1996.

Costo, Rupert, and Jeannette Henry Costo. *The Missions of California: A Legacy of Genocide*. San Francisco: Indian Historian Press, American Indian Historical Society, 1987.

Debo, Angie. *A History of the Indians of the United States*. Norman: University of Oklahoma Press, 1970.

Gibson, Arrell M. *The American Indian: Prehistory to the Present*. Lexington, Mass.: D.C. Heath, 1980.

Hoxie, Frederick E., and Peter Iverson. *Indians in American History: An Introduction*. 2nd ed. Wheeling, Ill.: Harlan Davidson, 1998.

Hurt, R. Douglas. *Indian Agriculture in America: Prehistory to the Present*. Lawrence, Kan.: University Press of Kansas, 1987.

Hurtado, Albert L., and Peter Iverson. *Major Problems in American Indian History: Documents and Essays*. Lexington, Mass.: D.C. Heath, 1994.

Josephy, Alvin M., ed. *America in 1492: The World of the Indian Peoples Before the Arrival of Columbus*. New York: Knopf, 1992.

Kehoe, Alice. *North American Indians: A Comparative Account*. 2nd ed. Englewood, N.J.: Prentice Hall, 1992.

Leacock, Eleanore Burke, and Nancy O. Lurie, eds. *North American Indians in Historical Perspective*. Prospect Heights, Ill.: Waveland Press, 1988.

McNickle, D'Arcy. *Native American Tribalism: Indian Survivals and Renewals*. New York: Oxford University Press, 1973.

———. *They Came Here First: The Epic of the American Indian*. Rev. ed. New York: Harper & Row, 1975.

Olson, James S., and Raymond Wilson. *Native Americans in the Twentieth Century*. Provo, Utah: Brigham Young University Press, 1984.

Prucha, Francis Paul. *American Indian Treaties: The History of a Political Anomaly*. Berkeley and Los Angeles: University of California Press, 1994.

Spicer, Edward H. *Cycles of Conquest: The Impact of Spain, Mexico, and the United States on the Indians of the Southwest, 1533–1960*. Tucson: University of Arizona Press, 1962.

Trigger, Bruce G., and Wilcomb E. Washburn, eds. *North America*. Vol. 1 of *The Cambridge History of the Native Peoples of the Americas*. New York: Cambridge University Press, 1996.

Waldman, Carl. *Biographical Dictionary of American Indian History to 1900*. Rev. ed. New York: Facts on File, 2001.

◆ IMAGE/STEREOTYPE

Bataille, Gretchen, and Charles L.P. Silet, eds. *The Pretend Indians: Images of Native Americans in the Movies*. Ames: Iowa State University Press, 1980.

Berkhofer, Robert F. *The White Man's Indian: Images of the American Indian from Columbus to the Present*. New York: Knopf, 1978.

Bird, S. Elizabeth. *Dressing in Feathers: The Construction of the Indian in American Popular Culture*. Boulder, Colo.: Westview Press, 1996.

Boehme, Sarah E., et al. *Powerful Images: Portrayals of Native America*. Seattle: Museums West in association with the University of Washington Press, 1998.

Deloria, Philip J. *Playing Indian*. New Haven: Yale University Press, 1998.

Dippie, Brian W. *The Vanishing American: White Attitudes and U.S. Indian Policy*. Lawrence, Kan.: University Press of Kansas, 1991.

Hauptman, Laurence M. *Tribes & Tribulations: Misconceptions About American Indians and Their Histories*. Albuquerque: University of New Mexico Press, 1995.

Hirschfelder, Arlene B., Paulette Fairbanks Molin, and Yvonne Wakim. *American Indian Stereotypes in the World of Children: A Reader and Bibliography*. 2nd ed. Lanham, Md.: Scarecrow Press, 1999.

King, C. Richard, and Charles Fruehling Springwood, eds. *Team Spirits: The Native American Mascots Controversy*. Lincoln: University of Nebraska Press, 2001.

Mihesuah, Devon A. *American Indians: Stereotypes & Realities*. Atlanta, Ga., 1996.

Moses, Lester G. *Wild West Shows and the Images of American Indians, 1883–1933*. Albuquerque: University of New Mexico Press, 1996.

National Museum of the American Indian. *The Changing Presentation of the American Indian: Museums and Native Cultures.* Washington, D.C.: National Museum of the American Indian; Seattle: University of Washington Press, 2000.

Rollins, Peter C., and John E. O'Connor, eds. *Hollywood's Indian: The Portrayal of the Native American in Film.* Lexington: University Press of Kentucky, 1998.

Slapin, Beverly, and Doris Seale, eds. *Through Indian Eyes: The Native Experience in Books for Children.* Los Angeles: American Indian Studies Center, University of California, Los Angeles, 1998.

Spindel, Carol. *Dancing at Halftime: Sports and the Controversy Over American Indian Mascots.* New York: New York University Press, 2000.

Stedman, Raymond W. *Shadows of the Indian: Stereotypes in American Culture.* Norman: University of Oklahoma Press, 1982.

◆ LAND

Berger, Thomas R. *Village Journey: The Report of the Alaska Native Review Commission.* Rev. ed. New York: Hill and Wang, 1995.

Clow, Richmond L. and Imre Sutton, eds. *Conservation and the Trustee: Environmental Essays on the Management of Native American Resources.* Boulder: University Press of Colorado, 2001.

Confederation of American Indians, comp. *Indian Reservations: A State and Federal Handbook.* Jefferson, N.C.: McFarland, 1986.

Fixico, Donald L. *The Invasion of Indian Country in the Twentieth Century: American Capitalism and Tribal Natural Resources.* Niwot, Colo.: University Press of Colorado, 1998.

Frantz, Klaus. *Indian Reservations in the United States: Territory, Sovereignty, and Socioeconomic Changes,* Geography Research Paper 242. Chicago: University of Chicago Press, 1999.

Hart, E. Richard. *Zuni and the Courts: A Struggle for Sovereign Land Rights.* Lawrence, Kan.: University Press of Kansas, 1995.

Johansen, Bruce E. *Shapers of the Great Debate on Native Americans—Land, Spirit, and Power: A Biographical Dictionary.* Westport, Conn.: Greenwood Press, 2000.

Kickingbird, Kirke, and Karen Ducheneaux. *One Hundred Million Acres.* New York: Macmillan, 1973.

LaDuke, Winona. *All Our Relations: Native Struggles for Land and Life.* Cambridge, Mass.: South End Press, 1999.

Sutton, Imre, ed. *Irredeemable America: The Indians' Estate and Land Claims.* Albuquerque: University of New Mexico Press, 1985.

Tiller, Veronica E. Velarde, ed. *Tiller's Guide to Indian Country: Economic Profiles of American Indian Reservations.* Albuquerque, N.Mex.: BowArrow Publishing Co., 1996.

Vecsey, Christopher, and William A. Starna. *Iroquois Land Claims.* Syracuse, N.Y.: Syracuse University Press, 1988.

White, Richard. *The Roots of Dependency: Subsistence, Environment, and Social Change Among the Choctaws, Pawnees, and Navajos.* Lincoln: University of Nebraska Press, 1983.

◆ LEGAL STATUS/LAW

Burton, Lloyd. *American Indian Water Rights and the Limits of Law.* Lawrence, Kan.: University Press of Kansas, 1991.

Canby, William C., Jr. *Indian Law in a Nutshell.* 3rd ed. St. Paul: West Pub. Co., 1998.

Clark, Blue. *Lone Wolf v. Hitchcock: Treaty Rights and Indian Law at the End of the Nineteenth Century.* Lincoln: University of Nebraska Press, 1994.

Cohen, Felix S. *Felix S. Cohen's Handbook of Federal Indian Law.* 2d ed. Charlottesville, Va.: Michie/Bobbs-Merrill, 1982.

Deloria, Vine. *Tribes, Treaties, and Constitutional Tribulations.* Austin: University of Texas Press, 1999.

Deloria, Vine, and Clifford M. Lytle. *American Indians, American Justice.* Austin: University of Texas Press, 1983.

Deloria, Vine, and Raymond J. DeMaille, comps. *Documents of American Indian Diplomacy: Treaties, Agreements, and Conventions, 1775–1979.* Norman: University of Oklahoma Press, 1999.

Falkowski, James E. *Indian Law/Race Law: A Five-Hundred Year History.* New York: Praeger, 1992.

Getches, David H. *Cases and Materials on Federal Indian Law.* 4th ed. St. Paul, Minn.: West Group, 1998.

Kappler, Charles J., comp. and ed. *Indian Affairs. Law and Treaties.* 7 vols. 1904–1971. Reprint. New York: AMS Press, 1972.

Norgren, Jill. *The Cherokee Cases: The Confrontation of Law and Politics.* New York: McGraw-Hill, 1996.

O'Brien, Sharon. *American Indian Tribal Governments.* Norman: University of Oklahoma Press, 1989.

Pevar, Stephen L. *The Rights of Indians and Tribes: The Basic ACLU Guide to Indian and Tribal Rights.* 2nd ed. Carbondale, Ill.: Southern Illinois University Press, 1992.

Shattuck, Petra T., and Jill Norgren. *Partial Justice: Federal Indian Law in a Liberal Constitutional System.* New York: Berg, 1991.

Wilkinson, Charles F. *American Indians, Time, and the Law: Native Societies in a Modern Constitutional Democracy.* New Haven: Yale University Press, 1987.

◆ LITERATURE AND POETRY

Alexie, Sherman. *The Business of Fancydancing: Stories and Poems.* Brooklyn, N.Y.: Hanging Loose Press, 1992.

———. *Indian Killer.* New York: Atlantic Monthly Press, 1996.

———. *The Lone Ranger and Tonto Fistfight in Heaven.* New York: Atlantic Monthly Press, 1993.

———. *Old Shirts & New Skins.* Los Angeles: American Indian Studies Center, University of California, Los Angeles, 1993.

———. *One Stick Song.* Brooklyn: Hanging Loose Press, 2000.

Allen, Paula Gunn. *The Sacred Hoop: Recovering the Feminine in American Indian Traditions.* Boston: Beacon Press, 1986.

———, ed. *Song of the Turtle: American Indian Literature, 1974–1994.* New York: Ballantine Books, 1996.

———, ed. *Spider Woman's Granddaughters: Traditional Tales and Contemporary Writing by Native American Women.* Boston: Beacon Press, 1989.

———, ed. *Studies in American Indian Literature: Critical Essays and Course Designs.* New York: Modern Language Association of America, 1983.

———, ed. *Voice of the Turtle: American Indian Literature, 1900–1970.* New York: Ballantine Books, 1994.

———. *The Woman Who Owned the Shadows.* San Francisco: Spinsters Ink, 1983.

Brant, Beth. *Food & Spirits: Stories.* Ithaca, N.Y.: Firebrand Books, 1991.

———. *Mohawk Trail.* Ithaca, N.Y.: Firebrand Books, 1985.

Bruchac, Joseph. *Survival This Way: Interviews with American Indian Poets.* Tucson: University of Arizona Press, 1987.

Bush, Barney. *Inherit the Blood: Poetry and Fiction.* New York: Thunder's Mouth Press, 1985.

———. *My Horse and a Jukebox.* Los Angeles: American Indian Studies Center, University of California, Los Angeles, 1979.

Conley, Robert J. *Mountain Windsong: A Novel of the Trail of Tears.* Norman: University of Oklahoma Press, 1992.

———. *The Way of the Priests.* New York: Doubleday, 1992.

———. *The Witch of Goingsnake and Other Stories.* Norman: University of Oklahoma Press, 1988.

Cook-Lynn, Elizabeth. *Aurelia: A Crow Creek Trilogy.* Niwot, Colo.: University Press of Colorado, 1999.

———. *I Remember the Fallen Trees: New and Selected Poems.* Cheney, Wash.: Eastern Washington University Press, 1998.

Cronyn, George W., ed. *The Path on the Rainbow: An Anthology of Songs and Chants from the Indians of North America.* 1918. Reprint, *American Indian Poetry: An Anthology of Songs and Chants.* New York: Fawcett Columbine, 1991.

D'Aponte, Mimi. *Seventh Generation: An Anthology of Native American Plays.* New York: Theatre Communications Group, 1999.

Dorris, Michael. *A Yellow Raft in Blue Water.* New York: H. Holt, 1987.

Erdrich, Louise. *Beet Queen.* New York: Holt, 1986.

———. *The Bingo Palace.* New York: HarperCollins, 1994.

———. *Love Medicine.* New York: Holt, Rinehart, and Winston, 1984; Bantam, 1985; new and expanded version, New York: H. Holt, 1993; HarperPerennial, 1993.

———. *Tracks.* New York: Henry Holt, 1988.

Geiogamah, Hanay, and Jaye T. Darby, eds. *American Indian Theater in Performance: A Reader.* Los Angeles: UCLA American Indian Studies Center, 2000.

———. *Stories of Our Way: An Anthology of American Indian Plays.* Los Angeles: UCLA American Indian Studies Center, 1999.

Glancy, Diane. *Firesticks: A Collection of Stories.* Norman: University of Oklahoma Press, 1993.

———. *Iron Woman: Poems.* Minneapolis, Minn.: New Rivers Press, 1990.

———. *The Voice That Was in Travel: Stories.* Norman: University of Oklahoma Press, 1999.

Hale, Janet Campbell. *The Jailing of Cecelia Capture.* New York: Random House, 1985.

———. *Women on the Run.* Moscow, Idaho: University of Idaho Press, 1999.

Harjo, Joy. *A Map to the Next World: Poetry and Tales.* New York: W.W. Norton & Co., 2000.

———. *In Mad Love and War.* Middletown, Conn.: Wesleyan University Press, 1990.

———. *She Had Some Horses.* New York: Thunder's Mouth Press, 1983.

Harjo, Joy, and Gloria Bird, eds. *Reinventing the Enemy's Language: Contemporary Native Women's Writings of North America.* New York: W. W. Norton & Company, 1997.

Hogan, Linda. *The Book of Medicines: Poems.* Minneapolis: Coffee House Press, 1993.

———. *Mean Spirit.* New York: Atheneum, 1990.

Kabotie, Michael. *Migration Tears: Poems About Transitions.* Los Angeles: American Indian Studies Center, University of California, Los Angeles, 1987.

Lesley, Craig, ed. *Talking Leaves: Contemporary Native American Short Stories.* New York: Laurel, 1991.

Lincoln, Kenneth. *Native American Renaissance.* Berkeley and Los Angeles: University of California Press, 1983.

Mathews, John Joseph. *Sundown.* 1934. Reprint. Norman: University of Oklahoma Press, 1988.

———. *Talking to the Moon.* 1945. Reprint. Norman: University of Oklahoma Press, 1981.

McNickle, D'Arcy. *The Surrounded.* 1936. Reprint. Albuquerque: University of New Mexico Press, 1978.

Momaday, N. Scott. *The Ancient Child: A Novel.* New York: Doubleday, 1989.

———. *House Made of Dawn.* New York: Harper & Row, 1968.

———. *The Way to Rainy Mountain.* Albuquerque: University of New Mexico Press, 1969.

Mourning Dove. *Cogewea, the Half-Blood: A Depiction of the Great Montana Cattle Range.* 1927. Reprint. Lincoln: University of Nebraska Press, 1981.

Niatum, Duane, ed. *Harper's Anthology of 20th Century Native American Poetry.* San Francisco: Harper & Row, 1988.

Ortiz, Simon J. *A Good Journey.* Berkeley, Calif.: Turtle Island, 1977.

———. *From Sand Creek.* Reprint. 1984. Tucson: University of Arizona Press, 1999.

———. *Men on the Moon: Collected Short Stories.* Tucson: University of Arizona Press, 1999.

———. *Woven Stone.* Tucson: University of Arizona Press, 1992.

———, ed. *Speaking for the Generations: Native Writers on Writing.* Tucson: University of Arizona Press, 1998.

Owens, Louis. *Bone Game: A Novel.* Norman: University of Oklahoma Press, 1994.

———. *Other Destinies: Understanding the American Indian Novel.* Norman: University of Oklahoma Press, 1992.

Rainwater, Catherine. *Dreams of Fiery Stars: The Transformations of Native American Fiction.* Philadelphia: University of Pennsylvania Press, 1999.

Rose, Wendy. *Bone Dance: New and Selected Poems, 1965–1993.* Tucson: University of Arizona Press, 1994.

Sarris, Greg. *Grand Avenue.* New York: Penguin, 1995.

———. *Keeping Slug Woman Alive: A Holistic Approach to American Indian Texts.* Berkeley and Los Angeles: University of California Press, 1993.

Silko, Leslie M. *Almanac of the Dead.* New York: Simon & Schuster, 1991.

———. *Ceremony.* New York: Viking, 1977.

———. *Gardens in the Dunes: A Novel.* New York: Simon & Schuster, 1999.

———. *Storyteller.* New York: Seaver Books, 1981.

Spatz, Ronald, ed. *Alaska Native Writers, Storytellers & Orators.* Anchorage: University of Alaska, 1999.

TallMountain, Mary. *The Light on the Tent Wall: A Bridging.* Los Angeles: American Indian Studies Center, University of California, Los Angeles, 1990.

Tapahonso, Luci. *Saanii Dahataal, The Women Are Singing: Poems and Stories.* Tucson: University of Arizona Press, 1993.

Tedlock, Dennis. *The Spoken Word and the Work of Interpretation.* Philadelphia: University of Pennsylvania Press, 1983.

Treuer, David. *Little.* Saint Paul, Minn.: Graywolf Press, 1995.

Vizenor, Gerald R. *The Heirs of Columbus.* Middletown, Conn.: Wesleyan University Press, 1991.

———. *Shadow Distance: A Gerald Vizenor Reader.* Hanover, N.H.: Wesleyan University Press, 1994.

———. *Wordarrows: Indians and Whites in the New Fur Trade.* Minneapolis: University of Minnesota Press, 1978.

Walters, Anna Lee. *Ghost Singer: A Novel.* Flagstaff, Ariz.: Northland Publishing, 1988.

———. *The Sun is Not Merciful: Short Stories.* Ithaca, N.Y.: Firebrand Books, 1985.

Welch, James. *The Death of Jim Loney.* 1979.

———. *Fools Crow.* New York: Viking, 1986.

———. *The Indian Lawyer.* New York: W.W. Norton, 1990.

———. *Riding the Earthboy 40.* New York: World Pub. Co., 1971.

———. *Winter in the Blood.* New York: Harper & Row, 1974.

Witalec, Janet, ed. *Native North American Literature: Biographical and Critical Information on Native Writers and Orators From the United States and Canada From Historical Times to the Present.* New York: Gale Research, 1994.

Young Bear, Ray A. *Black Eagle Child: The Facepaint Narratives.* Iowa City, Iowa: University of Iowa Press, 1992.

♦ ORAL TRADITION

Bullchild, Percy. *The Sun Came Down.* San Francisco: Harper & Row, 1985.

Clements, William M., and Frances M. Malpezzi. *Native American Folklore, 1879–1979: An Annotated Bibliography.* Athens, Ohio: Swallow Press, 1984.

Erdoes, Richard, and Alfonso Ortiz, eds. *American Indian Myths and Legends.* New York: Pantheon Books, 1984.

———. *American Indian Trickster Tales*. New York: Viking, 1998.

Garter Snake. *The Seven Visions of Bull Lodge*. Ann Arbor, Mich.: Bear Claw Press, 1980.

Margolin, Malcom, ed. *The Way We Lived: California Indian Reminiscences, Stories, and Songs*. Berkeley: Heyday Books, 1981.

Norman, Howard A., trans. *The Wishing Bone Cycle: Narrative Poems From the Swampy Cree Indians*. Expanded ed. Santa Barbara, Ca.: Ross-Erikson, 1982.

Quam, Alvina, tr. *The Zunis: Self-Portrayals, By the Zuni People*. Albuquerque: University of New Mexico Press, 1972.

Swann, Brian, ed. *Coming to Light: Contemporary Translations of Native Literatures of North America*. New York: Random House, 1994.

———. *Smoothing the Ground: Essays on Native American Oral Literature*. Berkeley and Los Angeles: University of California Press, 1983.

◆ POLICY

Castile, George P. *To Show Heart: Native American Self-Determination and Federal Indian Policy, 1960–1975*. Tucson: University of Arizona Press, 1998.

Castile, George P., and Robert L. Bee. *State and Reservation: New Perspectives on Federal Indian Policy*. Tucson: University of Arizona Press, 1992.

Deloria, Vine, Jr. *Behind the Trail of Broken Treaties: An Indian Declaration of Independence*. New York: Dell, 1974.

Deloria, Vine, Jr., ed. *American Indian Policy in the Twentieth Century*. Norman: University of Oklahoma Press, 1985.

Dippie, Brian W. *The Vanishing American: White Attitudes and U.S. Indian Policy*. Middletown, Conn.: Wesleyan University Press, 1982.

Fixico, Donald L. *The Invasion of Indian Country in the Twentieth Century: American Capitalism and Tribal Natural Resources*. Niwot, Colo.: University Press of Colorado, 1998.

———. *Termination and Relocation: Federal Indian Policy, 1945–1960*. Albuquerque: University of New Mexico Press, 1986.

Green, Donald E., and Thomas V. Tonnesen, eds. *American Indians: Social Justice and Public Policy*. Milwaukee: Institute on Race and Ethnicity, University of Wisconsin System, 1991.

Horsman, Reginald. *Expansion and American Indian Policy, 1783–1812*. East Lansing: Michigan State University Press, 1967.

Joe, Jennie R., ed. *American Indian Policy and Cultural Values: Conflict and Accommodation*. Los Angeles: American Indian Studies Center, University of California, Los Angeles, 1986.

Josephy, Alvin M., Jr., Joane Nagel, and Troy Johnson, eds. *Red Power: The American Indian's Fight for Freedom*. 2nd ed. Lincoln: University of Nebraska Press, 1999.

Legters, Lyman H., and Fremont J. Lyden, eds. *American Indian Policy: Self-Governance and Economic Development*. Westport, Conn.: Greenwood Press, 1994.

McNickle, D'Arcy. *Native American Tribalism: Indian Survivals and Renewals*. New York: Oxford University Press, 1973.

Mihesuah, Devon A. *Repatriation Reader: Who Owns American Indian Remains?* Lincoln: University of Nebraska Press, 2000.

Philp, Kenneth R. *John Collier's Crusade for Indian Reform, 1920–1954*. Tucson: University of Arizona Press, 1977.

———. *Termination Revisited: American Indians on the Trail to Self-Determination, 1933–1953*. Lincoln: University of Nebraska Press, 1999.

Prucha, Francis P. *The Great Father: The United States Government and the American Indians*. 2 vols. Lincoln: University of Nebraska Press, 1984.

Prucha, Francis Paul, ed. *Documents of United States Indian Policy*. 3rd ed. Lincoln: University of Nebraska Press, 2000.

Satz, Ronald N. *American Indian Policy in the Jacksonian Era*. Lincoln: University of Nebraska Press, 1975.

Sheehan, Bernard W. *Seeds of Extinction: Jeffersonian Philanthropy and the American Indian.* Chapel Hill: University of North Carolina Press, 1973.

Snipp, C. Matthew. *Public Policy Impacts on American Indian Economic Development.* Albuquerque: Institute for Native American Development, University of New Mexico, 1988.

Trennert, Robert A. *Alternative to Extinction: Federal Indian Policy and the Beginnings of the Reservation System, 1846–51.* Philadelphia: Temple University Press, 1975.

Washburn, Wilcomb E. *Red Man's Land/White Man's Law: The Past and Present Status of the American Indian.* 2nd ed. Norman: University of Oklahoma Press, 1995.

◆ PREHISTORY

Aveni, Anthony F., ed. *Native American Astronomy.* Austin: University of Texas Press, 1977.

Dixon, E. James. *Bones, Boats, & Bison: Archaeology and the First Colonization of Western North America.* Albuquerque: University of New Mexico Press, 1999.

Fagan, Brian M. *Ancient North America: The Archaeology of a Continent.* Rev. and expanded ed. New York, N.Y.: Thames and Hudson, 1995.

Fowler, Melvin L. *The Cahokia Atlas: A Historical Atlas of Cahokia Archaeology.* Rev. ed. Urbana, Ill.: Illinois Transportation Archeological Research Program, University of Illinois, 1997.

Gibbon, Guy. *Archaeology of Prehistoric Native America: An Encyclopedia.* New York: Garland, 1998.

Jennings, Jesse D. *Prehistory of North America.* 3rd ed. Mountain View, Calif.: Mayfield Pub., 1989.

Jennings, Jesse D., ed. *Ancient Native Americans.* San Francisco: W.H. Freeman, 1983.

Shaffer, Lynda. *Native Americans Before 1492: the Moundbuilding Centers of the Eastern Woodlands.* Armonk, N.Y.: M.E. Sharpe, 1992.

Snow, Dean R. *The Archaeology of North America.* New York: Viking Press, 1976.

———. *The Archaeology of North America.* New York: Chelsea House Publishers, 1989.

◆ RELIGION

Beck, Peggy V., and Anna L. Walters. *The Sacred: Ways of Knowledge, Sources of Life.* Flagstaff: Northland, 1990.

Black Elk. *Black Elk Speaks: Being the Life Story of a Holy Man of the Oglala Sioux.* 21st-century ed. Lincoln: University of Nebraska Press, 2000.

Bonvillain, Nancy. *Native American Religion.* New York: Chelsea House Publishers, 1996.

Coffer, William E. *Spirits of the Sacred Mountains: Creation Stories of the American Indian.* New York: Van Nostrand Reinhold, 1978.

Deloria, Vine, Jr. *For This Land: Writings on Religion in America.* New York: Routledge, 1999.

———. *God is Red: A Native View of Religion.* 2nd ed. Golden, Colo.: North American Press, 1992.

Gill, Sam D. *Native American Religions: An Introduction.* Belmont, Calif.: Wadsworth Publishing, 1982.

———. *Native American Religious Action: A Performance Approach to Religion.* Columbia: University of South Carolina Press, 1987.

Hall, Robert L. *An Archaeology of the Soul: North American Indian Belief and Ritual.* Urbana: University of Illinois Press, 1997.

Harrod, Howard L. *Becoming and Remaining a People: Native American Religions on the Northern Plains.* Tucson: University of Arizona Press, 1995.

———. *Renewing the World: Plains Indian Religion and Morality.* Tucson: University of Arizona Press, 1987.

Hittman, Michael. *Wovoka and the Ghost Dance.* Expanded ed. Lincoln: University of Nebraska Press, 1997.

Hultkrantz, Ake. *Native Religions of North America: The Power of Visions and Fertility.* San Francisco: Harper & Row, 1987.

Loftin, John D. *Religion and Hopi Life in the Twentieth Century.* Bloomington, Ind.: Indiana University Press, 1991.

McLoughlin, William G. *The Cherokee Ghost Dance: Essays on the Southeastern Indians, 1789–1861*. Macon, Ga.: Mercer, 1984.

Mooney, James. *The Ghost-Dance Religion and the Sioux Outbreak of 1890*. Lincoln: University of Nebraska Press, 1991.

Powers, William K. *Oglala Religion*. Lincoln: University of Nebraska Press, 1977.

Stewart, Omer C. *Peyote Religion: A History*. Norman: University of Oklahoma Press, 1987.

Sullivan, Lawrence E., ed. *Native Religions and Cultures of North America*. New York: Continuum, 2000.

Treat, James, ed. *Native and Christian: Indigenous Voices on Religious Identity in the United States and Canada*. New York: Routledge, 1996.

Vecsey, Christopher. *Handbook of American Indian Religious Freedom*. New York: Crossroad, 1991.

Zolbrod, Paul G., trans. *Dine Bahane: The Navajo Creation Story*. Albuquerque: University of New Mexico Press, 1984.

◆ SOCIOLOGY

Champagne, Duane. *American Indian Societies: Some Strategies and Conditions of Political and Cultural Survival*. Cambridge, Mass.: Cultural Survival, 1989.

———. *Social Order and Political Change: Constitutional Governments Among the Cherokee, the Choctaw, the Chickasaw, and the Creek*. Stanford, Calif.: Stanford University Press, 1992.

Faiman-Silva, Sandra L. *Choctaws at the Crossroads: The Political Economy of Class and Culture in the Oklahoma Timber Region*. Lincoln: University of Nebraska Press, 1997.

Fixico, Donald L. *The Urban Indian Experience in America*. Albuquerque: University of New Mexico Press, 2000.

Guillemin, Jeanne. *Urban Renegades: The Cultural Strategy of American Indians*. New York: Columbia University Press, 1975.

Kurkiala, Mikael. *Building the Nation Back Up: The Politics of Identity on the Pine Ridge Indian Reservation*. Uppsala: Uppsala University, Department of Cultural Anthropology, 1997.

Ross, Luana. *Inventing the Savage: The Social Construction of Native American Criminality*. Austin: University of Texas Press, 1998.

Sorkin, Alan L. *The Urban American Indian*. Lexington, Mass.: Lexington Books, 1978.

Thornton, Russell. *We Shall Live Again: the 1870 and 1890 Ghost Dance Movements as Demographic Revitalization*. New York: Cambridge University Press, 1986.

Weibel-Orlando, Joan. *Indian Country, L.A.: Maintaining Ethnic Community in Complex Society*. Rev. ed. Urbana: University of Illinois Press, 1999.

White, Richard. *The Roots of Dependency: Subsistence, Environment, and Social Change Among the Choctaws, Pawnees, and Navajos*. Lincoln: University of Nebraska Press, 1983.

◆ URBANIZATION

Danziger, Edmund J. *Survival and Regeneration: Detroit's American Indian Community*. Detroit: Wayne State University Press, 1991.

Fixico, Donald L. *The Urban Indian Experience in America*. Albuquerque: University of New Mexico Press, 2000.

Guillemin, Jeanne. *Urban Renegades: The Cultural Strategy of American Indians*. New York: Columbia University Press, 1975.

Lobo, Susan, and Kurt Peters. *American Indians and the Urban Experience*. Walnut Creek, Calif.: Altamira Press, 2000.

Neils, Elaine M. *Reservation to City: Indian Migration and Federal Relocation*. Chicago: Dept. of Geography, University of Chicago, 1971.

Sorkin, Alan L. *The Urban American Indian*. Lexington, Mass.: Lexington Books, 1978.

Stanbury, W. T. *Success and Failure: Indians in Urban Society*. Vancouver: University of British Columbia Press, 1975.

Waddell, Jack O. and O. Michael Watson, eds. *The American Indian in Urban Society*. 1971. Reprint. Lanham, Md.: University Press of America, 1984.

Weibel-Orlando, Joan. *Indian Country, L.A.: Maintaining Ethnic Community in Complex Society*. Rev. ed. Urbana: University of Illinois Press, 1999.

◆ WOMEN

Albers, Patricia, and Beatrice Medicine. *The Hidden Half: Studies of Plains Indian Women*. Washington, D.C.: University Press of America, 1983.

Allen, Paula Gunn. *The Sacred Hoop: Recovering the Feminine in American Indian Traditions*. Boston: Beacon Press, 1986.

Alvord, Lori Arviso, M.D. *The Scalpel and the Silver Bear*. New York: Bantam-Doubleday Books, 1993.

Bataille, Gretchen M., ed. *Native American Women: A Biographical Dictionary*. New York: Garland, 1993.

Bataille, Gretchen M., and Kathleen Mullen Sands. *American Indian Women, Telling Their Lives*. Lincoln: University of Nebraska Press, 1984.

Benedek, Emily. *Beyond the Four Corners of the World: A Navajo Woman's Journey*. Norman: University of Oklahoma Press, 1998.

Boyer, Ruth McDonald, with Narcissus Duffy Gayton. *Apache Mothers and Daughters: Four Generations of a Family*. Norman: University of Oklahoma Press, 1992.

Green, Rayna. *Native American Women: A Contextual Bibliography*. Bloomington: Indiana University Press, 1984.

Green, Rayna, ed. *That's What She Said: Contemporary Poetry and Fiction by Native American Women*. Bloomington: Indiana University Press, 1984.

Harjo, Joy, and Gloria Bird, eds. *Reinventing the Enemy's Language: Contemporary Native Women's Writings of North America*. New York: W. W. Norton & Company, 1997.

Klein, Laura F., and Lillian A. Ackerman, eds. *Women and Power in Native North America*. Norman: University of Oklahoma Press, 1995.

Landes, Ruth. *The Ojibwa Woman*. 1938. Reprint. Lincoln: University of Nebraska Press, 1997.

Perdue, Theda. *Cherokee Women: Gender and Culture Change, 1700–1835*. Lincoln: University of Nebraska Press, 1998.

Peters, Virginia. *Women of the Earth Lodges: Tribal Life on the Plains*. Norman, Okla.: University of Oklahoma Press, 2000.

Powers, Marla. *Oglala Women: Myth, Ritual, and Reality*. Chicago: University of Chicago Press, 1986.

Schweitzer, Marjorie M., ed. *American Indian Grandmothers: Traditions and Transitions*. Albuquerque: University of New Mexico Press, 1999.

Shoemaker, Nancy, ed. *Negotiators of Change: Historical Perspectives on Native American Women*. New York: Routledge, 1995.

Sonneborn, Liz. *A to Z of Native American Women*. New York, New York: Facts on File, 1998.

Spittal, W. G., ed. *Iroquois Women: An Anthology*. Ohsweken, Ont.: Iroqrafts, 1990.

◆ CANADA

Adams, Howard. *Prison of Grass: Canada From a Native Point of View*. Rev. ed. Saskatoon, Sask.: Fifth House, 1989.

Asch, Michael. *Home and Native Land: Aboriginal Rights and the Canadian Constitution*. Toronto and New York: Methuen, 1984; Vancouver: UBC Press, 1993.

Barron, F. Laurie, and James B. Waldram. *1885 and After: Native Society in Transition*. Regina, Sask.: Canadian Plains Research Center, University of Regina, 1986.

Boldt, Menno, and J. Anthony Long, eds., in association with Leroy Little Bear. *The Quest for Justice: Aboriginal Peoples and Aboriginal Rights*. Toronto: University of Toronto Press, 1985.

Brown, Jennifer S.H. *Strangers in Blood: Fur Trade Company Families in Indian Country*. Vancouver: University of British Columbia Press, 1980.

Cairns, Alan C. *Citizens Plus: Aboriginal Peoples and the Canadian State*. Vancouver: UBC Press, 2000.

Canada. Royal Commission on Aboriginal Peoples. *Report of the Royal Commission on Aboriginal Peoples.* 5 vols. Ottawa, 1996.

Carter, Sarah. *Lost Harvests: Prairie Indian Reserve Farmers and Government Policy.* Montreal: McGill-Queen's University Press, 1990.

Castellano, Marlene Brant, Lynne Davis, and Louise Lahache. *Aboriginal Education: Fulfilling the Promise.* Vancouver: UBC Press, 2000.

Clark, Bruce A. *Native Liberty, Crown Sovereignty: The Existing Aboriginal Right of Self-Government in Canada.* Montreal: McGill-Queen's University Press, 1990.

Coates, Ken S., and Robin Fisher, eds. *Out of the Background: Readings on Canadian Native History.* Toronto: Copp Clark, 1996.

Dewdney, Selwyn H. *They Shared to Survive: The Native Peoples of Canada.* Toronto: Macmillian of Canada, 1975.

Dickason, Olive P. *Canada's First Nations: A History of Founding Peoples From Earliest Times.* Norman: University of Oklahoma Press, 1992.

————. *The Myth of the Savage and the Beginnings of French Colonialism in the Americas.* Edmonton, Alta.: University of Alberta Press, 1984.

Frideres, James S., with Lilianne Ernestine Krosenbrink-Gelissen. *Aboriginal Peoples in Canada: Contemporary Conflicts* 5th ed. Scarborough, Ont.: Prentice Hall Allyn and Bacon Canada, 1998.

Getty, Ian A. L., and Antoine S. Lussier, eds. *As Long as the Sun Shines and Water Flows: A Reader in Canadian Native Studies.* Vancouver: University of British Columbia Press, 1983.

Grant, John W. *Moon of Wintertime: Missionaries and the Indians of Canada in Encounter Since 1534.* Toronto: University of Toronto Press, 1984.

Innis, Harold A. *The Fur Trade in Canada: An Introduction to Canadian Economic History.* Rev. ed. Toronto: University of Toronto Press, 1956.

Isaac, Thomas. *Aboriginal Law: Cases, Materials and Commentary.* Saskatoon, Sask.: Purich Pub., 1999.

Jenness, Diamond. *Indians of Canada.* 7th ed. Toronto: University of Toronto Press, 1977.

King, Thomas, ed. *All My Relations: An Anthology of Contemporary Canadian Native Fiction.* Norman: University of Oklahoma Press, 1992.

Krotz, Larry. *Indian Country: Inside Another Canada.* Toronto: McClelland and Stewart, 1990.

Little Bear, Leroy, Menno Boldt, and J. Anthony Long, eds. *Pathways to Self-Determination: Canadian Indians and the Canadian State.* Toronto: University of Toronto Press, 1984.

Long, J. Anthony, Menno Boldt, eds., in association with Leroy Little Bear. *Governments in Conflict? Provinces and Indian Nations in Canada.* Toronto: University of Toronto Press, 1988.

Lowes, Warren. *Indian Giver: A Legacy of North American Native Peoples.* Penticton, B.C.: Theytus Books, 1986.

Manuel, George, and Michael Posluns. *The Fourth World: An Indian Reality.* Toronto: Collier-McMillan Canada; New York: Free Press, 1974.

McMillan, Alan D. *Native Peoples and Cultures of Canada: An Anthropological Overview.* 2nd ed. Vancouver: Douglas & McIntyre, 1995.

Miller, Christine, and Patricia Chuckryk, eds. *Women of the First Nations: Power, Wisdom, and Strength.* Winnipeg, Man.: University of Manitoba Press, 1996.

Miller, David R., et al. *The First Ones: Readings in Indian/Native Studies.* Craven, Sask.: Saskatchewan Indian Federated College Press, 1992.

Miller, James Rodger. *Shingwauk's Vision: A History of Native Residential Schools.* Toronto: University of Toronto Press, 1996.

————. *Skyscrapers Hide the Heavens: A History of Indian-White Relations in Canada.* Toronto: University of Toronto Press, 1989.

————., ed. *Sweet Promises: A Reader on Indian-White Relations in Canada.* Toronto: University of Toronto Press, 1991.

Morrison, R. Bruce, and C. Roderick Wilson, eds. *Native Peoples: The Canadian Experience.* 2d ed. Toronto: McClelland and Stewart, 1995.

Morrisseau, Norval. *Legends of My People: The Great Ojibway.* New York: McGraw-Hill Ryerson Press, 1965.

Pelletier, Wilfred, and Ted Pool. *No Foreign Land: The Biography of a Northern American Indian.* New York: Pantheon Books, 1974.

Perreault, Jeanne, and Sylvia Vance, eds.*Writing the Circle: Native Women of Western Canada: An Anthology.* Norman: University of Oklahoma Press, 1993.

Peterson, Jacqueline, and Jennifer S. H. Brown, eds. *The New Peoples: Being and Becoming Métis in North America.* Lincoln: University of Nebraska Press, 1985.

Price, John A. *Indians of Canada: Cultural Dynamics.* Scarborough, Ont.: Prentice-Hall of Canada, 1979.

Ponting, J. Rick, and Roger Gibbins. *Out of Irrelevance: A Socio-Political Introduction to Indian Affairs in Canada.* Toronto: Butterworths, 1980.

Purich, Donald. *Our Land: Native Rights in Canada.* Toronto: Lorimer, 1986.

Ray, Arthur J. *I Have Lived Here Since The World Began: An Illustrated History of Canada's Native People.* Toronto: Lester Publishing and Key Porter Books, 1996.

———. *Indians in the Fur Trade: Their Role as Hunters, Trappers and Middlemen of the Lands Southwest of Hudson Bay, 1660–1870.* Toronto: University of Toronto Press, 1974.

Redbird, Duke. *We Are Métis: A Métis View of the Development of a Native Canadian People.* Willowdale, Ont.: Ontario Métis & Non Status Indian Association, 1980.

Russell, Daniel. *A People's Dream: Aboriginal Self-Government.* Vancouver: University of British Columbia Press, 2000.

Smith, Donald B. *Sacred Feathers: The Reverend Peter Jones (Kahkewaquonaby) & the Mississauga Indians.* Lincoln: University of Nebraska Press, 1987.

Tennant, Paul. *Aboriginal Peoples and Politics: The Indian Land Question in British Columbia, 1849–1989.* Vancouver: University of British Columbia Press, 1990.

Trigger, Bruce G. *Natives and Newcomers: Canada's "Heroic Age" Reconsidered.* Kingston: McGill-Queen's University Press, 1985.

Waldram, James B., Ann D. Herring, and T. Kue Young. *Aboriginal Health in Canada: Historical, Cultural, and Epidemiological Perspectives.* Toronto: University of Toronto Press, 1995.

Warry, Wayne. *Unfinished Dreams: Community Healing and the Reality of Aboriginal Self-Government.* Toronto: University of Toronto Press, 1998.

Weaver, Sally M. *Making Canadian Indian Policy: The Hidden Agenda 1968–70.* Toronto: University of Toronto Press, 1981.

Occupation Index

Subject Index

Personal names, place names, events, organizations, and various subject areas or keywords contained in *The Reference Library of Native North America* are listed in this index with corresponding page numbers indicating text references. Page numbers appearing in boldface indicate a major biographical profile. Page numbers appearing in italics refer to photographs, illustrations, and maps found throughout the *Reference Library.*

C

F

G

H

I

M

N